CW01665003

PHILOSO
OF EAST AND WEST

PHILOSOPHERS OF EAST AND WEST

The quest for the meaning of existence in Eastern and Western Thought

E. W. F. TOMLIN

Foreword by Kathleen Raine

Published by Oak-Tree Books Limited
11 Rosemont Road, London NW3 6NG, England

© E. W. F. Tomlin 1986

All rights reserved. No part of this publication may be reproduced, stored in a retrieval system, or transmitted, in any form or by any means electronic, mechanical, photocopying, recording or otherwise, without the prior permission of Oak-Tree Books Limited.

Philosophers of East and West—the quest for the meaning of existence in Eastern and Western thought is a revised and corrected version.

Great Philosophers of the East—First published in 1952.
Second impression 1968, Third impression 1969.
The Great Philosophers: The Western World—First printed in 1950.
Second impression 1954, third impression 1968.
Printed in America in 1967 by Harper & Row

ISBN 0 948059 06 0 (Hardback)
ISBN 0 948059 07 9 (Paperback)

Photoset, printed and bound by
Redwood Burn Limited,
Trowbridge, Wiltshire

Foreword

by Kathleen Raine

The publication of E. W. F. Tomlin's important *Philosophers of East and West*, now recast and extensively revised, is for more than one reason timely. First, a survey of the thought of human civilization from the earliest recorded times is an essential work for whoever wishes to understand the underlying assumptions about the meaning and values of life from which successive cultures have emerged. The intelligent common reader, the student of some special field of history, or literature and the arts, or of religion, will find in this book what is needed in order to relate these to a context of the seminal ideas from which they flowered. Such students will find not only clear statements of the thought of the principal philosophers, but just, and never merely negative, evaluations of their contributions. The author has understood that ideas cannot be taken in isolation from the men who expressed them; and has a particular respect for those philosophers who have been prepared to live, or to lose their lives, for the sake of truth as they understood it; as were Spinoza or Kierkegaard no less than Socrates or Sohravardi.

A second reason is more apparent now than when this work first appeared. There are few nowadays to whom it is not clear that our most urgent present problem is neither political nor economic, but a crisis of our value-systems: what is man, and what is the meaning and the purpose of our life? Since the stone age there has probably never been a time in which this was less clear. Whatever Utopian hopes were once vested either in Marxism, or in the Western 'democratic' humanist versions of mechanistic materialism, our world now seems nearer to the possibility of total destruction than to a secular millennium. How has Western civilization, for all its energy and good intentions, its material knowledge and power, lost its way? We are aware of living at a time of moral crisis affecting alike our relations with the transcendent, with the human, and with the natural world. Those prepared to re-examine the value-systems by which humanity has lived in other times and places may hope to find some lost clue which may even now enable us to re-orient our individual lives, even to change our world somewhat for the better. Mr. Tomlin, who so strongly stresses the life as the expression and measure of the truth of what a man thinks, presents to the reader, with an unfailing seriousness we cannot disregard, the moral issues. He is, in this field of ethics above all, himself a philosopher to be respected.

Presenting each philosopher and his thought with commendable impartiality, Mr. Tomlin leaves it to the intelligence of the reader (and he rates the intelligence of his readers and their capacity to think things out for themselves more highly than is at present customary in press or media) to reach his own conclusions. His own reading of the history of ideas clearly fills him with deep concern for the coarsening and decline of values that has gone hand in hand, it seems, with the growth of power to manipulate 'nature'. Modern philosophy has lost its roots in the sapiential doctrines which, in India and the Far East, as in our own Hellenistic and Christian past, have been the ground of philosophic thought. Little by little philosophy has narrowed and lowered its aims until it has become a mere exercise of the discursive reason on natural phenomena, with a corresponding loss of meaning and value. Philosophy, once a true search for wisdom, has become a word-game. René Guénon, the French metaphysician whose following today is considerable, has called this time 'The Reign of Quantity'; Mr. Tomlin would not dispute this.

His own values are, however, more positive. He belongs to the generation whose thought was formed by the works of A. N. Whitehead, R. G. Collingwood, Christopher Dawson, who in the name of wisdom made their stand against logical positivism and other reductionist materialist formulations. Of this moment Mr. Tomlin's friend T. S. Eliot has given us the poetic expression. Without confusing philosophy with religion, Mr. Tomlin nevertheless points out that the greatest philosophers (whether of the East or of European Christendom) have always been aware of what he calls 'the divine connection'—the Egyptian *Maat*, the Tao, the Way, the 'righteousness' of Israel; in India the separation of philosophy from its roots in spiritual reality is inconceivable. Now that, East or West, we live in one world, in which all alike are endangered by the destructive power of a mechanistic science in the hands of ignorance, it seems inevitable that the West should pay serious attention to the oriental philosophies, still, however under threat, a living tradition in India and in some Buddhist countries. We must again discuss those values for which Socrates died and Gautama Buddha renounced his kingdom. But Mr. Tomlin would be the last to suggest that we should therefore discard our own inheritance, since wisdom and truth are one for all humankind.

Readers aware of the continuity in the West of an alternative philosophic tradition, however disregarded or excluded by the dominant naturalistic thought, cannot fail to notice certain exclusions. Plotinus, Proclus and the other Neoplatonists are mentioned only in passing; so is Meister Eckhart (whom some would consider the equal of Shankara) and Scotus Eriugena. Coleridge, though a poet, was surely a greater philosopher than Hume or his precursors. (Berkeley is included, respectfully if a shade apologetically). What all these have in common is a recognition of the primacy of 'facts of mind' (Coleridge's phrase) as against the phenomena of nature, which have been the starting-point of so much Western philosophy, to the point of a virtual identification of 'reality' with the material world. This materialist bias, which might be traced back to Aristotle himself, has reached its term in Logical Positivism, Behaviourism and the like, and in Marxism has become a world-religion. We have surely reached a crisis, a point of that reversal of the 'gyres' of history of which Plato wrote in the *Laws*, and more recently W. B. Yeats in *A Vision*—a change not in conclusions or deductions from agreed assumptions, but of those assumptions themselves, the premisses on which our civilization is founded. There have been such times of change before, and painful as it may be to live at such a time, it may nevertheless be a moment of exhilarating freedom. Yeats wrote of his excitement as 'the new gyre begins to stir', when 'the limit itself has become a new dimension, that this ever-hidden thing which makes us fold our hands in awe has begun to press down upon multitudes'. Mr. Tomlin is himself alive to this stirring of change, and is in some measure one of its spokesmen, not at all through assertion or argument, but from the steady clarity of a certain moral wisdom.

Mr. Tomlin writes from a rich background of knowledge gathered not from books alone but from having lived in many countries both of the East and of the West (and especially in Japan). I will only add that readers will find it a delight to read a book written in a style that is the fruit of the author's clear understanding of complex thought, his respect for the dignity of men and of man, and a steady and mature concern for human values which places him with A. N. Whitehead, Arnold Toynbee at his best, with A. E. Taylor, with T. S. Eliot, and within the age-old order of true 'lovers of wisdom'.

Other books by E. W. F. Tomlin:

Philosophy
The Approach to Metaphysics
Simone Weil
Living and Knowing
R. G. Collingwood
Man, Time, and the New Science
Psyche, Culture, and the New Science
The Concept of Life (in preparation)

Literary
Charles Dickens: a Centenary Volume
Arnold Toynbee: an Anthology
Wyndham Lewis
Wyndham Lewis: an Anthology of his Prose
T. S. Eliot: a Tribute from Japan
T. S. Eliot: a Friendship (in preparation)

Travel and History
Turkey, the Modern Miracle
Life in Modern Turkey
Japan
The Last Country: My Years in Japan
In Search of St. Piran
The World of St. Boniface
The Church of St. Morwenna and
St. John the Baptist, Morwenstow: a Guide and History
The Tall Trees of Marsland

'The initiation of all wise and noble things comes and must come from individuals: generally at first from some one individual.'

JOHN STUART MILL

'One can tell for oneself whether the water is warm or cold. In the same way, a man must convince himself about these experiences, then only are they real.'

I-Ching

'Like an image in a dream, the world is troubled by love, hatred, and other poisons. So long as the dream lasts, the image appears to be real, but on awakening it vanishes.'

SHANKARA: *Atma Bodha*

'Truly, philosophers play a strange game. They know very well that one thing alone counts, and that all their medley of subtle discussions relates to one single question: why are we born on this earth? And they also know that they will never be able to answer it. Nevertheless, they continue sedately to amuse themselves.'

JACQUES MARITAIN

'So long as the bounds of logical possibility are respected, it is not for the philosopher to set any limits to the marvels of nature.'

SIR ALFRED J. AYER: *Philosophical Essays* (1954)

Contents

Illustrations

Introduction

'The curse of ignorance,' Socrates is made to say in Plato's dialogue called the *Symposium*, 'is that a man without being good or wise is nevertheless satisfied with himself: he has no desire for that of which he feels no want.'

By ignorance Socrates did not mean to imply simply lack of information. He meant lack of wisdom. And the wisdom in which he found his fellow-men to be most deficient was that concerning their own hearts and minds. How, he asked, can you be satisfied with yourself if you do not know who you are and what, being here in this world, you are meant to do with your lives? The satisfaction of a man who is ignorant in this sense is poor satisfaction indeed. The road to happiness, like the road to virtue, is the road not of self-satisfaction but of self-knowledge.

Few of us are really satisfied with ourselves in the way that Plato described. Even those who appear to display excessive self-conceit are forced by their very over-assertiveness to betray an inner disquiet. Almost everybody at some period of his life is prompted to ask himself such questions as: What am I? and why am I here? And this curiosity sometimes gives rise to the reflection that as these questions have never been satisfactorily met, the human mind is perhaps incapable of answering them. Before we confess our complete mental bankruptcy, however, we must attempt to discover what are the limits, if any, of our knowledge. And this in turn may lead us on to enquire what knowledge is and wherein it differs from, say, imagination and belief.

Such inner questionings—which, if the individual stifles them in one form, will reappear in another—are the beginnings of philosophy. And, having made a beginning, we must choose whether to allow our minds simply to drift, to accept our conclusions at secondhand, or to think things out to some sort of conclusion, even if the conclusion be that we must go on thinking.

Our covert respect for philosophy is revealed in everyday speech. Of a person who resolutely endures misfortune we say that he has 'taken it philosophically'. By this we mean that he has faced with courage the situation in which he finds himself, that he has made the best of a bad job, and that he has refrained from giving vent to rancour either against his fellows or against the providence of which he is temporarily the victim. When the Roman consul Boethius (470–526) was condemned to imprisonment and death on an unjust and indeed imaginary charge, he wrote a book of sublime and noble thoughts to which he gave the title of *The Consolation of Philosophy*. Such, then, are the rewards of the philosophical attitude: courage and consolation, in a world that never ceases to call for the first and so often fails to provide material for the second.

The Great Philosophers are merely those for whom the impulse to enquire into the nature of things has become a passion. Thought is the profession from which they never retire. Almost all such men have been distinguished by the nobility of their lives, and particularly by that form of courage which is needed to plough a lonely furrow, to voyage through 'strange seas of thought alone'. For philosophy is essentially the flower of solitude; it is the unstill and unstillable small voice in each of us which we can ignore at our peril. It is conscience resurgent, exchanging the rôle of plaintiff for that of judge.

That the frank, open and essentially humble attitude of the greatest philosophers should so often have been exchanged for its opposite—namely, an attitude of clever, showy logic-chopping, designed to bewilder and to befuddle the laity—is perhaps no more than evidence of a profound philosophical truth, namely, that the corruption of the best is the worst. Certainly it is one of the curses of philosophy that so many books should have been written making difficult problems more difficult still: or, worst of all, obscuring the comparatively simple problems with which philosophy begins by a parade of conundrums, paradoxes, pseudo-problems calculated to put the innocent reader into a state of alarm and despondency. One of the reasons why the term 'academic' is so often associated with arid pedantry is that the commentaries and exposés of those of purely academic training seem often to lack appreciation of what the problems they claim to be treating actually are. The subject, as we say, is of 'purely academic interest', which is as much as to imply that it is of no real interest at all—at least to those ordinary folk who have a job to do and a living to earn.

For this reason, if for no other, there is something to be said for relating to philosophy to the lives of the great philosophers: lives that so often remain unknown even to those who can discourse at length upon the problem of universals, cause and effect, the '*a priori* synthesis', and so on. For we are too ready to assume that thought is something produced in a vacuum, a process that can operate independently of any particular mind, and consequently something that can be ignored by people who have to employ their thoughts upon more practical matters. We do not realize, in fact, that a great philosopher makes his own age the subject of his thoughts and, in so doing, becomes a kind of keeper of the public consciousness; that the great philosopher, like the great historian (who, as we are seeing today, must be a kind of philosopher), is a man who reveals to humanity its own state of mind and thus makes not merely progress but equilibrium possible; and that, in short, all the science and art, the inherited skill and technique, which we assume to be our inalienable possession, and without which our whole civilized life would disintegrate in a short time, are upheld by the kind of knowledge of which the philosopher in all of us, and above all the great philosophers among us, are the chief sustainers. To know more about these unacknowledged leaders of men is not merely entertaining but instructive.

Most people, if drawn to the subject at all, pick up what philosophy they can through books that happen to come their way. The rise of radio and television, though greatly extending the appetite for entertainment, has provided a unique opportunity for instruction too; but apart from programmes directed at schools, the time devoted to any form of higher learning has always been extremely limited. That is perhaps the reason why the few experiments in this sphere tend to achieve prominence. During the last war, the BBC initiated a radio programme called The Brain's Trust. It did not start out as a popular programme: popularity was thrust upon it. This was due to what C. E. M. Joad—one of the best remembered of the participants—defined as a vast unsatisfied seriousness among the general public. The seriousness should not be underestimated. Bryan Magee, who thirty years later compered a TV series of philosophical interviews called 'Men of Ideas', spoke of receiving letter after letter saying 'at last an adult programme'. The reaction was not unexpected. Here were mature people talking interestingly about subjects of universal concern. Once more, popularity was thrust upon a series which its inaugurators had launched with some trepidation. What had been considered essentially a visual medium, with exclusively eye-catching appeal, showed itself adapted to a quite different technique. Many people, who had never opened—or dreamt of opening—a philosophical book, must have had their interest stirred by the series. The interviews were repeated and followed by others on the history of thought. Due partly to the personality of the compère and partly to his facility in expressing ideas better than some of the participants themselves, the series proved a milestone in popular education.

Many people approach works on philosophy as if about to undergo an ordeal. This attitude is not confined to the uninstructed reader. A modern American philosopher has admitted: 'I find I usually read works of philosophy with all the defences up.'[1] The present books, now combined in one volume, were written in the belief that such defensiveness is unnecessary.

This study is one of the few attempts to outline the philosophical quest from the 4th millennium BC to the present day. It argues that Western philosophy is the richer for recognizing its roots in Eastern philosophy, which concentrates on the meaning of life rather than on the meaning of meaning—or of meaninglessness, for in the West there is a very powerful tendency to deride the concepts of meaning and purpose. We pursue the common ground between the philosophers of the last 5,000 years. Western civilization has never needed their wisdom more than it does today.

In view of the fact that our study begins with the oriental tradition, it is worth pointing out that since the turbulent 1960s there has been a new interest in Eastern philosophy, belief and practice. That is what

[1] Robert Nozick, *Philosophical Explanations* (1981).

may lend the following account of oriental thought—placed first because of its antiquity—a relevance which did not previously attach to it. At the same time, a Westerner—even if, like the author, he has spent many years in oriental countries—must remain aware that his understanding of the oriental mind is necessarily conditioned by his upbringing. For if there is any truth in the thought of Karl Marx, it is that everyone is influenced (which is not the same as being determined) by his social and economic background. There have been remarkable people, such as Lafcadio Hearn, who have transformed themselves into orientals without apparent difficulty. But Hearn, due to the circumstances of his birth, was to start with somewhat *deraciné*; and when, as Koizumi Yakumo, he wrote about Japan, it was as a Western intellectual, much influenced by Herbert Spencer, that he did so. Nevertheless, a Westerner who has devoted much time to expounding, through the spoken and written word, European ideas, must come to realize, as the author assuredly does, that the Western tradition, for all its richness, has tended, especially in recent years, to lose sight of a dimension to which the oriental tradition has stubbornly clung; or rather that the direction of the thought of Ancient Greece, followed by the ideals of medieval scholasticism, have been succeeded by 'modern thought' which, while commendably repudiating superstition and obscurantism, has tended increasingly to throw doubt upon the legitimacy of the philosophical quest itself. This in turn has produced its own reaction. It has given rise to the cultivation of arcane doctrines, the revival of astrology, spiritualism—than which nothing can be more materialistic—and witchcraft, even among a branch of the intelligentsia. In short, there is a crisis in Western thought: a repudiation of rationality and commonsense which must be viewed with alarm. For if man's *raison d'être* is to be found in this direction, then he is a creature of the dark rather than of the light; and the civilization and culture which he has painfully evolved over the last few thousand years might never have been achieved, if that had been suspected to be their necessary outcome.

This is not to belittle the movement known as Analytical Philosophy, which has dominated the academics in Anglo-Saxon countries throughout much of the present century. It has proved hygienic and, so to speak, antiseptic, and viewed in perspective, its influence has on the whole been salutary. But, to paraphrase George Santayana, whose thought we shall be examining, there is a difference between polishing the lens of one's telescope and looking at the stars.

Let us then recapitulate what, in the two great world traditions, the philosophical quest amounts to. It is an enquiry with two main branches. First, it is an attempt, through the unfettered use of reason, to elucidate the meaning of existence. Secondly, it seeks to understand how a satisfactory life should be led. For it is generally assumed that, in so far as we find the world intelligible, or of a certain nature, so we shall be able to decide how best to live in it. These two branches are usually known as *philosophy* and *morals*, or *metaphysics* and *ethics*.

To embark on these enquiries, however, is at once to enter into controversy. There have, as we know, been philosophers who have denied that their task were to elucidate the meaning of existence. There have been others who have denied that morals or ethics formed part of philosophy. In our final chapter this subject will be taken up afresh. Here we need only point out that, if the meaning of existence and the nature of moral conduct are held not to form part of philosophy, then, since these problems will not go away, we must either invent a new name to cover such insistent problems or deny to the sceptics (as we may call them) the monopoly of a word which, for the greater part of history, has been assigned to them. To search for ultimate meanings may be difficult and even presumptuous, but it cannot be repudiated in advance. In one of the earliest works of literature dealing with ultimate matters, namely the Sumerian *Epic of Gilgamesh,* which dates from at least the 3rd millennium BC, the eponymous hero, resolved to discover the meaning of life and death, is told by a goddess: 'You will never find the life for which you are looking. When the gods created man, they allotted him death: life they retained in their own keeping.' What might have been Gilgamesh's answer is: 'Maybe, but I shall go on searching for the meaning of both.' And he does, even though he dies unsatisfied. Thus, when F. H. Bradley coined his celebrated epigram that 'philosophy is the finding of bad reasons for what we believe upon instinct', he was careful to add a less-quoted qualification: '*but the finding of those reasons is no less an instinct*'. You cannot abolish an instinct: you can only divert it, and then usually only temporarily. When the skirmishing is over and the dust has settled, the true task of philosophy reasserts itself. In Sir Karl Popper's words, 'There is at least one philosophical problem in which all thinking men are interested, the problem of understanding the world in which we live, including ourselves, who are part of that world.'[1] Moreover, Wittgenstein, in a letter to a friend, wrote: 'What is the use of studying philosophy at all if all that it does for you is to enable you to talk with some plausibility about some abstruse questions of logic, etc, and if it does not improve your thinking about important questions of everyday life?'[2] Those who associate Wittgenstein with precisely such 'abtruse' thinking as he here mentions, would do well to take that passage to heart.

In short, philosophy raises questions with which, in Popper's words, all 'thinking' people are concerned. If you reflect, in Wittgenstein's words upon the 'important questions of everyday life', you arrive in due course at ultimate—that is, philosophical—questions. You cannot avoid doing so.

This book, in its two parts, covers the life of philosophical thought in both East and West, and seeks to emphasize continuity. We have adopted no hard and fast rule as to how the 'life' and 'thought' should be related, the tendency being for later chapters to combine philosophy and biography in the way best calculated to illuminate both. For while we have assumed no initial knowledge of philosophy on the reader's

[1] Proceedings of the Aristotelian Society, October 31st 1958, pp. 1–2.
[2] Quoted in *Ludwig Wittgenstein* by Norman Malcolm (1958).

part, save such general notions as have prompted him to embark upon the reading of this book, we have assumed that he will be able to take his philosophy in stronger doses as the book proceeds. For the same reason, we have scrupulously avoided introducing a false simplicity into the exposition of the various systems of thought; for we believe—and the belief is based upon experience—that those who are genuinely interested in philosophy are not likely to tolerate being 'written down' to, since the difficulty in 'writing down' is that of knowing just how far down, and such oversimplification usually leaves us in a trough of puerility where nothing worth while can be said at all.

In the case of thinkers whose ideas are so often presented in abstract form, and who are sometimes in danger of being regarded almost as disembodied intellectuals, the approach through biography, where material for such treatment is available, has that much more to recommend it. Nor do we allow the reader to forget that the greatest thinkers, especially those of the Orient, expound their thought more effectively in their lives.

A question that must have occurred to everyone at one time or another—perhaps lying awake in the small hours—is whether, given the millions of years mankind is likely to remain on this earth—or indeed on more suitable planets, leaving the earth as a kind of planetary park to which a few will return for sentimental reasons—he will ever reach the truth, either about the universe or about himself. It is not perhaps easy to say what 'the truth' in this context means. If it means arriving at some final explanation as to why we are here: why our life-span, in the light of astronomical time, is so ludicrously brief and 'meaningless': and why the universe, if finite, came into existence with the prospect of vanishing one day for ever, as if it had never been, the answer is that such explanation, if forthcoming at all, is likely to be postponed for a considerable while. Indeed, the question posed first by Leibniz 'Why is there anything at all?' is unanswerable. This suggests that mankind must be content in the meantime with fragmentary knowledge, which is all that he has ever had to go by. But he cannot postpone the enquiry how he should live. Metaphysics can wait, but not ethics. This was the lesson of the Buddha in *The Fire Sermon*. It is the lesson of the *Baghavad Gita*. It is the lesson of the scriptures of Judaeo-Christianity. As to the larger metaphysical question, the small-hours-speculation may yield one tentative conclusion. Is it *credible* that a process begun so many millions of years ago—if we are to accept the Big Bang theory—should, at a certain point and without any obvious preparation, have become 'conscious of itself' for a relatively brief period, as if a light were suddenly switched on and then as swiftly extinguished, to be followed by the inevitable playing out of the Second Law of Thermodynamics until the 'heat death' of the universe? Most people, though not all, would be disposed to murmur, 'it is not credible'. Perhaps, therefore, the mystics were right. Man is obstructed in the understanding of his destiny—to use the old rhetorical term—by 'a cloud of unknowing' or a 'veil of Maya'. To the fourteenth century mystic who wrote a book with the former title, the cloud could be penetrated not by some telescopic instrument but by the 'dart of love'; and Immanuel Kant, in his final philosophical treatise, maintained likewise that reality could be penetrated not by the intellect but by the moral consciousness or ethical intuition. As a modern interpreter of Kant has observed, 'the moral life imposes an intimation of transcendent reality'.[1] Without this intimation, man would be less than man: with it, he shows that he can be more. All are capable of that transcendent experience, if they choose: and the choice can be now.

The philosophical quest would therefore seem to have reached its climax in the work of those who, whatever their origin or place in time, have pointed to a dimension which may be called spiritual. But spiritual does not necessarily mean supernatural: many humanists are prepared to speak of man's spiritual nature, as we see in the case of George Santayana. In the Orient, with a few exceptions, such a dimension is taken for granted. The separation in the West between the sacred and the secular, which also dates from about the seventeenth century, has tended to obscure this circumstance. It is often assumed that an academic philosopher, if he has any beliefs at all in a regligious sense, ought to keep them strictly to himself, bringing to the lecture-room a thoroughly 'sanitised' philosophy, guaranteed to hurt no one. Furthermore, as we have said, few thinkers in the West feel it incumbent upon them to 'live' their philosophy: some because it would be too complicated or too embarrassing, and others because, if philosophy is no more than analysis or the clearing up of linguistic 'confusions', the question does not arise. It is the author's hope that the following examples of the philosophical quest, outlined as simply as possible and without any hidden advocacy, may enable readers to make up their own minds on the question of truth or validity. At the very least they may acquaint themselves with what philosophy is about. And they may learn something else. The patient working out of an argument, or the scrupulous analysis of a theory which appears uncongenial, should induce a mood of tolerance and honest candour—a frame of mind in which sympathy and understanding, rather than hostility and rancour, predominate. For if there is one attitude with which philosophizing in the true sense is incompatible, it is fanaticism. The disputatious wranglings in which some philosophers—though never the greatest—have indulged, do not strictly belong to philosophy: they belong to ideological politics, the politics of irreconcilability. A genuine critique is never hostile, but in many respects the reverse. 'Comprehension is inseparable from criticism', wrote R. G. Collingwood, 'in the sense that the one necessarily leads to the other.... If (therefore) criticism must go with comprehension, and if comprehension means sharing the author's experience, criticism cannot be content with mere disagreement: and, in fact, whenever we find a critic systematically contradicting everything an author says, we are sure that he has failed to understand him. There are no doubt occasions when a reader may say of a book, "For my part, I do not propose to spend time on it: it seems to

[1] Roger Scruton, *Kant* (1982), p. 77.

me a mere tissue of errors and confusions." But this is not criticism. Criticism does not begin until the reader has overcome this attitude, and one has submitted to the discipline of following the author's thought and reconstructing in himself the point of view from which it proceeds. When this has been done, any rejection is of necessity qualified by certain concession, a certain degree of sympathy and even assent.'[1]

If, finally, some readers should feel that they have no capacity for philosophical speculation, and can very well get on without troubling themselves about 'ultimate' matters, that in itself is a philosophical position. What we would ask of such persons is that before setting down the burden of thought, they should resolve not to listen to the siren voices of the irrationalists, with their promises of secret knowledge or occult powers. That would be a betrayal. Meanwhile, they cannot do better than turn the page. . . .

E. W. F. TOMLIN

[1] *An Essay in Philosophical Method* (1937), pp. 218–19.

PART ONE

PHILOSOPHERS OF THE EAST

1

THE ORIENTAL VISION

The richest vein

Approach to oriental thought

The aim of this part is twofold: to provide a straightforward account of the life and work of the great thinkers of the Orient, and to attempt to show, in terms intelligible to the ordinary reader, with what remarkable insistence the greatest of these thinkers dwell upon common themes. The account that follows is to be regarded neither as a formal history nor as a source book, still less as a scaffolding upon which the author has attempted to erect a private system of his own. In the case of thinkers whose ideas are presented so often in abstract form, and who are sometimes in danger of being regarded almost as disembodied intellects, the approach through biography, where material for such treatment is available, has much to recommend it. We propose to maintain the general expository approach: we do not allow the reader to forget that the greatest thinkers, especially those of the Orient, expound their thought more effectively in their lives.

It has sometimes been maintained that philosophers, as distinct from other people, ought not to have any private lives: or if, as in the case of Peter Abelard, private life and public life were inextricably intermingled, that this was a regrettable aberration, which the serious student of philosophy should either regard with amused tolerance or else ignore. This is surely a mistaken attitude. Failure to 'practise what they preach' is a reproach frequently levelled at Western philosophers. To say that the great oriental sages were too busy living their philosophy to write about it is perhaps not far from the truth. Apart from the fact that the Buddha, Christ and Mohammed wrote nothing, their disciples have to a great extent repaired this deficiency, and their later followers have perhaps overcompensated for it.

This raises the question of philosophical language and style. Although the language of science must necessarily contain technical terms, the language of philosophy needs to be as free from technicalities as possible. As Schopenhauer pointed out, 'the first rule, indeed by itself a sufficient condition, of a good style is *to have something to say*'. Style is not a framework into which a particular context has to be fitted. Only when language is transparent to thought, so that it no longer obtrudes itself, can it be said to be truly philosophical.

Some readers may protest that their way of understanding the world, and themselves as part of that world, is not through thought and language at all, but rather through feeling and intuition; that they would rather go to the poets, the artists, the musicians (''Tis we musicians know,' as Browning said in *Abt Vogler*), or to the mystics for enlightenment than to professional philosophers; and that, in their view, some things are by their very nature beyond the scope of philosophy. Such a protest must be taken seriously. In their preference for an aesthetic or intuitional rather than a purely rational approach, they have on their side some of the greatest minds in history. Indeed, in so far as their grasp is successful, they are not to be ridiculed but to be envied. Nor are they mistaken in their ultimate aim. There is a limit to what can be grasped by reason alone. All the great philosophers, but above all the oriental sages, have recognized the fact: and Wittgenstein, who was a sage in his way, observed at the end of the *Tractatus Logico—Philosophicus*, 'of that whereof we cannot speak we must be silent'. As William Barrett has observed: 'The positivists ... who profess to follow Wittgenstein took this silence to be a sign that there was nothing there at all to talk about. For them indeed there was nothing there; the part of life Wittgenstein valued most simply did not exist for them.'[1] There is a Hindu saying that 'the use of words is to get beyond words'. Indeed, what other use have they? The faculty beyond and above reason used to be called intellect, a faculty of higher intuition at the opposite pole to the sensory intuition, until the meaning of that term was altered, like so many others, in the seventeenth century. But this does not exempt us from pursuing the exercise of reason as far as it will go. For, despite evidence to the contrary, man remains the rational animal; and it is only by the plodding exercise of his reason that he has achieved the degree of civilization that he has. Moreover, given this always precarious achievement, it seems clear that his reason, rather than anything else, will prevent him from throwing it away. For, as a great historian has said, man has gone back, but he has never gone the whole way back.[2]

Immersion in oriental philosophical writing over a period of years has led the author to believe that much of its attraction for Western readers resides first in its exotic terminology, and secondly in its apparent and to some extent inevitable vagueness. Words such as *Nirvana, Karma, Vedanta*, and *Maya* produce, it seems, an effect very much like hypnosis, above all perhaps upon those to whom their meaning is unknown. Admittedly few ideas of this order can be rendered into English with the precision demanded by Western philosophers for their own concepts. We have therefore refrained from introducing more than the minimum of technical terms, even where the temptation proved strongest, as in the sections on the *Upanishads*, the Yoga systems of Patanjali, and the Hindu doctrines or *darshanas*. And secondly, we have throughout endeavoured to bring home to the reader that ideas which need to be rendered in vague or general terms are often the reverse of vague in the original. If, as Patanjali main-

[1] *The Illusion of Technique* (1979).
[2] Arnold Toynbee.

tained, there are thirty-six forms of consciousness, or, as Kapila maintained, twenty-five 'realities', we are bound to miss endless subtleties of meaning by rendering their thought in the half dozen terms available at most in English.

How ought we to approach oriental thought? In the case of some of the more 'difficult' Western thinkers, such as St. Thomas Aquinas, Kant, or Hegel, we have formed the habit of approaching their works indirectly. We have climbed scaffolding of our own construction and peered with awe at the immense edifices before us. Such surveys and distant scrutinies are not without their utility—or, glancing at some of the pages ahead of us, we may presume to hope as much; but it would be regrettable if, from fear of intellectual vertigo, we were to rest content with such external appraisal. This book would not have assumed its present form, nor acquired any merit that it may possess, if the author had not based his study as far as possible upon the original texts. These are now largely accessible to anyone who takes the trouble to seek them, for the translation of the Eastern scriptures has reached in our day a high pitch of excellence.

Even so, the reader must not presume to imagine that by reading the *Vedic* Hymns, a few select *Upanishads*, some of the Jataka Books, the *Analects* of Confucius, and some *suras* of the Koran, he has assimilated the chief products of oriental thought. The corpus of Eastern literature is enormous; it is said—to take a minor example—that only one ten-thousandth part of T'ang poetry has been translated[1] What Mr. Gai Eaton calls in his recent book the 'richest vein'[2] will not be quarried in our lifetime. We have so far merely scratched the surface. At the same time, it is evident that people in the Occident are becoming increasingly alive to the necessity of studying oriental thought. That the condition of oriental studies still remains far from satisfactory is generally admitted. When the government signifies its alarm on the subject, we may fairly assume that a criticial stage has been reached. The findings of the Scarborough Commission as set forth in its Report published in 1947 were such as to spur the authorities to strengthen the oriental departments of our universities. And although such provision was pronounced to be desirable in the 'national interest' and as part of our 'imperial responsibilities'—a somewhat belated recognition in view of the powerful movement towards autonomy in Asia—the motives behind it are on the whole good: for Asia is more than half the world in terms of population, and the Western domination is now at an end.

The history of India, for example, sheds a flood of light upon the problem of what it is that constitutes a civilization or culture: for while India has been conquered and dominated again and again, its distinctive philosophy or metaphysics has survived not as a curiosity or a 'cultural heritage' (as the classical Western philosophy has survived within our own civilization) but rather as the means whereby a

[1] The T'ang dynasty (AD 618–905) was China's most civilized epoch.
[2] *The Richest Vein: Eastern tradition and modern thought* (Faber, 1949). The phrase is Thoreau's.

vast community has preserved its conscious identity. The resulting unity, to quote that remarkable Orientalist, René Guénon, is a 'doctrinal unity'. Now that the Western domination is at an end, it is incumbent upon us to treat with respect that which we tended formerly to regard with aloof patronage. In short, we have ceased to teach; it is time that we should learn.

It is often assumed that a people may be best understood by reference to its political history and geographical situation. The efforts of modern nations to understand one another are dictated to a large extent by a latent fear: and when international conflicts periodically break out, frantic appeals are launched for the services of missionaries, modern language teachers, historians and archaeologists. We know only too well how, in spite of these efforts, nation can still fail to understand nation to an extent that may spell disaster. The truth is that a people consists in that in which it believes. While we may find it difficult to discover what its beliefs are—and for such investigation scepticism and infidelity are as important as faith itself—all other information or evidence as to a people's likely behaviour is insufficient, and may prove misleading. It is possible that much of the turmoil associated with the 'British connection' in India was due to a failure to appreciate the importance of this aspect of the Indian character, if aspect is not too slight a word: the failure in India may have been at bottom a religious failure.[1] Even if religion were the 'illusion' that Freud declared it to be, as distinct from the oriental view that all is illusion except religion, the fact of belief would need still to be taken into account: for if a man thinks something to be true, this conviction, however preposterous, will inevitably influence his conduct. The words of Georges Sorel are particularly relevant to a study of the oriental mentality: '*Les religions constituent un scandale particulièrement grave pour l'intellectualiste, car il ne saurait ni les regarder comme étant sans portée historique, ni les expliquer.*'[2]

Characteristics of oriental and occidental thought

Those who approach the philosophers of the Orient after a deep study of Western thought cannot fail to be struck by one salient feature. Whereas so many Western philosophers, especially of the modern era, dwell upon minute technical problems and appear to avoid generalizations about the universe as a whole, the great philosophers of the Orient never lose sight of the fundamental problem, namely that which concerns life's meaning and purpose. From the oldest of coherent philosophical speculations in the Hindu *Vedas* and *Upanishads* to the sages of modern India, the quest not so much for certainty as for truth has continued without relaxation. Nor has this preoccupation been confined to a few men of distinction, learning, or piety in each generation; it has exercised the minds of those anonymous, patient, toiling millions with which, to the Western eye, the Orient is

[1] Cf. T. S. Eliot, *Notes Towards the Definition of Culture* (London, 1948), pp. 64–5.

[2] *Réflexions sur la Violence.*

peopled. Hence the much-quoted and commonly accepted distinction between 'Western materialism' and 'Eastern mysticism'.

When we come to examine closely the thought of the oriental philosophers, we find that such a generalization needs to be qualified. Eastern thought has its materialistic aspect, just as Western thought has its strong vein of mysticism. Furthermore, an extreme form of idealism such as involves the denial of the reality of matter itself is likely, by way of reaction, to turn into its opposite. For example, a theory which repudiates the existence of the human body is found upon examination to be largely concerned with the preservation of physical health. Buddhist mysticism, commonly supposed to be among the purest and most exalted forms of idealism, is linked with a theory of knowledge that would satisfy the most diehard Western materialist or positivist. Finally, in contrast to the upright and noble Confucius, the Orient can produce more than one distinguished 'moralist' whose cynicism and cunning go far beyond anything preached by Machiavelli himself.[1]

Those elements common to both Eastern and Western thought should confirm us in the belief, so often repudiated, that the human mind is everywhere one and the same, or at least that it operates in the same way. We should therefore avoid overdoing distinctions. That an Andaman pigmy and a Middle West farmer in the United States should employ a different system of logic is inconceivable, though they clearly start from very different assumptions. What lends to the study of Eastern thought its particular fascination is the fact that it is not merely vastly older than Western thought but that it represents far more of a continuity. To survey the long history of human thought is to observe that Western philosophical enquiry is merely an offshoot, though a flourishing one, of the oriental parent tree, just as Europe (in the phrase of Paul Valéry) is merely a tiny cap jutting off Asia. This is no doubt the reason why European thinkers such as Schelling and Schopenhauer and also Goethe and Tolstoy have been struck, on making acquaintance with Eastern philosophy, by its amazing profundity. It is indeed profound; and its profundity is that which results from having deep roots.

Presuppositions of oriental thought

The remarkable continuity of oriental thought, the long-hallowed tradition of speculation upon ultimate values, have been responsible for a further popular notion, namely that the oriental mind is essentially static. Here again the phrase may have meaning when applied to industrial organization, or methods of hygiene, or even diplomatic practice; it requires considerable qualification when applied to the oriental conception of life. That conception is not static; it were better described as rhythmical. It does not repudiate changelessness, but rather it is obsessed with the idea of eternal recurrence. To try to determine that which originally gave rise to philosophical speculation

[1] E.g. Kautilya Chanakya, adviser to the Indian ruler Chandragupta (*c.* 322–298 BC); also Yang Chu (*c.* 390 BC), and Hsun-Tze (305–235 BC). For the latter, see Chapter 8.

in the world, and when first it took systematic form, is no doubt a dangerous and possibly a futile game; but as far as the Orient is concerned, the process of animal and human generation, the rhythm of sowing and reaping, and likewise the daily miracle of the sun's birth and death, would appear to have suggested at least one ancient metaphysical doctrine, namely that of the 'transmigration of souls'. This doctrine indeed has been preserved by Indian thought from remotest antiquity.[1] Accepting it with neither question nor proof, such innovators as Gotama Buddha merely sought to deepen its significance and to prescribe means of diminishing its terrors; for it is a doctrine at once terrible and sublime. Nor did a sceptic such as Mahavira, founder of the Jain religion (599–527 BC), succeed in loosening its hold on the common people. For what after all is the doctrine of transmigration save a belief that the law applying to almost everything in nature applies likewise—and perhaps pre-eminently—to the soul of man?

So thoroughly has the oriental mind been preoccupied with this notion of reincarnation, or the sempiternal rebirth of the human soul in an infinite number of guises, that the chief task of every great Eastern prophet has been to show how such intolerable recurrence might be avoided. And since so great an evil could hardly be expected to yield to an early remedy, it was felt that the annihilation of desire—if possible at all and even if possible only after repeated experiments—was not too high a price to pay for final release from consciousness. Instead of being calmed and soothed by the notion of perpetual tranquillity, the Eastern mind is merely tantalized by it. What the Eastern sage or fakir remains most clearly aware of, at least this side of the condition of *Samadhi*,[2] is the storm and stress of instinct, passion, and desire. Men do not perpetually talk of inward peace if they already have it as an inalienable possession.

In the history of Western thought there is a thing called philosophy and there is a thing called theology; and it has usually been possible, except during certain periods such as the Middle Ages, to distinguish between the two. In the history of Eastern thought there is only a thing called theology. This is true even of the humanist thought of Confucius and Mencius, which is merely an ethical doctrine become detached from the religion providing its sanction. Philosophy pursued as a secular game, a technique to be acquired at a university or extramural seminar, a recipe to enable the student to be formidable in argument, is not merely a Western product, but a product of quite recent date. In the Orient it is impossible to be a philosopher without being also a sage. In the Occident it is not only possible, it is highly to be recommended. For it is difficult to be a sage in Europe except on a very high income.

Although we have stressed the futility of seeking to explain the origins of philosophical thought, it is not unreasonable to suppose, following the Italian philosopher Giambattista Vico, that such thought or

[1] Some of the reasons why it should for so long have obsessed the oriental mind are analysed in Chapter 5.

[2] The state of final release from consciousness. See page 233.

systems of thought originated in an ambience of myth.[1] There is a logical, if not a temporal, priority of imagination to thought; and so long as philosophy remains associated with religion or with mysticism, so long will it remain wedded to myth. In Western thought the divorce between philosophy and myth took place at least as early as Aristotle's reaction against Plato; and no doubt the importance assigned to myth in Plato's philosophy has led certain commentators to suppose him to have been immersed in Eastern lore, and even to have undertaken secret journeys to Babylon and Persia. As Western philosophy developed, Christianity filled the gap created by the expulsion of the pagan deities, or at least their retreat, as it were, 'underground'. And when, at the close of the Middle Ages, the intellectual influence of the Christian faith began to wane, the purely mythical impulse reasserted itself, but thereafter in association with the adventures of the new scientific hero called Matter. No doubt the philosophical impulse properly so-called, i.e. the disinterested enquiry into reasons, causes, and evidence, first took its origin from the clash of tribal myth, whether as a result of conquest, natural fusion for defence against man or nature, travel, or exogamy.[2] The claims of rival deities, then as now, had to be debated and assessed in human courts. The growth and refinement of man's reasoning faculty is the consequence of divine multiplicity.

It is tempting for the historian of Western thought to attribute the peculiar mental qualities of the Ionians, their curiosity and aptitude for enquiry, to the factor of environment and environment alone. Now environment is a blanket word; we are never quite sure how much it is intended to cover. If, however, environment means simply geographical conditions, then these are never a 'cause' in any orthodox sense of the word. To assert that man is the product of his surroundings, is to say he is part of them, in which case there is nothing positive to be surrounded. Environment in the strict sense is the cause of that which man chooses to make out of it. When the romantic Hellenist has drawn our attention to the idyllic beauty of the Greek countryside and coast, suggesting that such firmness, clarity of outline and atmospheric 'numinousness' provided direct inspiration to the early Ionian thinkers, he fails to explain how it is that only with Thales of Miletus in the 6th century BC did the Greeks begin to respond to this particular form of stimulation.[3] Communities living in circumstances no less propitious have been remarkable for their lethargy and lack of achievement. The mixture of races, the growth of trade, the experience of seafaring—these were presumably the decisive factors in the emergence of the Ionian spirit of enquiry: for what people having made contact successively with Egyptians, Phoenicians, Chaldaeans and Babylonians, nations so diverse in customs, language and type, could have failed to make comparison one with the other, and having compared, to judge, and having judged, to co-ordinate?

[1] For further treatment of this subject the reader is referred to the extremely interesting essay entitled 'Myth and Reality' in the volume *Before Philosophy*, ed. Frankfort (Penguin Books, 1949).

[2] i.e. compulsory marriage outside the tribe.

[3] We would refer the reader also to the chapter on Islam.

The Unitive Vision

We should therefore look upon Western thought as the point at which the oriental imagination became articulated into action, just as the churches of Christendom are the practical manifestation of Eastern mysticism. The growth of applied science is similarly an inevitable accompaniment of the Western philosophical approach; for we can act only in a world that we believe to be both real and worth inhabiting. Now characteristics such as reality and value are precisely those which Eastern thought, with certain exceptions, refuses to ascribe to the natural world. Similarly, the philosophers of the Occident, with even fewer exceptions (such as Schopenhauer), assume that man's primary duty is to cultivate his conscious life, to increase his awareness of the world of sense, with the object of achieving mastery over his environment. Compare the oriental attitude. So far as Hinduism and Buddhism are concerned, the aim is to effect an escape from consciousness, to obliterate awareness of the self, to doubt even to the point of negation the reality of the world of sense. An exception is that of Chinese thought, which is on the whole individualist, humanist, almost egocentric, certainly familocentric. Nor can we ignore the paradox of the Hindu sage or fakir who, by his very isolation and eccentricity, comes in time to assume that very 'individuality' which he is striving so obstinately to renounce.

In the chapters that follow we shall undertake to survey the history of oriental thought from the earliest times, using as our landmarks the great figures who have deserved, more even than in the Occident, the name of leaders and sages, and of whom a great number seem more than human in their personality, and some few of almost divine-human compound. The Western mind has tended to separate the various faculties of man, just as it has separated the sciences, the literary *genres*, and the various professions. A man is a poet or an aeroplane fitter. Biology is a science in its own right. This piece of verse is a lyric. We have a category into which everything can be fitted, and knowledge is sometimes identified with the capacity merely to read the labels. The Orient has eschewed this tendency to separation. Its philosophers are at once poets, moralists, statesmen. Its religion is a blend of poetic myth and precise reasoning. Knowledge is more than a collection of information; it is a species of visionary wisdom. We in the Western world have for too long remained blind to this unitive viewpoint.

The Morning of Reason

Writing at the time of the French Revolution, Thomas Paine expressed his conviction that 'a morning of reason' had dawned in Europe, and that the dark night of superstition was being finally rolled back.[1]

When was the first 'morning of reason'? That is a question which has never ceased to puzzle historians, anthropologists, philosophers, and psychologists. It must have taken place, if the expression is at all accu-

[1] Cf. *The Rights of Man* (1791).

rate, long before the earliest recorded history, and possibly earlier than such pre-history as we are able to deduce from rock painting, implement, menhir, or barrow. 'I want to know,' said Voltaire in his *Essai sur les Moeurs*, 'what were the steps by which men passed from barbarism to civilization.' So indeed do we all. In spite of great progress in archaeological investigation, whereby at least half a dozen civilizations—Egyptian, Sumerian, Babylonian, Hittite, Cretan, and Dravidian—have been uncovered, we are no nearer to answering that question than was Voltaire: we merely know how much farther we have to go back—to find men already to some extent civilized.

The evidence of art is misleading. The cave pictures and even the sculpture of the Paleolithic or Old Stone Age (from *c.* 100,000 BC) is superior, judged on present evidence, to anything produced during the New Stone Age (*c.* 5000 BC or earlier), save perhaps in respect of pottery; and not merely may the cave paintings of the Dordogne and Andalusia be accounted exquisite masterpieces, but they are clearly part of a tradition already of some antiquity. We cannot imagine them as either isolated 'sports' or the works of some extraordinary genius. It is possible that the works of genius have perished, and that these are merely the conventional efforts of journeymen.

Of the earliest writing we must speak with similar reservation. Whether script was used first for recording numbers, symbolized by plain strokes or fingers (digits), or was merely an abstraction from some kind of gesture-pictography such as the Chinese *Ku-wan*, we may legitimately assume that its development and perfection presupposes a considerable unwritten, unrecorded, prealphabete civilization. An eminent authority, Dr David Diringer, believes that the Alphabet as we now know it must have been invented in Syrio-Palestine about the middle of the Second Millenium BC, but the Egyptians were using an alphabet as early as 3000 BC. That writing was originally an art or craft for the few, or at least for recording recondite and select subject-matter, may be deduced from the antiquity of the word *Hieroglyph*, which means literally a 'sacred carving'. Nor has the activity of writing altogether lost its arcane significance in a society which, like that of the present day, still respects the literary as opposed to the merely literate, those who 'write' as opposed to those who can write. Finally, it is misleading to draw inferences from the mental condition of tribes or peoples contemptuously labelled 'savage', if only because our conception of savagery has lately undergone considerable revision: partly as a result of the emulation by some civilized peoples of methods hitherto regarded as primitive, and partly because the progress of anthropological studies has disposed of certain persistent notions concerning the 'irrationality' of much primitive culture.

Moreover, the 'savages' whose habits have been studied in recent times are those already undergoing corruption by contact with Western civilization: a contact that has tended first to demoralize them and then as often as not to bring about their extinction.[1] Certain practices

[1] Anthropologists have devoted insufficient attention to ascertaining the 'savages' own definition of 'savage'. The results might be illuminating.

conventionally associated with primitive culture, such as magic and even sorcery, are now regarded as by no means confined thereto, but rather as forming an element in all civilization. Indeed, their absence or neglect, or worst of all their deliberate eradication by rationalist-minded persons, may be the cause of serious harm to a civilization's stability. And that is another reason why Western readers should seek a better understanding of the thought of the Orient, where the dissociation of religion and philosophy, magic and science, has been achieved with much less violence than in Europe and America.

The Notion of a Golden Age

Sooner or later the enquirer into the origins of enquiry itself finds himself speculating upon the possibility of some kind of fall from grace, some cataclysm whereby mankind, hitherto the child of nature, was obliged to fend for himself, to 'stop and think', to assume the burden of freedom. From such a moment, it would seem, philosophical speculation must have begun its limping career. The story of the Flood, regarded by our devout ancestors as a legend, has become for their sceptical successors a historical reality; and if the researches of Sir Leonard Woolley in Iraq do not prove the Biblical account of Noah and the Ark, at least they suggest its symbolic truth.[1] For our present purpose we need not ask whether the so-called Fall of Man was a historical occurrence, or whether, as the Higher Criticism tended to suggest, it was a purely spiritual one (whatever that may mean). What we need to ask is whether the society anterior to this Fall represented, as is usually assumed, a kind of Golden Age. Why the natural or uncivilized should necessarily be more peaceful, serene, or desirable than the 'unnatural' or civilized is assumed more often than proved. In some very interesting books Professor Perry has stated a case for supposing there to have existed a pre-civilized condition of mankind, not too incredibly remote, in which war, even inter-tribal scrapping, was entirely unknown.

Such a theory, if true, does not necessarily entail the view that social life was one prolonged idyll and had remained in this condition from the beginning. From inspection of the earliest known (and therefore probably quite 'late') legal code, that of Hammurabi, for instance, we obtain an impression not of simple dealings or straightforward human relationships, common disputes or obvious means of redress, but very much the reverse: a contentious, right-conscious sophisticated community, in which men quarrelled and had always been known to quarrel as much as they do now, and probably took the law into their own hands more frequently. The rule of 'an eye for an eye and a tooth for a tooth' was probably the common law of antiquity, though not the only law, if we may judge from the earliest known legal document (now in the Egyptian section of the British Museum), dealing with a case of disputed inheritance. The more 'natural' human life may be, the more painful in many respects it becomes. If we find hints

[1] For an account of the various Flood legends, see Chapter 3.

in Hesiod or even Plato of a remote Golden Age, we need not accept their implied suggestion that it was a life of undiluted bliss and serenity. The Golden Age, as H. J. Massingham finally concludes in his brilliant little study,[1] is mankind's vague memory of its own youth: hence we must locate it at no particular point in time. But if we could recapture in their identity the feelings experienced in youth, we should recognize that period for what it is, namely a time of mental and physical distress from which we longed to be delivered. The Golden Age is golden only in retrospect, and merely gilded upon examination.

[1] *The Golden Age: the story of human nature* (London, 1927).

2

The Egyptians

Thus was Ptah satisfied after he had made all things and every divine word

A Young Science

The insight gained during the last century into Egypt's past has altered our whole conception of history. We may also ask to what extent it has altered our conception of moral and philosophical thought. For apart from its antiquity, the civilization of Egypt differs from all other known civilizations in at least two respects, in its length and in its continuity.

As the story of Eastern philosophy begins with such speculations as have been preserved in Egyptian records, we are now in a better position to enquire how far back in the past man's efforts at ordered thought can be traced. For we are curious to know what evidence there is of *civilization*—meaning thereby an ordered system of society dominated by a coherent view of life—having antedated the existence of written records, and by what conceivable stretch of time.

In order to answer these questions, it will be useful to touch for a moment both upon the rediscovery of ancient Egypt, or in other words the history of the young science of Egyptology, and upon the reasons for the fact, now largely accepted by historians, that Egypt was the birthplace of philosophical speculation as we know it.

Apart from the extremely interesting and largely accurate account of Herodotus, the Greek historian (484–425 BC), and of certain other Greek and also Roman writers, very little contemporary information about Egyptian life and culture has come down to us. It is true that we may derive much valuable information from both Testaments of the Bible, and we shall later be able to observe the extent to which Hebrew civilization was based upon that of Egypt. Unlike Greece, Rome, and Israel, however, Egypt produced no great historians and few reliable chroniclers. Of the latter, an Egyptian priest named Manetho, who lived between 300 and 250 BC compiled a list of Egyptian kings from all but the earliest times; or rather, since his work has survived only in fragments and transcripts, this list of rulers is the one contribution to knowledge with which he may fairly be credited. It took the form of a division into dynasties, such as our history books and museums have made tolerably familiar; but this division, which was never very enlightening to the non-specialist, has proved misleading. In the first place it suggested, what was not necessarily true, that the kings grouped in a particular dynasty belonged invariably to the same family. Secondly, it failed to make clear that certain dynasties, instead of preceding or succeeding one another, were, in consequence of political rivalries, contemporaneous. Thirdly, being based upon incomplete evidence, it began to number the dynasties from the beginning of what historians now call the Second Union (roughly 3500–2631 BC), thereby omitting to take account of any previous social epoch such as that which has now come within the purview of Egyptologists as the First Union.

The modern study of Egyptology was the by-product of a venture inspired by motives far removed from those conventionally associated with research. When Napoleon invaded Egypt in 1797 he took with him a large party of *savants*, chiefly scientists and archaeologists. With whatever degree of sincerity Bonaparte himself embraced oriental ideas—at one point he proclaimed his intention of becoming a Moslem, and it appears that in spite of certain disqualifications (the authorities finally decided that circumcision was not an indispensable condition of embracing Islam) he was officially admitted to the faith—his band of research workers made good use of their time. The publication in 1809 of their learned *Description of Egypt* is evidence of this. Perhaps the most valuable result of the expedition, however, was the discovery by a French officer, who happened to be working at Rosetta in the Nile Delta, of a basalt stone bearing an inscription in three different scripts. As one of these scripts, Greek, was known, the scholars were able to translate forthwith what proved to be a decree issued by Ptolemy V Epiphanus (205–181 BC). The presumption, which in due course proved correct, was that the other two scripts, namely Hieroglyphics and a more popular cursive script called Demotic, carried a faithful rendering of the Greek version. Nevertheless, the process of transliteration and translation raised a variety of difficulties. Published in its entirety in the above-mentioned report, the inscription on the Rosetta Stone, which is now in the British Museum, long exercised the intelligence of scholars in every European country, particularly Germany, England, and France. But it was to a young French student of Egyptology, Jean-François Champollion (1790–1832), that we owe the inscription's final decipherment.

Something of the magnitude of Champollion's achievement may be judged from two circumstances. In the first place the text ran on without regard to division between words; and, secondly, neither Champollion nor any other contemporary scholar knew at the outset whether hieroglyphic signs represented ideas, sounds, or syllables: in short, whether they were ideographic, phonetic, or merely syllabic. Nor did the experts realize, save after prolonged deliberation, that the hieroglyphic script was in fact based upon a combination of ideographic and phonetic characters, some of the latter acting merely as aids to comprehension rather than as elements in pronunciation, a fact which Champollion originally deduced from the preponderance of hieroglyphic signs over the Greek. To mention all the problems with which Champollion was confronted is unnecessary; we may merely note that it took him fourteen years to 'break' the hieroglyphic code, and another ten to acquire sufficient familiarity with the language to compile a grammar and dictionary—and incidentally to kill himself with overwork. By 1822, the learned world was put in possession of the means of understanding, however partially, the mind of ancient Egypt. Not since the closing of the Egyptian temples in the second century AD had access to such riches been possible.

Egypt as the Cradle of Civilization

The story of Egyptian excavation, which naturally received fresh impetus from the mastery of hieroglyphics, has been a record of patience and surprise, with no small admixture of romance. Moreover, it is a story to which new chapters are being added year by year. A new discovery on the banks of the Nile seldom fails to provide material for journalists, since Egyptian archaeology has received a good press in both Europe and America; nor is any European museum regarded as complete without its painted coffin or even its tattered mummy. Beyond the fact that the Egyptians practised the art of embalming and built enormous pyramids, the general public is not always aware of what it is that these industrious people achieved. No doubt the origins of thought and the first awakening of a moral and social conscience are less dramatic than the unearthing of a tomb or the prising open of a sarcophagus.

For our purposes we are interested in the Egyptians as being the first people, the first nation even, to debate those moral issues—issues of good and evil as applied to life itself, and issues of right and wrong as applied to human conduct—with which we are equally concerned today. Although man had perhaps been in existence as much as a million years before the first recognizable 'literature' was produced, we cannot in the present state of our knowledge conceive there to have been any similar attempt at coherent philosophizing before that of the Egyptian sages. The Babylonians, as we shall see, were in certain respects original thinkers and even more original scientists; but their religious speculations early assumed a superstitious character from which few positive or fruitful conclusions issued. Finally, the civilization of Elam probably antedates by several hundred years that of both Babylon and Egypt; but, apart from the potter's wheel, we know of no specific contribution to civilization made by that obscure people.

Why, then, Egypt? Can we explain how it was that a country so oddly endowed, if not victimized, by nature should have become the 'cradle of civilization'?

Without entering into physiographical details, we may begin by pointing out that after the slow desiccation of North Africa at the beginning of the Neolithic period (*c.* 5000 BC) Egypt remained a comparatively protected area. That the Nile valley has been inhabited by man from the very earliest times is now generally believed. Excavations begun as long ago—or as recently—as 1894 have furnished us with a good deal of information concerning the prehistoric inhabitants of the Nile valley. Many of these people must have sought that fertile region as drought overtook them and their flocks. Of the characteristics of the Paleolithic[1] inhabitants of Egypt we know little, though archaeologists do not despair of finding a skeleton from which the 'original' Egyptian might be known. Such cemeteries as have been unearthed suggest that the Egyptians of the Neolithic period and onwards were assured of at least one of the conditions of civilization, namely a continuity of food supply. No other people on earth had, it appears, enjoyed this privilege before. Furthermore, they had learned both to work metals and to domesticate animals; and from their burial customs it seems that they nourished that unshakable belief in an after-life for which, as their culture developed, they sought by diverse means to equip themselves. In due course we shall see how their attitude to this world and the next affected the development of moral ideas.

Ever since Herodotus called Egypt the 'gift of the Nile', it has been customary to regard that country as the happy product of purely physical conditions, as if man had scarcely a hand in the matter. This is a serious misapprehension. Egypt is an oasis (itself an Egyptian word). Now anyone familiar with desert country knows that such oases, however well situated, depend for their survival as inhabited areas upon the exertions of man. Where man chooses to live, there he makes life tolerable, and where he is forced to live, there he will make life possible. That the fertility of Egypt depends upon a regular inundation, caused by rainfall upon the hills of Abyssinia swelling the White Nile from June onwards, is only a half-truth. Such a gross surcharge of water and mud, though varying in quantity from year to year, would prove as much of a menace as a blessing were it permitted to reach the Nile Delta unchecked. Indeed, we know from various ancient records that the Nile, its flood waters assuming unusual proportions, has several times brought havoc upon the land. The ten plagues described in the *Book of Exodus* probably represent, as Flinders Petrie has well shown in his book *Egypt and Israel*, successive phases of such a catastrophe. In short, the survival of Egypt is due to a work of man, namely irrigation. That is as true today as it was five, ten, and perhaps a hundred thousand years ago.

Traces of the irrigation system of ancient Egypt show it to have been a highly intricate organization. And when we consider that the land, being 2,000 kilometres long and only a few kilometres wide, contained no more than 30,000 square kilometres of cultivated soil (i.e. 3·5 per cent), we perceive that the problem of irrigation is nothing but a problem of government, and vice versa.[2] To ensure not merely the control of the yearly inundation but its equitable distribution, the govern-

[1] i.e. the enormously long period preceding the Neolithic Age, and beginning about 500,000 BC.

[2] On the narrowest part of the Nile at Kummeh (east bank) may be seen the mark of the river's level made by a Twelfth-Dynasty Pharaoh 4000 years ago. It is about 30 feet *higher* than the level reached today.

ment of Egypt needed to be both strong and centralized. That is to say, the Pharaoh was obliged to use all possible means, including the assumption of divinity, to ensure his political authority. From the point of view of administration, however, the land divided itself naturally into small districts or *nomes*, of which there were forty; and more than one ancient papyrus affords us an insight into the tyranny which local rulers, believing themselves secure from governmental supervision, might occasionally wield.[1] A common danger, which in Egypt's case was the danger of extinction, is an unfailing means of unification. Thus it happened that Egypt, once the sources of its strength and weakness were understood by its people, developed not merely the first major social organization (the population of ancient Egypt was probably about seven millions), but, as we have pointed out, the most enduring human society so far known. Precisely how early the first unification of Egypt took place was not realized by those who, accepting the original order of dynasties, dated the reign of King Menes from about the year 3300 BC. It is to modern archaeologists such as Flinders Petrie and Breasted that we owe our knowledge, such as it is, of the First Union, which is thought to date from at least 4000 BC.[2]

It is the custom to honour the astronomer who detects a new planet, the chemist who isolates a new element, the physicist who propounds a new law of nature. For reasons which are not apparent, we seldom appreciate the achievement of the archaeologist or historian who discovers a new age. This is regrettable, because nothing is at once more exhilarating and chastening to the mind than the opening of a new vista in the past. If we cannot yet say how or why civilization began, we are at least better able to tackle these questions once we know, as we now think we do, when it began.

No writer has done more to throw light upon the origins of civilization and the development of thought than the American archaeologist J. H. Breasted. A life devoted to excavation in the Middle East, and particularly in Egypt, puts him in the best position to undertake that revision of historical perspective which recent discoveries, both his own and other people's, had rendered necessary. In defining what he called, not inaccurately, the New Past, Breasted drew attention to the fact that civilized life, as we understand it, must have grown up in the thousand years between 3500 BC and 2500 BC, the period of the Second Union. To grasp so remote an epoch is not easy; but some idea of its uniqueness may be appreciated from the fact that Europe, at this time and for many centuries after, was still in the Stone Age. By 'civilization' Breasted primarily implied two things: first a social organization based upon some measure of law and order, and secondly a conscious purpose animating that order, whereby the citizens, or at least a group of them, seem bent upon pursuing certain ideals of conduct, even if the latter should be more honoured in the breach than in the observance.

[1] See the story of the Eloquent Peasant, page 41–2.

[2] On a fragment of the royal annals in the Cairo museum, Breasted discovered representations of kings of the pre-Dynastic period wearing double crowns, symbolic of this early union.

This general definition is important, because the archaeologist's spade has turned up evidence of several civilizations older than, or at least as old as, that of Egypt: for example Sumeria, Elam, and Babylon. Of these we shall have more to say in due course. In the meantime we may examine Breasted's contention that Egyptian civilization not merely outlasted and perhaps outshone every other, but substantially contributed, through its influence upon the Hebrews, to the development of our own. During this unique thousand years the civilization of Babylon was likewise developing, though with nothing like the same continuity and along much less intellectual lines. But what does our Western civilization owe to the thought of Babylon? Little enough, save that which was appropriated by the Hebrews, including the story of the great flood, which, as we saw, was probably less of a myth than a real calamity in the Mesopotamian basin.[1] The code of Hammurabi, in spite of its enlightened provisions, does not represent a milestone in ethical thought as do the remarkable Egyptian documents to which we are about to turn.

Civilization written and unwritten

It will be clear that the civilization to which we refer is exclusively a written civilization. Some historians have maintained, or at least assumed, that civilization began with the invention of letters. There is no reason to suppose that this was so. The impulse to collate, to compile, to record, probably finds expression at the point at which civilization, as hitherto defined, is already some way advanced, perhaps even beyond the stage of maturity, certainly many centuries after birth. If, for example, we are right in assuming that the First Union in Egypt dates from about 4000 BC, it is hardly surprising that no written records should be found until at least 1500 years later. Moreover, no public monuments belonging to this epoch have been discovered. But we should consider a further point: how many years of experiment, of temporary or abortive alliance, of diplomatic manœuvre, of competition for leadership, of the ousting of rivals, of the expulsion of foreigners,[2] must have passed before that first national union, so evidently precarious, was itself achieved? We possess no materials for answering these questions. All we can say is that the civilizing process, having come to so early a climax, must have started earlier than we can at present conceive, or so early as not to have had a start at all, if by that we presuppose an epoch of human life devoid of even the most elementary organization. If, however, we presuppose such a condition of mankind, we are faced with the further mystery of how man should have succeeded in issuing from it: a mystery almost as difficult to solve as that of the evolution of man from animal creation.

These matters, apart from their inherent difficulty, hardly come within the scope of our study. What is more relevant, though equally

[1] See also Chapter 3, page 78.

[2] The Egyptians made a distinction between 'men' (i.e. themselves) and 'foreigners', just as the word for the 'land' of Egypt also meant the 'earth' (i.e. the civilized world).

involved in difficulty, is the question as to why man, having evolved a technique for recording his thoughts, should have proceeded to develop them with such rapidity that within a few thousand years he should have acquired his present control over nature. More interesting still, if a great deal less reassuring, is the problem of why his moral vision, which apparently awakened five thousand years ago, should have failed to keep pace with his technical accomplishments: a fact so indisputable that the very statement of it has become a platitude. It is true that material progress had enjoyed a start of several hundred thousand years, and that the development of writing was as much a stage on its journey as the development three thousand years later of printing, and the discovery five hundred years later still of radio. But, as Breasted has pointed out in his book *The Dawn of Conscience*, the evolution of moral thought in Egypt during the Second Union represents the farthest point to which such speculation can go in the absence of religious revelation. In this millennium of ethical reflection, we have something that had never taken place before. Men were systematically meditating on their destiny for the first time. To their implements, adornments, and techniques, they were now adding something totally different from any of these, namely a moral conscience.

The Memphite Drama

How old and important an oral tradition of philosophizing there must have been, at least in Egypt, can be inferred from the 'oldest written thoughts' known to us. These are embodied in what is called the Memphite Drama (from Memphis, the ancient capital of Egypt), which was written, so Breasted thinks, by priests from Heliopolis in the middle of the fourth millennium BC. We do not possess the full text of this remarkable piece of literature; and its preservation, even in mutilated fragments, is the result of happy accident. Its history is briefly as follows. The Ethiopian Pharaoh Shabaka, who reigned in the eighth century BC (he was a contemporary of Isaiah, and is called So in the Old Testament), ordered the ancient text to be copied from an old papyrus and inscribed on a black stone, where such a valuable 'work of the ancestors' (for so he significantly called it) might the better be preserved for future generations. This block, now in the British Museum, was unfortunately used for many years as a nether mill-stone, so that along with the corn of many generations part of its message was ground away. Even so we possess enough of the text to enable us to judge to some extent what is omitted.

That the most ancient recorded thoughts should be concerned with a discussion of 'right' and 'wrong' is a fact of very great interest. Nor is it without significance that the discussion should be conducted partly in dramatic form, thereby tending to confirm the religious origin of drama. But what, at first reading, strikes us most forcibly about this production is its extreme complexity. Here, we have to remind ourselves, is the beginning. Here is the infancy of thought. Here, more than two millennia before Thales, is the expression of an ordered view of life, yet couched in language suggestive of a tradition many centuries old. In other words, here is something very like mature philosophy: thought which, formulated by many minds, is so much a common possession as already to be anonymous. These circumstances alone prove that, long before writing was invented, organized and systematic thought had begun. What writing chiefly served to do was to establish an orthodoxy, a norm. It thus became a necessary agent of social stability, a means whereby the communal mind was informed and directed. Without writing we should view the past not as historians but as archaeologists; it is in the latter capacity, indeed, that we survey the development of man from the Paleolithic period until the age of which we speak. Writing is a means to spiritual continuity, and spiritual continuity is a condition of history.[1]

The piecing together of the text of both the Memphite Drama and the highly abstruse philosophical discussion that follows it has been a triumph of multi-national scholarship. We cannot here do more than summarize its contents, which, properly understood, throws light not merely upon the mentality of the Egyptian people of that distant age, but upon the development of philosophical speculation. There is something peculiarly exciting about examining a work of such extreme antiquity, the very nature of which was unknown until a few years ago. A new country of the mind is thereby revealed to us.

The piece begins with an invocation to the god Ptah. Now Ptah was the local god of Memphis. Originally, as one among many gods, he served as the patron saint of craftsmen but eventually he assumed a pre-eminent position, no doubt as a result of being identified with making or creation in general. When King Menes subdued both Upper and Lower Egypt, it appears that he promoted Ptah to a position hitherto occupied by the Sun-god himself. The reason was that Memphis had become, and was long to remain, the capital of united Egypt, in the forming of which Ptah had shown himself a master-builder.

How was it that the Sun-god had traditionally wielded such influence? The question is easily answered. Egypt owed her geographical survival to two natural forces, the waters of the Nile and the rays of the sun. Consequently her people came to deify both. The Sun-god, Re, whose headquarters were at Heliopolis (Greek: 'Sun Town', originally called On), was traditionally represented by a falcon, the bird that was thought to fly nearest to heaven. As a convenient symbol, a winged disc was often employed. The Nile god, on the other hand, was god not merely of water but of the fertility that the river was known to produce; and as the power of this god increased with the perennial evidence of his bounty, so he came to rival the Sun-god, and to assume many of the latter's characteristics. The name of this rival was Osiris.

To return to the newly-promoted god of Memphis, was the invocation addressed to Ptah merely a matter of form, a conventional

[1] Cf. 'Language makes it possible for man to *be* historically' (Hölderlin, quoted in Heidegger's *Hölderlin and the Essence of Poetry*, 1936).

reverence? It appears not. For the qualities ascribed to him are highly original. Ptah is described as 'the heart and the tongue of the gods'. Why, precisely, 'heart' and 'tongue'? Are these merely stereotyped metaphors? Scholars would suggest otherwise. By 'heart' the Egyptians meant something very like 'mind' or 'understanding', while by 'tongue' they referred to 'speech' or 'expression', particularly that form of expression which is official or *ex cathedra.* To be both 'heart' and 'tongue' is therefore to be not merely the interpreter of the gods in plenary session, but the divine mind itself engaged in the act of creation by giving concrete expression to its thoughts.

Such a notion may seem rather abstruse. It undoubtedly is. It becomes more intelligible, however, if we try to understand what the priests, in issuing such statements, had in mind. From inspection of the whole text and from what we know of early Egyptian thought, it seems clear that the priestly authors are engaged in a discussion of how the world began, i.e. what originated it. Now whatever we may think of their manner of expression, we cannot deny that they were tackling an eminently reasonable problem—a problem to which the early Greek and Hebrew thinkers likewise addressed themselves and to which we in our day have been able to give no ready answer. The beginners of thought at least began at the beginning.

It is to the nature of their answer to this question that the modern student may be inclined to take exception. Most textbooks of the history of philosophy begin with the speculations of the pre-Socratic thinkers of Greece, whose object it was to discover the original element, or group of elements, from which the world of nature was derived. Thales maintained that the world was ultimately derived from water; Anaximander that it was derived from a kind of mist; Anaximenes that something even vaguer, called 'the boundless', was that from which all things originated. To our sophisticated minds these answers appear elementary, far more so no doubt than they really were, for the Ionian philosophers must not be considered simple just because they put forward simple solutions. Nothing is less simple than genuine simplification. The Egyptian thinkers, who lived about thirty centuries earlier than the Greeks envisaged the problem in very different terms. They maintained—and we must not dismiss the answer as absurd without giving it careful attention—that the universe originated from *thought*: not so much thought in general as a particular kind of thought, a realized, objectivized, or incarnate thought.

Before commenting upon this apparently novel idea, let us look once more at the text. Here, as later, we quote from Breasted's translation. Ptah, we are informed, acting on behalf of all the other gods, 'pronounced the names of all things, created the sight of the eyes, the hearing of the ears, the breathing of the nose, that they may transmit to the heart. It is he (the heart) that causes that every conclusion should come forth, it is the tongue which announces the thought of the heart... Every divine word came into being through that which the heart thought and the tongue commanded; and thus the stations (official positions) were made, and the functions (of government) were assigned, which furnished all nutrition and all food.' And later: 'Thus was it found and perceived that his (Ptah's) strength was greater than all gods, and thus was Ptah satisfied after he had made all things and every divine word.'

The above extracts summarize an idea, which, like many similar notions in Egyptian literature, undergoes considerable repetition. Boldly vested with the Sun-god's functions, Ptah is proclaimed the Creator and Mover of all things. His creative organs are heart and tongue, the respective seats of intelligence and expression. Everything in the world, therefore, is the embodiment of *realized intelligence*, whereby it 'came into being'. The world, we may note, was not created as if by magic; nor was it created merely according to an intelligent plan; it came into being and is continually sustained in being by the active operation of intelligence, which is the breath of god. Moreover, Ptah, surveying his handiwork, was 'satisfied', i.e. like the God of *Genesis*, he 'saw that it was good'.

In order to understand ancient philosophy we need to be prepared to do two things: first we must learn to become accustomed to unfamiliar terminology and secondly we must be ready to believe that our ancestors were in most respects as adult and mature as we are. There is much heedless talk about the 'childhood of the race', as if men had remained for centuries or even millennia in a condition of infancy, from which they struggled to adolescence about the time of the Renaissance and have since grown up. That the brain-power of *homo sapiens* has undergone any marked increase since the earliest times has yet to be proved. If mere size should be a reliable criterion, we have the startling fact that the cranial measurements of the Cromagnon man (about 20,000 BC) reveal a brain fifty per cent larger than that of his successors. We live in an age which, impressed with the power of technics, tends to approach the problems of existence from a materialist angle; but we have only to reflect for a moment to perceive that much of our intellectual background has been formed from very diferent traditions. The priestly authors of the Memphite Drama are not, upon closer examination, so fantastic in their speculations as they at first appear.

An Early Version of a Familiar Idea

For nearly two thousand years the congregations of Christian churches have listened, with varying degrees of attention, to the opening of the Fourth Gospel, 'In the beginning was the Word, and the Word was with God and the Word was God'. How many realize the history behind these words—those particular words, that is to say, apart from the new meaning which they are given in the Gospel? For, as we know, the writer goes on to make a statement which, given the conventional philosophical ideas of the time, must have seemed both new and challenging. Having declared that in the beginning 'the Word was with God' and indeed '*was* God', he proceeds to claim that as a result of the Christian revelation the Word has become incarnate and 'dwelt among us'. Now although the authorship of the Fourth Gospel has been ascribed to St John, we do not know for certain who wrote it. Nor do we know for certain when it was written. We assume, on the basis of the pre-war discovery of a fragment of papyrus,[1] that it was known in Egypt early in the second century AD; which is much earlier than some experts had supposed. On the other hand, we think we know for certain why it was written. Composed originally in Greek like the other gospels, the Fourth Gospel was intended primarily for Greek readers. It therefore employed the kind of terminology with which the intelligent Greek would be naturally familiar. Moreover, it invoked a particular tradition of thought into which the Christian gospel was henceforth to be integrated. In the beginning was the Logos, and the Logos was one with God. Now, however, the Logos had been made flesh and was one with man. Hence the incarnate Logos, Christ, was also Immanuel, 'God with us'.[2]

What meaning attaches to the term 'Logos' in Greek philosophy? It occurs first in the fragmentary speculations of Heraclitus, and there it means a creative principle, a kind of fertilizing thought, an agent of divine energy. We find it later in Plato, who uses it to denote that aspect of God's creative power which results in the multiplicity of His works; the Logos is the *agent of variety*, but of ordered variety, not mere profusion. The concept of the Logos also had its parallel in Hebrew thought, sometimes personified as the Divine Wisdom. Indeed, it appears that this Wisdom idea, though reinforced by Greek thought, had already a long and authentic Hebrew history; and this prompts us in turn to ask whether the Hebrews, who experienced so much Egyptian influence, did not owe some part of the idea to early Egyptian thinkers. In short, the authors of the Memphite Drama, being priest-metaphysicians, were probably the first elaborators of the Logos concept. What we do not find preposterous in Plato, in Philo of Alexandria, and in the Gospel according to St John, should hardly cause us surprise and perplexity in these early Egyptians. If surprise there is, it is not so much associated with the idea itself as with its remarkably early expression. Man's first written thoughts are concerned with the power of thought itself.

If the Memphite Drama and discourse contained no more than a series of metaphysical statements, the interest of these works would be limited. But there is a great deal more to the text than that. Just as we have here the first metaphysics, so we have the first ethics, or morals. Since that is a gigantic claim to make in respect of any ancient inscription, we must remind ourselves that written words must long ago have been spoken, and longer still debated in the mind. In the case of moral questions, we must presuppose many generations of varied human experience; for men do not begin systematically to reflect upon problems of conduct until they have become aware of a conflict of loyalties, and can readily distinguish between obligation and self-interest. Even today this distinction is not always recognized, and

[1] Cf. *An Unpublished Fragment of the Fourth Gospel*. Ed. by C. H. Roberts, 1935.
[2] This idea is discussed further in the Conclusion.

there have been philosophers to whom its denial has been a matter of passionate concern. What strikes us as particularly interesting about the Memphite philosophers is that they are seeking to establish a divine sanction for moral conduct. 'Life,' says the text, 'is given to the peaceful and death is given to the guilty': a statement which, though ambiguous, is clarified to some extent by the later definition of the peaceful as 'he who does what is loved' and of the guilty as 'he who does what is hated'. In endeavouring to reconstruct the message of such early thinkers we are naturally dependent upon a rendering which we trust, but do not know, to be exact. The greatest scholars, with characteristic humility, admit as much. Thus Breasted's master Erman, one of the greatest of Egyptologists, suggested that 'he who does' should read 'he who makes'. This interpretation would alter the sense of the passage by introducing the notion, not in itself unreasonable, of a god who *created* good and evil. Sethe, another German Egyptologist, prefers to believe that the role of God is that of distributor of rewards and punishments, giving life to those that do his will and death to those that do not. If, as Breasted thinks likely, this interpretation is correct, we may gain some insight into the prevailing moral ideas. In the first place, it is clear that morality is already a *social* thing, and therefore susceptible of social regulation. Of two possible lines of conduct, one only is approved by the city and therefore by the city's god. Secondly, it follows that God is the kind of being to whom the conduct of human creatures is a matter of real concern. He is not simply a figurehead, a champion, a civic patron, still less a vague metaphysical entity like the God of Aristotle. He is a judge and guide, the friend of the good and the enemy of the unrighteous.

At this point we must issue a word of warning. Conduct ordained by a god, or prescribed by priests or rulers, and demanding perhaps no more than external observance, is admittedly not what we mean by morality. It is rather social custom, an outward thing. This distinction is important. The Memphite priests possessed no doubt a very strong vested interest in the maintenance of custom, or, given their status as servants of a new master, in the establishment of new custom. But what is distinguishable is not necessarily different. Features that became clear and articulate in morality are already present implicitly in custom. Like many a later ruler, the Pharaoh may have camouflaged his own personal wishes by representing them as having been ordained by God from all eternity. Hammurabi did the same. We know from the inscriptions on tombs and pyramids that the greater the Pharaoh's claim to divinity, the more intensely the people worshipped him. Whereas the popes of a later civilization claimed to be the vicegerents of God, the Pharaohs of the early dynasties claimed to exercise powers so far-reaching that nature herself was subject to their influence. Nor need we assume that all absolute rulers, yesterday as today, are animated by motives of cynicism, cloaking their power with extravagant propaganda in which they do not personally believe. In the majority of cases the Pharaoh was as convinced of his own divinity as were his subjects. The latter were obliged to obey him; he was obliged to obey himself. To sustain his immense responsibilities, however, he needed the support of a priestly caste engaged in the perpetual assertion of his divinity. We shall see in due course how the one Pharaoh to rely exclusively on his own belief in himself was very soon deprived of power.

The Memphite Drama, if correctly interpreted, shows the world of nature or the cosmos to be the product of divine intelligence. Both agriculture and government are therefore the revelation of such intelligence. God, in fact, has not merely thought man into being, but, in thinking him, thinks through him, and thereby guides him in the acquisition of such techniques as those of cultivation and husbandry. The divine origin of arts and crafts, together with skill in exploiting natural phenomena such as fire, is reflected in the mythology of almost every known culture. But the Memphite Drama is concerned with more than God's infinite creative powers; it is concerned likewise with the duty of man towards God. God actively thinks man; man, in turn, must actively think God. He must maintain his fellowship with God through prayer; for prayer, as the dictionary tells us, is not merely the making of a request, but a summoning to one's support.

Here it may be worth pointing out that Western philosophy, especially that of the last three hundred years, has almost completely lost sight of this communion of intelligence with intelligence, which is at the basis of so much ancient thought, even that which appears at first sight to be purely materialistic, such as the religion of the hunter of North America, with its visions and asceticism but obvious utilitarian aim.

The Role of the Pharaoh

There are few religions, and few cultures likewise, that do not look back to some pre-eminent human figure, the founder or rather the interpreter of its faith. This figure may be a personified force of nature, like Re the Sun-god; or wholly mythical, like Prometheus; or a historical figure, like Christ or Confucius; or semi-historical, like King Arthur. Similarly, he may have lived once, or he may be subject to reincarnation or palingenesis. Such a figure was the Egyptian Pharaoh. His person was doubly sacred: he was the embodiment of the Sun-god and therefore a religious figure, and he was the symbol of United Egypt, and therefore a political one. Moreover, he was the object of a mythology so ancient and elaborate that even in the time of Herodotus the rites connected with his person were already shrouded in mystery. Today, although we still know very little about Egyptian religion, we understand much that puzzled former generations, whose ignorance of hieroglyphics was frequently combined with an approach best described as 'positivist'. That is to say, they were inclined to dismiss as ignorant superstition anything which failed to conform to their notion of what was progressive and enlightened. We now know that the so-called primitive mind was the reverse of simple and childish, just as we realize that primitive art was often more subtle and skilful than that of the so-called Western 'primitives'. Modern savages, if carefully interrogated, will be found to believe not that civilized mankind is cleverer than they, but that it is simply more wicked and corrupt, the slave of evil powers. If we examine the mythology that surrounded the person of the Pharaoh, we shall find much to excite curiosity but little to cause derision. This mythology will not merely shed light upon the origin of ethical thought; it will explain how such highly elaborate metaphysical systems as that of the Memphite Drama came to be formulated.

Most ancient of the gods of Egypt was Horus, the falcon or hawk god. Like many other gods of Egypt, he was originally a local deity, the divinity associated with the town of Edfu in Upper Egypt. Even so, he was not simply a god of provincial significance; he was the local embodiment of the Sun-god himself, pictorially represented, as we have seen, first by a falcon and later by the winged sun-disc. If the falcon was the sun, then too the sun was a falcon, traversing the sky from east to west in the course of each day: an image later employed with numerous variations, the dead Pharaoh and his heavenly barque sometimes taking the falcon's place. The earliest Egyptian legends known to us are concerned with a titanic struggle between Horus and his enemy Seth or Set, who is usually portrayed as a dog or an ant-eater. This is presumably a symbolism of the struggle, renewed every twelve hours, between night and day, in which the eye of day is repeatedly put out. Hence the later myths concerning the miraculous powers which this particular member could confer, and the frequent appearance in Egyptian paintings and tomb engravings of a stylized image of an eye, the celebrated 'eye of Horus'.

The process of transformation—or, perhaps more strictly, transmogrification—whereby Horus became identified with the son of Osiris is as fascinating to trace as it is difficult to explain. All we can say is that Osiris, originally a god of vegetation or perhaps even a tree (his mother was Nut, the sky-goddess), seems to have come in time to symbolize the idea of fertility in general. He was associated with the underworld because of the upthrust of natural life from the nether regions, and he was on the same analogy associated with the Nile itself, as being both the source of Egypt's prosperity and, like the sun, believed to parallel its worldly course by traversing the underworld. In the earliest legends the dead Osiris was brought to life by receiving the eye of Horus, his son. In time the figure of Osiris was represented as possessing the power not merely of communicating life to others but of absorbing into himself the power of other gods, until his prestige almost exceeded that of Re. A school of theologians finally arose whose object was to impose the worship of Osiris over that of all others.

This deliberate imposition may be traced in the numerous hieroglyphic inscriptions in the pyramids of Sakkara, which are known as the 'Pyramid Texts'.[1] First brought to light in 1880 with the

[1] It is worth noting that, except for those at Sakkara, the Egyptian pyramids contain neither inscriptions nor diagrammatic carvings. The attempt by certain religious sects to foretell historical events from the pyramids, especially the Great Pyramid or Pyramid of Cheops at Gizeh, is based upon measurements of passages, chambers, etc, from which wholly arbitrary deductions are made.

exploration of the pyramid of Pepi I, these texts date from about 2600 BC; but Egyptologists are agreed that they contain material belonging to a much older period, for certain words and expressions are so archaic that we possess no clue to their meaning. What interests the student of Egyptian theology, however, is that certain texts originally composed in praise of the Sun-god have evidently been later rewritten to praise Osiris. There is frequent evidence of actual substitution of one name for the other. In certain pictures, for instance, we find Osiris holding court and issuing judgment from a throne situated in heaven, which is frank evidence of usurpation. Nor was the elevation or apotheosis of Osiris merely the result of a theological argument in which the solar theologians of Heliopolis were temporarily defeated, as happened in the case of Ptah. Everything for which Osiris stood—the rhythm of the seasons, the reality of death and renewal, the functions of the 'good' earth—was the daily experience of the common people. Consequently, Osiris was their god, a god whose habits they understood, and whose favours they might ask with some hope of requital. Osiris became in effect the god-king of Egypt, the president of a country that was itself a sort of recurrent miracle.[1]

To suggest that the worship of Osiris altogether overshadowed and excluded that of the Sun-god would be to misunderstand the workings of the religious consciousness, particularly in ancient Egypt. In cases of this kind—and such parallels may be found in every civilization—there is no absolute exclusion, but merely the blending of functions and characteristics: in this instance the Osirianization of the Sun-god and the solarization of Osiris. Theology lays down a terminology and believes that it has established uniformity of worship; but what is worshipped, is worshipped in the freedom of the individual conscience, and few theologians have been able to withstand the pressure of popular devotion consecrated by time and responding to an instinctive need. When at a critical moment in Egyptian history an attempt was made to impose a new and purified form of sun worship, the experiment was short-lived, not because the Pharaoh responsible for this innovation was devoid of character, but because the doctrine was too clear-cut to permit of that latitude and ambiguity whereby the common people, though nominally orthodox, are able to continue their cherished worship. The Egyptian *fellaheen* were not the only people in history, nor the most primitive, to pay lip-service to the sun, while privately propitiating a god of earth and water, virility and fecundity, darkness and terror.[2]

If we were writing a detailed account of Egyptian mythology, we should need at this point to retell the story of Osiris's death, the floating of his corpse down the Nile, its rescue by Isis, his sister and wife, its

[1] The Egyptians were the one people who would not have accepted the statement of Jean Cocteau that, '*un miracle qui dure cesse d'être considéré comme tel*'.

[2] In the earliest of the Pyramid Texts, Osiris is represented as being no friend to man.

dismemberment by his brother Seth (whose mutilation of Horus we have already described), his restoration by Isis and his consequent return to life. This story, which survived Egyptian civilization and became part of the mythology of Greece and Rome and did not perish with the Christian era, assumed various forms. In most of them, indeed, Osiris comes to life only to renounce his rights in favour of his son Horus. Having abdicated, he then descends to the underworld. But the traditional antagonism between Horus and Seth still continues; and when Horus proclaims himself Pharaoh, Seth brings what is virtually a legal action against him at a trial at which all the gods are present. This challenge is directed not so much against Horus's title as ruler over Egypt as against his claim to be the son of Osiris. The point is interesting, because early versions of this and similar legends clearly date from a time when paternity was not properly understood. Thus a son such as Horus could be born impossibly long after his father's death. When the myth came to be rationalized, the revival of Osiris was made to serve the secondary purpose of enabling him to beget Horus in the normal manner. His presence is thereafter no longer required outside his nether kingdom.

The Pharaoh, then, was Horus, and the new Pharaoh was simply Horus reincarnate. Because he was Horus incarnate, the Pharaoh was the source of national life and health; and, since the existence and prosperity of Egypt were dependent upon a seasonable rhythm, the Pharaoh was obliged to perform such ceremonies as would ensure the regularity of inundation and ebb, and even of night and day. Never, as we have said, was a ruler so weighed down with responsibility as was the Pharaoh, and never were a people so concerned with their ruler's welfare as were the Egyptians. Nor did their solicitude end with death: it merely assumed a new form. Since the dead Horus needed food, implements, means of transport, and even entertainment, the pyramids were built to ensure his preservation for as long as the world was thought likely to last. The purpose of these gigantic structures was not so much to keep the Pharaoh imprisoned as to provide him with an earthly *pied à terre* to which his soul could return at will. Every pyramid was therefore provided with vents for entrance and exit, together with a lifelike statue, which the soul on its visits to the earth could inhabit, or at least use as a means of self-identification. The entrance of the Great Pyramid points directly to the Pole Star, for the dead were supposed to inhabit that region of the sky.

From the Pyramid Texts we learn a great deal about the Egyptian conception of immortality. At first it appears that the Pharaoh alone could attain to everlasting life. Indeed, the extraordinary inscriptions on certain of the pyramids suggest not merely that the Pharaoh was regarded as deserving immortality as of right, but that the repetition of this fact must necessarily help to promote his future well-being.

As Breasted has pointed out,[1] the Pyramid Texts, though mortuary

[1] *The Dawn of Conscience*, Chapter 5.

inscriptions, mention the word death only in two sorts of context: first to deny its reality as applied to the Pharaoh, and secondly to assert it as the inevitable fate of his enemies. The Pharaohs are addressed with almost frantic ejaculations, as in the case of King Pepi: 'This King Pepi dies not. Have ye said that he would die? He dies not. This King Pepi lives for ever. This King Pepi has escaped his day of death. Raise thee up, O this King Pepi, thou diest not,' and so on. Apart from such rhetorical phrases, which were carved in the stone with a delicacy and precision that still excites our wonder, there are graphic accounts of the manner in which the Pharaoh, having renounced human life, ascends to heaven. As Horus, this ascension may seem unexpected. Should the Pharaoh not rather descend to the nether world and become one with Osiris? He should and he does—at least in the earliest Egyptian myths. The headquarters of the Sun-god was Heliopolis, and the Heliopolitan priests, the authors of the Memphite Drama, acquired increasing influence with the Pharaoh at Memphis.[1] During the Pyramid Age it became the convention to represent the deceased Pharaoh as being 'ferried over and set on the east side of the sky' (i.e. the side from which the sun was born every day and whence came all similar gods), though admittedly he might also fly heavenwards or ascend upon a golden ladder. Thus one text reads: 'O men and gods! Your arms under King Pepi! Raise ye him, lift ye him to the sky! To the sky! To the great seat among the gods!' And the final goal of this journey, however undertaken, was first his meeting, and, after due trial and judgment, his actual identification with the Sun-god. While the Pharaohs clung to their official solar religion, however, the reputation of Osiris was growing among his people, until it gave rise to precisely that re-editing of the Pyramid Texts to which we have referred. After the close of the Pyramid Age, Osiris, being no longer confined to the nether world, is himself translated to the skies and becomes the supreme judge. In the latest Pyramid Texts, as Breasted shows,[2] he is sometimes represented as climbing the ladder to heaven. Now this is a double promotion. Not merely is Osiris about to greet his mighty rival the Sun-god, but he has taken the place of the traditional climbing figure of the Pharaoh. The two faiths have telescoped.

This meeting of two streams of beliefs is not a mere compromise engineered by theologians. It has a more profound significance. Although we cannot hope to penetrate the innermost thoughts of those whom Herodotus called 'the most religious of all men', we can refrain from extreme assumptions regarding their mentality. Partly through the influence of history primers long out of date, and partly through unwarranted inferences from surviving relics of the past, we are inclined to assume that a monarchy such as that of Egypt must have been a monstrous tyranny; that structures such as the pyramids could have been built only by a system of slave-driving of unparalleled severity; and that the evidence both in Egypt and elsewhere (such as Sumeria) of wholesale public sacrifice excludes the possibility of these

[1] Memphis is only twenty-five miles from Heliopolis.
[2] *The Dawn of Conscience*, Chapter 8.

communities having enjoyed the smallest degree of social liberty. Such assumptions ought to be questioned.

When we represent the pyramids as having been constructed by slaves, cowed and driven by force, we ought to ask ourselves what undertakings of this magnitude are achieved without compulsion, whether wielded by a single master, which is rare, or by a guild or union, which, though formed perhaps with the object of combating despotism, comes to exercise in course of time a measure of constraint. In such communal undertakings force is employed not so much in achieving the object directly, as in inducing men effectively to associate together for that purpose. At the one extreme there is slave labour with its problem of association; at the other extreme there is the free group with its inevitable proportion of grumblers. Nothing great is achieved wholly voluntarily. Even the solitary worker bent upon work to which he is passionately devoted will have his moments of lassitude and discouragement when (to employ the obvious expression) he must take himself to task. Believing implicitly in the sacredness of their ruler, and regarding his dead presence among them as more significant—more beneficent even—than his living one, the people of Egypt no doubt erected the pyramids by a common effort of will, an upsurge of devotion.

And if the sound of the lash and the knout were heard to mingle with that of chant and incantation, so the building of the great Christian cathedrals cannot have been achieved without much goading and verbal blasphemy. In a conscript army there must always be many who would prefer not to fight: but such elements must experience the extremes of resentment before they start shooting their officers.[1]

We have already observed that the Pharaoh, before approaching the realm of the Sun-god, was obliged to face the judgment of the gods. Earlier still, in the legends of Horus, the idea of trial and judgment was no less clearly conceived. To ascribe so great a measure of responsibility to the most powerful man in the land may seem unusual, since we find a tendency throughout later history for the strong and powerful to evade this burden. Although there have been rulers such as Marcus Aurelius, Ashoka, and Saint Louis who have taken their job extremely seriously, they are the exception rather than the rule: responsibility has been attributed lower down in the social scale. That moral obligation was early recognized at the summit of Egyptian society may have something to do with the stability and duration of that society: for if Toynbee's 'challenge and response' theory of history is right, the society most morally tough will clearly be in a position to respond effectively to any challenge. What the student of thought will find particularly interesting is the easily traceable process whereby moral responsibility underwent a sort of democratization, the ordinary individual gradually becoming conscious of personal re-

[1] It is interesting to note that of the three great pyramid builders, Cheops, Chefren, and Mykerinus, we know extremely little. On the basis of the statement 'Happy is the country that has no history', we may venture to believe that their reigns were not eventful. This would appear to preclude any violent social upheavals or unrest.

sponsibility for the first time in history.

How did this moral awakening occur? No satisfactory explanation has yet been given, though we shall suggest some explanations in due course. We cannot legitimately say that human thought shows a process of development from concrete to abstract speculation. It does not follow, therefore, that ethical concepts, being abstractions, must have arisen at a certain stage in social development. The earliest recorded thought cannot have been evolved without the most thorough grasp of abstractions: nor does the fact that the Egyptians tended also to express their thought in concrete images prove that their hold upon abstract thinking was precarious. We have reason to believe that, psychologically speaking, one capacity goes hand in hand with the other. Furthermore, we have been able to trace what may be regarded as the first abstract ethical concept evolved by humanity, namely the Egyptian concept signifying 'Righteousness' or 'Justice'. And of one thing we may be sure: when this concept first appeared it had already enjoyed a long history not merely as a vague notion or impression but, to use the terminology of David Hume, as a genuine 'idea'.

The concept of Justice

The word employed by the Egyptians to signify Justice, Goodness, Righteousness, or Truth (probably it signified or included all four notions, like Plato's Form of the Good) was *Maat*. The word *Maat* does not occur in the surviving fragments of the Memphite Drama. There is nothing particularly mysterious about that. The concept is clearly much older than the sophisticated theological argument of the priests of Heliopolis; for moral thinking must long have antedated theological thinking. Something of the antiquity and veneration in which *Maat* was held may be judged from the fact that justice, as thus conceived, was regarded as the daughter of the Sun-god himself. Hence its diffusion from above—a further resemblance to the Platonic Form of the Good, which was compared to the sun on account of the latter's power both to lighten and to sustain life. This is sufficient to show that *Maat*, whatever its individual features, was not just a simple quality, a label to be pinned on to something worthy of praise. It was the spirit behind, or permeating, the universe: 'the Way' in the sense so often employed in oriental thought. For the Hebrews, *Maat* became Wisdom; for the Christians, Love—again not merely love of one's neighbour or one's country, but the *Amore* of Dante, 'the love which moves the sun and the other stars'.

Some time before the beginning of the Eighteenth Dynasty certain Egyptian scribes copied from an old manuscript a work to which they gave the title 'The Instruction of Ptah-hotep'. Composed most probably about 2880 BC, so far as our present knowledge suggests, this work forms a kind of political testament. Its author, a Governor of Memphis and Prime Minister to a king of the Fifth Dynasty, decided, upon relinquishing office, to compile a summary of precepts concerning not merely good government but—what interests us for the moment more—the good life. In a preface to his work, he asks permission of the king to transfer to his son the authority he can no longer exercise; and it is evidently for the new Prime Minister that the precepts are primarily intended. Addressing the king, Ptah-hotep declares his firm intention to 'speak the words of them that hearken to the counsel of the men of old time, those that once heard the gods', wherein we obtain a momentary glimpse of a tradition of thought already regarded as exceedingly ancient and in need of scrupulous preservation, together with hints of a period of time in which gods and men were on terms of familiarity and even intimacy, as we see also in the early chapters of *Genesis*. The wisdom itself, or such of it as has been preserved, bears a distinct resemblance to that which Polonius imparted to his son, or Benjamin Franklin to the readers of his autobiography.

It is at once shrewd, pithy, incontrovertible, worldly; and this essential worldliness, this surface brilliance or (in the literal sense) superficiality, reveals something of the nature of the civilization of the time. Whatever its corruption and its foundation in servitude, this civilization must have exhibited a good measure of stability and order, or else the precepts of the minister would have been irrelevant and even meaningless. In such precepts as 'Beware of making evil with thy words ... Overstep not the truth, neither repeat that which any man, be he prince or peasant, saith in opening the heart', or 'Silence is more profitable to thee than abundance of speech', or 'Consider how you mayst be opposed by an expert that speaketh in Council: it is foolish to speak in every kind of work', we obtain insight into a world not destitute of manners and social graces, a society in which the art of pleasing and gaining influence needed as careful cultivation as now. It is a society in which words and deeds are equally important, if not on occasion identical. Social vices do not differ very much from one age to another.

Save that they are the first moral statements of their kind to be preserved, though certainly not to have been uttered, the maxims of Ptah-hotep do not exhibit particular profundity. What impresses us is their urbanity. They are the fruit of the experience not of one man only but of many generations of men in office; they may even be rehashed from a commonplace book. Now it is much more interesting that the earliest recorded moral maxims should be trite than that they should be of staggering depth: for nothing suggests more forcibly that civilization is a great deal older than we ordinarily believe. Nevertheless, the 'Instructions' are not without their moments of sublimity, even if such sublimity is merely an example of the conventional rhetoric of the time; witness the following phrase, which stands out from the rest with peculiar force: 'Great is *Maat*: its dispensation endureth, nor has it been overthrown since the time of its maker.' In short, the foundation, the ground of all these injunctions to virtue, is a power enduring through the ages, an eternal value, a force operating not merely in the individual soul, but in society itself. Now this power, though embodied in the Pharaoh,[1] is conceived as an abstract concept. Perhaps it is the first such concept to be evolved in human thought.

That the maxims of Ptah-hotep became part of the traditional wisdom of Egypt is shown by the fact that they were invoked about four hundred years later in a document of remarkable similarity. This document, a papyrus at present in the museum at Leningrad, is known as the 'Instruction addressed to Merikere'. Who was Merikere? Unfortunately we know very little about him. He was the son of a king of Heracleopolis, the town about seventy-five miles south of Memphis. One of these kings, having overthrown the ruler in Memphis, assumed the title of Pharaoh. A period of great disorder followed. The country split up into warring provinces. The Old Kingdom disintegrated. The result was the collapse of that political union of Egypt which had already endured for a thousand years. The king of Heracleopolis who drew up this particular document seems to have been the most able, or at least the wisest, in his dynasty, for the latter has no other claim to distinction; and despite the fact that the usurpation of his family had done much to destroy the traditions of the Old Kingdom, he displays a deep veneration for the wisdom of the past. Characteristically, the king begins his address with a reference to *Maat*: 'Truth comes (to the wise man) well-brewed, after the manner of the ancestors. Imitate thy fathers, thy ancestors . . . for lo, their words abide in writing'—a reference to the wisdom of Ptah-hotep which is confirmed a few lines later. There follows much strictly political advice, first on the subject of foreign policy and later on internal affairs. How, asks the king, can a just system of government be preserved? He proceeds to answer his own question—by ensuring the material prosperity of those whose business is to administer justice. 'He who is wealthy in his own house does not show partiality, for he is a possessor of property and is without need. But the poor man (in office) does not speak according to his righteousness (*Maat*), for he who says 'Would I had' is not impartial; he shows partiality to one who holds his reward.'[2] But although the king declares 'Make great thy nobles that they may execute thy laws,' he is careful to add: 'Increase the new generations thy followers, equipped with possessions, endowed with fields, entrusted with herds. *Exalt not the son of an important* (i.e. '*well-connected*') *man above a humble one, but take for thyself a man because of his ability.*'

Such an approach to the problems of administration might suggest that Merikere was to concentrate on the means rather than the end. But this is not so. As the admonitions unfold, we find the king anxious to drive home an important lesson. 'It shall go well,' he says, 'with an impartially-minded sovereign, for it is the inside (of the palace) which conveys respect to the outside'; and he thereupon commits himself to what Breasted rightly calls 'one of the noblest observations in ancient

[1] Cf. The Pyramid Texts, 'King Unis comes forth to righteousness (*Maat*) that he may take it with him,' etc, etc.

[2] The idea was shared by many others. Cf. for example the inscription on the tomb of a noble called Mentuwoser who lived in the reign of Sesostris (or Senusret) I (2192–2157 BC), 'I was one who heard cases according to the facts, without showing partiality in favour of him who held the reward, *for I was wealthy and goodly in luxury.*'

Egyptian moral thinking': 'More acceptable is the virtue of the upright man than the ox of him that doeth iniquity.' We may remember that his utterance, so reminiscent of a later wisdom, was written more than two thousand years before the composition of the Hebrew psalms, i.e. a period longer than that separating us from the birth of Christ.

The immortality of the Pharaoh has already been shown, and his moral responsibility emphasized. But the assumption of immortality is not automatic; his deeds in this world must still be weighed in the balance. Whereas Ptah-hotep had not considered this fact worthy of attention, the King of Heracleopolis gives it due emphasis. No doubt this change in attitude represents a development of the moral conscience. 'Set not thy mind,' says the king, 'on length of days, for they (the Judges) view a lifetime as an hour. A man surviveth after death and his deeds are placed beside him like mountains. For it is eternity which awaits man there and a fool is he who despises it.' The idea of immortality underwent a progressive deepening of significance in Egyptian thought, until it was regarded as the reward of any man of righteous disposition. 'He who comes (to the other world) without having committed sin, shall live like a god, going onward freely like the lords of eternity.'

It was perhaps the gradual realization that *Maat* alone could assure eternal life to the individual that led to a popular revulsion against the values of what we have here called the Pyramid Age. The Pharaohs of that period clearly trusted to powers other than *Maat*; they built and equipped their tombs on such a scale as to ensure themselves at least permanent material habitation, almost as if they intended to rid time itself of victory over change. We have seen, too, that they caused their servants to cover the walls of these tombs with a kind of insistent verbal conjuration. The Pharaohs sought to take the kingdom of heaven by a storm of incantation and rhetoric. To us today there is something absurdly ironic in the fact that the object of all this elaborate construction of stone and chisel, musk, pigment and ambergris is the one thing that has in many cases failed to survive, namely the kingly body itself. Only the vessels, the food, the toilet requisites, the furniture—and the texts—remain.

The collapse of Materialism

The common notion that the Egyptians were people who spent all their time building pyramids and embalming their dead obscures the interesting fact that, during centuries and even millennia of Egyptian history, men looked back on the great pyramids as archaic monuments, as remains of a civilization whose ideas and values had long been repudiated. It is true that Egyptian kings continued to be buried with elaborate ceremony up to the time of the Macedonian conquest (333 BC); but the Pyramid Age ended about 2500 BC, and soon the enormous area covered by the pyramids (about sixty miles in length) was nothing but a waste of sand-strewn masonry. Caesar and Napoleon, looking down upon these monuments, reflected on the transience of human glory and pride. So also did the Egyptians. To them the sight was even more poignant, because it was their own history that lay in ruins before them. No wonder that such contemplation could inspire poetry of great depth and dignity. An example is the remarkable 'Song of the Harp Player', which was sung both at funerals and, as a *memento mori*, at banquets. Composed some time during the Old Kingdom (2200 BC?), this song is not known to us in its entirety. It has survived in two fragments, one on a papyrus and the other on the walls of a tomb at Thebes.[1]

How prosperous is this good prince!
The goodly destiny has come to pass,
The Generations pass away,
While others remain,
Since the time of the ancestors,
The gods who were aforetime,
Who rest in their pyramids,
Nobles and the glorious likewise departed,
Entombed in these pyramids. . . .

Behold the places thereof
Their walls are dismantled,
Their places are no more,
As if they had never been.

None cometh from thence
That he may tell us how they fare,
That he may tell us of their fortunes
That he may content our heart,
Until we too depart
To the place whither they have gone.

Encourage thy heart to forget it,
Making it pleasant for thee to follow thy desire,
Whilst thou livest.
Put myrrh on thy head,
And garments on thee of fine linen
Imbued with marvellous luxuries,
The genuine things of the gods.

Increase yet more thy delights
And let (not) thy heart languish
Follow thy desire and thy good,
Fashion thine affairs on earth
After the mandates of thy own heart.
Till that day of lamentation cometh to thee,
When the silent-hearted hears not thy lamentation,
Nor he that is in the tomb attends the mourning.

Celebrate the glad day
Be not weary therein,
Lo, no man taketh his goods with him.
Yea, none returneth again that is gone thither.

[1] The slab is now in the Leyden Museum.

The extract here quoted fails to convey the sombre majesty of even those fragments that remain; but the reader who is sensitive to beauty of image and depth of feeling will be struck by two things. Firstly the essential thought of the poem has survived translation from a language as far removed from English as Chinese, and secondly the thought itself (though not the primary element in any poem) anticipates that of some of the world's great poetry. To suggest that the original of this poem may compare at times with the great monologue of *Hamlet* to which so much of the subject-matter is common, as the translation compares almost at times with a well-known passage in *Isaiah*, is not perhaps an exaggeration.

In the above version, which is that of the papyrus, we have the expression of a pessimism so profound that nothing save oblivion can overcome it: 'Encourage thy heart to forget it'. In the version preserved on the wall of the Theban tomb, which is that of Neferhotep, a priest of Amen, a more positive note creeps in. Here the living are enjoined, in addition to 'following their desire wholly', to

> Give bread to him who hath no field
> So shall thou gain a good name
> For the future for ever,

indicating the value to posterity of a good example, but not seeking to discern the ultimate sanctions of moral conduct. What we have here, in fact, is a variety of *humanism* such as usually follows the collapse of orthodox religious faith: a humanism which, while advocating sensual enjoyment of a refined kind, pays due respect to conventional morality chiefly for the 'good name' that it gives a man. If we wish to find a later parallel for this attitude of mind, which is a recurring one, we may point to that of such nineteenth-century figures as T. H. Huxley, Matthew Arnold, and Emerson. Huxley, for example, while repudiating traditional religious belief, clung steadfastly to traditional ethical belief, chiefly perhaps for the 'good name' with which it invested those who conformed to it. Such an attitude may not suggest the most profound view of morality; but it does suggest an essentially social view of morality, because a 'good name' means nothing if not a 'good name' among men. Moralists tend to regard the 'social conscience' as something that developed only recently, with the abolition of slavery and the removal of disabilities on certain religious sects. From these fragments of Egyptian literature we see that the social conscience is as old as history. What is paradoxical about the social conscience is not so much its astonishingly early emergence as the fact of its survival among men whose instincts are predominantly anti-social.

In the light of the above, what may be said to constitute ethical or moral progress? One view held strongly until very recently was that first came a few moral men, and later, largely through their influence, a moral or semi-moral society. To say that this view was wholly mistaken would be absurd: we all know that such a thing as public opinion can be cultivated, and that nothing influences public opinion more than the eloquence (in deeds or words) of a man of vision. But the more attention we pay to the organization of primitive society, and the more we study comparative religion and culture, the clearer it becomes that social beliefs, taboos, and habits are equally things against which the individual leader rebels as things for which he is personally responsible. Both theories hold. Society needs to be influenced towards greater social responsibility, greater efforts towards mutual aid: it also needs to be shaken out of collective lethargy and public indifference. In a society like that of Egypt, with its extremely elaborate hierarchy of functions, its rigid social organization based upon material necessity, and its complex mythology and religious beliefs, the remarkable fact was not that a man should have a social conscience but that he should have an individual one. What the French sociologist Durkheim called social *pression* was felt by the ordinary Egyptian at every point. It is the inner experience, the drama in the soul, the individual at war with himself, for which philosophers in search of the origins of genuine moral perception look. Such an experience was that of Job. Another was that of the hero of the *Bhagavad-Gita*.[1] Do we find anything comparable to such dramas of conscience, at least as regards subject-matter, in the early literature of Egypt?

We certainly do. We find it, moreover, full one and a half millennia earlier than Job and Prince Krishna. The work in question, which has been preserved on a papyrus now in the Berlin Museum, dates from as early as 2000 BC; but we should bear in mind that a work committed to papyrus probably needed to be of established antiquity before such permanent form would be conferred upon it. It is only modern literature that receives almost immediate imprint and distribution; the classics are almost all transcripts. The text to which we refer has no title; but Breasted, possibly having in mind Plato's definition of philosophy as 'the dialogue of the soul with itself', calls this piece of 'existentialist' philosophy 'The Dialogue of a Misanthrope with his Own Soul', which is an appropriate description. The Misanthrope in question appears not to have been so from birth; what warped his temperament was the series of calamities that befell him. Of the precise nature of these calamities we are ignorant, because the relevant part of the papyrus has been lost: we can only infer that, like Job, he suffered accident, sickness, the loss of friends, property, and finally reputation, until it appeared to him that nothing remained but to 'curse God and die'. At the point at which he begins seriously to consider taking his life the papyrus resumes the story, but in a novel form. The unhappy man and his soul are made to confront each other. The soul begins to argue with the man. To die, it declares, is a misfortune; but to die in circumstances of misery and public execration is a calamity without parallel. Why is this so? Because a man deprived of means and deserted by his friends will have neither tomb nor mourner—a fate which to an Egyptian of this epoch could hardly bear contemplation.

Even so, the richest funeral is at bottom a mockery, as the neglected

[1] See Chapter 4.

tombs of the Pharaohs and the nobles prove. 'My soul opened its mouth and answered what I had said: If thou rememberest burial, it is mourning, it is bringing of tears; it is taking a man from his house and casting him forth upon the height.[1] Thou ascendest not up that thou mayest see the sun. Those who build in red granite, who erect the sepulchre in the pyramid, those beautiful in this beautiful structure, who have become like gods, the offering tables thereof are as empty as those of these weary ones who die on the dyke without a survivor.' If, in other words, the physical death of the Pharaoh is as sordid as that of the anonymous slave who helped build the royal pyramid, no one of sound mind would willingly hasten his end. Appropriately, then, this part of the dialogue concludes with a phrase reminiscent of the 'Song of the Harp Player': 'Follow the glad day and forget care.'

In order to appreciate both the merit and the originality of this document, we have to 'think away' four thousand years of literary and philosophical achievement. This involves considerable mental effort. Even so, the Misanthrope, though shrewd and free from sentimentality, has advanced to no deeper spiritual insight than the author of the 'Song of the Harp Player'. But the manuscript does not end here. It continues in a form of even greater originality. The prose introduction is succeeded by four poems, each of which conveys a stage or phase in the writer's spiritual progress towards enlightenment. With self-loathing rather than self-pity, the first poem dwells upon the theme of loss of reputation and good name in the manner of the 'Harp Player'. The image of stinking fish is employed as an analogy, for the Egyptian would as naturally compare a bad name to the stench of 'the catch when the sky is hot' as we today might refer to a name as 'stinking in men's nostrils'. The second poem stresses the Misanthrope's disgust with life from another point of view. What manner of man, it asks, can be trusted? Even brothers may prove false, while 'friends of today are not of love'. Wickedness abounds, but the malefactors are not brought to book. 'The gentle man perishes, the bold-faced goes everywhere.' Worse still, evil conduct excites not so much disgust as a tolerant amusement. Social life is a scandal, because 'there are no righteous' to whom to make appeal. Monotonously, but with the kind of insistent emphasis reminiscent of the Psalms, the first line of each verse of this poem runs, 'To whom do I speak today?', just as a modern prophet or artist might ask: 'What public shall I address? Who will listen to my message?'

In the last two poems, which are unquestionably the best, death is contemplated first with tranquillity as the final release from care, and secondly with confidence as the source of divine justice. Thus the mood of the early part of the manuscript is dispelled, and the injunction to forget death gives place to the counsel to accept the inevitable in the hope that it may lead to something more than mere physical dissolution. Of these poems, the third is undoubtedly the most beautiful, as the citation of even a few lines will show:

[1] The funeral plateau (Breasted).

Death is before me today
Like the recovery of a sick man
Like going forth into a garden after sickness.
Death is before me today
Like the odour of myrrh,
Like sitting under the sail on a windy day . . .

where on one of the few occasions in any literature the contemplation of death evokes images the reverse of horrific, morbid, or distressing. In contrast to the conventional ideas of this and later times, we have the approach of death compared to the recovery of a man from sickness. The entry into the unknown world is likened to stepping from the shuttered sick-room into a garden, and so on. This mood of awakening faith, conveyed in poetry at least equal to that of the 'Song of the Harp Player', provides a fitting transition to the final poem, which is concerned not so much with the fact of death as with the dead themselves. In this final phase of the Misanthrope's spiritual pilgrimage the immortals 'who are yonder' are regarded as judges and punishers of the wicked after death. If there is no justice on earth, then at least there is justice in heaven. Death is not the end, nor is it a passing into forgetfulness. It is rather the beginning, an entering upon a mode of living in which good and evil receive their due. Already, in other words, we have arrived at a stage at which all men are held responsible for their actions, at which conscience has become democratized, and at which a man's 'dialogue with his own soul' is becoming a recognized theme for literature. Nor does the concentration upon personal experience indicate the absence of a 'social conscience'. It is simply a form of social conscience, man's thoughts being 'driven inwards' on account of the corruption of society.

In the same way, Job was a public figure, a man of substance and reputation, who, having lost everything capable of making life worth living, was obliged to consult his own soul as to the meaning of life and suffering. What is remarkable about the experience of the Egyptian Misanthrope is not merely that it antedated that of Job, but that it forms part of the social conscience of a people lacking the profound spiritual endowment of the Hebrews. To this subject we shall return in due course. It is perhaps sufficient to remark that the Misanthrope, who no doubt died 'full of years' like Job, seems to have arrived at the condition of faith entirely on his own. Unlike Job, he sought and obtained no interview with God. There was no whirlwind conference. Nor, at the conclusion of his trials, was he 'blessed more than his beginning' with material possessions. For him, faith was literally 'the substance of things hoped for, the evidence of things not seen'; for we must remember that with all his belief in the supernatural and in tutelary deities, the Egyptian of this epoch had no conception of a religious revelation open to all mankind. Faith had nothing but itself to stand upon.

The Defence of Maat

That other documents surviving from this age should reveal a similar mood of disillusion cannot be accident. The student of modern literature, intent upon tracing a particular line of thought or trend of feeling, succeeds by judicious selection in finding all the evidence he needs; but the selection must necessarily be rigorous and it may sometimes be arbitrary. Hence the reversal in each generation of the judgments and valuations of the immediate past. In this section of our study the situation is totally different. No arbitrary selection need be made. The corpus of Egyptian literature, though much bigger than is usually supposed, is manageable, uniform, and now for the most part accessible. We need not juggle about with it to prove our theories. We may accept it as it is. A progressive deepening of moral and spiritual awareness crystallizes out of all the writings from the Memphite Drama to the time of *The Book of the Dead.* Since almost all these fragments of literature were preserved by the court and the priesthood, a good deal of careful editing was no doubt undertaken. Even so, for this body of writing to have survived is still remarkable, and perhaps all the more so for its evidence of increasing spiritual insight on the part of both authors and editors: material which, so far as we can tell, had been assembled for the first time in history.

Two very interesting examples of this increasing insight into the nature of morality date from roughly the period of the Misanthrope. The first is a meditation by a priest at Heliopolis called Khekheperre-soneb. This text was copied by a scribe of the Eighteenth Dynasty on to a board which is now in the British Museum. To this shrewd observer of his fellow-men, the old standards of morality have broken down. Unlike the Misanthrope, he appears to nourish no personal grievance, but rather a professional concern for the neglect of *Maat* and the wisdom of the ancestors. 'I am meditating,' he writes, 'on what has happened (i.e. his is no imaginary denunciation). Calamities come to pass today; tomorrow afflictions are not past. All men are silent concerning it (although) the whole land is in great disturbance.... Long and heavy is my malady. The poor man has no strength to save himself from him that is stronger than he.' And so he proceeds in the same vein for many lines, expressing social disillusionment all the more bitter and dark because it appeared to be without precedent. The rise and fall of empires and civilizations is a theme to which our modern historians increasingly address themselves, until we have come to regard the dissolution of our own civilization as merely a matter of time, so convinced are we of its inherent weaknesses. Khekheperre-soneb and his companions were facing the hitherto unthinkable: the disintegration of a social system regarded as ordained by God from all eternity and sustained by His living representative the Pharaoh and the power of *Maat.* The phrase 'I am meditating on what has happened' evidently refers to the contemplation of what had never happened before.

The second example is altogether more original. This is the story of the 'Eloquent Peasant', a lengthy piece of writing preserved on a papyrus roll now in the Berlin Museum. At first sight this tale, together with the moral which it points, provides a most damaging criticism of the upper and especially the official classes; for the story relates how a poor peasant, driving his mules one day near the estates of the king's Grand Steward, was tricked by a wily official into trespassing and permitting the beasts to nibble the master's corn. The peasant's goods and chattels are seized and he is arrested, but he determines to plead his cause before the Grand Steward himself. He does so in a series of nine lengthy speeches, each more eloquent and bold than the last, in which the high officials and even the king are reminded of their duties. To the earlier speeches the Grand Steward either lends a deaf ear, or, goaded to fury by the impertinence of the suppliant, replies by ordering him to be soundly beaten. Such chastisement merely prompts the peasant to greater feats of eloquence. Addressing the Grand Steward in impassioned phrases, he brings his argument to a climax with these words:

> Be not light, for thou art weighty,
> Speak not falsehood, for thou art the balances,[1]
> Swerve not, for thou art uprightness.

To drive home his point, he stresses the fact that justice is not dependent upon human inclination or whim, but, being eternal, survives neglect, defiance, and corruption. 'Justice (*Maat*),' he declares, 'is from all eternity: it descendeth with him that doeth it into the grave.' After this series of lessons from the least of his subjects, the Grand Steward becomes convinced that justice has after all been abused. He therefore arrests the guilty official and restores the peasant his property.

Whether or not this story was originally intended as propaganda, it sheds a vivid light upon the common notions of the time. What impresses us most forcibly is the fact that, in spite of its central theme of justice, there is at no point the smallest suggestion that the social order should be *subverted*. Unjust officials should be replaced by just officials, but peasants aspire to be nothing more than peasants: that is the underlying assumption of a story not devoid of wit and something often approaching humour. Secondly, and perhaps in consequence of this acceptance of an immutable social hierarchy, there is nothing inherently absurd in a peasant either reminding his masters of their social obligations or in possessing sufficient education to do so. In a country in which responsibility had rested upon the ruler for so many centuries, there must have been considerable force in the peasant's arguments. Throughout later history there is much denunciation of the rich and powerful merely on account of their riches and power: the preservation of the story of the Eloquent Peasant suggests that it was regarded less as subversive literature than as a reminder of what an enlightened king expected of his officials. We have here one of the few social documents in which the duties of masters to servants are regarded as the primary source of social stability. Almost every other civilization, having assumed the duties of servants to masters, proceeds to demonstrate its humanitarianism by making 'concessions' to the lower orders. The only concession for which the Eloquent Peasant

[1] In Egypt the balances were always the symbol of Justice. Justice is still usually represented as carrying them.

made plea was that justice should be done him as a man performing his duty in his particular station. He makes the distinction between that which may be conceded as a result of power, and that which should be granted as a result of obligation. We concede what we must, but we grant what we ought.

Those who caused the story of the Eloquent Peasant to be preserved and transcribed had evidently perceived the insufficiency of the maxim laid down in the 'Instruction to Merikere'—that an official will tend to do justice provided he is well paid. If, as it now seemed, the only guarantee of just action was the existence of a just ruler, the problem of how to find a just ruler admitted of no clearcut solution. It was a matter of chance. Moreover, with the collapse of the old order and the neglect of the traditional wisdom, there was an increasing danger that even the best-intentioned ruler or official would be corrupted. The traditional wisdom had been a bulwark against the grosser abuses of power. Now that such a guarantee was removed or weakened, what could take its place?

The men who sought to answer this question, or whose answers happen to have been preserved, were very different in outlook from those whose thoughts we have been considering. There was good reason why they should be. Ptah-hotep and the authors of the 'Instruction to Merikere', the 'Song of the Harp Player' and the testament of the Misanthrope were either worldly commentators on life or stoic contemplators of death. Finding mankind full of iniquity, they look to the after-world to redress the balance of good and evil. After the collapse of the Old Kingdom, however, we find certain thinkers whose disillusionment, though extreme, is nevertheless tempered with hope in a new social order: not an order to be obtained by the dispossession of the ruling classes or the accession to power of new social elements, but an order to be established by a ruler divinely guided to restore the power of *Maat.* This is more than 'social idealism' in the modern sense; it is, as Breasted has pointed out, the first hint in history of *messianism.* While the greatest of the Prophets were those to appear in Israel—greatest by reason perhaps of their continuity of message, for which there exists no parallel—the ancient world did not lack prophets of another order, whose utterances strike us as less impressive only because of the absence of some evident fulfilment.

When we read the sombre pronouncements of the Egyptian sage called Ipuwer, we are driven to wonder how many other men equal in insight have missed the accident of record: for man who voices a feeling common to many in the same generation must do so in a language that has already expressed much in the same tenor. You can initiate thought; you cannot initiate the language in which it is expressed. Ipuwer is more than a shrewd commentator on society; he is concerned, as every great philosopher is concerned, with the human condition, then as now hardly conducive to optimism. In what are called his 'Admonitions', he refers to the social evils of his time in terms not of political propaganda but of philosophic disillusion. He is in fact the first philosopher to identify the decline of civilization with what Gilbert Murray has called, in connection with a similar moment in Greek history, the 'failure of nerve': that is to say, a collapse of the will to believe, issuing in doubt concerning the benevolence and even the reality of the gods.

The sages before Ipuwer lament the decay of standards, and wring their hands over the impending collapse of their culture. Ipuwer probes deeper. For he perceives very clearly that once such doubts become widespread, once they eat into the soul, the very nature of life becomes abhorrent: not perhaps life itself but rather that characteristic of life which is least open to explanation, namely the vain and wearisome repetition of its functions. 'Would,' he exclaims at one point, 'that there might be an end of men, that there might be no conception, no birth!' This, indeed, is the first recorded note of a theme which is to run through Eastern thought to this day; but it is followed by a passage of strangely reminiscent beauty, composed, like the rest of Ipuwer's 'Admonitions', in a metre later made familiar in the Hebrew psalms, and hinting at the advent of a saviour or benevolent conqueror to whom, as we shall see, almost all ancient literatures make reference: for men had not yet discovered any science upon which they could nourish their illusions, or any art with which to beguile them. 'He' [and this can refer only to some such deliverer as we have mentioned] 'brings cooling to the flame. It is said he is the shepherd of all men. There is no evil in his heart. When his herds are few he passes the day to gather them together, their hearts being fevered.' So he continues in lines that remind us of Isaiah and Ezekiel, prophets for whom the theme assumes a greater significance fifteen hundred years later.

Faced with utterances such as the above, certain historians seek hastily for a materialistic explanation of its prophetic content. At all costs, it seems, these ancient sages must be shown not to mean what they say. It is not at all impossible that Ipuwer, like the priest Neferrohu,[1] had in mind a real person. Observing that the men of his day were accustomed 'to go ploughing bearing a shield', and being horrified at the thought of civil war (which, as he shrewdly says, 'pays no taxes'), Ipuwer may well have placed his hopes in a foreign ruler, probably from the south, whose spokesman he chose or was persuaded to become; or he may have invented an imaginary figure in the hope that it might later become incarnate. The attitude is none the less messianic. For we know that the people most possessed with messianic ideas, the Jews, were always divided, and are so to this day, as to the exact form which their deliverer should take.

Decadence

To the Eloquent Peasant, *Maat* was a spiritual possession to which all

[1] Neferrohu writes in terms of disillusion similar to Khekheperresoneb, but the saviour to whom he looks forward is almost certainly Amenemhet I, founder of the Twelfth Dynasty about 2030 BC. The latter did not achieve what was expected of him. He left a testament to his son Sesostris, in the course of which he said: 'I gave to the beggar, I nourished the orphan; I admitted the insignificant as well as him who was of great account. But he who ate my food made insurrection: he to whom I gave my land aroused fear therein.'

men had access. The fact that this story enjoyed official approval, as we cannot doubt that it did, shows that the spiritual growth observable in the sages had been accompanied by relative popular enlightenment. If the peasant was more than usually eloquent, he was in other respects typical of his class. But this democratization of *Maat* had its attendant dangers: first, because the exalted 'solar' theology became increasingly blended with the cult of Osiris, the people's natural faith; and secondly, because the admission of the Pharaoh's subjects to the heaven originally reserved for the king conferred greatly increased powers upon the priesthood. The priestly caste in Egypt—for caste it was—had enjoyed an immense reputation from the earliest times.

Herodotus, who learnt most of what he knew about the mind of the Egyptians from the priests he questioned, speaks well of this branch of the theocratic government. According to him, the priests were for the most part both highly skilled and upright in character. The 'mysteries' they supervised were in one sense as mysterious as the Nile inundation; and in another sense as practical as the control of this overflow by irrigation and the timely harvesting of crops. A lofty, metaphysical religion without any immediate connection with practical life would have been unintelligible to an Egyptian, who at certain seasons of the year was obliged to do overtime for his faith. Such powers and responsibilities were naturally a source of great temptation. It might even be suggested that the chief cause of corruption in the priesthood was not so much idleness, sloth, indulgence—the usual breeders of decadence—as too greater pressure of work. The elaborate ceremonial connected with a royal tomb might occupy the lifetime of groups of priests over a period of centuries. Temples needed to be staffed and maintained. Property accumulated by purchase or pious bequest had to be managed. Archives, more precious and revered then than now, required careful storage and occasional editing. Schools for scribes and catechumens were a condition of the profession's continuity. Above all, the people's needs, requests, and superstitions had to be attended to with patience, and perhaps with guile. If the people were to be satisfied they must be given that in which they were prepared to trust, whether it took the form of a charm, or an incantation, or a sacred scroll of unintelligible script. And if they sought help to cast out demons in this world and the next, the most reasonable reaction was not to deride their credulity but to furnish them with the necessary spells at the appropriate price.

It would be totally inaccurate to say that such methods worked only among the people: credulity of this kind is found among all classes of *Homo credens*. During the so-called Middle Kingdom (2065–1580 BC) powerful and wealthy officials used to arrange for their coffins to be covered inside with texts and inscriptions, mostly setting forth spells and magical formulae.[1] Studied carefully, such inscriptions betray evidence of having been used not for the sake of their intellectual con-

[1] These inscriptions have been collected and published under the title of '*Coffin Texts*', by Breasted chiefly.

tent, which is in most cases small, but as a kind of verbal protection for the body against demons and spirits. Consequently there is a great deal of repetition and error in their composition, and many passages are left incomplete, suggesting the rapid and mechanical work of funerary scribes whose task was to adorn the entire interior of the wooden box with writing.

In addition to these magical clichés—which, as Sethe pointed out, were evidently intended to 'read themselves'—there were a large number of papyrus rolls of similar characters[1] which could be purchased from the priests and deposited in tombs. These texts form what has come to be called *The Book of the Dead*. Assembled officially during the period of the Ptolemies about 400 BC, *The Book of the Dead* has sometimes been mistakenly termed the 'Bible of the Egyptians', whereas it is in large part a Demonology of a particularly gruesome kind. Here we find such odd official spells as those for 'refusing serpents', for 'repulsing crocodiles' and other beasts of prey, and also a variety of formulae of a negative and (to us) ludicrous kind, such as 'for not walking head downwards', to 'avoid losing one's mouth or heart', to 'prevent drinking-water turning into flame', etc. The latter category of spell evidently provided a harassed priesthood with infinite possibilities of magical prescription; for if both the dying or the companions of the deceased wished to make provision against the remotest as well as the most obvious contingencies, there was bound to be a sale for almost any formula whatever.

Less grotesque but equally negative in spirit are a series of written acts of personal contrition to be found not merely among the Coffin Texts in *The Book of the Dead*, but also as inscriptions on the walls of tombs. These so-called 'negative confessions' sometimes assume a wheedling form, as if the soul had hopes of coming to terms with the judge Osiris by a kind of settlement out of court. At other times they reveal a depth of moral understanding which not merely disposes of the view that the sense of sin is something instilled into man by his rulers, but shows that eternal life was regarded as a prize to be earned by righteous conduct in this world. The tomb of Ameni, Baron of Beni-hason, is inscribed with the following typical phrase, 'There was no citizen's daughter whom I misused, there was no widow whom I afflicted, there was no peasant whom I evicted.' Likewise the mortuary texts contain statement after statement of the following nature: 'Hail to Thee, Great God, Lord of Truth and Justice! I have come before Thee, My Master ... I have not committed iniquity against men. I have not oppressed the poor ... I have not defaulted, I have not committed that which is abomination to the gods. I have not caused the slave to be ill-treated of his master. I have not starved any man, I have not made any to weep, I have not assassinated any man,' and so on in an endless protest of innocence, culminating in the repeated phrase, 'I am pure, I am pure, I am pure.' We employ other people to write our obituary notices.

[1] About 2000 of these have been discovered.

Ikhnaten: the 'Great Schismatic'

In referring to the worship of Osiris, we mentioned the later imposition of a new and purified religion by an Egyptian ruler of more than usual distinction of character. The brief reign of this Pharaoh, who came to the throne under the name of Amenhotep IV in the year 1380 BC, has attracted more attention from historians than any other Egyptian king save, for more accidental reasons, his son-in-law Tutankhamen. Deservedly so; for Amenhotep was not merely one of the most remarkable men that has ever lived, but, as historians have pointed out, the first real *individual* known to history. (Some have reserved this title for the earlier Imhotep, the doctor and architect to King Zoser, who lived about 3150 BC; but Imhotep, who is incidentally mentioned in the 'Song of the Harp Player', is too obscure a figure to qualify for this distinction. Indeed, he was later worshipped as a god of knowledge, like another 'individual' whose personality has become blurred by veneration, Pythagoras.) Much of what we know about the 'heretic king', as he was later called, is derived from the works of art and literature associated with his reign, all of which are remarkable for their innovations in form, style, and content. What remains less explicable to the point of mystery is why this revolution, which was by no means confined to art, should have taken place at all.

When the Egyptian capital was established at Thebes by the Pharaohs of the New Empire (1580 BC onwards), the priests of Amen, the Theban equivalent of Re, began steadily to acquire power in the land. Possibly because he regarded such influence as a threat to his political authority, or because he abhorred the corruption of the Amen cult, Amenhotep IV seems to have lost no opportunity of showing his hostility to the orthodox priests. Such a policy of opposition to the most powerful caste in the country was attended by great risk. The high priest of Amen was chief among all Egyptian priests, and, given the excuse, he could mobilize more wealth than the Pharaoh himself, and also if necessary summon substantial aid from abroad. Indeed, at the end of the Nineteenth Dynasty (*c.* 1200 BC), a High Priest of Amen actually usurped the throne. Such considerations did not deter the young Pharaoh. With amazing self-confidence he resolved upon a course of action which, instead of simply purging or reforming the Amen cult, put the entire priesthood out of work. He declared Amen to be a divine impostor and proclaimed his worship blasphemy. Although the motives animating the young reformer have remained obscure, we can suggest various explanations of his extraordinary conduct. In the first place, his attack upon Amen was not simply iconoclastic. In abolishing one form of worship, he was ready to replace it with another. The cult of his choice was that of Aten, the Sun-god, whose worship he declared himself to have embraced as the result of a personal revelation. How true this is we shall never know. If he did not actually experience such a revelation, his conduct suggests that he believed himself to have done so on frequent occasions throughout life. In such cases, as William James pointed out in his *Varieties of Religious Experience*, the distinction between a man's claim to have felt something and his having actually done so, disappears: the claim may be the form that the feeling took. But is this all we can say? Perhaps the circumstances of the king's life serve to throw light upon this crucial phase of his development. Now that we have for the first time in this book a life to study, the question assumes particular interest.

From the vivid pictorial records that survive from this period, we observe that the young devotee of Aten was accustomed to appear in public accompanied by his wife and his mother. Such a practice, novel at the time, possessed an added significance on account of the personality of these two women. Both were evidently remarkable, particularly the wife. Nefretete, for such was her name, differed from most other royal consorts in that she was a foreigner, an 'Asiatic'. From early times it had been the custom for the Pharaoh to marry his sister, just as Osiris married Isis. In ancient Egyptian, the words 'brother and sister' may also be used to imply the relationship of love. Ikhnaten was one of the first to depart from this ancient tradition. His wife came from Syria, which, though part of the Egyptian Empire, was a land of mystery and strange cults, which it remains to this day. Now the Syrians, too, worshipped the sun; and it is not impossible that Nefretete, in becoming the Pharaoh's wife, brought with her the particular form of sun worship to which she had been accustomed. Of her great influence over her husband we have abundant evidence. Her exquisitely beautiful face was everywhere reproduced in painting, carving, and sculpture; and if, as we may suppose, the new realisitic tendency in art dealt with her as faithfully as it did with others, as well as with animals and natural objects, she may be accounted the most beautiful queen in history, not excluding Cleopatra or some of the Circassian slave-women whom the Ottoman Sultans took to wife. She was invoked in reverent and affectionate terms in the Sun Hymn, reputedly composed by her husband: she is therefore the only wife of a founder of a religion to be associated on equal terms in the routine worship of the cult. Finally she became her husband's partner not merely in private life but in public affairs. Not merely was she the first lady in the land, but she became the protagonist of her sex in general, encouraging her seven daughters to adopt a similar role in society, and remaining, as far as we can tell, on the best of terms with her mother-in-law. Even allowing for rhetorical exaggeration, it is possible to impute something approaching domestic perfection to one who could be described by her husband as 'Mistress of his happiness, at hearing whose voice the king's heart rejoices'. That Ikhnaten should have been attracted and finally converted to her faith is more than probable.

Since Nefretete brought personal happiness to her husband, though not a son and heir, and since he must have acquired from her a particular respect for women, nothing was more likely to rouse his antipathy to the Amen cult than its practice of sacred prostitution. At the great temple at Karnak, not far from his own palace, special quarters were set aside for the priestesses appointed to minister to the needs of the god. It is unlikely that the king would have objected to this practice, which was common throughout the world and, in sublimated form, has been a feature of most religions, including Christianity. But it was an open secret that the vestal virgins were also employed upon secular duties, in which the priests of Amen were associated. No doubt the manner in which the god was worshipped, rather than the nature of the Deity himself (who was, after all, the Sun-god too), induced the young king, already encouraged by his wife, to declare the cult an abomination. Another reason my be found in the nature of the new cult of Aten.

In suggesting that Nefretete imported the faith which her husband was persuaded to embrace along with herself, we do not mean to imply that Aten was an alien god. He was an Egyptian god. His name, together with the symbol of the sun disc,[1] appears in the earliest Egyptian records, including the Pyramid Texts. Moreover, he had been worshipped for generations as a Sun-god. How was it, then, that the substitution of a Sun-god (Aten) for a Sun-god (Amen), leaving the supreme Sun-god (Re) apparently unchallenged, produced such a complete revolution in social life? The answer to this question lies in the form taken by the worship of Aten. This, for Egypt, was thoroughly original. In the first place the devotee of Aten was obliged to renounce all other gods; Aten alone was to be worshipped. Secondly, the worship of Aten consisted not simply of sun worship; it was worship of the sun's life-giving properties, as the great Hymns make abundantly plain:

> Creator of the germ in woman
> Maker of the seed in man
> Giving life to the sun in the body of its mother . . .
> Nurse even in the womb
> Giver of breath to animate every one that he maketh.

The word Aten, indeed, means strictly 'heat which is in the sun', and the sun disc was intended to represent, as it is sometimes accompanied by, the sun's rays, the life-distributing antennae. That sun worshippers had hitherto stressed this aspect of the solar deity is not certain: a hot climate may not persuade men that the sun's influence is uniquely beneficial, still less the source of life. But it is clear that the worshippers of Aten were chiefly preoccupied by the beneficence of solar energy. Thirdly, and this was so marked a departure from Egyptian religious custom as to point to an Asiatic origin, the true temple of Aten was the open air itself. Dispensing with statues and shrines, the devotees of the new faith adored Aten in person and basked themselves in his bounty. God was to be worshipped in spirit and in truth.

Although the young king seems to have shown a marked preference for dreams as opposed to realities, poetry to diplomacy, he was well aware that the religion he had established could not be made to flourish without material support. Nor did he ignore, though he evidently grossly underestimated, the latent opposition of the devotees and priests of Amen, most of whom were unemployed, though a few of them apparently rallied to the new faith. He therefore took stern practical measures to prevent a resumption of Amen worship. He ordered

[1] One of the signs representing Horus. See page 27.

that the name Amen should be erased from every public inscription in the country. Such inscriptions ran into thousands. And since the new faith was monotheistic, a similar campaign was launched against all public references to 'gods' as opposed to 'god'.[1]

That the name Amenhotep, his own, contained the hated syllable naturally did not escape his notice. Accordingly it was changed to one embodying the name of the new god. Henceforth the king called himself Ikhnaten, meaning 'Aten is satisfied'. As the same objection applied to the name of his dead and revered father, the royal tomb was reinscribed along with the rest. Most of the erasures and alterations are still visible.

In order to complete his dissociation from the cult of Amen, Ikhnaten finally decided to abandon Karnak, which was too closely identified with the past, and to establish himself in a town specially dedicated to his god. He chose for his new capital the site now known as Tel el-Amarna, which was several hundred miles down the River Nile and roughly half-way between Thebes and Memphis. Upon it, as upon everything else, he conferred an Aten-name Akhet-aten, which means literally 'Horizon of Aten'. From this site archaeologists have unearthed most of the written testimony concerning Ikhnaten's reign. Not content with one Aten town, however, Ikhnaten decided to build two others, one in Nubia and the other in Asia: for he was resolved to demonstrate that Aten was the god not merely of Egypt but of all the world, or at least the Egyptian Empire. There would likewise be a special significance in establishing such a town in that part of the empire from which the queen herself came.

In the enthusiasm of the new faith, life at Akhet-aten seems to have been both prosperous and contented. As Egyptian society had always been accustomed to look upon its Pharaoh as the fount of blessings, the presence of a royal family so united and devout must have been regarded as a special mark of God's favour, a sign of Aten's appreciation of the new respect he had acquired among men. In the sphere of art, as we have said, the freedom of the Aten faith produced a remarkable liberating effect. Men and women are portrayed naturalistically as never before. The king permits the scenes of his domestic life to be recorded with almost photographic exactitude, including one which represents him embracing his queen. The delicate and somewhat effeminate portrait that has survived suggests that Ikhnaten, scorning the conventional flattery of court artists, wished to be portrayed exactly as he was—not as a warrior or even a man of authority but rather as a poet or seer. (The only puzzling feature about this human portraiture, suggesting perhaps a subtle flattery, is the fact that most of the figures appear to have deformed legs, which, as this cannot have been the case with so many, may possibly have been the case with one, whose feelings were in this way respected.) But perhaps the most beautiful survival from this other-worldly interlude is the great Sun Hymn itself, with its passages reminiscent of the 104th psalm ('O

[1] It is interesting to note that, apart from this, no gods except Amen were officially declared impostors.

Lord, how manifold are thy works! in wisdom has thou made them all'):

How manifold are thy works!
They are hidden from before us,
O sole god, whose power no other possesseth,
Thou who didst create the world according to thy heart,

and with its direct reference to the royal pair:

Thou didst establish the world
And raised them up for thy son...
Ikhnaten whose life is long;
And for the chief royal wife, his beloved
Mistress of the two lands,
Nefer-nefru-aton, Nofretete,
Living and flourishing for ever and ever.

Unique in literature and probably more beautiful in the original than we can easily imagine, this hymn may provide us with a clue to the strength and weakness of Ikhnaten's revolution. Composed in everyday language, it was simple, ecstatic, and intellectual. That it can ever have been popular, as hymns should be popular, is extremely doubtful. If the faith which it expressed was intended as a universal faith, its poetic expression was that of a solitary, almost a recluse, like the author of certain of the Hebrew psalms:

Thou art in my heart,
There is no other that knoweth thee
Save thy son Ikhnaten.
Thou hast made him wise
In thy designs and in thy might.

So he thought. However great his sincerity and the depth of his spiritual experience, this tendency to seek God in the quiet of his bed-chamber, this extreme subjectivism, was probably the cause of the lack of hold which the new faith had on his people. For, whatever their respect for Ikhnaten and his family, the ordinary man neither abandoned his old beliefs nor in most cases imagined that he was required to do so. A change of name meant very little to him, as little as the new theology itself. Curiously enough, the literature produced during Ikhnaten's reign makes no mention whatever of Osiris. Was this because the ban on Amen worship was assumed automatically to refer to Osiris too? Or was it because no innovator, not even Ikhnaten, would have been foolish enough to forbid the public devotion to Osiris, which was less a religion than an inveterate social habit? At any rate, the cult of Aten, being (so to speak) too free from superstition to compel the attention of the masses, made no headway in displacing the great Judge of the Underworld. The public must have its underworld, and the lofty realm of Aten provided no substitute for it. Finally, the Aten cult was primary one of adoration, of sheer worship; whereas a religion cannot take root, cannot be practised, unless it is practical. Just as morals must be buttressed by religion, so religion must become incarnate in morals.

The immediate threat to Ikhnaten and to the new social gospel came not from the discontented priests of Amen and their followers, still less from the common people, to whom social revolt was unthinkable, but from outside the country. Ikhnaten had hoped to govern Egypt by an idea, a dream; but an empire, however benevolently administered, must be defended and protected by force. Certain historians have maintained that Ikhnaten, though not a warrior like Thutmos III, sought to further the imperial interests of Egypt by the more subtle method of conquering the minds of his subjects: hence the cult of Aten was a form of propaganda. The winged sun disc was certainly a more easily exportable symbol than any other Egyptian insignia, and the Sun Hymns could be accepted anywhere, though it was a novelty for a national or imperial anthem to be at the same time ravishing poetry. The province of Syria was the first to raise the signal of alarm. The enemy came originally from Asia Minor—a fierce, hardy, dour people, though, as we are rapidly discovering, not without culture. Those people, the Hittites, had acquired numerous allies on the borders of the Egyptian Empire. The first incursion into the imperial territory was made by the King of Kadesh, who occupied northern Syria. This attack was followed swiftly by an advance of the King of the Amorites to the wealthy and strategically vital ports on the Phoenician coast, including Byblos. Frantic appeals for aid were sent to Ikhnaten from his distracted but loyal political officers. Reluctant to use open force, the Pharaoh sent a trusted official to Phoenicia on a fact-finding commission. The emissary, who no doubt acted in the spirit of the instructions given him by Ikhnaten, informed the King of the Amorites that he might stay where he was. It was hoped that he would later come to regard himself as a vassal to Egypt. The invader, agreeing to this arrangement for the time being, held his ground.

But the attacks continued from other quarters. The Bedouin, rising in revolt, seized the town of Megiddo (Armageddon) near Jerusalem. 'The Assyrians came down like a wolf on the fold ...' Finally, the King of the Amorites, who had hoped to turn vassalage into independence by discontinuing his nominal tribute to Egypt, was confronted with his old allies the Hittites, and obliged to sign away his nearly-won freedom. His governors deposed, his envoys insulted, his coffers empty of tribute, Ikhnaten suddenly found himself powerless abroad and friendless at home; for the opposition party had naturally become bolder in its protests as the situation abroad deteriorated. Much of the débâcle must be put down, it seems, to sheer political and diplomatic ineptitude on the Pharaoh's part. From the hundreds of cuneiform tablets discovered between 1855 and 1893 by Flinders Petrie at Tel el-Amarna (the 'Tel el-Amarna Letters'), we know that Ikhnaten's foreign representatives not merely kept him fully informed of what was happening but begged him earnestly to send them military aid.[1] Disloyalty there may sometimes have been; but such desperate

[1] Cuneiform was still the language of diplomacy, a relic of the traditional power of Babylon.

appeals suggest that many of the provincial governors, though not always Egyptians by nationality, were willing to stick to their posts. In the end, Ikhnaten lost nearly the whole of his empire without a fight.

A man can survive defeat, but a national god cannot. Of the end of Ikhnaten's life and reign we know little, because the evidence is obscure. Still less than thirty years of age, he appears to have broken down under the strain and humiliation of the national reverses: an older man might have borne these trials more philosophically, if he had had a more realistic philosophy upon which to rely. Whether, as is suggested, the king renounced the worship of Aten and returned to that of Amen, and if so whether he did so voluntarily, as a condition perhaps of being able to retain the throne, we cannot say. As for Nefretete, we gather that she remained at Akhet-aten but refused to renounce the Aten cult: a further indication that she had been brought up in its spirit. Had she borne a son, the latter would now have ascended the throne. Instead, Ikhnaten appointed the husband of her eldest daughter Semenkhare to rule jointly with him, perhaps at Thebes and perhaps as nominally repentant devotees of Amen. If so, the two must have died within a short while of each other, for the next Pharaoh to be proclaimed was the boy-husband of the second daughter.

This lad, who had remained with Nefretete at Akhet-aten, was called Tutankhaten. After three years' reign he abandoned the Aten capital, returned to Thebes, declared the Aten cult illegal, restored the Amen priests in their former offices, and, ridding himself of all vestiges of the old regime, changed his name to Tutankhamen.

Both Aten and his prophet received the same treatment at the hands of Tutankhamen as the Amen priests and their god had done under Ikhnaten. Inscriptions were once more changed, and the name of the late Pharaoh was banned even from conversation. If reference to him became necessary, it was as the 'great criminal', or the 'great schismatic'. By what luck or cunning Nefretete succeeded in remaining at Tel el-Amarna we do not know. Her enemies accused her of seeking the support of the Hittites against her own son-in-law. If this was the case, the wonder is not that she did so but that her activities, known to be directed against the new regime, were not more carefully watched. It is possible that, in her isolation, she was considered incapable of doing much harm.

Meanwhile the political misfortunes of Ikhnaten's reign were being repaired, not indeed by his successor, who seems to have lacked initiative, but by one of the latter's generals, Horemheb. In a series of remarkable campaigns, the latter not merely restored Egypt's fortunes but successfully made his own. Married to one of Ikhnaten's daughters, Horemheb finally ascended the throne as the last ruler of the Dynasty he had done so much to preserve; but with extraordinary arrogance and some ingratitude he insisted upon dating the beginning of his reign from the death of Amenhotep III, thus effacing from record the reigns of Ikhnaten, Tutankhamen, and Ai (married to

Tutankhamen's widow), who were considered to have brought disgrace upon their ancient line. As a restorer of his country's fortunes, however, he was no doubt justified in his claim, otherwise with little basis, to be the real founder of the Nineteenth Dynasty; for, having grown old in ceaseless military action, he decided to consolidate his achievements by arranging for the throne to be occupied by a comrade-in-arms, Rameses I (1320 BC), the immediate successors of whom, above all Rameses II,[1] justified his foresight by their immense achievements in building and foreign conquest. Nevertheless, these triumphs were the prelude to disaster. The Amen priesthood, now more firmly in the seat of power, succeeded during the reign of the last of the Rameses in putting one of their number on the throne itself. There was now no check upon corruption. Political decisions were determined as much by omen as by reasonable argument. Superstition, instead of being a creeping and inevitable growth of the spiritual underworld, was allowed freely to proliferate. The maxims and charms of *The Book of the Dead* invaded the sphere of the living, until a condition of mind was reached in which it was not considered preposterous that a sorcerer, bent upon extracting some favour from the gods, should threaten not merely to betray their names to the demons but to tear out their hair 'as lotus blossoms are pulled from a pond'. This mentality was neither blasphemous nor foolish; it was simply decadent—a state of credulity in which the devout are persuaded that God can be mocked at will.

The New Insight: Conclusion

Although the reign of Ikhnaten was a comparatively brief interlude—and, according to Horemheb, an interlude that disgraced the national annals—it would be a mistake to assume that the worship of Aten did nothing to affect the life and thought of Egypt, still less that its official interdiction erased it altogether from men's memories. Whatever their political naivety, Ikhnaten and his wife had unquestionably influenced the people by their example of personal devotion to a god, or at least to an ideal. There is evidence too strong to discount that after this golden moment of delight in life—for realism of the kind displayed in art was as genuine a reflection of such delight as realism of another kind is a reflection of disgust—strength and beauty of character was increasingly recognized to be a value in itself, perhaps for the first time in history. That is the reason why Ikhnaten, despite the fact that we know much less about him than we should wish, stands out as an individual in a world of types and figureheads, or mere shadows. The great sages who preceded him—ministers, governors, and priests, men wise in their generation—were content to expound the wisdom of the ancients, enjoining others, usually their sons, to follow it.

In contrast to these venerable figures, Ikhnaten, having received wisdom into his soul, lived it. On that account alone the Aten inter-

[1] Considered by some to have been the Pharaoh who figures in *Exodus*. Apart from this, he was a man of character. Reputed to have had several hundred wives, he assembled a family so large that it became for the next few centuries a clan of its own.

lude is a significant moment in history. Like the few other interludes with which it may be compared, such as the reign of Ashoka,[1] its chief value is to have shown that the effort towards human perfection can be made in any age and simply by the power of human aspiration. And if such interludes appear to belong to poetry rather than to history, to imagination rather than to action, then that is because history is merely the material that fills in the tedious gaps between such bright periods: which explains why all histories, including that of the Western world, begin with an interlude of poetry which is consequently also a prelude to a new kind of life.

Such a new life is perceptible only at certain levels and always at rare intervals. It is interesting to notice, however, that coupled with the dawning appreciation of human character went a new attitude towards human imperfection or sin. *The Book of the Dead* was largely composed of recipes for avoiding judgment hereafter, for concealing one's shortcomings, for cheating the gods. In spite of the orgy of sorcery, magic, and thaumaturgy to which we have already referred as heralding the collapse of Egyptian culture, we notice here and there a new note. This is a note not of protest of innocence but of admission of guilt, a genuinely expressed mood of contrition, a humility wholly absent from the conventional obituary inscriptions of rulers and governors, intent upon self-justification even in death.

This attitude, which is the sense of the Christian gospel, is nowhere more clearly expressed than in the works of the sage Amenemope, who lived about 1000 BC and whose work has survived in a papyrus now in the British Museum. Of all the works of the Egyptian sages, those of Amenemope are the most striking and the closest to us in spirit. Indeed, they provide us with the most fitting transition to the wisdom of the Hebrews, whose recorded thought, though dating from a later period, bears numerous traces of Egyptian influence. In places, fragments of Egyptian wisdom appear in the Hebrew scriptures in word-for-word translation. Some of Amenemope's writing, for instance, is reproduced, as Breasted demonstrated so convincingly, in at least one place in the Old Testament, namely *Proverbs*, Chapter xxiv. We know that Amenemope's wisdom was translated into Hebrew and was presumably circulated throughout the Middle East along with other Egyptian writings. We know likewise that Hebrew leaders and prophets were familiar with such writings, among them Moses, whose opportunities for making their acquaintance were obviously great, and no doubt also Amos and Hosea.

When Ptah-hotep and Merikere enjoin their children to revere *Maat*, we are in the presence of the wisdom of a civilization considered to be both unique and everlasting: wisdom, to use the definition of a Western philosopher, was a 'settled habit', since the laws of social life in Egypt were supposed to have been established by Thoth for ever and ever.[2] When Amenemope observes that 'God is in his Perfection, and

[1] See Chapter 6, page 177.

[2] Thoth was god of Wisdom. His reign, lasting 3000 years, was supposed to have begun about 18,000 BC.

man is in his insufficiency', however, we are in the presence of the wisdom of a civilization the very reverse of settled, a civilization in course of formation in bondage, a civilization on the march. In short, we are in the world of the psalmist, whose insufficiency is his daily preoccupation, and for whom insight into the majesty of God is to be attained not through enlightened maxims but through anguish of soul.[1]

We now take our leave of the civilization of Egypt. In most books dealing with philosophy, it is the custom to begin with the pre-Socratic philosophers and to proceed to the great thinkers of Greece: after which, if the author happens to be interested in theology, he turns to a consideration of the ideas of the early Christian Fathers, leading through St Augustine to the great mediaeval thinkers. In Part Two of the present volume, such an orthodox approach is adopted, for our concern is to trace the development of a westward-moving tradition of thought. The present part gives us an opportunity of studying a philosophical tradition starting from a somewhat similar point but moving in another direction. In observing this contrary movement, however, we shall be covering certain ground common to both traditions, while in these first few chapters we have been studying a culture not merely older and more lasting than any that is yet known, but more important as a cultural influence than has been recognized. Throughout the journey already accomplished we have constantly been obliged to remind the reader that what he is faced with is, if not the beginning of wisdom, then at least its beginnings; that these brief specimens of thought about God, man, immortality and the good life are the first of their kind to be recorded; that the earliest metaphysical treatise known to us, the Memphite Drama, would seem to presuppose a tradition of thought already ancient by 2500 BC; and that we cannot yet attempt to say why, at a moment to which no accurate date can be assigned (but at least a million years from man's first appearance on the earth), civilization should have arisen at all.

In an age in which the idea of progress has been dismissed as an illusion it is refreshing to observe that an advance in moral and spiritual apprehension is not merely hinted at, but, on the material available, incontestable.[2] Naturally, this does not mean that as time went on men behaved better and better. Unfortunately conduct lags behind precept in a way that secular moralists must find wholly baffling. Such progress is the result, we may suppose, of man's beginning

[1] It is perhaps worth pointing out for the benefit of those interested in Existentialism, a collective name for a variety of different and often conflicting theories, that the Hebrew psalms reveal a point of view distinctly existentialist. There is the same consciousness of man's utter helplessness before powers outside his control, the same realization that his freedom comes through action and service, the same preoccupation with degradation and death. The theme of the psalms, or at least the great majority of them, is *Angst*. In fact, by a paradox, the psalms approximate in spirit less to the religious existentialism of Gabriel Marcel than to the nihilistic or atheistic existentialism of Jean-Paul Sartre.

[2] 'Progress is real if discontinuous. The upward curve resolves itself into a series of troughs and crests. But in those domains where archaeology as well as written history can survey, no trough ever declines to the low level of the preceding one, each crest outtops its last precursor' (Gordon Childe, *What Happened in History*).

to reflect systematically upon questions to which, for material reasons, he had not addressed himself before: he was too busy keeping alive. If moral insight is a faculty to be attained, man's first attempts to acquire it are likely to have been made along with logical stages of its acquisition. Hence the steps of his progress from mere obedience to divine law, to a sense of duty to society, and finally to the exploration of his own conscience, entailing the acceptance of moral responsibility—a progress which, in the Pyramid Age, seems nearly to have taken a wrong turning, as kings endeavoured to build enormous bulwarks against death—have become visible landmarks on this distant rim of history. Such a development is remarkable for yet another reason: it was virtually completed before any other civilization, including that of the Hebrews, took up the theme on its own. And if no civilization of a later age exhibits a comparable development, this is simply because none other started, as it were, from scratch.

We must conclude this section upon a note of warning. Impressed by the wealth of material made available by excavation in Egypt, and its extreme antiquity, certain able thinkers—above all Flinders Petrie, Elliot-Smith, and to some extent Breasted himself—arrived at what has been termed the 'diffusionist' theory of culture, according to which all civilization in the world originated from developments in the Nile valley. That Western civilization owes an immense debt to Egyptian influence is incontestable; there is likewise a good deal of evidence to suggest that Egyptian influence extended to parts of the world where it might least have been expected.[1] But while acknowledging that Egyptian civilization must have exerted profound influence in every quarter which it penetrated, we can hardly accept the 'diffusionist' theory until it can be supported by more definite proof and less pure guesswork.

We might also point out that the Egyptians, though an imperialist nation for several centuries, made little serious attempt to export their culture. On the contrary, they guarded that culture with extreme care, resenting the intrusion upon their soil of anyone likely to threaten its existence. As early as the second millennium they had erected what they called the Wall of the Ruler, 'in order to prevent the foreign herds from coming down again to Egypt, so that they should beg after their fashion for their cattle to drink'. The Egyptian gods, likewise, were not merely ultra-nationalist but inhabitants of a realm which, save for the obvious disadvantages attendant upon terrestrial life, bore the closest resemblance to the 'Land-of-the-Nile'. There was a sacred Nile in the sky, and upon this river the deified Pharaoh sailed in his barque. There was also a Nile in the nether regions upon which Osiris sailed. All the descriptions of immortal life represent such exist-

[1] To go no farther than Cornwall, T. F. G. Dexter maintained with some plausibility that the ancient form of Cornish Cross is not merely of pagan origin but a development of the form of the Egyptian 'Ankh', symbol of fertility, and that certain customs still preserved reveal Egyptian ritualistic influence. These theories were developed not as a result of any *parti pris* but in consequence of extensive archaeological research in Cornwall. See his *Cornish Crosses, Christian and Pagan* (Longmans, 1938).

ence as merely a heightened form of life in everyday Egypt. It is almost as true to say that heaven was a replica of life on earth as to say that earth was at least in intention modelled upon life in heaven. When an attempt was made by Ikhnaten to export Egyptian culture in the only effective way in which a culture can be exported, namely by diffusing its religion, the faith in question was a highly abstract version of the god-crowded, mystery-ridden religion of Egypt, having been deliberately denationalized for the purpose. Hence the Nile itself becomes for the first and only time in theory what it was later to become in fact, namely an international highway. In Ikhnaten's Sun Hymn the alteration in spirit is quite evident:

> There is a Nile in the sky *for the strangers*
> And for the cattle *of every country* that go upon their feet.

But we know that the mission of Ikhnaten was as much a failure abroad as it was at home. What the world owed to the genius of Egypt was what the world borrowed from Egypt; but the borrower must possess another kind of genius in order to put to good use the things he has appropriated. Henceforth civilization is a shared possession.

3

Babylonia and Israel

If I forget thee, O Jerusalem,
let my right hand forget her cunning

Hammurabi

In the section of the Louvre in Paris containing antiquities from the countries of the Middle East, the visitor's attention will be struck by a glass case situated in a central position which contains an object of curious shape and somewhat forbidding appearance. This object is a shard of black diorite standing about eight feet high and two feet in diameter. On closer inspection, the stele, though in places smooth and polished and even emitting a faint gleam, is seen to be striated with notches and wedge-shape marks arranged in long vertical columns. Forty-four in number, these columns, bearing here and there evidence of deliberate defacement, consist of cuneiform script of remarkable legibility, seeing that it was cut nearly four thousand years ago. At the top of the pillar some carving is visible. A bearded and seated figure, presumably that of a god, is presenting a gift to another, who, though portrayed standing in an attitude of respect, possesses the bearing and wears the robes and helmet of a king. What is this gift? It is evidently something intangible but of surpassing importance. It is in fact the substance of that which is written on the lower flank of the column. For the seated figure is the Babylonian sun-diety Shamash, the recipient of his gift is Hammurabi, King of Babylon, and the gift itself is the oldest legal code in the world.

It is a far cry in both space and time from that glass mausoleum in the Louvre to the site where the shard was first erected. When Hammurabi caused it to be fashioned in the eighteenth century BC[1] he decided that it should be set up in a spot where everyone might be able to inspect it. Such a place was the temple at Sippara, a town not far from Baghdad, the capital of modern Iraq. Temples in Babylon were built to command a view of the surrounding buildings, their foundations being level with the roofs, and were used also as law courts. There the admonitory pillar remained for nearly a thousand years, during which time the laws inscribed upon it still continued to command the respect and obedience of the Babylonians—as indeed was the case for another five hundred years: a period of authority equalled by few other legal

[1] There is still considerable divergence of opinion concerning the exact dates of Hammurabi's reign. W. F. Albright suggests—*c* 1728–1686BC.

codes promulgated by a single individual. About 1100 BC it was captured and removed by a king of the neighbouring region of Elam, who was responsible for the wanton defacement of five of its columns. We say wanton, because whereas it was customary for Egyptian kings to deface monuments with the object of inscribing them afresh, the damage to Hammurabi's code was apparently purposeless. The cylinder then disappeared for nearly three thousand years, concealing from men's minds almost everything there was to know about Hammurabi and his contemporaries. Finally, in 1902, a French archaeologist, de Morgan, discovered it when digging at the Aeropolis at Susa in modern Persia. In turning up this block of stone he helped to bridge a void in our historical knowledge measuring over a thousand years.

It might be maintained that the development of law, being a branch of politics or economics, should have no place in a book concerned with philosophy. In a sense this is perfectly correct, especially with regard to modern legislation. But a book on the history of thought can no more neglect the earliest attempts to frame a legal code than it can neglect the rudiments of medicine or art. Law implies a law-giver; and it is not an accident that around the personalities of most of the great law-givers of history there has been woven a fabric of myth, almost a religious aura. Whoever imparted wisdom to mankind must likewise have imparted law, the wisdom of living the good life in community: or, if this important item of knowledge had been omitted, someone responsible and of trust in the tribe was obliged, like Moses, to go and fetch it. The apparent sacred origins of law, or the fact that law-givers such as Hammurabi considered it necessary to invest their codes with divine authority, are of considerable interest to the philosopher, who, being concerned with questions of value, wishes to ascertain what it is in particular that men hold sacred.

There is a further reason why the student of philosophy should take special interest in the nature of law. Law is a matter of words—or perhaps it would be more accurate to say, a form of words. Once written, it becomes identified with and resolves itself into the words in which it is expounded. If you introduce the smallest alteration in the wording you simultaneously alter the law. (The legal quibble is therefore an inescapable and even indispensable element in all jurisprudence, to the exasperation of the laity, who, in resenting the fact that law cannot be made to mean what they want it to mean, demonstrate the absolute necessity for law.) Now the only effect means of bringing home to people that law could not be changed without ceasing to be law, was to write it down; and this act of committing law to stone or potsherd, or whatever was likely to prove most durable, was another way of reinforcing its sacredness, since writing was itself a sacred art.

As an arcane and difficult acquirement, such writing was understood only by a privileged few, though probably by no fewer than those who understand our present legal codes. To say that law had to await the invention of writing before being recorded would be to suggest that law was originally nothing but unwritten custom. Of certain elements in law this may be true, but it is not true of law in general. The laws that are written down are usually those for which custom has made no provision. Hammurabi caused to be written down 285 such laws. Conversely, if custom had long held certain actions in abhorrence, such prohibitions need not necessarily be mentioned in the legal code. Among those crimes not specially mentioned in the code of Hammurabi, for instance, is that of murder.

Now apart from its concern with value, philosophy is preoccupied with the relation of thought to expression and in consequence with the definition and interpretation of words. What the lawyer undertakes in the course of a juridical enquiry into a particular set of circumstances, the philosopher undertakes in the course of a philosophical enquiry into a particular set of problems. Philosophy is a form of intellectual jurisprudence.[1]

A short motor trip from modern Baghdad takes the sightseer to what remains of ancient Babylon. Surrounded by arid desert, the capital of Hammurabi and later Nebuchadnezzar has now shrunk to a few crumbling mud-brick ruins and mounds. Less traces remain of its former opulence than have been unearthed at the more ancient site of Ur of the Chaldees, once the home of Abraham, which is situated several hundred miles to the south. Who were the Babylonians? They were a blend of two neighbouring peoples: the Sumerians, a non-Semitic tribe, who inhabited the extreme south of Mesopotamia in such towns as Ur, Uruk (called Erech in the Bible), Larsa (Ellasar), Lagash, and Nippur, and the Akkadians, the inhabitants of Agade farther up the River Euphrates, a distinctly Semitic people.

The blending of these two peoples, whose existence was practically unknown before the middle of the nineteenth century, was achieved as the result of a struggle from which the Akkadians appear to have emerged victorious. As a language, Babylonian was inevitably a composite formation. It contained Sumerian and Akkadian words written chiefly in Sumerian script, which represented not letters but syllables; but gradually the Sumerian element gave place to a vocabulary predominantly Semitic, and Sumerian itself became a classical language studied only by scholars and priests. In subduing both Sumeria and Akkad, Hammurabi was faced with the task of welding these nations—themselves composed of numerous petty princedoms—into a unity. From the evidence of seals and various inscriptions that have been deciphered we gather that Hammurabi was primarily a man of action; but although he freely boasted of his military exploits, he was no less anxious that posterity should learn of his civil achievements in building and irrigation. Whether because he lacked the callous streak so easily acquired by victors, or because he considered himself strong enough to dispense with such means of arousing terror in his enemies, he left no catalogue of massacre and destruction such as has survived from the reigns of other ancient conquerors. Boasting of his destruc-

[1] For a development of this line of thought, whereby the methods of philosophy and history are shown to form in combination what is known as 'metaphysical' enquiry, the reader is referred to the author's *Approach to Metaphysics*.

tion of Elam, Ashurbanipal, who ruled in Assyria several centuries later, declared: 'For a period of one month and twenty-five days I devastated the districts of Elam... Sons of the kings, sisters of the kings, members of Elam's royal family, young and old, prefects, governors, knights, artisans, as many as there were, inhabitants male and female, big and little, horses, mules, asses, flocks and herds more numerous than a swarm of locusts—I carried them off as booty to Assyria... The voice of men, the steps of flocks and herds, the happy shouts of mirth—I put an end to them in its fields, which I left for the asses, the gazelles, and all manner of wild beasts to people.'[1]

Hammurabi, on the other hand, put the following on record: 'When Anu and Enil (gods of Unek and Nippur) gave me the lands of Sumer and Akkad to rule, and they entrusted this sceptre to me, I dug the canal of Hammurabi-nukhush-nishi (Hammurabi-the-wealth-of-the-people), which brings copious water to the land of Sumer and Akkad. Its banks on both sides I turned into cultivated ground: I heaped up piles of grain, I provided unfailing water for the lands... The scattered people I gathered: with pasturage and water I provided them: I pastured them with abundance, and settled them in peaceful dwellings.' Indeed, his reign of forty-two years seems to have been one of comparative prosperity, progress, and—once he had eliminated his rivals—peace.

It is easy to interpret a statement such as the above in more ways than one. In declaring that the gods Anu and Enil 'gave' him both Sumer and Akkad and 'entrusted' him with the royal sceptre, Hammurabi may simply have been conveying with subtlety what other conquerors preferred to announce with perfect frankness, namely that he seized by force what he proposed to hold by the same means. Hammurabi introduces his Code with a no less pious claim: 'When the lofty Anu, King of Anunaki, and Bel,[2] Lord of Heaven and Earth, he who determines the destiny of the land, committed the rule of all mankind to Marduk,[3] when they pronounced the lofty name of Babylon; when they made it famous among the quarters of the world and in its midst established an everlasting kingdom whose foundations were firm as heaven and earth—at that time Anu and Bel called me, Hammurabi, the excellent prince, the worshipper of the gods, to cause justice to prevail in the land, to destroy the wicked and the evil, to prevent the strong from oppressing the weak ... to enlighten the land and further the welfare of the people. Hammurabi, the governor named by Bel, am I, who brought about plenty and abundance ... the governor of the people, the servant, whose deeds are pleasing to Anunit.'

While mankind is accustomed to fine phrases, especially in mani-

[1] This, by the way, is a comparatively mild example of the claims of Ashurbanipal (Sardanapalus, as the Greeks called him) to be remembered by posterity.

[2] Baal, god of the earth.

[3] The national god of Babylon. Originally a Sun-god, like Shamash: later called Bel-Marduk to signify that he had assumed the deities of the other gods. Originally there were thousands of these gods, many lacking all personality and receiving no individual worship. As they almost outnumbered men, Babylonian religion represents the farthest remove from Monotheism in history.

festos or as a prologue to constitutions, and is no doubt also accustomed to their remaining a dead letter, we need not suppose that these words of Hammurabi were simply a cloak for the violence and cupidity characteristic of the actions of absolute rulers. Accustomed to survey the outcrops of violence that jumble the territory of the past, historians adopt often enough a cynical attitude towards human motive, whereby all great men are branded as either scoundrels or hypocrites. Possibly, if such were the case, our dealings with our fellow-men would be greatly simplified. But clearly the assumption goes beyond the bounds of common sense, because if all motives were suspect there would be no such thing as suspicion, just as if all men were hypocrites the masks would automatically fall from their faces as being no longer of use. The significance of Hammurabi's claim to have established justice and peace in Babylon lies not so much in whether he actually did so, but in the fact that he considered it a commendable thing to have attempted. Nor would he have taken the trouble to place the fact on record had he not believed that his people and his successors would have registered approval. Consider, again, the manner in which he ends his Code: 'I am the guardian governor... In my bosom I carried the people of the land of Sumer and Akkad ... in my wisdom I restrained them, that the strong might not oppress the weak, and that they should give justice to the orphan and the widow... Let any oppressed man who had a cause, come before my image as king of righteousness! Let him read the inscription on my monument! Let him give heed to my weighty words! And may my monument enlighten him as to his cause, and may he understand his case! May he set his heart at ease [saying]: Hammurabi indeed is a ruler who is like a real father to his people ... he has established prosperity for his people for all time and given a pure government to the land... In the days that are yet to come, may the king who is in the land observe the words of righteousness which I have written upon my monument!'[1]

This passage, it will no doubt be agreed, is even more significant than that with which the Code opens, because it not merely makes claim to have established justice, but it invites any man to put this claim to the test. Wisely enough, Hammurabi is careful to specify that the man must have a *prima facie* case. If a suitor was found to be wasting the court's time he was likely to suffer severe penalties, especially in the case of a felony. 'If a man brings an accusation against another,' the first item of the Code reads, 'and charges him with a presumably capital crime, but cannot prove it, the accuser shall be put to death.' Thus one of the chief curses of a society in which legal redress is within reach of all, namely excessive litigation, was removed by a somewhat more drastic method than the imposition of high costs, the usual modern deterrent.

If Hammurabi is to be taken at his word, it would follow that he was the originator not merely of the first legal code but, in certain respects,

[1] The Code of Hammurabi may be studied in the edition of R. F. Harper, University of Chicago Press, 1904, from which the above rendering is taken, or in C. H. W. John's *The Oldest Code of Law*, 1903.

of the most enlightened and liberal code that the world has known. Before arriving at such a remarkable conclusion concerning a system created nearly four thousand years ago, we must examine some more of its detailed provisions. These are at once primitive and progressive. Savage punishments and reasonable fines (varying sometimes according to the status of the plaintiff: it cost more to strike a patrician than a plebeian) are imposed for crimes of greater or less seriousness. Both the *lex talionis* of Rome and the Mosaic Code of 'an eye for an eye and a tooth for a tooth'[1] are not merely anticipated but worked out with anatomical scrupulousness. By insisting that the criminal should suffer the precise equivalent of the harm inflicted upon his victim, a man who killed a boy was punished by the execution not of himself but of his son, and so forth. Nevertheless, among these startling edicts there stand out ordinances which are in advance of anything that has yet been given legislative form: for example, the law that a man who has fallen victim to unidentified robbers shall, upon making 'an itemized statement of his loss' and swearing a suitably solemn affidavit, be recovered from public funds. Clearly, Hammurabi did not think out all these measures *in vacuo*. Being a clever conqueror, he most certainly arrived at his system by careful compilation and co-ordination of the laws of provinces recently subdued.

While the Code of Hammurabi contains many enlightened measures, it betrays not the least concern for the rights of the individual against the state. Admittedly, the absence of such provision is probably due not so much to conscious despotism as to the fact that neither Hammurabi nor his subjects had envisaged a situation in which such rights could be exercised. Babylon, like Sumeria, was a theocracy. The king, though not himself a priest, donned priestly robes at his coronation, thereby signifying the absolute unity or identity of church and state. Taxation was imposed not in the name of the king but in the name of Marduk, who was considered owner of the soil of Babylon; and most of the money went to the priests. If the king needed financial help, and was not engaged in warfare that seemed likely to yield loot, he was obliged to apply for help to the Temple treasuries, though he was usually reluctant to do so unless in extreme difficulties. Moreover, in this country of law and order, no professional lawyers existed. Legal business was discharged by priests, who used the temples as assizes. The courts of the Lord—an expression made familiar to us by the Bible—were therefore also the courts of men. While the kings of Babylon were not regarded as actuating the course of nature as well as the processes of government, they remained divinely appointed governors, fathers of their people, distinguished from mere magistrates by being vested with ancestral authority, against whom rebellion or even contention was an act of impiety.

Thus, if Hammurabi's people possessed no means of asserting their rights against the system of government in force, they enjoyed within that system a considerable measure of material advantage and protection against molestation. Property, marriage, business, trade, and

[1] For the influence of Hammurabi's Code on the Mosaic Code, see page 80.

labour were regulated in a manner that suggest a busy, almost sophisticated social life: for it is obvious that Hammurabi's regulations must have been formulated at an epoch when commerce and industry, though often controlled by priests, had reached a high stage of development. Nor have we any reason to suppose that Hammurabi was interested exclusively in promoting the material welfare of his people. To the Babylonians we probably owe the beginnings of astronomy, mathematics, and medicine; and we know from the literary remains that have been found that they were assiduous scholars and, to use a slight anachronism, bibliophiles. Every temple of importance contained its library, which consisted of brick tablets stored in jars as in a columbarium. On a series of such tablets, found in the library of King Ashurbanipal at Nineveh in 1854,[1] is engraved the Babylonian story of the Creation. These tablets form but seven of 30,000 others which, copied by the Assyrians from originals now lost, have provided us with more detail concerning Babylonian society than we possess of nations much closer to us in time. The majority of these tablets represent routine business correspondence, including contracts, receipts, and even IOUs.

To most people, a glance at history a few hundred years BC induces a kind of chronological vertigo. The sense of proportion is deranged for want of landmarks in time, or fixed stars in the historical firmament. Roughly contemporary with Hammurabi was that lonely priest Neferrohu, who, having lamented the collapse of moral standards in the Egypt of his day, hailed the advent of a saviour-monarch whom we have presumed to be Amenemhet I (2061–2013 BC). We have referred to the dispute among historians of ancient civilization concerning the relative moral advancement of such countries as Egypt and Babylonia. In many ways the development of the sciences and the arts run roughly parallel: the problems of writing, mathematics, and government are worked out as necessity engenders invention. While the Egyptian conception of life, and above all the good life, matured earlier by perhaps a millenium than that of Babylon, and developed with greater continuity and consistency, we should not underestimate the enlightenment of a society of which the ruler freely undertook, without indulging in a idle boast, to 'prevent the strong from oppressing the weak, to enlighten the land and further the welfare of the people'. For there is evident here a sense of *abstract justice* upon which later pronouncements of this kind do not present a conspicuous improvement. Our own century, to exclude the past altogether, has seen the open advocacy of theories of governments in which the rights of the weak against the strong—or, what comes to the same thing, of the minority against the majority—have been not so much ignored as derided. Once again, it may be argued that practice does not always conform to theory. This is true: but if we are interested in estimating moral or ethical growth, a man's moral standards must be judged by what he thinks he ought to do as well as by what he does. It is the 'spirit of the laws', to use the phrase made famous by Montesquieu,

[1] Sennacherib sacked Babylon in 689 BC. Ashurbanipal reigned from 669–626 BC.

that counts. By this standard Hammurabi and his associates stand out among the early champions of justice.

Just as we knew little of Hammurabi before the discovery of the potsherds or *ostraka* and the Code itself, so it is possible that archaelogists will one day unearth evidence of mature legislation belonging to a much earlier age. Perhaps they have already done so. Nearly a thousand years before Hammurabi (about 2903 BC), Yrukagina, King of Lagash, introduced a series of reforms into his country, the general aim of which was to 'protect the weak against the strong'. In the view of many archaeologists, an investigation of the Mesopotamian region as intensive as that made in Egypt during the last century would reveal a civilization older in origin, though not necessarily more mature, than that of ancient Egypt. Unless supported by a series of discoveries in the cultural sphere, however, the opening of such a new perspective would not therefore invalidate the general point of view here maintained. As in evolution we observe creatures which, though possessed of human characteristics, have remained inexplicably undeveloped, so in history the intimations of civilization are constantly surprising us by their early appearance. This is especially true in art, the frontiers of which are being thrust farther and farther back in time. What counts in history, however, is continuity united with fecundity. Hammurabi's claim to attention is not merely that he complied the first great legal code, but that his work exerted a profound influence upon later peoples. One such people was to accomplish a historical mission far greater than that of either Egypt or Babylon. It is to this people that we now turn; and we begin by turning south.

Abraham

The final stage of Hammurabi's conquest of the Mesopotamian region was his overthrow of his powerful rival Rim-Sin, King of Larsa, a town south-east of Lagash and north of Ur. Rim-Sin, who had been a capable and munificent ruler in his day, was now an old man. Hammurabi, on the other hand, had proved himself an energetic young commander of marked administrative capacity. Unable to retain the loyalty of the princedoms under his control, Rim-Sin suffered the first defeat of his career. The Sumerian kingdoms surrendered. Ur, a Semitic city and no doubt sympathetic to Hammurabi, did not even put an army in the field. She quietly declared herself under the protection of the King of Babylon. The Semitic influence in both culture and commerce was now dominant throughout Babylonia.

We now enter, though with much greater confidence than would have been possible fifty or even thirty years ago, upon the realm of conjecture. Among the subjects of Rim-Sin was a man to whom three of the great world religions still look back as their Patriarch, the father of their faith. Abraham, for such was his name, inhabited the town of

Ur, known in the Bible as 'Ur of the Chaldees'[1]; and it was from here that, according to *Genesis*, Chapter xi, verse 31, he 'went forth', accompanied by his entire family, 'to go into the land of Canaan'. That journey, for reasons that we shall show, was one of the most momentous ever to be undertaken.

The so-called Higher Criticism of the Bible did not arise, as many suppose, in the nineteenth century. It was initiated by the Jewish philosopher Spinoza (1632–77), who was ousted by the local synagogue for criticizing, though not necessarily rejecting as false, certain claims made by Holy Scripture.[2] In the last century, however, critical scholarship of biblical sources, together with the archaeological investigation of sites associated with the Bible, made considerable progress. The revelation of inconsistency, though bewildering to the pious, need not injure faith: for if faith can move mountains—which it may do, as on a journey the resolute traveller puts them one by one behind him—it can no doubt also overcome logical contradiction. *Credo quia impossibile est.* But to the sceptic the revelation of inconsistency is conclusive evidence of error. When, therefore, the critics drew attention to contradictions and anachronisms in scripture, the biblical narratives, though remaining 'magnificent literature', were frequently dismissed as fiction.

By clearing away irrelevances and exposing slipshod scholarship, the Higher Criticism achieved much that was of value. To say that it has been largely superseded is true. It has given place to what, consistently enough, is a still higher criticism. This Higher Criticism seeks not merely to arrive at facts through a haze of myth; it also seeks to examine and analyse the mythical element itself. To the old criticism, for instance, the fact that such figures as Abraham or Moses are surrounded by a penumbra of legend was sufficient to prove that these figures were themselves legendary, as if greatness of reputation and posthumous fame were sufficient to cast doubt upon the reality of the person to whom they attached. This attitude had certain odd consequences. Denying the reality of the man but being obliged to accept that of the myth, such critics—among whom are some distinguished psychologists—proceeded to evolve a theory whereby myths, especially those relating to leaders of men, played a part in history best described as organic or catalytic. Such myths either set history going or enabled it to restart. Of certain figures associated with early civilization this interpretation is plausible, though it is still the persons concerned with originating the myth that provide the dynamic elements in history, not anything impersonal or 'archetypal'. In the case of men whose reputed deeds have been handed down by oral tradition over a period of centuries, and then recorded by scribes, a different approach is necessary, especially if archaeology can meanwhile

[1] The title 'of the Chaldees' is an anachronism. The Chaldeans belong to a later epoch. Visitors to Urfa in southern Turkey, a town difficult of access, are shown a cave reputed to be Abraham's birthplace. The claim is due to a confusion of names. Urfa was known as Edessa in the early Christian epoch.

[2] See page 356.

establish the accuracy of circumstantial detail. According to this approach, a penumbra of legend is regarded as likely to surround historical personalities whose achievements, because they were authentic, invite such embellishment. When enthusiastic members of the Academy circulated the story that Plato was the son of Apollo, and that bees had settled on his infant lips in anticipation of his honeyed words, they were not striving to show that Plato did not exist; they were striving to show, in the fashion of the time, what a great man he was.

Although excavations began at Ur under the direction of the British at Basra in 1854, and were resumed systematically in 1922 under Sir Leonard Woolley, not a single inscription among the great wealth of material brought to light has been found to contain a reference to Abraham. When we consider the meagre references to be found to persons living thousands of years later—Shakespeare, for instance—this absence of direct testimony need not greatly disturb us. What leads us to suppose that the Abraham of the Bible really existed is the fact that the biblical account is consistent with our knowledge, most of it very recently acquired, of the people to whom he is said to belong.

Who were these people? The first-known mention of the Habiru, whom scholars now agree to be identical with the Hebrews, is to be found in the reign of Rim-Sin, Hammurabi's old rival. The reference is not casual. The Habiru are accorded a vivid, if terse, description. In the Sumerian script they are represented by an ideogram which, translated broadly, means nomads, brigands, or cut-throats. Now although in *Genesis* xiv, 13, Abraham himself is described as a Hebrew, his nephew Laban (xxv, 20) and, later on, Jacob are referred to as Syrians or an Aramaeans, a tribe undoubtedly identical with, or related to, the Amorites. That the Amorites enjoyed the same reputation as the Habiru of Rim-Sin's reign is proved by a variety of references. A Sumerian hymn praising the 'gods of the west', of which the date is about 2000 BC, makes direct reference to these Amorites who roamed the Western hills. This tribe, says the hymn, 'known no submission, eats raw flesh, has no home in its lifetime, and does not bury its dead kinsfolk'. According to a later Egyptian source, the Amorite is described no less vividly as 'the miserable stranger... He does not dwell in the same spot, his feet are always wandering. From the days of Horus, he battles, he does not conquer, and is not conquered.' With this we may compare the prophecy of Balaam in *Numbers* xxiii, 9, 'Behold a people that dwells alone, and amid the nations is not accounted.' The construction by the Babylonians of the so-called Wall of the West as early as the third millenium BC has been due to a desire to prevent the infiltration of these unruly folk. Where such measures proved ineffective, local governors did their best to put the nomads to useful work. Either they were employed at stock-raising[1] or, to exploit their warlike qualities, they were enlisted in the army, though in special battalions in the manner of mercenaries or minorities. Rim-

[1] Apart from forced labour, this was the main occupation of the Jews during the Egyptian captivity.

Sin, himself a soldier, seems to have preferred the latter method of discipline.

In that repository of odd information, the 'Tel el-Amarna Letters', to which we have already referred in connection with Ikhaten's imperial problems, we read of a people called the Habiri. Their sporadic raids into Palestine from the desert were causing concern to the local governors holding office under Pharaoh. For a time scholars were in doubt as to whether to identify Habiru and Habiri. Now they are inclined to do so. For if we recognize that the Habiru were not necessarily an ethnic group but simply one of a variety of tribes united by love of wandering, the identity is more easily acceptable. But the 'Tel el-Amarna Letters' disclose a fact more interesting still. Mention is made therein of both Habiri and Aramaeans: but the ideogram here employed for Habiri is precisely that which conveys the notion of cut-throats and brigands. Now it is possible, and even likely, that a governor reporting to his superiors an attack by foreigners upon imperial territory would lump the whole band together as brigands, just as we used to talk of Huns; but what emerges is that the Habiri were associated with a group of people to whom the general name Aramaean attached, and that this group led a life similar to that of the modern Bedouin.

According to the account in *Genesis*, Abraham's first halting-place on his journey to the land of Canaan was Harran, a town now situated in the south of Turkey near the Syrian frontier. That such a northward movement of a Habiri family was usual at this period does not destroy the uniqueness of Abraham's journey: the uniqueness lies in that to which it gave rise. A northward migration had in fact been going on for some time: tablets of the fifteenth century BC found not long ago at Kirkuk, the oil-town in the north of Iraq, refer to the Habiri as frequently to be met with in the upper regions of Mesopotamia. Now there are two possible causes to which these migrations can be ascribed. In the first place, it is nothing surprising in a nomad people to betray evidence that they wandered. In the second place, they may have had reason to believe that their services, whether military or civil, might be better employed elsewhere than in the south. We have seen that large numbers of Amorites served in the Sumerian army. Being mercenaries, their primary reason for changing their allegiance would presumably have been a mercenary one: better pay and conditions were reported to be obtainable up north. Not merely did Hammurabi appear to offer immediate benefit. As potential master of the whole of Mesopotamia, he offered as good a chance of permanent employment as any mercenary troops could desire. We have no particular reason to suppose that Abraham's family belonged to the military caste, though *Genesis*, Chapter xiv, reports a desert scrap in which Abraham and his men clashed with the forces of 'Amraphel King of Shinar', who is thought by some to have been Hammurabi. But such an incident, even if isolated, would not be unusual in a nomadic body, especially as the story mentions that substantial booty was secured. It is more likely that Abraham's family were rich camel-owners, and that Harran—a town with which they were probably already in touch[1]—seemed, for reasons shortly to be mentioned, to offer better trading prospects than Ur.

On this point negative information is almost as valuable as positive. The *Genesis* narrative later refers to the large number of camels Abraham had at his disposal: but none of the thousands of business records found at Ur mention the camel. A probable explanation, upon which modern conditions shed considerable light, is that the camel business was altogether outside the normal affair of the town. Populated by as many as a quarter of a million people, Ur had for years been a thriving centre of business. The society that thronged its narrow streets was, to quote Sir Leonard Woolley,[2] 'highly individualistic, enjoying a great measure of personal liberty, materialistic and money-making, hard-working and most appreciative of comfort and the good things of life'; in short, a sophisticated, urban society in violent contrast to the tribal society outside its confines. While a camel-owner might be both extremely rich and as familiar with urban life as any other merchant, the source of his wealth would be, as it were, extra-mural, and might even be expressly concealed. Even today the use of camels within inhabited areas in some Middle East countries is subject to restriction, and the passage of these animals through the streets is limited to night-time.

To complete the picture, which must be drawn with precision if we would understand the revolution in thought for which Abraham was responsible, let us revert to the point from which we began: namely the collapse of Rim-Sin's Sumerian Empire. While the ordinary inhabitant of Ur or Larsa cannot have realized how critical the situation was, the simultaneous surrender of all the great Sumerian towns must have seemed to him a disaster greater even than the ruthless sack of Ur by the Elamites in 2170 BC. If he did not judge it to be the end of Sumerian political hegemony, his confidence in the national powers of recovery must have been put to severe strain. But supposing that this anonymous citizen of four thousand years ago was not a Sumerian but a Semitic nomad, his attitude might have been very different. He had never really been wanted. That was clear enough from the epithets customarily applied to him. He, in turn, had never really 'belonged'. That was a consequence of his race, his habits, and the trade in which he was engaged. Furthermore, it is the custom, as we know, for nations in defeat to seek scapegoats among the minorities to which they have formerly given protection. The nomadic Habiru, whose loyalty may often have been in doubt, would be only too likely to incur some portion of blame and recrimination. In these circumstances, his decision to leave, even if already taken for economic reasons, would no doubt have been hastened.

All this may account satisfactorily for the journey of Abraham's family from Ur to Harran. It does not yet throw light upon the circumstances in which we are chiefly interested. If Abraham is still looked

[1] The name Harran means 'way' or 'caravan', indicating a place or junction where caravans met and parted.
[2] Woolley: *Abraham*, p. 131.

upon as the father[1] of three out of the half-dozen great religions of the world, at what point in his career and simultaneously with what spiritual experience did he abandon the beliefs of his forefathers and render homage to the One God? Such a change in outlook cannot have been effected without some kind of spiritual crisis, perhaps a family crisis; because a conversion in the conditions of a theocratic state, with its enormous pantheon of national, local, family, and nature gods, all demanding due allegiance, would be a much more drastic affair than its equivalent today. Without informing us of the religion in which Abraham originally believed, the Bible asserts (*Joshua* xxiv, 2) that his family 'served other gods'. What other gods? Surely the gods of Sumeria, and in particular the gods of Ur. Now the civic god of Ur was Nannar, a Moon-god. Another town dedicated to a goddess of the moon was, curiously enough, Harran. This latter goddess was named Terah. So was Abraham's father. Is it possible, perhaps, that Terah, coming of a family of moon worshippers, was named after the diety of a town with which the family, or at least the roaming tribes to which the family belonged, had established close associations? If so, that might explain why he set out in time of adversity for the place most likely to afford him protection.

That Terah and his son should have left one 'moon' town to live in another suggests not a weakening of belief in the family god but the determination to continue the same form of worship. The choice of a place to live, which today is dictated by economic rather than sentimental reasons, meant a great deal to our forefathers. At every level, even that of business and trade, religious considerations would be given their due weight, as no doubt they were by the leader of the party. But while the family would be dominated by the father, nothing would prevent Abraham from professing other beliefs once he succeeded Terah as head of the clan. Now we know that Terah died and was buried at Harran. And it was after his decease that, according to the biblical account, Abraham received his first direct message from 'the Lord'. The message, in this case, took the form of a command. Abraham was to lead his people to Canaan and there to establish a new community.

What happened at Harran after the death of Terah? For it was then, if at all, that the conversion must have taken place. Of its nature the Bible affords no direct clue. We do not even know the exact name of the God who, without apparent warning, issued the command to strike camp. Nor did Abraham's family know Him by any other title than that of the 'God of Abraham' or (as the family acquired other heads) the 'God of Abraham, Isaac and Jacob'. This anonymity was preserved for much longer than is generally realized. It continued for several centuries, perhaps for as long as a thousand years, until, at a dramatic moment in the history of the same clan, God disclosed His identity to Moses. In an age when the names of gods, and indeed the names of anything, were of particular significance, this deliberate reticence on the part of Abraham's god seems to us as strange as Abraham's own acqui-

[1] Though not the founder. See p. 84.

escence in it.

If we approach this problem from a somewhat different point of view, we may be able to explain not merely its baffling aspects but the nature of the conversion which Abraham must have experienced. Although the conversion assumed a drastic form by reason of the complicated polytheistic faith against which it was a reaction, such an experience might have been less obtrusive at Harran than at Ur. It might even be a consequence of deciding to leave Harran, a place known to the clan, for Canaan, a place unknown but promised.

As we have seen in the case of Aten, gods do not usually survive the political defeat of their worshippers. To affirm as much is not to adopt the condescending attitude of the rationalist historian to 'primitive' beliefs. A god to whom a town looks for protection, encouragement, and defence cannot dissociate himself, unless he is a special kind of god, from public misfortune or disaster. Just as the citizen of Sumer must have witnessed the national reverses with foreboding, so his confidence in the civic gods must have undergone corresponding deflation. If he was by nature devout, the one form of pessimism would have been impossible to distinguish from the other. Experience in other epochs and at similar times of stress leads us to believe that minorities, even if of different religious persuasion, may be no less attached to the gods or, as we might say, principles of the country of their adoption than the nationals themselves. Their attachment or respect may be particularly strong, witness the feats of agents of non-British origin during the last war. Thus the Habiru clans, though treated as outcasts, may have contained cultivated individuals, who, priding themselves on being good citizens, shared to the full the disillusionment following Sumer's fall. Among these the family of Terah would be numbered. In abandoning Ur, and in seeking a town of better omen, we may well imagine a fundamental difference in attitude between the old, conservative father, seeking a place of retirement under the protection of his personal god, and the son, eager to rebuild his fortunes. Pursuing our conjectures to the limit, we can picture Abraham at the death of his father as a man who, conscious of the great responsibilities that had fallen upon him, considers what he can salvage from the past to sustain him in his future wanderings.

Although the biblical narrative withholds until the appropriate moment all direct information about the 'God of Abraham', we know that He possessed a characteristic that distinguished Him from others. This characteristic was that He moved about. Almost all other gods were stationary or attached. This applied especially to the gods of Sumeria. At Ur the Moon-god, Nannar, had his own private apartments in the Temple; while his wife, Nin Gal, had her own bedchamber. The couple lived at Ur, nor did they leave the capital except under compulsion, as happened when the Elamites 'captured' them by removing their statues to Susa. Likewise, all nature gods were rooted in the soil, or in groves, mountains, or rivers; they could not move, unless for some reason the natural objects did themselves, as when a river overflowed or a volcano erupted. From some interesting Hittite inscriptions of a later period we learn of certain gods called *Iani Habiri*, which may be translated either as 'gods of the Habiru' or, more likely, 'Habiru gods'. By referring to Habiru gods in this fashion the authorities were no doubt emphasizing a characteristic for which such gods were well known, namely their habit of accompanying the clan in its wanderings.

Of the God of Abraham, two features now stand out: firstly, that He was nameless, and secondly, that He was peripatetic. With regard to the latter characteristic, we know that, though unattached, He still had His temple in the tent-tabernacle set up at every major halting-place; but no proper temple was erected in His honour until the time of Solomon (974–937 BC).

In describing the God of Abraham as an unattached god, we have been understanding the word attached in the sense of fastened to something static. But naturally it is possible to be attached to something non-static, to something that moves. The God of Abraham was attached to Abraham and his family. Why, then, should 'He' not have been a family god? Given Abraham's situation at Harran, family considerations would inevitably have been uppermost in his mind. The civic gods of Ur, the national gods of Sumeria, had been left behind; but whether they had failed him or not, such local civic gods could not be removed or, being removed, retain their power. Nor, after Terah's death, was there much inducement to test the beneficence of the civic gods of Harran: a place to die in for the father was not necessarily a satisfactory abode for the son.

When at this moment the Lord said to Abraham (*Genesis* xii, 1), 'Get thee out of thy country,' meaning Mesopotania, the Lord who thereby attached 'Himself' to Abraham may, for all that is said to the contrary, have been stressing an attachment of long standing. The conversion may have been a form of reversion.

If the family god hypothesis is to be sustained, we must be able to show not merely that such gods were cultivated in Sumeria but upon what grounds, in this instance, the god remained nameless. To Sir Leonard Woolley we owe some valuable information on this as on most other points in the history of Abraham. From the researches made by the Joint Expedition of the British Museum and the University of Pennsylvania, it became abundantly clear that the Sumerians, while paying respect to an immense number of official gods, were accustomed also to worshipping tutelary deities, like the *lares* and *penates* of the Romans. These 'household gods' were usually represented by figurines or, as the Bible calls them, 'teraphim'. But such representation differed from that of other gods by being purely conventional; the god itself exhibited no particular characteristics.[1] Another custom of universal observance, as the excavations testify, was that of burying the bodies of ancestors directly beneath the little chapel attached to every private house.[2] In this domestic chapel, therefore, reverence

[1] The prohibition of representing God has remained permanent among the Jews. Likewise the word Jehovah is always read 'Adonai'.

[2] Woolley: *Abraham*, p. 220.

for ancestors would be combined with worship of the household god who watched over the family, both living and dead. Prayers, led by the head of the household, would be said regularly and offerings made, usually in the form of food; but it is an interesting fact that none of these chapels contains any inscription or sign whereby the domestic god can be named.[1] He was evidently regarded as a power whose identification other than as god of the family, past, present, and to come, was considered unnecessary. That he was identified *with* the family was all that mattered. If, as we may suppose, these ancient people, with their pronounced religious sense, derived genuine consolation from some at least of the innumerable forms of worship at their disposal, we may conclude that it was in the domestic chapel rather than in the public temple that such emotions were most often stirred.

The family god lives with the family, moves with the family, does not desert the family in its vicissitudes. It is the one god whose reputation undergoes no change when misfortune visits the little group, so intimately is it identified with its life through many generations. To a Habiri clan such as that of Abraham it would no doubt be much dearer than to more settled families; but not until the break with Ur and its gods effected by the death of Terah did it appear to Abraham, perhaps in a flash of insight or perhaps as something very simple (the Bible suggests the latter), that it was the one stay left. Forsaking all others, the family should allow itself to be guided by the god who had steadfastly accompanied it up to that moment. At that realization, God spoke.

To have followed the account in Chapter 1 of Egyptian religion and thought, followed by the outline of ideas current in Babylon four thousand years ago, will have confirmed our initial observation, namely that in studying the mind of the Orient we are unable to separate, if not to distinguish, religion and philosophy. There has sometimes been a tendency, not unrelated to the school of Higher Criticism, to suggest that the two not merely can but must be distinguished if we are to isolate what ancient man 'really thought' from the tissue of 'beliefs' with which, for reasons left to be explained, he encumbered himself. A more scientific approach is that which regards the beliefs themselves as what he 'really thought', and proceeds to enquire how such beliefs came to be entertained. This is history; the rest is prejudice thinly disguised as scientific impartiality. To endeavour to peel off the belief, whether supernatural or merely 'numinous', as if it formed a kind of chrysalis concealing and constricting the butterfly of fact, is to do violence to the state of mind of men not necessarily more irrational than ourselves, and to render our understanding of them much more difficult than it need be. Hence our attempt to reconstruct from the available evidence what Abraham, in initiating a new development in the outlook of man, thought he was doing.

XX To trace the process whereby the family god of Abraham became the

[1] Cf. Martin Buber: *Moses* (1946), p. 205. But Buber, following Kaufmann (*History of the Hebrew Religion*, 1, p. 675), says that these gods received no worship. This would seem to be incompatible with the existence of domestic chapels and votive offerings.

'Most High God' of Israel is to show, first of all, that there is no obvious contradiction between a private god becoming a public one if the public group is simply an expansion, as in the present case, of a private unit. The family of Abraham was already a clan; it developed into a tribe in the natural process of moving as a unit across vast stretches of desert. Naturally, Abraham and his near relations would still form a kind of central nucleus, as it was the custom for the elders to remain an inner clan of their own. Thus in the fourteenth chapter of *Genesis* we learn that among Abraham's followers there were a number of 'bondsmen', men presumably who had agreed to bind themselves to him as a natural leader. Such stray adherents, who attached themselves casually and finally decided to throw in their lot with the chief, were common enough in desert life. Even the 'stranger within their gates' is in Moses' time permitted to enjoy all the communal privileges, such as resting on the Sabbath. The tribe must be prepared against attack—'And when Abraham heard that his brother was taken captive, he armed his trained servants, born in his own house, three hundred and eighteen, and pursued them into Dan' (*Genesis* xiv, 14). And with every desert encounter the tribal unity was strengthened, the reputation of Abraham enhanced, the God of Abraham magnified.[1]

To conceive of the family God of Abraham on the analogy of the diminutive modern family, conditioned by the semi-detached house, hire-purchase and state allowances, is to form a grotesquely inaccurate picture of its size and complexity. The God of such a 'snowball' band was already God of a community, hence a God of potentially universal appeal. The transition was both natural and inevitable. Above all it was historical. The cathedrals of Europe, the parish churches of England, the chapels and meeting houses of America, the missionary huts of Africa and Asia, represent the gigantic projection of that process in time.

Abraham the bearer of civilization

This is not the place to enter into biblical controversy by debating the relative importance or antiquity of this or that passage in the Old Testament. In view of recent archaeological discoveries, the subject is of great fascination; but our object is to trace man's early ideas about life and death, good and evil, and in pursuance of this task we must now turn to another aspect of Abraham's character of which little was suspected until the beginning of the present century. In short, we must study Abraham as the transmitter of civilization in the form of both myth (using that word in no derogatory sense) and law. Woolley has pointed out that not until the story of Abraham begins to unfold does the Bible truly become alive. What precedes this story is mere chronicle, a hotchpotch of legend and imaginative speculation thrown together with little regard for consistency. Much of this material owes

[1] Abraham would not accept payment for military aid rendered to others. See *Genesis* xiv, 23.

its origin to pre-Hebraic sources; and, where an indubitable Babylonian source can be proved, we are inevitably led to enquire how such accounts can have been handed on from one civilization to another.

The seven tablets discovered at Nineveh in 1854 record one by one the days of the creation of the world according to Babylonian tradition. On the first of these tablets it is related how Apsu, the Ocean, father of all things, and Tiamat, Chaos, the mother, mingled together. At a time when,

> No field was formed, no marsh was to be seen,
> When of the gods none had been called into being
> And none bore a name and no destinies were ordained,
> Then were created the gods in the midst of heaven.

As a result of this huge gestation, order began slowly to form as the gods assumed control of their respective spheres. But before much progress could be made, Tiamat, suddenly resolving to make an end of her progeny, engulfed all the gods save one, Marduk. According to the fourth tablet, Marduk 'stood upon Tiamat's hinder parts and with his merciless club he smashed her skull'. Then, intent upon rendering her for ever innocuous, he 'devised a cunning plan; he split her up like a flat fish into two halves'. Having thus dispatched and divided her, 'one half of her he established as a covering for heaven', and the other half 'he spread out under his feet to form the earth'. Then, so the fifth tablet relates, he resumed the task of setting the universe in order:

> He made the stations for the great gods,
> The stars, their images,[1] as the stars of the Zodiac he fixed.
> He ordained the year and into sections he divided it,
> For the twelve months he fixed three stars...
> The moon-god he caused to shine forth, and night he entrusted to him.

Finally, deciding to make a creature who should not merely enjoy this stupendous work, but give thanks to the gods who fashioned and sustained it, Marduk proceeded to create man. This achievement is the burden of the sixth tablet: 'My blood will I take and (presumably by mixing it with earth) bone will I fashion ... I will create man who shall inhabit the earth.'

According to Babylonian tradition, the early condition of mankind was the reverse of simple and idyllic. Man was a creature as yet uninstructed in the arts and crafts of life. Just as the Egyptians, who held a similar view, regarded Thoth as the first teacher of man and in particular the inventor of writing. so the Babylonians attributed man's capacity to fend for himself in a hostile world to the instruction of a creature called Oannes, a kind of enormous fish-man. Even so, since man did not prove an amenable creature, the gods resolved in due course to destroy him. A flood of unprecedented dimensions, overwhelming the entire earth, promised to annihilate all natural creatures. But Ea, god of Wisdom, whom Marduk had consulted before making man ('He opened his mouth and unto Ea he spoke'—sixth

[1] An idea to be found also in Plato.

tablet), seems to have regretted the god's decision. He decided to save a man called Shamash-napishtim and his family, who under his guidance set to work to build an ark.

The story of Shamash-napishtim is told in a remarkable epic poem which was inscribed on twelve tablets found in the same library as that from which the Creation story was recovered. This is the *Epic of Gilgamesh*, a poem which some experts believe to date from as early as 3000 BC. Gilgamesh, King of Uruk, was a descendant of Shamash-napishtim, whose adventures are related in the course of the poem. As in the Biblical account with which we are familiar, the most precise details are first given of the size of the ark under construction. Shamash speaks in the first person:

On the fifth day I drew its design
In its plan 120 cubits high on each of its sides.
By 120 cubits it corresponded on each edge of its roof.
I laid down its form, I enclosed it,
I constructed it in six storeys,
Dividing it into seven parts . . .
Three sars of bitumen I poured over the outside,
Three sars of bitumen I poured over the inside.

Having finished the vessel, 'I put on board my family and relatives, the cattle of the field, the beasts of the field,' and when 'the appointed time arrived and the ruler of darkness at eventide sent a heavy rain, I entered the ship and shut my door'. For seven nights the storm continued:

The wind blew, the flood, the tempest overwhelmed the land.
When the seventh day drew near, the tempest, the flood,
Ceased from the battle in which it had fought like a host.
Then the sea rested and was still, and the wind storm and the flood ceased,
I opened the window and daylight fell upon my face.

Soon land was sighted, and 'the mountain of the land of Nisir held fast the ship and suffered it not to stir'; whereupon

I sent forth a dove and let her go,
The dove went to and fro,
But there was no resting place and she returned.

So Shamash tried first a swallow and then a raven. The latter, 'beholding the abatement of the water, came near, wading and croaking, but did not return'. Shamash then gave the order to disembark, and, camping on the peak of the mountain, made sacrifice and offered a libation. Apparently the recession of the flood was due to the fact that the gods, once having decided to destroy man, realized that they would now cease to be worshipped and thus be deprived of burnt offerings. For when Shamash makes it his first duty to offer thanksgiving, 'the gods smelt the sweet savour, the gods gathered like flies about him that offered up the sacrifice'.

What is remarkable about this account, which we know to have already been *in writing* during the time of Abraham, is its resemblance not merely in outline but in actual phrasing to that given in *Genesis*, Chapters vii, viii, and ix. Even the offer of sacrifice (ix, 20) is reproduced, with the comment that God 'smelt the sweet savour', though the entire theological aspect has been subject to revision in conformity with Hebrew monotheism. That the 'mountain of Nisir' should have been changed to that of Ararat is natural, as the latter would be the highest peak in the 'world' known to inhabitants of Palestine and northern Syria.

Now the story as related in the *Epic of Gilgamesh*, which records incidentally how Shamash-napishtim was made immortal for assisting the preservation of man and other forms of life, is not a pure essay in imaginative writing. Whereas the main story of the *Epic*, of which we possess only a fragment, is concerned with the adventures in love, battle, and the search for truth of the hero Gilgamesh, it is no more completely a work of fiction than the *Iliad* or *Odyssey*. Just as Troy was a real place and its siege an historical engagement, so we have reason to believe that the Flood described in the *Epic* forms the memory, however vague and distorted, of an historic episode. In the course of their excavations at Ur, Woolley and his colleagues succeeded, by sinking deep shafts into the soil, in exposing the levels at which the town was successively rebuilt in the four thousand years of its history. At a certain level the layers were found to be interrupted by an immense quantity of silt. This could be explained only by the onset of a catastrophic inundation (milder forms of which were as common in this area as in the Nile valley); for lying immediately beneath the deposit were further ruins in layers similar to those nearer the surface. Woolley had also drawn attention to the authenticity of much of the local colour of the story: the comparative shallowness of the inundation, so familiar and welcome at other times, the caulking of the ark with bitumen, a local product of proved utility, and so on. Nor need we suppose that this flood, though very likely to have been the Flood, was the first of its kind: such disasters represented a recurrent threat to a land dependent for its fertility upon a highly complicated, man-devised system of irrigation, traces of which remain over much of modern Iraq.

In the Creation myth we have something entirely different. This is not the story of a historical episode, but a plain allegory. As an allegory, it is admittedly a great deal cruder than the Memphite Drama, with its remarkable excursion into metaphysics; but the reader will no doubt have observed in it a gleam, however faint, of something more profound, something that lifts it above being a more blood-and-thunder myth. Tiamet and Apsu are monsters. And the product of their union so closely resembles a monstrous birth that the chaos-mother is moved to destroy it in self-loathing. She in turn is killed, not without brutality, by Marduk, who is himself a kind of monster. Before Marduk creates man, however, he consults, not another monster like himself, but the god Ea, the embodiment of Wisdom. It is likewise Ea who, observing the imminent return of chaos, intercedes for man and ensures his preservation. According to these early bardic-philosophers, therefore, man's existence and survival have something to do with the power of an intelligence comparable to the Egyptian *Maat*, the Chinese *Tao*, and the Greek *Logos*: a power perpetually at war with the forces of disorder, barbarism, and chaos.

This perception of the divine principle at work both in the world and in man is apparent in other parts of the *Epic of Gilgamesh*, overlaid as the poem is with much extravagant fantasy and grotesque adventure. At the conclusion of the fragment, Gilgamesh, mourning the death of his friend Engidu, is driven to reflect upon the nature of life and death. Having sought out and communed with Shamash-napishtim, his immortal ancestor, he finally decides to seek a personal interview with Engidu. Although this must naturally entail the latter's emergence from the underworld, Gilgamesh prays fervently to the appropriate gods and Engidu finally appears. When he is asked by Gilgamesh to unfold the secrets of death, however, he replied, 'If I were to tell thee that which I have seen, terror would overthrow thee, thou wouldst faint away.' Gilgamesh's answer, which in effect concludes the fragment, is as follows, 'Though terror should overwhelm me and I should faint away, yet tell me.' This spirit of obstinate enquiry, apparent in a folk-tale five thousand years old, is perhaps the sole power capable of carrying man through the next five thousand years, if in the meantime he does not unlock the secrets of nature to his own destruction.

When, we may now ask, did the Hebrews first learn of these legends? Was it not during their 'captivity', which dated from about 586–538 BC? So it has often been surmised. But there are a number of grounds for rejecting this view. We know from the biblical account—and we would in any case assume—that the Babylonian captivity was a time of great heart-searching and recall to the basic principles of faith. There had been a marked tendency to compromise with the rulers, and even to neglect the traditional worship. At such a time the compilers and guardians of the sacred lore would have taken steps to see that nothing but orthodox and accredited material were placed on record. While they might well have corrected and rewritten the story of the Creation and the Flood, it is unlikely that they would have chosen that particular moment to incorporate such stories from outside. In view of the extreme exclusiveness of Hebrew tradition, the contemporary popularity of such stories in their original form would have been a reason for rejecting rather than for accepting them. The fact that they are embodied in the Old Testament at all suggests that they were already part of the traditional sacred writings. Biblical scholars now hold that the early books of the Bible are based upon sources which not merely date from as early as 1000–900 BC, but represent the first written record of an oral tradition of greater antiquity. These sources, three in number, are known as P, J, and E. Source P hardly concerns us. It is so-called because it forms a kind of priest's code, with details of ritual and ecclesiastical law as practised at the end of the Babylonian captivity. The other sources are distinguished one from the other by the different words they employ for God: J calls

'Him' Yahweh and E Elohim, a word in the plural number. Both represent accounts of Hebrew history and religion from the point of view of what we may call the common man. As both J and E contain distinct versions of the Creation and the Flood stories, and as both are thought to date from a period prior to the Babylonian exile (J certainly does in the opinion of most scholars), the case may be considered proved.[1]

What we may further suggest, though without the same show of proof, is that these particular stories were among the elements of Sumerian and Babylonian tradition brought to Palestine by Abraham and his followers. There exists incidentally a tablet in the dialect known as Hurrian, which was that spoken at Harran, recording a version of the Flood story in which the hero is called not Shamash-napishtim but Nah-molet. Now the name Noah, which bears a resemblance to no other name in the Bible, may well have been derived from at least the first syllable of the 'Hurrian' name.[2] We have at least proof here that the story was circulating in a place with which Abraham and his family were closely identified over many years. Nor, on this basis, would the insertion of Ararat—the nearest high mountain after the Taurus peaks—be difficult to explain.

Code and Covenant

We have spoken of Abraham as the transmitter of some of the world's great myths; we have now to speak of him as the transmitter of some of the great legislative principles in history. The Code of Hammurabi formed, as we suggested above, a compilation of various legal codes or customs in force among the peoples whom the great King of Babylon wished, after subduing, to unite. The task of co-ordination and collation must have engaged the attention of a large number of experts, working first in the field and later in groups. Whenever the ancient world speaks of an achievement as due to one man, we may suspect the united labour of a number of expert assistants.

The Code of Hammurabi represents a great triumph of committee-work. Among the legal systems to which particular attention must have been paid was that of Sumeria, where law and litigation had already reached a high degree of development and complexity. Every plea and counter-plea was scrupulously recorded on tablets, and judicial procedure was established on a rigid basis. Now when the Code of Hammurabi was rediscovered and translated early in the present century, the extraordinary resemblance between its provisions and those of the Mosaic Code or Book of the Covenant became immediately apparent. Many of the individual items were identical, while the wording of many more was similar. In view of the notoriety acquired by the Mosaic edict of 'an eye for an eye and a tooth for a tooth', which

[1] The isolation of the three accounts from the material available has been a triumph of analytical scholarship.

[2] See an article in the *Journal of the Royal Asiatic Society*, 1925, by Father Burrows.

Christ singled out expressly as summing up the Spirit of the Old Dispensation, it is interesting to quote the literal rendering of Hammurabi's law on the subject: 'If a man destroy the eye of another man, they shall destroy his eye. If the man knock out the tooth of a man of his own rank, they shall knock out his tooth.' That the Mosaic Code should owe nothing to that of Hammurabi on the ritualistic side is hardly surprising. It is on the social side that the resemblance is most impressive.

These indisputable similarities dispose of the view that the Code was invented by Moses. No legal code was 'invented' by anyone. Moses himself must have gone to a good deal of trouble to co-ordinate the laws already in force among the tribes under his leadership. His work did not stop there, nor was such co-ordination its most important aspect. What he chiefly sought to do was to put his followers in mind of their old traditions, which their prolonged sojourn in Egypt had blotted out.[1] He himself had already had a taste of desert life among the Midianites. Much of his efforts, therefore, would have been directed to a revival, compatible with the new conditions, of the legal customs of that period in Hebrew history in which the tribes were, as then, on the march. During his journey from Ur to Harran, and from Harran to Palestine, Abraham had maintained order by means of the legal customs in which he had been brought up. Changes appropriate to a desert life must naturally have been introduced: nevertheless 'there is in the Old Testament concrete evidence for the fact that the tent-law of (Abraham's) family was actually the law of Sumer'.[2] If, in other words, Moses had drawn up his Code of Laws before reaching the Promised Land, he—a man 'learned in the wisdom of the Egyptians'—could not possibly have compiled the Book of the Covenant, as described in *Exodus*, in language reminiscent of the laws of Hammurabi: he would more likely have been tempted to introduce elements from Egyptian law.[3] In bringing the tribes to a better understanding of the God of Abraham—a task which, in spite of the miracles of preservation already experienced by them, he apparently found extremely difficult, judging from their inherent tendency to idolatry—Moses would have sought to revive as much as possible the law to which Abraham had conformed all his life.[4] The law in question was that of Hammurabi. Although Hammurabi's Code remained authoritative in Mesopotamia for several centuries after the death of Moses, we cannot imagine that it was assimilated by the Hebrews at a later period. As in the case of the Creation and Flood legends, a later borrowing was incompatible with the desire of devout editors to preserve, not to say

[1] See especially Martin Buber's *Moses*, chapter on 'The Sabbath'. It must be remembered likewise that the stay in Egypt lasted probably about 400 years.

[2] Woolley: *Abraham*, p. 183.

[3] The same argument disposes of the view that the Hebrews acquired their law from the inhabitants of Palestine among whom they had come to settle. Palestine had long been part of the Egyptian Empire.

[4] For further evidence that Abraham acted according to Sumerian law, particularly in the case of Hagar, see Woolley: *Abraham*, Chapter 5.

insulate, authentic Patriarchal traditions from those likely to exert a direct threat to their purity.[1]

Earlier in this chapter we showed that as the domination of Babylon by Hammurabi and his successors became complete, the old Sumerian culture gave place to that of the conquering people. Thus the language of Sumeria gradually assumed the status of a classical language, to be studied in schools for its 'cultural' value, as we study Greek and Latin. In one sphere only, it remained alive.

The temple services of Babylonia were performed not in contemporary speech but in Sumerian: a practice resembling that adopted by the Roman Church in its performance of the Mass, and also by the Moslem use of classical Arabic for religious practice. Such Sumerian religious literature as has survived suggests that its *corpus* must originally have been immense, perhaps as great in proportion as that of the Hindus, who are quantitatively the most religious of peoples. Much of the Sumerian scriptures consist of magical lore and treatises on demonology: there is a great deal of such matter on the tablets from the library of Ashurbanipal. Of all the literature that has survived, nothing is more interesting than the series of poems best described as penitential psalms. Composed in Sumerian, as was to be expected, these psalms might well be included in the Christian biblical canon without exciting the least suspicion as to their origin. In form they exhibit that 'parallelism of numbers', peculiar to hymnography, which seems to have first been employed in the hymns of the early Pyramid Texts. Breasted maintains that the Hebrews borrowed this technique (which suggests an antiphonal mode of performance) direct from the Egyptians. It is equally possible that the Hebrews derived it from the Babylonians, whose religious temperament was much closer in spirit. Although not all these psalms are strictly penitential, the themes of abasement before God and the weight of sinfulness are those which prompt the psalmist to most eloquent expression:

> Mankind is perverted and has no judgment:
> Of all men who are alive, who knows anything?...
> O Lord, do not cast aside thy servant:
> He is cast into the mire, take his hand!
> The sin which I have sinned, turn to mercy!
> The iniquity which I have committed, let the wind carry away!
> My many transgressions tear off like a garment!
> My god, my sins are seven times seven ... etc.

Such utterances, even in a bald translation, are perceived to differ radically from the 'mock' penitential rhymes from *The Book of the Dead*. The mood prevailing is one of spiritual anguish. Except in rare instances, *The Book of the Dead* is an anthology of religious humbug, like the rules of a celestial game of forfeits. From what we know of Babylonian social life we may also be reassured on another point:

[1] An example of a prohibition all the more necessary in view of the influence of foreign practice was that concerning images. The Egyptian practice of representing their gods must have been a perpetual temptation to the Hebrews: hence the second commandment of the Decalogue with its absolute ban upon image-making.

these psalms were not simply a verbal channel for the off-loading of the individual's emotions. Babylonian 'sin catalogues', wherewith the individual worshipper took regular soundings of his spiritual condition, have survived. Moreover, the theme of penitence was carried into everyday life. Certain days in the year, for instance, were set aside for the purposes of penitential reflection. The word *shabattu*, which applied to these particular days, was also applied to the middle of the month. Four other days, the 7th, 14th, 21st, and 28th, significantly separated by intervals of seven,[1] were regarded as *dies irae* on which the high officials from the king downwards refrained from carrying out their normal duties. The word *shabattu*, from which is derived Sabbath, carries the meaning of 'calming of the heart'. The notion survives, with a difference in orientation, in the statement in *Genesis* that 'God rested the seventh day and hallowed it'. In *Exodus*, Chapter xxxi, 17, we find a phrase suggesting that, after the creation of the world, God 'rested and breathed freely'. 'Calming of the heart' may also mean propitiating the regularly-incurred anger of the gods, as if every so often they called to mind their remorse at having created man. In borrowing the word *shabattu*, the Hebrews proceeded to apply it to precisely those days of the week which the Babylonians regarded as 'cursed'. Significantly enough, the Hebrew conception of the Sabbath was altogether more serene than the Babylonian; and this may explain why, in seeking a word for it, they took over (perhaps unconsciously) that which applied in Babylon to a specially holy day. For the mid-month festival was that of the full moon, the day on which Nannar or Terah appeared in the highest perfection of beauty.

Whether we shall ever possess enough insight into Babylonian psychology to discover why, and how early, certain days were regarded as of bad omen (or, to use our modern shirking word, unlucky) is more than doubtful. Like many other peoples, the Babylonians held seven to be a sacred number. If, as is possible, they were the first to believe the world to have been created in seven days, whatever they may have meant by 'day', the isolation of every seventh day in the month as an occasion for national humiliation suggests the commemoration of an event of cosmic significance. Nor would this hypothesis be nullified if it were proved, as has often been suggested, that the idea of seven-day creation was the consequence rather than the cause of the universal veneration for this number.

As the Babylonians were the originators, so far as we know, of the lunar month of twenty-eight days,[2] it seems clear that the black days were those connected with the phases of the moon. But we should need to penetrate the depths of their minds, as we have succeeded in penetrating the ruins of their houses, in order to understand why they insisted upon punctuating their lives with such intervals of self-

[1] Cf. also the term 'sabbatical year'. A relic of the same notion may perhaps be found in the expression 'seventh heaven'.

[2] They were also the first to divide the day into twelve hours, and the hour into sixty minutes, though they also experimented with an hour divided into thirty minutes.

castigation.[1] Such a tendency may be the result of the growing rigidity of custom, which seems to cast an atmosphere of solemnity over that which it no longer, or only half, understands. Certain persons, in England at least, deplore the tendency towards the 'continental Sunday', forgetting that there has likewise been a tendency towards something equally removed in spirit from the original 'Sunday', namely the kind of dismal festival represented on occasion by the Scottish Sabbath. Thus the Babylonian days of abasement may be as much a perversion of early moon festivals as the Hebrew Sabbath of the New Testament—for the violation of which Christ was reproached by the Jews—was a perversion of the original Sabbath introduced or revived by Moses. For we cannot help observing the oddity of the situation described in *John* v, where, so far as healing the sick is concerned, it is apparently permissible for the angel to 'trouble the waters', but blasphemy for Christ to trouble the Sabbath.

Just as it is impossible to invent a legal code, so it is impossible to invent a religion. We constantly hear of new religions, especially in countries like the United States where there is a good deal of unexpended female mental energy, but such gospels are sure to reveal, upon examination, familiar and even banal characteristics. A man may decide to worship a colour, but that was done long ago in Syria, where a sect still worships the colour blue; or himself, but that was done by a Roman emperor. In our account of Abraham we have failed of our purpose if we have given the impression that he personally invented the faith which, for the next two thousand years, goes by the name of Judaism. He did nothing of the kind. 'The men whom we call founders of religions are not really concerned with founding a religion, but wish to establish a human world that is subject to divine truth: to unite the way of the earth with that of heaven.'[2] That is a statement the importance of which, for reasons we hinted at in our first chapter, has tended to be obscured in the Western world. It remains the plain truth about the oriental world, the key to its spiritual mentality. Except in very rare instances, the oriental mind does not argue about the existence of a divine realm. Such a realm is accepted as a fact. If there is any argument at all, it is concerned with the degree to which the natural or material world falls short of this realm in respect of truth and reality.

In the light of these considerations, it is no less misleading to describe Moses as the true founder of Judaism than so to describe Abraham. Like Zoroaster or Buddha, both Abraham and Moses were engaged in establishing or re-establishing the 'divine connection'. Connection, in both their cases, involved also connection with the past. They innovated to conserve; the one to keep his family, the other his tribe, together. This is the explanation of the so-called Covenants (*berith*) which Abraham and Moses, and later Josiah, are reported to

[1] Micea Eliade, in his book *Le Mythe de l'Eternel Retour*, maintains that '*la durée des nations exigeait la répétition périodique d'actes cosmogoniques et que tout sacrifice* répète *le sacrifice initial et coïncide avec lui*'.

[2] Martin Buber: *Moses* (1946), p. 82.

have concluded with Yahweh. Such covenants are sometimes described on the analogy of contracts or even political agreements. The Jews were free at last from the authority of Pharaoh. In the desert they began to exhibit a tendency towards anarchy, as people suddenly released from political despotism are inclined to do. The other form of rule available to them was that of the desert wanderer, the Bedouin, whom they had already encountered in their brush with the Amalekites, kept at bay so long as Moses held aloft his hands (*Exodus* xvii, 8).

The object of the Covenant was to assert the authority of a different form of rule, that of Yahweh Himself. In another of its aspects the Covenant was a way of establishing that permanent relationship between God and man first announced in *Genesis* after the survival of Noah, and of which the symbol was the bow in the clouds. If the Covenant needed later to be renewed, as was often the case, that was due to man's repeated failure to realize the implications of such a relationship. Such a human-divine pledge was not unique. The more we study the Archaic culture the more we discover that Covenants between man and God form part of the traditional mythology of ancient races. Covenants can be made with the devil too; we have yet to see whether the modern world's covenant with science and technology is not of this diabolical character.[1]

A study of man's early conceptions of good and evil cannot ignore, in discussing the history of Israel,[2] certain arguments tending to diminish the spiritual insight attributed to the Old Testament Jews. In philosophy we cannot slur over difficulties or ignore criticism: these must resolutely be faced. It has been said that Yahweh, instead of being the invisible, unrepresentable God who first disclosed His true identity to Moses, was in fact a god already well known in the district where He was first encountered. The Sinai peninsula, it is true, shows evidence of volcanic activity of, geologically speaking, recent occurrence. Such phenomena inevitably gave rise to notions of the presence of spirits or local deities. Yahweh, it is held, was a fire or volcano god. And Moses' first genuine encounter with Yahweh took place on the mountain where He permanently resided.

This theory is extremely plausible. Even if true, it is not necessarily damaging. The naming of a god may originally have been as accidental, or as little to the purpose, as the naming of a person, though admittedly this is not likely among people to whom naming was a serious matter. But, as far as we know, the name Yahweh was not attached to any god honoured on Sinai.[3] Like most volcanic regions, Sinai could presumably boast of a volcano god, and such a god was bound to receive homage from local inhabitants. The Hebrews were neither local inhabitants nor, according to our argument so far, did they

[1] It is worth remarking that the outstanding characters of the Bible do not mix with the gods. Humanity and divinity are always separate. The reference to giants on earth in *Genesis* vi, 4, is obviously an interpolation.

[2] The meaning of Israel is 'God rules'. Cf. Islam, 'submission (to God)'.

[3] See Montgomery: *Arabia and the Bible* (1934), p. 10, and Buber: *The Prophetic Faith* (1949), p. 25.

regard Yahweh as an 'attached' god. He temporarily inhabited Sinai as He temporarily inhabited the Burning Bush, which, because of its momentary inmate, 'was not consumed'—and indeed as He had temporarily inhabited the desert spring perceived by Abraham's maid Hagar (*Genesis* xvi, 7, 13). This momentary investment of natural objects proved not so much His kinship with ordinary nature gods, whose essence was to remain in one place, as His absolute difference from them. By taking up positions all along the line, as it were, He made mock of their fixity.

If Mount Sinai harboured a god, as we have suggested, what was he called? We do not know. But we do know that a tribe called the Kenites inhabited this region, or, since they may have been a wandering people, frequently visited it. This tribe probably helped to work the neighbouring copper mines; some of them were ore-smelters or travelling smiths. Their god may well have been that of Sinai, whose activity on a grand scale so closely resembled their own. We cannot suppose that Moses' wife, a Midianite, had not spoken to him of the mountain god of this district. The subject is bound to have arisen in a household in which theological discussions must have been frequent. And when her father Jethro visits Moses at Sinai and is informed (*Exodus* xviii) of what Yahweh had done for the people of Israel, his exclamation, 'Now I know that Yahve is greater than all the gods,' resembles the episode in *Genesis* (xiv), in which Melchizedek makes a similar declaration to Abraham. In the first case, the god is called El'Elyon, the name of Melchizedek's god, for which Abraham deliberately substitutes the 'Most High God' of his fathers. In the second episode, the word Elohim is used, which, as explained above, is a word meaning gods as well as God. Now the statement of Jethro (who is here described as a priest) is sometimes taken to suggest not merely that he attributed Israel's fortune to the bounty of his own god, before whose sanctuary the company were encamped, but that thereafter Moses and his people were converted to this same god, whose name was Yahweh. What happened was precisely the contrary, as the later history of Israel proved. Both incidents describe the kind of Covenant, human as well as divine, whereby Yahweh became through His representative the God of peoples other than Israel, until in the time of the prophets He was pronounced a God universal in both power and appeal: in short, a God not of nature but of history.

The Prophets

After wandering in the desert for as long as forty years—a period which, though apparently excessive even for a heterogeneous group, might well have elapsed in the case of nomads—Canaan was finally conquered, and an era of settlement followed. The history of this settlement, with its disturbances and upheavals no less serious than those of the desert trek, must briefly be passed over. Israel was governed first by judges and then by kings, of whom Saul, David, and Solomon were the most distinguished, the last two being men of unusual vision and wisdom. Nothing is recorded of either Saul or David outside the Bible, but part of the *Book of Kings* has been confirmed from inscriptions found in 1935 at Tel Ad-Duweir. After Solomon's death in or about 937 BC, Israel was convulsed with civil war. As a result, the country split into two kingdoms, a northern kingdom of Ephraim with its capital at Samaria, and a southern kingdom of Judah of which the capital remained at Jerusalem. That such social unrest was partly due to the extravagance of the great kings, particularly Solomon, is very probable. We learn that the Temple took seven years and immense quantities of material to erect, and that Solomon thereafter devoted thirteen years to building himself a palace. Public works of this kind are usually either an attempted palliative for labour troubles or a very potent cause of them. When finally the Egyptian Pharaoh Sheshante invaded Judah, sacked the capital, and seized most of Solomon's accumulated gold, it may well have seemed that God was executing divine judgment on His people.

At this critical stage in Israel's history, something of the old guidance was required. The religion of the Patriarchs stood in need of preaching afresh. Under the kings there had been wealth, wisdom, and (if we accept David as the author of some at least of the psalms) art. But neither David nor Solomon had been disinterested followers of Yahweh. Their reputation had been immense, their personal example less impressive.[1] Only their great power had enabled them to maintain their position as leaders. Such power was evident in the case of Saul and Solomon, but in the case of David there was something more than power, namely genius. After Ikhnaten, and much more vividly, David is the ancient world's great 'individual'. His character is too subtly and yet frankly depicted to be that of any but a living person. (To cast doubt upon his authenticity by pointing to the lack of evidence for it outside the Bible is to forget what an important testimony the Bible itself provided, as archaeologists are discovering; it is like questioning a series of facts because it is nowhere mentioned outside the *Encyclopædia Britannica*.) Who, then, were to be the keepers of the moral conscience of Israel? In whom, to put the question in the form appropriate to our enquiry, did the development of the moral sense in man seem most clearly perceptible?

The word Prophet or *Nabi* does not necessarily mean one who fortells the future. It means one who 'announces', a spokesman of news. Such is likewise the meaning of the Greek word *prophetes*. If we bear this sense of the word in mind, we perceive the error of asserting that at a moment of disruption in Israel's life the prophets appeared. They did not appear. They reappeared. Naturally, like everything else that reappears, they did so in a new form, a form appropriate to the time. Instead of being accredited leaders of men they were usually persons who, with nothing but a burning conviction to sustain them, arraigned the authorities for their wickedness and blindness to facts. Sometimes they were men of family and substance. Sometimes, poor to

[1] Solomon, for example, did not scruple to build altars and temples to alien gods, such as Astarte and Chemosh.

the point of destitution, they roamed the wilderness, where the reverberation of their cries symbolized the heedlessness that so often greeted their message. Sometimes they were men whose personalities we can easily understand: occasionally they remain mere mouthpieces of vatic denunciation. For in their message we observe a resumption of the theme of oppression of the weak by the strong at a point where the Egyptian sages and such isolated figures as Hammurabi tended to leave off. These men are neither intellectual critics nor the earliest preachers of doctrinal socialism. They are self-elevated public figures enraged by social injustice. With no men earlier and possibly only with Socrates later can they bear comparison.

The most important fact about the prophets, and one which tends to be obscured if we regard them simply as radical spokesmen for the proletariat, is that they claimed divine inspiration: 'The spirit of the Lord is upon me.' In the ancient and to a great extent in the modern oriental world, the idea of possession by spirits is nothing remarkable. It does not happen to everyone, but to some it may happen by nature. The Holy Man is not a curiosity; the village idiot or his equivalent must be accepted as such. At what point in the history of the Western world the capacity for 'seeing visions' and speaking with tongues (i.e. permitting another to speak on one's behalf) became atrophied, only manifesting itself during religious revivals or in attenuated form as aesthetic inspiration, we cannot say. If T. S. Eliot is right to suppose that a certain form of disciplined dreaming common in Dante's time has ceased within the last six or seven hundred years,[1] we cannot wonder that the last few thousand years should have witnessed a decline in susceptibility to other forms of visionary experience, disciplined or otherwise. No study of the oriental mind can ignore the fact of supra-sensible experience. To some thinkers—and Aldous Huxley in his distinguished book *The Perennial Philosophy* counts himself among them—the norm of oriental speculation is simply the mystical grasp of a transcedent order of being, leaving 'philosophy' in the Western sense to explore the foothills of knowledge. If you deny the possibility of such knowledge you must at least take upon yourself to explain how the oriental mind, which does not lack subtlety, should have expended so much energy towards its attainment. Even if the oriental mystic, or any mystic for that matter, is under a misapprehension concerning the nature of this form of communion, it would be interesting to lay bare the causes of such a radical departure from common reason. Without pursuing this question, which we shall treat in detail later, we must accept the fact not merely that the prophets claimed to be divine spokesmen but that they were the most distinguished, judging from contemporary records, of a group of persons gifted with similar insight.

In almost every language the word for 'spirit' and the word for 'breath' are, if not identical, related: *pneuma*, *spiritus*, and in Hebrew *ruah*. A prophet—or prophetess, for there are women spokesmen or announcers too, especially in Israel—is one through whom the breath of divine knowledge blows, and whose words are consequently

[1] See *Dante* (1925).

'inspired', or drawn from the reservoir of spirit which is God. From the earliest times we have evidence that such inspiration can be of several kinds, only one being truly authentic: for falsity and fraud are often to be distinguished by variety. There is the prophet uniquely and consciously persuaded of his vocation to deliver a message. There is the man who, without proper understanding, is made a vehicle for such information: Balaam was evidently such a person. And finally there is the 'false prophet', common enough in Israel, whose message, whether understood or not, is wholly mischievous. Common to all is the breath, the afflatus, that upon which the message is borne. A true prophet breathes weighted eloquence. A falst prophet is merely a windbag.

According to Mohammed, no great prophet has ever lived who did not begin life as a shepherd. Amos was a shepherd. Living in the days of Uzziah, King of Judah, he described how, though 'neither a prophet nor a prophet's son but a herdman and a gatherer of sycamore fruit', the Lord 'took him as he followed the flock', and said to him, 'Go prophesy unto my people Israel.' Having visited the town of Bethel, he there 'sat at the gate' and poured forth a fierce denunciation of its citizens and of all Israel for its extravagance, exploitation, and neglect of God. His words are all the more effective in that he preserves the imagery of his original calling, 'Woe to them that are at ease in Zion ... that lie upon beds of ivory, and stretch themselves upon their couches, and eat the lambs out of the flock, and the calves out of the midst of the stall: that chant to the sound of the viol and invent to themselves instruments of music, like David.' And later, more bitterly and to the point, 'Thus saith the Lord, As the shepherd taketh out of the mouth of the lion two legs or a piece of an ear, so shall the children of Israel be taken out that dwell in Samaria in the corner of a bed in Damascus on a couch.'

This attack upon those who 'swallow up the needy, want to make the poor of the land to fast', and who 'falsify the balances by deceit', is a great deal more violent in its effect than the only other surviving piece of denunciatory literature with which it may be compared, namely the Egyptian story of the Eloquent Peasant. The peasant reminds the authorities of their duties. 'Thou art the balances,' he cries to the Grand Vizier; but he does not suggest that this instrument shall be struck from the ruler's hand. He wishes it to remain there. Speaking on behalf of Yahweh, Amos threatens with utter destruction the society that has always understood itself to be the 'peculiar people' or 'treasure' of the Lord. Two remarks in *Amos*, viii, make this abundantly clear. 'The end is come upon my people Israel,' God is made to say. 'I will not again pass by them any more.' Thus the very hymns and psalms of the temple 'shall be howlings in that day', and, more dreadful still, the means whereby Israel's deliverance was originally effected shall be turned against an ungrateful and heedless people. 'It shall rise up wholly as a flood, and it shall be cast out and drowned as by the flood of Egypt.'[1]

If the message of Amos were purely destructive, it would deserve no

[1] A threat repeated in Amos ix, 5.

more than passing attention. But his prophecy, together with that of another prophet roughly contemporary with him, Hosea, seemed to have been justified in the event. 'They that sow the wind shall reap the whirlwind,' Hosea proclaimed. Ephraim and Judah were soon at war one with the other. Feeling herself threatened, Judah sought aid from Assyria. The latter country sent an army which not merely routed Judah's enemies, but, determined to exploit its success, turned upon Judah herself and swept up to the gates of Jerusalem, almost capturing the city. Even so, such apparent fulfilment of the words of the prophets was not the most important part of their mission. In the work of Amos we observe a development of thought concerning God which reveals the prophets as initiators of a new stage in the moral consciousness of mankind. Having denounced Israel and threatened its virtual extinction as a nation, Amos reminds his people of something which, in their conceit, they had tended to ignore. By establishing a Covenant with Israel, God had singled them out as 'His' chosen people. At the same time this choice laid upon them particular responsibilities. Not merely must they deserve the trust placed in them, but they must realize that they are not the only people in whom God is interested. 'The whole earth,' He declares, 'is mine.' He even taunts them for supposing that, by delivering Israel from the house of bondage, He was undertaking something absolutely unique: 'Are you not as children of the Ethiopians unto me, O children of Israel?' saith the Lord. 'Have not I brought up Israel out of the land of Egypt? And'—to drive home the irony—'the Philistines from Caphtor, and the Syrians from Kir? ... For lo ... I will sift the house of Israel among all nations, like as corn is sifted in a sieve' (ix, 7, 9).

Such is the climax of a story which, beginning with the compact with Melchizedek and Jethro, ends only with the Christ's injunction to preach the gospel to every creature. The gradual development and widening vision to which the Old Testament, with all its inconsistencies, bears steady and convincing witness, has appeared to some critics to suggest a series of accidents from which the world faith of Christianity emerged more by chance than by design. Leaving aside the question of the 'truth' of this or any other system of belief, the onus rests upon such critics to suggest some other way in which a universal faith can emerge than by its gradual dissemination from small beginnings. The Kingdom of Heaven is not to be advertised by a mailed circular: its origin is a grain of mustard seed.

The point of view of Amos and Hosea was further developed by a remarkable man who personally witnessed the Assyrian assault on Jerusalem. This was Isaiah, the author of at least thirty-nine chapters of the book bearing that title. Sharing the opinion of his fellow-prophets concerning the unworthiness of Israel, he sees in her possible destruction or defeat a means whereby her iniquities may be chastened. If the God of Israel is a universal god, He will 'use' Assyria and indeed any other nation to work out His purpose. Thus a new attitude to history is born. To the Egyptians, Pharaoh's enemies not merely deserve defeat but are doomed inevitably to suffer it. Death and destruction, which we saw to exist only for the enemy, were invented expressly for such as challenged the power of the sacred descendant of Horus. To Isaiah, who is the first of a series of such seers, this attitude is one of childish pride. The children of Israel must resist the national enemy within as well as without. Justice at home is an obligation no less than resistance to foreign enemies, whose cupidity has usually been inflamed by the prospect of looting a disordered and unruly kingdom. So Isaiah, having advised King Hezekiah to resist Sennacherib to the best of his ability, forthwith turns upon his own nation with words that express for all time the *saeva indignatio* of a just man. 'What mean ye that ye beat my people to pieces and grind the faces of the poor? ... Woe unto them that join house to house, that lay field to field, till there be no place... Woe unto them that decree unrighteous decrees to turn aside the needy from judgment, and to take away the right from the poor of my people, that widows may be their prey and that they may rob the fatherless!' The traditional worship, the regular offering up of sacrifice, even the orthodox prayers, are not sufficient. 'I am full of the burnt offerings of rams and the fat of fed beasts. Your appointed feasts my soul hateth... And when ye spread forth your hands (in prayer) I will hide mine eyes from you; yea, when ye make many prayers I will not hear; your hands are full of blood.'

Although he was the most eloquent of the prophets and perhaps of all his eloquent race, Isaiah did not exhaust his listeners with mere diatribes. He issued them with precise instructions as to what to do to be saved. 'Seek judgment (meaning, see that justice is done), relieve the oppressed, judge the fatherless, plead for the widow.' But these precepts, vigorous though they are, do not form the most original part of his message. Like his attitude to the political struggles of his day, this message is essentially historical. Suddenly switching his attention from the present, he peers into a future which, though distant, is not to be regarded as inconceivably remote. The troubles of Israel and of Israel's neighbours, which occupy the whole of his attention, are realized to be too deep-seated for any immediate cure. Only the 'gathering up' of history in an event both in and out of time would herald the end of discord, lust, and war. Such an event is the inconceivable (and therefore unconceived) birth in human form of the hitherto imageless, unrepresentable, God of the Fathers. The climax of the 'shewings' of God from that at Sinai onwards would logically be His actual appearance upon earth, his taking human flesh, His Incarnation. And as the successive revelations had hitherto been made to the holy and privileged people, so the birth of this Saviour would naturally spring from the 'stem of Jesse'. Except for the brief passage of Ipuwer, the meaning of which must always remain obscure, the following words are the first of their kind to be uttered:

'Behold, a virgin shall conceive, and bear a son, and shall call his name Immanuel...[1] For unto us a child is born, and the government shall be upon his shoulder, and his name shall be called Wonderful,

[1] See p. 40.

Counsellor, the Mighty God, the Everlasting Father, the Prince of Peace... And there shall come forth a rod out of the stem of Jesse... And the spirit of the Lord shall rest upon him, the spirit of wisdom and understanding, the spirit and might, the spirit of knowledge and the fear of the Lord... With righteousness shall he judge the poor, and reprove with equity for the meek of the earth... And righteousness shall be the girdle of his loins, and faithfulness the girdle of his reins. The wolf also shall dwell with the lamb, and the leopard shall lie down with the kid, and the calf and the young lion and the fatling together; and a little child shall lead them... And they shall beat their swords into ploughshares and their spears into pruning-hooks. Nation shall not lift up sword against nation, neither shall they learn war any more.'

It is difficult to judge with what measure of understanding the Israeli royal house, the priesthood, and finally the people, whose needs were here for the first time declared, received this impassioned prophecy. The Bible—and in some generations such as Puritan England the Old Testament in particular—has become a sacred book for millions, as well as a book respected by millions more. Yet orthodox Christians would do well to reflect upon the explosive material assembled within that richly-bound volume, which, reposing so often in the quiet of a church or on an obscure bookshelf at home, assumes an outward appearance of innocuousness. If we were to bind together the most violent political denunciations of the rich and powerful, the fiercest satires upon conventional morality, the most penetrating commentaries upon the vanity of life, together with the best poetic expressions of our civilization and its wittiest maxims, we should not have collected an anthology one-tenth part as disrupting of complacency as that eclectic handbook of the 'Old Dispensation'. We may wonder how the prophets managed to escape with their lives, and how their message, with its inflammable content, did not meet with drastic censorship or even total suppression.

The wonder is increased by a reading of the message of Jeremiah. In 639 BC Josiah had ascended to the throne of Judah. His reign is of particular importance for two reasons. As a result of the preaching of the prophets the priesthood was becoming gravely concerned about the condition of the orthodox faith, which was in danger of both pollution and neglect. It was time to return to first principles, or in other words to renew the Covenant of Moses. The discovery in the Temple either by chance or of set purpose of a scroll purporting to have been written by Moses himself caused a profound sensation throughout the country, and marks the beginning of the deliberate putting together of the sacred writings that now form the Pentateuch.[1] But, in spite of Josiah's reforming zeal, the political fortunes of Israel reached an extremely low ebb. The power of Assyria admittedly disappeared with the fall of Nineveh in 612 BC; but one enemy soon gave place to another, and Josiah himself was killed at Megiddo in an attempt to stem an Egyptian invasion. The next threat came from Babylon,

[1] Greek: 'Five Rolls', the first five books of the Old Testament.

whose king, Nebuchadnezzar, twice attacked Jerusalem, first placing a puppet king called Zedekiah on the throne, and later, when the puppet sought to be something more by pulling strings on his own, deposed Zedekiah, reduced Jerusalem to ruins, and deported most of its inhabitants to Babylon. The so-called Babylonian Captivity followed.[1]

This was Jeremiah's opportunity. His mission had begun immediately prior to the Exile. Declining to sustain public morale in the orthodox sense, he set himself up as the scourge of an incorrigibly idolatrous people. Like the first Isaiah, he declared that the domination of Babylon must not merely come about but that it should be endured as the will of Yahweh. The Jews, he maintained, had brought this terrible fate upon themselves. If the rules of justice had been observed, if internal oppression and corruption had not increased, Yahweh would surely have come to the aid of His Holy People; but (the passage reminds one of God's attitude to the inhabitants of Sodom) 'Run ye to and fro through the streets of Jerusalem, and see now, and know, and seek in the broad places thereof, if ye can find a man, if there be any that executeth judgment, that seeketh the truth, and I will pardon it.' At a time of acute national crisis, when futile recrimination is usually silenced, Jeremiah insisted upon the priority of justice and righteousness even over national safety. As a reward for his frankness he was pilloried on a high gate, consigned to a filthy dungeon, and all but put to death; but the king, reluctant to add the reputation of martyr to that of prophet, stayed his execution. On forcing the gates of Jerusalem, Nebuchadnezzar found this reluctant ally under protective arrest in the king's palace. Zedekiah he executed; but he spared Jeremiah, nor did the latter follow his people into exile.

In the days before the siege, as part of his stock-in-trade, Jeremiah had worn a wooden yoke round his neck, symbolizing the fate due to overtake Jerusalem. In old age he wrote a series of *Lamentations* in which that fate was mourned in sombre, though magnificent, poetry. Just as his exiled countrymen were required by their taskmasters to 'sing one of the songs of "Sion",' which they did in the superb psalm beginning 'By the waters of Babylon', so Jeremiah, an exile in the ruins of his own home, was prompted to dwell upon the same theme, but with even greater penetration and therefore increased disillusion. The question of the Egyptian Misanthrope is here raised afresh, as it is raised by the discerning in every age: 'Righteous thou art, O Lord, when I plead with thee, but'—and this is the fundamental issue between man and God—'*let us talk of thy judgment*: *Wherefore doth the way of the wicked prosper?* Wherefore are all they happy that deal treacherously?' This theme receives its most profound treatment in the *Book of Job*, which must have been composed about 450 BC.[2]

'If I forget thee, O Jerusalem, let my right hand forget her cunning,'

[1] This deportation had been preceded by a transfer of 10,000 Jews to Babylon after Nebuchadnezzar's first attack on Jerusalem.

[2] Some fragments of Babylonian literature on the same subject are thought to have influenced this composition. The protagonist is Tabi-utal-Enlil, a ruler of Nippur.

was the burden of the earliest among the exiles. But the conditions that made it difficult 'to sing the Lord's Song in a strange land' made it easy to grow lax in religious observance, or, more destructive of communal morale, to 'go whoring after strange gods'. Of the latter, Babylon had a large variety. The Babylonian Exile, though shorter and on the whole less burdensome than the Egyptian, proved in many ways more damaging to a people united by a faith born of bondage and persecution, yet gifted with powers of assimilation above that of any other people. In these circumstances the mission of the prophet proved more important than ever. Ezekiel, one of the few prophets to have been a priest (or so he declares), set out to continue the work of Jeremiah. Unlike the latter, he knew in direct fashion the bitterness and demoralization of exile, having been among the first of the Jewish deportees to Babylon. True to the *Nabi* character, he describes how he was 'among the captives by the river of Chebar in the land of the Chaldeans' when the hand of the Lord was set upon him, and he saw, through the opening of the heavens, 'visions of God'. These visions assumed many strange forms. Anyone who has visited the country in which Ezekiel was obliged to toil can detect in much that he wrote a hallucinatory quality born of long spells of exposure to intense heat, whereby an impression is obtained of the sky giving forth images as he records them in the opening verses.[1]

Unlike Jeremiah, Ezekiel concludes upon a message of hope. If the children of Israel will renounce their political divisions (especially that into the two kingdoms of Ephraim and Judah), if they will cease 'defiling themselves with their idols', and other 'detestable things', Yahveh will cleanse them, and they shall once again be His people.

If, as the Jewish people have thought, the prophetic books of the Old Testament do not reach fulfilment in the New Testament, their successive message—for it is one message delivered by many mouths—reveals a progress in spiritual discernment, a deepening grasp of the nature of God, to which no other tradition, religious, literary, or historical, can be compared. If they do not anticipate a Saviour, or at least the Savious who was Jesus of Nazareth, they may well anticipate each other: the torch of enlightenment is not merely handed on but, as it is grasped afresh, seems to grow brighter. They may not, if you like, prophesy the supreme Prophet; but, in the person of the so-called Second or Deutero Isaiah, they prophesy the consummation of Prophecy. For it is in the work of this latter writer, whose identity we do not know, that the true nature of the God of the Fathers is apprehended in the purest light. Ezekiel, as we have seen, concluded on a note rarely struck by his predecessors (whose obsession with the vengeance of Yahweh could be described in our modern jargon as pathological): 'I will make a Covenant of Peace.' In the same way, the second Isaiah

[1] A later writer can often bring to life a passage of past literature, or at least render it still more moving. This is the case with T. S. Eliot's poem *Ash Wednesday*, in Part II of which the valley of Ezekiel forms the background. Ezekiel is said to have been an epileptic: but the suggestion may be based upon the modern assumption that the capacity to see visions is usually the result of illness.

begins his message with almost startling mildness, like a sudden calm after a storm of unparalleled severity, 'Comfort ye, comfort ye, my people, saith your God.' Declaiming in the traditional manner that the spirit of the Lord is upon him, he thus announces the terms of his mission, 'The Lord has appointed me to preach *good tidings* unto the meek: he hath sent me to bind up the broken-hearted, to proclaim to the captives, and the opening of the prison to them that are bound.' No one in Israel or anywhere else had spoken quite like this before.

The mood of exaltation which is sustained throughout almost the whole of the second part of *Isaiah* loses its force if we regard it merely as fine literature. Fine literature in the sense of ringing words without content, or with a content that is pronounced unacceptable to educated readers, is mere 'sounding brass and tinkling cymbal'. 'The Bible to be Read as Literature', to quote the title of a much-heralded publication, is the Bible to be left largely unread and finally neglected, as all literature severed from its living message deserves to be. The second *Isaiah* is fine literature because its message of hope and forgiveness, even if nourished upon an imaginary historical consummation, is the noblest message that man had hitherto delivered to his contemporaries in the few thousand years of civilized life. If its proclamation at that epoch is not to be regarded as a matter of history, as part of the achievement of the human mind in its slow evolution, then the matter of history is assuredly dead matter, and all our civilized values would seem to be based upon illusion.

The literature of hope and the literature of messianism go hand in hand. We have observed an occasional note of hope in the literature of Egypt: in the literature of Babylon practically none. Oppressed by a stern theocratic society without and by the pressure of 'sin consciousness' within, the men of the mid-oriental archaic world seem to us to have lacked almost everything that makes life worth living. In fact we know that as far as day-to-day happiness is concerned the men of one age are hardly better off than those of another. Historical records, being by necessity abbreviations, do not record *la vie quotidienne*. Yet there is another form of happiness, that which not only makes life worth living but also death worth dying. This is the product of faith in the meaningfulness of life itself, and if of human life, then of all life. Such a faith, for reasons beyond our present understanding, seems to have been communicated to, or evolved by, man within historical memory, but even so gradually and step by step. That the second Isaiah should have recorded his messianic vision perhaps contemporaneously with the Buddha in India may suggest either a similar, though unrelated, preoccupation in several regions of the world at the same time, or, since such preoccupation is permanent, a more than usual series of attempts to meet it. To the Christian the following passage must naturally appear to make more sense than to those who reject revelation, but it is still not senseless: 'The voice of him that crieth in the wilderness, Prepare ye the way of the Lord, make straight in the desert a highway for our God. Every valley shall be exalted and every valley or hill shall be made low, and the crooked shall be made straight and the rough places plain. And the glory of the Lord shall be revealed, and all flesh shall see it together... O Jerusalem that bringest good tidings, lift up thy voice with strength... Behold the Lord God will come with a strong hand, and his arm shall rule him, behold, his reward is with him and his work before him. He shall feed his flock *like a shepherd*: he shall gather the lambs with his arm and carry them in his bosom, and shall gently lead those that are with young.'

Here we have three invocations: the promise of the originally nameless and imageless God of the Fathers being finally revealed to his people; the invocation of Jerusalem not in the scarlet terms of Jeremiah and even Ezekiel but as a bride awaiting her husband; and finally the metaphors of the early shepherd prophets brought to a climax of pastoral beauty.

Although Isaiah speaks in the loftiest strains, he possesses as acute a political sense as his namesake. The delivery of the Jews from Babylon was not simply a matter for messianic hope. It was a practical matter. Introducing the passage in which he makes one of his most important theological statements, he declares boldly, 'Thus saith the Lord to his appointed, to Cyrus, whose right hand I have holden, to subdue nations before him, and I will loose the loins of the kings.' Cyrus, King of Persia, seemed to Isaiah to be the only man capable of overthrowing Babylon and of securing the passage back to Jerusalem of the exiles. He proved to be right. Cyrus not merely entered Babylon in 539 BC, but restored to the Jews all the money that Nebuchadnezzar had appropriated from the Temple. For the journey home he ordered the Babylonian families who had employed Hebrew slaves to provide them with food and money, including a subscription towards rebuilding the Temple. 'Whosoever remaineth in any place where he sojourneth,' said Cyrus, 'let the men of his place help him with silver and with gold and with goods and with beasts, besides a freewill offering for the house of God which is in Jerusalem.' The exiles were soon organizing their departure; but on returning to Jerusalem they found an alien and hostile people awaiting them. A generation passed before the Temple was rebuilt, and another century before national life was consolidated on the principles of the Law of Moses. This Law was re-edited and re-affirmed in 444 BC, by the priest Ezra, who entertained the people to a reading of the sacred scrolls lasting seven days.

What is the consummation of prophecy of which we spoke? It is the vision expressed by the second Isaiah of a God not merely of Israel but of all mankind, and secondly of God claiming absolute allegiance. In the Decalogue, God is made to refer to 'other gods' whose relative power by claiming superiority He implicitly acknowledges: 'Thou shalt have none other gods but me.' In *Isaiah* He is made to declare: 'I am the Lord and there is no one else, there is no God beside me... I have made the earth and created man upon it... I have raised him up in righteousness and I have directed all his ways.' And again: 'Behold the nations are as a drop of a bucket, and are counted as the small dust of the balance... And Lebanon is not sufficient to burn, nor the beasts thereof sufficient for a burnt offering. All nations before him are as nothing, and they are counted to him less than nothing and vanity... Hast thou not known that the everlasting God, the Lord, the Creator of the ends of the earth, fainteth not, neither is weary? There is no searching of his understanding. Even the youths shall faint and be weary, and the young men shall utterly fall. But they that wait upon the Lord shall renew their strength; they shall mount up with wings as eagles, they shall run and not be weary, and they shall walk and not faint.' Furthermore, the consciousness of sin and death, which runs like a swollen vein through the archaic mind, an inexplicable dread, is accorded for the first time some prospect of relief: 'Surely he hath borne our griefs and carried our sorrows... The Lord hath laid on him the iniquity of us all.' This is already the sense of the Christian Gospel.

Summary

If, turning our backs upon the events of the next three or four centuries (the second Isaiah wrote about five hundred years before the birth of Jesus), we contemplate the archaic world, we observe two supreme efforts at self-knowledge, like the mounting curves of a graph. There is the Egyptian challenge to death, first in the materialism of the Pyramid builders and later in the perception of the absolute value of *Maat* as reflected in individual conduct; and secondly there is the Hebrew challenge to the nature gods of antiquity by the vision of a God of righteousness, justice, and mercy, originally conceived on a family and tribal basis and finally as a God supreme over all men. Between these upward thrusts of moral aspiration there are thoughts equally debased and degraded: the gross trafficking in indulgences of *The Book of the Dead* and of the Babylonian manuals of theurgy, the incurable idolatry of the Israelites, the worship of Baal and Moloch, and so forth.[1] There are also such blind alleys as the sun worship of Ikhnaten, and the myths of Tammuz and Ishtar, touched with a strange beauty which suggests that no religion can dispense with an element of poetry.

Cyrus, the king who had supervised the return of the Jews from Babylon, showed the greatest respect for the religion of these ex-captives. He even seems to have acknowledged the God of Israel as the true God. 'The Lord God of Heaven,' he declared in a royal proclamation, 'hath given me all the kingdoms of the earth, and he hath charged me to build him a house at Jerusalem, which is in Judah... He is the God.' One would suspect that, like Napoleon in Egypt, he professed beliefs that served his political ambitions. To the Babylonian priesthood he was equally respectful. A conqueror in those days was obliged to admit, as Alexander in turn soon discovered, that peoples will not change their religion so easily as kings. In 334 BC, this young Achilles,[2] arriving in Palestine, accepted the surrender of Jerusalem from its high priest and continued Cyrus's policy of toleration. Three

[1] 'Then they came to Baal Peer and dedicated themselves unto that shame-idol, and became (the same) beings of abomination as that which they loved' (*Hosea* x, 10).

[2] Alexander's conception of himself.

years later, after capturing Babylon, he became master of the entire Middle East. Judea, midway between Egypt and Persia and therefore a perpetual invitation to foreign conquest, next came under the domination of Rome. In the reign of Caesar Augustus, at a time when the Roman world was stable enough to warrant the taking of a census of the population, Jesus was born in the outhouse of a crowded *hahn* in Bethlehem, in the region of Judea, when Herod was King of the Jews.

The origin and diffusion of that extension and to many minds completion of Judaism, called the Christian faith, does not come within the scope of this book, which halts upon the threshold of revelation. The preaching of the gospel of Jesus Christ and the foundation of His Church are matters to which neither philosophy nor history can remain indifferent. The birth was a registerable fact, the death a consequence of juridical proceedings, and the foundation of the Church a reality, as we know not so much from its survival in history as from its being in great measure the history that has survived. This projection of a new scale of values, a *vita nuova*, into the historical process raises philosophical considerations of great importance; but the working out of the new philosophy was undertaken chiefly in the Roman and Byzantine worlds, first by an isolated figure such as Philo of Alexandria (a contemporary of Christ but not a Christian), then by the early Christian fathers of both East and West, and finally by the great mediaeval theologians. To affirm that the Christian faith exerted negligible influence upon the oriental world, however, would be both a serious and, from the point of view of understanding Zoroastrianism and Islam, a disastrous error. Few religions are self-enclosed. All great faiths interpenetrate. Church may persecute church, and every so often a church is obliged to expel from its orbit an element of danger and disaffection, as the Catholic Church expelled the Catharist heresy, and Islam that of the Mu'tazilites. But the impulse behind every faith—even the most crude and primitive, such as the furtively cultivated worship of luck and fortune which will survive as long as human nature—is, as we have hinted, identical. We may therefore find it convenient, during the rest of our survey, to drop the world religion altogether as too much enveloped in vague and misleading associations, and to adhere to the more illuminating definition. Religion will thus be viewed not as the competitor or even the extension of philosophy, but as the basic element in Perennial Philosophy.

4

Zoroaster

The first perfection is good thoughts, the second good words, and the third good deeds

A Figure Shrouded in Legend

The King of Persia who displayed such toleration of the faiths of his subject peoples was officially a Zoroastrian. The three wise men of the East who, according to Gospel tradition, arrived at Bethlehem saying 'Who is he that is born king of the Jews for we have seen his star in the East and are come to worship him,' were possibly priests of the same faith. Who was Zoroaster?

As with most other religions, one school of thought maintains that he did not exist at all. We certainly know less concerning his life than about the founder of almost any other faith, though the legends of his birth, upbringing, and conversations with God are numerous. Modern scholars, no less than ancient devotees and historians, are equally divided as to the date of his birth. The earliest date to which he has been assigned is 6000 BC. We need not for a moment suppose him to have lived as early as that. To have preached a gospel three thousand years before the earliest known kings of Egypt, when most of the world was no further advanced than the Bronze Age, would have been to preach into a kind of historical void. (There is no reason why men of wisdom should not have lived much earlier, but we are unlikely ever to learn what they said.) Berosus, the Babylonian historian who lived in the fourth century BC, committed himself to the opinion that Zoroaster lived about 2000 BC; but we are never sure with early historians, even with the great Herodotus, upon what basis they are calculating time. This is true even of such original and painstaking mathematicians as the Babylonians. Today, scholars are inclined to believe that Zoroaster was born no earlier than 660 BC, which brings him to within a few years of some of the greatest thinkers of the world.

Whereas we possess the means of verifying certain events in the lives of such figures as Ikhnaten, Abraham, Buddha, and Christ, we enjoy no such facilities in the case of Zoroaster. There are no known or credible events to verify. The career of Zoroaster is shrouded in a tissue of legend so fantastic, and to Western minds so preposterous, that he appears at first sight to belong to the order not of human beings but of mythical heroes. But we must not be too hasty in making inferences. Let us consider first of all the marvellous stories connected with his birth. Such stories seem invariably to attach themselves to religious leaders, and also to those who are regarded with something approaching religious awe—Plato, for instance; for the world is reluctant to allow men of outstanding personality to have come to birth in the manner of normal human beings. These legends do not prove a man never to have existed; but while they certainly do not prove the contrary, their existence and persistence may, as we have said, be accounted for by there having been some outstanding personality to eulogize. Oral tradition is not necessarily less reliable than written record. Today, with our dependence upon written testimony, we underestimate the power of communication by word of mouth, which served mankind for perhaps as much as a thousand times as long as writing. We can justifiably assume that where there is legendary smoke there is a spark at least of factual fire.

The name Zoroaster is the Greek rendering (Zoroastres) of Zarathustra, which Nietzsche adopted in his famous poetic fantasy *Also sprach Zarathustra*. He was born in Persia. To unravel from the Pahlavi Texts the precise details of his birth is extremely difficult, as the discourse has a habit of running on like a kind of divine gossip. We gather that some archangels 'framed together on a stem of Hom (the *haoma* plant), the height of a man, excellent in colour, and juicy when fresh', which Zoroaster's guardian chose to enter. Six white cows were then led up to the plant, and two of them, though virgin, became full of milk. These two cows ate the *haoma* plant, so that 'the nature of Zarathustra came from that plant to these cows, and mingled with the cow's milk'. Then a young girl of noble birth called Dukdaub was persuaded by the priest Porushaspo to milk the cows, whereupon Porushaspo pounded the *haoma* plant and mixed it with the cow's milk. Both he and the girl 'drank up that Hom and milk, when they were mingled together and announced to Ahura Mazda; and here occurred a combination of the glory, guardian spirit, and bodily nature of Zarathustra into a manchild'. Even so the evil spirits did their best to prevent the normal gestation of the child in his mother's womb; but she prayed to Ahura Mazda and became well. On the day Zarathustra was born the village of Porushaspo was suffused with a kind of divine illumination, 'the fire being in every crevice'; but the greatest marvel of all was that 'on being born he laughed outright. The seven midwives who sat round him were quite frightened thereby; and those terrified ones spoke thus: "What is this, on account of grandeur or contempt, when, like a worthy man whose pleasure is due to activity, the manchild so laughs at the birth owing to him?" But Porushaspo replied proudly: "Bring out this manchild to the sheep-skin clothing which is soft. The affair was owing to thee, owing to the virtue of thee who art Dukdaub, that the advent of glory and the coming of radiance to this manchild was openly seen when he laughed outright at this birth."'

The events attendant upon Zoroaster's birth were nothing to the trials and adventures that beset his boyhood. The demons and evil spirits sought by every means to destroy him. They tried to strangle him by appointing a nurse to perform this act on their behalf, to throw him under galloping horses, to burn him to death by placing him on a pile of ignited firewood, to have him seized and eaten by wolves. In each case he was rescued unharmed. On the last occasion, this was due to the fact that, 'Vohumano and Srosh the righteous brought a woolly sheep with an udder full of milk into the den, and it gave milk to Zarathustra, in digestible draughts, until daylight.'

As a very young child, likewise, he was reported to have 'looked a long while upwards, downwards, and on all sides round'.[1] On being asked what he was doing, he replied that he was seeing visions of the blessed ascending to heaven, and the wicked descending to hell, while at the same time he prophesied the dissemination of a new gospel throughout the earth.

The divine mission

Like Jesus, Zoroaster began his mission about the age of thirty years. This mission opened with a kind of spiritual examination undertaken by the good spirit Vohumano. Having challenged Zoroaster one day to declare 'what was his foremost distress, about what was his foremost endeavour, and for what was the tendency of his desire', the young man replied, 'About righteousness I consider my foremost distress; about righteousness my foremost endeavour; and for righteousness the tendency of my desire.' Being in due course admitted to the company of spirits, Zoroaster was able to put questions to Ahura Mazda himself. 'In the embodied world,' he asked, 'which is the first of the perfect ones, which the second, and which the third?' To which Ahura Mazda replied, 'The first perfection is good thoughts, the second good words, and the third good deeds.'

At the outset of his mission, Zoroaster seems to have lived the life of a recluse. Like John the Baptist, he took to the wilderness and subsisted upon nothing but cheese and roots. Then came temptation. Whereas Christ's tempter was Satan, Zoroaster's was a female demon, Spendarmad. The meeting took place not in the wilderness but among ordinary men, whose habits Zoroaster had resolved to study: 'Zarathustra proceeded to the habitable and friendly world, for the purpose of fully observing that beaten track of the embodied existence. Then the fiend came forward—a female, golden-bodied and full-bosomed. Companionship, conversation, and co-operation were requested by her from him.' Being aware that her charms were utterly deceptive, he requested her to turn her back. She replied, 'O Zarathustra of the Spitamas, where we are, those who are females are handsome in front but frightfully hideous behind, so do not make a demand for my back.' He insisted, and after she had protested a third time she consented to turn, upon which there issued from her a loathsome progeny of serpents, toads, lizards, centipedes, and frogs. The real ordeal, however, came later in the form of devilish assaults upon him, among which was the injection of molten lead into his stomach. But nothing succeeded in shaking his faith in the righteousness of the god with whom he

[1] The same was reported of the young Buddha at birth.

had enjoyed communion, Ahura Mazda. Finally, as a reward for his stoic devotion, Ahura Mazda presented him personally with a Book of Heavenly Wisdom later called the *Avesta*. This was the gospel of which he had dreamed as a boy. The missionary now had his Bible.

Although his preaching fell at first upon deaf ears—for the Persians already had their gods and nature cults—Zoroaster gradually began to make converts. When finally a Persian prince called Vishtaspa or Hystaspes decided to embrace the new faith, a powerful movement of religious conversion began; for this prince at once declared his intention of spreading the Zoroastrian religion throughout his kingdom. The usurping successor of Cambyses, a devotee of the old Magian gods, endeavoured to stamp it out; but with the accession to the throne of Darius I in 521 BC, Zoroastrianism was officially proclaimed the religion of Persia. Some historians believe that Hystaspes, the prince who first befriended Zoroaster, was none other than the father of Darius. If so, that would prove Zoroaster to have been born at the latest date claimed for him.

According to tradition, the death of Zoroaster, which is supposed to have taken place in his seventy-eighth year, was accomplished with as much drama as his birth, though more quickly. A flash of lightning enveloped him, and he was borne up to heaven.

Such a brief account of Zoroaster's life, despite its picturesque anecdotes, may not strike the Western reader as either particularly convincing or particularly edifying. Of the personality of Zoroaster we learn next to nothing. He is without doubt the most shadowy of all the spiritual leaders whose lives we shall have occasion to study. The marvels attributed to him, or associated with various phases of his life, verge often upon the grotesque. Whatever their effect upon the people of his time and upon his later devotees, they tend not so much to magnify him in our eyes as almost to exclude him from the front rank of men of superhuman vision. That is our first impression.

It is true that if you know little enough about a man you can make him into any sort of person you wish. Whatever our ignorance of Zoroaster, we can be certain that he was a very different person from the genial sage, the German professor on holiday, that Nietzsche made him out to be. Indeed, the figure of Zarathustra presented in the work already mentioned is merely a prop upon which to hang samples of the Nietzschean philosophy of the superman. For no other great figure of antiquity was sufficiently free from historical trappings. Our only hope of attaining to understanding, however modest, of the significance of Zoroaster is to view him against the background of his time. We are dimly aware of a great change in the spirit of the civilization to which he belonged—a change that is associated with the evangelistic work of a great teacher. To examine the new teaching is to approach as far as it is possible to an understanding of the man. The result may be surmise, but what history beyond a certain era is not? This line of enquiry would seem worth pursuing.

The pre-Zoroastrian gods of Persia bear a striking resemblance to those of the Hindu *Vedas*. Indeed, it has often been maintained by Indian scholars that the *Avesta* owes almost all its essential teaching to the *Vedas*, including its name. The pantheon contained two major deities: Mithra, god of the sun, and Anaita, goddess of the earth and of fertility. The importance of the cult of fertility was further emphasized by the worship of the bull-deity Haoma, whose blood was supposed to confer immortality upon those who drank it. The *haoma* herb, as we have already seen, was that into which the spirit of Zoroaster first entered on its devious journey towards birth. Found chiefly in the mountains, *haoma* possesses intoxicating properties: the worship of the bull-god consisted of drinking the plant's juice as being equivalent to the life-giving blood. The Hindu god Soma is probably the same as Haoma. Among these early peoples we also find distinct traces of ancestor worship: a religion whose disappearance in civilized times has left a void which is filled by such abstract substitutes as nationalism, the only religion that the West has presented to the East.

We have mentioned that the Zoroastrian scriptures to have survived, namely the *Avesta* and the Pahlavi Texts,[1] make difficult reading for the Western student. No doubt this is because there is almost nothing in Western literature with which they may be compared. In fact, the surviving texts are but fragments of a much larger body of scripture, some of which perished when Alexander the Great destroyed the royal palace at Persepolis, while other parts were lost during the Moslem conquests in the seventh century AD. The *Avesta*, with its collection of stories, hymns, and prayers, bears a certain resemblance to the Old Testament: what it appears to lack is a continuous theme, which is one of the most remarkable characteristics of at least the Pentateuch. Nevertheless, once the repetitions, obscurities, and unusual terminology of the Zoroastrian writings are discounted, a general message begins slowly to emerge, and the reader who has approached them determined to be baffled remains to surrender to their spell. Nor is the word 'spell' employed without deliberation. The prose literature operates upon the imagination with the force of incantation. To look for logic is to look for something that was apparently never meant to be there (or at least that is not apparent in translation), except in passages of epigrammatic wisdom such as we associate with the Chinese sages. Curiously enough, the Western reader may find proportionately more content in the poetry. The Zoroastrian Hymns or *Gathas*, with their moral and sometimes metaphysical argument, contain a good deal more substance than the Sun Hymn of Ikhnaten and the exquisite hymns of the *Rig-Veda*.

Content of the Faith

What general impression do we derive from these miscellaneous essays on righteousness and justice, these reports upon interviews with the Lord of Light, these accounts of the creation of the world and the propagation of the human species, and finally these outbursts of

[1] The *Avesta* were written in Zend (hence the title *Zend-Avesta*) and the Texts in a dialect of Hindu origin from which the modern Persian language is derived.

ecstatic poetry? It is an impression of delight in life and nature, a faith not so much of a materialist as of a vitalist character, but shot through with a sense of awe and dread of the power of evil.

In other words, the old fertility worship is still there, exercising its powerful and not-to-be-denied pressure, much as the worship of Osiris continued to maintain its hold in Egypt side by side with that of Re. In an agricultural nation, this was no doubt natural. 'Unhappy is the land that has long lain unsown with the seed of the sower and wants a good husbandman, like a well-shapen maiden who has long gone childless and wants a good husband.'[1]

What Zoroaster seems to have done was to purify the fertility cult of its grosser aspects. Similarly, Moses had tried to stem the inherent tendency of the children of Israel to engage in extravagant rites. From the biblical narrative it is possible to infer (though the inference has been hotly disputed) that Yahweh's refusal to allow Moses to enter the promised land may have been due to his failure, particularly at the last moment, to keep these demoralizing instincts in check.[2] We are told that at the very threshold of their new home, which merely to have sighted ought to have convinced the ordinary individual that Yahweh was the true God, large numbers of the men entered into illicit relations with the women of Moab, whom we assume to have solicited their co-operation in the performance, not in itself 'immoral', of a fertility rite. No doubt Zoroaster endeavoured to wean his countrymen from the worship of Haoma for the same reason that Moses strove, though often in vain, to suppress the worship of the Golden Calf: not for what it was, namely a graven or molten image, but for what it stood for, namely a bull, the most obvious fertility totem. For the same reason Zoroaster's emphasis upon the transcendent character of Ahura Mazda may have derived from a conviction, which was entertained equally by Abraham and Moses in respect of Yahweh[3] that such elevation would place Him 'above sexuality'. Ahura Mazda and Yahweh were, and remain, masculine only for grammatical purposes. They inhabit a different level from that of the ancient god-goddess pantheon, which is likewise invaded by animal or half-animal deities, whose sex is interchangeable.

One of the most interesting passages in the *Vendidad* (Chapter 2), which is that part of the *Avesta* forming the priestly code of the modern Parsees, contains an account given by Ahura Mazda to Zoroaster of the first 'holy man'. His name is Yima.[4] The fair Yima' was a shepherd with whom Ahura Mazda had conversed before he revealed himself to Zoroaster. When Ahura Mazda invited Yima to be 'the preacher and bearer of my religion', the latter declined on account of his rudimentary education. To this Ahura Mazda replies, 'Since thou dost not consent to be the preacher and bearer of my religion, then make thou my world increase, make my world grow: consent thou to nourish, to rule,

1 *Vendidad, Fargard* III.
2 The refusal was clearly on account of some omission of duty. See *Deuteronomy* xxii, 51.
3 Cf. Buber: *Moses*, p. 194.
4 Cf. the Hindu Yama.

to watch over my world.' Yima agreed, promising that as long as he ruled the world there should be 'neither cold wind nor hot wind, neither disease nor death'. He was true to his word. After the passage of three hundred winters the abundance of 'flocks and herds, with men and dogs and birds and blazing red fires' was so great that the earth could not hold them all. When Ahura Mazda drew Yima's attention to this crisis, the young king proceeded to press the earth with a golden seal and to bore it with a poniard (the insignia of his office), whereupon it miraculously increased in size by one third. This process was repeated every three hundred years, the earth being enlarged correspondingly on each occasion. We observe here a preoccupation, even an obsession, with natural abundance and increase, either reflecting the territorial expansions of a tribe of herdsmen and tillers of the soil, or depicting in language of exaggeration the condition of the world before some disaster equivalent to the Babylonian Flood.

The same theme reappears in the Zoroastrian accounts, two in number, of the Flood itself. In the first of these, Yima the shepherd reappears in the role of Noah or Shamash-napishtim. The flood is caused on this occasion by the melting of mountain snows. 'Upon the material world,' Ahura Mazda informs Yima, 'the evil winters are about to fall, that shall make snowflakes fall thick on the highest tops of the mountains... Before that winter, the country will bear plenty of grass for cattle, before the waters have flooded it. Now after the melting of the snow, O Yima, a place wherein the footprint of a sheep may be seen will be a wonder of the world.' Accordingly, Ahura Mazda bids Yima lay out a garden 'long as a riding ground on every side of the square, and thither bring the seeds of sheep and oxen, of men, of dogs, of birds and of red blazing fires'. Within this enclosure or compound (*Vara*), presumably raised to a certain level, Yima is instructed to undertake the cultivation and procreation of men, beasts, and plants in such manner as to eliminate all imperfection. In the case of men, 'there shall be no humpbacked, none bulged forward there; no impotent, no lunatic, no one malicious, no liar, no one spiteful, none jealous, none with decayed tooth, no leprous to be pent up, nor any of the brands wherewith Angra Mainyu stampt the bodies of mortals'. All this was accordingly done, and the episode, which we have here shorn of its repetitions, closes with the observation that 'the men in the *Vara* which Yima made live the happiest life; since they conform in every detail to the precepts of the religion of Ahura Mazda as interpreted by Zarathustra'. Like every earthly paradise, however, it is doomed to interference and destruction by the powers of evil.

Whereas the first Flood story accounts simply for the preservation of the species and provides an opportunity for mankind's improvement, the second from the *Bundahis*[1] strikes a note of greater profundity. Here we find stated in relief the essence of the Zoroastrian theology, which is the world-wide conflict between the forces of good and evil, light and darkness, Ahura Mazda and Ahriman, the Evil One. Instead of the Flood being sent by God as a punitive measure, as it is in both

[1] A surviving fragment of the *Avesta*.

the *Epic of Gilgamesh* and in *Genesis,* the Zoroastrian catastrophe was deliberately engineered by the powers of darkness for the overthrow of Ahura Mazda. The conflict of wind and water forms merely a background to a gigantic duel between Ahura Mazda and his allies, and Ahriman. Only by endowing Tistar, the star-god, with 'the strength of ten vigorous horses, ten vigorous camels, ten vigorous bulls, ten mountains, and ten rivers', did the powers of Good manage to prevail.

If we now turn to the Zoroastrian legends concerning the origin of mankind, we observe this same conflict at work in the Zoroastrian equivalent to Adam and Eve, who are called Mashya and Mashyoi or Matro and Matroyao. We may note in passing that, as in *Genesis,* man was sixth in order of creation. According to the *Dadistan-i-Dinik,* Ahura Mazda produced the material of man from light, but for the space of three thousand years this creature neither spoke nor ate, existing only for the purpose of reflecting upon 'the righteousness of the perfect and true religion, the desire for the pure glorification of the creator'. Birth, as we know it, was the consequence of an evil design on the part of 'the contentious promise-breaker', but we are not told how this misfortune came about. All we know is that 'a burdensome mortality' was conferred upon the person of Gayomard, who, with the co-operation of an angel, transmitted at his death the seed from which Mashya and Mashyoi, 'brother and sister of mankind', were born. The story is now taken up by the *Bundahis.* The brother and sister, here called Matro and Matrayao, were physically united, the waists of both being 'brought close and so connected together that it was not clear which was the male and which the female'.

To this twin-individual Ahura Mazda issued a solemn warning. 'You are,' he said, 'a man, you are the ancestry of the world.' He thereupon enjoined 'them' to obey the laws of his religion, and to remain pure in thought, word, and deed. Above all they were to worship no demons. For a time all went well. They enjoyed the delights of nature, and worshipped Ahura Mazda as the Lord of Creation. Then the demons decided to act. 'Antagonism rushed into their minds and their minds were thoroughly corrupted', so much so that they began to attribute creation not to Ahura Mazda but to the evil spirits themselves. For this wickedness, their souls were later consigned to hell 'until the future existence'. Gradually their bodily appetites asserted themselves. They milked a white-haired goat by applying their mouths to its udder, and they relished the taste for its own sake, not attributing its deliciousness to the Creator. Next they killed a sheep. By blowing upon the wood of the Loteplum and the boxtree, they produced fire and set the sheep to roast. On this occasion, being more thoughtful of the gods, they threw three handfuls of the meat into the fire, as its share: three handfuls at the sky, as the share of the angels. Meanwhile a vulture appropriated a share for itself. Later they acquired skill in weaving cloth and sewing garments. They dug a pit in the earth, obtained iron, smelted it, and made an axe to cut wood. They even set up a wooden shelter.

With increase in skill came contention. They had their first quarrel. Being attached one to the other, their disputes were unusually violent. They cuffed each other, scratched each other's cheeks, and tore out each other's hair. This was the demons' opportunity. They called upon Mashya and Mashyio to surrender their souls completely to Ahriman. In this way, it was promised, their 'demon of malice' would be quietened.

In consequence of this steady falling away from God, the pair soon became unbearably conscious of carnal desires. For fifty years such instincts had lain dormant. Now they became imperious. The couple entered into union. After nine months twins were born, but the parents promptly devoured them, a practice that might have continued but for Ahura Mazda's intervention. Hence man was born in sin and lived thereafter on divine sufferance.

That the first man and woman were either one creature or very closely connected is an idea by no means peculiar to Zoroastrianism. It is found, as we shall see, in the *Rig-Veda,* where Yama and Yami children of Vivasat, are represented as twin brother and sister. Likewise in *Genesis,* Eve is made by God from the rib of Adam. In the *Symposium,* Plato puts into the mouth of Aristophanes, a legend concerning the origin of mankind from a two-headed creature which was later split in half: from this division he explained the passion of love, which is the desire of either creature to find the complement from which it had been severed. This aspect of the subject, however, is trivial. What is more significant is the fact that each story, save that of Aristophanes (which is intended to be fanciful), describes the origin of the sexual impulse as being associated with sin, or with some kind of fall from grace. Even the conception of Zoroaster was associated with guilt: the couple Porushaspo and Dukdaub 'start up ashamed' when their 'embrace with desire for a son' is interrupted by the evil spirits. For the moment it would be unwise even to speculate as to why this idea should have such widespread currency, or how it has come to be so deep-seated. That is a subject to which we shall revert after studying the profound notions of the Indian sages, whose preoccupation with generation and birth assumes primacy over all other interests.

Good and Evil

It is idle to seek an explanation as to why Ahura Mazda, though nominally supreme, should have been subject through all eternity to the challenge of Ahriman. Zoroastrianism has no legend of Lucifer, though its equivalent to Satan must certainly have influenced Christian thought. We notice that Satan figures more frequently in the later books of the Old Testament, while in the New Testament he is an accredited member of the *Dramatis Personae.* Yahweh's early competitors are not emissaries of Satan but simply other gods. In the Zoroastrian theology we are merely told that Ahriman 'preferred the practice which is iniquitous'.

In the *Zad-Sparam,* an extremely vague allegorical account is given of the original antagonism between Ahura Mazda and Ahriman. We are told in terms reminiscent of early *Genesis* that at the beginning of time 'light was above and darkness was below, and between those two was open space'. Ahura Mazda inhabited the light realm, Ahriman the dark. Whereas Ahura Mazda 'was aware of the existence of Ahriman and his coming for strife', however, Ahriman was not aware of the realm of light overhead. One day, loitering along in the gloom, Ahriman by chance emerged from the nether regions and 'a ray of light was seen by him', and because of its antagonistic nature to him 'he strove to reach it, so that it might also be within his absolute power'. At this point Ahura Mazda approached the boundary. What then occurred was not a struggle, such as took place between the Herculean Tistar and the powers of darkness, but the expulsion of Ahriman by 'pure words' (cf. Zoroaster's first interview with Ahura Mazda), whereby his witchcraft was 'confounded'. Again, in the *Vendidad,* Ahura Mazda is made to explain to Zoroaster how the evils and defects of life have originated. He begins by pointing out that he has made every land, 'even though it had no charms whatever in it', dear to its people; otherwise the whole world of men would have long ago invaded the *Airyana Vaejo*, the Aryan land, or home of the race from which both Persians and Indians are descended.[1] After the creation of this most beautiful of lands, Angro Mainyu (Ahriman's other name) proceeded to 'counter-create' all the unpleasant aspects of it. The list is 'prolonged to include sixteen lands or districts, in each of which Angra Mainyu has wrought such evils as serpents, ants, locusts, pride, tears, witchcraft, burial,[2] unbelief, oppression, monstrous births, excessive heat, and above all winter—the latter being described at each mention as 'the very devil' ('a work of the *daevas*').

Such allegories are clearly invented to satisfy the minds of a simple people. We need not thereby belittle their importance. All religions have recourse to such allegories, which have the supreme advantage of keeping a faith concrete. Metaphysical religions, such as that of Aristotle, are not intended for popular consumption. Just as the national religion of Egypt was kept before the minds of both the young and the mentally young by allegories of the dead Pharaoh and his golden barque, or the adventures of Osiris, so the religion of Zoroaster was brought home to the humblest peasant or nomad (Iran has always been a land of tribes) by means of stories of the strife of ogres and the mischief of *daevas*: terms in which the teaching could enter into the living tissue of everyday experience. There may be a good deal to be said for the view that theological truths, having an inherent tendency to fly off into remote abstractions, are better rendered in allegory than in any other medium. To express them at all is to express them as

[1] Herodotus observed that the Persians regarded nations as inferior according to their distance from Persia.

[2] Described as 'the sin for which there is no atonement'. The modern Parsees strictly refuse to bury their dead; the corpse is exposed on what is called a 'Tower of Silence' for birds to consume.

myth. Myth, in other words, is not false religion, but rather its particular way of being true.[1]

In speaking of the faith of Ikhnaten we emphasized the necessity for every religion to have as a complement to its theology a clear-cut system of ethics. You may teach men in general terms what is good and what is evil; but if you would hold their allegiance you must make absolutely clear to them what is right and what is wrong. Most religions find it necessary to couch these ethical maxims in negative terms. This was so in Babylon. Of the Hebrew Decalogue eight of the items are negative. The Zoroastrian teaching, though shot through with negations and antagonisms in its theology, is on the whole positive in its injunctions. The ethical system is outlined most succinctly in the *Zad-Sparam,* one of the Pahlavi Texts, which consists of two parts, one concerned with 'Dispositions' and the other with 'Admonitions'. The five Dispositions, which are described as specially for the attention of priests, lay down rules of ceremonial and of right conduct in office. The Admonitions, of which there are ten, are applicable to all. The first is to maintain what is called good repute, so that you may win respect not merely for yourself but for your teachers or guardians. The second is to refrain, for the same reasons, from acquiring the least element of evil repute. The third is not to beat your teacher, or to annoy him by repeating that which he has not taught you. The fourth is to accept the best of your teacher's instructions humbly, as if they were a loan instead of a gift.[2] The fifth is to see that the law of punishing malefactors and rewarding the righteous is kept for the sake of progress. The sixth is to keep open house to all men of righteousness and goodwill. The seventh is freely to confess the sins you have committed, so that by expelling what is evil you will keep your mind pure. The eighth, which resembles the former, is to keep away all occasions for sin. The ninth is to do your utmost to spread the true religion, and to help restore its authority should it be subject to reverses. The tenth and last it to give due obedience to the ecclesiastical hierarchy.

From this list of Admonitions it is easy to see in what the whole duty of man consists. It consists in being devout and pious, obedient to both teacher and priest, and an example to all. Nor is the least duty that of propagating the gospel.[3] In an account of the Resurrection given in the *Bundahis* the faithful are warned that it is their special duty to see that the erring friends are given every chance of amendment. If, for example, a wicked man complains on the judgment day that his righteous friend 'did not make him acquainted with the good deeds that he practised himself', then the righteous friend will receive appropriate punishment. Moreover, although in the last day the 'wicked man becomes as conspicuous as a white (*sic*) sheep among

[1] Cf. Schelling: 'The myth is not based on a thought, as the children of an artificial education suppose; but is itself a kind of thinking, which imparts a conception of the world, but imparts it in a sequence of events, acts and sufferings.'

[2] Certain of these maxims are obscure. We have tried to bring out what we consider to be the essential meaning.

[3] It is curious, however, that the modern Parsees admit no converts to their faith, and therefore do not proselytize.

those which are black', the good will not be able to escape grief. 'They suffer,' the account goes on, 'everyone for his own deeds, and weep, the righteous for the wicked, and the wicked about himself'; for though the father may be good, the son may be bad, and so forth. Nor is the experience of hell anything to make light of. For the fear of most other things is more than the thing itself, but 'hell is a thing worse than the fear of it'. We are told that at the Resurrection all those judged righteous will have the sensation of walking perpetually in warm milk, while the wicked will have the sensation of walking in molten metal.

Such scrupulous piety implies the regular worship of God according to consecrated rites. As the centuries passed, the simple ceremonies of the Zoroastrian faith became complicated, just as its lofty monotheism became studded with polytheistic ornaments. A god is accorded sole worship. He is endowed with every perfection. In due course these virtuous characteristics become detached and receive special veneration. God is nowhere. Therefore He is everywhere. So He is in everything, and everything contains God, and therefore becomes a god. Hence the original unity gives place to a granular polytheism. The *daevas,* expelled, return as *fravashis,* or guardian spirits.

That Zoroaster's chief object was to purify rather than to overthrow the traditional faith of his countrymen is suggested from many sources. Mithra, the Sun-god, far from being expelled, was both worshipped as a Celestial Fire and praised in most of the Zoroastrian hymns. Haoma the Bull may be excluded from the Pantheon; but the plant in which his power was worshipped plays its part in the prophet's creation.[1]

The early followers of the new faith built neither temples nor idols, but they erected altars upon which fires were lit in honour of Ahura Mazda. Fire, to which so frequent mention is made in Zoroastrian literature, soon came to be worshipped as a god, as did the sun itself, until these deities almost usurped the place of Ahura Mazda.[2] The custom of maintaining a perpetual fire in the home became part of a man's daily religious observance: for the hearth was especially sacred in a faith that glorified family life. Incidentally, the rainbow, that substitute for the sun, was regarded by the Zoroastrians in much the same way as it was in *Genesis*, as 'a sign above from spiritual to earthly beings'.

Just as the followers of Zoroaster were allowed no temples, so they were forbidden to have idols. Something of the power which idol worship and belief in demons exerted over the common people may be judged from the elaborate Mazdayasnian creed which is to be found in the *Yasna* (the liturgy of the Zoroastrian priests). Here we have a lengthy formula of abjuration directed chiefly at expelling the influence of the *daevas,* 'Off, off, do I abjure the *daevas* and all possessed by them, the sorcerers and all that hold to their devices, and

[1] The juice was also drunk as a religious act even after Zoroaster's time.

[2] It is incorrect, however, to describe the modern Parsees as 'fireworshippers'. The lighting of fires is merely a rite.

every existing being of the sort; their sorts do I abjure, their words and actions, and their seed that propagate their sin; away do I abjure their shelter and their headship.' Such repudiation of the enemies of 'the most imposing, best, and most beautiful religion that exists' is extended throughout much repetition, but its drift, especially in the mouth of a priest, is clear. It is sometimes maintained that Zoroaster, in asserting the supremacy of Ahura Mazda, intended to deny the reality of the demons or *daevas*. Whatever he may personally have believed, it is clear that his followers were loth to abandon such cherished notions. The Pahlavi Texts introduce the personified powers of evil into every phase of the life of Zoroaster, as in that of the good angels his confederates.

Evolution of the Faith

Some idea of the quality of the faith preached by Zoroaster may be gained by considering the vicissitudes of its history. Any religion whatever, indeed any political creed, will prevail for a time if it is imposed by order of an authoritarian ruler. In this respect the edict of Darius I resembles that of Ikhnaten. The religion became law, impiety being equivalent to treason. One suspects that the creed of Zoroaster, as originally preached, imposed too great or too sudden a strain upon a people not yet educated up to the level of pure monotheism.[1] The old gods crept back; the demons were already there. Gradually the pre-Zoroastrian priesthood, the Magi, who had been excluded from favour as rigorously as the priests of Amen, returned to power. Mithra, as we have seen, shone more brightly: indeed the cult of Mithra became, in due course, so popular with the conquering Roman legions that it spread to countries so inferior to, by reason of their distance from, Persia as Britain. Although the Sassanid kings of Persia (AD 226–651) tried to restore Zoroastrianism as the state religion, the impetus of the once pure faith was exhausted. Small groups continued to maintain the old worship; but today, except for a tiny group of adherents in Fars, Zoroastrianism as a faith is extinct in the country of its origin. It survives, however, as the religion of the Parsee inhabitants of the Bombay Presidency. This people has done its best to keep the faith pure, and their present enlightenment may afford some idea of the impact of the founder's personality upon his contemporaries.[2]

Zoroastrianism was given the *coup de grâce* by Islam. The militant faith drives out the less belligerent, less missionizing, religion of the elements. Nevertheless it would be wrong to assume that the religion of Zoroaster left no permanent traces either in Persia or elsewhere. We have already drawn attention to the possible influence upon the Old Testament of Zoroastrian ideas concerning the personified evil spirit. Similarly, the Zoroastrian conception of life after death may well have exerted influence in the same quarter, because we find little or noth-

[1] There has been no later development of the *theology* of Zoroastrianism.

[2] During the last few years a new Mazdayasni creed has been started in Bombay by an American millionairess. The faithful, it appears, are occupied chiefly with special breathing exercises and *la cuisine*.

ing of such a notion in the early part of the Bible. The ideas of a seven-day creation, of an earthly paradise, of the fall of man from grace, and of a 'prehistoric' catastrophe threatening the existence of the human race, are common to more faiths than Judaism, Christianity, and Zoroastrianism, though in the latter we find some interesting and original modifications. If there is nowhere reason to suggest that Zoroastrian religious practices directly influenced those of the Hebrews, we can legitimately assume that such practices were among those with which the Hebrews, ever prone to religious flirtations,[1] were instructed to have nothing to do. Indeed, if it is not to the practice of fire-worship by disciples of Zoroaster that the following passage from *Ezekiel* refers, then it is difficult to see the point of the vision so meticulously described: 'It came to pass ... as I sat in my house ... that the hand of the Lord God fell upon me. Then I beheld, and lo a likeness as the appearance of fire: from the appearance of his loins even downward, fire; and from his loins even upward, as the appearance of brightness, as the colour of amber. And he put forth the form of a hand, and took me by a lock of mine head; and the spirit lifted me up between earth and heaven, and brought me in the vision of God to Jerusalem, to the door of the inner gate that looketh towards the north... And he brought me to the inner court of the Lord's House, and behold, at the door of the temple of the Lord, between the porch and the altar, were about five and twenty men, with their backs towards the temple of the Lord and their faces towards the east: and they worshipped the sun towards the east. Then he said unto me, Hast thou seen this, O son of man? Is it a light thing to the house of Judah that they commit the abominations which they commit here?' If Zoroaster lived at the end of the seventh century BC we can well imagine that the enthusiastic practice of his doctrine in countries bordering Persia, such as Mesopotamia, may have been common in the time of Ezekiel (*c.* 580 BC).

A credible figure

To appreciate the full nature of Zoroaster's faith, with the object of comparing it with the few others that have achieved at least comparable success among men, a prolonged treatment of the surviving scriptures against the background of their composition would be required. In this chapter we have naturally done little more than sketch the essentials of the creed. Even so, the impression with which we started may well have undergone a degree of modification. A not altogether incredible figure seems to advance through the shadows. The grotesque elements fall away, become inessentials, froth. The creed that was passionately preached, energetically practised for a period, and then allowed to fall into relative neglect, was the creed of an individual to whom an experience similar to that of the prophets must surely have been vouchsafed. The nineteenth century theory of the importance of the individual, which was so aptly summed up by Emerson

[1] Even as late as Joshua's assumption of leadership, the children of Israel had to be asked to make up their minds whether they wished to worship Yahweh or 'other gods'.

in his statement that 'history is the lengthening shadows of great men', may have been exaggerated; but there is a point beyond which it cannot be scaled down without producing an opposite error. And those who deny the possibility of that which has been so unfortunately named 'religious experience' (as if it were possible to entertain religious belief without experiencing it) need not suppose that what has never happened to them cannot in any circumstance happen to other people. We perceive at the origin of the worship of the Lord of Light one of those great leaders of the spirit of whom we have spoken; a master of simplification, like all such leaders, who pictured the struggle in the individual soul as mirroring *in parvo* a great cosmic struggle between Good and Evil; who was essentially a lover of nature not in the superficial scenic sense popularized by the Romantics but in the deeper sense which sees in the fundamental instincts of the body something holy, since they were implanted there by God and are turned to evil only because dark powers seek to appropriate that which belongs to the world of light; who consequently conceived a particular tenderness towards the young, the fecund and the new-born,[1] and not least the animal creation;[2] who saw in the family the most precious safeguard of the unity of society, and who conceived the unity of the family to be impossible without respect for the household gods and the souls of the ancestors (*Fravashis*); and who evidently envisaged a time albeit distant by three thousand years and in consequence of the work of other prophets, when the forces of evil should be utterly overthrown, and mankind should be restored to its ancient paradise. Few men, it seems, and few religious leaders, have been so completely free from the unwholesome and the morbid.

Of the Christian mystics, no one save perhaps St Francis and Thomas Traherne approaches Zoroaster in his adoration of creation: 'He who recites the praise of Holiness, in the fullness of faith and with a devoted heart, praises me, Ahura Mazda. He praises the waters, he praises the cattle, he praises the plants, he praises all good things made by Mazda, all things that are offspring of the good principles' (*Yast* fragment). Finally, we detect in the faith of Zoroaster an element overshadowed, but by no means superseded by emphasis upon personal repute and obedience to authority, namely a stress upon inner experience manifested above all in the priority given to 'good thoughts' and a righteous disposition:[3] There is no surer sign of spiritual enlightenment. Nor is this preoccupation with the interior state of sanctity a mere temptation to quietism. The truth faith demands constant exertion both in the form of self-discipline and in the form of social action. Above all there must be an end to bigotry, the most obvious danger to which an official creed is subject. There are few passages in the scriptures of the world's faiths at once so dignified and

[1] 'It lies with the faithful to look after every pregnant female, either two-footed or four-footed, two-footed woman or four-footed bitch' (*Vendidad*).

[2] This was particularly true of cattle and dogs. Cf. the *Vendidad*: 'Whosoever shall kill the dog kills his own soul for nine generations.'

[3] See especially the *Prayer for Guidance*: 'Tell us how you may come to us with good disposition.'

inspired as this from the hymn called the 'Farvardin Yast': 'We worship this earth, we worship those heavens: we worship those good things which stand between the earth and the heavens and that are worthy of sacrifice and prayer, and are to be worshipped by the faithful man. We worship the souls of the wild beasts and the tame. We worship the souls of the holy men and women, born at any time, whose consciences struggle, or will struggle, or have struggled, for the good.'

5

Hinduism

He who sees the inaction that is in action, and the action that is in inaction, is wise indeed

The Vedas

At the conclusion of the chapter on Babylon and Israel we made, as the reader will remember, a resolution. This resolution was to drop the word religion in so far as religion was to be distinguished from philosophy. We now approach the study of a philosophy in which the purpose of this repudiation of a distinction so dear to the Western mind will become clear. Hindu thought, in practically all its aspects and throughout its long history, has remained indifferent to the distinction between religion and philosophy.

To eliminate a superfluous term from our intellectual vocabulary is no doubt a matter for congratulation. The human mind has too many terms that accomplish too few significant operations. Unfortunately, the study of Hindu thought makes it abundantly clear that in identifying religion and philosophy the Indian sages were not prompted by any marked economy in the use of terms. On the contrary, the philosophical terms in their vocabulary exceed in number those of any other form of intellectual belief. No language of ancient or modern times contains more philosophical terms than Sanskrit. Similarly, in 'pricking' the distinction between religion and philosophy, the Hindu sages show no corresponding reluctance to draw distinctions in other fields. Indian thought arrives at subtleties of distinction so varied and acute that the uninitiated and unprepared reader may well receive the impression that Indian philosophers enjoy the use of half a dozen intellects instead of one. We are accustomed to the idea of scientists constructing artificial brains to effect calculations which neither a single individual, nor a team of individuals devoting a lifetime to the task, could hope to achieve. The elaborate system of certain Indian philosophers sometimes appear to be the product of such socially-constructed intellects. This impression is deceptive. Just as the electronic brain is made by men to do what lies beyond man's power, so the great systems of Eastern thought were evolved by thinkers trained in a tradition of speculation that seems to overshadow but in fact enhances their individual contributions. 'Hercules had not more muscles than we,' said Paul Valéry; 'they were only larger muscles.'

While we need not allow these gigantic thought-structures to overawe us, it would be foolish to pretend that merely by taking thought we can understand in them all there is to be known. According to authoritative Indian scholars, there are certain terms and therefore arguments in Hindu and oriental philosophy in general which remain virtually untranslatable into European languages. A thorough acquaintance with oriental tongues, therefore, would be a condition of our being able fully to understand Eastern thought: added to which we must presuppose a marked talent for speculation. Such a combination of talents has appeared in a William Jones, an Edwin Arnold, a Rhys Davis, but we must admit that it is an occurrence of once or twice in a century. Meanwhile, men of high intelligence have confessed, after devoting much time to oriental research, that if they were to arrive at complete understanding of Eastern philosophy they would need to abandon Europe altogether and begin life again as an Oriental as Guénon did. It is possible that the reverse is also true, though the spectacle of so many Indians, Chinese, and Japanese adapting themselves successfully to the life of the Western hemisphere would seem to disprove it.

What may well enable us to pursue a middle course between arrogance and helpless inferiority is the consciousness of the great movement of understanding and sympathy that seems to be uniting Orient and Occident. Of this movement, with its attendant dangers, we shall have more to say in the sequel. That the East has in the past borrowed some of the least desirable features of Western civilization is a commonplace. While deliberate borrowings from the East by the West have been rare, Eastern influences have percolated unconsciously into the Western mind for centuries. Today we are witnessing something to which the past offers no parallel: that is to say, a sudden awakening on the part of Western scholars, including poets and artists, to the infinite riches of oriental and especially Indian culture. Like several others of its kind, this movement has been going on for some time without attracting much notice; for political events and prejudices have often obscured its real nature. Attempting to raid unfamiliar material in search of 'new thought' or 'secret wisdom', cranks have tended to bring discredit upon it. But it advances. And the ordinary man may find, to his surprise, that the thought thus made accessible not merely enables him to understand aspects of the oriental mentality about which he has entertained the most superficial notions, but throws much light upon questions that have long perplexed him.

Exponents of Indian philosophy are usually anxious to draw attention first to its profundity and second to its antiquity. Concerning the former there has never been any doubt. If India has not ascertained the secret of life, it has probably framed by far the most searching questions on the subject. When precisely it began asking such questions is a matter about which experts disagree. The oldest known Indian religious literature is the series of hymns that form the *Rig-Veda*. As far as we can tell, these were written between 1500 and 1200 BC. That lends them sufficient antiquity: we need hardly repeat what we have stressed so often, that the *impulse* from which they originate must date from a much earlier time. But let us look for a moment at the history of Egypt. By 1500 BC two long and eventful civilized epochs had passed away, the Old Kingdom and the Middle Kingdom. A profound and extensive philosophical and religious literature had been composed. By 1200, to take the later date, Ikhnaten's revolution had come and gone, and the great moral effort of which we have spoken at length had been almost completed. Or let us take the civilization of Western Asia. By 1500 Babylon had produced all the literature and art that it was to produce, the Code of Hammurabi was established over the whole of what is now the Middle East, Abraham had turned a family into a tribal nation or 'portable fatherland', as Heine called it, and the Hittites had developed the civilization that begins only now to yield its secrets. By 1200, again, the Jews had conquered Canaan. For the present (and this qualification must be stressed for reasons that will soon appear) it seems beyond question that Egyptian and also Babylonian religious and philosophical speculation of an advanced kind antedates that of India by many centuries.

We must hasten to add that such priority in time does not mean that Egyptian thought necessarily exhibits greater profundity or indeed enjoys any other intellectual advantage over that of India: but in a survey such as the present we must maintain our historical bearings, and above all we should be on our guard against the chauvinism of scholars, which can sometimes assume unexpected intensity.

It is one thing to correct misleading impressions about the antiquity of Indian speculative thought; it is another thing to compare the relative antiquity of Indian and other traditions of social life. On this subject recent archaeological investigations have thrown a most interesting and even startling light. If in due course the earth could be made to surrender all its archaeological treasures, we may envisage a series of revolutions in historical perspective necessitating the scrapping every few years of hundreds of authoritative text-books. That might be all to the good. If a work is to remain useful for as long as most works of exposition can expect to remain, it must seek to avoid too close an identification with any contemporary school of archaeological doctrine. On the other hand, it must not omit to report the latest conjectures: one of the difficulties of such reporting is precisely that these may have shifted and been replaced by others during the composition of the book itself.[1]

The archaeological discoveries to which we refer are those undertaken since 1924 by Sir John Marshall and his Indian colleagues at Mohenjo-daro and Harappa on the lower Indus, now Pakistan. These investigations brought to light the remains of a series of 'cities'—the word is used deliberately—built one upon the ruins of the others. Five

[1] We mention this circumstance because it happens that during the late 1940s two extremely interesting discoveries were made: first, the finding of the earliest Old Testament manuscripts near Jericho, and secondly the unearthing at Kara Tepe in Cilicia of the inscribed Hittite bas-reliefs. The past is a great deal more fluid than the present.

such cities have so far been unearthed, and it is possible that more will in due course be found.[1] The buildings show every evidence of having been several storeys in height. There are hundreds of them, suggesting a thriving city life very similar to that which flourished at Ur. What has been recovered from the buildings themselves is more interesting still. Pottery, jewellery, furniture, inscribed seals, weapons, tools, and toys; these have been found not merely in great quantity but of a quality which is often unsurpassed. Curiously enough, the lower levels of excavation have revealed a number of objects superior, judging by artistic canons, to those found higher up. But for the fact that some of the weapons are of stone, others of copper, and still others of bronze, we should be led to doubt whether our conventional prehistoric categories any longer applied. Sir John Marshall believes that the cities of Mohenjo-daro belong at least to the third millennium BC, and perhaps even to the fourth. How long they took to grow into flourishing cities we cannot tell: the presumption is that their origin must belong to a period to which we have so far denied the title of civilized. It seems certain, in other words, that Mohenjo-daro was the scene of brisk commerce, trafficking, and gracious living at a period assigned by the Egyptians to mythical kings such as Scorpion. This places Mohenjo-daro, for the present, at the head of all the civilizations of the world.

The more we know about archaic culture the more we become aware of links, borrowings, and influences. The fact that many of the seals and some of the pottery found at Mohenjo-daro resemble those found in Sumeria cannot be an accident. What is more remarkable is that these particular seals belong to different phases of their respective civilizations: the products of the very earliest phase of Sumerian culture match those found in the later epochs of Mohenjo-daro. This presumably suggests not merely that the Indus civilization was in touch with that at Sumeria, but that the latter owed a great deal—perhaps even its existence—to the former. Or, perhaps, as some archaeologists believe, both civilizations owed their existence to a third situated somewhere between. Possibly when we learn to read, if we ever do, the pictographic writing adorning some of the poetry found at Mohenjo-daro, we shall become aware of something else, even if only indirectly: the existence of a tradition of thought taking us back to and even beyond that of the Memphite Drama. And that will mean another drastic revision of current preconceptions.

Reference to these early civilized settlements in the Sind region was necessary even if only to dispel the impression, derived inevitably from history books, of a sudden and therefore inexplicable arrival of thought, art, and science in India. Such things do not arrive suddenly, though they may be suddenly extinguished. They must be viewed against their own receding background. Their apparent isolation in time must be discounted. When the so-called Aryan invaders descended upon north India they found the country occupied by a people of whose existence traces have been found at Mohenjo-daro itself.

[1] The lowest foundations are unfortunately waterlogged.

These people are known as Nagas and they worshipped the serpent. Now the serpent symbol is found upon seals unearthed from Mohenjo-daro. It is likewise found upon some of the seals that we have mentioned as belonging to the earliest Sumerian (or pre-Sumerian) civilization. Today it remains the symbol of that strange devil-worshipping people, the Yezidis, who inhabit the region of Arbil in northern Iraq. Another people, of whose civilization we have evidence, were met by the Aryans in their invasion of the Deccan region to the south. These were the Dravidians.

Where did the Aryans come from? It seems almost certain that their home country was precisely that *Airyana Vaejo* (Aryan Home) of which we have already heard in Zoroastrian scriptures, particularly the area of Persia bordering the Caspian Sea. Possibly this area is the cradle of civilization. Entering India about 1600 BC, they took a long time penetrating so vast a country; but, by following the great rivers, they finally mastered a very large part of it.[1] In calling themselves Aryans they meant to convey the impression, reinforced by success, of racial or class superiority: for Aryan derives from the Sanskrit term meaning 'noble'. Being likewise a small if powerful minority, they were evidently determined to preserve their purity of race. Intermarriage between Aryan and Naga or Dravidian was rigorously forbidden. This measure was the origin, at first purely ethnographic, of that system of social discrimination which is known as Caste.[2]

Although the 'Vedic Age' is usually considered to have started about 2000 BC, the world of the *Vedas* is that of the early Aryan conquerors. For this reason they reflect two worlds at once: that into which Aryans had ventured, with its strange and sometimes uncouth gods, and that which the conquerors themselves introduced. The word *Veda* means in Sanskrit 'knowledge'. Of the original number of these Books of Knowledge we are ignorant. Judging from the four that have survived they must have formed a very considerable body of sacred literature, which was the transcript of a still greater volume of memorized lore. Like all religious scriptural material of any antiquity, the *Vedas* contained a great deal of purely ecclesiastical data and the inevitable portion of *arcana*, magical and hermetic lore, etc. In the history of human thought, only one of the *Vedas* is of importance, namely the *Rig-Veda*, a collection of 1028 religious hymns or *mantras*. *Rig* means 'verse'; *Rig-Veda* may therefore be rendered by some such title as 'Songs of Spiritual Knowledge'.

The *Vedas* were intended to be committed to memory. Recitation from memory was originally a religious act. Even today we speak of 'learning by *heart*', and not by mind or brain: no child was ever taught to read his prayers. So important was it that the *Vedas* should be transmitted orally (and learning by heart depends upon oral practice) that they were not committed to paper until long after writing became

[1] i.e. the area known as Hindustan, from the Persian word *Hindu*. This meant the whole of the north.

[2] The only mention of such social division—very elementary at this stage—is in the *Vedic* 'Hymn to Purusha' (Book X, 90).

widespread in India. As this transcription took place perhaps as late as the ninth century BC, we can judge to what extent early Indian religious thought depended upon communal memory. Some critics have suggested that this long dependence upon oral tradition makes nonsense of the claim that the *Vedas*, being supposedly communicated to man by God, have been preserved without modification from time immemorial. Without subscribing to the divine authorship of the *Vedas* (unless by that we mean authorship dictated from 'above', such as that which produced the Decalogue and, if we are to attach any significant meaning to 'above', every other piece of inspired writing), we may still accept the view that they have undergone comparatively little change. For, as we remarked in connection with the *Zend-Avesta*, oral transmission in days when this was either the sole or the most revered method of communication was probably as reliable as written. Even today the things that for convenience we commit to memory—the alphabet, for instance—are not observed to suffer appreciable corruption in the process. Alterations and interpolations in tales and sagas are another matter. These are due, as Aristotle remarked, to the idea entertained by all story-tellers that exaggeration renders a tale more exciting.

Like the great poetic works that succeed them, the *Vedas* are composed in Sanskrit, the most ancient of the group of languages from which English itself derived. But the Sanskrit that we study today was not the language of the early Aryan invaders of India. Arriving in groups or tribes, these invaders probably spoke a variety of dialects. It is possible that Sanskrit may not originally have been a vernacular tongue at all: the word itself conveys the notion of something which is reserved for special purposes, probably sacred ones. Just as Hieroglyphic means 'sacred writing', so Sanskrit means 'sacred speaking'. The composition of the *Vedas* in Sanskrit is another indication of their antiquity; it is also an indication of the esteem in which they were held. The classical, sacral language would be used only for that which was considered holy and worthy of preservation.

Of the religion of the pre-*vedic* age we know extremely little; all we can do is to make inferences about it. We know that the worship of animals, including the serpent, was prevalent, and from this we can assume the practice of fertility cults. There were also gods of trees (*yakshas*) and plants. One such tree, the *Bodhi* tree, seems to have been regarded as sacred from remotest time. When Buddha, sitting under it, received the sense of his mission, he was stationed at a spot at which such experiences, though less remarkable, were regarded as natural and appropriate.[1] One such plant, the *soma*, and in particular its intoxicating juice, has long been revered in both Persia and Hindustan. When Zoroaster was said to have been brought into the world through its agency, his sacrosanct nature was thereby demonstrated or confirmed. A new religion is rendered the more holy by having chosen to avail itself, in its formative years, of the salient features of the old; for repudiation is a political rather than a religious weapon. In

[1] See Chapter 5.

the *Vedas* we find hymns addressed to almost every aspect of nature, and particularly to those objects whose influence could directly be felt by man; the sun, wind, water, fire, light, and that imperative force that resides in men themselves, ensuring their increase. Addressed directly as personalities, the gods of the *Rig-Veda* form a kind of ordered hierarchy: which suggests that the hymns are approved elements of a canon established by priests. We may therefore assume that they are concerned with a selection rather than a collection of gods. What may strike the European as a crude, polytheistic attitude to life is no doubt the most refined abstraction from popular animism and totemism.

Like the compilers of the Old Testament, the editors of the *Rig-Veda* anthology were careful to preserve intact material belonging to different epochs. We are thus able to trace the development of the early Aryan religious consciousness, just as a reading of early and later parts of the Bible affords us an enlarged conception of the nature of the Hebrew Yahweh. There is wisdom in this refusal on the part of priestly guardian to suppress the primitive elements of their faith; for these are better kept well before the eye than allowed to fester, as the result of excision, in that uneasy corner to be found in the most devout conscience. Some of the *Vedic* hymns are merely satirical, such as that addressed 'To Frogs', which is considered to be a satire on the priesthood; or straightforward *vers de société*—such as that on 'The Gambler', of whose dice ('dearer than *soma*') it is said:

> Downward they roll, and then spring quickly upward, and, handless, force
> The man with hands to serve them.
> Cast on the board, like lumps of magic charcoal, though cold themselves,
> they burn
> The heart to ashes.

Others consist of fanciful or naive speculations, such as why the sun travels through the heavens without falling down, or imaginary dialogues such as that between the first man and woman, Yama and Yami (cf. Yima of the Zoroastrian scriptures), debating whether or not to start the human race, an initiative for which Yama shows some reluctance. If the *Rig-Veda* contained nothing but verse of this kind, it would still be a curiosity of great interest and a historical document of a period otherwise obscure; but its value would be on a level with that of the *Atharva-Veda*, with its charms and formulae to grow hair, cure sterility, confound witchcraft, and encourage the crops.

The great value of the *Rig-Veda* lies in those *mantras*, mostly to be found in the tenth book, which deal with philosophic themes. Let us take first the great Creation Hymn, which Max Müller described as the 'first word spoken by Aryan man'. (That may be true; but if so, Aryan man must have thought a good deal before he spoke.) The hymn begins with an attempt to represent the world or universe as it was before creation started. At that time, says the poet, only 'That One Thing, breathless, breathed by its own nature: apart from it was nothing whatsoever.' The notion of That One Thing is further illuminated, or obscured, by a line further on which states that 'the gods are later than this world's production'. What, we may ask, is meant by That One Thing? The Sanskrit word for it is *Tatekam*. Now *Ekam* means 'The One' or 'Unity', and *tat* is the neuter personal pronoun. The concept of a Power beyond, behind and yet between all things, and finally before all things, is fundamental to the understanding of Indian thought. Sometimes called *Purusha*, but more frequently *Brahman*, this Power is nameless, beyond our mental grasp, because infinite, and also the origin of all things human and divine, because creative. The first description of it in this early hymn may give an impression of extreme vagueness, to which the poetic content no doubt lends colour; for poetry in the Western world has been regarded since the Romantic Revival as a medium in which accuracy and precision are obstacles to enjoyment. In our study of Indian thought we need to remind ourselves that the *Vedic* hymns, the *Upanishads*, and indeed all the important sacred writings of Hinduism, are in point of fact striving after an accuracy beyond that of normal everyday experience. Vagueness is neither the aim nor the result; it is the enemy. The difficulty with a concept such as That One Thing is not that it is vague, but that it represents the extreme of *abstraction*. Unfortunately the word 'abstraction' is used often in two senses: the sense in which a notion is stripped of its qualities, and the sense in which a notion is freed from error or adulteration. To strip a thing of its qualities is like peeling an onion; you end up with nothing, no hidden nucleus. To free a notion from imperfection, error, and illusion is less an intellectual than a spiritual operation; and that is what the Indian mystics attempted to undertake on a scale never before practised.

The hymn in which this primary concept is first promulgated does not content itself with mere statement. It ponders how creation started. First of all, there was 'desire, the primal seed and germ of spirit'. This idea, to which Buddha and later Plato devoted so much attention, is not here elaborated, for the poet is concerned primarily with the awe and wonder of creation, not with its detailed mechanism. Indeed he concludes with questions that are deliberately rhetorical:

> Who verily knows and who can here declare it, whence it was born and whence comes this creation?
> The gods are later than this world's production. Who knows then whence it first came into being?
> He, the first origin of this creation, whether he formed it all or did not form it,
> Whose eye controls this world in highest heaven, he verily knows it, or perhaps he knows it not.[1]

Although this hymn and the others of the same nature are concerned to illuminate philosophic themes, we must bear in mind that, being poems intended for declamation, their primary purpose is to put the devout listener in the correct frame of mind. They form elements in a liturgy, which is none the less intellectual for having an overtly emotional purpose: people do not go to church to learn to worship. This

[1] Cf. the Zoroastrian *Prayer for Guidance*, which contains a similar series of questions.

W. F. Mansell

Ikhnaten

W. F. Mansell

Hammurabi

W. F. Mansell

Zoroaster
From a bas-relief at Persepolis

Picture Post Library

The child Krishna and his foster-mother Yashoda
By Asil Kumar Haldar

Picture Post Library

Japanese Buddha

W. F. Mansell

Lao-Tze and his Disciples
Chinese painting (sixteenth century)

Picture Post Library

Confucius

Picture Post Library

Mencius

may throw light upon an element of apparent scepticism in some of the most profound of the hymns, such as that addressed to Prajapati (X, 121), the Lord of all Living Things, who long enjoyed an immense reputation among the people. This hymn, for which the title *To the Unknown God* was suggested by Max Müller, sings of the 'giver of vital breath, of power and vigour, he whose commandments all gods acknowledge', but concludes nine of its ten verses with the tantalizing phrase 'What god shall we adore with our oblation?' There is an apparent contradiction here; but if we realize that the same distinction is being made as in the Creation Hymn, between the ultimate Unity (with which Prajapati was later associated) and individual deities, the point of the repeated question becomes clearer. The emphasis, as always, is on the inadequacy of the human mind to comprehend the meaning of life. In the last verse we have a clue to the general argument: 'Prajapati! Thou only comprehendest all these created things and none beside thee. Grant us our hearts' desire when we invoke thee.' The hymn is designed to produce a condition of mind not of scepticism but of intellectual humility.

The gods whose power and bounty are hymned with particular fervour in the *Rig-Veda* are Agni, god of fire in all forms, and Indra, the 'Heaven pervading' storm god. To the latter, a quarter of the hymns are dedicated. Towards the end of the collection the reputation of both of these gods suffers something of an eclipse, which suggests that they were gods associated with the days of the original conquest of India rather than with the period of consolidation and settlement. In the powerful *Hymn to Indra* in Book II (12), we may note the phrase 'without whose help our people never conquer', and also the remark in verse 5 to the effect that Indra's existence and power have lately been subject to doubt. A most interesting light upon the relations between Persia and India is shed by the reputation enjoyed in the two countries by both Indra and that other important god, Varuna. Indra, the god of storm and thunder, becomes in Persia a demon. Recollecting the low repute in which winter was held among the followers of Zoroaster, we can scarcely wonder that the god whose activities contributed so largely to the defects of that season should have been pronounced diabolical. Varuna, however, the god of the heavens—'who, standing in the firmament, hath meted the earth out with the sun as with a measure'—was a figure to undergo marked development in both India and Persia. In Persia, for reasons that will appear, he was regarded as identical with no less a figure than Ahura Mazda himself. In India, from being a god of the high heavens, 'the universal encompasser', he gradually came to be associated with the universality of moral and ethical order in the world. This order went by the name of *Rita*. *Rita* began by being a kind of moral thread or current running through the universe, keeping it not merely harmonious but suffused with the radiance of goodness. In due time *Rita* was conceived as also weaving its path through the souls of men, being present to the individual as a kind of throb at the depth of his self, which, duly attended to, indicated his oneness with the universe. We shall see to what length the Indian thinkers pushed this conception of ultimate self-hood when we come to discuss the *Upanishads*, with their concept of *Atman*. As guardian of this precious law—the Hindu equivalent of *Maat* and *Tao*—Varuna is thus described in an early hymn (V, 85):

> In the tree-tops the air he hath extended, put milk in kine and vigorous speed in horses,
> Set intellect in hearts, fire in the waters, the sun in the sky and Soma on the mountain.

In precisely such terms the Zoroastrians sang the majesty of Ahura Mazda.

The Upanishads

At one end of the *Rig-Veda* we have the terrible might and fury of Indra—'impetuous as a bull' (I, 32). At the other end we have a world of personified abstractions: Creativity, Liberality, Speech, Faith, to each of which at least one hymn is devoted. We seem to be moving forward to a sphere of thought in which the sonorous verse and emotional intensity of the *Vedas* will need to be sacrificed, as too much of a luxury, later to return in the elevated poetry of the *Bhagavad-Gita*. What is to happen in the meantime? The intervening period is to be filled with the deep speculations of which we have already hinted, those of *Upanishads*.

That it is misleading to regard the *Vedas* as having been composed at a kind of 'morning of the world', as the phrase of Max Müller would suggest, we have duly emphasized. What is more probable is that they reflect, like most other creative movements, a renewal of vitality, one of those sudden renaissances of the spirit, the regular succession of which in the past makes history an intelligible story instead of a mere log-book. To what causes such movements can be ascribed we can hazard only guesses. Possibly soil erosion accounts for a good many of the major displacements of population in history, or the lure of more temperate climates, or the decline of an established trade. Such material causes do not determine the nature or quality of the results. Just as the movement of a tribe through Mesopotamia started a religion of righteousness, so the advance of a race through Baluchistan started a religion of knowledge. Needless to say, such invasions or penetrations may be completely sterile: certain nations, otherwise distinguished, do not seem to have possessed the gift of fruitful invasion.[1]

In one of the last of the *Rig-Veda* hymns (X, 151), it is asserted that 'man winneth faith by yearnings of the heart', and the same poem concludes with the words 'O Faith, endow us with belief'. The *Vedas* are rich not merely in faith—for the mere perception of beauty is a token of faith: faith in the value of that which is seen—but in the kind of enquiry which, by endeavouring to penetrate behind that which is seen, leads to belief in a profounder sense. In the *Upanishads* the 'yearnings of the heart' assume an intellectual guise. From a sweeping

[1]See the interesting analysis in R. G. Collingwood's *New Leviathan* (1943), section on 'Barbarism'.

contemplation of the world the sages turned to an inward scrutiny. In so doing they withdrew from all publicity and contact with men. Retiring to the forests and jungles for the sake of secrecy, they engaged in deep discussion; sage and saints in solitude, like the later Desert Fathers in Egypt, sage with sage exchanging the results of their meditations, master and pupil in the work of initiation and instruction. For the 'highest mystery in the *Vedanta*, delivered in a former age', as the *Svetasvatara Upanishad* says, 'should not be given to one whose passions have not been subdued, nor to one who is not a son, or who is not a pupil'. The element of debate and exchange of view has been preserved in the word *Upanishad* itself, which is made up of *upa*, near, and *shad*, to sit. To 'sit at the feet of' is still the phrase we use to convey the notion of receiving wisdom, as opposed to mere information, from a teacher of high repute. The *Upanishads* are the confidential reports of such secret sessions.

To contemplate is ultimately to become aware of the distinction between oneself and the object. The self here and the world there: the self with its egoistic desires, and the world with its apparently unrelated and impersonal laws: and thus arises the need to establish some relation between the one sphere and the other. This is the strategy of the *Upanishads*. Upon these problems the forest saints and sages devoted their lives to reflecting. We would give much to know about the men (and women) who were thus addicted to a passion for thought. Of some we know the bare names. As for their daily life, this was devoted entirely to meditation, leaving no time for the 'action' with which other people, terrified of being left to their own reflections, cram their waking hours. Nevertheless, as we shall see, such mental labour does not deprive them of vitality and character. In due time they come alive and acquire a reality greater than that of more strenuous individuals.

How did the sages work out the 'problem' that we have stated? To answer this question is to plunge directly into that celebrated argument concerning the Self and the Divine Ground of existence—*Atman and Brahman*—which was first raised in the creation hymn of the *Rig-Veda*. To some people, this argument represents the highest point to which human intelligence has ascended. It forms the crux of all philosophical enquiry. Not to grasp its meaning and import is to fall short of the kind of experience that renders life significant and meaningful. There is no choice, such people maintain, between living according to this fundamental truth and living according to a 'simpler' or more 'comfortable' doctrine. The choice is between living according to this doctrine and not living at all. This only is reality. This only is truth: wholeness: *it*.

We may add in parenthesis that this celebrated problem is not merely a philosophical, still less an academic one. Bearing in mind what we have said about the identity in Indian thought between philosophy and religion, we perceive that it is concerned precisely with the establishment of that 'divine connection', that uniting of the way of earth with that of heaven, which is the essence of the religious quest. Moreover, it is accorded a solution to which all the great religious subscribe. A faith which refuses to accept it in general terms is one that has failed to realize the implications of its own claims to truth.

The proposition with which the sages start is as follows. Our ordinary world, with its material objects and its individual minds or consciousness, is a world of imprecision, incompleteness, finitude. Being incomplete and unstable, it is neither self-reliant, nor self-supporting: in other words, it depends for such reality as it possesses upon a realm of totally different character. This other realm is the Ground of all existence. It is That One Being of which the *Vedic* hymn speaks. The 'things' of which our existence and experiences are composed form manifestations of this Ground. Their 'thinghood' is precisely that which, rendering them separate and distinct one from another, gives rise to their imperfection. 'Wise men only,' says the *Katha Upanishad*, 'knowing the nature of what is immortal, do not look for anything stable here among things unstable.'

An important fact to which students of the *Upanishads* do not always pay sufficient attention is that among the individual things in the universe deriving their reality from the ultimate and Divine Ground are the gods themselves, or at least the gods as conceived in the limited way characteristic of human beings. This is true even of the notion of *Brahma*, which, in contrast to *Brahman*, means God as creator.[1]

This first proposition, which resembles distinctly that of Plato in defining the world of phenomenon as only partially real, is not stated without some show of proof. The proof lies in our own experience. This does not mean that to most people such a statement appears immediately obvious. What is immediately obvious differs according to the level to which the individual's experience has attained. Part of the grounds for supposing the statement to be true is derived from the manner in which its truth comes at length to be perceived. In other words, the fuller our experience—the older we are in knowledge of life—the better equipped we shall be to acknowledge that statement as a true statement. Now what sort of knowledge is it that we acquire from ripening experience? Surely it is an increased perception of the unsatisfactory character of everything belonging to the natural plane. Only maturing experience could disclose such knowledge, such progressive *disillusion*. Nor, unless the maturing mind were simultaneously in process of acquiring a new form of apprehension, could the disclosure have been vouchsafed. The new form of apprehension is that relating to a sphere of reality from which defect, error, and illusion are absent. Without some such insight into perfection we should be unable to perceive the extent to which our everyday experience fell short of it. This ideal sphere of reality is the Divine Ground of existence. A 'Ground', on this basis, is that by which ultimately everything is what it is, just as the ground (or grounds) of an argument is that upon which the argument hinges, its *raison d'être*.

[1] Cf. The *Bhagavad-Gita*: 'All the worlds, and even the heavenly realm of *Brahma*, are subject to the laws of rebirth. But for the man who comes to me (Krishna), there is no returning' (Book VIII). Shankara later developed this view.

Such knowledge is acquired by the process known as inference. From one condition we argue logically to the existence of another. But the sages of the *Upanishads* believe that knowledge of the Divine Ground can be acquired in a more direct fashion. This is due to the nature of the Ground itself, which is necessarily difficult to define. Although it is beyond the reach of our everyday faculties, it is nevertheless sufficiently akin to the soul to be within its grasp. By the faculty of intuition the human mind may apprehend the Ground as something with which it enjoys a special relationship. And this act of intuitive apprehension, if pure and direct, effects an immediate union between the mind and that which it apprehends. Even so, as the Ground is in its wholeness beyond human grasp, the sages have a special term, *Ishwara*, to denote that much of the Ground which the intellect can know. *Ishwara* may be regarded in much the same light as the 'personal' God of Christianity.

Such an act of union would be impossible if the self consisted simply of the phenomenal self, the natural ego. But every individual, even the most corrupt and self-obsessed, possesses another and deeper self, the Eternal Self. It is by discovering within himself this deeper Self that man is able, if he chooses, to apprehend the Divine Ground. And as this deeper or Eternal Self is simply the divine Ground immanent in human beings,[1] the union of one with the other is simply the recognition of Identity. Such state of union which the sages call *Nirvana*, is not to be reached without discipline, renunciation, and indeed complete self-surrender.

Granted the existence of the Divine Ground, and assuming that in every individual there exists a deeper, inner or noumenal Self which partakes of the nature of this Ground, then it must necessarily follow that the duty of all men here on earth consists in entering into the state of divine union. Not to render themselves fit for such union is to frustrate the purpose for which they were put into the world. Worse than that: it is to condemn themselves to a prolongation of their state of separation and misery, and perhaps to an intensification of it in another existence or series of existences. 'For them who depart from hence without having discovered the Self and those true desires, for them there is no freedom in all the worlds.' But those who depart from hence, after having discovered the Self and those true desires, for them there is freedom in all the worlds (*Chandogya Upanishad*).

To the Divine Ground the sages give the name of *Brahman*. Now *Brahman* cannot be translated exactly as God. It is rather a kind of undifferentiated Godhead. The inner Self is called *Atman*, which is *Brahman* immanent in man. The *Upanishads* employ a particular phrase to describe the fundamental identity between the self and the Ground of existence, between *Brahman* and *Atman*. This is the tense, startling observation upon which the whole argument hinges, 'Thou art that.' In other words, the 'inner' Thou is not merely equivalent to, but identical with, the objective That. The eternal Ground flows under both the

[1] 'When we consider *Brahman* as lodged within the individual being, we call him the *Atman*' (*Bhagavad-Gita*).

phenomenal world and the phenomenal self, uniting in reality that which is considered separate in the world of opaque experience; for that which is of the surface does not know itself to be superficial unless irradiated by wisdom. 'He (the Ground) is the beginning, producing the causes which unite the soul with the body, being above the three kinds of time, past, present, future, he is seen as without parts, after we have first worshipped that adorable god, who has many forms, and who is the true source of all things, as dwelling in our mind. He is beyond all the forms of the world and of time, he is the other, from whom this world moves round, when one has known him who brings good and removes evil, the lord of bliss, as dwelling within the self, the immortal, the support of all' (*Svetasvatara Upanishad*).

To illustrate the doctrine of the *Upanishads* by introducing here and there a brief quotation, however carefully chosen, must inevitably give a false impression of both their profundity and even their charm. We must not imagine them simply as consisting of a series of aloof, dogmatic, and sometimes highly disputable utterances, delivered by those who considered themselves already to have achieved the measure of renunciation necessary to sanctity. Much of the interest of the *Upanishads* is that of following the stages of the argument: equally impressive is to observe the intellectual humility of both teacher and pupil. What they claim to have achieved is not sanctity or deliverance but the knowledge of the way to these things. Some scholars have maintained that, 'it is not for the systems they build or for the truths that they can be said to have discovered that these scriptures are to be so greatly prized, but rather for the simplicity and earnestness with which great problems are approached.'[1] Such an approach is certainly to be recommended in preference to the arid disputation with which philosophical discussion has so often come to be associated, especially in academic life; but this attitude to the *Upanishads* remains open to the same objection as that which withholds praise from the Bible except as 'fine literature'. The disciples of the sages, both contemporary and in later times, regard the *Upanishads* not as exercises in thinking but as repositories of divine thought. The truth of the identification of *Brahman* and *Atman* is regarded as a fact, even a revelation. To the student whose philosophical knowledge is confined to the Western world the tendency is to accept as normal in a professional philosopher the famous doctrine of Kant, who claimed that he taught his pupils not philosophy but how to philosophize. The logical conclusion to such an attitude, at least in less capable hands, is the cultivation of philosophy as a superior kind of game, played in the lecture-room or at meetings of learned societies, where the intrusion of truth or wisdom as a guide to right conduct is considered almost a scandal. We make a great mistake if we suppose that such a superficial attitude is characteristic of the mind of India. Nor have we any reason to think that the new India will in this respect differ from the old.

Perhaps the most illuminating of these discourses, from the point of

[1] Dr Nichol MacNichol: Introduction to *Hindu Scriptures* (Dent, 1943).

view of human interest, is that which is entitled the *Brihadaranyaka Upanishad*. The story is there related of the departure from home of the sage Yajnavalkya, the so-called 'Lord of Sacrifice', who is reputed to have written some of the most revered Hindu scriptures. Before leaving to adopt a hermit life, he announces that he wishes to make a settlement between his two wives, Maitreyi and Katyayani. We are told that one of these wives 'possessed such knowledge only as women possess', whereas the other, Maitreyi, was a woman of fine perceptions with an understanding, if not direct experience, of *Brahman*. Maitreyi, to whom he announces his intention of departing, takes the opportunity of asking him whether in his opinion wealth, such as perhaps she may one day possess, will bring immortal happiness. He assures her that it will not. Still detaining him, she then solicits his views upon immortality. As 'thou art truly dear to me,' he replies, 'and speakest dear words, come sit down and I will explain it to thee.' He then embarks upon an exposition of the doctrine of human love according to the meditations in which he has engaged. Human beings and natural things cannot, he maintains, be direct objects of love. When we love them, our love is directed not at, but through them. Love being of the Self (*Atman*), it seeks in its activity that which will bring it once more in contact with eternity (*Brahman*); and this it does by embracing the Self in another. Such an activity, being possible only if it renounces all commerce with the world of *Maya* or illusion, is the reverse of selfish or sensual. Love on the natural plane seeks only to possess, to multiply and cultivate illusions. Love on the eternal plane seeks only to renounce, and, having renounced, to merge with the Godhead. The complete union sought by lovers on the natural plane increases their separation both from each other and from the Divine Ground. Such union is possible only in the mutual recognition of the true Self in each individual, which results in the possession of lasting happiness in the shape of release from desire (*Moksha*).[1]

Yajnavalkya illustrates his argument by a long series of statements of which the following are typical: 'Verily a husband is not dear, that you may love the husband; but that you may love the Self through the husband, therefore a husband is dear. Verily a wife is not dear, that you may love the wife, but that you may love the Self through the wife, therefore a wife is dear... Verily creatures are not dear, that you may love the creatures; but that you may love the Self through the creatures, therefore are creatures dear... Verily, everything is not dear, that you may love everything; but that you may love the Self through everything, therefore everything is dear.' He then proceeds to illustrate by means of analogy the nature of the Godhead or *Brahman* to which he would direct the attention. Here, again, we observe how such analogies serve to keep concrete and full-blooded a doctrine that must otherwise remain dim and remote. 'As all waters find their centre in the sea, all touches in the skin, all tastes in the tongue, all smells in the nose, all colours in the eye, all sounds in the ear, all precepts in the

[1] Cf. 'Love between persons means that each wants the other to be more himself' (*The Mind and Heart of Love*, by M. C. D'Arcy, S.J. (1945), p. 166).

mind, all knowledge in the heart, all actions in the hands, and all *Vedas* in speech; as a lump of sugar, when thrown into water, becomes dissolved into water, and could not be taken out again, but whenever we taste (the water) it is sweet—thus verily, O Maitreyi, does this great Being, endless, unlimited, consisting of nothing but knowledge, rise from out their elements and vanish again in them. When he has departed there is no more knowledge.'

But Maitreyi is still puzzled. 'Here thou has bewildered me, sir,' she protests, 'when thou sayest that having departed, there is no more knowledge.' To which the husband replies: 'O Maitreyi, I say nothing that is bewildering. This is enough, O beloved, for wisdom. For when there is as it were duality, then one sees the other, one smells the other, one hears the other, one salutes the other, one perceives the other, one knows the other; but when the Self only is all this, how should he smell another, how should he see another, how should he hear another, how should he salute another, how should he perceive another, how should he know another? How should he know him by whom he knows all this? The self is to be described by No, no![1] He is incomprehensible, for he cannot be comprehended. He is imperishable, because he cannot perish. He is unattached, for he does not attach himself; unfettered, he does not suffer, he does not fail. How, O beloved, should he know the knower? Thus, O Maitreyi, thou hast been instructed. Thus far goes immortality.'

In the above passage, with its repetitions characteristic of an age of oral tradition, Yajnavalkya is seeking to emphasize three points of capital importance for the *Upanishad* doctrine. The first is one to which Plato later (but not so very much later) gave expression in his statement, never perhaps surpassed in pregnancy of meaning, that 'Love is the desire and pursuit of the Whole'—i.e. The All, the *Brahman*. The second point is that human values, such as love and beauty, are important not in themselves but in their revelation, however intermittent, of a more fundamental and eternal love and beauty. Their reality resides in that which they 'let through' from the eternal source of value which is *Brahman*. The third point is that the object of knowledge is attained not through vain learning and academic study, but through a kind of willed-for ignorance, a draining of the mind of the conceit of worldly erudition. 'Not by learning is the *Atman* attained, not by genius and much knowledge of books ... Let a Brahman[2] renounce learning and become as a child.' The whole world, suggests Yajnavalkya by his similes, is as it were suffused with *Brahman*, dissolved in Spirit; but only those whose taste is not corrupted and jaded can become aware of the fact. The same truth is conveyed in another brilliant simile from the *Svetasvatara Upanishad*, namely that *Brahman* is 'like a fire that had consumed its fuel'. When the individual has disciplined his soul sufficiently and attained to a knowledge of truth, he will issue forth in the childlike state defined by

[1] Sanskrit *Neti, neti*, 'Not this, not that': in other words the Self cannot be defined in ordinary terms.
[2] The word here means a member of the caste of priests.

another faith as a condition of entering the Kingdom of Heaven. When the individual is one with Reality, the inherent division of ordinary existence, with its mind-body and pleasure-pain duality, will have been healed, as the wake of a ship closes up without trace. If, to preserve the marine metaphor, we think of Being as an ocean, the waves are creatures that assert a momentary individuality and are then drawn down once more into the depths.

How, it may be asked at this point, can we suppose any husband to have addressed his wife in such terms as these, even though the husband was one of the world's great sages and the wife a woman of more than ordinary intellect? What couple can be imagined as having devoted the last hour of their domestic life together to such high-flown discourse? Naturally, the *Upanishads* as they have come down to us are stylized, formalistic documents; they are more rigid in their composition even than the *Dialogues* of Plato. Nevertheless, they transmit across all these centuries an experience that we recognize to be at bottom authentic. To the Western mind, such an experience may not come alive without violent imaginative readjustment. We have to put ourselves in the place of men and women whose conditions of life brought them face to face with naked reality, almost with essences; whereas the machine-punctuated life of the modern man shows him reality several times removed.[1] Had they been accessible, the reports of these elemental experiences would have been more easily appreciated by the pre-industrial generations, for whom the rhythm of life had undergone negligible change since the Neolithic epoch. Our modern lives are notched with such intervals as pay-day, the year's holiday, the receipt of a government pension. We find it hard to conceive of a life controlled by the more plastic but apparently endless rhythm of the seasons: a life brooded over by an eternity of natural recurrence, and alternately drenched by heat and torrent. Such materially sheltered existence has rendered us correspondingly less exposed to those spiritual truths which stare the oriental in the face—namely the vanity of egoism, desire, and attachment to objects of sense.

Granted this thoroughly disillusioned view of the nature of existence—'this patched-together hiding-place', as Yajnavalkya describes it—we find it hardly surprising that the origin of mankind should have been regarded by early Hindu philosophers as an event of shame and evil. In the hymn of the *Rig-Veda*, to which we have already referred, Yama and Yami's mating is concluded in an atmosphere of guilt. 'Shall we not do,' says Yami, 'what we never did aforetime? We who spoke righteously now talk impurely?' Since Yama and Yami were brother and sister, the feeling of guilt may partly be accounted for by horror of incest; but in the first of the *Upanishads* (fourth *Brahman*) we find a story of the Creation which is equally coloured by feelings of guilt. In the beginning, according to this account, was the Self, the *Atman*, which, feeling no delight in a solitary existence, 'made his Self fall into two, and thence arose husband and wife'.

[1] We return to this point in the Conclusion.

After the first embrace, however, the woman, experiencing a sudden feeling of shame, feels she must hide herself. This she does by becoming successively most of the animals of creation, down to the ant. Each time, the husband, following suit, became the male animal, with the result that the entire fauna of the world were brought into existence. Even allowing for the latitude of allegory, this particular story borders on the ludicrous; but we may observe that it exhibits two points in common with most of the other Creation stories. The first is that woman is born from part of man. The second is that the act whereby mankind is begotten produces an immediate sense of shame. We are here dealing with a feeling deeply implanted within the human mind. Consciousness of sex and consciousness of sin are somehow interrelated, no man knows why: but particularly is this the case with the act from which sprang humankind. It is interesting to note that modern psychology has no more succeeded in explaining this human obsession than any other science; indeed, what modern psychology has done is merely to confirm its existence at every mental level. Undoubtedly the Hindu attitude, which received impressive confirmation at the hands of Buddha, was the result of its horror of rebirth. To be born was forthwith to step into the realm of desire and attachment—to enter upon a career that might last for ages, if not for all eternity. In these circumstances, the act from which such infinite evil might spring must itself be evil, while most evil of all would be the initial act of our first ancestors. Upon the latter (as they apparently recognized) a terrible responsibility rested.

If life, and in particular birth, represented so great an evil, however, why did not the sages recommend either the prevention of the continuation of the race or the universal practice of suicide upon attaining years of discretion? We shall see in due course that a certain school of thinkers, more logical perhaps than the forest sages, advocated and adopted precisely these measures.

The Bhagavad-Gita

The ancient hymns of the *Rig-Veda* were considered, as we saw, to have been communicated to man by God Himself. Although such divine origins were not ascribed to the *Upanishads*, the latter were, and still are, regarded as sacred writings or *Sruti*. Today they remain as precious to the devout as they were in the centuries of their composition and compilation, which was probably between 800 and 500 BC. If the Western reader finds the *Upanishads* dull or remote he can usually assume that he has failed, even though he may have tried, to make the imaginative readjustment of which we have spoken. He may be reassured, however, by the knowledge that even the most orthodox Hindus regard the *Upanishads* as, if not deficient, then at least in need of completion by a less purely intellectual doctrine. Just as they benefit from being preceded by the imaginatively rich *Rig-Vega*, so they gain immeasurably by being followed by the far richer *Bhagavad-Gita*. 'The *Upanishads*,' wrote Rabindranath Tagore, 'though they measured the highest reaches of the philosophic imagination of our people, were yet incomplete in their answer to the complex longing of the human soul. Their emphasis was too intellectual, and did not sufficiently explore the approach to Reality through love and devotion.'[1]

Indian philosophical tradition has fully recognized the different degrees in wisdom to which the three great elements of Hindu scripture approximate. In the first place there is the so-called Path of Activity, or *Karmamarga*. To this path belongs the *Vedas*, songs to be chanted in public as a stimulus to effort: the anthems of a people engaged in a communal exploit needing for its accomplishment a burning faith in its mission. In the second place there is the so-called Path of Knowledge, or *Inanamarga*. To this path belong the *Upanishads*, explorations by the mind in secret conclave of that which is permanently knowable behind the world of appearances and illusion. In the third place there is the so-called Path of Devotion, or *Bhaktimarga*. To this path belongs the *Bhagavad-Gita*. This epic within an epic retails the story not of the Philosopher-King but of someone rarer still, the Philosopher-Hero. It demonstrates for all time the possibility of serving *Brahman* wholeheartedly in a situation very different from that chosen by the authors of the *Upanishads*. Obsessed by their problems the forest sages often failed to see the wood for the trees. Arjuna, the hero of the *Gitas*, makes the great reconciliation between immediate duty, dictated by material and political considerations, and the ultimate obligations of a devotee of *Brahman*. It is perhaps the only convincing solution to a problem that faces sometimes a whole generation, but of which few perceive the true nature.

The *Bhagavad-Gita* is a poem unique in the world's literature. In the first place it belongs as much to philosophy as to literature, and as much to the social life of India as to its spiritual heritage. As a document revered as sacred or *Smriti*[2] by all Hindus, it is still employed for taking oaths. As a work of literature, it forms an acknowledged masterpiece; the best translations convey enough of its beauty of expression to suggest something of the perfection of the original. And compared with the scriptures of any other religion, it excels all except the New Testament in its sustained exposition of spiritual truth.

The title *Bhagavad-Gita* is best rendered in English as *The Lord's Song*. Although it forms an epic poem in itself, it is in point of fact a digression of considerable length in another epic of much greater dimensions. The *Mahabharata*, as this gigantic 200,000-line poem was called, dates from about 500 BC. We do not know who wrote it. All we know is that it was added to and elaborated over a period of many centuries; that it received its present form about AD 400 under the great Gupta kings, and that at some point in its compilation the *Bhagavad-Gita* was included within it, forming what is now Book VI.

[1] Tagore's verdict, always worthy of the greatest respect, is in this case indisputable; but his view of the *Vedas* as being the product of a 'childlike' approach to reality seems to be based upon assumptions about human progress learnt from the West: a danger to which lesser intellects of the Orient are the more obviously exposed.

[2] *Smriti*, as opposed to *Sruti*, means writing or teaching of saints or prophets. It amounts to 'indirect' *Sruti*.

No wonder that the only author to be associated, if not credited, with its composition should have borne the name of *Vyasa*, which means literally compiler or editor. The *Mahabharata* (or 'Great Bharata') is the last place in which one would expect to find a piece of writing such as the *Bhagavad-Gita*. Bharata, son of the great Indian heroine Shakuntala, is the father of two tribes, the Kurus and the Pandavas. The rambling story opens with an account of the jealousy of the Kurus for the more enlightened and god-fearing Pandavas, culminating in a gambling match in which Yudishthira, King of the Pandavas (whose only weakness was love of the dice), lost the whole of his kingdom, including his wife Draupadi, to his rival. The latter, who has employed loaded dice, now decides to eliminate the Pandavas for good and all. He is restrained by the pleas of his blind father, Dhritarashtra, under whose roof the Pandavas had themselves been educated, and agrees finally to banish them for a period of twelve years. At the conclusion of this term, which the Pandavas have spent in the forest acquiring wisdom, Duryodhana, breaking his word, refuses to restore the Pandavas their kingdom. The exiled clan have by this time acquired numerous sympathizers throughout northern India. War is declared. Among the Pandavas is the warrior Arjuna, a kind of Hindu Achilles. He chooses as his charioteer Krishna, the incarnation or *avatar* of the God *Vishnu*. Realizing that he is about to fight his own kinsmen, Arjuna hesitates on the field of battle whether to proceed to the attack. Krishna, whose identity is disclosed, argues with him, and the *Bhagavad-Gita* is the record of their remarkable conversation together. Stationed at the side of the old king, Dhritarashtra, the courtier Sanjaya is specially endowed with extra-sensory perception in order to provide a running commentary upon the proceedings.

The gospel of Krishna, the Lord whose Song it is, marks the culmination of Hindu thought starting with the *Vedas*. Those for whom the *Upanishads* are cold intellectual documents will find warmth and sublimity in the *Gita*. Its general point of view, though less consistent, is more acceptable to the Western mind. Furthermore, Krishna's arguments dispose of the view that the Orient lacks a doctrine of action. Of the passive resistance or *Satyagraha*,[1] preached at a later date, there is here no hint. Even pacifism itself, of which Arjuna is at first the spokesman, meets with rejection by Krishna as incompatible with the doctrine of *Brahman*. In its day the poem no doubt provided an answer to those who feared that the *Upanishads*, with their quietist doctrines, might tend to demoralize the people. Thus although the *Gita* forms perhaps the loftiest religious epic in the world, infused with the spirit of renunciation and contemplation, it is at the same time a shrewd and noble apology for action. Whereas it probably began as a heroic poem of the *Kshatriya*, or warrior caste,[2] it was gradually moulded under Brahman influence into a 'high history', like the somewhat similar legend of the Holy Grail. The highest virtue rquired by the *Upani-*

[1] The doctrine espoused in particular by Mahatma Gandhi.
[2] To which the Buddha and Mahavira belonged.

shads is to be saintly. In the *Gita* the highest virtue enjoined upon Arjuna is devotion (*Bhakti*). Now devotion is best exemplified in selfless attachment to a person. It is Arjuna's devotion to Krishna that places the *Gita* above the *Upanishads* in point of realism and humanity. Seeing that the *Brahman* of the *Upanishads* represented an entity beyond human understanding, it was impossible that such a Supreme Being should command devotion of the personal kind lauded in the *Gita*. 'The path of the Unmanifested,' says Krishna in the poem, 'is hard for the embodied to reach.' Men talk of dedicating themselves to honour, virtue, and even love; what it is to which they declare themselves attached is always something endowed, or at least credited, with personality. Men cannot adore an abstraction. The evolution of the impersonal *Brahman* of the *Vedas*, which is often referred to as 'It', into the God-Man Krishna of the *Gita*, represents a natural and inevitable process. The desire to see the human incarnation of God has been a feature of every religion, above all of Christianity. Allowing for obvious differences of message, no person in history—not even the Buddha himself—spoke more in the manner of Christ than Krishna.

Although the profound wisdom of the *Gita* is discernible to us only by studying the poem as a whole in good translation, we can follow the gist of the argument by citing certain salient passages. In his first mood of dejection, Arjuna, turning to Krishna, exclaims: 'Seeing these my kinsmen, O Krishna, annoyed, eager to fight, my limbs fail and my mouth is parched, my body quivers, and my hair stands on end, Gardiva [his bow] slips from my hand, and my skin burns all over, I am not able to stand, my mind is whirling, and I see adverse omens, O Kesave ['enlightened one']. Nor do I see any advantage from slaying kinsmen in battle ... killing these desperadoes, sin will but take hold of us ... Although these, with intelligence overpowered by greed, see no guilt in the destruction of a family, no crime in hostility to friends, why should we not learn to turn away from such a sin, O Krishna, who sees evils in destruction of a family?' Krishna does not reprove Arjuna for this natural reluctance to engage in slaughter. He even applauds his wisdom, but he goes on to point out that his grief is misplaced. To be truly wise, he says, is to grieve for neither the living nor the dead. The present evils are both temporary and ephemeral. The human soul will outlast these and every other occurrence in this world. Therefore the evils of life must be borne with equanimity. To be moved and cast down by human sorrow is to display conduct the reverse of that which deserves immortality. The immediate duty, which is resistance to the enemy, must be squarely faced. Arjuna must fight. The true Self, the *Atman*, being birthless, deathless, and changeless, will thereby come to no harm. In any case, as Krishna later points out (Book XI), Arjuna, in fighting his enemies, will only 'seem to slay'. In point of fact these men are already dead, having been ordained to be killed by Krishna himself. No man really kills or is killed by another, for such actions have no real significance. Regret at what is unavoidable is misplaced. If death is the outcome, heaven will be the reward; if victory, a kingdom to which Arjuna is legally entitled. Victory and defeat amount in the end to the same thing. To engage in battle in a mood of holy indifference is to rid oneself of sin.[1]

Having expounded to Arjuna the true nature of the Self, according to orthodox *Upanishad* teaching, Krishna proceeds to elaborate a doctrine which, though frequently misunderstood, has perhaps enjoyed more popularity in the Western world than any other of oriental origin. This is the doctrine known as *Karma Yoga*. Although we shall discuss Yoga in detail later, it is important to understand at the outset what is meant by these two terms. *Karma*, a word to which reference is increasingly made, is not easy to translate into English. It means primarily 'deed' or 'work'; but it can also mean both the results of a particular deed and the chain of causes and effects that links various deeds together. It is in the latter sense that the word is now most frequently employed. *Karma* is the law which is brought into operation by our least act in this life; for what we do in the present world is not merely the result of what we did in some past existence but the cause of what we shall do in another. The meaning of Yoga is less simple. Literally a 'Yoke', it can mean the state of union with *Brahman* which is the end or goal of life. Another and more usual meaning is that of rule or path whereby this union is achieved. As there is more than one path to such union, so there are several kinds of *Yoga*. That Krishna should expound to Arjuna the principles of *Karma Yoga* is appropriate, since *Karma Yoga* is concerned with action that results from self-dedication to a personal God such as Krishna represents.

At this point in the *Gita* we become aware of a tendency to humanize the rather stringent asceticism advocated by the *Upanishads*. To approach the latter in a mood of humility, which is the correct attitude, is to be overwhelmed by the demands made upon a human nature easily tired by two minutes' concentrated thought. Salvation, it may seem, is to be acquired at a price not merely too big but beyond anything ordinary men can afford. In the *Gita*, on the other hand, Krishna repeatedly stresses the value of even a brave show of effort and will. 'In this Yoga,' he says, 'even the abortive attempt is not wasted. Nor can it produce a contrary result. Even a little practice of this Yoga will save you from the terrible wheel of rebirth and death.' The first requisite is to despise and ignore the fruits of action. 'You have the right to work but for the work's sake only. You have no right to the fruits of work . . . Perform every action with your heart fixed on the Supreme Lord. Renounce attachment to the fruits. Be even-tempered in success or failure; for it is this evenness of temper which is meant by Yoga.' Then follows a shrewd analysis of that form of conduct which, being attached to the fruits of action, lands a person in frustration and discontent. 'Thinking about sense-objects will attach you to sense-objects; Grow attached, and you become addicted; Thwart your addiction, it turns to anger; Be angry and you confuse your mind; Confuse your mind, you forget the lesson of experience; Forget experience, you lose discrimination; Lose discrimination, and you miss life's

[1] One calls to mind a line of a war poem written in 1940 by Herbert Read: 'To fight without hope is to fight with grace.'

only purpose.' Those immersed in the life of the senses naturally believe they are enjoying the richest experience that life has to offer. To such people, the detachment of the seer appears as a kind of befuddlement. The truth is quite otherwise. 'The recollected mind is awake In the knowledge of the *Atman*, Which is dark night to the ignorant: The ignorant are awake in their sense-life, Which they think is daylight: To the seer it is darkness.'

It is in the third section or 'lesson' of the *Gita*, specially concerned with *Karma Yoga*, that the new doctrine of action is most clearly expounded. Arjuna draws Krishna's attention to an apparent contradiction in the philosophy of *Brahman*. If, as the *Upanishads* suggest, knowledge is the highest goal of man, and if the contemplative is the highest type of human being, how can action be justified at all, let alone action involving both violence and slaughter? To this question Krishna replies that the distinction between knowledge and action is at bottom a false one. Knowledge is a form of action, because action can include the operations of the mind. In other words, we never cease to act for one moment, even in sleep.[1] Hence 'freedom from action is never achieved by abstaining from action.' What is required of the true devotee is not passiveness but selfless action. It is that to which *Karma Yoga*, properly followed, will lead.

The exposition of the principles of *Karma Yoga* leads Krishna to explain how so great a wisdom, though preached from the beginning of time, has been neglected. The evil instincts of men, by mistaking the senses for organs of true knowledge, have obscured the knowledge of *Brahman*. For this reason Krishna is obliged from time to time to visit the world in bodily form. But unlike Arjuna, who has also experienced many forms of existence, Krishna is endowed with the capacity to remember each of his incarnations. 'I seem to be born,' he says, 'but it is only seeming.' Only when evil appears to be gaining the upper hand, 'I make myself a body.' (We are given to understand that Krishna's human embodiment at this time represented the eighth incarnation of Vishnu.) He then issues his first clear statement of his mission as the saviour of mankind: 'He who knows the nature of my task and my holy birth Is not reborn. When he leaves this body he comes to me. Flying from fear, From lust and anger, He hides in me, His refuge, his safety: Burnt clean in the blaze of my being, In me many find home. Whatever wish men bring me in worship, That wish I grant them. Whatever path men travel Is my path: No matter where they walk It leads to me.' He then sums up his teaching about action in a fashion that, though paradoxical, contains truth even on a lower level than that of which he speaks, 'He who sees the inaction that is in action, and the action that is in inaction, is wise indeed.'

After some detailed instructions concerning the practice of Yoga, which we shall study in connection with the philosophy of Patanjali, the *Gita* returns to the question of the weakness of human nature, for which these practices entail such rigorous discipline. Arjuna asks what becomes of those whose will-power is too feeble to enable them to

[1] Arjuna incidentally was supposed never to indulge in this relaxation.

follow the proper directions. For if a man fails to attain a knowledge of *Brahman*, does he not in effect miss both lives: the present which he has renounced in favour of the future life of the spirit, and the future life of the spirit which he has not attained? On both these points Krishna reassures him. Such a man, who must on no account be confused with the backslider, is lost to neither world, because 'no one who seeks Brahman ever comes to an evil end'.[1] Those who, having embarked upon the practice of Yoga, cannot sustain the effort of self-discipline, will still reach 'the heaven of good deeds', where they will remain for a considerable time. Then, being reborn by the so-called *Pitri-Jana*[2] into a good and enlightened home, they will strive towards perfection from the point at which they left off. They may even have the good fortune—but this is not very common—to be born into a family of enlightened Yogis (practitioners of Yoga). Through a series of births they will finally succeed in escaping from further rebirths by attaining to knowledge of *Brahman*.

In the seventh section of the poem, where Krishna further enlightens Arjuna on the subject of who is to be saved, we observe a marked widening of outlook, a universal vision of faith, such as occurred in Judaism only with the second Isaiah. Krishna accepts the fact that men of different ages, countries, and temperament will adopt different rituals and even worship different gods. This does not greatly matter. So long as a man has faith, even if he is wicked he is worthy to be admitted to the number of the devout. By an act which Christian theology was later to describe as one of grace, God will in due time make that faith, however misplaced, unwavering, so that 'endowed with the faith I give him, he worships that deity, and gets from it everything he prays for. In reality, I alone am the giver.'

Perhaps the climax of the *Gita*'s teaching is reached in the eighth Book, in which Krishna answers Arjuna's question as to how, at the hour of death, God reveals Himself to those who have been faithful to Him. Introduced at a similar point in one of the greatest of modern religious poems,[3] this sublime passage alone would make the *Gita* a work of surpassing value. 'Whatever a man remembers at the last, when he is leaving the body, will be realized by him in the hereafter: because that will be what his mind has most constantly dwelt on during life.' We may venture to say that all the bitter and tortuous arguments concerning 'faith' and 'works' that were to darken the next two thousand years, especially in Europe, are here exposed as vanity. Both forms of argument are to be rejected simply because they are arguments; for there is no arguing oneself at the last moment into salvation. It is the spiritual level upon which a man is accustomed to live that will determine at the moment of mortal interruption his fate hereafter. Admittedly this level is not always easy to assess from external observation. One suspects that much overt piety, much in-

[1] Cf. Socrates: 'No harm can come to a good man in this or the next world' (Plato: *Apology*).
[2] The 'path of the fathers', as opposed to the *Deva-Jana*, the 'path of the bright ones', who attain direct to a state of *Nirvana*.
[3] T. S. Eliot's *East Coker*, the second of the *Four Quartets*.

sistence upon outward performance of duty, serve to conceal a mind unused to higher aspiration. And here we may appreciate once more the convenience of defining 'religion' as the maintenance of the 'divine connection': for it is this connection which, as Krishna says, the soul not merely establishes but, if deserving of salvation, maintains within himself. Thus the summit of each world faith is on a level with that of the others. At the highest point to which the Hindu spirit attained we observe that insistence upon the spiritual disposition which is found equally in Zoroastrianism, in Buddhism, and in Judeo-Christianity. The same insistence upon inner sanctity distinguished, as we saw, the apex of Egyptian moral speculation. We are beginning to learn something of the mind not of one or two nations or peoples, but of mankind as a whole.

The majesty of the *Gita*'s message is to be discerned likewise in its view of the nature of Knowledge. The knowledge of God for which the forest sages sought was an intellectual thing. It resembled the supreme knowledge spoken of by the great European philosopher whose 'God-intoxicated' spirit most nearly resembled that of the forest sages, Benedict Spinoza. It was in fact an *amor intellectualis Dei*, an 'intellectual love of God'. The knowledge of God of which we learn in the *Gita* is more than that. It is devotional love. Hence the literal meaning of *Bakhti*, Devotion, is 'loving faith'. A modern English philosopher[1] has well remarked that true knowledge is to be distinguished from mere belief 'by being vision'. This visionary quality, though not always sustained to the degree apparent in the *Gita*, is that which places a work of literature in the category of inspired utterances, the work of the *Nebiim* among mankind who are the only leaders that matter because their message is of permanent validity. In the light of such prophetic testimony, even theology reveals its inadequacy. 'To the *Brahmana*, the knower of Faith, all the *Vedas* are of as little use as a small water-tank during the time of a flood, when water is everywhere.'

A précis of a poem may, by a modest aim, do less harm than a more ambitious attempt to convey its excellences. In the brief account given above of the *Gita* we have been concerned solely to distil its message, a legitimate endeavour in the case of a poem which, in addition to being a work of art, possesses an evident didactic purpose. We have refrained from entering into explanations of difficult philosophical terminology; the *Gita*, like *The Divine Comedy*, has its technical vocabulary and requires a sheaf of notes and an occasional diagram. Similarly, we have omitted, as outside the scope of this book, all detailed comment upon its dramatic qualities. A literary approach would certainly need to dwell upon the magnificence of Book X, in which Krishna, ceasing momentarily to act as Arjuna's charioteer, assumes the aspect of an omnipotent god, magnificent and terrifying, like the apparition in the *Book of Revelation*, and having a voice like that which addressed Job from the whirlwind.

What is the outcome of Krishna's counsel and revelation to Arjuna?

[1] A. E. Taylor

Arjuna, calm but heartened, resolves to fight. Indeed, his own nature, however reluctant at the outset, dictates this course of action. 'If, in your vanity, you say: "I will not fight", your resolve is vain. Your own nature will drive you to the act. For you yourself have created the Karma that binds you. You are helpless in its power. And you will do that very thing which your ignorance seeks to avoid.' And the poem ends with Krishna's bidding to Arjuna to renounce all fear of life or death, all explanation of reward, all attachment except to God. Here, again, the message is addressed not simply to Arjuna but to all. 'If any man meditated on this sacred discourse of ours, I shall consider that he has worshipped me in spirit.'

Thus concludes the work which Wilhelm von Humboldt, to quote but one spokesman from many, described as, 'the most beautiful, perhaps the only true, philosophical song existing in any known tongue'. That verdict may possibly be exaggerated; but there is clearly something remarkable about a poem which, during the centuries in which it has been accessible to Europe, has prompted to exaggeration so many thinkers whose views are entitled to respect.

The Sceptical Backwash

India has often been contrasted with China by saying that India has too much religion, China too great an obsession with ethics.[1] The preoccupation of India with the meaning of existence has admittedly been more intense than that of any other country: it has certainly been more prolonged. Preoccupation with the meaning of existence, however, does not always make for 'belief' as commonly understood. It may make equally, or at least periodically, for scepticism. From too great a concentration upon ultimate problems the mind may spring back in exhaustion or even disgust. The divine connection, however passionately sought, may appear as either beyond man's capacity to discern, or else as something that in the nature of things cannot be established. The first conclusion, though not in itself productive of scepticism, may easily collapse into one that is. In the composure of the faculties to despair there is experienced a kind of tranquillity (we talk of 'happy agnosticism'), whereas the realization of a basis for belief opens up bewildering vistas of effort and concentration, at least until the final attainment of union. The very fury of resolve displayed by the forest sages, their itch to arrive at certainty, their hunger of explanation, even of trivial matters—and there is triviality in certain of the *Upanishads*—indicate a state of mental turmoil persisting not for a lifetime, an 'age of transition', but for several centuries. If the secret of life had been known to them, there would have been no need for 'secret doctrine', nor would the mystery of *Brahman* and *Atman* have needed unravelling in solitude by men with 'hair grown white and having seen their son's son'. The gospel of Krishna would have amounted to the revelation of banality. In short the *philosophia perennis* is

[1] See for example *The Wisdom of India*, edited by Lin Yutang, p. 17.

shadowed by its opposite, an *anti-philosophia*, equally perennial and with the greater fecundity of the weed over the flower.

In point of fact we become aware of scepticism not only as shadowing the fluorescent doctrine of the *Upanishads*, but also as growing up in its midst. The *Chandogya Upanishad*, for instance, consists of a long meditation on the significance of the sacred syllable *OM*.[1] Employed at the beginning and end of the *Vedas*, and considered as an aid to meditation if repeated or meditated upon, *OM* may be rendered as 'peace' or even as *Brahman*. We very soon come to perceive how it can be abused. When the sage Glava Maitreya went to repeat the *Veda*, we learn that a white dog appeared before him, and other dogs followed, saying, 'Sing and get us food, for we are hungry.' The dogs later 'came on, holding together, each dog keeping the tail of the preceding dog in its mouth, *as the priests do when they are going to sing praises*... After they had settled down, they began to say *Hin* (Prajapati). *OM*, let us eat! *OM*, let us drink! *OM*, may the divine Varuna, Prajapati, Savitri, bring us food! Lord of Food, bring hither food, bring it, *OM*!' Other *Upanishads* reveal not merely a critical attitude to the priesthood, but a frank scepticism about all the higher values, the gods, and the scriptures. Similarly, in the *Gita*, Krishna warns Arjuna against those 'demoniacal men' who contend that 'the universe is without truth, without basis, without a god, brought about by mutual union, and caused by lust and nothing else'.[2] There is no doubt that this passage refers to ideas current at the time. Moreover, we can be reasonably sure of the school of thinkers to which it refers. These were the *Nastiks*, or those who 'said no'—Nihilists, as we should call them. Such a negative attitude can manifest itself in a number of ways, ranging from conventional agnosticism, which does not know 'either way'—whether there is a God or whether there is not—to complete materialism, which, proclaiming no law save that of chance, reduces the world to a fortuitous assemblage of bits of matter: a point of view to which the puzzling *Swasanved Upanishad* approaches. Downright materialism of the latter kind is admittedly rare in philosophy, and rarer still in life. The mind cannot easily be made to entertain, except for polemical purposes, a theory which, like a boomerang, returns to shatter to pieces the instrument that launched it: for the mind on such a theory is as chance a concentration as anything else, with the result that its conclusions are equally accidental. A genial agnosticism, especially if combined with a talent for logic-chopping, is both more common and more socially acceptable. Nothing in the modern world can be compared with the practice, as common in ancient India as in Greece, of holding public philosophical contests,

[1] Compressed from the letters AUM, which symbolize the three chief *Vedas*.

[2] Attention may perhaps be drawn here to the fact that Krishna directly relates bad conduct to a false view of the world: 'Holding evil ideas through delusion, they engage in action with impure resolves.' Today, such is the divorce between metaphysics and ethics, we rarely regard a man's conduct, good or bad, as having anything much to do with his conception of the nature of the universe.

sometimes under official and even royal auspices, and sometimes purely freelance.[1] We learn of such debates in the *Upanishads*.

Likewise there existed a number of philosophical 'pedlars' or *Paribbajaka*, who, like the Greek Sophists, made a profession of engaging in argument for the sake of argument, or sometimes of purveying a specious kind of wisdom, mental cures or sedatives, like quack psychologists: for every community contains its mental as well as its physical hypochondriacs. Sometimes the cure prescribed was that which entailed purging the mind of the illusion of faith, for, as we pointed out above, men are not necessarily more happy as believers than otherwise. Such a denouncer of the 'opium of the people' was Brihaspati, who ridiculed the sanctity of the *Vedas* and preached a philosophy of 'Eat, drink and be merry'. Of his life and work we have little direct knowledge; but his influence was great enough to start a school of sceptical materialists, the Charvakas (so-called after one of the most distinguished of their number), who anticipated and out-did the sceptics of the modern world in the rigour of their destructive analysis. Whereas the faith of the *Vedas*, the *Upanishads*, and the *Bhagavad-Gita* repudiated the evidence of the senses as productive of illusion, these *Nastiks* (to resume the general term for the sceptical school) contended that men, having nothing but their senses upon which to rely, were foolish to seek a sphere of experience behind or beyond that of momentary sensation. Both *Atman* and *Brahman* were figments of the imagination: their identity in that respect was unquestioned. Furthermore, the discipline of Yoga represented an outrage against nature, the invention of a twisted mentality. Not the renunciation or uprooting but the acceptance of instinct should be regarded as the true law of life. Everything that would delude men into thinking otherwise, above all the domination of the Brahman caste, was a menace to society. There was no 'divine connection'. The world was maintained by a nexus of atoms. Soul and body were therefore composed of the same material.

Mahavira

Orthodox belief is supposed to induce social torpor; but, as we have shown, there is also a quietism that comes from the profession of certain forms of scepticism, mild rather than bitter. The communal mind can be roused and quickened by two quite opposite influences: that of a revolutionary and transcendental faith such as that of Ikhnaten or Zoroaster, or that of a ferociously ascetic belief such as that which, without warning, captured the minds of a small group of zealots in fifth-century India, not many years before the more profound but less stringent faith of Gotama Buddha. The faith of Mahavira, the founder of Jainism, is perhaps the most perplexing of all that we shall study in this book. That anyone should have devised such an extravagant

[1] The B.B.C. Brains Trust is our nearest equivalent. The great success of this institution, especially in its initial stages, revealed an obvious interest in serious public disputation. Possibly the gradual evolution of the Trust into an entertainment deprived it of its attraction for many people.

belief is as remarkable as that anyone should have followed it, for at first glance it appears not merely incredible but impracticable. Like most other extreme faiths, it has modified itself in course of time into something in which it is possible to believe. The faith of the Jains, which denies life to the extent of regarding suicide as the most sacred act of which man is capable, has survived and even prospered for over two thousand years.

Mahavira, who probably lived from 549–477 BC,[1] came of a family belonging to the *Kshatriya* or Warrior caste, which for centuries was regarded as superior to all others, including that of the Brahmans or priests.[2] He was born in the town of Vaishali in modern Bihar. From the beginning his upbringing was unusual. His father, one of the leaders of the *Lichchavi* tribe and a man of considerable wealth, was an adherent of a religious sect which professed a doctrine staunchly opposed to that of the *Vedas*. If the beliefs of this sect were not exactly materialist, they were certainly nihilist or *Nastik*. Sharing the common Vedic horror of rebirth, they enjoined a particular method of avoiding it. This was by voluntary suicide. The aim was not to induce a violent end, but, by preference, slowly to drain away vitality by means of starvation. Only thus would the life-force be reduced to a degree of inanition rendering it incapable of further transmigration. It appears that Mahavira's father converted his wife to the same belief, and in due course shared with her the martyrdom to which they were thereby committed. Possibly they may be pronounced guilty of a certain measure of procrastination or sloth, for at the time of their fast unto death their son was already in his thirty-second year.

The death of his father and mother reduced the young man to a state of extreme dejection. Being in his prime, he instinctively clung to life while at the same time sensing and suspecting its futility. Before following the parental example, however, he determined to embark upon a quest for wisdom more thorough than that undertaken by any of his contemporaries or predecessors. Rejecting current orthodoxy and heterodoxy alike, but subscribing at least to the principle of self-purification and renunciation, he left home and adopted the life of a vagrant. To demonstrate his complete withdrawal from civilized life he dispensed with every amenity and property, including clothing. For thirteen years he roamed the country of western Bengal practising austerities of the most extreme variety. In a land of strange sects and practices, such conduct would not at first have attracted undue attention; but such was the powerful personality of this young man that he soon began to acquire followers and disciples. A tradition dating from remote time held that mankind, plunged in corruption and sin, was periodically afforded enlightenment by the appearance of Saviours, Redeemers or, as they were called, *Jinas* ('Conquerors').[3] Upon the small group of disciples of the naked wanderer there gradually

[1] This date has been questioned.

[2] It was in fact the second caste in the Hindu hierarchy. The first, that of the Brahmans, was exempt from all taxation.

[3] Or Jainas.

dawned the conviction that their master was none other than the latest of these *Jinas*. Accordingly they gave him the new name of Mahavira, which means 'Great Hero'. As followers of this new leader they called themselves Jains, hero-worshippers.

In spite of the ascetism of his life, Mahavira lived to the age of seventy-two. At the time of his death there were about 14,000 Jains, some of whom had formed themselves into monastic communities, male and female. Nor did the death of the *Jina* halt the spread of his doctrine. On the contrary, the faith won converts rapidly, attracting rather than repelling by the severity of its impositions. That it should ever become a world faith was impossible; but whereas many a belief of less rigour has run into the sand, Jainism, despite schisms and fierce controversies, can still claim almost a million and a half followers.

The original beliefs of the Jains have undergone a good deal of development since their first formulation by Mahavira. Sharing the family belief that the *Vedas* were not the word of God, Mahavira was one of the first men on earth to proclaim a faith nominally without an Object. In his view, the search for absolute knowledge of *Brahman*, as for absolute union with that infinite Being, was futile. The universe was not created or started by a god: it was self-subsistent and always had been so.[1] Far from men presuming to know the ultimate truth, their very finitude renders this impossible. Just as six blind men might consider an elephant to be half a dozen totally different things by touching different parts of its body, so individual men, reflecting upon their own little facet of experience, arrive inevitably at different conclusions about the nature of the world. Truth is indeed revealed to men, but only by the *Jinas* whose appearance is recognized by the faithful. Free from the chain of Karma and rebirth, these *Jinas* win for the truth in each generation a minority of saints or *Arahats*, who remain for ever exempt from reincarnation. Of lesser though substantial merit were the 'high souls' or *Paramatmans*, whose blameless conduct permitted them a temporary interruption of the birth-cycle.

Although Mahavira denied the existence of a god and even of a god-pool, he was unquestionably one of those whose mission in life was to unite the way of earth with the way of heaven. His repudiation of *Vedic* beliefs did not lead him to materialism, nor did it prevent his later disciples from constructing an entirely new pantheon composed of the saints of Jainism. It is difficult to know whether the oriental mind is capable of subscribing to a creed of absolute brute materialism. Even where the claim is made, we cannot be sure that it is being carried out in practice. Clearly, the doctrine of the transmigration of souls is incompatable with materialism even of a refined or dialectical kind. And without the doctrine of the transmigration of souls the whole point of Mahavira's self-laceration is lost. For even if your primary wish is to avoid the cycle of rebirth, you must steadfastly believe in the reality of that process in order to justify your precautions.

[1] Such a view, as we shall see, is not necessarily 'materialistic'. Aristotle held a somewhat similar view, as do our Emergent Evolutionists.

From the so-called *Jaina Sutras*[1] that have been preserved for the enlightenment of the faithful it becomes clear that the most striking feature of the Jain faith, its advocacy of suicide, is hedged round with certain conditions. It is not an act to be undertaken lightly. Defined as 'the incomparable religious death', it cannot be achieved by mere forthright self-immolation. The proper frame of mind for such a sacred act must be induced, and this may paradoxically require a lifetime's cultivation. Among the emotions that need severely to be disciplined is that of desire or longing. Therefore you must not long for death or release. You must manage to bring about your extinction in a mood beyond both desire and aversion. Among the instincts of life to be eradicated, therefore, is the instinct to leave it. In the *Bhagavad-Gita* there are passages to suggest that the sages were not unaware of the dangers of exaggerated self-discipline. They had observed, possibly among the Jains themselves and their related sects, a too great—almost a voluptuous—indulgence in asceticism. 'Yoga is not for him who eats too much or for him who fasts excessively. It is not for him who sleeps too much, or for the keeper of exaggerated vigils, etc.' (Book VI). In the *Akaranga Sutra* of the Jains, however, we read that 'there are no degrees in control'. This is followed by a terse summary of the kind of mental discipline expected of the devout Jain: 'He who knows wrath, knows pride. He who knows pride, knows deceit. He who knows deceit, knows greed. He who knows greed, knows love. He who knows love, knows conception. He who knows conception, knows birth. He who knows birth, knows death. He who knows death, knows hell. He who knows hell, knows animal existence. He who knows animal existence, knows pain. Therefore, a wise man should avoid wrath, pride, deceit, greed, love, hate, delusion, conception, birth, hell, animal existence, and pain.'

The admonition to avoid pain may appear a trifle incongruous in a creed prescribing the extremes of bodily suffering; but the emphasis here, as always, is upon the word 'avoid'. Nothing must deliberately be either sought or desired. Thus, in the instructions given in the same *Sutra* for the attention of 'the wise ones who attain in due order to one of the unerring states in which suicide is prescribed', we are given details of three methods by which the monk or *fakir* should compose himself for death. The first method is to spread out straw upon a piece of ground free from living beings of every kind. Without food the Jain should lie down and endure such pains as attack him. 'When crawling animals, or such as live on high or below, feed on his flesh and blood, he should neither kill them nor rub the wound: though these animals destroy the body, he should not stir from his position.' The second and 'more exalted method' is to lie on the bare ground and, without any comfort or food, 'strive after calmness', being unttached both internally and externally. While this method permits movement if absolutely essential, the third method, or that which conforms to 'the highest law', is to lie down flat and 'not to stir from one's place while checking *all* motions of the body'. By this means the holy man will

[1] *Sutra*: literally a string or thread, i.e. a series of verses or maxims on recurrent themes.

gradually, inevitably, and mindlessly—except in so far as to reflect that patience is the highest good—permit his physical dissolution. Such an end, in other words, must not be contrived; it must be the incidental consequence of having drained the mind of all forms of volition. The will, utterly deflated, sinks, dragging the body down with it. Thus the soul passes serenely into *Nirvana*.

The reference in the above rules to the avoidance of causing death to living creatures introduces another important tenet of Jain belief. The Jain was obliged to take five vows. The first of these vows was that of *Ahimsa*. No living creature, except the first person singular, was ever to be deprived of life. To fulfil this vow effectively it was necessary to consider not occasionally but perpetually the five ways in which it might be broken: namely in thought, word, deed, eating, and drinking. In other words, nothing must be thought, no intention formulated, that might lead to an act involving the death of living beings. Nothing must likewise be said leading to the same result. Nothing, such as thoughtless walking or carelessly laying down the begging bowl, must be done directly to destroy living creatures. This means also that no Jain can engage in agricultural pursuits. Finally, before eating or drinking vegetarian food—for no other was permissible—the Jain must examine it carefully to see that he does not destroy life in the process.[1] This strict general prohibition became also a feature of Buddhism. The other four rules of conduct laid down for the Jains were the prohibition of lying, of taking that which is not a gift (this applied in particular to the ground upon which he sat begging), of all sensual pleasures, particularly those of sex, and of all forms of attachment, even if it be the attachment of the ear to beautiful sounds or the eye to a lovely sight.

Literal fulfilment of such rules would clearly restrict the number of the faithful below the limit necessary to maintain a sect intact. No faith has survived in its original purity, for survival inevitably means compromise and adaptation. The great schism in the ranks of the Jains occurred in the first century AD, when a dispute arose concerning the necessity or propriety of going about naked. Those who insisted upon the latter principle were thence on called *Digambaras* or 'sky-clad'. Those who chose to wear clothes were called *Shwetambaras* or 'white-robed'. Further schismatic movements later divided these sects into numerous others. Nevertheless, the major principles of Jainism, having been stated and on more than one occasion lived to their logical conclusion, will probably continue to haunt the imagination of a minority of mankind for whom the great world religions leave too much room for the practice of the extremes of *askesis*. There is a spiritual athleticism which requires restriction rather than freedom for its exercise. Nor, as we know, has the figure of the emaciated naked fakir, periodically threatening starvation and defying the authorities to stop him, ceased to fascinate and to disturb modern India.

[1] The Jains were some of the first to set up veterinary hospitals.

6

The Buddha

Work out your salvation with diligence

The Birth Story

Within a few years of Mahavira there was born at the foot of the Himalayas, on the frontiers of Oudh and Nepal, a man whose life and personality have left a more lasting impression on the oriental world than any other. Gotama Buddha was one of those great innovators of thought whose career has become so encompassed with legend and poetry that he appears, at a remove of more than two thousand years, to be more than mortal. At the same time, this superhuman figure seems not merely to have preached but to have possessed to a degree, without precedent, the qualities which, no doubt with a certain irony, we call human: gentleness, kindness, tolerance, humility. Like most other apostles of the divine connection, his birth has been made the subject of elaborate and, to our minds, unnecessarily complicated legend. And like all the *Nebiim*, his mission was the result of a supposedly divine revelation. Like them all, except Christ, he was regarded by his disciples as merely one among a number of other saviours of mankind, or Buddhas. Finally, and in this respect resembling only Mahavira, he preached a faith in which there is nominally no place for a god. It is as difficult to account for the appearance on earth of a man such as Gotama Buddha as it is to imagine what would have filled the historical void if, instead of forsaking the world, he had assumed the high office for which his inheritance had prepared him.

Like Mahavira, Gotama Buddha was a man of high birth. He, too, was a member of the *Kshatriya* caste. But he was more than that. His father, Suddhodana, was a king, the ruler of Kapilavastu, a town a hundred miles north of Benares, and member of a tribe renowned for its independence and spirit, the Shakya. From the particular clan to which he belonged, the Gotama, his son Siddhartha was later known. The exact date of Gotama's birth is the subject of dispute. Most scholars now believe it to have been 563 BC. As to the manner of his birth, this was the subject of the most extraordinary legends.

In writing the life of Buddha it is impossible, even if it were desirable, to omit these legendary accretions. While we may find it difficult to imagine a devout Buddhist of reasonable education literally believing the account of Buddha's conception as given in the first of the

Jataka Books, we should be foolish to ignore even the most preposterous of the various 'Birth Stories'. In the first place it is extremely interesting to observe, in stories primarily intended for the common people (like the Egyptian legends), what kind of fact or fancy was thought most likely to stimulate popular wonder and awe. And in the second place it is important to realize that such stories, which characterize every world faith, were intended to be accepted in a mood not so much of credulity as of suspended belief and disbelief. To say that these legends amount simply to poetry is not therefore to suggest that they are false; they are no more false than the hyperbolic utterances of a lover to his mistress. In a situation of this kind, both sides are in a conspiracy to regard such utterances as a means of expressing that which would otherwise remain unsaid or unsayable. We exaggerate the intellectual level of mankind, just as we no doubt overrate the capacity of intellect, if we suppose that belief can be sustained purely upon the basis of fact. In inviting the common man to believe in the supernatural, the leaders of a faith must accustom him to ideas in which the laws of nature are liable to frequent suspension. If art and poetry are the religion of the natural, religion is the poetry of the supernatural.

About seven hundred years after the birth of the Buddha, the various legends concerning his conception and birth were first written down. In the introduction to the *Jataka Books* we learn that history is divided into three great cycles separated from one another by varying stretches of time. The renewal of a cycle of time is heralded by an event which can best be translated by the word disturbance or, literally, 'uproar'. The first of these disturbances, which took place after the world had been in existence for a hundred thousand years, entailed the complete destruction by fire of the earth 'as far up as the Brahma heavens'. The third and final disturbance would be the establishment on earth of a universal monarchy. Between these great historical disturbances, and occurring about a thousand years after the cataclysm precipitated by the first, the central fact of history took place: namely the birth of an omniscient saviour or Buddha ('Blessed' or 'Enlightened One'), whose task was the salvation of the world.

When the time came for the guardian angels of the world to proclaim 'The Buddha uproar', we are told that the 'gods of all ten thousand worlds came together in one place', and, having ascertained who was to be the Buddha, publicly acclaimed him as such. After announcing the circumstances in which he proposed to be born, and apprising the gods of his successor Maitreya, the Buddha thereupon died and was conceived on earth in the womb of Queen Maha-Maha, the eldest of Suddhodana's two consorts. The chronicle then enters into the following details. 'At that time the midsummer festival had been proclaimed in the city of Kapilavastu, and the multitude were enjoying the feast. And Queen Maha-Maha, abstaining from strong drink, and brilliant with garlands and perfumes, took part in the festivities for six days previous to the day of the full-moon. And when it came to the day of the full-moon, she rose early, bathed in perfumed water, and dispensed four hundred thousand pieces of money in great largesse. And decked in full gala attire, she ate of the choicest food, after which she took the eight vows, and entered her elegantly furnished chamber of state. And lying down on the royal couch, she fell asleep and dreamed the following dream: The four guardian angels came and lifted her up, together with her couch, and took her away to the Himalaya mountains. There, in the Manosila tableland ... they laid her under a prodigious sal-tree, seven leagues in height, and took up their positions respectfully at one side ... Not far off was Silver Hill, and on it a golden mansion. There they spread a divine couch with its head towards the east, and laid her down upon it. Now the future Buddha had become a superb white elephant, and was wandering about at no great distance, on Gold Hill. Descending thence, he ascended Silver Hill, and approaching from the north, he plucked a white lotus with his silvery trunk, and trumpeting loudly, went into the golden mansion. And three times he walked round his mother's couch, with his right side towards it, and striking her on her right side, he seemed to enter her womb. Thus the conception took place in the midsummer festival.'

According to the story, the queen did not awake until the next day, when she at once recounted her dream to the king. He was naturally concerned to discover its significance. Accordingly he summoned in council sixty-four of the most learned Brahmanas (Brahmans) in his kingdom, and having both entertained them to a sumptuous feast and made them costly presents, he recounted the queen's dream and asked for an explanation of it. After due deliberation, the Brahmanas came to a unanimous conclusion. 'Be not anxious, great king,' they said: 'a child has planted itself in the womb of your queen, and it is a male child and not a female. You will have a son. And he, if he continue to live the household life, will become a universal monarch; but if he leave the household life and retire from the world, he will become a Buddha, and roll back the clouds of sin and folly of this world.'

Directly the earthly conception of the Buddha became known in heaven, an immense commotion took place. Thirty-two manifestations and prognostics were enumerated. The ten thousand worlds were suffused with a radiance never before seen. Cripples and invalids were suddenly healed. In all the hells of the universe the fires were extinguished. Horses neighed and elephants trumpeted 'in a manner sweet to the ear'. Musical instruments, without the intervention of an executant, played celestial tunes. The ocean turned sweet. Lotuses grew in the air. And so on. Although the queen was forty-five years old, the period of gestation passed in the most satisfactory manner. Not only did she feel unusually well, but she remained perpetually aware of the presence of the future Buddha in her womb, 'like a white thread passed through a transparent jewel'. When the birth was nearly due, she experienced a strong desire that the child should be born in the home of her family in the city of Devadada. The king, who was anxious to grant her every wish, ordered that a special highway should be constructed for her to pass along. Borne on a magnificent palanquin and accompanied by a thousand courtiers, she reach in due course a point in the road which was called Lumbini Grove, just outside the city gates. The sight of so beautiful a scene—for 'the grove was one mass of flowers from the ground to the topmost branches'—captivated her. She expressed a desire to halt there. Wandering through the sylvan loveliness, she approached a great sal-tree in the middle of the grove. As she reached out her hand towards it, one of the branches inclined towards her, and, to her surprise, the moment she touched it the birth-pangs started. Thus it came about that, still holding the branch of the sal-tree, she brought forth the young Buddha 'flashing pure and spotless, like a jewel thrown upon a vesture of Benares cloth'; for as he emerged from the womb, four angels, arriving opportunely from heaven, received him upon a golden net, while two jets of water from the sky performed the office of the ritual bath. This scene has frequently been depicted in Buddhist art. As to the queen herself, she died on the seventh day of her son's life, since 'the womb that has been occupied by a Buddha is like the shrine of a temple and can never be occupied or used again'. The boy was therefore brought up by his aunt, Maya-Prajapati.

It is reported that upon entering the world the young Buddha, facing east, surveyed the entire universe as if it were spread out before him 'like a great open court'. Like the young Zoroaster he turned his gaze deliberately and solemnly in every direction with the object apparently of ascertaining whether anyone in the world could equal him. No rival being found, he took seven strides forward and proclaimed himself, in a noble voice, the Lord of Creation. This infant 'shout of victory' may be compared with the loud laugh which was uttered by Zoroaster at his birth. The scripture informs us at this point that simultaneously with the birth of the Buddha there came into existence the famous *Bodhi* or Bo-tree, which was to play so important a part in Gotama's career.

The four signs

The Buddha's birth, like his conception, was hailed by both gods and men as an event without parallel in history. A heavenly chorus resembling that which greeted the birth of Jesus sang the praises of the young child. Buddhist tradition likewise records an event very similar to that of the visit to Bethlehem of the Three Wise Men. A saintly man called Kaladevala, well known to King Suddhodana, was accustomed after his daily meal to engage in a period of rapt meditation. On the day of the Buddha's birth he noticed that the gods with whom he was holding communion were in a state of unusual excitement. Upon his enquiring the reason, he was told that their merry-making was due to the fact that, 'a son has been born to King Suddhodana, who shall sit at the foot of the Bo-tree and become a Buddha and cause the wheel of doctrine to roll'. On receiving this information, Kaladevala, who was the Simeon of Buddhism, hurried to the royal palace and asked to see the baby. Delighted to comply with this request, the king ordered that the young prince should be dressed in his best clothes and brought in.

It seemed appropriate that the baby should be made to do reverence to so holy a man, but this was not to be. No sooner was the Buddha carried up to Kaladevala than he planted his feet firmly among the matted locks of the venerable ascetic, thus showing that there was no one on earth before whom he was prepared to do obeisance. Kaladevala at once realized that he was in the presence of a divine creature, and noticing certain sacred marks on the child's body, such as that of the 'wheel of the Law' on his foot, the old man made haste to genuflect. The king was astounded. Never had he observed such a reversal of the rules of etiquette as that a saint should pay homage to a new-born child. But his eyes now being opened, he made haste to follow Kaladevala's example.

The king thereupon called to mind the prophecy of the Brahmanas whom he had consulted about the queen's dream. How would it be revealed, he asked Kaladevala, whether the boy was to become a universal monarch or a Buddha? In reply, Kaladevala declared that the child's future destiny would be determined by four signs. If the boy were to see in due order a decrepit old man, a diseased man, a dead man, and finally a monk, then he assuredly would become a Buddha. The king reflected. He was privately resolved that his son, instead of retiring from the world, should become the ruler of a great kingdom. This young prince, he felt, was destined to rule the world. Accordingly, so as to ensure that he should not be thwarted in his design, the king ordered that guards should be posted in every direction with explicit instructions to refuse admittance to any suspicious visitor, but especially to the four types of men of whom Kaladevala had spoken.

For some years the prince lived a happy, heedless life at the royal palace. The elaborate precautions taken by his father appeared to have been effective. There was nothing that the boy lacked, no enjoyment of which his young life was deprived, no cloud of grief to overshadow an existence that came near to being idyllic. Even so, legend records that, while still a schoolboy, the prince, observing labourers at work in the fields, was suddenly overcome by the sight of human drudgery, and also of the destruction of insect life caused by the disturbance of the soil. At the age of nineteen it was decided that he should marry. The choice of a bride for such a prince was a matter of great importance; but in conformity with his upbringing he was given an opportunity of exercising his own judgment. Out of five thousand exquisitely beautiful young women he selected one who happened to be his cousin, the lovely Princess Gopa. Fearing lest a prince so accustomed to luxury might lack the virility expected of a satisfactory husband, Gopa's father invited him to undergo certain tests of strength and manliness, which he passed without difficulty. The match proved a very happy one. King Suddhodana breathed more freely. It seemed that by this new and firm attachment, which was supplemented by a number of concubines, the prince was assured a future of worldly power and prosperity. The dreaded signs had not appeared. The auspices, such as they were, pointed to a happier destiny.

One day the prince decided to go on an excursion through the immense royal estate. This was the moment for which the gods had been waiting. For they had decided that the prince's enlightenment must now begin. One of the gods, disguising himself as an old man, crippled and shaking, stationed himself on the path along which the prince and Chauna, his charioteer, were due to pass. No sooner did he catch sight of this grotesque and pitiful figure than the prince was shocked beyond measure. Never in his young life had such an object come within his view. Chauna, to whom the visitation was also vouchsafed, thereupon explained to him the nature of old age and decrepitude. For the first time the prince experienced a feeling of intense revulsion at human life and at birth in particular, to which such a horrible outcome must be attributed. Abandoning all thought of further pleasure that day, he hurried home.

The king, who was surprised at this early return, enquired of the prince's charioteer what had happened. On learning that the prince had met an old and decrepit man, he was filled with a mixture of fear and rage: emotions that were further aggravated when he learned to what depths of despondency the prince had been moved. Orders were at once given that the guard round the palace should be strengthened, and that everything should be done to prevent the prince from indulging in morbid reflections. Unfortunately, although the king watched over his son with great care and solicitude, the first ominous sign was followed in due course by the other three. In short, the prince and his charioteer encountered in succession a man riddled with disease, a corpse, and finally a monk. On each occasion Chauna was obliged to explain to his young master the nature and meaning of disease, death, and, most significant of all, renunciation. Although familiar with the first two, the charioteer knew nothing of the life of monks, for such a mode of existence was to derive its significance from the mission of the future Buddha. Nevertheless, the gods, who had impersonated the four figures in question, put it into Chauna's head to acquaint the prince with the true meaning of retirement from the world and also to recommend it as the life of greatest merit.

Perplexed and almost in despair, the king could think of nothing but how to continue to beguile the prince with amusements, distractions, and other pleasures. He realized too late that such artifices merely served to feed the young man's discontent. The proximity of a world of pain, disease, and death had wholly alienated his thoughts from common enjoyments. His past and even his present happiness had suddenly become meaningless. Gradually the attraction of a different mode of life began to assert itself : a life not of attachment to things and people but of detachment and contemplation, in which the true meaning of existence might become clear.

The great retirement

The crisis occurred soon after the birth of his first child. Devoted as he was to his young wife, the news of the birth of their son prompted him to bitter reflections. 'An impediment has been born, a fetter has been born,' was his only comment on first hearing news that filled the whole kingdom with joy. The king, who set great store by all that his son said, pondered this remark. 'Let my grandson be called Rahula (impediment),' he declared, in a mood half of fun and half of apprehension. And the boy was so named. Nevertheless there were celebrations in the city, not merely to greet the birth of the boy, but to hail his father as the most fortunate of mortals. Such frivolous jollity only made the prince's heart more heavy. The sight of a troupe of dancing girls, sprawling at rest on the floor, filled him with sudden disgust. Weary of such meretricious allurements, he had fallen asleep during the performance. Now he awoke with the feeling of one who is told that his house is on fire. He realized it was time to make what he called 'the great retirement'.

Of the prince's silent leave-taking of his family, the Jataka contains a record of moving simplicity. We can well understand how this and other episodes in the life of Buddha have come to assume a place as sacred and memorable in the mind of orthodox Buddhists as the gospel story in the mind of Christians. There is nothing in Hindu scripture, except perhaps certain episodes in the *Bhagavad-Gita*, to compare with it in respect of unaffectedness and grace of expression. Even allowing for differences in intention, the famous leave-taking of Yajnavalkya and Maitreyi in the *Upanishads* strikes the reader in contrast as absurdly intellectual and formal. 'Now the future Buddha, after he had sent Chauna on his errand (to saddle his horse Kanthaka), thought to himself, "I will just take one look at my son," and, rising from the couch on which he was sitting he went to the suite of apartments occupied by the mother of Rahula, and opened the door of her chamber. Within the chamber was burning a lamp fed with sweet-smelling oil, and the mother of Rahula lay sleeping on a couch strewn deep with jasmine and other flowers, her hand resting on the head of her son. When the future Buddha reached the threshold, he paused and gazed at the two from where he stood. "If I were to raise my wife's hand from off the child's head, and take him up, she would awake, and thus prevent my departure. I will first become a Buddha, and then come back and see my son." So saying he descended from the palace.'

Mounting his great steed Kanthaka, and instructing Chauna to hang on to its tail, the prince left the city. In order to muffle the noise of the horse's progress and of the sound of its neighing, the gods took special measures; 'at every step he took they placed the palms of their hands under his feet'. On arriving at the gates of the city a formidable obstacle presented itself. The gates, which had been specially constructed to prevent the prince from leaving the city unknown to his father, required a thousand men to move them. The scriptural account informs us that the future Buddha, being providentially endowed with 'strength that was equal when reckoned in elephant-power to ten thousand million elephants', could without difficulty have either opened the great leaves of the doors, or lifted himself, his horse and his faithful charioteer collectively over them. This feat proved unnecessary, for the god who inhabited the gates, realizing that the future Buddha wished to leave the city, opened the portals to let him pass.

Scarcely had the prince ventured into open country when he was assailed by a formidable temptation. The Prince of Darkness, Mara,[1] assuming visible shape, informed him that within seven days he was due to become the great ruler of whom the Brahmanas had spoken. Renouncing all intention to seek enlightenment in the forest, he must turn back and prepare to govern an empire. The prince scorned such advice, declaring that he did not covet earthly sovereignty. 'I am about to cause the ten thousand worlds,' he said, 'to thunder with my becoming a Buddha.' Mara was not deterred. 'I shall catch you,' he threatened, 'the very first time you have a lustful, malicious or unkind thought.' Accordingly, like a shadow, Mara followed the young prince on his wanderings, never despairing of winning him from the sacred mission to which he was dedicated. Thus, at the outset of his career as the saviour of men, the Buddha, like Zoroaster and Jesus, was assailed by forces of evil intent not so much on destroying as on corrupting him. And in each case the bait offered was that of temporal power.

When the prince had reached the forest to which so many holy men and ascetics had retired, he dismissed his faithful charioteer, after presenting him with the now unwanted ornaments and rich clothes. A god, disguised as a hermit, provided the young man with rags appropriate to a beggar. Chauna had also expressed a wish to retire from the world, but his master insisted that such was not his vocation. Then Gotama, professing ignorance of their way of life, asked the forest sages to instruct him in the various methods of acquiring wisdom and sanctity. He had already heard vague stories of their rigorous discipline: how some lived on a few grains of corn, others on grass, others still, like the snakes, apparently off air.[2] By submitting to various degrees of pain, the ascetics believed themselves near to attaining moral perfection: 'pain', they declared, 'is the root of merit'. This attitude towards life and suffering, while impressing the future Buddha, failed to satisfy him. He saw in such striving after merit a powerful impulse of attachment, a covert hope of being reborn, a subtle clinging to life; whereas since his first glimpse of the aged man, the cripple and the corpse, he had nourished the conviction that birth itself was evil, a thing to be brought to an end. Action bred life. And however near they came to snapping the last vital thread, these ascetics were still men of action. The ascetic path, it seemed, was a road leading not to *Nirvana* but back again to the world of illusion and rebirth.

With courteous expressions of appreciation on both sides, Gotama quietly left the sage Arata and his community of ascetics and embarked once more upon his wanderings. Meanwhile, when Chauna arrived home with Kanthaka, the news of Gotama's departure for the great retirement spread rapidly among the courtiers. Most inconsolable of all was the young prince's wife, who called to mind the very different conduct of former seekers after truth. 'If,' she declared, 'he wishes to practise a religious life after abandoning me, his lawful wife, widowed—what is his religion, who wishes to follow practices without

[1] The English 'nightmare' is a derivative of this word.
[2] An ancient superstition.

his lawful wife to share them with him? He has surely never heard of the monks of olden times, his own ancestor, Mahasudarsa and the rest—how they went with their wives into the forest—that he thus wishes to follow a religious life without me... Surely it must be that this fond lover of religion, knowing that my mind was secretly quarrelling even with my beloved, lightly and without fear has deserted me thus angry, in the hope of obtaining heavenly nymphs in Indra's world.' Her thoughts then turned impulsively to the young baby Rahula, and it seemed as if her lord had committed a double outrage in thus deserting both mother and son.

On arriving at a place of great beauty called Uruvela, about fifty miles south of Patna, the future Buddha decided to resume his meditations. To divest his mind of distracting thoughts, he resolved to begin a fast of steadily increasing rigour. He tried the experiment of living on jubjube fruits or a few grains of sesame and rice, steadily diminishing his daily diet until he confined it to a single grain. His flesh sagged and wasted until it scarcely stretched over his protruding bones. 'The mark of my seat,' he later confessed, 'was like a camel's footprint, through the little food. The bones of my spine, when bent and straightened, were like a row of spindles through the little food. And as, in a deep well, the deep low-lying sparkling of the water was seen, so in my eye-sockets was seen the deep, low-lying sparkle of my eyes through the little food. And as a bitter gourd, cut off raw, is cracked and withered through rain and sun, so was my skin withered through the little food. When I thought I would touch the skin of my stomach, I actually took hold of my spine.' In order that no one should accuse him of having failed to practise self-mortification in earnest, he pursued these austerities to a point just short of suicide.

Living thus scarcely above subsistence-level, Gotama spent as long as six years seeking to arrive at sanctity by way of absorption in self-denial. Finally it occurred to him that, despite his feats of mental concentration, he was following a course little better than that of the ascetics for whom he had expressed such contempt. His very absorption in the practice of self-denial was nothing but a form of absorption in the Self. Moreover, the fury of his efforts at mortification, far from inducing a mood of composure, bred instability and irritation. As long as he continued to toy with life, or to flirt with death, by following the path of extreme ascetism, the goal he sought eluded him. He must recover his balance. To do so, however, he must recover his strength. Mental calm must be sought along a path midway between extreme self-denial and self-indulgence. 'True meditation,' he concluded, 'is produced in him whose mind is self-possessed and at rest.' A young peasant girl, Sujata, opportunely brought him milk and rice. By resuming a normal, if still frugal diet, he at length acquired the robustness of the prince to whom nothing had been denied. But his change of attitude alienated the five disciples who had gathered round him.

Enlightenment

In abandoning the spectacular austerities of the hermits and sages of his day, Gotama did not renounce his spiritual exercises. With the return of bodily vigour, he embarked upon a further course of meditation. On this occasion he realized that his search must either bring him within sight of his objective, or end in futility and disillusion. An unshakable decision must be made. 'Then he sat down,' records the *Buddha-Charita* (Book XII), 'on his hams in a posture immovably firm and with his limbs gathered into a mass like a sleeping serpent's hood, exclaiming, "I will not rise from this position on the earth until I have obtained my utmost aim".'

The tree under which Gotama sat was the famous *Bodhi* or Bo-tree which had come to life at the moment of the prince's birth. The word *Bodhi* means literally knowledge: the tree itself was a fig-tree to which the people gave the name of Pipal. This revered spot is now called Bodh Gaya, situated in Bihar, where about AD 500 an immense temple was built. Nearby stands a fig-tree, possibly a descendant of the sacred Bo-tree itself. While sitting at this spot, Gotama experienced the second and most violent of the series of temptations by Mara. The god of evil and darkness had mobilized all his friends throughout the universe. There came demons of every conceivable shape, all of equal horror, whirling in the air, at once threatening and cajoling: for after the assault of the demons, with their volley of projectiles, came a host of aerial temptresses, hoping by contrast to stir his sensuality. So vivid and yet horrifying is the description of this host from hell that we are made to realize its symbolic purpose: Gotama, on the point of making up his mind, is assailed for the last time by the doubts and uncertainties, as well as the pleasures and allurements, of human existence. It was the last step, the mountaineer's final heave to safety, when for a moment all seems in danger of being lost. True to his vow, Gotama refused to be distracted. The compass of his will trembled, but was not deflected. As his mind gathered itself for a supreme effort of concentration, suddenly, at the first hint of dawn, 'the shell of ignorance was broken,' and he attained to perfect knowledge. He became, 'the perfectly wise, the Bhagavat (Lord), the Arahat, the king of the law, the Tathagata, he who has attained the knowledge of all forms, the Lord of all Science.' This insight followed close upon a vision of all eternity in a single flash, with the entire chain of births at every level of existence strung out before his eyes.

Gotama's experience beneath the Bo-tree represents the authentic—to some millions of mankind the most authentic—moment of illumination of the *Nabi*, the prophet of divine connection. To the Western mind, the curious feature of this particular vision is that it appears to illuminate a void: there is no God to hold, as it were, the other end of the string.[1] It is true that there is no God. On the other hand there is such a thing as divinity, and by the law of *Karma* there is divine punishment and retribution. This amazingly complicated law is operated from a realm outside time and beyond human scrutiny. Gotama did not invent it; he accepted it without question as the most important fact of experience. Like all prophets, Gotama's mission was not so

[1] This point is discussed again in the Conclusion.

much to introduce a new law as to reaffirm, to recall, to re-establish old communications.

Believing himself at last to have found the secret of man's deliverance from illusion, Gotama forthwith became conscious of his Buddhahood. Such consciousness did not entail the belief that he was the first 'Enlightened One' to be born among men. There had been former Buddhas or Jainas. There would be others, such as Maitreya. Like Mahavira and Zoroaster, Gotama embarked upon his mission in the belief that enlightenment had been conferred upon him at a particular time for a particular purpose. To his disciples and their successors may be traced the conviction that his mission, though one among others, was unique.[1] Of the great religious prophets, only Jesus seems deliberately to have excluded a later incarnation of God, except in so far as he hinted at his own return to supervise the liquidation of history.

According to the scriptures, Gotama's assumption of Buddhahood cast the evil powers of the universe into utter dejection. It is said that Mara, feeling his power to be on the point of extinction, snatched at a last expedient for frustrating the Buddha's mission. This was to persuade him to ascend at once to heaven. 'O holy one,' he accordingly addressed Gotama, 'be pleased to enter Nirvana, thy desires are accomplished.' By refusing this subtle invitation Gotama became in the eyes of one school of Buddhists not merely a Buddha in the orthodox sense but a Bodhisattva, or one who for the sake of saving the world abstains voluntarily from entering Nirvana. 'I will first establish in perfect wisdom,' he said, 'worlds as numerous as the sand, and then I will enter Nirvana.' Thus the forces of evil were permanently held in check by the Buddha, who deferred by eighty years his passage to extinction.

A few weeks after receiving Enlightenment, the Buddha left for the holy city of Benares, making several converts on the journey. While orthodox theology conceives of the Buddha as a majestic and kingly figure, the man who was to change the outlook of so many millions went about in his lifetime as a beggar living on alms. Moreover the assumption of Buddhahood conferred upon Gotama no particular gift for influencing his fellow-men, save that of example and eloquence. His mission possessed nothing in common with that of the magician or medicine man. Instead of curing suffering, he merely preached the truth about it. The disciple, having been enlightened, needed to achieve his own salvation. Nor did enlightenment involve any particular exercise of the intellect. None of the great prophets or *Nebiim* have been metaphysicians, except perhaps Krishna (whose arguments in the *Bhagavad-Gita* may have received later elaboration). 'The assurance of Nirvana,' said the Buddha on one occasion, 'is not an assurance of numbers nor logic; it is not the mind that is to be assured but the heart' (*Lankavatara Sutra*). The Buddha not merely despised metaphysical speculation; he regarded it at best as a distraction, an unnecessary refinement, like acrobatics, and at worst as an obstacle to

[1] He is sometimes declared to be the ninth incarnation of Vishnu (by the Brahmans who succeeded Buddhism).

the apprehension of simple, if unpalatable, truths. The prophet of divine connection does not need metaphysics to convey the nature of divinity. Metaphysics is the product of a disputatious discipleship.[1]

In the north of Benares is a Deer Park which, like Bodh Gaya, remains a place of sacred associations for Buddhists. It was to this quarter that the Buddha, havisng crossed the Ganges by a form of levitation, directed his steps. Perhaps he knew that there he would find the disciples whom he had recently alienated. When they saw him approaching, they felt a common resentment. 'This is Gotama,' they said one to another, 'the ascetic who has abandoned his self-control. He wanders about now, greedy, of impure soul, unstable, and with his senses under no firm control, devoted to enquiries regarding the frying-pan. We will not ask after his health, nor rise to meet him, nor address him, nor offer him a welcome, nor a seat, nor bid him enter into our dwelling.' The Buddha perceived their hostility but ignored it. The simplicity of his approach, begging-bowl in hand, disarmed them. They found themselves rising to their feet. 'Know that I am Jaina,' he said quietly, 'and that I have come to give the first wheel of the law to you.' And having received the five men into a new mendicant order, he proceeded to preach to them the first of his great sermons, that which is entitled the 'Discourse of setting in motion the Wheel of the Doctrine', sometimes regarded as the Buddhist equivalent of the Sermon on the Mount.

First teaching

The Wheel of the Doctrine or the Law was so-called because it is concerned with the 'wheel' of human life and rebirth. Without enlightenment, existence is nothing but a succession of futile lives, a treadmill of mortality, *samsara.* How, then, was enlightenment to be attained? The Buddha's sermon opens with an exposition of the two extremes to be avoided. The first and obvious extreme is that of sensual pleasure. Nothing causes the Wheel to turn so much as indulgence. For pleasure increases our dissatisfaction not merely with everything else but with itself: faced with this void, we need more of the same kind to fill it, so that we proceed to engage in a process akin to borrowing ourselves out of debt. The other extreme to be avoided is that of excessive mortification. According to the Buddha, this extreme was no more profitable than the first, for it not merely results in the increase of agitation but leads logically to extinction before any real merit has been acquired. Such was the objection that the Buddha, had he known it (and it is possible that he did), would have preferred against the teaching of Mahavira. The true object to be attained is that of calmness and composure, the condition and usually the sign of wisdom. Following the great sages of whom we have written, the Buddha defines the means of inducing this frame of mind as the cultivation of an attitude of 'right-

[1] We do not agree with Bishop Gore when he says in his *Philosophy of the Good Life* that Buddha's 'appeal was in the highest degree intellectual, and such as the uneducated or those who were unversed in abstract speculation could not have understood'. Buddha eschewed abstract speculation.

ness'—a rightness which derives its exactitude by being the product of a 'middle path' between extremes. The 'noble eightfold path', as it is called, consists of right views, right intent, right speech, right conduct, right means of livelihood, right endeavour, right mindedness, right meditation. By the cultivation of this balanced attitude we shall attain to the cessation of that pervasive suffering which is the inevitable result and accompaniment of *craving*. Craving, as the Buddha remarks with characteristic insight, is that which causes 'the renewal of becoming'.

The Buddha's analysis of craving has come to be known in scripture as the Four Noble Truths. They form an acute summary of pain, the product of craving. Firstly, comes the definition of what is painful, birth, age, sickness, sorrow, despair, ugliness and so on. Secondly comes the definition of the cause of pain, which is craving. Thirdly comes the definition of how pain is to be overcome, which is by non-attachment. Fourthly comes the definition of the doctrine whereby non-attachment may be attained, which is the Eightfold Path.

Beginning with the five ascetics or *Bhikkus*, who became the first genuine Buddhist monks, the Buddha proceeded to make converts by the hundred, by the thousand, and in due course by the million. Accredited missionaries were sent throughout Oudh, Bihar, and Bengal, but in effect every monk with his begging-bowl was a missionary, a witness to enlightenment. 'Go your rounds,' was the Buddha's daily order to his monks, 'for the salvation of many, for the happiness of many, with compassion for all, for the good of gods and men.' Although the Buddha both preached and practised the virtues of gentleness, humility, self-discipline, and forbearance, it will not do to imagine him as lacking in energy, fire, or even passion. Some of the Buddha's recorded sermons are instinct with the kind of gentleness and sweetness that we associate not always accurately with St Francis of Assisi. Others, particularly the famous Fire Sermon or the 'Sermon on the Lessons to be drawn from Burning', one of the greatest of his utterances, exhibit the kind of passion that we find in the major Hebrew prophets, besides being conveyed in language that poets have not always sustained at such a pitch of intensity. The Fire Sermon ought not to be quoted in excerpts: it forms one long passage of incandescent expression. Never before, and in no other part of the world except perhaps Babylon among the captive Jews—for Buddha may have been a contemporary of the second Isaiah—had human nature been, as it were, branded with such eloquence:

> All things, O priests, are on fire. Forms are on fire. Eye-consciousness is on fire. Impressions received by the eye are on fire. And whatever sensation, pleasant or unpleasant or indifferent, originates in dependence on impressions received by the fire, that also is on fire. And with what are these on fire?
>
> With the fire of passion, say I, with the fire of hatred, with the fire of infatuation. With birth, old age, death, sorrow, lamentation, misery, grief, and despair are they on fire.
>
> The ear is on fire. Sounds are on fire . . . The nose is on fire. Odours are on

fire ... The tongue is on fire. Tastes are on fire ... The body is on fire. Things tangible are on fire ... The mind is on fire. Ideas are on fire ... Mind consciousness is on fire. Impressions received by the mind are on fire. And whatever sensation, pleasant or unpleasant, or indifferent, originates in dependence on impressions received by the mind, that also is on fire. And with what are these on fire?

With the fire of passion, say I, with the fire of hatred, with the fire of infatuation. With birth, old age, death, sorrow, lamentation, misery, grief, and despair are they on fire.

Perceiving this, O priests, the learned and noble disciple conceives an aversion for the eye, conceives an aversion for forms, conceives an aversion for eye-consciousness, conceives an aversion for impressions received by the eye; and whatever sensation, pleasant or unpleasant, or indifferent, originates in dependence on impressions received by the eye, for that also he conceives an aversion ... And in conceiving this aversion, he becomes divested of passion, and by the absence of passion he becomes free, and when he is free, he becomes aware that he is free; and he knows that rebirth is exhausted, that he has lived the holy life, that he has done what it behoved him to do, and that he is no more for this world.

It may be wondered how a philosophy based almost wholly upon aversion for everything human and natural should have become the 'view of life' of hundreds of millions of persons. Would not the logical conclusion of such repudiations of life be the self-starvation of the Jaina? Evidently not. Having deliberately experimented with such extreme asceticism, Buddha renounced it as a spiritual blind-alley. The professional *fakir* tends to be an exhibitionist. His rigours are displayed for all the world to see. The attitude to desire preached by the Buddha excludes such demonstrativeness. The struggle to overcome desire and craving is an inward thing. And whereas in the Buddha we find a rejection of the flesh, this rejection is not accompanied by the hysteria of much Western puritanism, which is simply evidence of covert attraction. To express unbounded loathing for the life of the senses is to add fuel to one of the 'fires' which needs most urgently to be quenched, namely the fire of hatred.

It was not merely in the fire Sermon that Buddha had recourse to the metaphor of fire. The image occurs again and again in his recorded sayings. We may recall that just before the Great retirement, when he was awakening from the sleep into which the palace celebrations had plunged him, he experienced the feeling of one whose house was on fire. In other words, practical measures for salvation were, in his view, more important than enquiries into the origin of life, evil, God. Whenever the Buddha was asked questions about God, his responses were evasive, equivocal, and sometimes frankly unsatisfactory.[1] On one occasion, for instance, someone asked him, 'Sir, is there a God?' To which he replied not with a statement but with the further question, 'Did I say there is a God?' The questioner, confounded, rejoined with, 'Then there is no God, Sir?' To which the Buddha quickly replied, 'Did I say there is no God?' Such an evasive attitude, extraordinary in a religious leader, is comprehensible only if we bear in mind a remark that he was

[1] We shall see that Confucius responded in the same way.

fond of making to his disciples, once more introducing the familiar image: 'When a house is on fire, do you first go and trace the origin of the fire, or do you try to extinguish it?' 'The Tathagata has no theories', sums up the mission of the Buddha very succinctly. He had only practice. In the great Buddhist epic poem called the *Dhammapada*, which some oriental scholars place higher than the *Bhagavad-Gita* itself, occur the words, 'How is there laughter, how is there joy, as the world is always burning?'

Homecoming

To trace the events of the Buddha's life from the moment of his Enlightenment, which occurred about the age of thirty-five, to that of his death about forty-five years later, is rendered difficult by reason of the variety of legends that has accumulated around his name. Of the great events of his life to which we can attach credence, his return to his home country and his family is perhaps the most dramatic. Whatever intelligence of his acts and conduct had reached the remote Himalayan kingdom, the old king and the still young wife were totally unprepared for the sight which finally greeted them, though they had frequently sent messages to the Buddha begging him to return. Modestly robed in yellow, like a conventional ascetic, with shaven head and beardless face,[1] the prince who had exchanged an earthly for a heavenly kingdom entered the town of his birth in the manner his family least expected. The Jaina, whom no woman could touch, was not to be greeted by his own wife. And so the townsfolk were amazed to see the princess standing aside as her husband moved towards the royal palace from which he had departed with such stealth.

The Buddha's visit was a time of great missionary activity. But although Gotama had renounced all earthly ties, he was scrupulous in paying respect to his family. He even made a special journey to the Lumbini Grove, where, to quote the *Buddha-Charita*, 'he saw the holy fig-tree and stood by it remembering his birth, with a smile'. This was the only occasion, it would seem, on which the subject of birth provoked in him something other than dejection. Having honoured the memory of his mother, he proceeded to receive into his Order a large number of his fellow-citizens, including members of his family, the chief being his wife, son, and brother. The brother, Nanda, was enticed into the Order by trickery, and forcibly shaved. The account of this press-gang operation is perhaps the only outright amusing episode in the scriptures of any faith. Thus Gotama's promise to return to his family was fulfilled, and the indignation of his wife gave way to lasting devotion. The Buddha never again returned home, though it is recorded that he undertook a spiritual journey to receive his father's dying breath, and on one occasion he spent three months in heaven instructing his mother in the Law.

Given his detestation of sex, the admission of women into his Order cannot have been made without considerable reflection. When he

[1] Cf. Edwin Arnold. *The Light of Asia*: 'Three plain cloths, yellow, of stitched stuff, worn with shoulder bare, a girdle, almsbowl, strainer.'

finally decided to permit women nuns, beginning with his aunt Maya-Prajapati, he is reported to have observed wryly that in so doing he was reducing by at least half, the period during which his religion would exert influence in the world. Apparently he estimated this period at five hundred years: Buddhism has already flourished for four times as long. But although he warned his male followers to have as little as possible to do with women, he personally showed no reluctance to frequent their company. When, for example, the well-known courtezan Ambapali met him in her private mango grove at Vesali, whither he had apparently deliberately repaired, he greeted her with extreme politeness and at once proceeded to 'instruct, arouse, incite, and gladden her with religious discourse'. When, further, she invited him next day to a meal at her house, he accepted the invitation (by preserving the silence that gave consent) and arrived in company with his brethren, including his favourite Ananda,[1] whom he was specially to warn against womenkind. On this occasion he likewise took the opportunity of preaching at length to his hostess, following which the latter, like Mary Magdalene, hailed him as a divine messenger to humanity and made him a gift of land. It would seem that the Buddha wished to demonstrate, by a show of indifference, that he observed no distinction among humankind, whether of sex or of caste, the righteous or the sinful. Nevertheless he took care to enjoin his disciples, whose weaknesses he realized, not to become friends, companions, or intimates of sinners. Similarly, although he expected his monks 'not to stop on their way to Nirvana', he knew as well as Zoroaster that the majority of mankind could be saved only by degrees. In the account of the Buddha's daily habits taken from the commentary by Buddhaghosha[2] on *Digha-Nikaya*, a collection of long Buddhist discourses, we read that: 'when he had finished his (morning) meal, the Blessed One, with due consideration for the different dispositions of their minds, would so teach them the doctrine that some would become established in the refuges, some in the five precepts, some would become converted, some would attain to the fruit of only one returning (to earth), or of never returning, while some would become established in the highest fruit, that of saintship, and would retire from the world.' The truth is that in spite of the extreme rigour of his doctrine the Buddha, like Jesus, possessed an unusual insight into human frailty; and his compassion was equal to his understanding.

Approaching death

After the stay in Vesali, where his conduct was naturally considered by some to be an outrage, Gotama, now in the forty-fifth year of his Buddhahood, decided to spend the rainy season in the village of Beluva. Meanwhile, he had dismissed the greater number of his disciples. When the rains had set in, he suddenly fell ill. He was racked with pain, and seemed to be on the point of death. Throughout this ordeal, one thought obsessed him: he could not permit himself to die

[1] Ananda was also a member of the Shakya clan, and a cousin of the Buddha.

[2] Lived fifth century AD.

without taking leave of the members of his Order. He therefore decided to prolong his life for a brief period.

Mustering his will in an effort almost as great as that which had carried him, all those years ago, from humanity to Buddhahood, he 'bent the sickness down again', and it temporarily retreated. The account of his subsequent conversation with Ananda is exceedingly moving. Ananda, who confessed that his own frame had wasted as soon as he learnt of his master's illness, rejoiced that it was still possible to receive a final benediction and farewell message. 'What does the Order expect?' replied the Blessed One. 'I had preached the truth without making any distinction between exoteric and esoteric doctrine: for in respect of truths, Ananda, the Tathagata[1] has no such thing as the closed fist of a teacher, who keeps some things back... Now the Tathagata, Ananda, thinks not that it is he who should lead the Brotherhood, or that the Order is dependent upon him. Why then should he leave instructions in any matter concerning the Order? I too, O Ananda, am now grown old and full of years, my journey is drawing to its close, I have reached the sum of my days, I am turning eighty years of age; and just as the worn-out cask, Ananda, can be kept going only with the help of thongs, so methinks the body of the Tathagata can only be kept going by bandaging it up.' He then enjoined Ananda to 'remain strenuous, self-possessed and mindful, having overcome both the hankering and the dejection common in the world'.

For a time the Buddha continued to lead his old mendicant life. One morning he invited Ananda to spend the day with him at the Chapola shrine. It was here that he received his last visit from Mara, the Evil One. Assuming a role superficially similar to that of Nicodemus, though animated by purely cynical motives, Mara hailed the approaching death of the Buddha as the final triumph of Good over Evil. The Blessed One, realizing the irony of Mara's invocation, answered him: 'O Evil One! make thyself happy, the death of the Tathagata will take place before long. At the end of three months from this time the Tathagata will pass away.' Having uttered these words, he decided to renounce that ingrained will to live upon which alone he had depended since the onset of his illness. As his hold upon life relaxed, the elements suffered a series of convulsions equal to that which had occurred at his conception. There were thunderstorms, earthquakes, and similar portents.

The last episode traditionally related of the Buddha is that concerning his visit to Chunda, the smith, who incidentally and unwittingly was responsible for the master's death. It is a curious story. The Buddha decided to stay for a while at Chunda's mango grove, where his host invited him to a meal of sweet rice, cakes, and truffles. When the Blessed One was seated with his brethren, he directed Chunda to serve the sweet rice and cakes to the others, and to reserve the truffles for himself alone. He went further. He stipulated that whatever truffles were left over should be burned. 'For I see no one,' he

[1] The title Tathagata literally means, 'he who neither comes from anywhere nor goes to anywhere'.

explained, 'on earth nor in Mara's realm, nor in Brahma's heaven, by whom, when he has eaten it, that food can be properly assimilated save by a Tathagata.'

Within a short time of leaving Chunda's mango grove, the already declining Buddha was once more taken ill, this time with an acute form of dysentery. He behaved as if this sudden malady was something for which he had been waiting. In his sufferings, however, he did not fail to take account of the feelings of his late host. Realizing that Chunda would be filled with horror and self-reproach at having been the indirect cause of the Blessed One's distress, he specially instructed Ananda to comfort and reassure him. To have provided the food whereby the Buddha should 'pass away by that utter passing away in which nothing whatever remains behind' amounted, he explained, to a kind of merit. Undertaken in good faith and as a token of respect, Chunda's act would earn for its perpetrator a remission of *Karma*, beginning with an extension of his life-span on earth and a substantial increase in fortune. So important an instrument of providence would be watched over by providence until the end of time. Thus was Chunda rewarded.

At a spot called the Sala Grove of the Mallas, by the River Hiranyavati, the Buddha, now wasted with illness, decided to prepare for his last moments. It is said that the beautiful Sala trees, perceiving the recumbent body of the Blessed One, rained down their blossoms, while heavenly music was wafted earthwards, 'out of reverence for the successor of the Buddhas of old'. Perceiving this tribute on the part of nature, the Buddha turned to Ananda and said: 'it is not thus, Ananda, that the Tathagata is rightly honoured.... But the brother and sister who continually fulfils all the greater and the lesser duties—it is he who rightly honours the Tathagata with the worthiest homage.' He then proceeded to specify the places of pilgrimage, four in number, at which the pilgrims and disciples should be encouraged to assemble after death had deprived them of a living master. These were to be the place of Buddha's birth, the place at which he had attained to the vision of reality whereby his Buddhahood was confirmed, the place where he began to establish his heavenly Kingdom, and the spot at which he was at that moment lying down to die. These places have been held sacred until this day.

It was chiefly to his faithful friend and disciple Ananda, the St John of Buddhism, that the Master confided his last thoughts, which have been recorded at length. If the Enlightened One did not bequeath any message longer than that which we have quoted, he left a series of miscellaneous instructions. It was on this occasion, for example, that he issued the warning to Ananda against women to which we have referred:

'How are we to conduct ourselves, Lord, with regard to womenkind?'

'As not seeing them, Ananda.'

'But if we should see them, what are we to do?'

'No talking, Ananda.'

'But if they should speak to us, Lord, what are we to do?'

'Keep wide awake, Ananda.'[1]

In addition to this stern admonition, the Buddha gave certain instructions about the future administration of the Order from which we may observe the beginnings of inequality and privilege: features originally absent from the Buddhist Order, which represented not merely a form of opposition to the Brahman caste but a tacit protest against caste in general. Whereas during the Buddha's lifetime it had been the custom for the brethren to address one another as 'Avus' or 'Friend', the Master expressed a wish that such familiarity should thenceforth be abandoned, and that the elder brethren, while continuing to address their juniors in the old manner or by name, must themselves be greeted with the word 'Sir' or even 'Venerable Sir'. On the other hand, the Buddha, who regarded his doctrine as likely to remain valid only until the arrival of another Buddha, in the true Jaina fashion, expressed a wish not to hamper his later disciples with rules and precepts likely to become out of date. Finally, he reaffirmed his faith in his disciples, whom he declared one and all—even the most backward—to have reached that stage of enlightenment at which rebirth into suffering was no longer necessary.

When he realized that his master was actually about to die, Ananda besought him to prolong his earthly existence for a while longer, and even, since it lay within his power, for as much as an eon. The Buddha reproached him almost sternly for expressing that which was contrary to the design of providence, and Ananda was finally persuaded to acquiesce in his master's bodily departure. 'Have I not formerly declared to you,' reasoned the Buddha, 'that it is the very nature of all things, near and dear unto us, that we must divide ourselves from them, leave them, sever ourselves from them? How, then, Ananda, can this be possible—whereas anything, whatever born, brought into being and organized, contains within itself the inherent necessity of dissolution—how then can this be possible that such a being should be dissolved?' So saying, he ordered Ananda to assemble all the brethren, to whom he delivered a brief address, his important last public utterance, in which he recapitulated the basic tenets of his doctrine, ending with words that have become famous: 'All component things must grow old. *Work out your salvation with diligence.*'[2]

Having finally severed communication with mankind, the Buddha sank into a condition of mystical possession, passing successively through the four states of *Jhanas* which culminate with the attainment of unitive vision. By entering these states the soul gradually shed, as it were, its superficial forms of consciousness, and attained to the condition of 'right rapture', the final stage of the famous Eightfold Path, the simultaneous possession of everything and of nothing, *Nirvana*. Thus the Bodhisattva, having excluded himself from heaven to save mankind from the tyranny of egoism and desire, signified the end

[1] It is interesting to note that in Buddhist mythology the goddess of love or desire, Rati, is represented as the daughter of Mara himself.

[2] Cf. the words pronounced by the doctor-psychiatrist in T. S. Eliot's play *The Cocktail Party*, Act II.

of his mission by returning to the realm of *Brahman*. The final 'life' which his *Karma* had reserved for him had taken its course.

In conformity with instructions given to Ananda, and as a token of the respect in which the people held him, the Buddha received a funeral worthy of the highest nobleman or ruler. His ashes (for his body was cremated) were divided among the members of his family and certain powerful men who had approved of his mission. An urn discovered at the end of the last century, and inscribed to the effect that it contained 'the remains of the exalted Buddha of the Shakya clan', is considered to be that which was deposited by his family under a monument still standing.

The Doctrine of Karma

At one time it was the fashion to cast doubt upon the existence of such great religious leaders as Zoroaster, Buddha, and Christ. No doubt history would be less perplexing if we could accept this view. But all the evidence suggested that such people really existed; and what is difficult to explain is not their historical authenticity but how their teaching, opposed as it is to certain fundamental instincts of mankind, should have obtained its prolonged hold upon the human mind.

The understanding of Gotama Buddha's thought is made difficult for the Western mind in two ways. Some of it is very nearly outside our comprehension, while that which is within the grasp of our intellects can still be misconceived. Whereas the Buddha distrusted 'metaphysics' as much as did Socrates, and discouraged futile speculation about the origin of the world, he held very definite views about cosmology, or the way in which life in the universe manifested itself. This Buddhist theory of the cosmos differed little in essentials from that which has been entertained in India from the earliest times; that is a point to which we have already drawn attention. Not once did the Buddha, or indeed any other known Jaina, refer to the origin or author of this extraordinary theory of conduct, one of the most comprehensive that has ever been formuated. He merely accepted as a fact not to be disputed.[1]

There would seem to be no reason why reincarnation or transmigration should not commend itself as a belief to the Western mind. Among the unproved and unprovable theories of morality, it is not merely the most ingenious but the most logical. The 'practical' Western man, with his strong sense of rewards and deserts, might have taken the idea to his heart more enthusiastically than the Oriental, with his strong sense of fatality (a very different notion).[2] Why, except in very isolated

[1] And not to be argued about either. Buddha listed it among four 'unthinkables' (*Kamma-vipako* in Pali).

[2] At times the Oriental fatalism overshadows the ethical aspect of *Karma*: cf. the *Vishnu Purana*: 'Birth, education, conduct, character virtue or connection avails not a man in this life. The effects of one's *Karma* and penance, done in a prior existence, fructify, like a tree at the opposite time, in the next.' True: but the exertions in the 'next' existence must presumably also fructify in their turn, or the burden of *Karma* would never be reduced.

cases,[1] has he never done so? The suggestion of the present writer is that the idea was never preached to him. In other words, it seems reasonable to believe that the doctrine of the transmigration of souls was conceived and preached in the Orient by a Jaina earlier than any of which we have record, perhaps earlier even than the 'gods' themselves, for the latter, as the Buddha was careful to insist, were just as much subject to its law as men and animals.[2] Now a doctrine may derive a large part of its stimulus, and achieve much of its effect, from the fact that it runs directly counter to the temperamental instincts of the audience. The idea of fatality, which represents the furthest remove from a just and logical view of the universe, needs to be corrected by an opposite notion. The Jaina or *Nabi* gives the people what it lacks. Hence the Eastern faith which has achieved least success in the Orient is Christianity, with its indifference to the theory of transmigration. And its prodigious success in the West may be due to its emphasis upon aspects of conduct which needed, and still need, perpetual reaffirmation for a civilization ever prone to materialist excess.

If, in consenting to be born into the world, the Buddha was voluntarily deferring his personal salvation, this does not imply that he was a 'perfect' man who, like Jesus Christ, abandoned heaven for the purpose of redeeming humanity. The Buddha had personally endured all the processes of transmigration. This had taken some time. What made the buddha 'enlightened' above all previous prophets was that he could remember all the phases of life through which he had passed. All that the unenlightened mortal knew was that his present existence, whatever its nature, was the result of his own contrivance in the sum of his previous existences; but his conduct then and there might either redress a balance seriously upset, or else still further disturb it. However brief, a lifetime of effort or sloth might effect changes of the most remarkable kind. A good man might so successfully 'work off' his *Karma* as to render further incarnation on earth unnecessary,[3] while a thoroughly bad man might be lucky to be allowed to remain within the confines of the natural world at all, but then only as some vile insect or reptile. For the wheel of existence might be eluded either by ascending to one of several different heavens, or by being consigned to one of the 136 hells of which later Buddhist theology speaks. Absolute good and absolute evil, both equally rare, would be rewarded by absolute salvation or damnation.

It is conventional to maintain that Buddhism is animated by an intense and ineradicable disgust for life. Certain statements of the Buddha, particularly in the Fire Sermon, might easily lend support to this view. As an aid to meditation, the Buddhist monks are instructed to keep before their minds such images as a skeleton, or a corpse in process of decomposition: attachment to bodily pleasures will thereby be reduced and finally repudiated. Nevertheless, the specific duties laid down for monks and mendicants were not necessarily obligatory for or-

[1] The idea appears, somewhat vaguely, in Plato.
[2] Shankara held a similar view. See p. 191.
[3] This was the avowed aim of the Yogi. See Chapter 7.

dinary laymen. Certain Christian mystics, St Catherine of Siena, for instance, were accustomed to engage in forms of 'self-discipline' of which the bare description may induce nausea; for a very effective way of 'divesting oneself of the love of created beings' (to quote the phrase of St John of the Cross) is to concentrate upon those aspects which reveal life at its most unaesthetic and humiliating pitch. Yet Christianity has always prided itself upon its freedom from the scabrous and the morbid. Likewise, the most attractive side of Buddhism is perhaps its attitude to natural beauty. If the human body was revolting, nature as a whole was beautiful. Consequently the first Buddhist monasteries were built in places of idyllic loveliness—'not too far nor too near the town, remote from the tumult and the multitude, places of repose and favourable to solitary meditation'. In such communities the brethren dwelt 'in perfect joy, without enemies in an otherwise unfriendly world'. 'Gaiety is our nourishment,' they declared.

To study Buddhism at all deeply is to become aware that what it repudiates is not 'the body' (as is the case, for example, with Christian puritanism) but *individuality*, of which the body is an obvious symbol. Hence the attraction to be 'alone with nature' was also that of being, in Shelley's phrase, 'at one with nature'. No longer was the individual lost and unattached. 'In the verdant forest,' says the monk, 'in an airy cave among the mountains, I wish to bathe my body, and I wish to walk alone in the vast and lovely woods. When in the sky the storm clouds clash their cymbals, when torrents of rain fill the highways of the air, and the monk, in a mountain crevice, abandons himself to meditation, there is no greater joy. On the flower-covered river-bank he sits in ecstatic meditation: surely there is no greater joy than that.'

Joy and ecstasy, far from being banished from the life of both monks and laymen, are regarded as the sign of an excellent spiritual disposition. Such a prevailing mood induced an attitude of gentleness towards all creatures. The Buddha's attack upon ritualism was the result of this attitude. Charity was superior to ritual sacrifice. 'There is a form of sacrifice easier than that of milk, oil, and honey: it is charity. Instead of sacrificing animals, let them go free! Let them seek grass, water and fresh breezes.' No wonder that the Buddhists were among the first to establish hospitals for animals. As the *Dhammapada* says, 'If a man for a hundred years sacrifices month by month with a thousand, and if he but for one moment pay homage to a man whose soul is grounded in true knowledge, better is that homage than a sacrifice for a hundred years.' Hence the double paradox of the teaching of Gotama. Life was both beautiful and ugly. Man must endeavour to root out of himself the desire for continued existence; but he might venerate to the point of sentimentality the life of natural things. He must endeavour to secure cessation of birth; but at the same time he must connive at the continuance of rebirth until the *Karma* of humanity shall have been worked out. Life, however burdensome, must go on until it is purged of sin and egoism. The disposition of the monk must be a kind of stoic benevolence. According to the Master, if a monk is injured by his enemies, he should say to himself, 'They are good, they are good, for at least they do not strike me.' If he is then struck, he should say to himself, 'They are good, they are good, for at least they are not killing me.' If, finally, they set about killing him, he should say, 'They are good, they are good, because all they are doing is to deliver me from this transitory life without imperilling my salvation.'

Certain scholars have described the assumption that life is inherently evil as a later corruption of the Buddha's teaching.[1] Save for certain of the images employed, the teaching of the Buddha does not suggest a nature morbidly obsessed with the fouller aspects of physical existence. Whatever the Buddha's personal temperament, he was as far removed from the hysterical and the neurotic as Mahavira may, from what we gather, have been the reverse. Moreover, a philosophy cannot be dismissed as wholly negative and despairing which offers, even though fleetingly and at a stupendous price, some modicum of hope: and the Buddha offered *Arahatship* here and now to those prepared to quench the fire of desire and passion in their hearts.

The two 'Vehicles': Ashoka

With the growth of a Buddhist system, and with the development of a church from a group of monks which was never intended to form a preisthood, the gentle and wise notions of the Buddha became hardened into precepts, until in due course the simple doctrine developed a rift which, far from the land in which the Buddha first preached, has persisted until this day. This rift was between so-called Hinayana Buddhism and Mahayana Buddhism, or the 'Little Vehicle' and the 'Great Vehicle', terms which do not in themselves prove very enlightening. Which of these two forms of Buddhism comes nearest to that preached by the Enlightened One is difficult to say at such great distance in time; but they differ from each other as profoundly as both differ from a further variation known as Zen Buddhism, which flourished chiefly in Japan. The history of these various schools is very instructive, but, like all histories of denominational strife, it can be depressing.

Buddhism had no Judas; but in the disciple Subhadda it had its doubting Thomas. On receiving news of the Blessed One's death, he is supposed to have remarked, 'Now we shall be able to do whatever we like; and what we do not like, that we shall not have to do.' This is a good summary of what happened. Even before the schism of the Little and Great Vehicle effected a broad geographical division of Buddhism, no less than eighteen different sects appeared. The process of disintegration, inevitable to some extent in every faith, might have ended in utter chaos but for the conversion to the Buddhist faith of one of the most remarkable rulers in ancient history, Ashokavardhana or Ashoka. It seems that no religion can survive without its imkperial champion; Ashoka, who began to rule the whole of India (except the very south) in 273 BC, was to Buddha what Constantine was to Christianity. Unless our conjectures are wholly mistaken, Ashoka represents one of the few rulers in history for whom absolute power did not spell

[1] Cf. M. Hiriyanna: *The Essentials of Indian Philosophy*, p. 75.

absolute corruption. Beginning as a monarch of conventional ruthlessness, he seems to have undergone in middle age an experience of revulsion from the life of alternate pageantry and slaughter which, for purposes of prestige, he was obliged to follow. Some say that this was due to the heroism of a Buddhist monk whom he had cast into his prison-inferno; others that it followed the news of one of his more sanguinary victories, that over the Kalinga, in which several hundred thousand persons were killed, maimed, or rendered homeless. All we know is that he suddenly decided to become a Buddhist lay-brother or *upasaka*, and that the rest of his life (he may later have become a monk) was devoted to governing his people according to Buddhist principles.

How far Ashoka was successful in turning Buddhism into a state religion, we cannot tell: he certainly went to great lengths to inculcate his people with moral teaching. Our modern efforts in political propaganda neither match those employed by Ashoka nor are likely to survive for so long. At carefully selected points throughout his kingdom he set up huge stone pillars upon which were carved, usually in the dialect of the region, the essentials of the Buddhist ethic. Similar inscriptions were cut upon numerous rock faces. Both the rock inscriptions and a number of the pillars may still be seen. As might be expected, these writings deal not so much with abstract theological matters (curiously enough they do not once refer to the Buddha by name) as with civic or social morality. In a society threatened with the danger of being split into irreconcilable sects, they make an earnest appeal for religious toleration. The Rock Edict No. 12, for instance, contains the interesting passage: 'A man must not do reverence to his own sect, or disparage that of another, without reason. Depreciation should be for specific reasons only, because the sects of other people all deserve reverence for some reason or another. By thus acting a man exalts his own sect, and at the same time does service to the sects of other people. By acting contrariwise a man hurts his own sect, and does disservice to the sects of other people... Concord is meritorious.' That is the statement of a man who, while understanding the violence of religious passions too well to engage in persecution, yet realizes the heavy responsibilities of permitting religious freedom.

A slightly sententious edict such as the above might suggest that Ashoka, though tolerant of religion, lacked a personal faith. The presumption is probably false. Like Ikhnaten Ashoka seems to have been a pious and sincere convert. As an administrator, he was a great deal more capable than the idealistic worshipper of Aten. He established monasteries by the thousand, and started veterinary hospitals. He held a gigantic Buddhist Congress and reformed the Church. And having thoroughly evangelized his own country from end to end, he embarked upon the organization of foreign missions. Ashoka's monks travelled over almost the entire known world, ranging as far as Greece in the West and, shortly after his death, carrying the gospel of enlightenment to Tibet, China, and Japan, where it later took permanent root.

The public inscriptions of Ashoka were not merely intended as exhortations to virtue; they often consisted of reports upon the results so far achieved. Even allowing for official exaggeration, these results seem to have been remarkable. Not merely had the officials acted with forbearance, but the people had shown qualities of virtue not to be left unacknowledged. Rock Edict No. 5 must have been cut at a moment of singular calm and prosperity: 'Now by reason of the practice of piety by his sacred and gracious Majesty the King, the reverberation of the war-drums has become the reverberation of the Law... As for many years before has not happened, now ... there is increased abstention from the sacrificial slaughter of living creatures, abstention from the killing of animal beings, seemly behaviour to relatives, seemly behaviour to Brahmans, hearkening to father and mother, hearkening to elders.' In short, there was something approaching public order and decency.

The final years of Ashoka's reign (which lasted forty years) are as obscure and confused as those of Ikhnaten. Failure and backsliding there must have been at all times, and possibly Ashoka insisted too much upon outward conformity, thus confusing 'seemly behaviour' with inner moral rectitude. Moreover, the maintenance of public virtue at a level considerably higher than that prevailing in any ordinary society must have required a great deal of exasperating inspection and vigilance; and whatever the humbler part of the community might have been prepared to endure, there were powerful influences working against the king's regulated virtue. Chief of these influences was that of the Brahmans, who, like the priests of Amen, awaited an opportunity to reassert their power, and incidentally to resume such forbidden customs as the sacrificing of animals. In the end, Ashoka was apparently deposed and succeeded by his grandson, though it may be that he withdrew from public life and, like the Emperor Charles V, devoted his last years to religious practices.

The apotheosis of The Buddha

Even though his system was abandoned, the Buddhist religion, somewhat modified, continued to win adherents at a rate unparalleled and no doubt on a scale greater than its originator anticipated. For just as there are two 'legendary' Buddhas, the young and brilliant prince and the humble apostle of gentleness and forbearance, so there were two conflicting Buddhist ideals, that of converting the whole world to *Arahatship*, and that of founding a gospel sufficiently durable, not to say flexible, to serve humanity until the arrival of the next Buddha. That Gotama seems to have regarded the caste system as a permanent feature of society, even though he may personally have flouted its conventions, is suggested by the fact that this next Buddha was to be of the Brahman class. To this point we shall return. In course of time the division between Mahayana Buddhism and Hinayana Buddhism assumed a territorial character. Hinayana, a creed which sought to preserve the simplicity of the Buddha's teaching, flourished for some time in the south of India, including Ceylon, whereas the Mahayana, a more sophisticated, took hold in the north, spreading thence across China, Tibet, and Mongolia to Japan.[1] As the simpler faith, Hinayana revered the Buddha as a great and even divine teacher; and the monastic communities continued to be organized on the lines indicated by the Master. Thus even today, in Ceylon, the monasteries probably preserve better than anywhere else the characteristics of the original Buddhist communities.[2] The Mahayana creed (or creeds) on the other hand, exalted the Buddha to such a degree that he came at length to be regarded as a god: with the result that the atheist prophet was in due course responsible for an elaborate system of theology and metaphysics. At a grand ecclesiastical council convened by the great Kushan ruler Kanishka (*c.* AD 120), who ruled an immense Indian and Asiatic Empire from his capital at Kabul, the doctrine of Mahayana was established with minute elaboration and scriptural wealth. Among the achievements of the delegates was the composition of three hundred thousand *Sutras* or theological essays, bearing upon almost every conceivable problem with which the faithful were likely to be confronted. Buddhism now formed the faith of a powerful established Church.

Was the 'Great Vehicle' constructed merely as a useful engine of government? There will always be historians for whom the 'development' or modification of a faith represents a departure from original innocence and truth, engineered as a rule for political purposes, or caused by the periodical disposition of human nature to flag and seek repose in dogma. A more profound scrutiny, however, while admitting degeneracy, will also recognize a certain advance, and sees nothing inherently absurd in the two processes occurring simultaneously. Coupled with the growth of ritualism, relic-worship, and an immensely complicated theology, went a more liberal and refined moral outlook. Instead of propagating the doctrine that none but the saint or *Arahat* could be saved, Mahayana Buddhism opened the way of salvation to all mankind. Furthermore, it conceived this way of salvation in a much less abstruse and negative manner than had hitherto been entertained. *Nirvana* ceased to mean (if it ever did mean) absolute *extinction*, and became an abode of blessedness and peace beyond the reach of the transmigratory process. This development, though accompanied by much superstitious or *tantric* (magical) ceremonial, bears a remarkable resemblance to that which took place in Egypt after the revolution of Ikhnaten and simultaneously with the compilation of *The Book of the Dead*. Perhaps the most interesting development of Mahayana, however, is the doctrine of Bodhisattvas: that is to say, Buddhas who abstain from entry into *Nirvana* in order to work for the promotion of universal deliverance. The veneration of these future Buddhas tends sometimes to obscure the revered name of the 'historical' Buddha. Instead of concentrating upon the attainment of *Nirvana*, the faithful tended to aspire towards one of two conditions: either that of rebirth during the lifetime of one of the Bodhisattvas, or, more

[1] The division is rough. Mahayana took hold likewise in Korea and also Hawaii.
[2] Cf. the article on Buddhism by de la Vallée Poussin in *The Legacy of India* (1938).

ambitious still, that of Buddhahood itself. As to the best means of achieving the latter end, theologians disagreed violently. Meanwhile it was natural that the devotee should seek to invoke the aid of saints, gods, and all the Buddhas who had ever existed; and hence the simple notions of Gotama were in due time swamped by an inrush of dogma and myth. Osiris and the *fravashis* cannot long remain in the background.

The Diffusion of Buddhism

One of the most extraordinary phenomena in history is the fact that several of the world's great religions—and there are usually agreed to be eleven of them—have flourished least readily in the place of their origin. This is particularly true of the Buddhist faith. Today, the number of professing Buddhists in India is negligible.[1] Why did so powerful a religion fail to take permanent root in the land that originally embraced it with such ardour? The answer lies in a fact often ignored or underestimated. Buddhism did not drive out the religion that preceded it. By its very looseness and tolerance, the Hindu faith survived and finally enveloped the younger and more exacting doctrine. For in so far as Buddhism accumulated superstitions and developed an intelligible if abstruse theology, so it approximated to the condition of a popular faith such as Hinduism had always remained, in spite of its intellectual appanage; until finally the Buddha himself came to be included among the gods of the Hindu pantheon. Secondly, owing to the Buddha's distrust of sacrifice, ritual, and ceremony, the *Sangha* or Buddhist brotherhood undertook few, if any, of the duties naturally incumbent upon priests: notably the performance of ceremonies connected with birth, marriage, and death, and the fulfilment of numerous other religious and civic functions. These offices continued to be performed as a matter of course by the Brahmans. Without this caste of respected if sometimes corrupt persons, social life in Hindustan would have lost its continuity. Although the Buddha had tacitly opposed the Brahmans, he seems not merely to have acquiesced in their priestly status, but assumed it to be a permanent feature of social life. The Buddha remained indifferent rather than hostile to the caste structure of society.

Although Brahmanism exerted so powerful an influence upon Indian society, the *Sangha* enjoyed a period of immense prestige. Indeed, there came a time when its attraction exerted such influence upon the young men of the Magadha (north-east India) that society seemed likely to perish from an excess of celibacy. Another debilitating factor was the strict pacifism of the Buddhist doctrine: for while a display of force may not necessarily destroy non-violent beliefs, it can often exert an influence upon where they shall be preached. Thus the expulsion of Buddishm from India was brought about by the arrival of a people inspired by a faith of militant fervour, the Moslems. And Islam has retained a firm foothold in India to this day. Even so, it has succeeded no better than Buddhism in ousting that extraordinary con-

[1] About three million.

glomeration of exalted metaphysical beliefs, myths, superstitions, and apparent obscenities, which make up the historical Hindu faith.

A history of Buddhism from its extinction in India until the present day may strike the Western reader as a prolix and bewildering process in which the pure faith of the Buddha almost ceases to be recognizable. Certainly the Buddhism of Asia, including Japan, is a faith that exhibits a great deal of internal variation. Surveying the history of Christianity in the West, an Eastern scholar would no doubt experience a similar impression of violent conflict, glaring disparity of profession and practice, and rank superstition. The purest Buddhism is perhaps that to be found in Burma, the least pure in Japan; but the test of a faith is finally in the lives of individuals. The literature of Zen Buddhism contains some pieces of great beauty and spiritual insight:

> Let others speak ill of me, I acquire the chance of gaining merit,
> For they are really my good friends;
> When I cherish, being vituperated, neither enmity nor favouritism,
> There grows within me the power of love and humility which is born of the unborn.
>
> From Yoka Daishi's *Song of Enlightenment*

Perhaps the most interesting form of later Buddhism, however, is that which began to flourish in Tibet from the seventh century AD. The conqueror Strong-tsan Gampo (629–50), having become master of this country of difficult access, set up his capital at Lhasa and, with rare wisdom, began to Buddhize his people with the help of missionaries specially summoned from India, such as the saintly Padma Sambhava. The faith quickly took root.[1] Two powerful authorities, the Dalai Lama ('the all-embracing priest') and the Tashi Lama, wielded theocratic rule over the country. Even today the successor of the first is considered to be the incarnation of a Bodhisattva, while the second is believed to be the *avatar* of a Buddha. The Lama theology is expounded in a voluminious series of scriptures. The faithful are believed to acquire merit by the strict performance of ritual, including the use of the prayer-wheel and the so-called 'trees of the law', long beflagged poles. In spite of this *tantric* aspect, however, the Lama wisdom contains teaching that calls to mind the wisdom of China or the *Book of Proverbs*.

> A foolish man proclaimeth his qualifications,
> A wise man keepeth them secret within himself.
> A straw floateth on the surface of water,
> But a precious gem placed upon it sinketh.

or more loftily:

> The path is one for all,
> The means to reach the goal must vary with the pilgrims.
> Thou shalt not let thy senses make a playground of thy mind,
> Hast thou attuned thy being to humanity's great pain, O candidate for light?
> For know, that the Eternal knows no change.

[1] It may have begun to penetrate Tibet much earlier.

7

The Hindu Systems

The only way to find Yoga is through Yoga

Kapila

In expounding the thought of India, even in the simple manner here adopted, we run the risk of both misrepresentation and omission, or worst of all, dilution. The monotonous abstractions of the *Upanishads* are with difficulty imagined as having moved men and women—whole multitudes of them—to devotional ecstasy, still less to the extremes of asceticism. But we know that they did. A bare account of the life of Mahavira, with its succession of macerations, does little to convey the fire and passion of the man, his frightful yet inspiring presence. Even the story of Shakyamuni,[1] the Buddha, embellished as it has been with legend and parable and augmented by accounts of his five hundred and fifty previous existences, fails to come alive unless we picture a man of infinite pity and gentleness, a wanderer, a lover of cave and ravine as well as of bathing-Ghat and the shaded grove, a solitary and yet a good companion, a preacher of uncompromising sternness and yet a man of wit and even humour. To understand Hinduism as a living faith we need to read the great epics such as the *Mahabharata* and the *Ramayana*. To enter into the spirit of the Buddhist gospel we must go to the *Dhammapada*.

When we approach the Hindu 'systems' proper,[2] the task of infusing life and spirit into abstract philosophical statements becomes one of extreme difficulty. These 'systems' are among the most complex thought-structures that have been invented. In Europe we have become unaccustomed to philosophical systems. To us, philosophy tends to be an abstruse game, a debate about definitions, words set to chase words. The faith or system or belief we live by—and we must live by something—is almost totally unrelated to the contents of philosophical text-books. The earliest philosophers appreciated the need of systematic or comprehensive thought; a philosophy that failed to embrace experience as a whole was a philosophy that had failed to complete its work. Obsessed with trifles, we may well arrive at a state of mind in which the notion of the unity of experience has been completely abandoned: a sensation experienced by anyone who listens to papers read before certain select philosophical assemblies.

[1] One of the Buddha's many titles, derived from the name of his clan.

[2] They are not strictly 'systems' but doctrines of one traditional System: cf. Réne Guénon. *Introduction to the Study of the Hindu Doctrines* (London, 1945).

What was the oldest of Indian philosophical doctrines? It is probably that which was known as Sankhya, of which the author was Kapila, a sage who may have lived as early as the sixth century BC.

It is no small merit for a man to sit down and endeavour to expound the whole meaning of life to his contemporaries and for posterity: and if, as we suspect, Kapila's work consisted largely in the codification of previous ideas, he does not for that reason become less remarkable a thinker. The principle from which Kapila starts is one with which our study of the *Upanishads* has made us tolerably familiar. Experience itself is not merely evil, but always painful. The aim of existence, therefore, is not 'fullness of life' or the 'enrichment of experience', as almost all Western philosophers (save Schopenhauer) implicitly believe, but the voiding of the mind of its entire contents, followed automatically by the collapse and dismemberment of the mind-structure itself. Experience is codified, labelled, and measured as a necessary prelude to its dismantling.

Kapila's analysis of experience is extremely thorough. He finds reason to sort reality into twenty-five categories. Hence one of the possible meanings of *Sankhya*, namely the 'science of numbers'. He begins rather like Spinoza by positing the existence of a general Substance called *Prakriti*. From this basic substance are derived three 'realities', or agents of reality, called *gunas*. The first achievement of these *gunas* (which act somewhat like catalysts in chemical reaction) is to create the intellect or, since the appropriate word is *Buddhi*, the enlightening power or perceptive faculty. The next stage in this process, which is an evolutionary one, consists in the articulation, again by means of the seminal *gunas*, of the faculty of perception into the five senses. These senses proceed to create the physical organs with which they are associated: sight created the eye, hearing the ear, sexual desire the generative organs. This may well seem a reversal of the proper order of things, though Schopenhauer and some of our modern evolutionists have followed Kapila. Finally, the *gunas*, operating upon the raw material of *Prakriti*, produce the constituents of the so-called 'external world': ether, water, earth, fire, etc. These are the result of what is called 'secondary evolution'.

Set over against this basic substance *Prakriti*, but not intervening in its individual activities, is its complete opposite: Spirit or *Purusha*. Whereas *Prakriti* is passive (though not static), *Purusha*, being spirit, is activating, though not exactly dynamic. Whatever is active in the world is spirit ('The spirit of God moved upon the face of the waters'): a 'man of spirit' is a man who does things. What *Purusha* does is to exercise a 'lure' (to employ the term of the modern English philosopher Whitehead) over *Prakriti*, so that the creative *gunas* are set in motion. As the Sankhya commentator of the second century AD, Ishvara Krishna, remarked, '*Purusha's* purpose is the sole cause of *Prakriti's* evolution.' In other words, *Purusha* is the sun which, directing its rays upon the rich humus of *Prakriti*, stimulates life and growth. Under the influence of this distant but vivifying power the 'things' in the universe came into being: a *nisus* or urge impels them to do so. Such a process might at first sight be thought to resemble that occasioned by Aristotle's Unmover Mover: but *Purusha*, in operating upon *Prakriti*,[1] is in fact working out its own purpose. 'The organ of sight comes into existence because it is necessary if *Purusha* is to see.'[2]

At first glance this account of the origin of life and mind may seem absurdly fanciful. Taken at its face value, what does it amount to but idle juggling with abstractions? Admittedly philosophies have been criticized for slighter faults: but when a form of thought has survived for twenty or so centuries, we cannot lightly dismiss it. Errors in practical everyday life may be brushed aside; in philosophy they must be accounted for. Error in philosophy is another word for opportunity; for every form of belief, however removed in spirit from that to which we are accustomed, represents a challenge. The Sankhya doctrine, at least in its general outline, bears a resemblance to certain modern philosophies of 'emergent evolution', such as those expounded by A. N. Whitehead and S. Alexander: so much so that it is best described in terms employed by these thinkers. Whereas the philosophy of emergent evolution is usually shot through with optimism, however, the Sankhya doctrine is a structure erected over a pit of nihilistic acedia. For instead of the evolution of matter and life being regarded as something good and wonderful, it is regarded by Kapila as the result of a gigantic cosmic error.

To expound the nature of this error, this evolutionary mistake, is by no means easy.[3] The argument borders upon the abstruse, a realm upon which no philosopher ever ventured and returned of sound mind. Instead of parading the sort of abstract argument which some Indian philosophers enjoy, we should bear in mind certain basic principles common to all Vedic or Vedantic philosophy. One of these principles is the evil of individuality. Individuality is an obstacle to enlightenment. Now the work of the *gunas* is precisely to individualize, or egotize: therefore one of the commonest illusions from which mankind suffers is to identify the work of the *gunas* with the goal of *Purusha*. It is like mistaking physical growth—obviously not a bad thing in itself—with the true and complete end of man, which is presumably a spiritual fruition: or perhaps to do something even more common, to confuse the beauty of an experience of physical (say sexual) origin with certain higher experiences, of which the former can at best provide an intimation. In short, the beginning of wisdom is to escape from individuality, because to do so is to escape from illusion. 'Liberation obtained through knowledge of the twenty-five realities (categories),' Kapila is reputed to have declared, 'teaches the one only knowledge, that neither I am, nor anything is mine, nor do I exist.' Such liberation involves an immediate perception of the fundamental difference between *Prakriti* and *Purushu*. When we have attained to the highest experiences of which the mind is capable we find mere physical enjoy-

[1] It is not, however, an 'agent' in the crude sense.
[2] Hiriyanna: *Essentials of Indian Philosophy* (1949), p. 119.
[3] Even Indian philosophers admit this. *Op. cit.*, p. 116

ments paltry by comparison. Unlike certain forms of Buddhism, the Sankhya doctrine does not necessarily condemn bodily pleasures as evil. The tendency of Hinduism, especially in its later development, is to assert the contrary: hence the preponderance of ritual and conduct which, as Gandhi once remarked, became 'obscene' only when the Western conquerors arrived to pronounce it so. Possibly the Orient was wiser to permit the open parade of such tendencies within the sphere of religious ritual than their covert parade through the dream-world, as in our Western consciousness. The worship of Shiva, with its undisguised emphasis upon the generative organs of both sexes, the *linga* and *yoni*, does not strike the Hindu, however young and innocent, as obscene: 'obscenity' might rather be attributed to the tendency found almost universally in the Occident, namely to associate sexual operation with other purely automatic activities.

Patanjali and Yoga

The doctrine of Kapila has been described by a great orientalist, Professor Garbe, as exhibiting for the first time 'the complete independence and freedom of the human mind, its full confidence in its own powers'. We now pass from an elaborate philosophical doctrine to something to which we should perhaps give the name of a philosophical technique. For everyone who has heard of the Sankhya doctrine there are a hundred—perhaps a thousand—who have heard of the system of Yoga. Of all the products of oriental thought, Yoga has perhaps exerted the greatest fascination over the Western mind. To account for this fascination is not difficult. The 'mysterious East'—or what Disraeli, in the person of Sidonia in *Tancred*, called 'the great Asian mystery'—seems to find its embodiment in the Yogi. Even allowing for differences of appearance and practice, such holy men represent the farthest remove from what to Western eyes is a useful or decent member of society. In the first place the Yogi does no work: that is to say, his intense exertions are devoted to nothing of apparent social utility. In the second place, he possesses, or claims to possess, powers beyond normal human attainment: a fact calculated to rouse immediate interest in a European and even more perhaps in an American. Dissatisfied with traditional religion and finding no exhilaration in the absence of faith (which was at one time supposed to be the condition most to be envied), many a lonely Western man or woman has sought in some oriental discipline the way to spiritual repose.

The principles of Yoga are deceptively simple. Their practice, particularly by anyone with a living to earn, is extremely difficult and inconvenient. Just as the appreciation of education is itself the consequence of education,[1] so 'the only way to find Yoga is through Yoga'. In his little book *A Confession*, Tolstoy records how, once the unsatisfactoriness of his unregenerate life became clear to him, he believed himself capable forthwith of embarking upon a career of the highest sanctity. Experience did not bear out this confidence. Similarly, the student of a new faith feels as if the bare assent to its prin-

[1] Lecky.

ciples, the mere expression of approval, will ensure his being at once admitted to its most profound secrets. What we find in reality is something rather less edifying. There is an initial enthusiasm, sometimes overwhelming and always infectious. In the absence of immediate and visible results, the novelty wears off. Finally, what was initiated with enthusiasm is abandoned with scarcely a regret. The seeker after faith may then turn, with the least show of embarrassment, to one of the many other systems of belief for which his suffrage is invited: until it will become clear to others, though rarely to himself, that what he desires is not so much to live steadily and earnestly by a faith as to enjoy the intoxication of surrendering to one faith after another, as to so many spiritual mistresses.

Detailed descriptions of Yoga exercises or an account of the habits of fakirs—a word used chiefly by Moslems to denote a man dedicated to poverty—may excite curiosity, but it will not necessarily promote understanding. If a half-naked or wholly naked hindu squats down on the ground and directs his gaze at the tip of his nose or at his navel, or if he persists in holding his arm in the air until, deprived of circulation, it begins to wither and atrophy; or if, preferring not to remain seated, he adopts a mode of progress that consists of rolling himself in the direction of some shrine or holy place; or if, the better to demonstrate his indifference to material wants, he starves himself to within an ace of death or nearly buries himself alive—or actually does so—we tend to dismiss these acts as mere wanton aberrations, the product of ascetic high spirits. Such a judgment is superficial. The practice of Yoga is not for everybody, but nor is the exercise of supreme command in the army, nor that of premiership or the pursuit of scientific research. Yet just as every society must have a few men prepared to work longer and harder than their fellows, otherwise certain urgent and necessary tasks would never be accomplished, so every religion must have its extremists—its prophets, saints, and martyrs—without whom certain urgent spiritual tasks would remain unfulfilled. The Yogi is simply a man who takes the Hindu philosophy to its logical conclusion. That such a man should be called an extremist, as well he may be, serves to show with what half-measures most people practise their professed religion.

What are the origins of Yoga? Undoubtedly they are of great antiquity. It is tempting, especially in the absence of definite proof, to compare these gymnosophists, these athletes of the soul, with the extraordinary figures in primitive society called *shaman*. The *shaman* is usually a recluse to whom strange powers are attributed. His withdrawal from society is both voluntary and lifelong. His 'social function' is not necessarily to prophesy or even to dispense advice: only modern societies require a man that he shall give, rather than simply be, something. The *shaman*, so far as we can judge, is permitted to engage in meditation because the community believes such activities to be useful in themselves. In northern Nigeria, for instance, a member of the Abuan tribe, questioned by an anthropologist about the social function of a figure called the Ak-Abuan, replied that such a man existed 'to be holy on our behalf, keeping all the laws that ordinary men have no time to remember because of their regular work'. If the Indian Yogi is not identical with the primitive *shaman* in all respects, he at least fulfils certain of the religious functions of that figure.

The practice of Yoga meditation was unquestionably familiar to the men who composed the *Vedas*. To the author of the *Upanishads* it is a recognized technique for arriving at knowledge of *Brahman*, while in the *Gita* Krishna prescribes its rules to the bewildered and distressed Arjuna. When, sometime between 300 and 150 BC, the sage Patanjali composed the *Yoga Sutras*, he was probably engaged in the codification of many ancient traditions. Men who devote a lifetime to the practice of ascetic meditation must evolve a great variety of techniques; but the comparative simplicity of Patanjali's rules must not blind us to the elaborate metaphysics upon which they are based. The practice, however scrupulous, of such rules of posture, breathing, etc., by the enthusiastic Westerner can scarcely do harm; but abstract gymnastics are no substitute for the arduous consecration of a lifetime to reflection, *askesis*, and worship. By learning to sit or breath properly, the Westerner thinks that he may inevitably acquire better health or poise; whereas to the genuine practitioner of Yoga, such ambition must appear paltry. Finally, 'Yoga powers are not obtained by wearing the dress of a Yogi, or by talking about them, but untiring practice is the secret of success' (Patanjali).

To put the matter briefly, Yoga is a technique for freeing the mind from attachment to the senses. Once freed, the mind does not wander aimlessly about in a world superior to nature; it actually becomes that which it is seeking. Now the quest of the soul or the *Atman* is for *Brahman*. Therefore the aim of Yoga is to effect a fusion of *Atman* with *Brahman*. Having passed through the successive states of Yoga discipline, the Yogi, though physically unchanged (or at least still present), is psychically transmogrified. Occasionally, it is claimed, he can be physically modified too. The Yogi can render himself invisible, engage in feats of levitation, enter another body, and remain buried in the ground for days at a time.

The Brahmans have always distrusted Yoga. Similarly, the priests of Christianity take care not to encourage mysticism, save in the case of those for whom it is evidently a vocation. Although the number of practitioners of Yoga is today between two and three million, we cannot suppose that more than a few of these adepts have consistently reached the final state of union or *Samadhi*. Not merely is such a state difficult to reach in itself; the Yoga ascetic ought not be content with its momentary or sporadic attainment. For what he is seeking to do is nothing less than to remove, in the space of one lifetime, the whole burden of *Karma* inherited from his previous existences. That which the ordinary man hopes, all being well, to eliminate in the course of a series of existences, the Yoga seeks to liquidate (if the word may be employed) in the space of one.[1]

What are the stages of attainment of *Samadhi*, or complete absorption? They are eight in number. These stages form the means whereby the five so-called 'hindrances', or obstructions to detachment, may be eliminated: that is to say, Ignorance (*Avidya*), the notion of personality (i.e. that man is a self-contained individual), desire, hatred, and attachment to the things of the senses. The stages are as follows. Firstly comes *Yama,* perhaps the most difficult stage of all and therefore that at which many an enthusiast turns back; it involves the extinction of desire and egotism and their replacement by charity and unselfishness. Secondly comes *Niyama* the stage at which certain rules of conduct must be adopted, such as the maintenance of cleanliness, the pursuit of devotional studies and the fulfilment of certain rituals of purification. Thirdly comes the stage to which greatest attention has been paid, namely *Asana*, or the attainment of correct posture. Just as the first stage of *Yama* involved the stilling of all desire, so the third stage involves the reduction to a minimum of all bodily movement. How is this to be done? To arrive at a satisfactory position, a great deal of experimentation must have taken place. The usual posture of the concentrating Yoga is familiar to most people from pictures. Resting his right foot upon his left thigh and his left foot upon his right thigh, the adept crosses his hands so as to be able to hold his two big toes, and, thus co-ordinated, lowers his head with the object of gazing either at his navel or at the tip of his nose.[2]

This is the kind of posture to which the Western body, unless taken in hand early, is ill-adapted, which probably accounts for its fascination: our office-existence is 'sedentary' only in a very artificial sense, and our bodies suffer for it. Alarmed at his slouching laziness, the Westerner may see in a strenuous course of gymnosophy a means of counteracting the harm done by his daily routine. This is to mistake the nature and purpose of *Asana*. The *Yoga Sutras* make it clear both that 'the posture assumed must be steady and easy', and that such steadiness and ease of posture is to be achieved through 'persistent slight effort'. It is not the purpose of this book to recommend the adoption of the belief and practice of any system here described: possibly it should be the author's duty to issue a warning against such conduct, which may end in disappointment and even disgust. In the case of those wishing to pursue such matters seriously, however, what is to be avoided above all is the furious enthusiasm of the novice.

Asana is not an end in itself; it is a means to the next stage, which is called *Pranayama*, the 'right control of the life-force' or breathing. By regulating the breath, the Yogi hopes to arrive at two conditions; that in which he concentrates upon the process of breathing alone, and that in which, after due practice, he all but ceases to breath at all. The first

[1] His exertions need not be directed exclusively to selfish ends. According to the Chinese treatise *I-Ching* (see Chapter 8), 'if you only meditate (according to the prescribed rules) for a ¼ hour, you set ten thousand aeons and a thousand births at rest'.

[2] According to Swatmaram Swami, this posture is called 'the Lotus seat' and destroys all diseases.

condition, by evacuating the mind of all outer impressions, enables him to attain to complete spiritual repose: this is a necessary prelude to the flooding-in of divine light. The second condition enables him, if necessary, to undergo feats of endurance, such as those of which we have spoken.

Having contemplated the foregoing stages of discipline, the amateur of Yoga may find it difficult to imagine through what further rigours he must brace himself to pass. But there are still four stages to come. *Pratyahara*, or abstraction, which means the mind's complete withdrawal from the world of sense, is followed by *Dharana*. Here an attempt is made to bring the mind to think only of one thing, or in effect to think of nothing specific at all. We have now reached a level at which it is difficult, without employing metaphors, to give an account of what is happening. Fortunately, Indian thinkers are equally aware of this difficulty. Having invited us to consider a mental state at which there is only one thing to think about, they are now obliged to give us some idea of what this is. At this point the teacher invokes the sacred syllable *OM*.

The reader will recall our references to *OM* in connection with the *Upanishads*. To provide the mind with subject-matter for meditation, the Yogi is recommended to repeat the sacred syllable, which thus generates a subject-matter otherwise inexpressible. 'Through the sound of the word and through reflection upon its meaning,' says Patanjali, 'the way is found. From this comes the realization of the Self (or Soul, *Atman*), and the removal of all obstacles.'[1]

No doubt the repeated invocation of the word *OM* induces a condition almost of hypnosis. Now the final stage of Yoga supervenes logically upon that which preceded it: for *Samadhi*, the eighth rung of this spiritual ladder, takes the form of a deep and complete trance. If we are to believe the experts, the trance state of *Samadhi* is a sign of the complete identification of soul with reality, *Atman* with *Brahman*. The soul in its individuality no longer exists: 'like camphor in the flame and like salt with the water of the ocean', it has merged with the ocean of Being. The Yoga philosophers delight to represent this ineffable state by such metaphors. 'The Yogi in highest meditation,' says Swatmaram Swami, 'is void within and without like a pot in the world-space. He is also like a pot in the ocean, void within and without.' Naturally, to one in such a condition, nothing evil can happen. 'A Yogi in *Samadhi* is invulnerable to all weapons; all the world cannot overpower him, and he is beyond the powers of incantations and magical diagrams.'

Of mysticism Bossuet observed that the genuine article was so rare a thing, and false mysticism so common, that the whole subject were best left alone by the laity. That is the view of an official. The official

[1] The repetition of the sacred syllable has sometimes been recommended on purely psychological grounds. The Rajah of Aundh, author of an instructive manual of physical exercises, suggests that certain bodily movements should be accompanied by the pronunciation of various Indian vocables, of which *OM* is the most important. At least this reveals the connection of the syllable with regulated breathing, which no one denies can be of therapeutic value.

attitude, whether in religion or politics, was defined by Burke as the knowledge of 'how much evil to tolerate'. The historian of philosophy is not concerned to keep the peace; he is concerned to understand, first, how men come to think as they do, and, secondly, whether what they think is reasonable and consistent. Mysticism is a fact. The endeavour to suppress it has on the whole failed. If on occasion its practice has given rise to serious abuses, this may be the least cogent reason for dismissing it as fraudulent. No one is likely to question the value of liberty on the basis of Madame Roland's remark as to the number of crimes, including her own execution, committed in its name. And the same may be said of the celebrated remark of Lucretius on the evils of religion. A system such as Yoga may prove a fearful weapon in the hands of those who, misusing its discipline, claim to exercise powers purporting to be divine; but unless such a claim is sometimes made, even by the unscupulous, Yoga is not worth the serious consideration that students of religion and psychology have agreed to give it. Without some rudiments of organization, it is difficult to imagine any religion surviving much beyond its founder's lifetime; but that same religion, contained within the ritual of a church, is faced with a more serious problem of survival if it cannot, every few generations, issue forth in some refreshing novelty, embarrassing no doubt to its official custodians but revealing to a profounder gaze something essential to its health. Mysticism interrupts religion for the purpose of asserting its continuity.

In studying Yoga it is tempting to raise the question of the relation of magic to religion. There have been times when the two were regarded as the same thing, as perhaps in Sumeria. There have been other times when the two were regarded as opposite things, as often in our own civilization. Leaving aside the trick-magic of our entertainers, it is possible to see in magic a necessary ally of religion. We tend to concentrate less upon the end of magic than upon the means. The end is to heighten our emotional life, to raise it to that level of concentration and impetus from which, and from which only, a leap into another dimension may be made. To deny the possibility of such another dimension in the name of rationalism or 'free thought' is to take a very narrow view of the capacities of reason, and to fail to explain how thought, thus circumscribed, can be free.

Shankara and Vedanta

In outlining the principal Hindu doctrines we have introduced the minimum of philosophical terms. A technical history of Indian philosophy would need, in speaking of Yoga, to go into detail concerning the pacification of the *chitta* or mind-stuff, the control of the *vrittis*, which produce false versions of reality, the detailed action of the *gunas*, and so forth. The mere parade of such terms cannot but bewilder the laymen, as well as exasperate, by their random introduction, the expert. All we can do is to emphasize, without elaborating, the complex theoretical foundation of this famous doctrine. We ought likewise to cite the attempts of modern psychologists, above all C. G. Jung, to relate some of their own theories to those of Eastern philosophers: for it is with the same reality that philosophers of every age have to do. An argument raised by one philosopher may be resumed in earnest many centuries later, as happened with Parmenides and Bergson, with Shankara and Kant, and possibly with many others of whom no record has been preserved: we have repeatedly drawn attention to the fact that the earliest extant philosophical documents must presuppose many centuries of speculation. Nevertheless, jargon has always been the enemy of clear thinking. From time to time the Indian doctrines have been denounced for their abstraction, their abstruseness, and occasionally their impiety. The doctrine (if such it can be called) of *Purva Mimansa* represented a protest against the impressive but covertly atheistic systems such as the *Sankhya*. The originators of such doctrines were careful to pay lip-service to the *Vedas*; but, having done so, they proceeded to indulge in speculations that have nothing to do with those inspired documents. Jaimini,[1] the founder of *Purva Mimansa*, was what we should today call a fundamentalist. He urges his countrymen to return to the word of God, to recognize the finitude of their intellects, and to practise charity instead of parrotting abstractions. Apart from duly recording his protest, however, there is little about his work upon which we need linger.

With Shankara we have to do with a philosopher of very different calibre: in fact we have to do with one of the greatest of all philosophers, whose work ought to be better known in the Occident than it is. Shankara's thought not merely effected a revolution in the Orient—for it was one of the causes of the disappearance of Buddhism from India; it assumed a direction (as we have hinted) almost identical with that later pursued by the German philosopher Immanuel Kant. The resemblance is so close as to invite speculation as to whether Kant could possibly have been acquainted with the work of Shankara. Not a shred of evidence has been produced suggesting even indirect influence: indeed, the debt, if genuine, would have been too great not to receive acknowledgment upon practically every page. We have to be content with the view, hardly less remarkable, that two major thinkers separated by a thousand years offered similar interpretations of reality. On reflection, what is strange is not so much that this should have happened once or twice in history, as that it should not have happened more often. If reality *is* of a certain nature, it is curious that men dedicated to its study should not have been more frequently disposed to agreement.

The system expounded by Shankara—and here the word 'system' is appropriate—is traditionally known as Vedanta. Strictly speaking, Vedanta means the conclusion or completion of the *Vedas*. Now the conclusion of the *Vedas*, as we have seen, is the *Upanishads*. What the *Upanishads* teach is the identification of *Atman* with *Brahman*: this teaching is not so much analysed or explained as dogmatically asserted. When you are obliged to defend your dogmas, either against criticism or against other dogmas, you must provide them with a

[1] Fourth century BC.

rational basis. The philosophy of Vedanta is that by which the *Upanishad* dogmas are supported by argument, demonstration, and proof. And just as St Thomas Aquinas was there to sustain Christian dogma by rational argument, so Shankara was there to perform the same service for Hindu dogma.

Shankara, or Sankaracharya,[1] lived from AD 788–820. These dates are striking in two ways. First of all they show that the great system-maker of India lived for only thirty-two years. Second, they reveal that Shankara lived a thousand years, and perhaps more, after the composition of the *Upanishads*. The shortness of Shankara's life derives its significance from the magnitude of his achievement. As to his separation in time from the sages whose ideas he systematized, this is hardly more remarkable than Aquinas's systematization in the thirteenth century of Christian thought originating in the second or third centuries. And just as Aquinas had the Christian Fathers and Augustine behind him, so Shankara was preceded by such men as Badarayana (second century BC), author of the *Brahman Sutra* (a composition of 550 aphorisms or apophthegms), Gaudapada (seventh century AD), and finally Govinda, who transmitted the doctrine of *Brahman* to Shankara himself.

Still to dwell for a moment upon resemblances, Shankara reminds us of Aquinas not merely in his place in history and his attempt at synthesis, but in the holiness of his life. Born in Malabar, he was a member of the caste of Nambudri Brahmans, who combined the twin ideals of the saint and the *savant*. Shankara appears early to have felt the call of renunciation and asceticism. He became a hermit-saint or *samyosi* at an age when other young men, far from rejecting the world, are busy tasting its pleasures. Nor did Shankara engaged in ascetic practices merely according to the routine laid down for hermits: it is recorded that he achieved as a matter of common experience the condition of *Samadhi*. Consequently, his lifelong opposition to both the *Sankhya* system of Kapila and the equally atheist ideas of the Buddha was dictated by reasons as much emotional as intellectual. A philosopher who regularly achieves union with the divine, or at least who thinks he does, is not likely to be content with the verbal carping and logical aridities of so much theological discussion; he will organize his thought upon a majestic basis, and recommend it the more effectively by living it.

It is sometimes maintained that the best debaters are those who do not believe in what they advocate. Such a view depends for its plausibility upon the level at which the debate is conducted. Those who believe strongly, passionately, are admittedly not always in the best condition to defend their arguments. Aware of their inward certitude, they see no reason to engage in elaborate disputation. The capacity to believe has been described, with justice, as a kind of genius. Such genius, united to unusual intellectual vigour, produces the great philosophical leaders of the world. Most generalizations about human nature have a superficial ring because they are based upon inspection

[1] 'Acharya' means a spiritual teacher.

of those who are 'above the mob but lower than the man of genius'. To suggest that Augustine, Aquinas, or Shankara would have been superior dialecticians had they been less convinced of their ideas is at once to make nonsense of belief and to degrade human intelligence.

Summoned by the Pope from a life of solitude and devotion, Aquinas arrived in Paris for the purpose of defending orthodoxy. In spite of his obvious preference for a hermit life, Shankara was obliged, while still a youth, to undertake a similar mission. The centre of debate was the holy city of Benares. Acting as a kind of representative of south India, Shankara proved himself a redoubtable champion of Brahmanism. Very soon his services were required at other centres. He attacked the demolished heresy wherever it might be found. Nor was the demolition merely rhetorical and dogmatic; it was characterized by subtle argument and reasoned apologetic.

We should give a great deal to possess a *procès-verbal* of some of the encounters in which Shankara distinguished himself. The writings attributed to him are voluminous: like the great *Summae* of Aquinas, and like *The Critique of Pure Reason* of Kant, they are confessedly not easy reading. We must remember that they represent no more than a skeleton or—if it is preferred—a blue print of Shankara's thought. It is unreasonable to expect that profound philosophical works should, to use the favourite criterion of interest, 'read like a novel', which may imply that they will as soon be forgotten. The greatest essays in philosophical enquiry are merely notes or memoranda, the basis of an actual or imaginary exchange of views. Only civilizations organized differently from our own, such as the city states of ancient Greece, have provided leisure enough for philosophers to record their thought in the way best suited to it, namely in the form of dialogue.[1] And what was thus recorded was not strictly thought but thinking.

While at Benares, Shankara wrote his famous commentaries on both the *Upanishads* and the *Bhagavad-Gita*. Synthesizing all that Badarayana, Gaudapada, and Govinda had maintained, these learned and elaborate works did more than anything to re-establish in India the intellectual ascendancy of Brahmanism. Shankara's approach to the Scriptures was fully as orthodox as that of Aquinas: he is not attempting anything in the nature of 'higher' criticism, which depends paradoxically upon an initial belittlement of the subject to be criticized. The task to which he devoted himself was that of finding a basis in reason for that which was given in revelation: an aim that appears impious only to those who fail to see in human reason a secondary channel of revelation.

The word secondary is important. Admittedly reason cannot take us all the way. It is an instrument which, though of great utility, may be used to further any cause whatever; it is not loaded in any particular direction. We need another and even higher faculty, a kind of intuition, whereby to discriminate between truth and error. This higher faculty is acquired through the cultivation of detachment, the with-

[1] Aristotle may be cited as an exception, but Aristotle wrote a number of dialogues, all of which have been lost.

drawal from the life of sense, and, if possible, a total absorption in *Brahman*. In short, the philosopher must be not simply a man given to reflection, still less a man endowed with keen wit and capacity for argument; he must be both pure in heart and a lover of wisdom. In the appointment of our own teachers of philosophy, such characteristics are not normally insisted upon.

Having made clear in what respect philosophy differs from other intellectual disciplines, Shankara proceeds to expound his system. The reader may conclude, from what has been said, that the argument is conducted upon a somewhat rarefied level. If we are to accept the view that none but the saint can be a true philosopher, and if philosophical knowledge is in effect the same as *moksha*—a kind of ignorance (or bliss) due to liberation from all other forms of ignorance—then philosophical enquiry is evidently beyond the reach of ordinary men. But no: Shankara is prepared, as we shall see, to begin at the beginning. He starts by asking the simplest, if most fundamental, questions. Having dwelt upon the majesty of knowledge at its supreme point, he turns aside to consider how knowledge, of whatever kind, is possible at all. Both his formulation of the question and the answer he gives to it put us immediately in mind of Kant.

According to Shankara, our knowledge of the external world is sense-bound: that is to say, our senses, in endeavouring to contact 'reality', inevitably adapt that reality to their own uses. The world that we see, hear, and feel is a world that appears to be extended and in movement, a world of changing phenomena. This phenomenal world is not merely the world that our senses apprehend; it assumes this phenomenal form precisely because our senses apprehend it. Extension and temporality are, in the Kantian phrase, 'forms of our sensibility'. In brief, the world accessible to our senses is in great part the world that our senses have constructed. In the external world we perceive that which we have contributed.

The external world, then, is a world of *Maya*. To render it satisfactorily in Western philosophical terminology is extremely difficult. If we here translate it as 'illusion', we shall be committing a serious error: for Shankara does not for one moment suggest that the world apprehensible by our senses is a world that is not, as it were, 'there'. A similar misunderstanding is frequently met in discussion of the theory of knowledge advanced, though in different terms, by Bishop Berkeley. *Maya* is perhaps better translated as 'delusion' rather than 'illusion'. On this assumption a world of *Maya* is a world pretending to be that which it is not. It is a world of half-lights and half-truths, of inexactitude and imprecision, of promise without fulfilment. Is there anything particularly startling or unfamiliar about such a world? Not at all: it is the world, surely, with which we are familiar in everyday life.

To introduce a further comparison, the world of *Maya* is much the same as the shadowy, phenomenal world described by Plato. Although only the eternal Forms are real, Plato's world of appearance is still very much 'there'. R. G. Collingwood used to explain the distinction very aptly. If Plato's world of appearance is a 'pack of lies', he pointed out, they are nevertheless lies that are 'really told'. *Maya* exists. We live in *Maya*. Ignorance, *Avidya*, sees no more in experience than this realm of *Maya*. Just as Plato asserted the existence of a world of Forms behind appearance, so Shankara maintained the existence behind and beyond *Maya* of a world of timeless Being.

How do we know that such a suprasensible realm exists? Indeed, what right have we to assume its existence? Certain philosophers, namely the so-called empiricists, declare that we have no right at all. All knowledge, they hold, is obtained through the senses. Now clearly the senses yield no knowledge of the realm of which Shankara speaks: how could they, seeing that such a realm is by definition above and beyond the sensuous plane? Nevertheless, as Kant argued, the world of phenomena logically implied another world, the noumenal world, the region of the 'thing-in-itself'. Appearance presupposes Reality. Such a world, therefore, necessarily exists. What remains to be determined is, first, what is its nature, and, secondly, how do we make contact with it?

Students of *The Critique of Pure Reason* will recall the ingenious answers given to these questions by Kant. The noumenal realm, he maintained, is a realm of Being rather than beings, because it is the nature of our senses to regard the world as a multiplicity: that is to say, the senses are so constituted as to perceive the world as a number of separate *things*. For practical purposes this mode of apprehension is both necessary and desirable. Not merely do our bodies form part of the sensuous or material world, but our perceptive faculty is composed of at least five separate 'senses'. A condition of 'sensing' anything is that it shall be sensed as one thing among others, and simultaneously as a unity composed of 'parts'. It follows that the reality behind and inaccessible to the senses will be not *Many* but *One:* a Thing-in-itself.

So much for the nature of the realm of Being. Now for the means whereby such a realm may be contacted. Again, Kant's answer will form a useful prelude to that advanced by Shankara. Let us refrain for a moment from speaking of material things, and observe the nature of personalities or selves. When we consider mankind we regard it inevitably as composed of a great number of different individuals. I am aware of myself as a distinct personality, and I assume everyone else to regard himself in the same manner. Such an impression, says Kant, is the result of our belonging in part, at least, to the world of phenomena. But there is more to us than that. My real self, or, as Kant calls it, my moral self, belongs to a different order. In exercising my moral will, I as it were pierce the world of phenomena, and make direct contact with the noumenal world of the Thing-in-itself. Indeed, my real Self and the Thing-in-itself are, in some mysterious way, the same thing; to know the one is to know the other. This is the answer to the second problem. We make contact with the realm of Being only when, disregarding the accidents of 'character' and 'personality', we attain to genuine Selfhood. To act thus morally is to act freely, and freedom is the shedding of the bonds of the senses. We might add, what has often been denied by the practitioners of that science, that the study of 'character' and 'personality' is the proper domain of psychology, since 'character' and 'personality' belong to the phenomenal realm: whereas the moral self is the domain of philosophy proper.

Now let us compare the Kantian view with that of Shankara. According to the latter, the Self in the sense of the ego belongs to the world of phenomena or *Maya*. We are under the impression, for instance, that our individuality, our passions, our opinions, are real things, capable of subsisting by themselves. Such an impression, however, is mistaken. The *Upanishads* teach that our real self is not the ego but the *Atman*, the reality lying behind appearances, the divine spark, the light that lighteth every man that cometh into the world. And knowledge of Reality, of eternal Being, is acquired, as we know, by realizing the identity of *Atman* with *Brahman*. In other words, we make contact with Reality by means of the true or moral self. Science, in the sense of the technique for analysis and measurement, is concerned solely with phenomena.

To hazard reasons why Shankara and Kant should have evolved a similar idealist theory of knowledge is, as we have said, tempting: but such a study hardly comes within the scope of the present work. Nor do we wish to enter into comparisons regarding the superiority in detail of the one philosophy over the other. The present account affords little idea of the ingenuity with which in both cases the argument is pursued. Nevertheless, to give the Western reader some notion of what is being discussed, we must emphasize that the subtleties of Kant, though difficult to underestimate, appear simple in comparison with those of Shankara. And although subtlety does not necessarily imply profundity, it must equally be admitted that Shankara is by far the more profound philosopher. Indeed, his profundity is to some extent the result of the extraordinary range of his thought, just as Kant's attainment just short of sublimity is the result of the voluntary limitation of his subject. The concepts which Kant expressly excluded from philosophical treatment were those of God, Freedom, and Immortality. In so doing he excluded almost everything that an Indian philosopher will think worthy of serious discussion.

Having given us an extremely ingenious theory of knowledge, Shankara naturally feels under the obligation to discuss the nature of God. In the case of so thorough a devotee of *Brahman*, it may appear surprising that he should have asserted the existence of two gods, *Ishvara* as well as *Brahman*. If, however, we examine why he did so, we shall see that he still remains a complete and absolute monotheist. The god *Ishvara* represents the god of what we are accustomed to call Natural Religion. As there is no such thing as a world without a god, the god of the world of phenomena is *Ishvara*. *Ishvara* is, in fact, the creator, the author of phenomena. And since the world of phenomena is a world of multiplicity, the supremacy of *Ishvara* is fully compatible with the existence of other, if lesser, deities. In short, the polytheism of the people to which Shankara was wise enough to defer is both the consequence and the correlative of the 'deism' of scientists and intellectuals.

It follows that God as both person and creator is a feature of the realm of *Maya*. But *Ishvara* is also something more: He is the purveyor of rewards and punishments, and therefore the arbiter of *Karma*. Is, then, the whole process of *Karma*, the fundamental tenet of the Hindu faith, illusory? Again, we must remind ourselves, not illusory, but simply a process pertaining to a level of experience short of the highest. In a sense *Karma* must belong to *Maya*, because the successive rebirths of the soul take place inevitably in the natural world. To escape from *Karma* is the same as to escape from *Maya*. Such escape involves at once release from the authority of *Ishvara* and absorption in *Brahman*.

If rewards and punishments are features of the world of *Maya*, so are the good and bad actions which elicit them. Those who think to obtain absorption in *Brahman* merely by doing good works, by behaving decently or inoffensively, and by keeping the laws, are under a serious misapprehension. Admittedly good conduct is at all times to be encouraged, because, in so acting, the chain of rebirth may be shortened. The people must be taught 'morals'. But social conformity is not the same as holiness. To the sage it appears immediately evident that the individual self which performs good or evil actions, and to which the law of *Karma* applies, enjoys no real or ultimate separateness at all. And to achieve this realization is to be delivered for ever from the bondage of reincarnation. Even among sages, however, such a degree of holiness is rarely to be attained.

Life as we commonly know it, then, is lived on the plane of *Maya*. And if life, then death. And if pleasure, then suffering. These are phenomena, without true substance. One of the most remarkable passages of Kant, which will also be quoted in the chapter on that philosopher, is that in which, almost in the manner of an Oriental thinker, he suddenly rises to a theme all too frequently obscured by the thickets of his concentrated argument. 'It is difficult to suppose that a creature whose life has its first beginning in circumstances so trivial and so entirely independent of our own choice, should have an existence that extends to all eternity. As regards the continuance here on earth of the species as a whole, this difficulty is negligible, since accident in the individual case is still subject to a general law, but as regards each individual it certainly seems highly questionable to expect so potent an effect from causes so insignificant. But to meet these objections we can propound a transcendental hypothesis, namely that all life is strictly speaking intelligible only, is not subject to change of time, and neither begins in birth nor ends in death; that this life is an appearance only; that is, a sensible representation of the purely spiritual life, and the whole sensible world is a mere picture which in our present mode of knowledge hovers before us, and like a dream has in itself no objective reality; that if we could intuit ourselves and things as they are, we should see ourselves in a world of spiritual beings, our sole and true community, which has not begun through birth and will not cease through bodily death—both birth and death being mere appearances.'

This passage is entirely in the spirit of the philosophy of Shankara. We may cite passage after passage from the latter in the same vein. The *Atma Bodha*, or 'Knowledge of Spirit', sums up Vedanta as follows.

'The spirit is smothered, as it were, by ignorance, but as soon as ignorance is destroyed, spirit shines forth, like the sun when released from clouds. After the soul, afflicted by ignorance, has been purified by knowledge, knowledge disappears, as the seed or berry of the *Kataka* after it has purified water.'

'Like an image in a dream, the world is troubled by love, hatred and other poisons. So long as the dream lasts, the image appears to be real; but on awakening it vanishes.'

'The world appears real, as an oyster-shell appears to be silver; but only so long as the *Brahman* remains unknown, he who is above all and indivisible. That Being, true, intelligent, comprehends within itself every variety of being, penetrating and permeating all as a thread which strings together beads.'

'In consequence of possessing diverse attributes, the supreme existence appears manifold, but when the attributes are annihilated, unity is restored. In consequence of these diverse attributes a variety of names and conditions are supposed proper to spirit, just as a variety of tastes and colours are attributed to water.'

'The body, formed by the union of five elements produced by the effect of action, is considered to be the seat of pleasure and pain... All that belongs to the body (must be considered) as the product of ignorance. It is visible; it is perishable as bubbles of air (on the surface of water); but that which has not these signs must be recognized as pure spirit, which says of itself, I am *Brahman*. Because I am distinct from body, I experience neither birth, old age, decrepitude, nor extinction, and detached from organs of sense, I have no longer any connection with their objects.'

To the Western reader passages such as the above may appear impressive and even moving. But do not they represent a kind of poetry, a mystical lyricism? How, it may be asked, do we *know* all this? Why should not the *Nastiks* and the *Charvakas* have been right to deny *Brahman*, and indeed all forms of suprasensible experience? As to the first question, it is impossible to deny that much of Shankara—and not Shankara only—can be read as poetry: that is to say, it can be appreciated for its emotional rather than for its intellectual appeal. But then, in addition to being a philosopher, Shankara was a poet, and a very accomplished one. Aquinas, it will be remembered, was also a poet. A further point to bear in mind is the following. Classical Indian philosophy remains indifferent to the distinction between poetry and prose: the fact that we tend to stress this distinction may indicate too hard and fast a separation between our intellectual and emotional life.

The *Vedas* are not merely inspired philosophy, but inspired poetry: the same is true of many of the *Upanishads*. Hindu thought reserves its prose for such documents as the *Ordinances of Manu*, with its laws and regulations mostly concerning morals and hygiene—the Hindu equivalent of the *Book of Leviticus*. As to the second question, Shankara, though as convinced as Aquinas of the truth of revelation, is prepared to argue at great length concerning the existence of *Brahman*. To Shankara it is not so much *Brahman's* existence that presents difficulty; what is far more difficult to imagine is how, in the absence of *Brahman*, anything else can be said to enjoy existence. If *anything* exists, then God must. In other words, you have to account for existence itself; and the consciousness of imperfection, vanity, futility, illusion, implies the capacity to apprehend, though not necessarily to enjoy, perfection. The 'problem of evil' may be difficult to solve on a spiritual view of the world. On a materialistic view it admits of no solution whatever; it has to be explained away in terms of 'environment', upbringing, etc.

According to the limited information we possess, Shankara ended his days in a monastery on the foothills of the Himalayas. His incessant labours in the service of the orthodox Hindu faith had rendered him not an old man before his time—because he seems always to have been adult—but a man for whom half a lifetime had consumed the energies normally expended in half a dozen. Ten religious orders quickly sprang up, dedicated to the propagation of his ideas. And these ideas, studied and taught all over India from the ninth century to the present day, have ensured the survival of the Brahmanical tradition in a manner that, given the strength of the forces opposing it, is truly remarkable. But those who despise metaphysics, like those who ignore it, must be prepared for it to outlive them.

* * *

A history of Indian thought would need to dwell upon the various attempts to synthesize and introduce harmony into so many conflicting traditions. To undertake this task, which is outside our scope, would require in itself a volume much larger than the present. In conclusion, however, we ought not to leave the impression that Vedanta, the completion of the *Vedic* tradition, has failed to undergo development since the time of Shankara. Nor must we dismiss as without significance the long line of saints and sages who, down to our own time, have kept the pure Vedanta tradition alive: for we are too apt to regard the oriental tradition as having become bogged in a slough of fanaticism and corruption, paying 'divine honours to the maniac and the fool'.[1] From time to time powerful rulers such as Akbar (1556–1605) have attempted to impose a synthetic state religion on the people. Other reformers, such as Kebir (1440–1518), founder of the very interesting religion of the Sikhs, have attacked and thrown back the tendency towards polytheism which is never likely to be wholly

[1] Disraeli: *Contarini Fleming*, Chapter 1.

eradicated. In the last century several men of powerful personality, such as Ram Mohan Ray, have felt the need to unite Vedanta with what they considered best in both Christianity and Islam. Perhaps the most attractive of these sages was Sri Ramakrishna (1836–86), who, having made a close study of both Christianity and Islam, finally returned to Hinduism, and whose disciples, Brahmananda and Vivekananda, have exerted almost as much influence abroad as in India herself. In these men we see the Vedanta faith at its noblest pitch: for they combined great intellectual force with personal humility. And we may perhaps see in Ramakrishna's lifelong devotion to Kali, the Mother goddess of the universe, a link with that form of worship which may have ante-dated the Aryan invasion of India, and which represents, however vaguely, a natural acceptance by man of life in all its aspects, the pain and destruction (for Kali, beside being Creator, was also Destroyer) as well as the rapture and fruition.[1]

There are only two ways in which man's part in the universe may be regarded: either he is a mischievous and predatory animal who must live by exploiting the natural world, or he is a creature for whom the universe, in spite of its immensity, is in some sense intended to be his home. Whatever he undertakes, he is implicitly adopting one or other of these attitudes. In the Western world it has usually been left to the poets and mystics to reveal the true path, while the philosophers have too often confined their attention to debating whether or not there are such things as chairs or tables. Only rarely do we find a thinker to whom it is obvious that, as a prelude to the 'divine connection', there must first be a 'natural connection'—a truth which is beginning to be appreciated in the sphere of agriculture, where failure to realize that nature is something *alive* has brought us to the brink of disaster, and which we dimly perceive, though more often misconceive, in relation to such a process as sexual love. The words of Marcus Aurelius, so often dismissed as a vague pantheism, are consistent with this view: 'Everything harmonizes with me that is harmonious with thee, O Universe. Nothing for me is too early or too late, which is in due time for thee. Everything is fruit to me which thy seasons bring, O Nature: from thee are all things, in thee are all things, to thee all things return.'

[1] Kali was the wife of Shiva, the Destroyer, who, according to Sir John Marshall, was worshipped in Mohenjo-daro. Shivaism may therefore be 'the most ancient living faith in the world'. Shiva is thus the Osiris of Hinduism, opposed to Vishnu, the Preserver.

8

The Chinese Sages

Govern a state as you would cook a small fish:
do it gently

A Peasant Civilization

'Men always have the greatest respect,' said Thucydides, 'for that which is farthest off.' He might have added—because it is still more true—'and fear', which is an element in respect. For many centuries the European attitude to China illustrated that maxim, as well as its corollary. Save for the visit of an occasional explorer and several missionaries (the earliest being the Nestorian Christians), European contact with China is of comparatively recent origin. Already in the seventeenth century, however, the intellectual world of Europe was evincing great interest in Chinese culture. How little it understood that culture may be surmised from the fact that we, with our much closer contact, still understand very little of it. To speak of contact between one country and another, even countries as near as England and France, is to refer perhaps to continuous contact only at the most superficial level—say the diplomatic level—supplemented by miscellaneous 'contacts' by individuals, business firms, or, at times of emergency, armed forces: which latter is by hypothesis the least typical of all. The first translations of Chinese classical literature, even more perhaps that those of India, exerted a profound influence upon the European mind, particularly the French mind of the eighteenth century. In his brilliant but forgotten study *The Illusions of Progress*, Georges Sorel shows how the French physiocrats regarded ancient China as a kind of idyllic commonwealth, governed by a Natural Law of right and justice, and providing the model from which 'decadent Europe' might learn salutary lessons. This impression while not without an element of truth, was the result of generalization from a few instances. The 'wisdom' of Confucius, for instance, is extremely refreshing and stimulating to the European mind. When it first became accessible it appeared to open up a new world of balance, maturity, and commonsense. It was the kind of message for which Europeans, weary of fanaticism and the wars resulting therefrom, had been waiting. That it should appeal to the French in particular was natural: a balanced, humanist culture was and still is the French ideal of life.

The fact remains that if Confucius had been 'typical' of the Chinese culture of his day, his career would have been very different from what we know it to have been. The apostle of balance and the middle way led a life of much greater struggle than the Buddha, whose ideals were far more difficult to attain. Inviting men to renounce the world, the Buddha moved from place to place at leisure and amid adulation; for men respond more readily to the call of the impossible than of the possible. Save for brief intervals of power and influence, Confucius not merely experienced the bitterness of long exile but died, as we shall see, a disappointed man. In due course he was worshipped. This alone was proof enough of his distinctness from ordinary men, for the day of the apotheosis of the Common Man was far distant. Of the Master, one of his disciples said: 'He is the sun, the moon, which there is no way of climbing over, and though a man desire to cut himself off from them, what harm does he do to the sun and moon? ... The impossibility of equalling our Master is like the impossibility of scaling a ladder and ascending to the skies.' The wisdom of China, like that of any other country, represents the best that country could do in the person of a few sages. Nor would these sages have taught as they did if the lives of their fellow-citizens had not fallen far short of virtue.

Knowledge, even more than love, is reputed to cast out fear: a generalization which is not perhaps so true in fact as it is supposed to be in theory. Certainly the distrust of 'orientals' is less prevalent than it was, perhaps as a result of closer contact. It is difficult, on the other hand, to say whether the traditional Oriental 'contempt' for Westerners, as being materialistic upstarts, has diminished, or has had any reason to do so. We must make due allowance for the fact that for centuries and indeed millennia the Oriental and the Occidental world grew up in complete isolation. The mind is the last thing about a person that one comes to know. The 'mind' of another culture, to use a vague term for an exceedingly vague relationship, cannot be known at all until it has become so penetrated by outside influences that it has changed its character. Much insight can be obtained from the study of past literature so long as such researches are pursued by men of imagination and sympathy (one of the misfortunes of civilized existence is that research is left to scholars, who, because of the time needed to learn the technique of their job, tend often to lose contact with normal life); and among such literature, works of philosophy or wisdom are of particular value as being the quintessence of that which many have vaguely felt but lacked ability to express.

Until the nineteenth century the Far East consisted of a gigantic peasant civilization. A peasantry is by nature conservative. You cannot change it; you can only break it up. The peasantry of China and Japan was broken up, or partially broken up, from outside. Europe discovered China and Japan and not vice versa; and having discovered these countries, Europe began to 'civilize' them, largely by force. The second dissolvent of a peasantry is a sudden rise in the standard of living: for what holds a peasantry together, and in particular what holds it down, is not government or police or excessive taxation, but natural adversity. The 'natural wisdom' attributed to so many peasants is due, as Tolstoy realized when he set out to enquire into the docility of the peasant mentality, to a realization that his situation, never much above subsistence level, is grounded in the nature of things. And until recently, until about a century ago, the nature of things was that most people in the world were obliged to endure a life of hard work with little return, punctuated by private misfortunes for which small provision could usually be made, and often reduced to a level of untold misery as a result of pestilence or war.

Apart from the physical circumstances of his existence, however, it would be a mistake to assume that the life of a Chinese peasant, even in the most arid districts, was necessarily brutish. Brutish is a relative term. The life of Squire Western in *Tom Jones* was probably a great deal more brutish than that of many of the servants on his estate. If brutish signifies a mixture of brutality and irresponsibility, then the life of the average Chinese peasant was certainly less brutish than that of many an overlord and many an emperor. A tradition of family solidarity and of filial piety had existed from (the cliché is apt) time immemorial. The Western world has known nothing like it. The family formed a miniature state of which the father was the ruler. Likewise the family formed an economic unit, every member contributing to the common welfare and having his particular function to fulfil—not least the old, for whom modern European civilization has found decreasing use. Finally, the family formed its own church, because reverence for ancestors was a cult stronger than devotion to any supernatural being. If we think of religion in the sense given to it in India, then China appears to have no religion at all: but if we define the religious instinct as that which prevails over such powerful instincts as that of sex and survival, then the Chinese can certainly be counted as profoundly religious. The bodies of ancestors, for instance, were buried in the plot of land belonging to the family. This plot was always small, but the ancestors were allotted the richest part of it as a matter of course.

The Idea of 'The Way': Lao-Tze

Sages such as Lao-Tze and Confucius are often regarded as having taught the people a new way of life. That is not how they conceived of their own mission. Their task—the task of the 'prophet', as we have come to understand it throughout this book—was to lead men back to the ancient wisdom. Confucius in particular did not claim any originality for his ideas. He merely regretted that, owing to neglect and ignorance, many of the old rituals had fallen into desuetude, with the consequent loss of the truths they had symbolized. He regarded himself as essentially a 'transmitter'. Like Lao-Tze, the older of the two, he set out to show men the road to virtue and contentment. This road was very properly called the Way, the *Tao*. As to how this Way might be found, however, Lao-Tze and Confucius differed markedly one from the other.

To translate *Tao* as 'Way' is reasonable so long as we do not identify it with a technique, a recipe for happiness, which is only a small part of its meaning. It means also the principle of the universe, that which maintains it and gives it motion and order. Just as the stars have fixed courses, so there is a course for man, a means whereby he may link his being with reality: a reality from which he has somehow become alienated. A *Tao* is the origin of all meaning in the universe, it is also responsible for all created things. But things have to be engendered, and creation is in fact brought about by two principles, called *Yin* and *Yang*. *Yin* literally means 'shadow'. It is represented pictographically by the north side of a mountain and the south side of a river, since in daytime the south of the river is shrouded in darkness. *Yang*, on the other hand, means 'light', and is represented in an opposite fashion. *Yang* is active, *yin* passive, the one male and the other female. But *Yin* and *Yang* do not form a dualism which splits the world in two. These principles characterize only the phenomenal world. At the core of reality is *Tao*, unity.

The first elaboration of these ideas of *Yin* and *Yang* was made, so far as we know, in a book of which the title is as obscure as its contents. It was called the *I-Ching*, or *Book of Changes*. Those who declare the Chinese mind to be incapable of metaphysical speculation omit to account for the immense prestige enjoyed by this book. Even Confucius, who otherwise took little interest in metaphysics, edited it and added his own notes. In due course this manual, with its list of sixty-four *hsiangs* or 'ideas' which in combination make up reality, became a source of trivial magic and divination. This was a further sign of its traditionally sacred character, because only books believed to contain genuine spiritual content are likely to be put to such use or abuse.[1] We have used the word 'trivial' deliberately: for if the original purpose of the *I-Ching* was astrological, as seems certain, this does not detract from its basic profundity. A great modern psychologist, C. G. Jung, has declared the *I-Ching* to embody the essence of Chinese culture. For what the modern rationalist dismisses—without understanding it—as astrological, and what modern science regards as sheer superstition, Jung sees as a form of knowledge older by thousands of years than our cause-and-effect technique which, with its dwarfing effect, we call science. To Jung, the *I-Ching* forms a treatise on what may be termed, in the words of modern psychology, 'psychic parallelisms', united by the principle of 'synchronism', or relative simultaneity: for the fundamental truth of astrology, or 'the summation of all the psychological knowledge of antiquity', is not so much that man's destiny is controlled by the stars as that 'whatever is born or done this moment of time has the qualities of this moment of time'.[2] We do not know with any exactitude how old a book the *I-Ching* may be; but we know that it was handed down from generation to generation as embodying precious wisdom. Such fate does not befall a mere compendium of abracadabra.

[1] Cf. the *Sortes Virgilianae* of the Middle Ages.

[2] *The Secret of the Golden Flower:* translated and explained by Richard Wilhelm, with a European commentary by C. G. Jung (Kegan Paul, 1945).

The first philosopher to be associated with the elaboration of the doctrine of *Tao* was Lao-Tze. He is the reputed author of a book called the *Tao-Te-Ching,* which means *The Book of the Way and of Virtue.* Lao-Tze is an obscure figure. Indeed, there is some doubt as to whether he existed at all. His very name may suggest a legendary personage, for it means simply 'The Old Master': but apparently he had another name, Li, which means a plum. On the other hand Confucius is said to have met him, and he is mentioned by several other philosophers. When historians dismiss a man as being legendary without producing any other evidence about him, all they usually mean is that they have not yet discovered another set of legends. At any rate, Lao-Tze is supposed to have been born in 604 BC in Honan province in Central China. Although brought up in a poor home, he rose to become curator of the Royal Library at Chou and lived to an advanced age. His reputation for wisdom was great, but he evidently failed to exert any marked influence outside a small circle. Towards the end of his life, believing that his native state was doomed to anarchy, he made up his mind to leave it. At the frontier, the customs official, recognizing the venerable sage, gave him permission to depart with all his goods on condition that he left one thing behind for the benefit of his country: namely his wisdom. Lao-Tze, to whom it had never hitherto occurred to write down his thoughts, consented. Setting to work at once, he condensed all his ideas into five thousand words, which must be a record in the annals of philosophy. Thus the *Tao-Te-Ching* came to be written. What happened to Lao-Tze after that not even legend says anything except to record the date of his death, which is put at 517 BC.

The philosophy of the *Tao-Te-Ching* is perhaps one of the most revolutionary that has ever been formulated. Interpreted literally, or as literally as we are able to understand it, it represents an attack upon everything that has gone to make up what is called civilization. Lao-Tze tells us to 'let things alone'. He tells governments in particular to let things alone: in short he sees nothing but evil in the idea of government. Unlike almost all other philosophers, he does not extol knowledge, nor does he identify it, as Socrates did a little later, with virtue. On the contrary he extols ignorance, which he identifies quite categorically with bliss. Again, the true sage refuses to argue. By following the *Tao,* he sets an example of simplicity and contentment which, being naturally infectious, produces a tranquillizing effect upon his fellows. 'The sage,' says Lao-Tze, 'carries on his business without action, and gives his teaching without words.' All the normal recipes for bringing into being a just society are dismissed by this philosopher as futile, even dangerous. We must refrain, because it is most dangerous of all, from inculcating righteousness itself, since all attempts to introduce goodness through legislation will produce the opposite of that which is intended. 'Do away with learning, and grief will not be known. Do away with sages and eject wisdom, and the people will be benefited a hundred times. Do away with benevolence and eject righteousness and the people will return to filial duty and parental love. Do away with artifice and eject gains, and there will be no robbers and thieves... Appear in plainness and hold to simplicity.' That is the substance of his message.

Just as Lao-Tze tells his fellow-men to 'let things alone', so he tells them to stay where they are. 'Without going out of the door, one can know the whole world. Without peeping out of the window, one can see the *Tao* of heaven. The further one travels, the less one knows. Therefore the sages know everything without travelling. He names everything without seeing it. He accomplishes everything without doing it.' The ideal society, therefore, is 'a small state with few people'. These few must be content with what they have. And they will be content with what they have if they do not seek to enlarge their horizon. 'Though the neighbouring states are within sight, and their cocks' crowing and dogs' barking within hearing, the people (of that small state) will not go near them all their lives.' No doubt this was strange doctrine to issue from one who, while committing it to paper (or split bamboo, as in fact was the procedure at the time), was in the very act of leaving his own country; but his point of view is interesting as being a solution which human beings, never having tried, can hardly condemn out of hand. Perhaps Lao-Tze's ideas on the art of government can best be summed up in a phrase typical in both expression and thought of all Chinese wisdom: 'Govern a state as you would cook a small fish: do it gently.'

Such teaching, expressed with remarkable compression and sharpness, has found an echo in every age, almost in every generation. There is no evidence that Jean-Jacques Rousseau knew the works of Lao-Tze; but his early ideas on society and government are very similar, with nature taking the place of *Tao*. The problem raised by such an ideal vision of existence is, needless to say, a practical one: what happens to the little state when, as must occur sooner or later, it meets with outside attack or interference? Lao-Tze was sage enough to have anticipated this difficulty. He also anticipated, alone of the thinkers of antiquity, the words of Christ. 'Recompense injury with kindness. To those who are good I am good, and to those who are not good I am also good; thus all get to be good. To those who are sincere I am sincere, and to those who are not sincere I am also sincere; and thus all get to be sincere... The softest thing in the world dashes against and overcomes the hardest... There is nothing in the world softer or weaker than water, and yet for attacking things that are firm and strong there is nothing that can take precedence of it.' And he adds, with justice: 'This all the world knows but does not practise... These are the words of truth, though they seem paradoxical.'

Why does Lao-Tze place such emphasis upon passivity, even going so far as to enunciate the further paradox, stated in slightly different terms by Krishna, that we should 'act inaction'?[1] It is not that he values paradox for its own sake, as we suspect certain of the Indian sages to have done. His doctrine of passivity follows logically from his conception of the nature of *Tao*. As we have seen, *Tao* is a conception very similar to the Egyptian *Maat* and the Greek *Logos*. It animates, it

[1] The term for this celebrated concept of 'inaction' is *Wu Wei*.

pervades reality: it also generates and becomes incarnate. Indeed, Chinese translations of the opening of the Fourth Gospel run, 'In the beginning was the *Tao,* and the *Tao* was with God and the *Tao* was God.' And just as at some point the 'Word is made flesh', so the 'light that lighteth every man' comes to recognize its kinship with the divine power. To translate this process in terms of Indian thought, *Atman* becomes *Brahman.* The Taoist philosopher conceives of a similar identification. The world is in a condition of misery, or rather man is not at home in his world, because he has failed to identify his *Tao* with that of the universe. The two are at loggerheads. Let him eschew learning, convention, even civilization, and harmony will be restored. The *Tao* in his innermost self will turn out to be the *Tao* that 'existed before heaven and earth, motionless and fathomless, standing alone and never changing, the Mother of the Universe'.

Kung-fu-tze: birth and upbringing

No two philosophers were more unlike each other in personality than Lao-Tze and Confucius. Given this difference in outlook, their influence was bound to be unequal. Taoism is still a living faith: the latest estimate is that forty-three million Taoists still live in China. This is a large number; but it is probably as little indicative of the intensity of the faith as to say that a similar number of people in France is Catholic. Moreover, it must be borne in mind, when speaking of China, that adherence to one form of belief does not exclude sympathy with another or several others. An educated Chinese, just because he is educated, is willing to accord respect to any congenial faith; what he holds in abhorrence is fanaticism and bigotry. Possibly the real religion of China, at its most intellectual level, is that of toleration. At the same time we must not imagine that willingness and ability to tolerate other beliefs is necessarily instinctive with the Chinese people (who are in any case too numerous to be summed up by a generalization of this kind): such an attitude is the product of long and deep-rooted tradition. And the founder of this tradition—one of the great traditions of humanity—is Confucius.

The name Confucius is the best that Europe, with its Latin culture, could make of the words *Kung-fu-tze*, which means literally 'Kung, the Master'. His real name was Kung-Chiu. Like the other great spiritual leaders of mankind, Confucius was credited with a miraculous birth, accompanied by celestial wonders. He was the illegitimate son of a father already well advanced in years. Born in 551 BC in the kingdom of Lu, now Shantung, he was described, presumably metaphorically, as having the lips of an ox and a mouth like the sea. More plausibly, he had an immense forehead: hence the name Chiu. As with Buddha, a jet of water sprang up to wash the new-born baby, who was delivered in a cave to which his mother had been directed by an annunciatory spirit. The boy's upbringing was hard. After his father's death he was obliged to support his mother by doing odd jobs after school hours. No doubt he was always old for his years: we can imagine the boyhood of almost all the great philosophers save Confucius—that immense forehead must have lent him premature adulthood. Even so, he was by no means a solitary or a book-worm. Sport he loved, particularly archery and fishing; and he was from earliest youth a passionate devotee of music, though his tastes—here as elsewhere—were conservative. He married at the age of nineteen. We do not know much about his married life. The lady, we gather, came from Sung, a neighbouring state. Some records suggest that the couple were divorced after four years; others that the parting came at the time of Confucius's exile, which was twenty years later. The sketchiness of the information at our disposal suggests that the marriage bond, having been entered into for conventional reasons, was preserved for as long as convention dictated. A son was born of the marriage, Kung Li, or, as he is called in *The Analects*, Po Yu. We know that Po Yu became a disciple of his father, but, strange to say, the two do not seem to have been united by any stronger sympathy. The disciple whom Confucius loved—the St John or the Ananda of Confucianism—was Yen Hui, whose life was a model of what the true sage should be.

Confucius entered upon his mission as a teacher or sage earlier in life than most spiritual leaders of mankind. By the age of twenty-two he was already well known both for his wisdom and for his upright life. Moreover, he had a marked gift of eloquence. Encouraged by a few enthusiastic associates, he decided to set up a school. What this amounted to was that his house was thrown open to anyone seeking instruction: fees were exacted according to the pupil's capacity to pay. Not that Confucius set out to purvey a kind of abstract wisdom. He undertook to teach definite 'subjects', above all history, poetry, and the principles of what he called decorum. Believing that society was suffering from neglect of the traditional wisdom, Confucius took great pains to instil into his disciples the meaning of the ancient rites and ceremonial Odes, to say nothing of such repositories of truth as the *Book of Changes*. Above all, he had a great belief in the efficacy of music as giving a last polish to a man's character; but he would have nothing to do with modern music—'the songs of Cheng'—which produced the opposite effect. Confucius's attitude to music was somewhat similar to that of Schopenhauer: he believed that it not merely typified the harmony of the universe but symbolized the concord which, given enlightened rulers, might prevail in the state. How he would have been perplexed by our modern educational curricula, where music is so often treated as an 'extra' or at best an added accomplishment. The neglect of the 'philosophy' of music may be the clearest sign of man's feeling of isolation in the universe.

Growing fame

As the number of his pupils grew, Confucius began to be a power in the land, because many of these young men soon obtained responsible positions. In 518 BC the Minister of Lu expressed the wish on his deathbed that his son should be entered at Confucius's school. From that moment Confucius became the equal, as well as the instructor, of princes. Hitherto he had been content to remain at his little academy, a conscientious pedagogue; now he felt the desire, and likewise received official encouragement, to travel. His first important excursion was to the capital of the province, Lo-yang, now in Honan. What he saw in this busy place fascinated him, especially the ancient court rituals and the ceremonies in the magnificent temples.

At Lo-yang, too, was another source of attraction for Confucius. Lao-Tze was there, then a man of eighty-seven. Less than half his age, Confucius, though duly respectful, seems to have made less impression upon Lao-Tze than upon most other people. In reply to some recondite questions about past history and ancient men of wisdom, the old man expressed himself both forcibly and frankly. 'Those about whom you enquire,' he said, 'have mouldered with their bones into dust. When the hour of the great man has struck he rises to leadership; but before his time has come he is hampered in all that he attempts. I have heard that the successful merchant carefully conceals his wealth, and acts as though he had nothing—that the great man, though abounding in achievements, is simple in his manners and appearance. Get rid of your pride and your many ambitions, your affectation and your extravagant aims. Your character gains nothing from all these. This is my advice to you.'

It appears that Confucius took these words seriously to heart, for when he returned to his school he conveyed his impression of the old exile in the following vivid phrases: 'I know how birds can fly, fishes swim, and animals run. But the runner can be snared, the swimmer hooked, and the flier shot by the arrow. But there is the dragon—I cannot tell how he mounts on the wind through the clouds, and rises to heaven. Today I have seen Lao-Tze, and can compare him only to the dragon.' Such was the tribute of the philosopher of humanism to the apostle of mystic naturalism: a tribute best described as that of respectful incomprehension.

If Confucius showed no personal disposition to mystical thought, he was aware of the fascination that such thought exerted over the mass of mankind. It was not that he denied the existence of a transcendental world of spirit; it was rather that he gave priority to considerations of human government and welfare. As in his teaching, so in his private speculations, he adopted the method of rational and logical enquiry. The cultivation of trance-states according to Yoga principles was something to which, after some early experiments, he refused ever after to apply himself. 'I have spent the whole day without food and the whole night without sleep in order to meditate. It was of no use. It is better to learn.' Again and again, when questioned about matters beyond immediate human experience, Confucius answered in terms more downright than the Buddha himself, though from very different motives. When his disciple Tzu-Lu asked him to discourse on man's duty to the spirits of the departed, he replied, 'While still unable to do your duty to the living, how can you do your duty to the dead?' And on another occasion, when asked about the nature of death itself, he answered, perhaps begging the question slightly, 'Not understanding life, how can you presume to understand death?' Frequently his disciples came under the criticisms and even the jeers of ascetic practitioners of the simple and reclusive life: for hitherto the true sage had been regarded as one who, the better to concentrate his thoughts, renounced all contact with the world. To such gibes Confucius always had a telling reply: 'I cannot herd with birds and beasts, and if I may not associate with mankind, with whom am I to associate? If right rule prevailed in the world, I should not be taking part in reforming it.'

In 517 BC a crisis occurred in the province of Lu. The duke, who had been oppressed by some powerful chieftains, endeavoured to reassert his authority. The *coup* failed. Confucius, thereby compromised, followed his master into exile. As they were making their way to the neighbouring province of T'si, the sage and his disciples came across an old woman weeping at a graveside. They asked her what had happened. She replied that at that same spot a triple tragedy had occurred: her father-in-law, her husband, and finally her son had all been killed by tigers. Having tried to console her, Confucius enquired why her family had nevertheless decided to settle in such a dangerous part of the country. 'There is no oppressive government here,' she answered. Turning to his pupils, Confucius remarked: 'Take note of this. Oppressive government is fiercer than a tiger.'

On arrival at T'si, the duke at once received Confucius in audience. The sage's observations on the art of government pleased him, and he considered appointing Confucius to high office. Opposition came from the other ministers. They ridiculed the little band of scholars as impractical pedants. As for Confucius himself, they regarded him as nothing but an eccentric busybody, obsessed with the niceties of etiquette. 'It would take generations,' they said, 'to exhaust all that he knows about the ceremonies of going up and going down.' Confucius stayed on for several years, but without obtaining even minor government employment. Finally, on learning that the situation in Lu was somewhat improved, he returned home.

The sage in office: exile

His patience was now rewarded. The new duke, Ting by name, decided to try the experiment of entrusting affairs of state to someone without overt political ambition. The man who had observed that 'I am not concerned that I have no place: I am concerned how I may fit myself for one,' was the obvious choice. In 501, Confucius became chief magistrate or governor of the city of Chung-tu. He forthwith set to work. In a very short time, we are told, an amazing social transformation occurred. The standard of morality reached a height never before attained; the Golden Age seemed to have returned. Public honesty was such that valuable objects dropped in the street were either left or returned to their owners: the people became astonished at their own virtue. Finding the burden of government considerably lightened, the duke promoted Confucius to the office of Minister of Public Works. The new minister, determined to be practical, introduced measures for surveying the land and improving agriculture. As a result, prosperity rapidly followed upon exemplary conduct. The duke, no less delighted than his subjects, saddled Confucius with further responsibilities. Having been advanced to the office of Minister of Justice and finally to that of Prime Minister, Confucius soon wielded an authority second in name, and far superior in practice, to that of Ting himself. At this point the Chinese records grow lyrical. 'Dishonesty and dissoluteness,' we read, 'were ashamed and hid their heads. Loyalty and good faith became the characteristics of the men, and chastity and docility those of the women. Strangers came in crowds from other states. Confucius became the idol of the people.' An exaggeration, no doubt: but we have the commemorative pillars of Ashoka to prove that, given a ruler of powerful personality, such changes are not impossible. What is impossible, given human nature, is that they should endure.

Nor did they—though Confucius can hardly be held to blame. The disruptive element came not from within but from outside. The rulers of states bordering upon Lu began to grow seriously alarmed. Confucius's achievement, which was even celebrated in poetry, might cause oppressed peoples elsewhere to insist upon the display of similar conduct on the part of their rulers. These despots were convinced neither of the benefits of public righteousness nor of the sincerity of its exponents in Lu. Feeling it incumbent upon him to do something drastic before the contagion of honesty spread, the Minister of T'si devised a scheme for setting Confucius and his master one against the other. One day the Duke of Lu received a sumptuous present. It consisted of eighty beautiful singing girls or courtezans, and one hundred and twenty horses. On learning the nature of this gift, Confucius ordered that the entire party should be lodged outside the capital. Unfortunately, one of the duke's officials, who slipped out to inspect them, returned with a glowing account of what he had seen. In spite of Confucius's protestations, the duke yielded to temptation, and the girls were taken into the royal harem. Festivities of a kind long abandoned ensued. Public business, including the ritual sacrifices, was interrupted. Ignored and humiliated, Confucius found he could do nothing. He chose the most dignified way of showing his disgust, which was to embark once more upon the life of an exile. His comment on this fiasco was apt. 'I have never met,' he said, 'one who loves virtue as he loves beauty.'

His wanderings lasted for no less than thirteen years. First of all he decided to pay a visit to the state of Wei, where he felt he could at least count upon the hospitality of his brother-in-law. The duke, Ling by name, welcomed him at first with great respect. Confucius was not merely feted as Plato was feted by the younger Dionysius of Syracuse, but he was offered a substantial pension in kind. In spite of this, he was to suffer the same disillusionment as Plato himself. On acquaintance, Ling proved to be more of a blackguard than Ting. Again Confucius decided to leave, but he met with such perils on the road that he was obliged to return, though with reluctance, to Wei. Evidently the court were in no mood to welcome him back, for the wife of the duke, Wan-Tzu, a lady of wanton character, had always strongly objected to him. There was once a statue in Paris of King Louis XV on horseback, surrounded by figures of the Four Virtues. The popular saying was, '*Les Vertus sont à pied, le Vice est à cheval.*' When Confucius drove in his carriage behind Wan-Tzu, the public comment was similar: 'Lust in front, virtue behind.' As soon as he could manage it, Confucius took his leave once more.

In company with the faithful disciple Tze-Kung, the now aging philosopher experienced the most severe of all his trials. Having incurred ridicule both from men of the world and from those who posed as being other-wordly, he found himself tempted to regard all men as potential enemies. From the highest office he had sunk to the condition of an outlaw, the butt of ridicule, the target of abuse, and on at least one occasion the object of violence; for the brother of one of his disciples nearly succeeded in killing the little party outright by pulling down a tree in their path. Although no one was hurt, the act was sufficient to scatter the alarmed disciples; for some time Confucius wandered about alone. When Tze-King enquired of some peasants whether they had seen the Master, the reply was that an old man 'disconsolate as a stray dog' had been observed in the neighbourhood. On being later informed of this description, Confucius laughed heartily. 'Well put,' he said. All his life Confucius seems to have retained a wry sense of humour.

With so many disappointments and rebuffs it is a wonder that Confucius did not despair of ever making himself permanently useful to his fellow man. But he never lost hope. 'If there were any princes who would employ me,' he once declared, 'in the course of twelve months I should have done something considerable. In three years the government would be perfected.' He was always willing to put his services at the disposal of anyone who required them, but he refused to accept offers that might involve a compromise with his principles. Thus although Duke Ling of Wei several times invited him to return, Confucius accepted no place of distinction at his court: absolute control or exile were the two poles between which his public career continued to move. We cannot blame his disciples for occasionally losing confidence in their Master, especially under the taunts or chidings of the hermits and ascetics whom they so frequently met in the course of their peregrinations. 'Rather than follow one who withdraws from this state and that state,' said one aged hermit to Tzu-Lu, 'had you not better follow those who withdraw from the world altogether?' It seemed plausible advice, but to Confucius despair of mankind was still the greatest of sins. Nor did he feel that his wandering life was altogether useless. The world now knew him as a sage of remarkable character and determination, whom governments could exile but not silence, and whose rejection by princes was a signal reproach to the waywardness of mankind. Unknown to the countrymen of Confucius, a figure of comparable wisdom was receiving even worse treatment in the city state of Athens. Except for a brief period, Socrates never enjoyed public office; but at his trial he claimed the right, as a man of wisdom and public spirit, to be supported at the public expense. They gave him a month in gaol as an example, and then, for economy's sake, poisoned him.

Recognition and retirement

In spite of its reputation for savagery, the Orient has tended to be less violent with its saints and sages than the Occident, which possesses a somewhat black record in that respect. The most power-crazed of oriental despots have stayed their hand when confronted with the *Nabi*. Croesus spared few of his rivals, but he spared Solon, and Nebuchadnezzar spared Jeremiah; whereas Socrates was done to death by the people to whom the Western world owes its highest ideals of culture, and Christ was crucified by the people to whom we owe our highest conceptions of law. Several local tyrants of China regarded Confucius as a menace to their authority or an obstacle to their enjoyment of the spoils of oppression; but no ruler dared to put him under arrest and cut off his head, though jealous ministers often contrived to expose him to ridicule. In the end, however, Confucius received a measure of recognition the more touching in that it was extended from his home-state, that of Lu. Duke Ting had long been dead of dancing-girls and other luxuries, and the throne was occupied by Duke Gae. The latter sent the sixty-nine-year-old philosopher some presents and an invitation to return home. Confucius was overjoyed. In accepting the invitation, however, he made it clear that the days of his power were over. He would advise, he would study, he would rest. Those who wished to listen to him could do so. He was a tired but also a resigned man.

He enjoyed five years of honourable and studious life at Lu before he died. The ministers consulted him but did not seek to disturb his repose. He was now able to undertake a work that he had so long deferred as almost to have lost hope of accomplishing, namely the editing of the famous 'Classics'. He also devoted his time to writing a history of his people, to reclassifying the traditional Odes, and to re-arranging the ceremonial music.

One morning the old man, now seventy-three, was observed to rise from his couch with more than usual difficulty, and to shuffle out of doors singing a sad song. The words were those of an Ode for which he had always shown particular affection, but on this occasion the disciples detected an ominous meaning in them:

> The great mountain must crumble,
> The strong beam must break,
> And the wise man wither away like a plant.

He then gave some directions as to how his body should be buried, being careful to specify the rites that were to accompany his funeral. That his mind should have dwelt upon the niceties of ceremonial was characteristic; but his last words to his disciples were to do with his mission, and might well have been spoken by the prophetic 'transmitters' of every age: 'No intelligent monarch arises: there is not one in the empire that will make me his Master. My time has come to die.' He returned to his couch, lay there for a week, and, without uttering another word, died. The disciples buried him with meticulous attention to his directions, and, by building little shacks by his tomb, prepared to mourn over his remains for several years. It is said that Tze-Kung, his most devoted follower, remained at the spot for as long as six years. The descendants of Confucius were in due course elevated to the rank of dukes, and the family flourishes in China to this day.

We may learn a good deal about Confucius, the man, from his recorded sayings or *Analects*. These sayings are terse, mordant, sometimes a trifle sarcastic, but never sentimental. That he showed great pity for human suffering we know; but he liked best to express his sentiments in action. When one of his friends had sustained a personal loss, he ordered one of the horses of his carriage to be loosed and presented to the mourning family. 'I dislike the thought,' he explained, 'of my tears not being followed by practical sympathy.' That was his habitual attitude. From the various descriptions we have of him, and also from the majestic image at the temple erected at his birthplace, we may assume that he was both physically and mentally tough. Indeed, no man of poor physique or weak will could have survived the ordeal of his various terms of exile. It is a curious turn of fate that the philosopher most attached to ideas of decorum, good form, and social grace, should have been obliged to spend so much of his life in the wilderness, deprived of civilizing influences, condemned to be a displaced person, and begging in vain to be employed to some purpose. Equally ironical, perhaps, was the fact that Lao-Tze, who reputedly despised urban life, should have been living, when encountered by Confucius, in one of the biggest towns in China. Confucius has been accused, against the testimony of his close friends, of overweening egoism. He certainly made some statements which, if not exactly egoistic, do not err on the side of modesty. 'In a hamlet of ten families,' he said on one occasion, 'there may be found one honourable and sincere as I am, but not so fond of learning.' More celebrated is his remark: 'At fifteen I set my mind upon wisdom. At thirty I stood firm. At forty my ear was still docile. At seventy I could follow the desires of my heart without transgressing the right.' We can only affirm that if a man has really attained to such a pitch of perfection, he is entitled to say so. There are today about 550 millions who believe him to have been justified despite Mao-Tse-tung's anti-Confucian campaign.

The 'Classics'

The canonical books of the Confucian faith—for so we may legitimately call it—are known as the Nine Classics. Five of them, called the Five *Ching*, were probably the work of his own hands, either in an author's or in an editorial capacity. They consist of the *Li-Chi* or *Book of Rites*, a repository of rules of propriety, designed to inculcate spiritual as well as physical deportment. The second was a commentary on the remarkable book to which we have already referred, namely the *I-Ching* or *Book of Changes*. The third was the *Shi-Ching* or *Book of Odes*, another piece of editorial work: these poems, though beautiful in themselves, were of obvious didactic purpose. The fourth and fifth, the *Ch'un Ch'iu* or *Spring and Autumn Annals* and the *Shu-Ching* or

Book of History, treated the past of the province of Lu and of the Chinese Empire as an inspiring record of heroism and order, thus bringing it into contrast with the prevailing anarchy. So much for the direct work of Confucius. The remaining four Classics are compositions which, though inspired by the Master, were written, so far as we know, by his disciples. Most famous of all are the *Analects* (or 'fragments') to which we have referred. These sayings, bearing the stamp of a single personality, are probably as accurate a record of what the Master said as the notes of Boswell. The next *Shu*, or Book, is that entitled the *Ta-Hsueh* or *The Great Learning*, which many scholars regard as the clearest summary of the Confucian creed: parts of it, indeed, may be by Confucius himself. The grandson of the sage, Kung Chi, is considered to be the author of the Third *Shu,* the *Chung Yung* or *Doctrine of the Steadfast Mean*. The last is the *Book of Mencius*, named after Confucius's great disciple.

In *The Great Learning*, the Confucian ethic is pared down to its bare essentials. There is probably more concentrated wisdom, more solid truth, in this remarkable work than in any other philosophical treatise, even though it may be wisdom of a wordly kind: Lao-Tze would have dismissed it as folly, the more so in view of its presumptuous title. 'Things have their root and their branches,' says the treatise, 'affairs have their end and their beginning. To know what is first and what is last will lead one near to what is taught in The Great Learning.' We are then told how the Ancients set about ordering their kingdoms according to virtue. In order to achieve public tranquillity, they discovered that they must first set a good example in their family life, which in turn led them to a kind of inquisition into their own souls, culminating in the realization that they must 'extend to the utmost their knowledge', until it penetrated to the heart of 'reality' or the 'nature of things'. In other words, good government is not to be attained by the imposition of external regulations: on the contrary, it is to be attained only by each individual, the governor as well as the governed, engaging in self-cultivation according to the natural law of life. A vague aspiration, some will say: for what is this natural law of life? That is a question to which Confucius was more reluctant to give an answer than Lao-Tze, who said that the law was *Tao*, or than Hsun-Tze, who said that no such law existed. But Confucius, when pressed to give an answer to this problem, left no doubt in anyone's mind that, like his great predecessors, he was an apostle of the divine connection. 'I seek *unity*, all pervading,' he once remarked *apropos* of nothing, but in reality of everything. The reality of which he spoke was not the less real for being inaccessible to the majority of mankind. We must remember that, according to his own admission, he was fifty-years-old before he understood 'the laws of heaven'.

To open a modern textbook of ethics (which surely no one would willingly do unless obliged to pass an examination) is to find oneself in a world totally different from that inhabited by the great sages. In the first place, most textbooks of this kind are occupied exclusively with enquiry into the meaning of terms, such as Right, Good, Duty, etc.:

feigning a kind of academic unawareness of what these notions can really convey, and frequently arriving at the conclusion that they do convey nothing at all. The conception of human conduct as somehow related to the world in which man lives, virtuous action being that which is in harmony with some divine purpose, has become so thoroughly alien to the Western academic mind as almost to seem preposterous. Yet such is the message, albeit sometimes difficult to decipher, of all the spiritual leaders of mankind: nor would it appear that past civilizations would have accorded a man this status unless he had made good his claim to provide such enlightenment. The last great moralist after Spinoza to preach a kind of universalism in ethics was Kant; but Kant's statement that we must 'act so that the maxim of our conduct shall become a universal law' is a pale abstract regulation, promulgated without reference to the purpose of nature and of a world superior to nature.[1] Confucius made a remark very similar to that of Kant. 'The Higher Man,' he said, 'behaves so as to make his conduct in all generations a universal law'; but he uttered this maxim against the background of the traditional wisdom that he did so much to keep alive. It was not for nothing that he should have spent the last years of his life studying the most ancient piece of Chinese metaphysical thinking, the *Book of Changes*. The *I-Ching*, as we have seen, is a treatise on 'the laws of heaven'; and if these laws, as thus interpreted, appear obscure, nobody before or since has pretended them to be otherwise. What is important is the recognition of their ceaseless, if imperceptible, operation. As we read in the *Doctrine of the Steadfast Mean*,[2] 'what heaven has conferred is called The Nature. An accordance with this Nature is called The Path of Duty.' The point is hammered home until it takes on the aspect of a platitude; but in fact it is a truth that counts above all others. 'Unroll it, and it fills the universe; roll it up, and it retires and lies hid in mysteriousness.' A platitude is a truth that mankind has been content thus to roll up and hide away. A platitude is the product of a conspiracy between human inertia and verbalism.

Compromise and the Mean

Like the Buddha, whose faith has proved the most powerful competitor to the doctrine of decorum and the Mean, Confucius was aware even to the point of over-simplification of the necessity of compromise. To the common people he preached a doctrine that might be understood without recourse to philosophical subtleties. He made allowance for the incapacity of most men to apprehend truths outside their immediate experience. 'To give oneself earnestly to the duties of men, and, while respecting spiritual beings, to keep aloof from them—that is wisdom.' It is, indeed, if you have in mind the bulk of humanity. With the same object of keeping within the normal range of experience, Confucius laid emphasis upon the virtue of family solidarity and

[1] The reader may wish slightly to qualify this remark in the light of our reference to Kant in the section on Shankara, Chapter 7.
[2] Rendered incisively by Ezra Pound as 'The Doctrine of the Unwobbling Pivot'.

in particular of filial piety. In the family he saw the natural unit of both order and continuity. It is here that virtue becomes concrete, duty a reality. The abstract theorist may reduce ethics to a few rules of expediency: common humanity will continue to respect the teachings of the sages, even if more in the breach than the observance. The Confucian teaching has entered so deeply into the Chinese mentality that all other doctrines have been obliged, by a kind of irony, to compromise with it. When historians and publicists speak of the futility of trying to conquer or subdue the Chinese people, they sometimes appear to have in mind the sheer vastness of the country. Strategists, speaking knowingly of 'long lines of communication', think they have thus settled the matter. But the difficulty of 'conquering' a people such as the Chinese (if the notion of conquest still retains any meaning) is the difficulty of breaking the power of a deeply-instilled and almost unconscious ethic. The 'long lines of communication' which play a vital part in such a process are the channels whereby a realist doctrine of social responsibility has been handed down for two and a half millennia. Break that, and you will have achieved a victory without parallel in history. But we have yet to see whether, at the moment that your 'pacification' or your 'communization' seems complete, it has not broken you.

After the death of Confucius, his teaching achieved a success far beyond the modest expectations of its founder: how great a success the violence of certain opposition movements can best testify. As the doctrines of the Mean, the Golden Rule ('do unto others as you would have them do to you'), and the ideal of Filial Piety seeped into the public consciousness, so a new aristocracy of Confucian scholars was gradually formed. Nor were these scholars necessarily men of retiring or hermit-like disposition: the ideal of the philosopher king, or rather the ministerial sage, was always before them. Likewise, the Master's example in founding a school was followed by men of public spirit all over the country. Such schools, though often reducing the living teaching to absurdly formal patterns, preserved art and learning and therefore civilization through many centuries of disorder and indifference. For civilization, never at any time in great public demand, is obliged at different epochs to be content with teaching itself to itself, just as the exiled Confucius kept up his spirits by rehearsing the Odes for his own amusement, and playing his lute. While a number of rulers adopted a nominal Confucian doctrine as the official creed of their state, others, following the susceptible Duke Ting, burked at the obligation to set a shining moral example to their subjects. They were content to proclaim rigorous laws and see to their enforcement upon others. The Emperor Shih Huang (221–211 BC), wishing to demonstrate that history began with himself and resenting the influence of Confucius's doctrines (as well as all others), ordered a gigantic 'Burning of the Books'. The act was largely symbolic: as an attempt to destroy learning it was futile. Many scholars had the Confucian scriptures by heart. Others, at great personal risk, hid the split-bamboo packets against a more enlightened reign. Having ruled for a brief period, Shih Huang-ti was fortunately succeeded by just the monarch for whom the scholars had been waiting. Wu Ti, by way of reaction, proclaimed the Confucian doctrine the official religion of the state in 136 BC. The Master was in effect elevated to the status of a divinity.

In due course Confucianism began to spread to other countries. Taoism and later on Buddhism exerted a profound influence on the Chinese mind; but whereas Buddhism has been driven from India by a more belligerent doctrine, its diffusion throughout China did not weaken to the same extent the hold of Confucianism, which proved too 'natural' and congenial a philosophy to be eliminated, and which will perhaps outlast every creed that seeks to take root in the minds of that most ethical, because Confucian, of people.

Wisdom Genuine and Counterfeit

A concentrated study of Indian and Chinese philosophy, viewed out of its historical context, may lead one to suppose that Hindustan and the Middle Kingdom[1] were crowded with little princelings round whom philosophers buzzed like gadflies, seeking to influence affairs of state, proffering gratuitous advice, and losing no opportunity for admonition. The impression needs to be corrected by reflecting upon the size of the country, the absence of communications and the comparatively small areas over which effective government could be exercised. Granted such conditions, however, we cannot help being once more struck by the fact that, in contrast to our own times, the five centuries preceding the birth of Christ saw the rise of more world philosophies than all the years that have followed. In a recent book, Professor Karl Jaspers has endeavoured to show that the contemporaneity, to employ the term somewhat loosely, of such men as Buddha, Confucius, Lao-Tze, Zoroaster, and the second Isaiah, indicates a common and related movement of thought throughout the oriental world. If so, such a movement has never been repeated; nor is it ever likely to be explained. There is one possibility, on the other hand, which the study of pre-history has rendered more plausible than it would have been considered a century ago: namely that the ancient world was perhaps less isolated than we sometimes suppose. Travel may have been difficult, hazardous, and above all slow; but immense distances were covered by both individuals and groups. The slowness may have been an asset; modern travel is too quick. Moreover, a long journey was something to be accomplished in stages; it amounted to taking up an abode at a series of points along a line not always predetermined. It consisted not so much of leaving your home as of moving it, or at least of establishing new ones. Nor were these interim dwellings necessarily as provisional as the camps of a tribe of nomads. Many of the castles built throughout the Middle East by the crusaders, to take a later example from European history, are good for another thousand years if we discount the possibility of deliberate demolition. The 'conquest of distance'—a victory not two centuries old—may have

[1] i.e. *Chung-Kuo*. China is sometimes called also *Chung-haw-kuo*–'Middle Flowery Kingdom'.

exerted from a psychological point of view much less influence upon bringing the right man and the right ideas together than the pioneers of locomotion and flight, and apostles of free trade such as Cobden, hoped. What distance has conquered is not ignorance but mature reflection, just as the invention of the typewriter has meant that we now write half a dozen letters instead of one. In short, pre-industrial travel may have been as effective a transmitter in space as the oral tradition was an effective preserver in time.

It follows that if the influence of individual philosophers has on occasion been exaggerated, we must not fall into the opposite error of underestimating such influence. We know that in India and China philosophy was respectable and respected, because it paid men to pretend to philosophical ability even when they did not possess it, except in a very debased form. Although modern rulers, especially in times of war, may sometimes consult psychologists, no Western ruler has ever been known to put himself under the tutelage of a major philosopher. The modern passion for administration, which produces committees of advisers on technical questions, has completely obscured the more fundamental problem of what is good government. In the centuries following the death of Confucius, Chinese society was much influenced by men resembling in their methods the Greek Sophists; the so-called Dialecticians and Logicians (*Pien Che* and *Ming Chia*, as their schools were respectively called). These men were not necessarily all charlatans, any more than our modern advertisers are all liars; but having set themselves up as purveyors of wisdom and experts in controversy they were obliged to lay claim to an omniscience which, had they been genuine spiritual leaders, they would have been the first to disown. Once you turn philosophy into a business, your aim ceases to be the pursuit of truth or the achievement of wisdom and becomes rather the maintenance of solvency. Such commercial philosophy provides convincing evidence of the prestige in which sagacity was held: the Western world tends to accord a similar pre-eminence to prosperity, in spite of the mild protest of the churches.

Among the sages that gravitated towards the city of Lo-Yang were some who more nearly conformed to the traditional idea of the sage. There were men such as Mo Ti (*c.* 450 BC) who, in addition to being a logician, preached a gospel of universal brotherhood based upon the contention that men are by nature good: his books, considered subversive of good government and authority, were burnt together with the works of Confucius by the Emperor Shih Huang-ti. There was Yang Chu (*c.* 390 BC), an opponent of both Confucius and Mo Ti, who believed that since life was inherently evil and pointless we should endeavour to extract from experience as much pleasure as possible, without regard to the feeling of others. His argument, stated more incisively than it has ever been since, was that the 'good name' of which the moralists speak is a figment. To whom is it good? For whom is it left behind? A man may toil and sacrifice, engage in fasts and prayer, perform innumerable good works. So far so good. When he dies he may be revered as a saint. Men may even begin to worship him. But of what use to *him* is all this posthumous adulation? He is not there to enjoy it. 'Such fame,' says Yang Chu, 'is what no one who cares for what is real would choose. Celebrate him—he does not know it. Reward him—he does not know it. His fame is no more to him than to the trunk of a tree, or a clod of earth.' On the other hand there may be men who, having the power and the means, live a life of unbridled self-indulgence. After their death their names are held in execration. They become models or epitomes of tyranny, rapaciousness, and lust. But what effect can such evil reputation have upon them? None at all. 'Reproach them—they do not know it. Their ill-fame is no more to them than to the trunk of a tree or a clod of earth.' In short, since good and evil reputation are equally meaningless, there is no point in concerning oneself with moral virtue in life. The only reality is the fulfilment of desire, here and now, and for oneself alone.

Mencius

To sages with a deeper sense of moral responsibility, such a gospel represented a serious danger to society. Like the idealism of Mo Ti, it could not be put into practice without bringing about anarchy. It is the ethical doctrine of the solipsist. Mencius, the great disciple of Confucius, regarded his life's work as an attempt to combat the two gospels, between which he saw little to choose: 'The words of Yang Chu and Mo Ti fill the world. If you listen to people's discourses about it, you will find that they have adopted the views of the one or the other. Now Yang's principle is "Each for himself"—which does not acknowledge the claims of the sovereign. Mo's principle is "to love all equally"—which does not acknowledge the peculiar affection due to a father. To acknowledge neither king nor father is to be in the state of a beast. If their principles are not stopped and the principles of Confucius set forth, their perverse speaking will delude the people, and stop up the path of benevolence and righteousness ... I am alarmed by these things and address myself to the defence of the doctrines of the former sages and to oppose Yang and Mo.'

The above passage reveals one of the outstanding qualities of Mencius; his sanity or, what comes to the same thing, his pursuit of the Golden Mean. We observe also another quality, humility: for Mencius claimed no particular originality for what he taught. All his life he sought to further the doctrines of Confucius, whom he regarded as the greatest teacher the world had known. He was of distinguished birth. By name Mang Ho, the imperial government later caused him to be known as Mang-tze, which means Mang, the Master. Having converted *Kung-fu-Tze* into Confucius, the Western doctors latinized *Mang-Tze* into Mencius. He was born in 372 BC, about a century after Confucius's death.

The formative influence in Mencius's life was his mother, whose husband had died when the boy was very young. She represents in Chinese tradition the model of motherhood, and her son the model of filial piety. Many stories are told of her devotion and care for her son's welfare. One one occasion, grieved to see him idle, she deliberately severed the thread of her shuttle as he watched her at work. He enquired the reason for this unexpected act. She explained that it represented his own failure to concentrate on his studies, so that his life consisted of unco-ordinated bits and pieces. The lesson proved effective. Mencius became a conscientious student, and in due course followed in his Master's footsteps by starting a school of his own.

The authorities from whom he profited most were themselves pupils of Confucius's grandson. Mencius forthwith determined not merely to live according to the wisdom of the Master but to follow a similar career. He lived to a great age, dying at eighty-four, and spent his active years at the courts of princes, sometimes holding office and sometimes merely seeking to influence those who did so. We gather that he met with many disappointments, though not more than Confucius himself or than his own contemporary, Plato. In old age he decided to set down the results of his reflections, and these form the fourth Confucian 'Classic', which, as we saw, is named after him.

At first sight the fundamental principle of Mencius's philosophy bears a strong resemblance to that of Mo Ti, for Mencius believed that human nature is at heart good. But he did not subscribe to the naive view that men, left to themselves, will automatically do what is right. What he maintained was that they have the capacity, well within their reach, to exercise benevolence and to train themselves to make the correct responses. 'Speaking realistically,' he wrote, 'it is possible for men to be good, and that is what I mean when I say that man's nature is good. If they become evil, it is not the fault of their natural powers. Thus all men have a sense of compassion, also a sense of shame over wickedness, a sense of reverence, and a sense of truth and error. The sense of compassion is equivalent to individual morality, the sense of shame to public morality, the sense of reverence to ritual propriety, and the sense of right and wrong equals wisdom.' He refers to these faculties as the 'four tender shoots' of human nature. The expression is apt. Man is inherently endowed with these good impulses; but they are sensitive growths which must be tended and cared for. Rough handling and an unfavourable environment will deform and even destroy them.

Because he believed that human beings were capable of organizing the good life in society, Mencius did not hesitate to advocate the overthrow of princes whose rule was inherently oppressive. 'The people,' he declared, 'are the most important element in a nation: the sovereign is the lightest.' A man needed to have courage to make such statements in public, and Mencius was supremely courageous. He argued the matter with kings. 'Suppose that the chief criminal judge could not regulate the officers under him, how would you deal with him?' The king said, 'Dismiss him.' Mencius again said, 'If within the four borders of your kingdom there is not good government, what is to be done?' The king looked to the right and left and spoke of other matters. The second principle to which Mencius gave emphasis was that of filial piety, the bulwark of the Confucian tradition, which was to bind Chinese society together for more than two thousand years. 'The desire of the child,' said Mencius, 'is towards his father and mother. When he becomes conscious of the attractions of beauty, his desire is towards young and beautiful women. When he comes to have a wife and children, his desire is towards them. When he obtains office, his desire is towards his sovereign... *But the man of great filial piety to the end of his life has his desire towards his parent.*'

Confucius and Mencius exerted permanent influence over Chinese civilization because their doctrine, for all its prudence, was essentially one of hope, based upon faith in human nature. Such faith can easily be belittled and made subject to ridicule: for human nature can always be invoked in discredit of itself. The most powerful criticism of Mencius's doctrine was that levelled against it by a contemporary called Hsun-Tze, who is thought to have died about 235 BC. According to this philosopher, human nature was thoroughly evil. While Mencius had pointed to the 'four tender shoots' of human nature, Hsun-Tze pointed to as many thorns. Above all he drew attention to the fact, difficult enough to confute, that human beings were animated by an ineradicable acquisitiveness, a desire for power and gain. Against such an instinct, what availed benevolence and kindness? 'There belongs (to human nature),' he said, 'even at birth, the love of gain; and as actions are in accordance with this, contentions and robberies grow up, and self-denying and yielding to others are not to be found. There belong to it envy and dislike; and as actions are in accordance with these, lewdness and disorder spring up, and righteousness and propriety, with their various orderly displays, are not to be found. It thus appears that to follow man's nature and yield obedience to its feelings will assuredly conduct to contentions and robberies, to the violation of duties belonging to every one's lot, and the confounding of all distinctions, till the issue be a state of savagery.'

What was Hsun-Tze's remedy for this state of affairs? He had none. He had merely a palliative. The acquisitive desires could never be rooted out. They might simply be kept within bounds. Institutions were necessary. 'The sage kings of antiquity, understanding that the nature of man was thus evil, set up the principles of righteousness and propriety and framed laws and regulations to straighten and ornament the feelings of that nature and correct them.' The European thinker who most resembles Hsun-Tze is undoubtedly Thomas Hobbes, who held a similar view of human nature and prescribed the same kind of remedies for its short-comings.

Chuang-Tze

We have no evidence to suggest that Hsun-Tze ever met the great Taoist philosopher Chuang-Tze, but the two were contemporaries, and they frequented the same courtly circles. We should certainly have heard of any such meeting, because it would have resulted in a disputation far more heated, we may suppose, than that in which Confucius and Lao-Tze engaged. Chuang-Tze has been called the St Paul of the Taoist faith, and the description is just. His work is a restatement of the doctrine of Inaction in terms at once profound and elegant, for

Chuang-Tze was a master of language and gifted with a poetic imagination. He was born in the province of Sung in the third century BC. Although several times offered important positions, he preferred to live a life of quiet teaching and meditation. To the emissaries sent by the Duke of Wei, who offered him the post of Prime Minister, he replied in terms which ensured that the invitation would not be repeated: 'Go away quickly, and do not soil me with your presence. I would rather amuse and enjoy myself in a filthy ditch than be subject to the rules and restrictions in the court of a sovereign.' It is reported that he did not trouble even to turn round from his fishing when the king of Khu sent two officials offering him supreme control of all his territories. In comparison, Confucius appears like an ambitious place-seeker.

Chuang-Tze attacked the idea of government even more vehemently than his master Lao-Tze himself. 'There has been such a thing as letting mankind alone,' he said, 'there has never been such a thing as governing mankind.' He quotes the answer of La-Tze to one of his disciples who enquired how, on such a theory, men were to be kept in order. 'Be careful not to interfere with the natural goodness of the heart of men. Man's heart may be forced down or stirred up. In each case the issue is fatal. By gentleness the hardest heart may be softened. But try to cut and polish it—'twill glow like fire or freeze like ice. In the twinkling of an eye it will pass beyond the limits of the Four Seas. In repose, profoundly still; in motion, far away in the sky. No bolt can bar, no bond can bind—such is the human heart.' An absolute quietism is recommended: 'Cherish that which is within you, and shut off that which is without: for much knowledge is a curse.' Consequently, all the conventional values are seen to be snares and delusions. 'Appeal to arms is the lowest form of virtue. Rewards and punishments are the lowest form of education. Ceremonies and laws are the lowest form of government. Music and fine clothes are the lowest form of happiness. Weeping and mourning are the lowest form of grief.' The true sage, on the other hand, 'places himself outside the universe, beyond all creation, where his soul is free from care. Apprehending *Tao*, he is in accord with virtue. He leaves charity and duty to one's neighbour alone. He treats ceremonies and music as adventitious. And so the mind of the perfect man is at peace.' Is such a condition the same as that which men call happiness? Yes, answers Chuang-Tze; but there is a counterfeit happiness of which we should beware. 'I make true pleasure, he says, 'to consist in inaction, which the world regards as great pain. Thus it has been said: "Perfect happiness is the absence of happiness: perfect renown is the absence of renown." Now in this sublunary world of ours it is impossible to assign positive and negative absolutely. Nevertheless, in inaction they can be so assigned. Perfect happiness and preservation of life are to be sought for only in inaction.' And the argument culminates in a passage of great beauty. 'Let us consider. Heaven does nothing, yet it is clear. Earth does nothing, yet it enjoys repose. From the inaction of these two proceed all the modification of things. How vast, how infinite, how vast, yet without form! The endless variety of things around us all spring from inaction. Therefore it has been said, "Heaven and earth do nothing, yet there is nothing which they do not accomplish." But among men, who can attain to inaction?'

We find in the work of Chuang-Tze a strong vein of mysticism. To some extent this is reminiscent of Buddhist thought; and perhaps the originality and fascination of Chuang-Tze resides in this blend of fancy and commonsense. 'Those who dream of the banquet, wake to lamentation and sorrow. Those who dream of lamentation and sorrow, wake to join the hunt. While they dream they do not know that they dream. Some will even interpret the very dream that they are dreaming; and only when they are awake do they know it was a dream. By and by comes the Great Awakening, and then we find out that this life is really a great dream. Fools think that they are awake now.' The passage ends with an image that blurs the distinction between reality and illusion. 'Once upon a time I, Chuang-Tze, dreamt I was a butterly, fluttering hither and thither, to all intents and purposes a butterfly. I was conscious only of following my fancies as a butterfly, and was unconscious of my individuality as a man. Suddenly I awaked, and there I lay, myself again. Now I do not know whether I was then a man dreaming I was a butterfly, or whether I am now a butterfly dreaming I am a man.'

Yet we must not suppose Chuang-Tze to have been lacking in shrewdness or even humour. Interspersed with the lyrical passages on the nature of *Tao* there is much brute commonsense—a toughness that is Confucian or, more accurately, that is inherently Chinese: witness the reply of Chuang-Tze to his disciples when they expressed the wish to give him an elaborate funeral. 'We fear,' they had said, 'lest the carrion kite should eat the body of our Master.' 'Above ground,' said the dying man, 'I shall be food for kites; below I shall be food for mole-crickets and ants. Why rot one to feed the other?' But what better summary of Chinese wisdom can be found than the words quoted by Chuang-Tze of his Master, 'The art of preserving life consists in being able to keep all in One, to lose nothing, to estimate good and evil without divination, to know when to stop, and how much is enough, to leave others alone and attend to oneself, to be without cares and without knowledge—to be in fact as a child.' All the profound, philosophies of the world boil down in the end to something like that, in violent contrast to the conclusions of the pseudo-philosophies. And Lao-Tze is reported to have gone on to elaborate what he meant by living as a child, arriving at the summit of Chinese wisdom: 'A child acts without knowing what it does; moves without knowing whither. Its body is like a dry branch; its heart like dead ashes. Thus good and evil fortune find no lodgement therein; and there where good and evil fortunes are not, how can the troubles of mortality be? Those whose hearts are in a state of repose give forth a divine radiance, by the light of which they see themselves as they are. And only by cultivating such repose can man attain to the constant. Those who are sought after by men are assisted by God. Those who are sought after by men are the people of God. Those who are assisted by God are His chosen children.

'To study this is to study what cannot be learnt. To practise this is to practise what can never be accomplished. To discuss this is to discuss what can never be proved. Let knowledge stop at the unknowable. That is perfection.'[1]

[1] Compare the similar remark by Wittgenstein (see page 4).

9

Mohammed

The religion of Abraham, the sound of faith, and not one of those who join gods with God, is our religion

The Uniqueness of Islam

Man's Faith in God or the gods is the one factor in human history about which it is dangerous to make prophecies. There have been periods—of which the present may be one—in which Christianity as an influence upon social life has suffered such spectacular decline that recovery seemed impossible. Whether Pope Leo X actually committed himself to the statement that 'the myth of Christ hath brought much gain' is doubtful. Sufficient evidence of the infidelity of the age lies in the fact that such a remark could be attributed, without a sense of outrage, to the vicegerent of God and successor of St Peter. Similarly, there have been periods in which the Islamic faith seems to have run into the sand from which, at an unexpected moment, it originally issued. But it has revived, and it has revived again to-day.

In many ways the faith of Islam is unique. It is unique not in the sense that it owes little to any other faith—for the reverse is true. It is unique in the same sense that it is the one post-Christian faith to have achieved and for centuries maintained world influence, while remaining alive and fertile in the land of its origin. The centre of gravity of almost every other faith has shifted, sometimes by many thousands of miles. The path to Rome, for example, is more frequently traversed by Catholics than the path to Jerusalem, which is crowded with the returning exiles of an earlier faith. But the pilgrimage to Mecca is still incumbent upon all true Moslems who can afford the journey, just as the ceremonial language of Moslems of every nation is still Arabic, whether the faithful can understand it or not.[1]

A further curiosity about the Islamic faith, or more strictly about its founder, is that it appears to have had no distinct precursors. Christianity is remarkable for the prophetic succession of which it forms, to the devout, the culmination or fulfilment. The Buddha was the Buddha of Buddhas, but not necessarily the last of his kind. The basic beliefs of Hinduism seem to be as old as the human race. Confucius was one, if the greatest, of a long line of Chinese sages. But Mohammed begins with himself. He had neither an Isaiah nor even a

[1] This applies to the 'set prayers'. An exception is Turkey, where Islam was 'disestablished' in 1928.

John the Baptist. Nor, apart from the Khalifs, had he any successors. Of all the great apostles of the divine connection he was the one whose great influence upon history might least have been anticipated.[1]

Such emphasis upon Mohammed's unique historical mission has received a sharp challenge in certain quarters. What, it is asked, is so remarkable about the career of this leader of men? A close study of the society in which he lived reveals that his 'religion'—if it was that, and not rather a political ruse—can be explained in very simple terms. It came at a time when its utility was most evident. It seems to have been devised to meet a particular set of conditions. In short, it was a historical necessity. That is one reason for disposing of the view that its origin is in some way mysterious. The second reason, perhaps more plausible because more in harmony with modern trends of thought, is psychological. The 'appeal' of Islam to a desert community is obvious. The conditions of the desert, we are often told, conduce to unity of thought, to concentration upon essentials, and therefore to an inclination towards monotheism.

Do they indeed? If so, the theory raises some curious reflections. Even allowing for a period in which the process of soil desiccation and erosion was much less advanced, the desert is a great deal older than Islam. It may be as old as the human race, which, however ancient as a species, has probably enjoyed about a million years of sub-civilization, and not less than ten thousand years of culture.[2] But the desert, it appears, had to wait until the seventh century AD before it 'generated' the monotheism that is appropriate to it. Such arguments, as we have already seen, explain nothing. To those who know it, the desert is a crowded, oppressive place. The terrors of loneliness are more likely to be experienced in the heart of a great metropolis.

The remarkable unification of the Arabian tribes for which Mohammed was responsible might suggest that in his day, or during his youth, Arabian society was particularly disunited. We must not forget, however, that even today Arabia is a country with few stable centres and a largely fluid population. In this respect it preserves, as few other countries have done, the conditions in which all human societies have existed for much the greater part of history. Only with the Industrial Revolution in the West, and then chiefly in England, has the average man ceased to be a countryman and become a townsman: we fail to appreciate how short a time he has had to become adjusted to urban conditions.

The earliest stable society in Arabia was that which existed at Saba in the modern Yemen. Even today the strong and stately castles of that epoch—gigantic window-pocked tenements of baked mud—remain standing. Like Ur, Saba was a town of which the titular governor was a god. The ruler held office nominally at the god's sufferance, though he (or she) sometimes chose to become identified with him. Not

[1] But see Arnold Toynbee, 'Did Islam lack antecedents?' (*A Study of History*, Vol XII, pp. 461–7).

[2] Or much more, if we take into account the twenty-five-century-old art of Lascaux in the Dordogne.

merely was the constitution of Sabaean society matriarchal, but some of its queens, such as Balkis, attained great reputation for wisdom and beauty. In contrast, the Bedouin tribes were, and still remain, rigidly patriarchal. From Saba, an important caravan centre, the tribes set out upon trading journeys to such cities as Petra, now in Jordan, and Palmyra in Syria, which served as links between the Roman Empire and the Sassanian Empire of Persia. So wealthy a city was Saba, in fact, that the Persians considered it worth capturing in AD 570. Along the trade-route to the north lay another flourishing city, Mecca, which had been dominated during the fourth century by a powerful tribe called the Quarash.

Mecca was not simply a commercial centre for the trading of spices, silk, ivory, and precious stones. Like Saba, it was a temple city of which the tutelary god was named Horbal. The shrine of this god took the form of a sanctuary containing a large black stone or cube, which was known as the Kasaba. In this temple, of which the Quarash were guardians, stood many hundreds of images. These were the gods, or their replicas, of the numerous tribes which visited the town, and their material presence enabled the traveller to worship conveniently his own particular deity. A nearby mountain, Arafat, was the centre of an annual pilgrimage as well as a sacred fair of great antiquity. The attraction of the Kaaba itself was that it was supposed to have come down from heaven at the time of Abraham. If, as many suppose, it is a meteorite, this tradition may have some foundation in fact. As for the association with Abraham, the interest of this will in due course appear.

The youth of Mohammed

Mohammed was born in Mecca about the year AD 570. His family, though belonging to the Quarash tribe, was poor, and he appears to have spent a lonely boyhood. Both his father and mother died before he was six-years-old, and he was entrusted to the care first of his grandfather and then of his uncle. In early youth he became a camel driver, and soon began to accompany his uncle on trading journeys, particularly to Syria. Realizing the boy's latent business abilities, his uncle sought to further his interests by obtaining for him employment in the service of a rich widow and business woman called Kadijah. This was the foundation of his fortunes. As his new work brought him into contact with merchants of many different nations, Mohammed was not slow to realize the backward state of his own country compared with the powerful empires ruled from Byzantium and Persia. No doubt he was impressed initially by the fact that order and stability promoted wealth; but, being of a reflective turn of mind, he was equally struck by the contrast between the religious beliefs of some of these foreign communities and the crude polytheism of his own countrymen. For just as he began to acquire knowledge of the great world empires, so he came to learn of the so-called world religions: it is certain that he mixed freely with Zoroastrians, Christians, and Jews. He may indeed have been attracted to one or other of these sects without penetrating very deeply into its tenets: or he may have been principally attracted by what was common to all three faiths, namely their grasp of certain basic spiritual facts, such as the struggle between good and evil forces, represented by Ahura Mazda and Ahriman, Jehovah and Lucifer, Christ and Satan. There were strong Jewish communities in southern Arabia and at Medina, while Christian ideas, especially in their monophysite form, had begun to penetrate Arabia in the fifth century. Mohammed describes both Jews and Christians as the 'people of the Book', but it is unlikely that he knew the Bible at first hand. There is reason to think that the same is true of some of his Christian contemporaries.

It is tempting, and indeed legitimate, to draw a comparison between Mohammed and Abraham. Both were inhabitants of a temple city, a civic theocracy. Both were early engaged in the kind of trade that enabled them to acquire both considerable experience of the outer world and marked independence of mind. Both were obliged, at a critical moment of their lives, to quit the city of their birth and to seek their fortunes elsewhere. Both felt the necessity, once this uprooting had taken place, of dissociating themselves from their formal convictions and following a different faith. Finally, each believed himself to be the vehicle of a special revelation from heaven. Now the faith in question was not necessarily a new faith; it was an old faith. The faith of Abraham was faith in the god of his fathers. The faith of Mohammed was the faith of Father Abraham.

Mohammed's youth and early manhood were overtly occupied with business. So assiduously did he serve his mistress that in due course she agreed, though fifteen years his senior, to become his wife. The marriage proved a success. Mohammed, now a rich man, established a large family. His worldly ambitions were satisfied. To the men of his race and community he represented the kind of being to whom the gods had been unusually bountiful: for those whom such gods loved enjoyed prosperity and died full of years. What other evidence could be found of divine favour?

The voice in the desert

In spite of the sudden revolution in Mohammed's conduct and beliefs about the age of forty, we need not necessarily assume that the 'revelation', when it came, was altogether unexpected. The theory of the 'sudden conversion', which has been exploited by certain revivalist sects, is not merely discounted by modern psychologists but regarded with suspicion by most spiritual directors: for that which arrives so suddenly can as suddenly depart, leaving the mind little changed for this momentary diversion. We may surmise that such fundamental spiritual changes begin at a level far below that of conscious reflection, for the compost of the psyche best generates its heat when left undisturbed. Consequently, a life of routine, particularly business routine, is in some ways more favourable to the regeneration of personality than occupations of a more reflective character; the depths of the mind are rarely engaged. Nevertheless, however long

Mohammed remained unconscious of these hidden forces, there came a time when the inner turmoil issued in an outer restlessness. Feeling an imperative need for periods of solitude and retirement, he remained alone for days at a time in the desert or in some remote cave. In due course he began to see visions and to hear voices, or rather one particular voice: for, like the daemon of Socrates, the voice that addressed him was invariably the same, the words falling into a rhythm that grew more and more compulsive. Between periods of great exaltation of spirits, he would fall into a dejection no less extreme.

At length Mohammed became convinced that the bearer of the messages was the Archangel Gabriel himself, and that the messages came from God. Such communications were made, he knew, only to one whom God has chosen to be his *Nabi,* his Prophet, whose task was to lead men back to a faith from which they had strayed. The feeling assumed the character of a burning conviction when one day he heard the voice of God say plainly: 'Thou art the man. Thou art God's new prophet to convert the people of Arabia.'

Did Mohammed really hear those words, did he imagine them, or did he fabricate the whole story of his divine revelation? These questions will always be asked, though, being unanswerable, they are idle enquiries. To those who regard Mohammed (or Buddha, Christ, or Joan of Arc for that matter) as having been at best the victim of an illusion, the difficulty is to give a coherent account of the later course of history. For, within a century of the supposed revelation, an Islamic Empire had been established which not merely threatened with destruction all the empires of the world, but continued for centuries to exert pressure upon Christian Europe from at least three fronts. At its height, this Empire stretched from India to the neighbourhood of Poitiers. By belittling the cause, rationalism renders itself correspondingly less able to explain the effect. It may finally be more reasonable, if less rationalistic, to admit the possibility of supernatural intervention than to pile upon naturalism a load greater than it can bear.

The fact that his mission as Prophet was announced to him by the Archangel Gabriel disposes of the view that Mohammed was commissioned to preach to mankind a new faith. While interested in the beliefs of the Jews and Christians, he regarded these beliefs as themselves deformations of the pure monotheism preached by the Father of Semitic religion, Abraham. If the Koran bears evidence that Mohammed misunderstood Christianity, it is at least as reasonable to suppose that the Christians whom he met were responsible for this misapprehension as that he was obstinately stupid. He believed that his mission was similar to that of the great Prophets who had succeeded Abraham: above all, Moses and Jesus. For a time, it seems, he imagined that 'the people of the Book' could be brought to a truer understanding of their own fundamental beliefs, thereby enabling his people to unite with others in worship of the true God. Only with the passage of years did he come to the view that it was his duty to give to his people a new Book.

First converts

It was to Kadijah that he first confided the substance of the revelations he had received. Filled with awe and enthusiasm, she forthwith became her husband's first convert and disciple. Other members of his family followed her example, above all his uncle's son Ali. His guardian, being essentially worldly in outlook, was less certain. An early convert outside the family circle was Abu Bekr, a man who exerted great influence in the Quarash tribe and who later came to succeed the Prophet himself. Even so, the faith made little headway at first among the bulk of the people of Mecca. Indeed, it met with considerable opposition, especially from Mohammed's fellow merchants. Since the temple city drew much of its revenue from religious dues and offerings, the attack on idols was thought likely to have an adverse effect on trade. There were others, less materialist-minded, who, learning of Mohammed's mystical transports, denounced him at best as a harmless poet and at worst as a false prophet. Among the tribes themselves, whose lives were largely taken up with vendettas and pillage, the doctrine, though simple and severe, made no immediate appeal. Bearing in mind the statements made concerning the aptitude of the desert-bound Bedouin for monotheism, we may recall with interest Mohammed's own opinion on this subject: 'The Arabs of the desert are most stout in unbelief and dissimulation, and it is not likely that they should be aware of the laws which God has sent down to his apostle' (Koran, *sura* IX). Mohammed, like Abraham, was at heart essentially a townsman.

Some idea of the slowness with which the faith made headway may be judged from the fact that during the next four years Mohammed made only forty converts. The mission of Christ, it may be remembered, was completed in three years. As men doubted Mohammed and his claims, so on occasion he doubted himself. He even abandoned Mecca, retiring for several years to a safe place in the country of his uncle's choosing; for the latter, though sceptical, stood by him in all his trials. His return, though indicating the passing of public displeasure, was followed by private misfortune. Both Kadijah and his uncle died. He suffered money troubles. It seemed as if the visions and the voice had altogether misled him.

Twelve years from the time of the first revelation, however, a significant event occurred. A group of pilgrims reached Mecca from the town of Yathreb, which was situated about two hundred and fifty miles to the north. They sought out Mohammed, whose fame had spread as far as the rival city, and pledged themselves to accept his doctrine, agreeing to renounce idolatry, fornication, the exposure of children at birth (a custom among those unable to afford their upkeep), and other pagan habits. This mission, numerically so insignificant, was followed by others. The men of Yathreb were eager both to learn and to spread the gospel among their fellows. Such enthusiasm was something to which Mohammed had not been accustomed. It dawned upon him that he might do well, if only as a temporary expedient, to leave Mecca and to establish his headquarters at Yathreb.

This decision and its accomplishment, undertaken in conditions of the greatest secrecy, marked the beginning of an era in the history of Islam. Mohammed's flight to Yathreb in the summer of AD 622 is known as the *Hegira* (or Flight), and from it Moslem chronology begins. Yathreb was thereafter known as Medinat al Nabi, the City of the Prophet, or simply Medina, the City.

The great welcome given to Mohammed in Medina was due to two causes. His teaching found eager disciples there, certainly: the celebrated saying of Christ concerning the honour denied to prophets in their own country applied equally to his great rival of the Christian era. But the men of Medina not merely agreed to provide asylum to Mohammed; they hoped to profit from his presence. They had cause to hate the people of Mecca, whose prosperity was purchased to a great extent at their expense; for they resented above all the fact that caravans passing across Arabia made their chief halting-place at the sanctuary of the Kaaba rather than at the equally fertile Medina. On more than one occasion these animosities had boiled over into open warfare. It is difficult to effect a serious aggression, however, without the aid of some exalted warcry. No one engages in immorality without thinking up some moral reason for so doing. Inflamed by Mohammed's summons to wreak God's vengeance on those who had rejected His Prophet, the people of Medina launched a crusade against Mecca and inflicted a series of defeats upon its defenders, though the town was not finally taken until later. The immediate task was to assume control over the surrounding country and its unruly tribes.

When Mohammed first arrived at Medina, he had expected to receive a particularly warm welcome from the Jews. Here he gravely miscalculated. The people who looked to Abraham as their father refused to take seriously the man who believed himself summoned by God to lead men back to the Patriarchal faith. Far from regarding him as the Saviour whom they awaited, they treated him as merely the latest of the false prophets. While Mohammed accused them of having departed from the faith of Abraham, the Jews accused Mohammed of attempting to manipulate that faith for his own uses. That the two doctrines had much in common was precisely the trouble, for the followers of two creeds dissimilar in certain particulars are more prone to enmity than those of widely-divergent doctrine.

The return to Mecca

In the end, Mohammed felt obliged to break with the Jews altogether. At one time he had ordained that his followers, when praying, should turn towards Jerusalem, the Holy City of the Jews. Now he decided that the faithful, a growing body, should turn towards the Holy City of the Arabs, which was Mecca. A radical change in his outlook occurred. In his youth it had seemed to him, an inquisitive but ignorant Arab, that enlightenment, learning, and civilization must all come from beyond the borders of Arabia. He betrayed the exaggerated respect of unsophisticated people for those of superior education and training.

He nourished the idea of civilizing Arabia from without. Not only did he become increasingly dissatisfied with the 'civilization' that he hoped to import (for he may have realized that by the time such a thing reached the cities of Arabia it had become considerably debased), but he grew to appreciate the true significance of Gabriel's message, and above all the manner of its delivery. The revelation had been made in the desert. It had been addressed to him as an Arab. It owed nothing to either Persia or Byzantium or Jerusalem. The enlightenment it provided was of a kind to which nothing in these civilized centres could show any parallel. Instead of civilizing Arabia from without, Mohammed now addressed himself to the high mission of enlightening the world from within. He might rule at Medina for some time—in fact he stayed there for as long as ten years; but his true task was to return in triumph to Mecca and so reconsecrate that city in the name of the one God.[1]

The God was Allah, and so the word 'god' is still translated. But there was a special reason why Mohammed should have employed this word. The Quarash tribe had two special deities, one male and the other female. Allah and Al-lat. By calling the God of Abraham Allah, Mohammed was not merely preserving a name with which his people, and above all the people of Mecca, were familiar; he was in effect identifying the 'new' God with the traditional God of his own family. Such an identification was no more arbitrary in his case than it was in the case of Abraham. One of the most remarkable differences in outlook between the Western world and almost all ancient civilizations is that modern man, in seeking spiritual guidance, tends to look to the future. Salvation, even on the plane of pure materialism, is thought to be achieved by following a path leading towards some distant but theoretically accessible goal. Hence Science, or rather the impulse behind scientific enquiry, comes to be regarded as almost a sacred process, since the pursuit of such enquiry (to which nothing seems impossible; another 'divine' characteristic) promises to remove all obstacles to happiness, even though final salvation may be reserved for a generation so far distant as hardly to interest us. The objection to such an outlook is that in freeing us from slavery to the past it delivers us over to another form of bondage, namely slavery to the future. Archaic man, who was more conscious of the need for guidance than we, first looked to the past.[2] Differing from us again in the strength of his group-loyalties, he would fall back in times of crisis upon tribal or family deities, whose worth had been put to the trial on occasions

[1] In order to break the tribal power, Mohammed introduced the custom of uniting pairs of men together in brotherhood, one being from Mecca and the other from Medina. The aim, soon to be established, was to found a Moslem brotherhood superseding ties of race.

[2] It may be suggested that the whole mission of the Hebrew Prophets contradicts this; but their mission was only indirectly with the future. 'The connection of the *Nabi* with the future is not that of one who predicts. To be a *Nabi* means to set the audience, to whom the words are addressed, before the choice and decision, directly or indirectly. The future is not something already fixed in the present hour, it is dependent upon the real decision, that is to say the decision in which man takes part in this hour.'—Martin Buber: *The Prophetic Faith* (New York, 1949, p. 2).

within every man's memory and with whom the ancestors were closely identified. Thus it is too simple an explanation to suggest that Mohammed called his god Allah so that the ignorant Bedouin, familiar with that pagan deity, should find the transition from one faith to the other easy. Mohammed wished to preserve continuity in his own spiritual development: another instance of the tendency of the great world faiths to avoid wholesale repudiation.

The final conquest of Mecca was achieved by a combination of violence and trickery. Mohammed did not hesitate to attack the Meccan caravans during the months of pilgrimage, though such action was regarded as sacrilege. That he dared thus to violate the truce of God, while shocking the few, served to increase his reputation among a people to whom power and success have always been objects of reverence.[1] Finally, at a great battle fought at Badr, AD 624, the power of Mecca was shaken, but it was six years before Mohammed was master of the two great cities of Arabia. Having removed the idols from the sanctuary of the Kaaba, he proclaimed himself civil and religious governor of the city, being at once priest, king, law-giver, and judge. Thenceforth the faith prospered as almost no faith had done before; for the spiritual energy released in that small Arabian city did not spend itself in the West until the armies of Islam were turned back by Charles Martel at Tour in AD 732. Had the decision been otherwise, it is possible that the whole of the Occident, including the American continent, would today form part of a gigantic Islamic Empire, and that the writer and readers of this book would be Moslems.

The rapidity with which tribe after tribe was enlisted in his service encouraged Mohammed in the hope that his authority might one day extend beyond the borders of Arabia, and that the rulers of much more powerful nations might come to accept Islam. He was therefore emboldened to address letters to both the Emperor at Constantinople and to the King of Persia inviting them to adopt the Islamic faith. The latter, not being accustomed to receive appeals of this kind, reacted in a most hostile manner. The emperor, who realized the wisdom of maintaining peace on his frontiers, responded more cordially. An appeal to the ruler in Egypt met with the most satisfactory response of all, part of it being made in kind: for Mohammed's envoy was sent back with two extremely attractive Egyptian women, whom the Prophet took into his harem.

In the year 632, feeling that his end was approaching, Mohammed decided to lead in person a gigantic pilgrimage to Mecca. The number of the faithful on that occasion was about forty thousand, probably the largest concourse ever assembled in the presence of the leader of a world faith. Having conducted the ceremonial prayers, the Prophet, surveying the people from a high hill, declared that his work was at last accomplished. In words very similar to those spoken by the

[1] In *sura* 2 of the Koran, such conduct is excused as follows: 'They will ask thee concerning war in the sacred month (i.e. Ramadan). Say: the act of fighting therein is a grave crime: but the act of turning others aside from the path of God and unbelief in him . . . is worse in the sight of God.'

Buddha on his deathbed, he declared that every man's task was steadfastly to work out his own salvation, submitting only to the will of God. Not long after this ceremony he contracted a fever, possibly brought on by the effects of poison, and died.

The Koran

Although Mohammed could neither read nor write, he showed great respect for the written word, as is proved both by his interest in the Bible and by his resolve to leave behind him a book of his own. The Koran (or *Qur'an*) is a collection of utterances, regulations, and legendary stories which Mohammed, claiming to be the mouthpiece of Allah, dictated over a period of more than twenty years. Recorded piecemeal on objects as various as stones and palm-leaves, the book was put together after the Prophet's death by Abu Bekr, who divided it none too skilfully into chapters or *suras*. To the orthodox Moslem it forms one prolonged inspired utterance, wheren provision is made for every contingency in life. That for which the Koran makes no provision is regarded as outside the experience of the devout. Thus the Koran (a word which means 'that which is to be read') is a book which the Moslem must either accept as inspired or not accept at all; but if he does not accept it at all, he cannot be counted a Moslem. All Moslems are fundamentalists.

To the non-Moslem reader, the Koran is a puzzling and somewhat unsatisfactory book. Whereas the Bible, or substantial parts of it, can hold the interest for many chapters at a time, preserving in spite of apparent irrelevancies a recognizable theme, the Koran can be entered at any point: it represents a static collection of religious lore. It is likewise distinguished from the Bible in that the history of its chief personage, the Prophet himself, remains outside it. If you imagine the New Testatment, for example, as containing only the sayings of Christ and not his acts, you would have a book very like the Koran. This deficiency was later repaired by the compilation of a book of almost equal interest, namely the *Sunna,* in which the life of Mohammed is fully recorded, though with exaggerations presumably intended to demonstrate his superiority to Christ. Mohammed is there portrayed as a wonder-worker of unexampled talent; and in order to show at least his equality with Christ, he is made to utter statements lifted from the New Testament. Furthermore, while the Koran is not devoid of sublimity,[1] and though Moslem scriptures contain passages of profound spiritual insight, especially in the works of the mystics and such poems as the Turkish *Mevlidi Sherif* and the *Mathnawi* of Mevlana, the Koran can show nothing comparable to the Sermon on the Mount, the Fire Sermon, or certain passages in the *Bhagavad-Gita.* Perhaps the explanation lies in the difference between that which is *required* of a Moslem as compared with a Christian, a Buddhist, or a Hindu. Whereas the Moslem is called to be a good man, the others are 'called to be saints'. It may be argued, as Dostoevski sugges-

[1] Particularly in its powerful language, charged with a poetry that only the Arabic scholar can appreciate.

ted in the famous Grand Inquisitor passage in *The Brothers Karamazov*, that the Christian, and by implication the Buddhist and the follower of Krishna, are being called upon to reach a standard beyond human attainment. At any rate, we can hardly imagine the Grand Inquisitor objecting to Mohammed as he objected to Christ. We can see ourselves as attaining without undue effort the standard of righteousness set by the Prophet, though whether, with such a moderate aim in view, we should think it necessary to go to the trouble of embracing Islam is another matter.

To suggest that Mohammed enjoined upon his disciples a few ritual practices, and no more, would nevertheless be grossly inaccurate. Like Zoroaster, he laid great emphasis upon the 'good disposition'. In the first place, the disciple must pass in his lifetime one fundamental oral test. This is to declare, 'There is no God but Allah and Mohammed is his Prophet.' He must utter this statement with both understanding and conviction: a mere verbal repetition will not suffice. If the disciple makes this declaration with complete sincerity, he need do so only once, for he has thus enrolled himself irrevocably among the believers. The second condition is that he must be circumcised: Napoleon, as we saw in the first chapter, was put in a dilemma by this ordinance. Thirdly, the believer must pray five times a day at certain intervals: before dawn, at noon, in the afternoon, at sunset and at nightfall, adopting a series of deep obeisances[1] and facing in the direction of Mecca. Here again the mere performance of ritual is not sufficient. On that point the Koran is firm. 'There is no piety in turning your faces towards the east or west, but he is pious who believes in God and the last day and the angels and the scriptures and the prophets; who for the love of God disburseth his wealth to his kindred, and to the orphans, and the needy and the wayfarer, and those who ask, and for ransoming; who observeth prayer, and payeth the legal arms, and who is one of those who is faithful to their engagements when they have engaged in them, and patient under ills and hardships and in time of trouble: these are they who are just, and these are they who fear God' (*sura* 2). In the same spirit, the fast of Ramadan and, if feasible, the pilgrimage to Mecca must be undertaken.

Mohammed and the Christians

Within two centuries of the Prophet's death the Moslem faith hardened into a rigid system. Although violent schisms occurred among the devout, the theology and law (*Shari'a*) of Islam have since remained unchanged. Whereas the Buddha regarded himself as merely one among a succession of Enlightened Ones, Mohammed was convinced of the finality of his mission. He claimed to be the 'Seal of the Prophets', the last and greatest of a line which included Adam, Noah, Abraham, Moses, and Jesus. His 'successor', therefore, was not another *Nabi* but simply the *Khalifat an-Nabi*, 'successor to the Prophet'. Consequently, much of the Bible scriptures are as sacred to

[1] Hence the adoption of the fez. The Moslem cannot pray in a brimmd hat: hence the outcry against Kemal Atatürk's 'Hat Law' in 1924.

the Moslem as to the Jew and the Christian. This applies above all to the Pentateuch (the first five books of the Bible), the Psalms of David, and even the Gospels.[1] It was not to Christ that Mohammed objected, but to Christians. Their theology, particularly as regards the Trinity, seemed to him to detract from the pure monotheism which he believed, with justice, to have been the faith of Abraham. We need not ridicule Mohammed for misunderstanding the Trinity. This 'rude human soul', as Carlyle called him (and indeed the Prophet would have made a strange visitor at Cheyne Row), had as good an excuse for failing to grasp the idea of trinity-in-unity as those learned doctors of the Christian Church who had wrangled with one another at the Council of Chalcedon in 451.[2] In a sense Mohammed was simply a Christian heretic.[3] God, he maintained, 'begetteth not nor is He begotten'. To declare otherwise was to fall once more into polytheism. The Koran sums up the matter as follows: 'They say moreover "Become Jews or Christians, that ye may have the true guidance." Say: "Nay, the religion of Abraham, the sound in faith, and not one of these who join gods with God is our religion."' Those who 'join gods with God' are the Christians.

So insistent was Mohammed upon his possession of the true faith that he imagines the covenant between God and Abraham to have presaged his own appearance as the final Prophet of God. There is an interesting passage in *sura* 2 of the Koran which makes this clear: 'And when Abraham, with Ishmael, raised the foundations of the house, they said "O our Lord! accept it from us: Thou of a truth art the hearer, the knower. O our Lord! make us thy Muslims (i.e. resigned to thee), and our posterity a Moslim people: and teach us our holy rites and be turned towards us . . . O our Lord! and raise up among them an apostle from themselves who may rehearse thy signs unto them, and teach them 'The Book', and wisdom, and purify them: of a truth thou art the Mighty and the Wise" . . . And this to his children did Abraham enjoin, and Jacob also, saying 'O my children! truly God hath chosen a religion for you: so die not without having become Muslems."'

The Khalifate and the sects

The development of a rift among the followers of Mohammed is remarkable not in itself but on account of its early emergence. The Sunnis are those who accept the spiritual authority of the first three Khalifs, or successors of Mohammed, namely Abu Bekr, Omar, and Othman.[4] To the Shiahs, on the other hand, these Khalifs are usur-

[1] Moslems accept the Virgin Birth and miracles of Jesus.

[2] 'In the church of St Euphemia at Chalcedon there were gathered all the forces that were henceforth to divide the Christian world. The rival forces of Egypt and the East shouted defiance and abuse at one another from either side of the nave, while the great officers of the Empire, seated in front of the chancel rails, with the Roman legates by their side, impassively dominated the turbulent assembly and guided it with inflexible persistence towards a final decision in accordance with the wishes of the Emperor and the Pope.'—Christopher Dawson: *The Making of Europe,* Chapter 7, 'The Awakening of the East'.

[3] The description was first used by St John of Damascus.

[4] All three, together with the fourth Ali, were members of the Quarash tribe but only Ali was related to Mohammed.

pers. Mohammed's true successor, they maintain, was the Prophet's cousin and son-in-law, Ali, son of Abu Talib and husband of Fatima. The Sunnis have always been the most numerous party, and their doctrine and ritual are preserved in the *Sunna,* from which they take their name. Nevertheless, the Shiah sect has likewise been powerful in many regions, and in modern Persia their beliefs are accepted as orthodox. As the simple doctrine of the Prophet underwent theological and juridical elaboration, various movements and sects arose dedicated to restoring the ancient simplicity. Today the most important of these sects is that of the Wahabis, fanatical puritans, of whom King Ibn Saud was the chief representative. An offspring of Shiism is the Babi[1] or Baha'i sect, founded by Mirza Ali Mohammed (1820–50) and continued by a second 'Messiah' called Mirza Huseyn Ali or Bahau 'llah (1817–92), and his son Sir Abdul Baha (1844–1921). Baha'ism, as it is called, has converts not merely in Persia, but in India, China, Japan, and also America and England.

The rapid résumé of the last paragraph leaves out of account many features of modern Islam to which the student and the scholar would need to pay careful attention. A faith which can claim adherents in every part of the world, and which within the last few years has been largely responsible for the creation of a new nation, Pakistan,[2] can hardly be considered either as moribund or even in need of artificial respiration. On the contrary, in its fundamentalist forms it has recently shown a new dynamism.

The Sufis

When we speak of 'The Prophets' we tend to think of a series of isolated figures whose message, though at first derided, won acceptance by a kind of imperious inner authority. We forget that among such people as the Jews, the 'prophet' was a figure only too familiar: indeed, he could often become a menace. In *Zechariah* xiii, for instance, we read: 'And it shall come to pass that when any shall yet prophesy, then his father and his mother that begat him shall say unto him, Thou shalt not live: for thou speakest lies in the name of the Lord: and his father and his mother that begat him shall thrust him through when he prophesieth. And it shall come to pass in that day that the prophets shall be ashamed every one of his vision, when he hath prophesied; neither shall they wear a rough garment to deceive.' Islam, like every other faith, has had its fill of false prophets; but there grew up a movement early in its history which, had it been suppressed (as for instance the Mu'tazilites were suppressed in the ninth century), might have deprived Islam of much of its later spiritual influence. This movement was associated with the Sufis, poets and mystics who were so-called because, like the men mentioned by Zechariah, they wore rough shirts of wool (*suff.*). The Sufis were not isolated figures; they belonged, as their scattered successors still belong, to a closed brotherhood, membership of which necessitated a period of initiation, strict training,

[1] From the Arabic *bab* (door).
[2] Literally, 'Land of the Pure', from the Urdu *pak,* meaning 'pure' or 'clean'.

and participation in special services of meditation called *dhikrs*. Most Sufis, having reached a particular stage of training, joined one of the famous Dervish Orders: the Mevlevis or Whirling Dervishes, the Rufais or Howling Dervishes, and the Bektashis or People's Dervishes (who were primarily poets). The Sufis would probably have remained in a condition of spiritual outlawry, a potential danger to orthodoxy, but for the adoption of their faith by one of the greatest intellects of Islam, al-Ghazzali (died in 1111). The latter was professor of theology and canon law at the Nizamiya College at Baghdad, and his conversion necessitated his resignation from that post.

While we may be tempted to see in Sufism traces of Buddhist and Vedantist thought, the influence of Christian mysticism is paramount. In his book called *The Precious Pearl,* al-Ghazzali imagines a group of poor people who were asked on the Day of Judgment why they had turned away from God. They answered that they had renounced their faith in consequence of their poverty. They were then asked, 'Who is the poorest, you or Jesus?' 'Without doubt Jesus,' they replied. 'That did not turn Him away,' was the rejoinder, 'from living according to the will of God Most High ... O reader, take Christ as your model, for it is said that He had no purse: for twenty years He wore the same shirt of wool (*suf*) ... In the work of al-Ghazzali, as in that of his successors such as Jalalu'l-Din-Rumi (1207–73),[1] Jesus, is regarded as the 'Seal of the Saints'. In view of the bitter hostility between Moslems and Christians, and the use of the word 'Giour' (pagan or unbeliever) as a term of abuse even by street urchins today, it is interesting to recall the passage from *sura* 5 of the Koran, 'Verily, those who believe, and the Jews and the Sabaeans and the Christians—*whoever of them believeth in God and in the last day,* and doeth what is right, on them shall come no fear, nor shall they be put to grief': a statement as elevated in its way as Krishna's words in the *Bhagavad-Gita.*

[1] Known in Turkey ('Rum') as Mevlana. He lived for most of his life in Konya, the old Seljuk capital.

PART TWO

PHILOSOPHERS OF THE WEST

10

Socrates

True philosophers are always occupied in the practice of dying.
Phædo

His Life
Western philosophy did not begin with Socrates. With Socrates, however, it not merely entered upon a new road but took the direction which, in spite of numerous setbacks, it has since followed. This remarkable man wrote nothing.[1] He had few possessions. For the greater part of his life he did not work for his living. Yet his influence upon a few contemporaries, some of them gifted statesmen and writers, was such that we know a fair amount about his character, his habits, and the events of his life. Above all we know something of the way he thought and the way he believed men should be trained to think. And we are aware that his ideas inspired not merely two other great philosophers in the next generations, but all those who have since endeavoured to think in a philosophical or orderly manner. Possibly no other man, with the exception of the founders of the great religions, practised what he preached so thoroughly and consistently as this intrepid, somewhat uncouth figure of fifth-century Athens.

From what sources do we learn about Socrates? We owe most of what we know about him to two men, Plato (427–347 BC) and Xenophon (430–357 BC). But, even so, our knowledge is limited. Both of these men were junior to Socrates by about forty-five years. Save for the last decade of his life, therefore, the authorities are few and of doubtful value. The great comedian, Aristophanes (*b.* 448 BC), introduces Socrates into one of his plays, *The Clouds*, with the object of poking fun at him. But the Socrates who is ridiculed by Aristophanes and his contemporary, Ameipsias, is already a man in his middle forties. Of Socrates as a youth we have no authentic picture. We have to go upon what he tells us, or rather upon the account put into his mouth by the two friends of his old age.

Socrates was born near Athens in the year 469 BC, ten years after the battle of Salamis, in which the Athenians, aided by the Spartans, crushed the sea-power of Xerxes, the Persian king. Socrates' father,

[1] Epictetus, the Stoic philosopher (first century), alone maintains that Socrates occasionally wrote down his thoughts (*Discourses*, Book II, Chapter I, 5). His poetic compositions in prison may have been purely extempore effusions.

Sophroniscus, is reputed to have been a sculptor, but on this point there is some uncertainty. (Our only authority for the statement is a third-century writer, Timon of Phlius.) That he was a friend of Aristeides, Commander of the Athenians at the battle of Platæa (479) and nicknamed 'The Just', we know for certain. His mother, Phænarete, was by occupation a midwife, or at least she was accustomed to act as one; and it is interesting to remember that, according to Plato, Socrates used to describe his method of extracting knowledge as a kind of intellectual midwifery. From later writers we deduce that, if in fact his father's calling was that of a sculptor, the son not merely followed the same trade but excelled in it. A sculptured group representing the Three Graces and preserved in the Acropolis was supposed to have been the work of the young Socrates, and was exhibited as such up to the time of Pausanias, the geographer (late second century AD).[1] So far as we know, Socrates followed no other profession except that for which he later became renowned. But the circumstances which induced him to become a 'freelance' philosopher—perhaps the last of that category and without doubt the greatest—will be described in due course.

If we possess scant information about the events of the life of Socrates, we do not lack impressive evidence as to his outstanding character. In the first place he seems to have been one of the toughest physical specimens of his time. Winter and summer, year in and year out, he apparently wore the same light garment, with neither shirt nor shoes. Accustomed to an outdoor existence, he was always to be seen either in the streets, in the market-place, or in the gymnasium, hobnobbing with young and old. Neither heat nor cold appeared to worry him. Even his bitterest enemies testify to his great physical courage. He served as a hoplite, or foot-soldier, in several military campaigns. He was at Samos, between 441 and 440 BC, at the battle of Potidæa (432–430 BC), at Delium (424 BC) and probably at Amphipolis (442? or 437–436 BC?). At Potidæa he saved the life of Alcibiades, the headstrong young Athenian politician, who repaid the compliment at Delium, and whose tribute to the philosopher's bravery is recorded in Plato's *Symposium*:

'I was wounded,' recounts Alcibiades, 'and he would not leave me, but he rescued me and my arms; and he ought to have received the prize for courage which the generals wanted to confer upon me on account of my rank, and I told them so, but he was more eager than the generals that I and not he should have the prize. There was another occasion on which his behaviour was very remarkable—in the flight of the army after the battle of Delium. He and Lactes were retreating, for the troops were in flight, and I met them and told them not to be discouraged, and promised to remain with them; and there you might see him, just as he is in the streets of Athens, stalking like a pelican, and rolling his eyes, calmly contemplating enemies as well as friends, and making very intelligible to anybody, even from a distance, that who-

[1] Diogenes Laërtius (third century AD), author of *Lives of the Philosophers*, records the tradition. Archæologists now suggest an earlier sculptor.

ever attacked him would be likely to meet with a stout resistance.'

Alcibiades also records how, one morning during the expedition to Potidæa, Socrates was pondering a problem which he could not resolve. 'He would not give it up, but continued thinking from early dawn until noon—there he stood fixed in thought; and at noon he was noticed, and the rumour ran through the wondering crowd that Socrates had been standing and thinking about something ever since the break of day. At last, in the evening after supper, some Ionians out of curiosity brought out their mats and slept in the open air in order to watch him and see whether he would stand all night. There he stood until the following morning; and with the return of light he offered up a prayer to the sun and went his way.'

Not merely did Socrates live in a condition of which many a slave would have been ashamed; he was for most of his life desperately poor. Indeed, his extreme poverty was the principal source of the mockery of contemporary comedians. Aristophanes goes so far as to represent him, most unfairly, as a mad, impoverished stargazer who was prepared to give instruction for money in a bogus kind of philosophy. As to star-gazing, both Xenophon and Plato witness to the great interest he displayed in astronomy and geometry, but, unlike the Sophists or professional teachers of philosophy, Socrates never taught for gain. On this subject he spoke feelingly to his accusers at the end of his trial: 'If I had gained anything, or if I had been paid for my preaching, there would have been some sense in my doing so; but now you see not even the imprudence of my accusers dares to say that I have ever taken or asked for pay from anyone; of that they have no witness. And I have sufficient witness to the truth of what I say—my poverty.'

In spite of his straitened circumstances, which the abandonment of a regular profession increased, Socrates was married rather late in life to a woman called Xanthippe. Of the character of this woman, who bore him three sons, we know little, though Xenophon declares that she was a hot-tempered creature.[1] A remark in Aristotle's book on Rhetoric suggests that the boys grew up to be nondescript men, without a spark of their father's genius. The last occasion on which we hear of Xanthippe is when she paid a brief visit to her husband in prison, bringing the youngest of her children with her. Although Socrates' attitude to his wife might suggest that his was a cold and reserved temperament, we learn from other sources, particularly Plato and Æschines, that the reverse was true. Even if we admit that he exercised considerable self-control, it is a mistake to regard him as a self-denying, ascetic kill-joy. He was by temperament ardent, prone to gaiety, with an irrepressible sense of humour (manifested not least in his final speech to his friends). He also had a healthy contempt for those who, like Antisthenes and certain disciples of Pythagoras, identified wisdom and sanctity with dirt, vermin and squalor.

But to return to the circumstances of his life. Between the first performance of Aristophanes' play *The Clouds* (423 BC) and the trial of

[1] He says that she was 'the most insupportable woman that is, has been, or ever will be' (*The Banquet*).

Socrates (399 BC), great changes had occurred in Athens. There had been a political revolution in consequence of which the Democratic party had returned to power. Although a firm supporter of democracy (he could hardly be otherwise), Socrates had a number of friends, like Critias and Alcibiades, who were associated with the old order. And so the gentle and not too bitter burlesque figure of Socrates in Aristophanes' play (which, being a failure on its first production, the author rewrote in somewhat stronger terms) was taken more seriously a quarter of a century later. Nor was Socrates under any illusion as to the harm done to him, albeit inadvertently, by Aristophanes; he deliberately referred to the play in his last speech, chiding his judges for repeating as literally true that which had been originally intended as jest.

Two questions concerning the relation between Aristophanes and Socrates are still a source of perplexity to us. The first is at what point their friendship, or at any rate their respect one for the other, began to cool; and the second is what Aristophanes, still a comparatively young man, was doing at the time of the trial of Socrates. We know that Aristophanes and Plato remained on terms of friendship long after Socrates' death—and this is surely incompatible with their holding opposite views about the man whom Plato, for one, regarded as 'the most righteous of the whole age'. It is possible that at the time of the trial Aristophanes was absent on military service. There is no record that he intervened or showed any particular interest in the shameful proceedings taking place in the court at Athens.

Although the motives for the final arrest of Socrates were probably semi-political, Socrates himself had throughout life taken little part in politics. As he pointed out to his judges, the holding of political office was directly contrary to his principles. A man so much in the public eye, however, could not avoid becoming involved indirectly in political controversies. For one complete year, 406–405 BC, he was a member of the Council of 500, where his influence was all for moderation. When the victors of the battle of Arginusæ were being tried, he alone opposed the condemnation of the generals. Under the Reign of Terror of the Thirty Tyrants in 404 BC, his stubborn refusal to agree to the arrest of Leon, who had incurred public displeasure at the time, nearly cost him his life. Had it not been for the counter-revolution of the Democrats, he would have been indicted for disobedience. And that is another reason why it cannot be maintained that he was a whole-hearted sympathizer with the old order.

Nevertheless, although the Democrats proclaimed a general amnesty soon after their return to power, and although Socrates was known to have had nothing to do with the outrages and tyrannies of the old regime, he was summarily charged with impiety in the year 399 BC on two main counts: first, that he had been responsible for 'corrupting' the youth of Athens; and secondly, that he had neglected the traditional gods by introducing in their place a variety of religious novelties. What exactly lay behind these allegations? To answer this question, we must go back to the time of his youth.

At what age Socrates first became conscious of the promptings of a divine or supernatural voice, rather like the traditional voice of conscience only much more authoritative, we do not know. Although he frequently referred to this mysterious power, he could never make up his mind when first he became accustomed to obey its injunctions. As in most cases of this kind, the experience probably began much earlier than he realized, growing more insistent with the dawn of adolescence, when the sense of right and wrong is sharpened. What distinguished the 'voice' or 'demon' of Socrates from other 'inner' oracles is that it afforded him warnings of a particular kind. It gave him negative information, never positive. It told him not to do things; it never told him what he should do. It was a check, not a prompter.

Thus, early in life, Socrates, otherwise the most humble of men and without riches or power save the friendship of certain distinguished contemporaries, became convinced that he was entrusted with a divine mission. Whatever his critics and later accusers might say, his belief in God and spiritual values, and even his reverence for the traditional deities of his country, were never for a moment in doubt. He was by disposition a religious man. Unlike the common people of his day, however, he refused to credit with literal truth the mythology and legend so deeply interwoven with the traditions of Greek society. Such tales of gods and goddesses he ascribed to poetic invention; but he saw no harm in their being handed down from generation to generation, just as he saw no harm in the poetic fancies they had inspired. And, sceptic though he was, he refused to ignore the testimony of supernatural signs and portents, oracles and seers, for was he not himself given to mystical transports, being to that extent a disciple of the cults of the Pythagoreans and of the Orphic mysteries?

Indeed, it was to the deliverances of an Oracle that he owed what he believed to be a striking confirmation of his missionary status. One day, he tells us, a friend of his, Chærephon by name, visited the famous Oracle at Delphi for the express purpose of asking whether any man was wiser than Socrates. Without hesitation, the Oracle replied that no one was wiser. Now the Oracle at Delphi was famous for a command that it issued to all those who came to seek its aid. This command was the single motto, 'Know Thyself'. In what sense, then, did the Oracle intend its statement about Socrates to be interpreted? Why was Socrates to be judged wiser than any man living (and perhaps dead)? The answer was not that Socrates knew everything, but that on the contrary he knew little or nothing. But the difference between Socrates and other people was that whereas they were ignorant but thought themselves wise, Socrates was ignorant and knew himself to be so. In other words, Socrates 'knew himself' in the true sense.

The Oracle's revelation caused Socrates to ponder deeply. If the statement were true, it must be acted upon; for the words of an Oracle represented a command, a summons to action. And so, after due reflection, Socrates made up his mind that his true vocation in life, the work to which he must henceforth devote himself, was to examine, analyse, and if necessary expose, the wisdom of those whom the world called wise.

And that was how the trouble began. His fellow-citizens did not welcome this relentless inquisition into what they believed or supposed themselves to believe. To them Socrates was the worst sort of busybody—a man who asked intricate questions with no other motive than that of satisfying an insatiable curiosity. It was this very 'disinterestedness' of Socrates that upset them most of all. What was the object of it? The man did no work. He had nothing to offer. His one object was to disturb people's preconceived opinions. And no one was proof against him.

As for Socrates himself, he realized early in his new career that he was likely to provoke much enmity. But this did not deter him. According to the account in Plato's *Apology*, he tried his first experiment upon a politician who was 'thought wise by many and still wiser by himself'; but he soon took his leave. 'Although I do not suppose that either of us has any knowledge of goodness and beauty,' he said to himself, 'I am better off than he is, for he knows nothing, and thinks that he knows: I neither know nor think that I know. In this latter point I seem to have slightly the advantage of him.' But, as a result of this difficult interview, the politician came to hate him bitterly, and so did many others who were in the audience at the time. Thoroughly baffled, he then went elsewhere to one 'who had still higher pretensions to wisdom', but fared no better and made another enemy in consequence. And so he passed on from one man to another, from the poets to the artisans and to those practising intermediate trades, probing and drawing out of them admission after admission as to the shallowness of their wisdom, exposing their downright ignorance, and on each occasion asking himself on behalf of the Oracle whether he would prefer to be as he was, 'neither having their knowledge nor their ignorance', or to be like them in both, and always answering that he was better off as he was.

However much they feared and hated him, the contemporaries of Socrates were finally obliged to admit that he was a very shrewd man. Yet this was not the impression he necessarily wanted to create. It was a constant source of embarrassment to him to find that his hearers always considered him to be possessed of the wisdom which he found wanting in others. In this they laboured under a misapprehension. 'The truth is,' he explained, 'that God only is wise; and by His answer' (*i.e.* through the medium of the Oracle) 'He intends to show that the wisdom of men is worth little or nothing; He is not speaking of Socrates, He is only using my name by way of illustration, as if He said, he is the wisest who, like Socrates, knows that his wisdom is in truth worth nothing.' And recalling the accusation that he was no better than the Sophists, he added: 'My occupation quite absorbs me, and I have no time to give either to any public matter of interest or to any concern of my own, but I am in utter poverty through my service of the god.'

The legal prosecutor of Socrates was a man named Meletus, a writer of inferior tragedies and a thoroughly worthless fellow, probably bribed to participate in this outrage, but the enemy behind the scenes was Anytus, a wealthy Athenian who had played a leading part in the overthrow of the Thirty Tyrants by the Democrats. Lycon, an orator by profession and a friend of Anytus, was another of Socrates' accusers. As for his judges—men with little public experience but with a number of private scores to settle—they had themselves not long returned from banishment. Nevertheless, it must not be supposed that Socrates' prosecution was simply the consequence of a political reversal of fortune. Under the rule of the Thirty Tyrants, he had fared little better. In fact, Critias, the leader, had gone so far as to issue a proclamation stipulating that Socrates, and indeed the Sophists in general, were to desist from the work of teaching; and we have already referred to those earlier occasions on which he acted contrary to the wishes and orders of the authorities. In the turmoil of political reaction, however, a man's precise status and reputation under the former regime are rarely assessed with impartiality.

To the credit of the Tribunal, the initial vote cast against Socrates after his 'trial' was very far from unanimous. Two hundred and eighty votes were cast against him, and two hundred and twenty in his favour.[1] The accusers thereupon asked for a sentence of death to be pronounced. In all cases of this kind, however, it was the custom in Athenian law for the accused to be allowed to make a counter-proposal, following which the judges might be induced to modify their sentence. Socrates took full advantage of this privilege, but in his own fashion. He suggested that, instead of being punished, he should first be proclaimed a public benefactor, and thereafter maintained, as was the custom with celebrities, at the public expense. As a 'token' fine, however, he suggested that he should pay 1 *mina*.

Couched in typically ironic terms, no statement was better calculated to arouse the wrath of Anytus and his colleagues. The feeling of the court immediately went against Socrates. Nor did the action of his friends in suggesting a fine of 30 *minæ* serve any purpose. The court had been insulted, the accusers made to look foolish, just as Socrates' interlocutors had in the past been held up to ridicule. Socrates was proving himself incorrigible. As a result, a greatly increased majority demanded the imposition of the death sentence.

Socrates entertained no fear of death. But he had made it clear that if by chance the judges should decide to let him go free, he would not merely revert to his previous mode of life but interpret the acquittal as a direct invitation to do so. If, on the other hand, they refused to tolerate his public teaching and interrogating, his probing into questions of justice and virtue, or his mixing freely with the impressionable young men of Athens, then, said Socrates, 'I should reply: Men of Athens, I honour and love you; but I shall obey God rather than you, and while I have life and strength I shall never cease from the practice and teaching of philosophy, exhorting anyone whom I meet and saying to him as my habit is: You, my friend—a citizen of the great and

[1] The jury consisted of 500, and Plato affirms that Socrates was condemned by a majority of 60.

mighty and wise city of Athens—are you not ashamed of trying to get as much money and honour and reputation as possible, while remaining careless and indifferent to wisdom and truth and the greatest perfection of your soul?... For I know that this is the commandment of God; and I believe that no greater good has ever happened to Athens than my service to God.'

Whether the moving speech delivered after the passing of the sentence was that actually spoken by Socrates, or whether it was put into his mouth by his disciple Plato, we shall never know. All we know is that the thoughts expressed therein are such as Socrates must certainly have tried to put into words, for they are in harmony with everything he is reported to have said and done in the course of his career. They represent not merely one of the greatest speeches ever uttered, but one of the profoundest statements of that view of life which, perfected in the Christian teaching, still forms the moral basis of our civilization. Socrates had reached the age when he no longer wished to prolong his life, if to do so meant enforced silence and ostracism. Consequently, his final words to his judges dwell upon the theme of death and the fear of death, and form a kind of summing-up of his life's teaching, and of what is sometimes called the 'perennial philosophy'.

'There is great reason to hope,' he said, 'that death is good; for either death is a state of nothingness and utter unconsciousness, or, as men say, there is a change and migration of the soul from this world to another... Now if death is like the former, I say that to die is gain; for eternity is then only a single night. But if death is the journey to another place, and there, as men say, all the dead abide, what good, my friends and judges, can be greater than this? If indeed, when the pilgrim arrives in the world below, he is delivered from the professors of justice in this world, and finds the true judges who are said to give judgment there ... that pilgrimage will be worth making. What would not a man give if he might talk with Orpheus and Musæus and Hesiod and Homer?

'I myself, too, shall have a wonderful interest in there meeting and talking with Palamedes, and Ajax the son of Telamon, and any other ancient hero who was unjustly sentenced to death; and there will be no small pleasure, I think, in comparing my own suffering with theirs. Above all I shall then be able to continue my search into true and false knowledge, as in this world so also in the next; and I shall find out who is wise, and who pretends to be wise and is not... What infinite delight would there be in talking with them and asking them questions! In another world they do not put a man to death for asking questions; assuredly not. For besides being happier than we are, they will be immortal, if what is said is true. So, my judges, you too should face death confidently and reflect on this one truth, that no evil can happen to a good man, either in life or after death. He and his are not neglected by the gods; nor is my own approaching end a matter of mere chance.

'I see clearly that the time has arrived when it was better for me to die and be released from trouble. And so I am not angry with those who condemned and those who accused me; they have done me no harm, although they did not mean to do me any good; and for this I may gently blame them. But I have a favour to ask them. When my sons are grown up, punish them and trouble them, as I have troubled you, if they seem to care about riches, or anything, more than about virtue; or if they pretend to be something when they are really nothing—then reprove them, as I have reproved you, for not caring about that for which you ought to care, and thinking that they are something when they are really nothing. And if you do this, both I and my sons will have received justice at your hands. The hour of departure has arrived, and we go our ways—I to die, and you to live. Which is better only God knows.'

With these calm and noble words Socrates passed out of public life. But fortunately we have a record, again due to the artistry of Plato, of what happened to Socrates and his small circle of loyal friends in the interval between his trial and his death. In fact we are much better informed about these last days than about the whole seventy-three years that preceded them.

It was the custom in Ancient Greece for a man condemned to death to drink a draught of hemlock within twenty-four hours. Such would have been Socrates' fate but for an interesting circumstance. It so happened that the sacred ship from Delos[1] had not yet returned, and there was no question of an execution taking place before its arrival.

In this way Socrates' life was prolonged by thirty days, during which time he devoted himself, with all his former enthusiasm, to philosophical speculation and also apparently to his first essays in writing poetry. The poetry, it is sad to say, has not survived; but the philosophizing is preserved in two immortal dialogues of Plato, the *Crito* and the *Phædo*. Crito was, next after Plato, Socrates' most loyal friend. He it was who had offered to stand surety for his master when the latter, half in earnest, had suggested that his sentence should be commuted to the payment of a fine. In a last passionate display of devotion, Crito now tried to persuade the condemned Socrates to make his escape, and went to great trouble to prepare a stratagem to deceive the gaolers. Somewhat to the surprise of his friends, Socrates refused to contemplate any such action. He proceeded to defend his decision by an argument concerning the duty of obedience to the laws of the state which, read out of its context, might strike the modern reader as unnecessarily submissive. He points out, however, that if a man has lived in a particular city, and has accepted its constitution and protection for the greater part of his life, he has no right to try to evade its ordinances when they are invoked, however unjustly, to condemn him to imprisonment or death. If he did not approve of the laws of his country, he could long ago have taken his leave and made his home elsewhere—a practice rather more open to a Greek, provided he had sufficient means, than to a modern national.

Having lived in Athens through so many different regimes and having survived them all, Socrates had no intention of taking flight at

[1] An island sacred to Apollo. The custom was to celebrate the deliverance of the city by Theseus.

the eleventh hour. 'Listen, then, Socrates,' he imagines the Laws as saying, 'to us who have brought you up. Think not of life and children first, and of justice afterwards, but of justice first, that you may be justified before the rulers of the world below... Now you depart in innocence, a sufferer and not a doer of evil; a victim not of the laws but of men. But if you go forth, returning evil for evil, and injury for injury, breaking the covenants and agreements which you have made with us and wronging those whom you ought least of all to wrong ... we will receive you as an enemy... Listen, then, to us and not to Crito.'

And so, reconciled to his fate and with a profound peace in his soul, Socrates made a habit each day of receiving his friends, in discoursing with them, and answering their questions. In due time, the sacred ship from Delos arrived; and Plato recounts in the *Phædo* how the loyal company assembled early the next morning, only to be kept waiting rather longer than usual. For the prison officials were closeted with their charge, giving him instructions as to his last moments, and taking off his chains. Xanthippe, his wife, had also been summoned to bid him farewell. When Crito and his friends entered (Plato, incidentally, was not able to be present on this last occasion, owing to illness), Xanthippe burst into loud lamentations and had to be led away. Socrates looked up at the visitors with a quizzical expression, slowly rubbing his bruised leg. The removal of his chains had set a train of thought going.

'How singular is the thing called pleasure,' he reflected, 'and how curiously related to pain; for a man never feels both at the same instant, and yet he who pursues either is generally compelled to take the other; their bodies are two but they are joined by a single head.' Warming to the theme, he went on to express his regret that Æsop had not composed a fable on this matter, showing how God, in order to reconcile the strife between pleasure and pain, had decided to fasten their heads together.

Soon the conversation took a more serious turn. The sense of death oppressed the company; Socrates alone, whose end was to come that same day, proclaimed his unshakable conviction that the soul, purged of its sins, was destined for immortality. His discourse on the subject, which is preserved for us in the *Phædo*, culminates in the statement that if a man shall 'cast away the pleasures and ornaments of the body as alien things which do him harm rather than good, and pursue the pleasures of knowledge', he may well be 'confident about his soul'.

By this time the day was wearing on, and Socrates suggested that he should take a bath, in order to save the women the trouble of washing his body after death. Crito, anxious not to waste a moment, begged him first to tell them whether there was anything they could do either for him or for his children. How, for instance, did he wish to be buried?

Socrates' reply was characteristically simple. He told his friends merely to 'take care of themselves', and to remember what he had tried to teach them. As to how he should be buried, he replied: 'In any way you like; but,' he added, with a touch of whimsical humour, 'you must get hold of me, and take care that I do not run away from you.' And, turning from Crito to the others, he remarked: 'I want you to go bail for me now, as at the trial he [Crito] went bail to the judges for me; but let the promise be of another sort; for he was surety for me to the judges that I would stay here, and you must be my surety to him that I shall not stay, but go away and depart.'

Then he got up and went into the next room, followed by Crito. Phædo and his companions stayed where they were, talking of their sorrow; for, as he observed, Socrates 'was like a father whom we were losing, and we were going to be orphans for the rest of our lives'. When Socrates had bathed, he received for the last time his family, commending them to the care of Crito; and finally, just when the sun was sinking, he returned to the others.

After the performance of these last rites, the atmosphere changed. Few words were spoken. Then, as if to break the tension, the jailer entered. He was clearly much affected by the scene, and addressed Socrates in a tone almost of apology. Accustomed to be greeted by an outburst of rage or grief on the part of the prisoner, he hardly knew how to disclose his mission to one whom he described, quite unaffectedly, as 'the noblest and gentlest and best of all who ever came to this place'. 'I am sure,' he added, 'you will not be angry with me; for others, as you are aware, and not I, are to blame. And so good-bye, and try to bear lightly what must needs be—you know my errand.' Then he suddenly burst into tears and hurried out.

Socrates remarked upon his courtesy. And then, turning to Crito again, he requested that the poison should be prepared.

Crito still saw no reason for haste. Most condemned persons, he pointed out, were accustomed to defer the fatal drink as long as possible, employing their last hours with eating and drinking and, in some cases, with other pleasures. Again Socrates shook his head. There was nothing, he insisted, to be gained by waiting. His life was already forfeit. And he had no wish to prolong unnecessarily the sufferings of his companions. He would therefore drink the hemlock without further ado.

Realizing that the old man's mind was quite made up, Crito directed one of the servants to summon the jailer once more. When the latter entered carrying the cup of poison, Socrates, still without turning a hair, said to him: 'You are an expert in these matters, my friend. Tell me what I must do.'

The jailer answered that, having drunk the poison, he must walk about the room until his legs began to grow heavy and then lie down. The poison would then do its work. So saying, he handed Socrates the cup.

Socrates received it quietly; but suddenly, as if in afterthought, he exclaimed: 'What about making a libation out of the cup?' meaning that he considered it appropriate to pour away some of its contents, as was the custom, in honour of the gods. When the jailer replied that he had prepared, according to official instructions, no more than was absolutely necessary, Socrates nodded in understanding, and, calling upon the gods to prosper his journey to the other world, he resolutely drank the poison in one draught.

It was a tragic moment. Those in the room who had hitherto managed to control their feelings could restrain themselves no longer.

Several minutes elapsed before they realized that one of their company had retained his full composure. This was Socrates himself. 'What are you doing, you strange people?' he asked. 'I sent the women away that they might not strike this false note. Be quiet then and have patience.'

These words, criticizing their demonstrativeness, calmed them in an instant. Then, almost incredulously, they beheld Socrates arise from his couch and begin to pace about the room, methodically acting upon the jailer's instructions. And so he continued, in the unbroken silence, until in due time his legs grew heavy, and he was obliged to lie down. Pressing one of his feet, the jailer asked whether he could feel anything. Socrates replied that he could not. The jailer continued to feel his limbs until it was obvious that a general numbness was creeping up his frame. Just before the poison took effect, however, Socrates, uncovering his face for an instant, murmured: 'Crito, I owe a cock to Asclepius; will you remember to pay the debt?' By this he meant that he wished to do honour to the god of health, in gratitude for having at last recovered from that prolonged malady, human life.

'It shall be done,' answered Crito, 'is there anything else?' To this question there was no reply. When they uncovered Socrates again, the life had ebbed completely.

In recounting the life of Socrates, the concluding words of the *Phædo*, addressed to a common friend, form the most fitting close: 'Such was the end, Echecrates, of our friend; of whom I may truly say, that of all the men of his time whom I have known, he was the wisest and justest and best.'

His Thought

More than any other man of his time, and possibly more than anyone before or since, with the exception of certain great religious leaders, Socrates lived his own philosophy. It was he, indeed, who, in criticizing the Sophists, laid such emphasis upon the necessity of realizing virtue in practice. Mere exhortations to moral virtue, so easy to give and so comfortable to listen to, were not enough. The injunction to 'Know Thyself' imposed upon the devotee of philosophy a discipline more rigorous than anything hitherto either recommended or followed. But it also implied a new theory of human conduct. Virtue, that is to say, was the consequence of self-knowledge; and moral goodness was the greatest value in the universe.

In following this line of thought, Socrates was, in effect, inaugurating a new departure in philosophy. During the centuries before he embarked upon his mission, many thinkers of great originality had appeared on the borders of the Ægean, though our records of their thought are scanty and in most cases garbled. We know enough of their ideas, however, to form a general picture of what it is that they were trying to find out about the world. We know that certain things interested them in particular, that certain problems baffled them, and that by certain aspects of reality they were left apparently unmoved. Above all we know that their attitude to the universe was characterized by an intense desire to discover the ultimate *constituents* of matter and life. They were in fact the first philosophers of Nature, or, as we should call them today, the first natural scientists.

Of Thales of Miletus, who lived about 600 BC, we know no more than that he was the first investigator of the natural world to work out a coherent, if elementary, science of matter.

His chief claim to fame is his assertion that the immense variety of the natural world ultimately sprang from one element or principle. To us, this way of regarding the world of Nature may not commend itself very strongly; but that is merely because we have been long accustomed to think of the universe, if not as composed of a single material, then at least as a coherent whole. To the early Greeks, this latter was an idea of brilliant originality. Now the element or ἀρχή from which everything else originated was, according to Thales, water. Water is that which envelops the earth. The earth, in fact, may be said to float upon an ocean infinite in extent, and to derive its nourishment, like a huge organism, from this circumambient flood.

A disciple of Thales, Anaximander, while accepting the view that everything in Nature derived from a single principle, differed from his master on the question of what this principle was. Instead of water, Anaximander maintained that the generative element was the boundless atmosphere itself, from which everything was formed by gradual separation and into which everything was finally resolved. Pursuing his speculations into what we should today call the Origin of Species, Anaximander made some suggestions as to the evolution of man which have a surprisingly modern ring; but with this aspect of his work we are not at the moment concerned. Yet a third philosopher, Anaximenes, also from the town of Miletus, modified the principle of Anaximander to the extent of calling the generative principle air or 'breath'. In other words, the philosophers of the so-called Ionian School were serious philosophers of Nature, and their overriding aim was to explain how Nature *came into being*.

The philosophers who followed these pioneer thinkers were concerned, as might be expected, with the problem of evolution itself. Whereas their predecessors had established, or at least postulated, the fact that all things developed from some primal substance or element, men such as Xenophanes (a contemporary of Anaximander), Parmenides, Zeno (fifth century BC), and Gorgias (485–380 BC?) concentrated upon the problem of how such development, process, or 'becoming', took place. Thus they set to work to analyse a concept which had been arrived at by the process of *abstraction*. Moreover, in the few fragments that we possess of the work of Parmenides (who expounded his thought in the form of a philosophical poem called *The Way of Truth and the Way of Belief*), we witness the first attempt of a Greek philosopher to engage in a form of thought which, for reasons to be discussed later, may be described as 'metaphysical'.

The conclusion at which Parmenides arrived, however, was the startling one that change was not a fact but an illusion. And he supported his contention by the logical argument that what exists can never either cease to exist or become anything different. For if it changes, it must have changed either from itself or from nothing. If it has changed from itself, however, it can have undergone no fundamental change at all; and as for the notion that it has come from nothing, that is preposterous. Being, therefore, must be eternal, infinite and unchanging. Zeno, who followed Parmenides' line of thought, illustrated the theory by the famous example of an arrow travelling through space. The arrow, he contended, must reach its destination by passing through an infinite number of successive points, each of which it occupies in turn. This can only mean that at every single point in its course the arrow is at rest. The 'movement' of the arrow is therefore something which exists wholly in our imagination. It has no reality in itself.

Zeno's pupil Gorgias carried this argument a stage farther. In fact, he tipped it over into the abyss of absurdity. It is all very well, he argued, to maintain that Being is both infinite and eternal. That which is both infinite and eternal obviously cannot be located anywhere, since to locate it in space would be to render it finite, while to locate it in time would be to render it temporal. If, therefore, Being is both infinite and eternal, it cannot enjoy any existence whatever. Hence Being and Nothing are identical.[1] Clearly this is the *reductio ad absurdum* of Parmenides' theory.

Now if you push an extreme argument far enough, it turns into its opposite. That is what happened with the argument that all change is an illusion. The philosopher Heraclitus, who lived at Ephesus in the fifth century BC, countered the ideas of Parmenides, Zeno and Gorgias with an argument that has exerted a profound effect on philosophical thought down to our own time.[2] It is perfectly true, he argued, that Being and Not-Being are the same, because changeless Being is itself an illusion. The world that we know is always in a state of change or flux; that is its most obvious characteristic. We can never grasp anything and say 'this is unchanging or stationary', because that which we intend to grasp has already suffered change by the time we are able to set our hands upon it. Reality is a stream into which we cannot plunge twice. Everything flows. We can arrest the flow only in thought. Consequently the idea of permanence is something that we ourselves have invented; but it would be foolish to imagine that reality exhibits any permanence beyond the fact that it is in a permanent state of flux.[3]

[1] This argument was revived, as we shall see, by the German philosopher Hegel.

[2] See the chapter on Bergson.

[3] Heraclitus also had some interesting things to say about the concept of unity in diversity and *vice versa*.

To outline the thought of all the pre-Socratic philosophers, of whom there were a great many, would take too long; but it is impossible to understand the work of Socrates, and the great revolution in thought that he effected, without referring to one more distinguished name, a name familiar to all, even schoolchildren: Pythagoras. Born at Samos in the early sixth century BC, Pythagoras was a man of such influence over his contemporaries that he inspired a school of philosophers who interested themselves in almost every form of speculation—mathematics, music, medicine, religion. This school or Order had flourishing branches at Crotona, Tarentum, and later at Athens and Thebes; and historians are still debating how far Pythagoras himself was responsible for some of the ideas defined by later historians and philosophers as 'Pythagorean'.

What chiefly distinguishes the Pythagorean School from that initiated by Thales is its emphasis upon mathematics as the 'key' to the nature of reality. Whereas the Ionian School had been obsessed with the *material* constituents of Nature, the Pythagoreans were more interested in the types of order or *form* to be found in Nature. The basis of geometry, astronomy and music was harmony and proportion; and harmony and proportion were ultimately reducible to Number. Number, in fact, assumed for the Pythagoreans an almost mystical significance.

Both Socrates and Plato were greatly influenced by the doctrines of the Pythagorean School, above all those concerning the nature and destiny of the human soul. With thinkers such as Democritus (460 BC), however, Greek thought took a decidedly materialistic direction. Born at Abdera (in Thrace), Democritus was the founder of the school of Atomists; and although most of his writings—and he is said to have written a great deal—have perished, we can learn something about his theories from the great poem of his disciple Lucretius, *On the Nature of Things*. According to Democritus, both matter and mind are composed of atoms; and these constituent atoms, though varying in shape, are by nature indestructible. Even the gods themselves are formed of combinations of atomic particles, their so-called immortality being due to superior and therefore more lasting combinations than those of mortals. Nevertheless, we cannot suppose that such combinations will last indefinitely; for death will one day overtake even the most transcendent of Beings. Only the individual atom, then, is assured of immortality. Although its partnership with other atoms may be dissolved, it will remain free to enter into other partnerships, and so on for ever. About 2405 years after the birth of Democritus, his theory of the hard, indestructible nature of the atom received striking refutation in practice.

The thinkers whose work we have outlined in the foregoing pages were not isolated figures, speculating in the void and exerting little influence upon the ordinary people of their day. Some, like Gorgias, held important public positions. Many were skilled in various sciences, such as medicine or astronomy, and became renowned for their spectacular cures and prognostications. Empedocles of Agrigentum (450 BC), poet, orator and seer, was such a one. Others, like Anaxagoras, who began teaching at Athens about 460 BC, were friends and advisers of the great statesmen of the time. In an age when the sources of knowledge were so few, the sage or wise man was a figure of eminence, whether he taught what was popular, or whether, like Anaxagoras and Socrates, he defied current beliefs and incurred the odium of the authorities.[1] The fame of a great teacher would spread so rapidly that young men, anxious to acquire wisdom, would travel great distances to attend his lectures, and sometimes to consult him upon subjects not always strictly philosophical. The Greek world was already famous for the wisdom of its Oracles. These philosophers were living, moving and sometimes equally expensive oracles. For there were not a few charlatans among them. Inevitably, in time, there grew up schools of *professional* wise men, or, as they were known by their contemporaries, Sophists: individuals who went into the business of purveying wisdom for gain, charging high prices for instructing pupils in the art of persuasion and rhetoric. At their best, the Sophists induced people to examine their own consciences, to revise their everyday assumptions, to curb their prejudices, and so to broaden their outlooks, with a view to influencing their conduct of affairs. At their worst, they imparted nothing more than intellectual 'sales talk', casuistry, logic-chopping and quibbling—in short, the art, so cruelly ascribed by Aristophanes to Socrates in *The Clouds* of 'making the worst cause seem the better'.

The first well-known figure in ancient Athens to impart knowledge and instruction for gain was a Sophist called Protagoras (481–411 BC), a friend of Democritus, about whom Plato wrote an entertaining and not too friendly dialogue. Plato pictures Protagoras as always surrounded by a group of earnest young men who listened in awe to his least remark, firmly believing that, in return for a moderate sum of money, he would make them wise. For the disciples of the Sophists appeared to labour under the delusion that wisdom, at least as possessed by these professional teachers, was a commodity capable of being transferred *en bloc* from one person to another. The teaching of Protagoras possessed all the attractions of being somewhat 'daring' and 'advanced'; hence its fascination for those who, like the smart young men of Athens, wished to emphasize their superiority over the masses. The promoter of scepticism is not necessarily an evil influence in society, for no society can afford to dispense with healthy criticism; what is important is that the critic shall be animated by the right motives. As for the Sophists, their motives were frequently tainted with mischief; for their aim was not so much to enlighten as to bewilder. They wished to inspire awe instead of respect, or to enforce a reluctant respect by a display of intellectual virtuosity.

According to Socrates and Plato, such was the underlying motive that inspired the Sophists Protagoras and his colleague Hippias. The scepticism of Protagoras took the form of casting doubt upon the power of the human intellect to arrive at truth; an entertaining but

[1] Anaxagoras's works were publicly burned in Athens in 411 BC.

dangerous doctrine. Every man, Protagoras argued, has nothing but his own senses upon which to rely; but your senses and mine may register different conclusions, and which of us is to claim that he is the more trustworthy in his impressions? The answer must seemingly be that both are right, because each has reached his own truth, so that there are an infinite number of possible 'truths'.

Such a theory, it is obvious, leads us nowhere. All authorities, being equally useful, become equally useless. Truth has been shattered into a myriad particles, each of which neutralizes and dulls the brilliance of the others. The result is not illumination but obscurity. And the student who sets out to find a sure guide to conduct retires in a state of mental befuddlement. In return for his money, he possesses nothing but a store of useless jargon. He has bartered good coinage for the 'snide' of intellectual conceit. Such was the effect of much of the Sophistic teaching.

Of Protagoras and his colleagues at least it may be said that they stumbled upon an important truth without knowing it. In their attack upon the lofty but vague speculations of their predecessors and contemporaries, they laid bare the fact, so rightly insisted upon by Socrates, that 'the proper study of mankind is man'. Where they erred was in their excessive emphasis upon that which distinguished and separated one man from another. When Socrates set out to discover the meaning of the Delphic Oracle's maxim 'Know thyself', or, more strictly, 'Know that thou art mortal', on the other hand, he began by considering human nature in general. His argument was as follows. To lay bare the secrets of the universe, its origin and destiny, must assuredly take centuries of patient investigation; perhaps those secrets will never be fully revealed to man, given faculties of such limitation as those which he possesses. But man can here and now embark upon the road to self-knowledge. He does not need complicated instruments for that. In reflecting upon his own conduct, in examining the discrepancy between what he is and what he ought to be—what he does and what he ought to do—he will find mental occupation sufficient to enlist his energies to the full.

Thus Socrates laid the foundations of a science which his successors, Plato and Aristotle, and their successors in turn up to our own day, have developed and debated, though never fundamentally altered; namely, the science of human conduct or, as the text-books call it, Ethics. To Socrates, the science of conduct was that to which man should devote his most earnest attention, because by no other path could true wisdom be found; and by calling Ethics a science, Socrates meant to imply that it was governed by principles of universal validity, so that what was good for one was good for all, and what was my neighbour's duty was my duty also. Socrates was therefore not merely the founder of the science of ethics; he was the first great opponent of the doctrine most destructive of rational morality, namely, ethical *relativism*

In seeking to prove the existence of a law for mankind transcending personal differences—a law valid at all times and places, and one which imposed its own rewards and punishments by conferring or withholding happiness—Socrates was in effect contending that, beneath the mass of opinions and prejudices entertained by mankind, something in the nature of a 'universal conscience' existed, and, despite external pressure, never ceased to carry weight and authority. The crucial problem was how to break through the overgrowth of opinion and prejudice and contact the root itself: to shut out the clamour and hear the 'still, small voice'.

Socrates claimed—and he made good his claim in action—that this could best be done by endeavouring to discover, through a technique of questioning, what precisely each man's personal opinions were, and how far he was prepared to go in backing them by argument. And the kind of individual whom he found to respond most satisfactorily to this treatment was he who imagined, at least to begin with, that his views were absolutely proof against argument: in short, the man who, far from wishing to acquire wisdom, was convinced that he already possessed it.

The Socratic method of examining men's everyday opinions (for these were good enough for his purpose) by means of a carefully elaborated system of questioning or, as Plato called it, dialectic, was not instruction in the ordinary sense. Socrates was concerned less with imparting knowledge—indeed, he claimed that he had none to impart—than with exposing and expelling ignorance. His object was to extract admission after admission from his interlocutor, until the latter, deflated in his initial belief that his ideas were sound and consistent, realized that in fact he knew very little.

'My art,' Socrates explained on one occasion, 'is like that of the midwives, but differs from theirs, in that I attend men and not women, and I look after their souls when they are in labour, and not after their bodies; and the triumph of my art is in thoroughly examining whether the thought which the mind of the young man brings forth is a phantom and a lie, or a fruitful and true birth. And, like the midwives, I am barren, and the reproach often made against me, that I ask questions of others and have not the wit to answer them myself, is very just—the reason is, that the god compels me to be a midwife, but does not allow me to have children... Dire are the pangs which my art is able to arouse and to allay in those who consort with me, just like the pangs of women in childbirth; night and day they are full of perplexity and travail, which is even worse than that of women.'

The method of approach entailed a view of education which differed profoundly from that commonly held at the time. Education, in Socrates' view, implied above all the stripping away of prejudice, the probing of superficial opinions, with the object of arriving at that hard *substratum* of knowledge which everyone, if sufficiently well examined, would be found to possess. For the truth is in all of us, only it needs to be brought to birth. Education, in short, can produce nothing that is not already latent in the soul. The 'idea' of justice, goodness, beauty and truth is common to all mankind; and if a man acts always with sufficient self-knowledge, he will inevitably act rightly. Those who have no 'sense' of what is right or wrong are beyond the reach of rational persuasion and must be pronounced abnormal.

In preaching his new gospel, Socrates was endeavouring to fulfil a social purpose, to serve his fellow Athenians. Against the view that philosophy deals with ideas divorced from practical, everyday life, he contended that the aim of philosophy was to purify the social conscience, and thereby to strengthen the 'morale' of the community. It needed strengthening then as now. In concerning himself with the problems affecting each individual man, the true philosopher helped the society in which he lived to become conscious of itself; by shouldering the burdens of his neighbours, he assisted in making their tasks lighter; by sacrificing his life for what he believed to be the truth—albeit the unpalatable truth—he ennobled the very people who were base enough to condemn him. For, as has so often happened, the unanimous indictment of Socrates gave place, within a short time of his decease, to a violent social reaction, in the course of which his prosecutors, once the idols of the mob, became the objects of universal execration, ending their lives by being stoned to death in that same market-place where a humbler leader had taught the principles of the good life.

11

Plato

The noblest of all studies is the study of what man is and what he should pursue.
Gorgias

His Life

Socrates was a man of the people, or more accurately of the middle-classes. According to all acounts, he was a person of grotesque, almost repulsive, appearance: short and stout, with a snub nose, large prominent eyes, thick lips, full of wit and irony, ready to take a joke against himself, a good mixer, no respecter of persons. Plato, his disciple, presented a complete contrast. By birth he was an aristocrat, in appearance dignified and handsome, brilliant and polished in speech, a man careful of his associates, a stately visionary and a visionary statesman. Yet, though so different in character from Socrates, Plato confesses that his meeting with this ungainly fellow inspired in him the desire to devote his whole career, which already promised great things, to the search for truth behind appearances, while not abandoning the hope that one day he might find a ruler great enough to unite philosophy and statecraft in a true Republic of justice and peace.

Concerning the date and even the place of Plato's birth there is still a great measure of uncertainty. It is presumed that he was born in either 429 or 428 BC, most probably at Athens, but possibly in the island of Ægina. As to the circumstances of his birth, there is an abundance of fancy and legend of which little need here be repeated, save perhaps the story that bees settled on the lips of the sleeping child in anticipation of the honeyed words that promised to issue therefrom. He was the son of Ariston and Perictione or Polone, the former of whom claimed descent from Codrus, the last King of Athens (1068 BC?), and the latter from Solon, the famous Athenian law-giver (born 638 BC?). One tradition insists that he was originally named after his grandfather Aristocles, but that the name Plato was substituted because of his gift for fluent speech (others say it was because of his broad chest). Whatever the value of these legends, it is clear that he belonged to one of the best and oldest of Athenian families, and that he was give a chance in life such as few enjoy and from which fewer still contrive to take advantage.

As a boy, Plato's interests and pursuits were those of a typical, though unusually talented, child of well-to-do parents. He was an athlete of no mean ability; in the Isthmian games on one occasion he won the wrestling competition. He indulged in the usual youthful 'scribbling', turning out a stream of epic and lyric poetry, and also some full-length tragedies, of which nothing but a few fragments has survived. That he displayed any particular interest in the activity of thinking for thinking's sake, or philosophy, we have no reason to suppose. Something had to happen, some powerful influence to be brought to bear, before his deepest creative instincts and his desire for knowledge and wisdom were stirred. Nevertheless, he probably became acquainted with the speculations of Heraclitus and Anaxagoras, because there were few subjects upon which he did not receive regular instruction from the best available teachers. When he was in his twentieth year,[1] however, he met Socrates and joined his little circle. Such a dramatic encounter might have been expected to call forth a special memoir, and later writers have commented upon the fact that nothing of this kind has been preserved. They are mistaken. Plato has left us a record of this meeting in his entire published works, for the hero and chief spokesman throughout is Socrates himself.

The fact that Plato put almost all his ideas into the mouth of Socrates, mentioning himself by name only a few times, does not necessarily imply that his thought is not original. There are several possible explanations for his unique method of exposition. Most of his works are in the form of dialogues, and Plato must early have been attracted to the technique of 'question and answer' that Socrates had brought to such a pitch of perfection. Nor did Plato wish to conceal the fact that both in form and in context his ideas were of Socratic origin. Even so, we have no reason to suppose that the development and working out of these ideas is not Plato's own: in fact, we need only compare the temperament and interests of master and pupil to perceive that the one was concerned to evolve a *method* while the other was endeavouring to erect a *system*. Socrates, as we have seen, did not write a line. Plato, on the other hand, not merely wrote a very great deal; he left behind him the first systematic body of philosophical literature that the ancient world had produced. Of the works of philosophers before Plato, we possess only a few fragments that can be described as genuine. Of the works of Plato, the genuine books are almost all known, though there are certain dialogues or fragments that may well be by other hands.

The meeting with Socrates was not in itself remarkable. No clever and cultivated young man of Athens at the time could have failed to be attracted within the Socratic orbit. The significance lay in what Plato made out of this association, which became closer and closer. For while it is true that without Socrates we should have had no Plato, or at least a very different sort of Plato, it is equally true that without Plato we should have had no Socrates, or at least only the Socrates portrayed by Xenophon, who is a far less interesting figure. At the same time, Plato is not a mere Boswell; and he exhibits an artistry and range of thought

[1] Perhaps earlier; but Diogenes Laërtius says twenty.

which, if Socrates did not himself possess them, it was his gift to be able to stimulate in others.

In pursuing his enquiries on the subject of virtue, Socrates had always before his mind the idea of a happier and better society which he hoped to persuade man to establish. Plato's interests were equally practical. He felt, with that half-conscious conviction and self-assurance characteristic of the young, that he was cut out to be a great statesman, a master of men. Those companions with whom he mixed—the great men of the time—encouraged him to nourish such ambitions because they realized his unusual distinction of mind. His future thus seemed assured. He had been born great. Honours were plentifully thrust upon him. It required but little effort, or so it appeared, for him to achieve greatness.

And then, at the critical moment of his career, his beloved master was arrested on the charge of worshipping false gods and of corrupting the young. To Socrates himself, now a weary old man, the event must have come as no great surprise; he had expected—almost courted—it. But the effect upon his small band of disciples was devastating. From Socrates, Plato had derived the emotional stimulus that he felt he would need to transform himself from a mere politician, a party manager, into a statesman of lofty ideals. He was to be the first man of his time to demonstrate the workability of a political plan based upon justice instead of self-interest. He was to be the instrument whereby the glory of Athens, now in danger from formidable external enemies, was to be regenerated from within. The democratic regime under which he had grown up seemed to be based upon false—that is to say, materialistic—values; and when in turn that régime was overthrown and a new government of thirty reformers (the 'Thirty') substituted for it, Plato, being personally acquainted with many of the latter, had sincerely believed that the Athenian state would now at last recover its soul.

'I thought,' he later explained in one of the most interesting of his letters, 'that it [the rule of the Thirty] would substitute the reign of justice for the reign of injustice, and so I gave it my closest attention to see what it would do. And I saw these gentlemen within a very short time make the democracy they had destroyed seem like a golden age! I was deeply disgusted and dissociated myself entirely from this deplorable government. Shortly afterwards the Thirty were turned out and their règime destroyed. Once again I was filled with a desire to take an active part in politics. It was not surprising that those revolutionary times resulted in personal reprisals of a violent character; but on the whole the restored democracy exercised considerable moderation. And yet, as ill-luck would have it, certain influential persons brought an action against Socrates. The charge was an outrageous one, of which Socrates was completely innocent. They accused him of irreligion, and on this count the jury condemned him to death.'

Henceforth Plato was to entertain towards politics and the profession of statecraft feelings of unconcealed revulsion. 'The more I considered it,' he wrote, 'and the older I grew, the more difficult appeared to me to be the task of decent government. Traditions of honesty and the actual observance of law alike were degenerating in Athens with surprising rapidity, and when I saw how chaotic the political situation was, I felt completely baffled... Finally I came to the conclusion that every state without exception is badly governed, and that the state of legislation is everywhere so deplorable that no improvement is possible without drastic reconstruction combined with some very good luck. And so I was forced to extol true philosophy and to declare that through it alone can real justice both for the state and for the individual be discovered and enforced.' And he concluded with the following profound observation: 'Mankind will find no cessation from evil until either the real philosophers gain political control or else the politicians become by some miracle real philosophers.'

True philosophy; real philosophers. Not, in other words, the philosophy that amounted simply to juggling with words (rhetoric) or juggling with ideas (casuistry); nor the philosophers who regarded their profession solely as a means to money-making. True philosophy, as Plato was henceforth to conceive it, was practical philosophy; but this practical philosophy was to be very different from that of the Sophists, who wished to press wisdom into the service of material advancement, and to use their tricks to gain control over men and their possessions, making the worse cause the better and the worst of all the best.

In other words, the task to which Plato—moved to the depth of his soul by the prosecution of Socrates—henceforth dedicated himself was that of laying the foundations, at first in theory only, of the ideal City. We are accustomed to Utopias, but for Plato's contemporaries the ideal was quite original, even startling. In Greece at that time the political unit was the City State, a unit much more manageable than our modern nation-states, and more easily reorganized as a result of conquest or revolution. But Plato was concerned with something more than a mere blue-print of a political system to be established in a particular locality. His vision was not provincial but universal. He wanted world revolution, but within the human heart.

He saw, as Socrates had taught him, that the most urgent and difficult of all reforms was that to be undertaken within man himself, a reform that should ultimately extend to all mankind, embracing both Greeks and barbarians, slaves and free men. That a truly just society could be established within measurable time he was too disillusioned to believe. A long period of education must prepare the way for any such millennium. Nevertheless, if his ideals were pronounced too lofty to be realized, he was convinced that no goal less lofty was worth pursuing. Greek civilization could survive, he believed, only through the kind of spiritual renewal that would render impossible a repetition of the scandal of Socrates's persecution. Indeed, the test of a just society was simply whether it would foster and honour its great reformers and teachers, or whether, out of crass ignorance on the part of the masses or from fear of exposure and ridicule on the part of a few tyrants, it would seek to muzzle them.

In order to equip himself for this self-imposed task, Plato decided upon a course of action that has recommended itself to many men similarly resolved. He travelled. Deep and prolonged meditation is not necessarily accomplished best in seclusion. The senses need to refresh themselves with new sights and sounds, the body to engage in unaccustomed exertions, in order that the mind, quietly disengaging itself from stale routine, may go freely about its business of self-examination. How frequently men of action have reported, in later years, that their minds were most at peace at the time when their physical being was subject to greatest agitation! In one sense, Plato's excursion abroad represented a kind of retirement and even exile. He was away from Athens for about eleven years. In the case of one so full of vitality, however, this long period was devoted to much else besides thinking, reading, and writing. As we shall see in due course, he twice became involved in complicated political affairs. Nevertheless, this departure from Athens marks the beginning of his creative period, the renewal of his zest for the pursuit of truth.

At first he withdrew to Megara, a town only twenty-six miles from Athens, and here he probably wrote some of his early dialogues. Possibly he formed one of a small band of disciples of Socrates, another of whom, Euclides (not to be confused with the mathematician of that name), composed similar works of which none have survived. Deciding to venture farther afield, Plato then set out for the town of Cyrene in North Africa (now in the Libyan province of Cyrenaica), perhaps at the invitation of the well-known philosopher Theodosius. The latter had been given the title of Atheist in consequence not so much of his denial of the gods as of his outspoken comments upon the religious beliefs and practices of the time. He was a man for whom, in the circumstances, Plato would have felt a special sympathy.

Later still, Plato visited Egypt and Sicily, and the flourishing Greek cities of Lower Italy, impelled both by an insatiable thirst for knowledge and by the desire, understandable in a young man of his nature, to make personal contact with the famous men of the day. Long after his death, these wanderings were made to assume a romantic colouring which, though no doubt justified in part, was on the whole greatly exaggerated. We have no reason to give credence to the stories—as fantastic as that which made him out to be the son of Apollo—concerning his mysterious journeys to the Hebrews, to the Babylonians, to the Assyrians, and even to the Magi, a religious sect of the Medes and Persians whose representatives made a journey to Bethlehem a few centuries later.

Of the details of his visits to Sicily, however, we have more reliable information. He went there first in 389 BC, when he was forty years of age. Here he soon won the respect and finally the friendship of Dion, brother-in-law of the tyrant of Syracuse, Dionysius. Already a man of upright character, Dion had but to come under the influence of Plato to conceive an immediate distaste for the life of dissipation, luxury, and sloth which he and his fellow-courtiers had been leading. Nevertheless, whereas Dion maintained good relations with Dionysius the Elder, he soon fell out with the latter's son, whose mode of life was characterized by excesses of an even more revolting kind, and to whom the newly-assumed austerity of his uncle Dion was both a reproach and a source of irritation.

Plato, unlike Dion, soon quarrelled with the elder Dionysius and is said by some historians to have been sold into slavery by him. This story is probably without foundation. We do know, however, that Dion, determined to gain influence over his nephew, the younger Dionysius, and believing that no one but Plato could effect his 'conversion', begged the philosopher to make a second journey to Syracuse, which he did shortly after the death of the Elder Dionysius, in 367 BC. On arrival, Plato was accorded a reception such as has rarely greeted a man renowned for wisdom, even in days when personages of this type were honoured to a marked degree. In spite of his strenuous efforts to win the young ruler to the cause of philosophy, however, Plato was obliged to admit failure. For he was faced with two forms of opposition, that resulting from Dionysius's early training, and that from Syracusan party politicians, who regarded such a disinterested mission on the part of a foreigner with undisguised hostility. And so, in the end, not merely was Plato forced to make a hasty retreat, but Dion, his host, was obliged to accompany him back to Athens, where he remained for some time in exile. Thus concluded Plato's second attempt to turn a statesman into a philosopher.

His third and last venture, which occurred in 360 BC, nearly cost him his life. It was concerned with the same ruler, Dionysius II. Now anxious to reconcile himself with Dion, Dionysius, who seems to have been a man of most changeable temper, invited Plato to act as mediator once more. But the man whose advice had been sought by both parties to the quarrel was again ill-paid for his efforts.

Dionysius, on receiving Plato at his unruly court, took it into his head to resent the very counsel he had so earnestly solicited; and had it not been for the intervention of Archytas, himself a philosopher of repute as well as a general, Plato might have spent the rest of his life in the diabolical quarry-prison of Syracuse, where, it is said, the tyrant has already incarcerated the poet Philoxenus for daring to ridicule some royal attempts at versification. Nevertheless, Plato had not altogether failed in his efforts to educate Dionysius II as the Philosopher-King. The royal disposition underwent another change. For a time all went well: the courtiers abandoned their dissipations and even set about studying geometry, tracing figures on the ground which had been specially strewn with sand for the purpose. Later (357 BC) Dion returned to Syracuse and ousted Dionysius. In 353 BC, however, Dion was himself murdered, and a great ruler was thus probably lost to the world.

After his return from his first visit to Syracuse, Plato had purchased a house and a garden in a suburb of Athens near the river Cephissus. Not far away was a plot of land which had originally belonged to Academus, the Attic hero. This had been later turned into a sanctuary and gymnasium, planted with plane and olive trees, and decorated with groups of statuary. Here, in what came to be known as the Academy, as well as in his own garden at Colonus, Plato began to teach and to lecture. He taught free of charge, and his pupils were at first a small circle of intimate friends. Above the entrance to his house he affixed the inscription: 'Let no one enter who is unacquainted with geometry.'

The disciples of Plato at this time were almost all persons of distinction. There was his nephew Speusippus, a keen student of philosophy who was to accompany him on his third journey to Syracuse. There was Xenocrates of Chalcedon, also a philosopher of some merit who, like Speusippus, later became president of the Academy. There was an extraordinary young man from Stagira called Aristotle, of whom we shall hear more. There was Heraclides Ponticus, mathematician and philosopher, Hestiæus of Perinthus, Phillipus and Arpuntian, and many others. Apart from this inner circle, however, there were men of wisdom and learning from all parts of Greece and sometimes beyond, who, hearing of the great abilities of Plato as a teacher, made journeys to Athens for the purpose of becoming acquainted with him.

Women, too, were among those who attended his courses of instruction. For although in Ancient Greece woman played practically no part in public affairs and enjoyed no higher education, Plato, almost alone among the thinkers of antiquity, advocated the equality of the sexes. As he declared in the *Republic*: 'If women are to have the same duties as men, they must have the same upbringing and education.'

Of the forty or so literary works said to have been written by Plato, thirty are today regarded as genuine. But even so his output was enormous. Except during his two eventful journeys to Syracuse after the foundation of the Academy, he was occupied with teaching and writing up to and including the day of his death.[1] This took place at the ripe age of eighty-two in 347 BC, fifty-three years having elapsed since the death of Socrates.

The removal of the leader, however, did not mean the breaking up of the philosophical conclave, still less of the Academy. In his will, Plato left his properties to the school he had founded, and its members faithfully preserved those hallowed places. In course of time they became a shrine, a centre of pilgrimage, where the anniversaries of the death of Plato and Socrates were celebrated year by year with true devotion. Finally the Academy passed into the hands of the Neo-Platonists, remaining open as a school of philosophical research and debate for more than five centuries into the Christian ear. Thus Plato's Academy was in reality the world's first university; and hence the word 'academic' is today inseparably linked with university life, though with slightly derogatory associations for which its originator was in no way responsible. Having been founded in 380 BC and closed by order of the Emperor Justinian in AD 529, it survived without a break for longer than any other university of which we have record. Meanwhile, the influence of Plato's philosophical ideas had spread to the confines of the civilized world, informing the thought of the Fathers of the Christian Church, penetrating and fertilizing the speculations of the peoples of the East, and inspiring every philosopher worth the name

[1] Plato's lectures have not survived.

down to our own time. A modern thinker, whose work we shall later discuss.[1] has even gone so far as to describe the course of Western philosophy since the fifth century BC as nothing but a series of 'footnotes to Plato'.

What was Plato like as a man? We know almost as little about Plato's private life and character as we know about Shakespeare: which means that of the two supreme men of genius of the Western world we know practically nothing. The bust that has been preserved, with its tangled beard and penetrating eyes, suggests a man of profound, almost fiery, temperament, presenting a marked contrast to the judicial countenance of Aristotle. There are suggestions, derived from Plato's own works and from those of his contemporaries and successors, that he was a man of ardent disposition. Ardent he must certainly have been; whether he exhibited the frankly erotic tendencies that have been attributed to Socrates is more than doubtful. Both the passionate love of intellectual beauty that animates all his work, and his reputation as a man of supreme wisdom and goodness, are irreconcilable with the notion that he (or Socrates for that matter) was merely another, though vastly more intelligent, Alcibiades. At the same time we have no reason to suppose that he was a prig or a recluse. The Academy was a place of good fellowship; and how striking is the difference between the modern word 'symposium', with its exclusively literary significance, and the original Symposium (literally 'a drinking together'), that greatest of all drinking parties of which Plato has left us such a lively record!

His Thought

If we devote more space to both Plato and Aristotle than to most of the philosophers of whom we shall be speaking, it is because the work of these two thinkers, master and pupil, has exerted such a profound influence upon everything that has since happened in the realm of philosophy. Their achievement represents the rock or foundation upon which subsequent thinkers have constructed their habitations, great or small, weather-proof or gimcrack. They drew up the Constitution, to which their successors have made amendments of varying importance.

Of Plato's use of the dialogue in expounding his ideas, we have already spoken. He was not the only thinker to use it. Zeno did so, and also Xenophon and Æschines (both acquaintances of Socrates), Antisthenes, founder of the school of Cynics, and Euclides. With Plato, however, the dialogue form took on a more significant aspect both as a literary convention and as a method of expounding ideas. From Socrates Plato had grasped what may seem to us a self-evident fact, namely, that the right way to acquire knowledge is to ask questions. Admittedly, in order to proceed in the correct way, we must know what questions to ask. It was Socrates' achievement to have made clear that there is, for those who seek it diligently, a correct order in thought, a natural unfolding of logical argument. Thinking, he said in effect, is

[1] A. N. Whitehead.

not just the 'hit and miss' activity which for most of us it remains throughout life. Or rather, it resembles the shooting at a target only in the sense that each shot is intended as a nearer approximation to the bull's-eye. It is a case of hit-and-near-miss, with the margin of error being steadily whittled down.

In other words, the dialogue form is admirably adapted to the view that truth is attained in a series of definite and recognizable stages. In most modern books concerned with the exposition of ideas, the argument flows on uninterruptedly from beginning to end, as if it were a string unwound from a ball. And this regular 'paying out' of ideas is something upon which the writer is inclined to pride himself. This may perhaps be called the 'horizontal' method of approach. Plato and some of his contemporaries used a different one, which might be called the 'vertical' method of approach. Convinced that the search for truth must be a slow, gradual process, Plato sets out to make clear the exact stage, at any one moment, that he has reached in his argument. This he does by making each conclusion the subject of a kind of bilateral pact between the persons engaged in the dispute. As a result, his dialogues sometimes give the impression of being a series of separate 'bones of contention', without these components ever forming a complete frame or skeleton; but the frame is being built up all the time, even though we do not easily perceive its formation while we are absorbed in the structure of a particular section.

There is a further reason why Plato, seeking for the most effective means of expounding philosophical arguments, decided upon the use of dramatic dialogue. He was intent upon showing, by literary means, that thought is a growing, living, almost organic, process. Why was he so concerned to show this? Because he had been given the unique opportunity of observing it thus developing, thus germinating, in the mind of a living person. He was seeking to put Socrates on paper: to preserve as best as artificial means could afford the creative spontaneity, the personal magnetism, of the master.

For us, living more than two thousand years after, philosophy chiefly implies a book, a treatise, or a paper read before a learned society: a thing written down, a topic of limited interest and application, a subject in an Honour School. We do not live our philosophy, or rather we do not live the philosophy that we read, if we read any at all; we observe a marked distinction between theory and practice, bridging the gulf as a rule by our sense of irony and humour. Such a state of affairs would have seemed odd, even deplorable, to Plato. Plato regarded Socrates as the first of a series of truly practical, because practising, philosophers, whose line should culminate in the messianic figure of the Philosopher-King. He was not to know that Socrates, while being the first of his kind, was also in a sense to be the last.

Since he could imagine no philosophy worth the name as being anything but the expression of a personality, the mainspring of conduct in some individual, Plato introduced into his dialogues real historical personages—Alcibiades, Protagoras, Critias, Parmenides. Into their mouths he put words and arguments which, if always 'in character', are not, so far as we know, verbatim records of speeches actually delivered. Like the historian Thucydides, who put long speeches into the mouths of historical characters without claiming that they were necessarily spoken in that form, Plato tried to expound various 'points of view' by the realistic method of assembling a number of typical spokesmen. Not merely had he observed Socrates living and working out his philosophy 'in the open', without recourse to books; he had observed his enlistment of other people, not as passive objects for experimental purposes, but as partners in the business of seeking ultimate truth.

The 'artistry' of Plato, of which so much has been written, is not merely the artistry of a man who, besides being a master-thinker, knows how to write. It is the artistry of a man who captures in writing the drama of a philosophy that was in essence a spoken and extempore philosophy. Moreover it had the advantage of being spoken and extemporized by one of the greatest of all talkers. How vast a gulf separates a 'spoken' philosophy such as that of Plato from our modern 'written' philosophies will be observed when we come to discuss the work of another master of philosophizing, Immanuel Kant. While acutely aware that thought and action was inseparable, Kant lacked the literary skill to transcribe his ideas in the language of everyday life, with the result that his writings tend to be as forbidding to the ordinary reader as his lectures and conversation were reported to have been stimulating.

Taking his clue from Socrates that the aim of philosophy is to prescribe the kind of life most likely to promote the happiness of man, Plato realized that such a subject of enquiry depends for its clarification upon the answer to the question: what kind of a being is this creature, man, that he should need to be concerned with his own happiness? What distinguishes him as a living entity from the rest of Creation? In seeking to answer these questions, Plato pursued his speculations to a point where Socrates, content to 'shelve' metaphysical matters, or at best to interpret them in an allegorical fashion, had called a halt. Never wholly forsaking his early political ambitions, Plato earnestly sought to combine his loftiest notions with plans for a social system or Republic wherein the human spirit, destined for immortality in another sphere, might develop its latent capacities.

In short, Plato's political theory was concerned not so much with a state that should promote the material well-being of its inhabitants (though he was interested, especially towards the end of his life, in this aspect also) as with a system capable of opening the way to the good life by providing the maximum incentive to it. Here again his attitude differs from that of most modern writers on so-called ethical questions. Today, a man's ideas of goodness and badness are generally supposed to be matters private to himself. The good life is something to be lived apart from, and often in spite of, the social system of the day. Religion, for instance, is a private affair, a matter for the individual conscience. To Plato, this division of life into a public and a private sphere was not to be tolerated. Politics and morals were the same. Bad politics lead to bad behaviour. The good life was possible only in the good state.[1]

Naturally, he was well aware how far short of this ideal of harmonious living his contemporaries and most of his predecessors had fallen: the extract from his letter already quoted shows that he had a shrewd idea what he was facing. But this yawning gulf between what was and what ought to be impressed him as something more than a mere accident of social life. It struck him as characteristic of life in general. It was part of the nature of things. Between the ordinary everyday world that we know and the world as it should be—between the information and knowledge with which we 'make do' in our normal routine of living and the true knowledge that should ideally be our guide—there is a serious discrepancy. At any given moment, we act not upon a true assessment of the situation but upon a rough compromise; we are content with beliefs and opinions. This is because the ordinary world in which we live is a world of imperfections and imprecisions, of half-lights and shadows.

These ideals, beliefs and opinions of ours are not necessarily to be regarded as the product of an inaccurate or distorted vision of the ordinary world; they represent a true and faithful reflection of it, such as it is. But this everyday world may not be the only world with which we can establish contact. It is simply the world which we perceive with our senses. In Plato's view, there is another and truer world, the world which we may perceive with our intellect. This alone is reality.

Plato is thus one of the first philosophers to assert and exploit the fundamental distinction between that which is perceived by our senses and that which is perceived by our intellect. Pythagoras, with his emphasis upon form and structure as opposed to matter or 'stuff', partially anticipated him; but Plato used the distinction as the basis for a theory which may be said to have exerted more influence upon later philosophical thought than any other: namely, his celebrated Theory of Ideas.

Plato's Theory of Ideas has frequently been misunderstood, or at least mis-stated, as a result of a failure to perceive how he arrived at it. In fact, there need be no mystery about it at all, for it developed logically and inevitably out of Socrates' technique of inquisition (though the influence of Parmenides is also apparent). Socrates's aim in discussing a subject was to reach agreement, by a series of interim arguments, upon what constituted the *essence* of that subject. Take, for instance, a virtue such as Justice. Socrates would try to establish what constituted the unique character whereby everything just was just. This was equivalent to establishing the Idea of Justice. To arrive at the Idea of a thing was the final stage of any discussion upon which Socrates decided to embark.

Ideas, therefore, are the goal of our intellectual faculty; only by intellectual analysis can we arrive at a knowledge that they exist. With another bolt stroke of originality, Plato then proceeds to explain how such analysis is made possible. In his view, the knowledge of Uni-

[1] For Plato, the state signifies the City State of his day.

versals (as the Platonic Ideas are commonly called today) is the result not so much of learning as of re-learning. We do not acquire such knowledge; we recollect it.

This is above all the case with the truths of geometry (which is no doubt why Plato caused the famous inscription to be put up at the entrance to the Academy). In his dialogue entitled the *Meno*, he shows with extraordinary skill how an untutored slave-boy, questioned by Socrates, is able to discover and apprehend for himself the truth of a geometrical demonstration. How, Plato asks, can knowledge of this sort be completely new? If we set out to acquire a certain kind of knowledge, the knowledge we wish to acquire cannot be wholly strange to us; for if it were strange, how, once acquired, could we recognize it to be that which we are seeking? We cannot 'entertain' a complete stranger. Now it is clear that if there are certain truths of which we have instinctive knowledge (usually termed in philosophical textbooks *a priori* knowledge), we must surely have acquired that knowledge in some realm other than that into which we were born. Knowledge recollected here must have been collected elsewhere. What realm can this be, then, in which pure and perfect knowledge is eternally assembled? Moreover, how did the soul of man, once having known this state of perfection, ever become alienated from it?

Plato's answer to this fascinating problem is couched in the language of myth. A myth, in the sense in which he uses the term, is an allegorical explanation, not a logical one. The myth to which we refer is an account of the 'history' of the soul, and we may retail this history in Plato's own words, taking from the dialogue called the *Phœdrus*.

'The nature of the soul is altogether a subject for large and more than mortal discourse, but to say what the soul resembles is a briefer and human theme. Let me compare it to a pair of winged horses and a charioteer. Now the winged horses and the charioteers of the gods are all of them noble and of noble descent, but those of other races (*e.g.* human beings) are mixed. One human charioteer drives his in a pair; and one of them is noble and of noble breed, and the other is ignoble and of ignoble breed; and the driving of them is necessarily hard and difficult. I will try to explain to you how the mortal differs from the immortal creature. The soul in her totality has the care of all soulless being, and traverses the whole heaven taking different forms; when perfect and fully winged she soars upward, and orders the whole world; while the imperfect soul, losing her wings and drooping in her flight, at last settles on the solid ground—there, finding a home, she receives an earthly body which appears to be self-moved, but it really moved by her power; and this composition of soul and body is called a living and mortal creature. For immortal no such union can be reasonably believed to be . . .

'And now let us ask the reason why the soul loses her wings! The wing is the corporeal element which is most akin to the divine, and which by nature tends to soar aloft and carry that which gravitates downwards into the upper region, where the gods dwell. The divine is beauty, wisdom, goodness, and the like; and by these the wing of the soul is nourished, and grows apace; but when fed upon evil and ugliness and the opposite of good, it wastes and is destroyed . . . The reason why the soul exhibits this intense eagerness to behold the plain of truth is that pasturage is found there, which is suited to the highest part of the soul; and the wing on which the soul soars is nourished with this.

'And there is a law of Destiny, that the soul which attains any vision of truth in company with a God is preserved from harm until the next period, and if attaining always is always unharmed. But when she is unable to follow, and fails to behold the truth, and through some ill-hap sinks beneath the double load of forgetfulness and vice, and her wings fall from her and she drops to the ground, then the law ordains that this soul shall at her first birth pass, not into any other animal, but only into man; and the soul which has seen most of truth shall come to the birth as a philosopher, or artist, or some musical or loving nature; that which has seen truth in the second degree shall be some law-abiding being or soldier or ruler; the soul which is of the third class shall be a politician, or business man, or financier; the fourth shall be a lover of athletics or a physician; the fifth shall lead the life of a prophet or hierophant;[1] to the sixth the character of a poet or some other imitative artist will be assigned; to the seventh the life of an artisan or husbandman; to the eighth that of a sophist or demagogue; to the ninth that of a despot; all these are states of probation, in which he who lives justly improves, and he who lives unjustly deteriorates his lot.'

From the above account it will be seen that in the hierarchy of beings that are in contact with true reality, the philosophers and the 'good king' are those placed at the summit, with the philosopher definitely taking precedence. The mere politician comes third, along with the business man and the financier. We can therefore understand Plato's preoccupation with the problems of just and wise government; for he had become convinced that no good could come to mankind until the two highest callings, that of philosopher and that of ruler, were merged into one: in short, 'until philosophers are kings'.[2]

With Plato's theory of the 'transmigration of souls'—an idea which he almost certainly borrowed from Pythagoras—we are not concerned. What interests us rather is his belief, novel in its orientation, that man is, in the words appropriate to a later doctrine, a 'fallen' creature. Realizing his sorry condition, man strives to improve it; and he may, if supremely fortunate, arrive at true knowledge, as opposed to mere belief or opinion, by the technique of recollection or—to use Plato's term—*mimesis*, which 'brings to birth' the wisdom with which he was formerly endowed.

For, as Plato remarks further on in the same dialogue, 'a man must have intelligence of universals, and be able to proceed from the many particulars of sense to one conception of reason; this is the recollection

[1] A priest of the sacred mysteries.

[2] This famous phrase occurs in *The Republic*, 473.

of those things which our souls once saw when following God, when regardless of that which we now call reality she raised her head to Reality itself... Once the beauty was clear to see, when in that happy company our souls saw the beatific vision and were initiated into what may be called the most blessed of mysteries, celebrated by us in our state of innocence, while we were untouched by evils to come, when we were admitted to the sight of visions innocent and simple, calm and happy, which we beheld shining in pure light; and we were pure ourselves and unstained by that which we carry about and call our body, imprisoned like shellfish in their shell.'

It is easy to dismiss such lofty passages as the outpourings of a mystic who was also a poet. A poet Plato most certainly was, in addition to being an inspirer of poetry in others. Wordsworth, writing two thousand years later, embodies such Platonic doctrines in his *Ode on the Intimations of Immortality*. But, even allowing for his superb use of imagery and metaphor, Plato is not indulging in mere rhetoric. He does not pile phrase upon phrase, period upon period, like the Sophists. He is not concerned merely to achieve an effect. He wants us to take his criticism of materialism seriously. He is inviting his contemporaries, and indeed all those who are to follow after him, to turn away from the kind of life which identifies happiness with indulgence in the pleasures of the senses, and to seek a more permanently satisfying mode of existence. No man had spoken quite like this before, except the man who had put him on the road to wisdom.

Plato's 'idealism' is nowhere more clearly revealed than in his account of the nature of art; for it is his contention that we come closest to apprehending the world of Forms when we gaze upon something or someone beautiful. Beauty, in other words, is the form most easily accessible to us, even to the least intellectual, because it manifests itself chiefly through the medium of vision. 'Of beauty,' Plato says, 'I repeat again that we saw her there' (*i.e.* in heaven) 'shining in company with the celestial forms: and coming to earth we find her here too, shining in clearness through the clearest aperture of sense. For sight is the most piercing of our bodily senses; though not by that is wisdom seen: for loveliness would have been transporting if there had been a visible image of her, and the other Ideas, if they had had visible counterparts, would be equally lovely. But this is the privilege of beauty, that being the loveliest she is also the most palpable to sight.'

Of the three noblest and most exalted Forms, Beauty, Truth and Goodness, the first is thus the doorway to the other two. If the eyes are the 'windows of the soul', then Beauty is the casement through which we are able to descry the more distant images of Truth and Goodness. Beauty, especially in its most exquisite natural manifestations, sets up an agitation in us that causes the baser souls to rush and possess, while it elevates those of clearer insight to a perception of that which lies beyond.

What, then is the highest of the Forms, the goal of human aspiration? It is the Form or Idea of Goodness. The influence of this Form may be justly compared to that of the sun. The sun gives light, but at the same time it feeds and nurtures the world that enjoys its radiance: it is king and minister together, not merely ruling creation but simultaneously bringing it to fruition. Similarly with the Form of the Good. Goodness is its ideal manifestation causes the hierarchy of Forms to glow with celestial incandescence. It irradiates them, and at the same time it exercises an attractive influence. Thus, all the Forms approximate and incline to the Form of the Good; but this approximation or inclination does not imply a temporal growth or evolution. The world of the Forms is a timeless and eternal world, and the natural 'leading' of one Form to another is a logical or ideal process, of which the change and growth in the sensible world are but a shifting and shadowy copy. Time, in other words, is the 'moving image of Eternity'.

That Plato casts no doubt upon the existence or substantial reality of the natural world (the world of our body and its senses), we have already explained. But there appears to be a difficulty here. If the world open to our senses is merely the world of opinion and not of knowledge, how in fact can we penetrate from this shadowy, imperfect realm to the world of light and perfection? By our intellects, says Plato. Yes, but mere intellectual reasoning, though necessary to the achievement of supra-sensible knowledge, cannot function unless impelled by force of another kind. Before we can know, we must desire to know. Before we can ascend the scale, we must be possessed with the right kind of impulse. What is this impulse and where does it come from? Plato's answer is simple. It is Love.

Love is the medium or 'catalyst' whereby the soul, tied for the period of its natural life to the body, frees itself from passion and sensual desire and, with strengthening wings, ascends into the empyrean and gazes upon the divine Forms. In order to explain where this impulse of love comes from, Plato reminds us of his account of the 'pre-history' of the soul. Love, as human beings know it, is simply the memory, made poignant by a sense of loss, of the soul's previous communion with these same Forms. The 'twinge' of sadness rarely absent from human experience of love is therefore the nostalgia of a lover separated from the object of his complete devotion. Likewise, the sense of expectancy and fervour, uppermost at other times, is simply the lover's hope of recapturing in its fullness and through attachment to some human object of desire, an experience of which he craves renewal. Love that is content to express itself solely upon the natural plane is doomed to perpetual frustration, for the mere satisfaction of the senses leads to early satiety and disgust. And this is the meaning of that much misunderstood thing 'Platonic love': not love that implies complete indifference to physical attraction, but love that has for its goal the satisfaction of the spirit in what Shakespeare termed 'the marriage of true minds'.

To sum up: Plato's theory of Ideas is the result of his attempt to do two things. It is first of all an attempt to show how knowledge of reality is acquired. Secondly, it is an attempt to show what reality is like. It is thus both a theory of knowledge and a theory of reality.

Plato's application of his theory to the problems of political and social life is very relevant for us today. In his book *The Republic*, he is engaged in discussing not merely the abstract idea of government, but the practical reforms needed to improve the Athenian state of his own time. He was worried about the way things were going, just as Socrates had been worried before him. We have shown already how fervently Plato desired to create a democracy fit for good men, and above all good philosophers, to live in. Now it seemed to him obvious that no state could be considered good and just that was not founded upon the Idea of the Good which the philosophers, as opposed to the Sophists, had apprehended in the course of their meditations.

In other words, what was good for society must follow from what was good in the realm of true knowledge. There was not one law for the world of Opinion and another law for the world of Ideas, because such order and logic as was manifested in the former must ultimately derive from the influence of the latter percolating through the intervening 'no-man's-land' of imperfection. How, then, could the influence of the Ideas be made to impinge more directly upon men's consciences? How could we 'let in the light', or induce men to raise their eyes to the source of divine energy? How could we cultivate in the soil of the spirit the love that, once inclined in the right direction, would put forth its leaves in a spontaneous effort to raise itself in the sun's face, there to burst into flower?

Plato's answer is pruned of all extravagant expectations. The way is difficult, and for many impossible. Those who cannot fare forward by their own unaided efforts must submit themselves to superior direction. Above all there must be a long and painful process of education.

When Plato ventured to speak of a 'Philosopher-King', therefore, he had in mind something more than a benign but rather ineffectual figure, given to meditation and study, but separated by his superior intellect and rarefied tastes from the common herd. His philosopher was to be a practical philosopher; his king was also to be a law-maker, an active statesman. He was to lay down the law with the authority not merely of his regal office but of his philosophical insight. In obeying the laws he proclaimed, the common people would thus be acting in conformity with the supreme good of the universe. Some of them would no doubt obey willingly, conscious of the wisdom of the lawgiver. Some would obey mechanically, conscious merely of the necessity of conforming to a common standard. Some would obey with an ill-grace, being so far corrupted and immersed in the natural world that the 'pull' of heavenly wisdom would be felt hardly at all. Plato's ideal Republic approximated in this respect more to an authoritarian system than to what we should call Democracy. In the last of his books, significantly entitled *The Laws*, he went to great lengths to show how rigid and disciplined must be the state of transition from the corrupt and chaotic system of his day to the ideal system of the future. This 'state of transition'—a phrase not unfamiliar to us—would be not so much the dictation of the proletariat as the dictation of an *élite*; and no one in his right mind would presume to say how long and with what degree of repression such dictation would need to be maintained.

The sub-title of Plato's book *The Republic* is *On Justice*. Now Plato employs the word Justice in a very wide sense. He identifies it with the Form of the Good, which is the same as God. (Plato's conception of God, incidentally, is very different from our own, and we shall examine this difference when we come to discuss the religious ideas of Aristotle.) He contends that by our just acts, rather than our 'good' acts (a vague term), we help to realize God's purpose in the world, because love of Goodness is after all a longing for order, proportion, measure, and symmetry—it is in fact 'the desire and pursuit of the whole'—and justice is nothing but the observance of order, measure, and symmetry in our dealings with our fellowmen.

Thus we talk of 'fair dealing' where the word 'fair' combines the notions of beauty and justice. To describe Justice as the 'mother of the virtues'—the human virtues, that is to say—is to come close to Plato's meaning: and in its capacity of progenitor, Justice provides each faculty of the soul with its appropriate offspring. To talk of 'faculties of the soul' may sound like philosophical jargon, and jargon it has become, because the distinction between thought, will, and feeling is frequently employed without due attention to the facts which it seeks to explain.

Among the faculties, Plato gives pride of place to Intellect or Intelligence because this faculty penetrates to the eternal Forms behind the shadowy world of sense. Now the 'justice' of Intelligence is wisdom; for a wise man is not one who knows many things but one who sees things in proportion. Second in order of importance comes the faculty of Will, of which the 'justice' is known as courage, because a will that is directed to noble ends must engage in ceaseless war against indifference and sloth, and this requires determination. Lastly comes the faculty of sensibility or Feeling. In this sphere justice takes the form of temperance: temperance, that is to say, not in its abused modern sense but in the sense of self-control or moderation (the 'nothing too much' of the French essayist Montaigne), because neither a starved nor a glutted sensibility is tolerable to the man of balanced mind.

This three-fold distinction between the faculties of the soul is applied by Plato to the constitution of society itself. Society is composed of three orders, or, as we should say today, classes. At the head is the class of philosophers or thinkers, who represent the Intelligence of the body-politic. Next comes the warriors or military class, whose task is to defend the state from outside enemies, and whose virtue is courage. Finally come the merchants and artisans, the agricultural labourers, the slaves and the servants, who, being concerned with men's material needs, represent the most physical element in the system, corresponding to the most physical part of the mind, namely the sense-organs, whose virtue consists in submission to the higher faculties.

Even philosophers may rule unjustly, as Plato readily admits. Philosophers are men, and liable to make faulty judgments; and the very eminence of their position is such as to render them susceptible to pride and love of power. Long before Lord Acton made his famous statement that 'power corrupts, but absolute power corrupts absolutely', Plato, who had seen such abuses at first hand, observed that 'no human soul in its youth and irresponsibility will be able to sustain the temptation of arbitrary power—there is no one who will not, under such circumstances, become filled with folly, that worst of diseases, and be hated by his nearest and dearest friends; and when this happens his kingdom is undermined, and all his power vanishes'.[1]

Moreover, the achievement of the balanced and mature character is something much more difficult than is commonly supposed: 'Quick intelligence, memory, sagacity, cleverness and similar qualities do not often grow together, and persons who possess them and are at the same time high-spirited and magnanimous are not so constituted by nature as to live an orderly and peaceful and settled life. Their vivacity drives them this way and that, and they lose their stability. On the other hand those steadfast natures which can better be depended upon, which are in battle impregnable to fear and immovable, are equally immovable when there is anything to be learned.'[2]

Although Plato frankly acknowledges the difficulty of living the philosophical life, and is not in favour of giving young people too much philosophical instruction in their early education—when, as he shrewdly remarks, 'the chief and special care should be given to their bodies that they may have them to use in the service of philosophy' (for 'youngsters, when they first get the taste in their mouths, argue for amusement, and are always contradicting and refuting others in imitation of those who refute them')[3]—he never loses faith in the importance of philosophy. As he points out in another part of *The Republic* (500), 'a man cannot help imitating that with which he lives in admiring communion; and the philosopher, in his communion with the divine order, becomes orderly and divine, as far as the nature of man allows: but, like everyone else, he will have his enemies'.

In order to reduce to a minimum the temptations of power to which the rulers or Guardians are subject, Plato proposes that they shall not merely be deprived of all personal property, but that even the blessings of family life shall be denied them. 'The community of wives and children among our citizens,' he says,[4] 'is clearly the source of the greatest good for the State. And this agrees with the other principle which we were affirming—that the governing class were not to have houses or lands or any other property; their pay was to be their food, which they were to receive from the other citizens, and they were to have no private expenses; for we intend them to preserve their true character of guardians. Both the community of property and the community of families tend to make them more truly guardians; they will not tear the city in pieces by differing about 'mine' and 'not mine' ... but all will be affected as far as may be by the same pleasures and pains because they are all of one opinion about what is near and dear to them, and therefore they all tend towards a common end.'

Thus it will be seen that Plato expounds a point of view diametri-

[1] *Laws*, 691.
[2] *The Republic*, 503 f.
[3] *Ibid.* 539.
[4] *Ibid.* 464.

cally opposite to that put forward centuries later by the economist and philosopher Adam Smith (1723–90), who declared that public benefit would automatically result from private interest. As for the system of Communism which Plato outlined in *The Republic*, this too differs from that which has been advocated by revolutionaries in our own time. For the communal life is intended only for the caste of Guardians, and has since been put into practice, if at all, by groups equally restricted in membership, such as certain religious communities. And in view of the past history and record of experimental communist societies it is doubtful whether they can survive unless inspired by intense religious fervour, as Plato was careful to emphasize.

Even so there must be a long and arduous period of initiation. 'When our rulers have reached fifty years of age, then let those who have won through and have excelled in every sphere of action and knowledge be introduced at last to their final task: the time has now arrived at which they must raise the eye of the soul to the universal light which lightens all things, and behold the Absolute Good' (*i.e.* the Supreme Form). 'For that is the pattern according to which they are to order the State and the lives of individuals, and the remainder of their own lives too, making philosophy their chief pursuit, but, when their turn comes, toiling also at politics and ruling for the public good, not as though they were performing some heroic action, but simply as a matter of duty; and when they have brought up in each generation others like themselves and left them in their place to be governors of the State, then they will depart to the Islands of the Blest and there dwell.[1]

That was all very well, in theory. In practice, as the ageing philosopher realized, men exhibit qualities that differ little as regards ferocity from those displayed by animals, and as regards cunning and duplicity have no parallel even in the brute creation. Naturally, some few persons of wisdom and integrity there will always be: 'those who belong to this small class have tasted how sweet and blessed a possession philosophy is, and have also seen enough of the madness of the multitude; and they know that no politician is honest, nor is there any champion of justice at whose side they may fight and be saved. Such a one may be compared to a man who has fallen among wild beasts—he will not join in the wickedness of his fellows, but neither is he able singly to resist all their fierce natures, and so seeing that he would be of no use to the State or to his friends, and reflecting that he would have to throw away his life without doing any good either to himself or to others, he holds his peace, and goes his own way.'[2]

Plato, for his part, would not hold his peace. He worked and hoped on until the end. But some part of him had died, and the generous enthusiasms of his youth were chastened. The writer of *The Laws* is a disappointed idealist, and the disappointed idealist is almost always a cynic. As we read that sombre blue-book, which is as dull and heavy in parts as a government report, we experience a feeling of having heard

[1] Ibid. 540.
[2] Ibid. 496.

these maxims, these grim counsels, before. We are in a familiar atmosphere, the atmosphere of our own time. Here is the very breviary of dictatorship, with its minute directions for mobilizing, swaying, and snooping upon public opinion; with its prisons for political offenders and those found guilty of 'irreligion' (had Plato so far forgotten the accusers of Socrates?), its reformatories and concentration camps—'to be situated in some wild and desolate region in the centre of the country'—where a super-inquisition called The Nocturnal Council exercised the functions of a Security Police; and with the forcible expulsion (already suggested in *The Republic*) of the poets and artists and all those who flourish in an atmosphere of freedom of expression.

However near to despair this supremely endowed philosopher came, he never for an instant lost sight of the end to which human life should be directed. He remained in doubt only as to the means by which this end should be attained. Perhaps he hit the nail on the head most surely in a passage which occurs towards the end of *The Laws*, where he states the problem that in later ages was to become the chief preoccupation of all men of goodwill. 'In no very long period of time,' he observed, 'an autocrat, if he wishes, can change the manners of a State; he has only to go in the direction of virtue or of vice, whichever he prefers, he himself indicating by his example the lines of conduct, praising and rewarding some actions and rebuking others, and degrading those who disobey. The quickest and easiest way for a State to change its laws is through the leadership of its masters: such changes never have and never will come to pass in any other way.' So far, so good; but, he continues, 'the real impossibility, or difficulty, is of another sort, and is rarely surmounted in the course of ages; but when once it is surmounted, every kind of blessing follows. *The difficulty is to find a divine passion for rational and just institutions.*' That indeed was the purpose of his life; and if he failed to achieve it, his failure was touched with sublimity. From Socrates he had learnt that virtue was the child of true knowledge, and for himself he arrived at the idea that true knowledge issued from communion with the Supreme Good. The crucial question was whether mankind, left to itself and in the absence of some prolonged emotional stimulus, could ever be brought to desire this supreme communion for its own sake. That same question was later tackled by the Christian philosophers with an insight that Plato could not have possessed. But those later philosophers in turn looked back to him as the most inspired of the thinkers of the old dispensation, whose doctrine of the love of Good was the nearest approach to the Christian Gospel of Love.

12

Aristotle

Almost all things have been found out, but some have been forgotten.

Politics

Plato had tried to reform a king who was already in his middle years. To Aristotle was given the privilege—if indeed he counted it a privilege and not an imposition—of supervising the youthful education of one of the world's greatest conquerors, Alexander of Macedon. It is not easy for us today to realize with what esteem and awe philosophy and philosophers were regarded in the ancient world, even by powerful rulers. Later philosophers enjoyed royal favour, and some, like Descartes and Leibniz, entered into correspondence with kings and princesses; but to no subsequent thinker was accorded an opportunity so remarkable as that which offered itself to Aristotle.

Aristotle was born in either 385 or 384 BC in the town of Stagira, in Macedonia. This little place is situated on the peninsula to which the name Calchis still attaches. Aristotle's father, Nicomachus, was a doctor of considerable ability, who finally rose to be chief physician at the court of Amyntas II, King of Macedonia. While in the latter's service, he wrote a number of books on medicine and natural science. Aristotle's mother, Phœstis, was a native of Calchis. By reason of his father's profession, the young boy became a member of the guild of Asclepiadæ (named after Asclepius or Æsculapius, the Greek god of medicine), since the medical profession was hereditary in that confraternity.

This early acquaintance with natural science in its most practical aspect exerted a profound effect upon Aristotle's whole life and way of thinking. Not merely did it turn his interests in a particular direction—the direction of analysis, experiment, and classification—but it caused him finally to strike out on an original line of his own. This new departure in thought has affected all subsequent enquiry, whether scientific, philosophical, political or ethical. For the ideas and conclusions of Aristotle have entered into our common traditions of thought, so that we speak with his idiom even though we may protest ignorance of his writings.

Concerning the youth of Aristotle we possess numerous odd scraps of information and much testimony of doubtful value. Some ancient biographers write as if the contemporaries of their hero, knowing him to be destined for fame, were constantly engaged in collecting evidence of that future achievement which they can at best have dimly surmised. The historians of antiquity were liberal in their use of anecdote. Consequently there have been almost as many anecdotes preserved about Aristotle as about Plato. We do not need to dwell upon the more ephemeral of these stories, which shed little light upon his boyhood and early youth.

For our present purpose, the age at which Aristotle becomes interesting is that of seventeen. It was then that he set out for Athens, with the intention, so far as we know, of entering the Academy of Plato (368 or 367 BC). In days when even a short journey was an adventure, this excursion by an unknown youth to the headquarters of the best-known teacher of the day was attended by many hazards. Moreover, it was an early age at which to secure admission to so select an institution as the Academy. Aristotle must already have shown evidence of marked, even precocious, ability in order to have been permitted by his guardian Proxenus (his father being dead) to undertake the journey at all. Then there was the question as to whether he would prove an acceptable pupil. On that score there seems to have been no doubt. He was at once admitted to the company. So the future 'master of those that know' was first of all a humble seeker after knowledge, content to sit at the foot of the man whom he was later to criticize, but whose memory he never ceased to reverence.

A man of such originality might have been expected soon to weary of discipleship, and to seek the earliest opportunity of organizing an 'opposition' school of his own. But, as it happened, Aristotle was content to enjoy the status of pupil and imitator much longer and with a greater measure of self-effacement than many a thinker of lesser stature. The majority of scholars and intellectual leaders serve an apprenticeship of three, four or five years at some seat of learning. Aristotle served as many as twenty in the Platonic Academy. Finally he left it for the only reason that might have been expected to prompt his departure, namely, the death of Plato in 347 BC.

It happened that he had chosen an interesting and even critical time to enter the Academy. For many years now the central figure of that institution, the spirit that animated its deliberations, and indeed the character whom Plato had invariably employed as a mouthpiece for his theories, had been Socrates. To Plato and his closest associates, the memory of Socrates was still the most vivid experience of their lives, just as his method was the most revolutionary that they had yet studied. But now a generation was growing up for whom the master was not Socrates but Plato, and to whom Socrates was scarcely more than a revered name, possibly somewhat too idealized to be quite credible. Although the figure of Socrates never gave place to any other in Plato's memory, there came a time when Plato's own thought began to develop in directions that Socrates had not merely failed to explore but regarded as definitely outside the scope of philosophy. In short, a new spirit was coming over the Academy, and Aristotle's arrival more or less coincided with its emergence.

If our chronology is not at fault, Aristotle must have put in his first appearance at Athens at a time when Plato was away at the court of Dionysius II. Thus he probably did not have an opportunity of meeting the master until he had already become a well-established academician. His first teachers of Platonism were among those members, who, like himself, enjoyed the status of disciples. Although Aristotle soon succeeded in proving his ability, the activities at which he excelled were not as yet (and were not for many years to become) those of original speculation; they were those of faithful interpretation of the master's own works. Aristotle's first writings, in fact, consisted not merely of dialogues in the Platonic manner but of expositions of Plato's ideas; and these expositions were so distinguished for clarity and persuasiveness that for many centuries after his death they were studied with greater eagerness than the works of Plato himself.

It seems probable that later thinkers, such as Epicurus (340–270 BC) and later still Cicero (106–43 BC), derived their knowledge of Platonism less from the works of the master, which were regarded as exceedingly abstruse, than from the works of the pupil, which were accepted as models of precise statement. We should give a great deal to be able to read these early dialogues today; but except for a few fragments and what can be deduced from a paraphrase here and there in the works of less gifted writers, they have all been lost: a fate which, as we shall see, nearly overtook the whole body of Aristotle's writings.

The change in spirit at the Academy was, to be precise, a change to a more complex and abstract point of view. Socrates always had his feet on the ground—his bare feet; and his aim was to discover exactly where he stood and where other people stood. He distrusted airy speculations. Plato was a more complicated person, with at least three aspects to his character. There was first the fervent disciple of Socrates, who endeavoured to continue his work of careful analysis and intellectual midwifery. Secondly, there was the ardent champion of social justice, who hoped to persuade reigning potentates to fashion their states according to eternal precepts. Finally there was the pure philosopher, who, disillusioned with politics and despairing of the efforts of enthusiastic reformers (himself included), sought to lift himself by intense mental concentration to a realm of perfection utterly removed from mundane affairs.

Nor is it true to assert that these three 'stages' of Plato's thought followed one another in strict succession. At some moments the Socratic element was uppermost; at some, the reformer; at some, the soaring idealist. Towards the end of his life, the two most 'contradictory' attitudes strove one with the other for dominance. For even the most earnest and high-minded person has his moods of reaction, depression and anti-climax. Thus the Plato who composed such abstruse and lofty dialogues as the *Theætetus*, the *Parmenides* and the *Philebus* was also the Plato who composed, and died while completing, the sombre treatise on *The Laws*. This was an object lesson for so observant a pupil as Aristotle.

The word 'abstract' fills certain people with alarm, though the literal meaning of the term—'to draw out'—need not suggest anything obscure. If 'abstract' is taken always to mean 'vague', then abstractions are to be shunned, since philosophical thought is above all an attempt to combat vagueness. In fact, however, the process of abstraction is one with which each of us is perfectly familiar and to which we have constant recourse. Whenever we make a general statement, we are distinguishing a number of instances from the rule or principle to which they conform. At a higher level, indeed, the distinction between the 'universal' and the 'particular' is constantly present in the kind of thinking that we call, sometimes with too great a sense of awe, scientific. The scientist is engaged in detecting the operation of uniform processes or laws in the natural world, and at the same time in recording such instances as are observed to conform to these laws.

Being ever in search of evidence of the truth of his theories, the man of scientific turn of mind is usually a great 'collector'. This applies even to such an apparently abstract thinker as the psychologist, who collects 'cases' as assiduously as the geologist collects specimens. Aristotle, one of the world's first collectors, and in consequence one of the pioneers of the science of classification, differed from most of his successors not so much in his method of enquiry as in the extraordinary breadth of his interests. Here his early association with men of science must have stood him in good stead. He imposed no limits upon his investigations save those which Nature herself imposed by having made him mortal; otherwise he would have undoubtedly pursued his researches into every field of knowledge accessible to human curiosity.

As it is, he examined nearly everything that there is to be examined, and collected nearly everything that there is to be collected. He set out to classify animals, vegetables, minerals, as well as virtues, passions, and mental faculties. He collected the names of past rulers and winners of international gymnastic contests, and he collected and classified constitutions. In spite of this passion for detailed research and enquiry, however, he never allowed his interest to become a mania. He did not collect for the sake of collection. He was above all interested in tracing the operation of a general law in nature, both physical and 'human'. This was the law whereby one thing or being turns into another thing or being—in short, the law of organic development.

Preoccupation with the idea of growth and development was not something that Aristotle learnt directly from Plato, because Plato's world was essentially a static world. Yet it is possible to say that Plato's very indifference to this aspect of nature, his obsession with ideal perfection, was indirectly responsible for Aristotle's 'shift' of interest to that which, lacking perfection, strove to attain it through trial and error, perseverance and persistence. Now the sphere of nature in which such striving is most apparent is that of living organisms. Aristotle's aim, therefore, resolved itself into the reconciliation of Plato's theory of Ideas with the facts of biological development.

This digression concerning the difference in spirit between the work of Plato and Aristotle is introduced because otherwise the period elapsing between his first arrival at the Academy and the death of Plato twenty years later remains an unintelligible blank. To understand Aristotle's development as a thinker we need to use our imaginations to fill this blank. These, as the conventional biographies say, were the 'formative years': years during which he produced, if not his masterpieces, then the material out of which his masterpieces grew. Above all, it was during this period that he came into contact with the foremost intellects of the age: men who, like himself, had journeyed from other lands and who were thus able to put him in possession of facts of which he would otherwise have been ignorant.

Such a man was Eudoxus of Cyzicus, a distinguished mathematician, who had a store of information concerning the technical achievements of the Egyptians and the peoples of Asia Minor, and who was therefore a source of precisely the 'facts' of which Aristotle was in search. Nor must we imagine that Aristotle, as leader of the younger generation, was engaged in the kind of study of which Plato and his bosom companions disapproved. 'Fact-finding' was in the air. Plato, as we have already remarked, had himself caught the contagion. The treatise on *The Laws* is in effect a concession to the new approach to the study of the world of man. Without it, Aristotle's treatise on *Politics* would probably never have taken shape as it did.

In the year 348–347 BC a great crisis occurred in Aristotle's life—or, to be more exact, a double crisis. First of all, Plato died. Almost at the same time, and more unexpectedly, a disaster overtook Aristotle's home town in Macedonia. During an attack upon the flourishing cities of the Chalcidic peninsula, Philip of Macedon gave orders for the complete destruction of Stagira, the philosopher's birthplace. Aristotle thus found himself suddenly isolated in both a spiritual and a physical sense. Although he had left Stagira as a youth with a feeling of exultation at escaping from a provincial atmosphere, he did not realize his affection for his birth-place until he was made aware that he could never find it as he had left it.

The young man who ventures into the world always has in mind to return, in the hour of success, to the place from which he set out unknown and underestimated; he even secretly entertains the hope that conditions will still be much as he left them, so that the contrast between his own achievement and that of his fellows will be the more pronounced. This ruthless act of Philip, with whose family Aristotle was later to become associated, affected him deeply for many years: until, by a turn of the wheel of fortune, he finally obtained restitution at the hands of the perpetrator himself.

The death of Plato plunged Aristotle into a mood similar to that which had overcome Plato himself at the death of Socrates: the difference being that while Socrates had been condemned as a dangerous criminal, Plato died full of years and honours. Nevertheless, the effect upon the most promising disciple was in each case the same. Plato left Athens, bound he hardly knew whither. Aristotle did likewise. His strongest tie with the centre of Greek learning had been snapped. Now an independent, freelance philosopher, his precipitate departure marks a break not only with his mode of life but also with his mode of thought. Henceforth he was to become an original exponent of philosophy, critical of the work of his contemporaries and even of Plato himself.

If Aristotle was Plato's most famous pupil, why, it may be asked, did he promptly desert the Academy when the master died? Some historians have suggested that the two philosophers had already become estranged. There is little evidence to support this view. It is contradicted at least by the beautiful elegy written by Aristotle at this time, the occasion of which was the death of a great and honoured friend whose identity, seeing that Aristotle was not easily roused to poetic composition, can hardly be other than Plato himself.

Throughout Aristotle's later writings, the references to Plato, however critical, are marked by a special tone of veneration. Far from Plato's presence at the Academy becoming increasingly intolerable to Aristotle, it was probably the one thing that kept him there. For he was not always on such good terms with his fellow-disciples. One of the chief reasons for Aristotle's departure was doubtless the appointment of his chief rival, Speusippus, as head of the Academy: a position which, if Aristotle did not exactly covet, he would have derived some pleasure from being able to refuse. In the circumstances, however, the appointment of Speusippus was understandable, because his succession kept the Academy in Plato's family. Aristotle was an outsider.

Whatever the reasons for his departure, Aristotle, accompanied by his colleague Xenocrates of Chalcedon, set out in 347 BC on a journey to Assos, the Æolian town situated on the Troad. The choice of this locality as a place in which to settle was not made by accident. Two ex-members of Plato's Academy were already stationed there: Erastus and Coriscus from the town of Scepsis on Ida, of which we shall presently hear more. During the latter part of his life, Plato had devoted much energy to the founding of small colonies of scholars, or little Academies; and of these the community which had been started at Assos was one of the most flourishing. Moreover, it owed its continued prosperity as much to the patronage of the local tyrant[1] as to Plato's own encouragement.

This tyrant, Hermias by name, had been persuaded by Plato to study philosophy, geometry and dialectic, and had even introduced a measure of constitutional reform into his domain as a result of his 'conversion' to philosophy. It must be admitted that Plato was a great deal more successful with him than he had been with the younger Dionysius. Hermias was so thoroughly in earnest, indeed, that he virtually presented Assos to the group of philosophers who had assembled there; and it is interesting to read the letter addressed by Plato to Hermias and his protégés, in which he urges them, almost in the language of a biblical epistle, to co-operate in the great work of reforming mankind according to the principles of justice. This combined effort to unite thought and action was on a relatively small scale, as efforts of this

[1] A tyrant in Greek history usually means an absolute ruler or dictator who owed his position to usurpation.

kind are doomed to be. But events were to demonstrate in the most striking fashion that there was nothing artificial or unreal about it.

To Assos came the young philosopher Theophrastus, the 'Divine Speaker' (a name supposed to have been conferred upon him by Aristotle himself), from Eresus in Lesbos. Theophrastus, once a disciple of Plato, was not merely one of Aristotle's most brilliant pupils but the faithful friend to whom the Aristotelian manuscripts were bequeathed in the master's will. This bequest was to exert an influence upon the history of philosophy that no one at the time could have foreseen.

Aristotle's relations with his patron were so friendly that the tyrant finally gave the philosopher his niece and adopted daughter Pythias in marriage. We know very little of Aristotle's married life, which suggests that on the whole it went smoothly. Pythias bore him a daughter to whom the parents gave her mother's name, and of whom we later hear in Aristotle's will. In endeavouring to make the philosopher's life appear somewhat more romantic than it really was—never did so extraordinary a man live so comparatively ordinary a private life—later writers spun tales out of their own imaginations about a dramatic elopement and flight from Assos. From recently discovered records, however, we gather that the alliance was concluded in the most orthodox manner, and that Hermias not merely approved but himself suggested it.

Sentimental historians actually diminish the romantic aspect of the marriage by making it out to have been an affair of secrecy and intrigue; for the romantic aspect of it surely was that a proud, if high-minded, ruler should have counted it an honour to link himself by marriage with a mere teacher of philosophy. Little did Hermias know that future ages would learn of his name solely as a result of this happy association, without which he would have remained undistinguished among a hundred other minor potentates.

Three happy years passed by, and then Aristotle undertook a journey to Mytilene in Lesbos, probably at the suggestion and invitation of Theophrastus, whose home country it was. Again, as always when Aristotle (or Plato) made a journey, rumours have later grown up about quarrels and estrangements. But whoever Aristotle may have quarrelled with, it was certainly not with his father-in-law Hermias, if the latter's subsequent conduct is any guide. The removal was merely to a neighbouring island; and it is probable that Aristotle went there in pursuit of one of his favourite hobbies, namely, collecting. Scholars have pointed out that his researches into marine biology, always thorough and accurate, are particularly illuminating in connection with the marine flora of the Æolic coast and its islands: so that if he did not go there with the express intention of exploring this aspect of nature, at least he appears to have occupied much of his spare time in such investigation.

In 343–342 BC, however, an important and highly confidential message reached him which abruptly put an end to his stay in Lesbos, bringing him once more into the limelight and affording him opportunities such as few men of his calling have enjoyed.

The message in question was from no less a person than King Philip of Macedon, the ruler whose high-handed action at Stagira had caused Aristotle such grief. Philip had a son, Alexander, then thirteen years of age, of whom much was expected and to whom Philip, not himself an intellectual man, had resolved to give the best possible education. To whom, then, should he turn for help and advice but to Aristotle, already renowned throughout the Greek world for his skill as an instructor? Aristotle, after some thought, decided to accept the invitation. And so during four out of the seven years that he was to spend in Macedon, he was in charge of the studies of one of the most remarkable men in history.

Not long after his departure from Assos, an event occurred which caused Aristotle great anguish of mind. It concerned his old patron and friend, Hermias. Philip had for some time been preparing hostilities against Persia; and it seems highly probable that between him and Hermias there existed a secret treaty or understanding, since a tyrant of such limited authority as the latter was compelled by circumstances to seek support from one of the great powers. Suspecting that Hermias was in the opposite camp, the Persian general Mentor resolved to crush him before he had time to become more powerful. His forces surrounded those of Hermias at Atarneus; and there, on pretence of inviting Hermias to a parley, he treacherously kidnapped him. Renowned for neither magnanimity nor mercy, the Persians treated Hermias in the most vile manner. In order to exact from him the details of his supposed alliance with Philip, they put him to the torture, and finally, unable to make him talk, crucified him.

Before the end, the Persian king ordained that he should be asked to state his last wish. Hermias's answer caused mild astonishment. 'Tell my friends and companions,' he declared, 'that I have done nothing weak or unworthy of philosophy.' If this report is authentic—and our knowledge of Hermias's character suggests that it may well be—it reveals the extraordinary influence exerted by the members of the Academy and above all by Aristotle over men of different, and often opposite, temperament.

Hermias, for example, was a man of low birth and little education. In his youth he worked in a bank, probably as a money-changer. He had made his way in the world by sheer force of character. But he possessed qualities of moral greatness which his association with Aristotle brought out and developed in the most remarkable manner. He had little to lose by disclosing his alliance with Persia's enemy save the respect of the man to whom he owed the alteration in his outlook on life. Such high-mindedness was not commonly to be found among the rulers of antiquity; and many a nominally Christian monarch met the trials of his faith with less dignity. Aristotle was deeply moved.

At Delphi today there stands a cenotaph to Hermias, for which Aristotle wrote a dedicatory epigram. There is also extant a hymn to the ruler's memory which the philosopher composed at this time. To indulge one's emotions in the safety of a powerful court may be all very well; but we must not forget that Aristotle's vindication of Hermias was itself an act of moral courage, for the Greek nationalists, especially those at Athens who followed the orator Demosthenes, were violently opposed to Philip and his grandiose imperial schemes, and were therefore not disposed to think well of one suspected to be in sympathy with them.

The story of Aristotle's first arrival at the court of King Philip at Pella was until recently the source of much dispute among historians. A number of writers of antiquity suggest that Aristotle left Assos after Hermias's capture by Mentor and as a direct consequence of it. This would lend colour to the idea that he ran away with Pythias, the tyrant's daughter. But we now have good grounds for thinking that he left Assos while Hermias was still living. Whether the 'alliance' between Hermias and Philip had anything to do with Aristotle's journey is of course a matter of conjecture. Possibly it had. It had also been pointed out that Aristotle, though already famous as a leader of thought, had family connections with the Macedonian court through his father; but this does not seem to have had much to do with his appointment. What we need to realize is that the Academy and those bodies associated with it had come in time to be world-famous institutions, like the old oracles. For the ancient world was a small world, and institutions of this kind have no exact parallel today; but that is not so much because the world has expanded as because wisdom has shrunk.

Although Aristotle had complete charge of Alexander during the latter's most impressionable year, it is easy to exaggerate the influence of master over pupil. Admittedly, with such a master and with such a pupil, a partnership unique in history might have been formed. There is no other record, perhaps, of a great man ever having been associated in this manner with a man equally great in a different sphere. How strange, therefore, that throughout Aristotle's writings there is a complete absence of enthusiasm for conquering kings of the type that his pupil ultimately became! If we are to judge from the scant attention he gives to them in his works, Aristotle might never have taken the smallest interest in the imperial developments occurring in his day. It is not that he was uninterested in political questions; he was passionately interested in them. Whereas his famous treatise on *Politics* is concerned with the structure of the *Greek City State*, however, he was living in an age in which much larger units of political allegiance were coming into being. These he mostly ignored; and when he did not ignore them, he disapproved.

To suggest that Aristotle exerted no particular influence upon the character of Alexander, however, would be untrue. Among the great conquerors of the ancient world, Alexander alone is distinguished for a breadth of character, a sense of high purpose, which seems to have been derived from the kind of philosophical training the Academy sought to instil. Like Hermias, but with greater opportunities, he tried to mould his conduct according to an ideal; and even if he were no more than a highly successful general, it was as the New Achilles—an up-to-date version of one of the great heroes of antiquity—that he saw himself. A man must be judged not merely by what he is but by the standard that he sets himself. Alexander may have been as much a 'scourge' to the countries he overran as Attila or Tamburlaine; but he believed himself to be the bearer of civilization and enlightenment.

The royal pupil never became his master's close friend or even confidant; but, except for one phase of their relationship of which we shall speak, they seem to have remained on excellent terms. Even when Alexander was engaged in the most gigantic of his military operations in the East, with princes bowing down to him and wealth and fame accumulating beyond his highest expectations, he did not forget the man who had tried to instruct him in logic and the nature of virtue. Among other tokens of his respect and affection—tokens not perhaps untinged with irony—he gave instructions that Aristotle should receive all the interesting geological specimens collected on the various campaigns. There is no doubt, too, that Aristotle's astonishing researches into animal life would not have been possible without the discoveries made by Alexander's men, and the reports and specimens which, on Alexander's instructions, they sent home for study and classification.

As for Philip, he showed his gratitude to Aristotle in even more tangible ways. He caused to be built a delightful gymnasium, called the Nymphæum, in a quite grove on the royal estates, where Aristotle could indulge in his reflections and investigations in peace, and where he could receive his young pupils (for we gather that, besides Alexander, several young noblemen had the honour to receive instruction from him during his sojourn in Pella). Of all Philip's acts of kindness, however, that which gave Aristotle the keenest pleasure and satisfaction was the rebuilding, under royal supervision, of the little town of Stagira. For thus was removed the one blot upon their friendship. It is almost a perfect act of justice for a man to be able to recompense another in the way that, being appropriate to his talents, best satisfies himself at the same time.

In 336 BC, an act of violence put an end to their association. While walking in procession to celebrate the marriage of his daughter, Philip was fatally stabbed by a young man called Pausanias, who is thought to have borne him a private grudge. The King, then no more than forty-seven years old, died in the twenty-fourth year of his reign. He was succeeded by Alexander, and this put an end to the latter's period of tutelage. As for Aristotle, he remained in Macedonia for about a year, and then, feeling the urge to be on his travels again, packed up and returned to Athens.

After thirteen years' absence, he found a very different city and a very different intellectual atmosphere in the Academy. He returned with a great reputation, perhaps the greatest philosophical reputation of the time, certainly the greatest since Plato. But, as before, he was still to some extent the stranger, and it was not to be expected that he should be received by his colleagues of the Academy as a long-lost brother. Possibly, assuming that his leadership in philosophical matters would be openly acknowledged, he believed that he would step into the President's place without more ado. For it happened that Speusippus had just died, and the choice of a successor was due to be made from among those thought most capable of maintaining the Platonic tradition. As it turned out, the presidency went not to Aristotle but to his old friend and companion, Xenocrates of Chalcedon; and Aristotle may well have experienced the sensation of finding it even more difficult to surrender a coveted office to a friend than to an enemy.

Whatever may have been his intimate feelings in the matter, the choice of another to do what he would have done equally well, if to the sacrifice of the leisure that he needed, no doubt proved a blessing in disguise. He resolved to devote himself henceforth to scientific pursuits. He could not wholly abandon teaching; for the itch to instruct, to enlighten, to arouse curiosity in others, was no less compelling than to indulge his own curiosity by research. But he found, as he grew older, that a teacher must adopt towards his pupils an attitude of increasing discrimination. On the one hand, there is a small circle that he can take into his confidence and treat as equals and friends. On the other hand, there is a much wider circle of disciples to whom he can communicate merely the superficial elements of his doctrines, without obtaining more than formal adherence. With the first group, the teacher is distinguished from the pupils merely by being the first among them; with the second, he remains the aloof leader while the rest follow—at some distance. Being engaged henceforth in research of the most specialized kind, Aristotle found himself under the necessity of giving two quite distinct series of lectures: one to his intimate disciples and the other to what we should today call the 'general public'. Hence arose the distinction between the 'esoteric' doctrines of Aristotle and the 'exoteric', the abstruse and the simple: which is not quite the same as the modern distinction between 'highbrow' and 'lowbrow'.

Although he never appears to have cut himself off from the Academy, Aristotle soon felt the need to set up an institution of his own. Near the beautiful temple of Apollo Lyceius in one of the north-east quarters of Athens stood a gymnasium, called appropriately the Lyceum, in which Aristotle proceeded to set up a kind of rival Academy. Needless to say, he soon attracted a group of enthusiastic followers, some of whom were apparently ex-members of the Platonic school.

We know something of the activities of the Lyceum. In the mornings, Aristotle used to lecture to a small gathering of his friends on such subjects as metaphysics. In the afternoons he concerned himself with the exposition of the simpler subjects, such as rhetoric and dialectic. It is traditionally held that he conversed with his friends walking up and down under the covered portico or *peripatos* of the gymnasium. Hence the name of 'peripatetic' was later given to the school that Aristotle founded.

Although he prospered and wielded considerable influence in

Athens, Aristotle was not so secure in the esteem of his fellows as to be able to live without a patron, especially as Demosthenes and the Athenian nationalists were still hostile to one of his sympathies and past associations. The man who befriended him and who later became his executor was Alexander's own Commander-in-Chief and Regent in Macedonia and Greece, Antipater. With such a patron, Aristotle had nothing to fear. But naturally Antipater's power depended upon that of Alexander, and the day came when the Regent found himself deprived of authority; and that was an evil moment for Aristotle.

For many rich and productive years, however, Aristotle worked, experimented, collected, and taught; and the substance of what he taught is still preserved in the numerous treatises that bear his name. These treatises, such as they are, were not written for posterity. They represent in most cases the notes of lectures delivered to a particular audience at a particular time. We have referred to Plato's attempt at reproducing in prose an essentially spoken or argued (dialectical) philosophy; Aristotle, intent upon teaching, left nothing so sustained and perfect as Plato's dialogues. But what he has left us are his own, not other people's notes; and here and there we come upon passages of such transcendent clarity and beauty that we are able to form some notion of the literary skill at his command, and of which his 'lost' dialogues evidently provided striking examples. No thinker remained throughout his career so indifferent to posterity, and yet no thinker came to exert such tremendous influence upon it. Or perhaps we should say that no thinker was more anxious that philosophical thought should prosper, and less concerned with his own reputation as its purveyor.

Absorbed in the work that he relished, Aristotle continued to regard the spectacular achievements of Alexander with ironic detachment. To certain aspects of the conqueror's policy, notably that which sought to break down the distinction between Greek and Barbarian, he was definitely opposed, though he admired the attempt to establish Greek colonies in Asia and Egypt, and even wrote a book on the subject (the treatise *On Colonization*, subtitled *Alexander*). In 327 BC, however, the relations between him and his old pupil became suddenly strained. A nephew of Aristotle, Callisthenes, had for some time been a member of Alexander's suite, with the office of recorder or historian of the conqueror's campaigns. He apparently performed this task very capably in a number of books that have since perished; but although he went out of his way to eulogize his master and to attack the old Macedonian conservatives at home who disapproved of the young King's foreign exploits, he seems to have been by nature rash and outspoken. He made no attempt, for instance, to conceal his scorn at Alexander's adoption of certain oriental customs, particularly that which required excessive adoration of the King's person; and this critical attitude finally brought him under suspicion.

When a plot to assassinate the King was later uncovered, he was immediately held responsible, though the true culprit turned out to be a page called Hermolaus. Alexander's execution of Callisthenes could not fail to anger Aristotle, since there had been little attempt to establish the victim's guilt. As it was suspected that Aristotle himself shared the opinion of Callisthenes regarding Alexander's conversion to oriental ways (which resulted in eighty of his generals being ordered at Susa to marry Asiatic wives, an example promptly followed by at least 10,000 of his Macedonian troops), the rumour circulated after the King's death in 323 BC that Aristotle had been concerned in a plot to poison him. No greater slander could have been circulated. Apart from the absurdity of attributing such base conduct to Aristotle, the death of Alexander was the last thing that, out of pure self-interest, he could have welcomed. It rendered his position extremely precarious. Indeed, it very nearly brought about his undoing.

No sooner had the news arrived that Alexander was dead than the Nationalist party at Athens, ever biding its time, rose up in rebellion. If Antipater had still been at Athens, Aristotle's prospects might have been a good deal brighter; but Antipater, having likewise incurred the displeasure of Alexander, was busy campaigning himself back to favour in Asia Minor. Knowing with what hatred the Nationalists regarded him, and what murderous passions the oratory of Demosthenes could on occasion arouse, Aristotle planned to make his escape from Athens. His flight was hurried, but not altogether undignified. He was as little concerned for his personal safety as Socrates; but, calling to mind the circumstances of Socrates' death, he decided that no good purpose could be served by his remaining in Athens, if the price of staying was the silence and censorship offered to his predecessor as an alternative to the hemlock. For he had a shrewd suspicion of what was coming.

In spite of rumours that had been deliberately put about, no evidence could be produced to show that Aristotle had engaged in political intrigues. He was a friend of Macedon, and that was enough to damn him in the eyes of the new rulers at Athens. As no particular crime could be attributed to him, the authorities resorted to vague and mischievous generalities. The ludicrous but familiar charge of 'impiety' was preferred against him by a demagogue called Eurymedon, who seems to have been as anxious to repeat the role of Anytus as he was confident of avoiding the latter's fate. The charge stung Aristotle to the quick. For this was more than a personal accusation; it was an attack upon his professional integrity. And, as he remarked at the time, '*he could not permit Athens to sin twice against philosophy*'.

He decided to retire to Chalcis in Eubœa, where he had inherited some property from his mother. His wife, Pythias, had died some years before, and he had since taken a slave-girl, Herpyllis, to live with him: a union which appears to have been as happy as that which preceded it, and which resulted in a son, Nicomachus. The daughter of his first marriage, Pythias, was still a young girl, but Aristotle had bequeathed her hand to Nicanor, the son of his foster-parents, and now his adopted child. From the will he composed about this time, we learn a great deal, not merely about Aristotle's character, but about the circumstances in which he was placed during the last period of his life.

He cites Antipater as his executor, and gives instructions as to how he shall be buried ('with Pythias') and how his children shall be educated. There is an interesting passage relating to the second wife, Herpyllis:

'The executors and Nicanor, in memory of me and of the steady affection which Herpyllis has borne towards me, shall take care of her in every other respect and, if she desires to be married, shall see that she be given to one not unworthy; and besides what she has already received, they shall give her a talent of silver out of the estate and three hand-maidens whomsoever she shall choose besides the maid she has at present and the man-servant Pyrrhaeus; and if she chooses to remain at Calchis, the lodge by the garden; if in Stagira, my father's house, with such furniture as they think proper and as Herpyllis herself may approve.' As to his servants, he directs that 'none who waited upon me shall be sold but they shall continue to be employed; and when they arrive at the proper age they shall have their freedom if they desire it'. Finally, as we have seen, he left all his manuscripts to Theophrastus.

Just as the Academy became a kind of sacred shrine after the death of its founder, so the Lyceum inevitably became identified with Aristotle. And we may judge in what high honour his memory was held by the fact that the very ground on which he taught was later bequeathed, by a special legal concession, to Theophrastus, though the latter, being a foreigner or 'metic', was not strictly entitled to hold property in Attica. This bequest was made to Theophrastus by his pupil Demetrius of Phalerum; and it is reasonable to suppose that his intention was to ensure that the man who had 'inherited' Aristotle's ideas should also inherit the place associated with their germination. The property consisted of a garden and several buildings: there was a library, a room full of specimens of all kinds, with maps laid out on boards, and a museum in which stood a statue of Aristotle, forming a kind of sanctuary. It had been the custom to hold monthly meetings at the Lyceum, at which there would be philosophical discussions followed (and sometimes accompanied) by eating and drinking. Some of these parties appear to have been very elaborate and convivial, and we possess details of regulations drawn up to ensure that a high standard of philosophical as well as gastronomic decorum was maintained.

Although none of the Lyceum gatherings have been immortalized like that which Plato describes in his *Symposium*, we know that they were both select and successful. A later President, Strato, took care to list among the properties of that institution the linen, crockery, and drinking-cups used on festive occasions. The custom may often have led to abuse. Under Strato's successor Lycon, for instance, some of the poorer students made complaints that while they could afford the instruction, they could not always afford the junketing that went with it.

To turn from the cold, impersonal and objective style of the great treatises on Metaphysics, Ethics and Logic to Aristotle's practical and yet almost tender testament is to catch a glimpse of the generous personality of the man himself. No doubt he realized that he had but a short time to enjoy his 'hermit life', as he described it. A disease of the stomach from which he had suffered intermittently took a serious turn within a few months of his arrival in Calchis; and after a day or two's illness he was dead. He had reached his sixty-third year and was at the height of his mental powers; and who can guess upon what further works he would have embarked had worry and misfortune not accelerated his end? That he died at peace with the world—especially the little world of his family—we know; but his last months must have been clouded by certain slights which his enemies, now openly hostile, chose to level at him.

In particular, he must have been hurt by the act of the Delphians in cancelling the honours bestowed upon him as a result of his compilation of the list of Pythian warriors; but he bore the insult bravely, and there was a touch of irony in his remark in a letter to Antipater: 'About the voting at Delphi and the depriving me of my honours, my feeling is that I am sorry, but not unduly so.' Delphi was a revered name in philosophy, and the double sin from which Aristotle had preserved Athens had now been committed by the people whose oracle had hailed Socrates as the 'wisest of men'. Fifteen hundred years later, Dante in his great poem bestowed upon Aristotle a title of almost equal majesty—*Il maestro di color che sanno*, 'The master of those who know'. And that is how the world has since regarded him.

His Thought

None of the adventures that befell Aristotle equalled those that befell his manuscripts after his death. When Theophrastus, their first custodian, died in 287 BC, he left all his private papers to a relation and pupil, Neleus of Scepsis. The collection included not merely the works of Aristotle and Theophrastus themselves but the extensive libraries of these two writers. Neleus took good care of his valuable property; and when he finally decided to sell the books to King Ptolemy II of Egypt, as an addition to the great library at Alexandria, he retained for himself the original manuscripts, which were his special heirlooms. These were passed on to his own heirs, who were subjects of a king of Pergamus.

Now this monarch's ambition was to build a library surpassing in size that at Alexandria; and in order to preserve the manuscripts from seizure by the bibliophile king's special agents, Neleus's family hid them in a cellar. Whether because they were too well concealed or because the owners lacked interest in their contents, they remained thus entombed for the next two centuries, the only attention paid them being that of the worms with which the damp vault was infested. Here they might easily have perished altogether but for the zeal of an Athenian philosopher and book-collector, Apellicon of Teos, who, in the century before Christ, made a special search for the original works of Aristotle.

Having finally discovered where the manuscripts were located, he entered into negotiations with the owners for their purchase, and is said to have acquired them very cheaply. With a view to producing a standard edition of Aristotle's works he thereupon started to edit them himself. But the adventures of the manuscripts were not yet over. When the Roman general, Sulla, captured Athens in 84 BC, he appropriated Apellicon's famous library and took it *en bloc* to Rome. Here, in the new centre of culture, another keen student of philosophy, Andronicus of Rhodes, published an entirely new edition of both Aristotle and Theophrastus, putting the manuscripts into the order in which they are now assembled. Both Andronicus and the remarkable scholar, Alexander of Aphrodisias, wrote detailed commentaries upon the works of Aristotle, but those of the former have been lost.

As for the Lyceum, its life fell far short of that of the Academy; but it survived until the reign of the Roman Emperor Marcus Aurelius (AD 121–180). Up to this time and indeed for many centuries after, Aristotle, though studied with attention, was regarded simply as the most distinguished of the disciples of Plato. Not until his writings had penetrated the oriental world and their influence had been reflected back to the West, did he become a master-philosopher in his own right. But of the history of his reputation we shall speak in due course.

Aristotle's numerous writings fall roughly into four sections: (1) Works on Logic and Dialectics; (2) Theoretical Philosophy (*i.e.* Metaphysics, Mathematics and Physics); (3) Practical Philosophy or Politics; and (4) Writings on Art or Æsthetics. For reasons already given, many of these treatises make difficult reading: without a commentary, the ordinary student is bound to find himself bewildered and befogged, not merely by the terminology but by the extreme concentration of the argument. There are few purple passages in Aristotle; and so he has never been able to command the degree of affection that Plato, with his superb gift of style, has inspired. Nevertheless, Aristotle has his moments; and there are phrases, and often single terms, that have become part and parcel of our everyday vocabulary.

We have seen how Aristotle, after spending years as a devoted disciple of Plato, broke away from the Academy and gradually evolved a new philosophical method. People break away from the society in which they have lived not merely because of some material compulsion but because they have come to think differently. Aristotle had come to think differently. And the subject upon which his thoughts had undergone change was nothing less than the cornerstone of Plato's philosophical edifice: namely, the theory of Ideas or Forms.

In defining the nature of the Ideas, Plato sought to emphasize their supremacy over everything else, *i.e.* their 'transcendent' character: Plato exalted the Ideal so far above the Actual that the latter, almost losing its reality, became a twilight sphere of imprecision. Aristotle, more of a realist by temperament, found this lofty idealism unsatisfactory. He wanted to demonstrate that there was reality on earth as well as in heaven. Furthermore, he wanted to prove that reality inhered in *particular* things, and that by examining such things the universal Ideas could best be apprehended. He believed he had discovered a technique or instrument by which these Universals could be elucidated, without dragging in a mystical sense or intuition such as Plato deemed necessary. This instrument was Logic. Logic, Aristotle sought to show, applied to everything. This, then, was the universal 'key' to truth which Plato had sought, and towards which his famous Dialectic was merely a groping.

Although Aristotle was disposed to accept Plato's theory that the nature of each particular thing depended upon its Form, his realism forbade him to maintain that the Form exerted its creative influence from outside, *i.e.* from some supernatural region accessible only to the purified soul of the philosopher. It was not, he held, a heavenly model which the material object sought, more or less successfully, to copy; it was already there, at work in the object, and by its influence serving to preserve that object as a unity. As Aristotle pointed out, we have no means of perceiving the Form of a statue—that by virtue of which it is a statue, and that by virtue of which it is *this* statue and not another—except by contemplating the finished work. The more 'finished' the work of art, the more completely does it succeed in embodying its Form. We must concentrate on the whole thing, the completed object, the fruition.

The effort manifested by each natural object to embody more completely the Form which determines it, is the cause of the pervading *movement* in nature. The early Greek philosophers, from Parmenides onwards, had been puzzled and often baffled by the problem of change. In our sketch of the philosophy of Socrates, we have mentioned some of the attempts made by his predecessors to explain this phenomenon. Aristotle explained it by the impulsion within each object to pass from one Form to another, by organic stages, until a phase of maturity or wholeness had been attained, after which a process of disintegraton set in and the determining Form 'lost its hold'. This so-called determining Form is described by Aristotle as the Final Cause of the object, since it is the end to which the whole process is directed. The various stages preceding maturity are those in which the object is *potentially* that which it is striving to be, as a bud is potentially a leaf and a youth potentially a man.

We can understand each particular stage, therefore, only by perceiving that it is engaged in turning into something else, which realizes more of its potentialities. The end explains the beginning and all that lies in between, and the beginning already hints at the end. A 'promising' child is one of whom we expect great things, or who manifests earlier than his fellows the qualities we expect to find in a fully developed adult. Thus Aristotle arrived at a view of Matter which makes of it something different from just 'stuff', in the common sense of that word. Matter is never wholly formless, because that which is wholly formless cannot exist at all; and we know that Matter exists. Matter is therefore the unformed, or rather the half-formed. Pure Form, at the other extreme, is something immaterial; and Aristotle had a name for this perfect and supreme manifestation of Form. He called it God.

Aristotle's theory of Form is not at all difficult to grasp once we realize the problem which he has set out to tackle. No philosophical theory—indeed no theory of any kind—can be grasped unless we understand that it represents the answer to a question or a series of questions. A philosopher, especially if he leaves us merely the notes of his conversation or lectures, does not always state explicitly what questions he is proposing to discuss: usually because he takes it for granted that his audience, having assembled to hear him, shares in some measure his interests, and therefore knows what questions he is likely to raise.

Aristotle's problem—his chief problem, that is to say—amounted to this. Here is a world of change, flux, and imperfection: a world to which part of us at least belongs, in so far as part of us (our physical make-up) is subject to the change, flux, and imperfection that we observe in nature. But there is another part of us, differently constituted, which possesses the capacity to make clear to us our shortcomings, and even enables us to prescribe remedies for them. This part of us we call our mind or spirit. Whereas our bodies belong to the natural world, derive their sustenance from it, and eventually perish in the manner of all natural things, our minds do not appear to be at home in this shifting unstable environment, even though they may be involved with it. On the contrary, they derive their nutriment from another and higher order of Being, which is subject to none of the deficiencies of the natural order. Plato had defined this higher world of Being as the realm of Forms; and with certain modifications Aristotle had accepted this definition. One modification, as we have seen, was that he regarded the Forms as *immanent* in nature rather than *transcendent*; another modification was that he held an entirely different conception of the nature of God.

It is a common belief that before the advent of the prophets of Israel, no one believed in the existence of God. This is a serious error. The difference between the pre-Christian and the Christian belief in God was not merely a difference concerning the divine nature; it was a difference concerning the relation between the divine nature and the world of man. A study of the history of religious thought reveals the interesting fact, not always sufficiently understood today, that the kind of God you believe in determines the kind of world you believe in. The early Greek philosophers held that the world in which they lived was a certain kind of world because they believed it to stand in a certain relation to the supreme Spirit, or God. The Christians, in their turn, held that the world in which they lived was a certain kind of world because they believed it to stand in a totally different relation. The transition between the early Greek view and the Christian view is best seen in Plato and Aristotle; and that is the reason why certain Christian theologians agreed to admit Plato and Aristotle to the company of 'honorary' Christians.

According to Plato, God created the world on the model of the eternal Forms. The Platonic God is therefore a kind of Demi-urge, for whom the Forms represent the general principles upon which the work of creation is based. According to Aristotle, God's role is altogether different. He is not in reality a creator at all. He is rather the cause of all the movement in the world, while Himself remaining immobile and self-absorbed. In other words, He is the supreme Final Cause towards which the whole of nature is drawn; but He remains indifferent to this ceaseless striving on the part of nature, because He is engaged in an eternal self-communion.

Who, then, created the world, and how did it come into being? The answer, according to Aristotle, is that the world, by seeking to imitate God, is occupied in creating itself. There was no beginning to this process and there will be no end, though it is just possible (Aristotle suggested) that there may be a regular cycle of changes dependent upon the movement of the stars in their courses.

This aloof, metaphysical God was postulated by Aristotle for logical rather than for religious reasons. In order to account for the change and development in the world, there must first be something static, changeless and eternal: in short, there must be an Unmoved Mover presiding over everything else in lonely majesty. Such a God is not a being to be worshipped: He is a Being to be descried. He is not the object of the adoration of the devout: He is the object of the respect of metaphysicians. Meanwhile, the purpose of science is not to speculate upon the nature and characteristics of God, for these it can never know; the purpose of science is to study the developing world of nature. Aristotle's Unmoved Mover is therefore unmoved in two senses: He is unmoved by any other force in the universe, because there is no force in the universe equal to His own, and He is equally unmoved by the efforts and yearnings of the world in which He excites such commotion.

That such a view of God should have been seriously entertained may seem strange to us; but this is due largely to the spiritual insight of an obscure Semitic tribe which claimed to worship a God of righteousness and justice—as 'jealous' but not a self-absorbed God—and which looked for the coming of a Messiah who should demonstrate God's essential concern for the world He created. The Christian revolution infused the cold metaphysics of the ancient world with warmth and life; it clothed the Supreme Being of Aristotle with flesh and blood by what is correctly called the Incarnation. But even so it did not sweep the philosophy of Aristotle away. When the doctors of the Christian Church undertook to construct a complete and systematic philosophy of existence (a task not attempted on a grand scale until the thirteenth century), they found in the newly-recovered works of Aristotle a wealth of material upon which they drew heavily, and which they pronounced to be the greatest achievement hitherto of human reason unaided by divine inspiration.

Like Plato, Aristotle maintained that the highest object of our intellects is the contemplation of eternal truth; but he shared none of Plato's indifference to temporal matters. On the contrary, he bids us seek for truth in what lies around and about us, considering it no lapse from dignity on the philosopher's part to spend much of his time collecting and dissecting specimens, collating manuscripts, and rummaging among old archives and records. Socrates questioned men; Aristotle went on to question things. He questioned in all directions, being the first great thinker to seek for an underlying connection between the various spheres of enquiry in which he interested himself. In short, he was the first modern scientist.

It requires an imaginative effort on our part, almost a mental somersault, to realize that the early thinkers of the Western world did not take for granted the fact that the world they lived in was essentially 'one world'. If we believed in the existence of a multitude of gods—some more powerful than others and each occupying a special niche in a divine hierarchy—we should naturally tend to think of reality as being composed of a number of separate domains, access to which would depend upon our being content to wait upon the good pleasure of the presiding deity. Successful living, in other words, would depend upon our possessing not so much the master-key to reality as a number of different keys to a number of different locks. For in practical life, as we know, it is the minor officials that have to be encountered, the local powers-that-be that must be placated.

The writer, D. H. Lawrence, who often grasped the essence of a philosophy better than some of his academic contemporaries, stated in his own way the early Greek attitude in his book, *Apocalypse*: 'Today it is almost impossible for us to realize what the old Greeks meant by God, or Theos. Everything was Theos; but even so, not at the same moment. At the moment, whatever struck you was God. If it was a pool of water, the very watery pool might strike you. Then that was God. Or a faint vapour at evening rising might catch the imagination: then that was Theos. Or a thirst might overcome you at the sight of water; then the thirst itself was a God... Even to the early scientists or philosophers, 'the cold', 'the moist', 'the hot', 'the dry', were things in themselves, realities, gods, theoi. And they *did* things.'

The belief or trust in minor deities or powers (modern writers talk of 'forces' in scarcely less anthropomorphic language) has never wholly died, though it has been driven underground, often into the subconscious; but the monotheism of Christianity has so shaped the minds of Western man that the idea of a 'pluralistic' universe, though frequently resuscitated, has never returned to favour. Nor can we imagine it doing so. Aristotle is halfway between the early Ionian thinkers and the Christian Fathers.

Although he personally practised the contemplative life that he enjoined upon other philosophers, Aristotle recognized that for the majority of men the intellectual vocation imposed too great a strain; besides which the ordinary man has a definite job to do. There are others, the slaves, who are by nature incapable of anything but manual labour. Plato, appalled by the frivolity and baseness of mankind, wished to guarantee freedom for the devotees of the spirit by subjecting the masses to iron discipline. He is not alone among the idealists of history who have ended by condoning a regime of censorship and compulsion, of the knout and the firing-squad.

Less exacting in his demands upon the run of men, Aristotle preaches an ethics of compromise. Shun extremes, he urges. Observe the 'golden mean' in your behaviour. Happiness will result from the avoidance of excess. When action is undertaken from 'a balance of considerations' and virtue becomes a 'settled habit', the formation of character is merely a matter of time: for character, instead of being something that a man possesses ready-made, is simply the pattern formed by his good actions throughout life. Here, as elsewhere, Aristotle lays emphasis upon the fact of development. The world itself is a process, man a process within that world, and moral character a process within man. Everything, as Heraclitus correctly affirmed, flows; but the flow has direction, aim and purpose.

Just as Plato wrote the *Republic* and later the *Laws* in order to expound his views on the relation between the individual and the State, so Aristotle wrote his treatise on *Politics* in order to show that the good life is essentially a social life, since man is by nature 'a political animal'. Although the State of which he wrote was the City State of his time (we have remarked how indifferent he remained to larger units), his observations upon the various types of government, and upon the art of government in general, are in many respects still valid. Reading this work for the first time, the modern student may recoil from some of Aristotle's conclusions, especially that which suggests that certain men are born to be slaves; and he may well be surprised to find democracy denounced as a form of tyranny, along with absolute monarchy and self-seeking oligarchy; but if he carefully follows Aristotle's argument, he will observe that the aim of the book is precisely to pursue a middle course between extreme forms of government, and to arrive at a conception of the state which is neither exclusively monarchical, nor oligarchical, nor democratic, but a blend of all three. This balanced state Aristotle calls a 'polity'.

Not content with analysing the conditions of the just society, Aristotle, like Plato, describes in detail the kind of education that its citizens should receive. Plato recommended the expulsion of artists from his ideal Republic; his argument was that artists, being concerned to depict the world as it is, are responsible for beguiling men's minds with that which is imperfect and compounded of illusion. (It has been pointed out that this indictment refers only to the so-called 'representative' artists.) In his treatise on *Poetics*, Aristotle dissociates himself from this attitude to art and artists. Art, he holds, and above all the art of Drama (of which his time saw many splendid examples), may fulfil an important and indispensable social function. In portraying human beings engaged in acts of heroism, villainy, justice and violence, and in revealing now their sublime qualities and now their ridiculous, the artist is able to exercise a most salutary effect upon the feelings and emotions of his audience. He does not merely excite to admiration or pity, pleasure or disgust; he purifies these emotions by a process akin to 'earthing' them. The ordinary man is usually inarticulate as regards feeling: the function of art is to enable his pent-up emotions to discharge themselves in the manner least likely to cause damage to his fellow-beings. This process of spiritual release Aristotle called 'catharsis', and his theory has exerted a profound influence upon art, literary criticism, and even psychology. Thus the liberating effect that

Socrates ascribed to the dialectical method of philosophy, Aristotle extends to the sphere of imaginative creation.

A final word about the influence of Aristotle's writings. Of their effect upon the Oriental world we have already spoken. The last of the Neo-Platonists paid particular attention to Aristotle's views on Physics, and some of the Neo-Platonic manuscripts at length came into the hands of Jewish and Moslem thinkers, chiefly by way of the Christian communities in Syria. Thence, via Baghdad, they circulated to Cordova, as a result of which they began to exert an influence upon Latin Christianity. Towards the end of the twelfth century AD and at the beginning of the thirteenth, Greek texts and Arabic translations of Aristotle's treatise on *First Philosophy* and other writings were studied by the doctors of the Catholic Church. The official Catholic attitude remained one of extreme reserve, however, until Albert the Great and Thomas Aquinas, authors of exhaustive commentaries, demonstrated that the metaphysical views of Aristotle were, with due modification, a reasonable basis for Christian theology.

Although Aristotle's influence became thenceforward more widespread than it had ever been, it did not exercise quite the 'dictatorship' that some popular histories of thought, whether philosophical or scientific, would suggest. With thinkers such as William of Ockham (*d.* 1350), John Buridan (*d.* 1360), Nicholas Oresme (*d.* 1382), and Albert of Saxony (*d.* 1350), a definite reaction against Aristotle's theories of physics set in; and out of this reaction developed the movement known as modern thought. Thus we have Francis Bacon (1561–1626) describing Aristotle as 'the vile plaything of words'; a most ungenerous phrase to use of one who, like Bacon himself, was passionately devoted to research and experiment. But a man cannot be held responsible for the extravagances of his disciples and commentators, who often endeavour to prove themselves more orthodox than the master.

Of some great men it has been said that they 'rule from the grave'; but even the most salutary exercise of mortmain cannot prevent their tomb from becoming a gaudy shrine, decked with the trappings of those who, out of misplaced zeal, confuse idolary with deference. If Aristotle went into hiding, it was not for the first time; and he has always managed to issue forth again. If he has been misunderstood, he has survived the most absurd travesties. His thought has thus become intimately bound up with the fortunes of our civilization, so that to eject him would be equivalent almost to dropping the pilot.

13

From Stoicism to Neo-Platonism

In sketching the life and thought of the philosophers that follow, we shall be building upon the foundations already laid. The great philosophers of mediæval and modern times make no attempt to conceal the debt which they owe to Socrates, Plato and Aristotle, even when they join issue with them most fiercely; for although their problems are so different, the methods they use and the very terminology they employ are those invented and worked out by the early Greek masters. This applies not merely to the sphere of metaphysics proper but to that of ethics or morals, political theory, education, economics, literary criticism, and above all the physical sciences. Even those who deplore the excessive attention still paid to 'the classics' in education, and who would substitute a more 'modern' scientific form of instruction in our schools and universities, do not deny that this 'classical tradition' is intimately bound up with what is known as Western civilization, and that the abandonment of this tradition (assuming such deliberate jettisoning to be possible) would leave a void not easily filled.

Today we realize more clearly than ever that civilization is not so much a material as a spiritual or intellectual inheritance; that we can ignore this inheritance at our peril; and that the decline and fall of empires has something to do with the 'morale' of the people composing them—this morale being strengthened or impoverished according to the grip maintained upon certain principles which have formed the basis of communal life. Hence the importance of that branch of history which is concerned with the history of speculative thought; and hence the interest that must centre round the lives of those who have revolutionized our mental conception of the world.

The death of Alexander the Great in 323 BC marks roughly the end of an era. The philosophical tradition that had grown up in the free city states of Greece now assumed a new guise. During the next few centuries, the Greek spirit of enquiry pervaded the whole of the Mediterranean region, and 'Hellenism' became a kind of world culture, though we should bear in mind that the world in question consisted of the area covered by the Macedonian Empire and later the Roman Empire. Naturally, the break-up of the old order, and the merging of small plitical units into a larger whole, profoundly affected and disturbed the life of the thinking individual. There were many who felt, not perhaps always consciously, that they had lost their bearings. The old traditions of local civic patriotism were falling into neglect.

New principles of conduct were needed. Strange and novel religious cults sprang up, and from them a handful of earnest devotees derived a transient satisfaction of the spiritual hunger within them. Even the rulers themselves felt the need of moral backing for their own achievements and experiments in government; for the most humble and obscure inhabitant of a great and far-flung empire is not so lonely at heart, or so much a prey to inner doubts and misgivings, as the man at the head of it.

To meet this need for guidance and certainty on the part of the individual, great or small, the Stoics and the Epicureans propounded their philosophies of life. Led by Zeno of Citium in Cyprus (*d.* 260 BC by his own hand[1]), Cleanthes from the Troad and Chrysippus of Tarsus, the Stoics were men of the world who endeavoured to influence the great ones of the age. They taught with equal zeal the importance of effort and that of indifference in face of both success and failure. Happiness consisted in accepting one's destiny, for there was an inner harmony in the universe which the truly wise man will discern and approve. The Epicureans,[2] on the other hand, while not advocating unlimited or habitual indulgence (as the term 'Epicurean' has since come to suggest), believed that pleasure was the goal of human endeavour; but only the sage will know which among the pleasures of life are those most worthy of pursuit, his preference being for such as agitate the soul least and enable us to live in tranquillity.

Both Stoics and Epicureans succeeded in grasping half of the truth while convinced that they possessed the whole of it; and thus their doctrines were attacked from various angles by a group of thinkers who, abhorring all dogmatism, maintained that happiness was to be derived solely from the suspension of all judgment. In this group were such men as Anaxarchus and Pyrrho of Elis (born 365 BC; hence 'pyrrhonism'), who were later to influence the sceptics Timon of Phliasius (c. 300 BC) and later still Sextus Empiricus (AD 180–210). There were others whose approach was more direct: Aristippus of Cyrene, for instance, who pointed out that if the Epicureans were right to suppose that pleasure was the end of life, they were implicitly justifying suicide, since the end of life, thus defined, is unattainable. Indeed, Pyrrho (so Epictetus records) used to say: 'There is no difference between living and dying.' A person asked him: 'Why, then, do you not die?' 'Because,' answered Pyrrho, 'there is no difference.'

The problem of how the world came into being had puzzled the Greek thinkers, who never really succeeded in answering it except in terms of myths (as in Plato's *Timœus*). There was another people, however, which believed itself to be specially gifted with insight into the way the world had originated and how it was related to the Supreme Spirit. This people, the Hebrews, believed that God had created the world out of nothing; that He was particularly interested in the work of His creation; and that He would one day announce His solidarity with mankind by sending a Messiah to assume the leadership of the

[1] But at the age of ninety-eight.

[2] Epicurus was born at Samos in 341 BC and died at Athens in 270.

chosen people. This 'Creation Myth' was outlined in the book of *Genesis*, and the idea of the coming of the Messiah found expression in a series of prophetic utterances for which no other religion has an equivalent. What the Greeks found intellectually unacceptable, if not inconceivable, the Hebrews believed with passionate intensity; but when the Christian Faith later began to win converts among every class of people, the need became apparent for a reasoned theology. Thus it was natural to have recourse to Greek categories of thought, because these were the forms in which reasoned argument most naturally found expression.

Some of the 'philosophies' produced at this time were a peculiar hotch-poch of pagan and Christian ideas: the most interesting being that of Philo the Jew, who developed the Greek notion of the 'Logos' or creative-principle in such a way as to foreshadow the 'Word-made-Flesh' theme of the Fouth Gospel of the New Testament. A group of philosophers and teachers who put up a determined resistance to the new faith was that of the Platonic Academy. They felt they had nothing to learn from a religion of such humble origins and dubious intellectual credentials. If men required an other-worldly faith, a liberation from the flesh and the devil, Plato had already supplied the answer. Not 'forward with Christ' but 'back to Plato' should be the watchword.

The thinkers of this group of 'Neo-Platonists', as they were called, were Platonists with a difference. In philosophical thought there is no 'going back' to anyone. The point of view that finds sympathy with a past thinker is itself the product of a new climate of thought. Whereas Plato never loses sight of the fact that his ultimate aim is the betterment of society, Plotinus (AD 203–270), the greatest of the Neo-Platonist philosophers, ignores the social needs of man and concentrates upon the mystical union of the soul with God. He is concerned less with justice or happiness on earth than with ecstasy in heaven—an ecstasy which is the product of mystical contemplation rather than (as with Aristotle) of intellectual research into causes. In his pantheism, Plotinus is a pagan; in his emphasis upon love and self-discipline he comes near to the Christianity which, in its orthodox forms, he rejected.

14

St Augustine

Wherever we are, there is no place where He is not whose we are

Augustine: last letter

His life

By far the most dramatic example of a pagan thinker who arrived, step by step and after many backslidings, at an acceptance of the Christian faith is that of Augustine. The personality of St Augustine, one of the most attractive in the history of thought, has cast a spell over thousands who have neither the capacity nor the inclination to study his writings on theology. Born at Tagaste in Numidia (North Africa) in AD 354, he came of a family which, though probably Roman, contained some Punic or Numidian blood, and was by tradition thoroughly Africanized. This fact is not without significance; it throws light upon Augustine's ardent and passionate temperament, his stormy youth, and also his energetic old age.

Determined to give him the finest education available, his parents sent him at the age of twelve to the Grammar School, or its equivalent, at Madaura, where a community of Roman veterans had settled. Here he received a thoroughly Roman education, for it was the principle in the colony that, being away from Rome, it was the more important to do as Rome did.[1] Five years later he was sent to Carthage, where, assisted financially by a wealthy patron named Romanianus, he took a course in Rhetoric, a subject then considered as useful to an enterprising young man as Social Science or Economics is today.

Carthage was the metropolis. Attracted by its wealthy, colourful, and by no means straitlaced society, Augustine at once fell a victim to its allurements. That he was by nature vicious we have no reason to believe. He was certainly no worse than the majority of his contemporaries. Nevertheless, his lapses were a source of constant pain to his mother, Monica, a Christian from birth and tireless in her efforts to rear him in the same faith. He formed a number of attachments, one of which resulted in the birth of a son, Adeodatus. In his later *Confessions* we find him bitter with self-reproach at these youthful indiscretions, from the consequences of which he was to suffer for many years. Recalling the days of his first contact with the follies and snares of an

[1] Augustine's later friend St Ambrose was incidentally the author of the famous phrase *Si fueris Romœ, Romano vivito more* ('If you are at Rome, live in the Roman style').

essentially pagan society, he uttered the famous words: 'To Carthage then I came, where a cauldron of unholy loves sang all about mine ears.'

For all his social entanglements, he was not an idle student. Thirsting for knowledge and intent upon discovering a faith to live by, though unwilling as yet to embrace the religion of his mother, he fell in with a group of clever but wayward intellectuals known as Manichæans. The Manichæans entertained the belief that good and evil, being equal in power, were engaged in a perpetual struggle from which evil, in this world, tended to issue triumphant: and for this reason it was prudent to placate the dominant force. Such a belief gave rise to abuses both of logic and of conduct; it was particularly demoralizing to a man of Augustine's temperament. So far involved did he become with the society of the Manichæans, and so persuasive were the arguments they used to compel his adherence, that he remained for the next nine years under the spell of this stupefying heresy, clinging rather to what appeared to excuse his dissolute habits than to what satisfied his pressing mental needs.

Then, at long last, came release. Faustus, the master exponent of the Manichæan doctrine, paid a personal visit to Carthage. Hoping to extract from him the answer to certain intellectual difficulties, Augustine eagerly sought his company and listened to his conversation. He was thoroughly disillusioned. The man was not so much an impostor as a simpleton—though an exceedingly pompous and plausible one. Augustine at once saw through him and his facile logic. But, having escaped his influence, he arrived no nearer to the solution of his problems. He had torn one veil aside but without revealing anything likely to point him on the right way. At least the Manichæan teaching had provided some sort of mental nourishment, however mediocre. Now he was left with a jaded palate and no sustenance at all.

Unable to stay longer in Carthage, where, as he confesses, he had lived 'seduced and seducing, deceived and deceiving, in divers lusts:—openly, by sciences which they call liberal; secretly, with a false-named religion; here proud, there superstitious, everywhere vain', he decided to make a journey to Rome. His motives for taking such a step were mixed. He wanted a change of scenery, but above all he wanted to taste the intellectual life of the great metropolis, which, as a Roman by sympathy, he regarded as his spiritual home. His family, except for Monica, accompanied him. For some months after their arrival Augustine sought an appointment in which he could exercise his now highly developed talents in Rhetoric. Disappointment attended him at every step; and, as he laconically put it, 'I found other offences committed in Rome to which I was not exposed in Africa.' By good fortune, however, or by what he termed the Providence of God, a post of teacher of Rhetoric fell vacant at that time in Milan. Augustine put in for the job, requesting the prefect of Rome, Symmachus, to set him a subject upon which to display his ability. He passed the test brilliantly and was appointed.

Installed at Milan, where his mother soon joined him, Augustine came into contact with one of the most influential figures of the age, Bishop Ambrose, who, after Monica herself, was the first upright Christian he had known. The teaching and preaching of Ambrose attracted him as no other teaching and preaching had done: not at first because of its matter, which he largely ignored, nor on account of its polish, which he admitted to be inferior to that of Faustus, but on account of the obvious sincerity of the man, and the friendship which, in spite of differences in age and status, grew up spontaneously between them.

Gradually, as their intimacy increased, Augustine was moved to accept as valid much that in Ambrose's teaching he had previously dismissed as mere poetry or self-delusion. 'While I opened my heart to admit "how eloquently he spake", there also entered "how truly he spake"; but this by degrees.' It dawned upon him, though no less gradually, that he must on no account force the pace of his own conviction. In this state of semi-belief, he decided to assume the status of a catechumen, that is, one studying for admittance to the Church by baptism, which Monica and her husband (who accepted the faith later than his partner) had long before arranged for him. He desired salvation; but the old life still held its attractions and caused him to falter more times than he cared to recall. 'Make me pure,' was his prayer, '—but not yet.' As for Monica, she realized that it would take time for him to pass 'from sickness unto health', and that such convalescence would most probably result from 'the access, as it were, of a sharper fit, which physicians call "the crisis".'

The crisis, in his case, was somewhat long in coming, perhaps because he awaited it too complacently instead of plodding steadily forward in search of truth. For at this stage it was honour, gain and happiness, instead of true sanctity, that he desired most fervently. The pursuit of happiness led him, as it has led others, into curious reflections. One day he noticed a beggar in the streets of Milan joking and laughing. The contrast between this simple wretch on the one hand and himself and his friends on the other, engaged in incessant mental stress and torment, made him realize how 'for that by all such efforts of ours, as those wherein I then toiled, dragging along, under the goading of desire, the burden of my own wretchedness, and, by dragging, augmenting it, we yet looked to arrive at that very joyousness, whither that beggar-man had arrived before us, who should never perchance attain it'.

Even the privileges of his office as Professor of Rhetoric sickened him. 'How miserable was I then ... when I was preparing to recite a panegyric to the Emperor (Valentinian the Younger), wherein I was to utter many a lie, and lying was to be applauded by those who knew I lied.' He toyed with the idea of marriage—a rich marriage, it went without saying—and, in other moods, of becoming a hermit or member of a monastic community. He separated, not without some measure of regret, from the mother of his child, only to form a liaison with a woman less worthy and by no means as constant.

Of his industry at this time there was no doubt. He was overflowing with energy. He studied the scriptures with growing zeal, and also such philosophers as Plato. His Christian friends, and particularly the learned Simplicianus, were gratified that his tastes in pagan philosophy were as refined as this, for, as he said, 'the Platonists in many ways led to a belief in God and his word'. From Simplicianus he learned of the conversion of the great teacher Victorinus, who, having risen high in the esteem of his fellow Romans, even to the extent of being honoured with a statue in the Forum itself, showed his courage by one day professing his new faith to the multitude. Here, then, was a man for whom honour and reputation, both so dear to Augustine, counted as nothing in comparison with the obscure blessing of humility. What prevented him, who had so much less to lose, from following this great example? Nothing but the sloth and paralysis that still held his will: 'for,' as he later wrote, 'of a froward will was a lust made; and a lust served became custom; and custom not resisted became necessity. By which links, as it were, joined together, a hard bondage held me enthralled.'

At length a day came when a friend, Pontitianus, paid a casual visit to Augustine and his friend Alypius. By birth an African like himself, but now a convert to Christianity, Pontitianus held high office at the Roman Emperor's court. Noticing a book lying upon Augustine's table and supposing it to be some text used by him in the course of his teaching, he turned over the pages and found it to be the writings of Paul the Apostle. This discovery, for which he had not been prepared, moved him to speak of the life and work of more recent followers of Christ, above all of Anthony, the illiterate monk of Egypt (*b.* AD 251), and of his companion desert sages.

These revelations of contemporary sanctity, achieved without the aid of subtle arguments and ponderous learning, shamed Augustine into a recognition of the great contrast between his own intellectual gifts and his spiritual poverty. A feeling of intense humiliation and anguish followed; and then, as if the scales had fallen from his eyes, he saw plainly and for the first time his cardinal error. His extravagant intellectual pretensions were, it seemed, the primary obstacles to his acceptance of the Catholic faith. The weapons of dialectic and logic, wherewith he had hoped to argue himself into certainty, had brought him nearer and nearer to complete scepticism. Turning impulsively to his companion Alypius, he exclaimed: 'Are we ashamed to follow, because others are gone before, and not ashamed not even to follow?' His friend became conscious of a great change in the speaker, who hurried out into an adjoining garden and there, with Alypius following, sat down.

For some moments Augustine remained completely inarticulate. In his mind the phrase 'Be it done now' echoed again and again, and, from the other side of his nature, the leering words 'Think you that you can do without us?' The inward tension then resolved itself in a flood of tears, during which he became conscious of another voice, as it were of a young boy or girl, saying gently: 'Take up and read. Take up and read!' Returning, now somewhat calmer, to where Alypius was sitting and seizing the volume of Paul which he had brought with him, his eyes fell upon the text beginning 'Not in rioting and drunkenness...' He felt his doubts already receding; and Alypius, continuing the same passage as far as the striking and appropriate words 'Him that is weak in faith, receive', experienced a similar sensation of release from perplexity. Their joint impulse, needless to translate into speech, was to go indoors and tell Monica what had happened. This was the moment which she had long awaited. For, as Augustine put it, his own sudden conversion was responsible for another in her: namely, 'the conversion of her mourning into joy'.

As a result of this momentous turning-point in his life, Augustine decided to abandon the profession of instructor in Rhetoric. He went into retirement in the country to make himself ready for baptism, Ambrose giving him the advice he needed. About this time his health broke down, so that the continuance of his profession might in any event have been rendered impossible. With him stayed Alypius and the boy Adeodatus, whose mental gifts, at barely fifteen years of age, were already remarkable: he and his father later wrote a book together called *The Master*. All three were baptized by Ambrose in AD 387. Soon after they decided to return, with Monica, to Africa.

The little company had travelled no further than Ostia, the port of Rome, when Monica fell ill. She was then in her fifty-sixth year. Her peaceful death soon after removed the best and most lasting influence upon Augustine's life. Not merely did she enjoy the good fortune of witnessing his entry into the Church; shortly before her death she found in him the companion that her husband, though nominally turned Christian, had never proved equal to being. Her patience and suffering received their due reward at the last in an experience which, though Augustine was to live to a great age, he himself treasured as the most precious of his life, and for which his own words must suffice:

'It came to pass, Thyself, as I believe, by Thy secret ways so ordering it, that she and I stood alone, leaning in a certain window, which looked into the garden of the house where we now lay, at Ostia; where, removed from the din of men, we were recruiting from the fatigues of the journey for the voyage. We were discoursing then together, alone, very sweetly; and forgetting those things which are behind, and reaching forth unto those things which are before, we were enquiring between ourselves in the presence of the Truth, which Thou art, of what sort the eternal life of the saints was to be, which eye hath not seen, nor ear heard, nor hath it entered into the heart of man. But yet we gasped with the mouth of our heart, after those heavenly streams of Thy Fountain, the foundation of life, which is with Thee; that being bedewed thence according to our capacity, we might in some sort meditate upon so high a mystery.

'And when our discourse was brought to that point, that the very highest delight of the earthly senses, in the very purest material light, was, in respect of the sweetness of that life, not only not worthy of comparison, but not even of mention; we raising up ourselves with a more glowing affection towards the "Self-Same", did by degrees pass through all things bodily, even the very heaven; yea, we were soaring higher yet, by inward musing, and discourse, and admiring of Thy works; and we came to our own minds and went beyond them, that we might arrive at that region of never-failing plenty, where Thou feedest Israel with the food of Truth, and where life is the Wisdom by whom all these things are made . . . and while we were discoursing and panting after her, we slightly touched on her with the whole effort of our heart . . . when my mother said: "Son, for my part I have no further delight in anything in this life. What I do here any longer and to what end I am here, I know not now that my hopes in this world are accomplished. One thing there was for which I desired to linger for a while in this life, that I might see thee a Catholic Christian before I died. My God hath done this for me most abundantly, that I should now see thee withal, despising earthly happiness, become His servant: what do I here?"'

A few days later she was dead.

The fame that Augustine had sought in youth and renounced upon seclusion, came to him, though in different guise, in old age. Having spent three years as a recluse, he was ordained priest in 391 by Valerius, Bishop of Hippo. Four years later he succeeded Valerius to the episcopate—a promotion as swift as it was merited. In 397 he began the composition of his *Confessions,* one of the most moving records of its kind ever written, and from which the passages quoted above are taken. Not that this autobiography was the only great work that he produced. He wrote numerous sermons, commentaries and treatises, some expository and others directed against heretics such as the Donatists and the Pelagians. Finally, about 413, he began to write the monumental work called *The City of God*, wherein he expounded his plan for a Christian Commonwealth sufficiently stable and enduring to survive the internal decay of the Roman Empire. As he grew older, so his rule tended to become more autocratic; but, as far as his spiritual life was concerned, he never turned aside from the path upon which, following his conversion and his mother's death, he had set his feet. He did not lack enemies, even among the ranks of Christians, the most cruel being those who took delight in reminding him of his youthful errors. Such taunts he bore with true humility, ever ready to acknowledge his faults and of sufficient uprightness not to repeat them.

He died in Hippo in 430, having completed *The City of God* four years earlier, with the Vandals already surging at the gates. Since his acceptance of the Faith of his mother, forty-three eventful years had passed; but, to the end, his attitude to the Church was summed up in the moving words from the 10th Book of the *Confessions: 'Sero te amavi pulchritudo tam antiqua et tam nova, sero te amavi'* ('Too late have I loved thee, O Beauty most ancient and most new! too late have I loved thee').

His Thought

For reasons already given, it was to Plato rather than to Aristotle that

Augustine, seeking for a philosophical basis for his maturing religious beliefs, instinctively turned: for indeed there was hardly anything of importance, or realized importance, of Aristotle to turn to. Apart from the subject-matter of his philosophy, Plato exhibited the qualities of mind that Augustine most admired and in great part shared: above all, a passionate desire to make contact with a reality transcending that perceived by the senses. Like Plato, he held that the function of science, or ordered knowledge, was to render us more capable of sanctity and hence salvation: *nulla est causa philosophandi nisi ut beati simus*. He echoed the words of the Apostle that the truth, as revealed in the Son of God, should make men free. Unlike Plotinus, for whom God was so transcendent a Being as to be beyond the reach of thought altogether, Augustine maintained that human reason, notwithstanding its limitations, was at least *capable* of apprehending God, though not necessarily of understanding Him.

To assert otherwise was unduly to belittle the faculty of Reason, and therefore to cast doubt upon the value of a gift of God. Indeed, this gift of Reason was the most precious with which man had been endowed, since it marked his superiority over the rest of creation. If, however, Reason occupied a position of such eminence in man's spiritual make-up, what of that other faculty upon which theologians were accustomed to place such emphasis as almost to accord superiority to it: namely, Faith? Augustine, be it noted, refused to regard Reason and Faith as faculties opposed one to the other, as certain theologians have done both before and since, and as Augustine himself is sometimes credited with doing. To Faith, admittedly, he accorded some primacy, as well as a certain priority in time; we must believe a thing—or rather believe *in* it—in order fully to understand it. *Credo ut intelligam*. Everyone has experienced the mental condition of being intellectually satisfied but not emotionally satisfied. But the condition in which the mind is completely at ease with itself and with the world is that of *knowledge:* and knowledge is a blend of both Faith and Reason, or rather a state in which these two are merged into a larger whole.

In maintaining that the human intellect could comprehend but not fully understand God, Augustine had in mind the fact that, in thinking of God, we become involved in a series of contradictions or, as they are sometimes termed, 'antinomies'. Thus God is the cause of all change, but He is immutable. He exists but inhabits no particular place. He is living but not in time. This is the consequence of our finite mind endeavouring, and failing, to grasp the nature of an infinite and immaterial object. It is precisely because God is immaterial (a 'spirit') that no material image, or set of material images, can do justice to Him. Hence the danger of interpreting the Trinity in a literal manner. God is Three Persons and yet One Person just as a human person is compounded of thought, will and feeling—distinct but united faculties. Augustine's most serious charge against the upholders of the Arian heresy was that they converted a *distinction* into a *separation*.

Unlike the Greek philosophers of antiquity, Augustine insisted, as his Christian beliefs obliged him to do, that God created the world by an act of free-will. That such creation presupposed a previous eternity of inactivity on the part of God, Augustine denied, though his non-Christian critics had put forward this hypothesis as an insuperable objection to Catholic theology. Prior to the act of divine creation, there was no 'duration', infinite or otherwise, because the creation of the world involved the creation of time as well: indeed, movement, which in time, cannot exist apart from finite things, and therefore in eternity there can be neither movement nor duration. This, as the reader will recognize, and as Augustine was ready to acknowledge, is pure Plato.

Where Augustine parted company with Plato was in his view of the Fall of Man and (of course) the Incarnation. Concerning the Fall of Man Plato speaks in the language of myth; but he clearly believes that such an event took place—or how do we account for the condition of imperfection in which man, despite his momentary glimpses of true reality, finds himself? As to whether Plato conceived the possibility of an Incarnation, it is difficult to say, though there is a passage to suggest that he thought the perfect man would, like Socrates, be done to death by his fellows. Augustine held that before the Fall man was guided solely by his reason; since then, this 'inner light' has been increasingly obscured by sin. Had man's soul remained thoroughly transparent to reason, the revelation of God in Jesus Christ would not have been necessary. Those who persist in maintaining that Reason alone can save the world (*i.e.,* the so-called Rationalists) are those who either ignore the fact of sin or explain it in terms of something else ('environment', 'heredity', etc.).

Oppressed by a sense of impending doom as a result of the degeneracy of the Roman civilization of his day, Augustine emphasized to a degree that some of his followers found excessive the absolute dependence of men upon divine grace. If man has become the slave of vice and sin, salvation could come only through a definite act of liberation. Thus, towards the end of his life, Augustine tended to adopt a more and more fatalistic attitude to men and affairs. The phrase, 'O Lord, thou pluckest me out', summed up his philosophy of salvation. It may be that he never forgot how near to being engulfed in the abyss of error he himself had come.

15

Peter Abelard

The only way to return to God is by neglecting the creature we have adored, and adoring the God whom we have neglected.

Abelard to Héloïse

The story of Abelard is well known (though not always accurately known) by millions whose acquaintance with philosophy is of the slightest, and who are totally unaware of the part played by purely philosophical controversies in his stormy career. Few people likewise realize how far his innovations in thought have since been accepted as just and reasonable, even by the Church whose representatives repeatedly condemned him for heresy. In writing of Abelard, therefore, we shall be writing of a man who lived in days when the correct formulation of a doctrine was a matter about which men not merely quarrelled but were prepared to shed blood (their own and other people's); when a philosophical definition or distinction was thus literally a matter of life and death; and finally when a man who had something to teach attracted pupils from far beyond the borders of the country in which he lived.

Today, it is possible for a man's words to be broadcast to all nations of the earth. In the twelfth and thirteenth centuries, with none of these means of diffusion at his disposal, a great teacher might exert an influence upon his contemporaries greater than that which is wielded by the most eloquent of modern publicists. And this influence was primarily of an intellectual character. The demagogue's success was purely local.

Born about 1080 in Pallet, near Nantes in Brittany, Peter Abelard came of noble stock. His father and mother seem to have been persons of culture and refinement, and to Peter, their eldest son, they gave the best education they could afford. We know little of Abelard's childhood and youth; but it is obvious that he grew up with a strong sense of independence and marked intellectual ability. His desire for learning finally became so inordinate that he resolved, after the manner of the time, to set out by himself in quest of those who could put him in the way of further instruction: for in those days education was a thing to be sought by travel and pilgrimage, not something accepted as a right. In quitting his home Abelard abandoned not merely his family but his own right of primogeniture; and like any other wandering student, he travelled light, though he had the advantage of a heavier purse than most of his companions.

The goal of all young men with his particular leanings was Paris; but it appears that before arriving at the capital, Abelard spent a year or two studying at Locminé under a well-known teacher, Roscellinus, Canon of Compiègne. Roscellinus taught philosophy or dialectics. He taught it well, but he did not always teach what the Church approved. He had in fact already been condemned for heresy both at London and at Soissons. This made him something of a notoriety; but he was not on that account deprived of influence, or of the wealth that came from having many pupils. Abelard was later to enjoy a similar status. Undoubtedly his contact with Roscellinus sharpened his independent spirit, for thereafter orthodoxy could never contain him. He studied everything, mastering all branches of enquiry save mathematics, for which he never displayed the smallest aptitude. At music he excelled; and he soon made a name for himself as a composer of songs.

We next find this talented, well-favoured young man sitting at the feet (the phrase is to be taken literally, for the students reclined on the straw-covered floor of the lecture-room, resting their notebooks on their raised knees) of another distinguished teacher, William of Champeaux, who at that time occupied the Chair at the episcopal school at old Notre Dame. William was a teacher of great influence not merely with his students (who were of all nationalities) but with the powers-that-be. His orthodoxy was unquestioned. Abelard recognized this, and immediately proceeded to question orthodoxy.

As it is impossible to treat Abelard's career apart from the philosophical disputes that served so largely to shape it, we shall here discuss the two together. Considerable mental adjustment is needed for us today if we would understand how it came about that a particular philosophical problem, seemingly so barren and superficial, should plunge the whole of Christendom into bitter dissension; but this is because our own quarrels and controversies are conducted upon a plane that obscures the clash of ideas at the basis of every problem, even the 'impersonal' problems of economics. The particular problem that agitated the minds of the thinkers of the twelfth century was a development of a logical argument already elaborated by Aristotle. This argument was concerned with the relation between *genera* and *species*—a subject innocent enough in appearance, but bristling with difficulties once we examine its implications. Briefly, it may be stated as follows. While there are individual beings called men, that by virtue of which they are men is not something individual but universal. The question is whether the universal 'Man' enjoys an existence similar, if not superior, to that of individual men.

Plato, it will be remembered, answered this question in the affirmative; he believed, in other words, that Universals or Ideas inhabited a region of their own—a region of pure, timeless Being—from which the world of sense was separated by a gulf. Aristotle, realizing the disadvantages of such a theory, contended that the Ideas were already in contact with natural things, providing them with a kind of internal impulsion to realize their fullest potentialities.

Abelard and his contemporaries knew nothing of Aristotle save that which they could derive from Porphyry's *Introduction* (translated from the Latin) to his works; but the logical problem of Universal and Particular struck them as especially relevant to the discussion of the central dogmas of the Christian Faith, such as the Trinity, Original Sin, and indeed the nature of the Church itself. Were the Three Persons of the Trinity separate entities, or three aspects or attributes of one entity? Was Original Sin simply a 'name' for a collection of individual sins, or did it refer to an essential Sinfulness characteristic of and pervading all human shortcomings? Was the Christian Church merely an assembly of individual churches—an ecclesiastical federation—or was it Catholic or Universal in the true sense, an ideal entity from which each individual church derived such spirituality as it possessed?

Roscellinus, who declared that Universals were simply empty names (the standpoint of the Nominalist), was promptly accused of heresy for denying the central dogmas of the Faith. William of Champeaux, on the other hand, was a stout defender of the Realist view that Universals enjoyed a reality of their own. Abelard, while rejecting Nominalism, found the Realist doctrine frankly incredible. Within a short time of entering the philosopher's classes, he therefore began openly to defy his master. To everyone's astonishment, William was first indignant, then baffled, and finally overwhelmed, though not convinced. Abelard's moral victory caused a major sensation; but, like all his victories, it was to recoil upon the man who achieved it. 'This,' he wrote many years after, 'was the beginning of my calamities.'

The view put forward by Abelard in contrast to that held by the Nominalists and the Realists is now known in the textbooks as Conceptualism. It is a reasonable doctrine, easily comprehensible to the ordinary man. The Universal, said Abelard, exists, but only *in* the individual. Every person partakes of the nature of Man, but we arrive at the idea of Man through studying this man and that man. Outside the individual, this universal man is merely an intellectual *concept*. The human mind is so made that it can entertain such concepts as if they enjoyed an abstract being. They do indeed enjoy such a being, but it is a mental being, an *ens rationis*. The glory of our human Reason is that it can deal in such abstractions, manipulating them at will. And since Reason is a gift of God (as Augustine himself affirmed), we should not be afraid to subject everything in heaven and earth to its impartial scrutiny.

Abelard's contentions, inoffensive as they seem to us, were regarded in his day with the utmost suspicion. In claiming so high a place for the human intellect, he was said to be crediting the finite with the capacity to understand the infinite. That was blasphemy. Whatever Augustine's attitude to Reason, he had firmly believed in the primary of Faith. Abelard was virtually saying: 'I understand in order that I may believe.' This was rationalism, and through rationalism lay the way to atheism.

Although scholarship exhibited considerable vitality at this time, its academic organization was much inferior to that of the present day. A teacher had to live by his wits; and if his pupils drifted away, he was usually ruined or at least thrown temporarily out of employment. William of Champeaux, however, was the adviser of princes as well as the instructor of youth. To incur his disfavour, as Abelard had done, was to run great risks. Not for the last time in his life, Abelard decided to quit the scene of his momentary triumph. He moved to the little town of Melun, thirty miles away, and there set up a rival school of Dialectics. Many of William's pupils followed him with enthusiasm. A little later, plucking up courage once more, the young rebel moved his informal 'Chair' nearer to Paris by about fifteen miles. His popularity increased daily, as did the flow of disciples, now only too eager to 'make a day of it' by walking to and from the village of Corbeil, the Opposition Headquarters. The roads and lanes echoed to the sound of youthful voices, with the clash of dialectical rapiers and the din of logic-chopping.

The strain of holding his own in the learned world, even though he had hitherto proved so successful, soon told upon Abelard's health, and he was obliged to retire to Brittany. He stayed in seclusion, though not in idleness, for some years. When he returned to the fray, he found William of Champeaux in retirement too, probably because he felt that his fighting days were over. Nevertheless the old man continued to teach Rhetoric in the priory of St Victor, and thither Abelard used to pay occasional visits, no doubt with the object of continuing the heckling he had employed to such effect in Paris. This time he was no less successful. Indeed, he succeeded better than ever. One day, to the astonishment of the learned world, William of Champeaux—it does credit to his intellectual honesty—announced that, after due reflection, he had decided to change his mind upon the subject of Universals. That he agreed wholeheartedly with Abelard he would not admit; but it was clear to everybody that his change of viewpoint was, if not a surrender to Conceptualism, then at least a compromise with it. Abelard's reputation soared. So did his ambition. Claiming the Chair at Notre Dame as part of the spoils of victory, Abelard actually occupied it for a brief period before being ejected by William's friends. To Paris he had come, however, and at Paris he intended to stay: and so, as he later wrote, 'we pitched our camp'—the expression is more than justified—'on the hill of St Geneviève.'[1]

Here stood an abbey already famous, or infamous, for the independent views and free behaviour of its inmates. Later critics and puritans spoke scathingly of the wealth, merriment and goodliving of the monks, who appeared to be on excellent terms with the 'cannonesses' of the nearby convent. In Abelard's time, the place was merely a trifle bohemian—a characteristic for which the locality (the modern 'Latin Quarter') is still distinguished. Abelard's temperament found just the stimulus there that it needed, though not for very long. As he was

[1] *i.e.*, where the Lycée Henri Quatre stands today.

again on the point of scoring a dialectical victory over the orthodox teachers of Notre Dame, his mother summoned him to Pallet, this time to inform him of her resolve to adopt the religious life following her husband's decision to enter a monastery.

When, in somewhat sadder mood, Abelard returned to Paris, he hesitated to resume the controversies for which he had now become famous throughout Europe. Instead he began to devote himself to the detailed study of theology. His motives are not easy to analyse. He may have been seeking ecclesiastical preferment. He may have been genuinely 'converted', though he was not known to be anything but a believer. Possibly he considered it wise to become master of a subject about which his orthodoxy was beginning to be questioned. He knew that his enemies, who were multiplying in high places, had only to trump up a charge of heresy against him for his career to be changed from success to failure. If once he were to learn the rules of the theological game, he was confident of his ability to beat the so-called professionals at it. Soon he was lecturing to enthralled audiences at Laon, and proving a match for his master, Bishop Anselm, who promptly suspended him.

But it was too late. By universal acclamation he was appointed to the Chair at Notre Dame, which had now fallen vacant. His magnificent oratory, his ready wit, his huge learning (not by any means confined to the works of Christian writers), his fine presence, his high birth—all these combined to make him an object of attraction more dazzling even than a royal personage. Thousands of students assembled to hear him (the great expansion of Paris during this century is said to have been due chiefly to the increased student population), while his reputation as a 'wizard', 'smiter', 'Proteus', and 'Prometheus' grew among those who had never entered a lecture hall in their lives. For he seems to have exercised a general fascination over women as well as men.

Did success turn his head? To some extent it may have done so. In his later autobiography, he speaks of being swollen with vanity and pride, thinking himself to be 'the only philosopher in the world', and fearing 'no further menace' to his position. Certainly he was not given to underestimating his abilities, or he would not have risen to the position of first teacher in France. There is no evidence to suggest that his private life was anything but blameless. Had it been otherwise, he would undoubtedly have added this to the other items of reproach which he later enumerated in an agony of self-chastisement. If we take into account the moral standards of the time, even in respect of the ecclesiastical hierarchy, he might almost be considered a paragon of virtue. Later writers, and also some of Abelard's reputedly pious contemporaries (including St Bernard of Clairvaux), represent Abelard as consistently a reprobate in both thought and deed. But the language of abuse at this time was much inflated, and intellectual heresy was usually associated with depraved conduct.

Possibly because he had devoted so much energy to intellectual matters, the emotional side of his nature seems to have lacked sufficient outlet. He was now in his thirty-ninth year, an age when many of the 'great lovers' of history have begun to weary of successive infatuations; but we gather that Abelard had hitherto known no woman either casually or in consequence of an 'affair'. A man of his tastes and temperament was not likely to fall victim to common women; but amid so much flattery and attention from female society, it was to be expected that he should become increasingly susceptible to feminine charm. The remarkable circumstance in Abelard's life was not so much that he should suddenly have fallen in love, as that the object of his love should have happened to combine precisely the qualities, mental and physical, that he most admired. Héloïse, even when Abelard first beheld her among the concourse of his students, was intellectually the match for all the women and most of the men of her day; she was also possessed of dignity and beauty. Even if not so dazzling as later writers have tried to suggest, she was clearly a woman of more than usual attraction.

A girl of about eighteen, Héloïse had received her education at the Benedictine nunnery at Argenteuil, near St Denis, and also from her uncle (or reputed uncle), Canon Fulbert. We do not know precisely where or when she and Abelard first met: possibly a meeting between two such paragons of learning was deliberately arranged by parties wholly innocent of ulterior motives. All we have to go upon is Abelard's own confession that within a short time of seeing her he was 'wholly afire with love of the maid'; that he sought her company; and that finally, to cultivate her further acquaintance and no doubt with the express object of winning her hand, he went to lodge at her uncle's house. The initial arrangement was that Abelard should receive board and lodging in return for a small sum, and a few hours' weekly instruction of Fulbert's niece.

Closer contact served but to increase Abelard's ardour. He admits that neither the expression of his affection nor the welcome it found in the heart of his pupil were long disguised. As he later put it, their lessons began to consist more of 'kisses than theses', being maintained with a thoroughness and regularity that his public discourses soon lacked. There were raised eyebrows, then whispered communications, and finally open gossip. No longer able to listen to his voice expounding divinity and logic, the swarm of pupils and admirers, crowding to Fulbert's house, rehearsed the songs that the master now composed in honour of a woman of unparalleled virtue and sweetness. 'Every street, every house, resounded with my name,' wrote Héloïse long years after.

Proud to be associated with the 'wizard of the Schools' and to have secured for his niece such a unique teacher, Fulbert may have mistaken the tenor of the public gossip; or he may have been unusually stupid. One day, probably as the result of a friendly tip, he suddenly realized what was taking place under his own roof. His fury knew no bounds. Abelard was driven from the house, and forbidden readmission. The association was to terminate at once.

So, indeed, it might have ended—at least for the time—had not Héloïse, seeking for an explanation of her condition from a treatise of Aristotle, realized that she was pregnant. Judging from the way in which she managed, by secret means, to convey the intelligence to her lover, this discovery delighted her beyond measure.

No doubt it would have delighted Abelard too, if he had had time to examine his feelings; but the expulsion from Fulbert's house had placed him in a dilemma. To marry Héloïse was to risk his whole career: for although Abelard was not at that time an ordained priest, it would seem that he was intent, as already hinted, upon ecclesiastical preferment. That Héloïse herself, a prisoner in the house of an outraged guardian, should regard marriage as the most desirable way out, seems obvious enough. But apparently she did not. This fact has puzzled both historians and psychologists. In spite of her strict upbringing and undoubtedly virtuous character (judging from her manner of life before and after the love-episode), she declared until the end of her days that marriage with Abelard was, in her opinion, less honourable a status than that of remaining his mistress. She admits it openly, and Abelard himself so reports it.

Directly he learnt of her condition, Abelard decided to take action. One night he managed to remove Héloïse from her uncle's house and carry her off, in nun's attire, to his home at Pallet. It appears that they stayed there together, free and undisturbed for the first time, until Abelard felt that some sort of reconciliation with Fulbert was worth attempting. He set out, alone this time, for Paris; but needless to say, he greatly overestimated Fulbert's willingness to let bygones be bygones.

The suggestion put forward by Abelard for Fulbert's consideration was that a secret marriage should be arranged. Besides appealing to the sense of decorum of both, the idea opened the way to the resumption of Abelard's triumphal career. Fulbert appeared to be co-operative. But both parties had again reckoned without Héloïse. She objected outright to the proposal, preferring, as she put it, to be united with Abelard 'by love alone, not by the compulsion of the marriage vow': a sentiment from which the birth of her child in no way deflected her. In spite of her earnest entreaties and learned arguments (she instanced the married life of Socrates as a warning to every true philosopher), Abelard remained firm. They must return to Paris, be married, and endeavour to start life afresh. Héloïse finally assented. Leaving the child Astrolabe behind with Abelard's sister, they eventually arrived in the capital, where they were formally united in marriage, with Fulbert and a few trusted friends as witnesses.

The plan, having begun well, miscarried. With so many idle tongues wagging, it was necessary for husband and wife to meet rarely and in secret. Their nerves were rapidly becoming frayed when Fulbert, whom Héloïse had always distrusted, began to gossip about the marriage. Asked point-blank by friends whether or not she was Abelard's wife, Héloïse continued to deny the fact vehemently. Her attitude infuriated Fulbert and his former doting was exchanged for open abuse. Abelard could endure the tension no longer. He made another rescue attempt, this time carrying his wife away to the convent at Argenteuil, with which she had been familiar from her childhood days. Here she assumed the conventional habit of the Benedictine nuns, except for the veil.

Abelard admits that their relations continued during this period, as the discipline of the convent was lax; and such behaviour was not the most shocking that had been known to take place there. The same life of subterfuge continued, with few compensations for the couple apart from that of being temporarily out of Fulbert's clutches. In fact, however, no arrangement was better calculated to inflame Fulbert's wrath; for directly he learnt that Héloïse had been confined to a convent he jumped to the conclusion that Abelard, who had originally wished to keep his marriage secret, now desired to terminate it. He resolved to take revenge upon the man who had deceived and now proposed to dishonour him.

Finally he fixed upon a plan that would put an end, as he thought, to Abelard's association not merely with Héloïse but with any woman whom he had in mind to put in her place. He hired some desperadoes, squared Abelard's valet, and instructed them to gain access one night to Abelard's bedroom. There, as the unsuspecting man lay sleeping, they entered and brutally emasculated him. Short of actual murder, no more fiendish act could have been perpetrated. In a single night, Abelard's life—and indeed his whole personality—underwent a complete and permanent transformation.

It was natural that a blow of this nature should have plunged Abelard into the deepest anguish and despair. In an agony of repentance for sins committed and presumed to be receiving divine punishment, he decided to enter a monastery. This decision was understandable. Less understandable and praiseworthy was his desire that Héloïse, having once taken the nun's habit in dire emergency, should now take it in earnest and for good. The girl's distress was acute enough without this added imposition, since hers was a temperament not easily subdued. Nevertheless, as her love underwent no change in consequence of the forced change in her husband, she obeyed. At the final ceremony in the convent chapel, her closest friends made a last bid to prevent her taking the veil; but in vain. Approaching the altar to receive it from the Bishop, she recited not a prayer but the words of the heroine of Lucan:

> 'Why hapless did I wed,
> If this the fruit that my affection bore?
> Behold the penalty I now embrace
> For thy sweet sake!'

The idyll was at an end. Sombre tragedy followed, and continued more or less unrelieved until the end of Abelard's life. But it was a tragedy not without episodes of majesty, and the story of Abelard and Héloïse was more remarkable perhaps after they had gone their separate and solitary ways than when they were together.

For Abelard, life was to consist of one long battle with those who, fearing the power of a mind now concentrated upon questions of faith, sought more energetically than ever to silence and subdue him. For Héloïse, henceforth a figure of heroic dignity, the battle was primarily an interior one, of which we have some record in the brief confessions of her letters.

During his retirement in the abbey of St Denis, Abelard set to work upon a treatise entitled *De Trinitate*. He also began to lecture again, finding that his old skill had not deserted him, but that on the contrary he had acquired an added subtlety. The students flocked in as eagerly as ever; the authorities pricked up their ears with the same attentiveness. Two other works, *A Dialogue between a Philosopher, a Jew and a Christian,* and a treatise on the works of the Fathers called *Sic et Non* ('Yes and No') made their appearance, both being characterized by the same impulse to submit even the most subtle articles of Faith to the scrutiny of Reason. The latter works achieved a fair measure of popularity, but the great book on the *Trinity* attracted most attention of all. Indeed, it attracted so much attention that its author was summoned to Soissons to answer for some of the more daring statements that it contained. His enemies had at last succeeded in pinning him down. It was now for him to extricate himself.

Abelard had hoped that the Council of Soissons would become the scene of his triumph. He would show the world that his spirit, unlike his body, was far from being maimed. The event turned out differently. He had no opportunity to defend himself. The verdict was a foregone conclusion. Accused roundly of 'tri-theism' (*i.e.,* of believing in the separate deity of the Three Persons of the Trinity), he was compelled to consign his own book to the flames.

After a period of virtual confinement in the abbey of St Médard, not far from Soissons, Abelard was allowed to return to St Denis; but before long his enquiring mind rendered him so unpopular with the monks that he was again indicted for impiety and was obliged to flee the abbey. As a deserter, he incurred still further ecclesiastical displeasure, and in desperation he journeyed to Paris, hoping to find sufficient friends at court to shield him from the malice of his colleagues. Finally, after appearing at what amounted to a mock-trial, with Louis the Fat presiding, he was 'pardoned' on condition that he consented to adopt a hermit life. This at least spelt freedom: and freedom was all that he desired.

In complete solitude, living in two huts and a small oratory built entirely by hand, Abelard spent a period of comparative rest at Nogent-sur-Seine, feeling that he had at last escaped from the persecution of the righteous. Again he was sadly mistaken. Directly his whereabouts became known, the influx of students and disciples began as usual, and the hermitage soon became the centre of a thriving community. And as his reputation was gradually rekindled, so the rumours spread of further heresies and forbidden practices. 'I had one enemy—echo,' wrote the distracted man in his later *Memoirs*. These rumours came to the ears of Bernard of Clairvaux and Norbert of Prémontré, stern watchers over orthodoxy. Abelard, his peace of mind once more broken and fearing another Council or synod, contemplated flight from the

'Paraclete', as his hermitage was called; he even toyed with the idea of deserting Christendom altogether and fleeing to the realm of the Crescent.

Then, as luck would seem to have it, he was offered a way of escape. The monks of the monastery of St Gildas in Brittany, having lost their abbot, invited Abelard to fill his place. He accepted. At the same time a happy thought struck him. He would install Héloïse, now Prioress of Argenteuil, in the Paraclete hermitage, which was his own legal property. In 1131, he was instrumental in raising her to the status of Abbess. Whenever he could, he visited the flourishing community, glad to absent himself from his own boorish flock at St Gildas, where, feeling the atmosphere appropriate, he had begun to write the *Story of My Calamities* for the consolation (as he tells us) of a friend.

It has been suggested that this remarkable document may have been written in the hope that its perusal by influential persons would lead to the author's restoration to favour. Whatever the truth of the contention, the MS. was circulated widely: and into whose hands should it eventually fall but those of the gentle Abbess of the Paraclete. Hence the famous *Letters* of Abelard and Héloïse, the only classic example of love-letters written from wife to husband after so broken a marriage. In this correspondence, first with reserve and later with a torrent of passion, Héloïse reveals the true state of her heart after years of self-abnegation and devotion to duty: and it is a heart that has not changed.

> I have not looked to the marriage-bond or dowry; I have not even yearned to satisfy my own will and pleasure, but thine, as thou well knowest. The name of wife may be the holier and more approved; but the name of friend—nay, mistress or concubine, if thou wilt suffer it—has always been the sweeter to me . . . I should deem it more precious and more honourable to be thy mistress than to be the queen of a Cæsar.

So wrote the Reverend Mother, Abbess of the Paraclete, to the man whom she knew to be incapable of the response she still dared to solicit. Abelard's replies, though not what she craved, show some measure of alarm at the violent emotions that he has caused to awaken and urge her to fix her thoughts upon other matters. The correspondence ends on a calmer note; and we find a concluding epistle addressed by Abelard to 'the virgins of the Paraclete' in which, having enclosed a number of hymns and sermons of his own composition (very different hymns, we may suspect, from those secular outpourings of his youth), he congratulates them upon having a 'mother' who is versed in Latin, Greek, and Hebrew. He also sends detailed and reasoned replies to forty-two 'problems of Héloïse' derived from the Scriptures. Some of these have a very modern ring.

The atmosphere of St Gildas becoming intolerable and even dangerous, Abelard left the abbey; and we are not certain of his movements until in 1136 he turns up once more at Paris. Again he is the centre of attraction. He finds the ancient skill unimpaired. And, as of old, he cannot keep his mouth shut. It is Bernard of Clairvaux who once more raises the alarm. Since no amount of admonition will serve to restrain him, the heretic must be finally crushed. This time Bernard is in deadly earnest. He sends for Abelard's new works—his *Theologia Christiana* and his *Commentary on the Epistle to the Romans*—studies them, decides they are the voice of Satan, and resolves to obtain Papal condemnation of their reprobate author. Arraigned before the Council of Sens in June 1141, Abelard himself decides to appeal to Rome, and sets off to obtain justice at the hands of the Supreme Pontiff. On 16 July, probably as a result of Bernard's letters of denunciation, Abelard is excommunicated at St Peter's, and condemned to imprisonment.

On the way to Rome, however, Abelard, now much broken in health, stopped at the great Benedictine abbey of Cluny, where the abbot, Peter the Venerable, received him with great kindness and at once interceded with Bernard (who had not yet published in France the Pope's indictment), so that the latter finally agreed to stay the persecution of his already failing enemy. Probably he was softened by an *Apology* which Abelard wrote to him from Cluny, where he also wrote a final and most tender letter to his 'sister Héloïse, once dear to me in the world, and now most dear in Christ'.

So Abelard became a monk at Cluny and passed out of men's sight. On 21 April, 1142, aged sixty-three, he died. Héloïse, who supervised his interment at the Paraclete, survived her husband by twenty years. Many centuries afterwards, the remains of these two courageous souls were removed; and in 1817 their ashes, commingled, were buried at the cemetery of Père Lachaise, on the outskirts of Paris, where they have since been preserved. In one of his last letters Abelard had written: 'I hope you will be willing, when you have finished this mortal life, to be buried near me. Your cold ashes need then fear nothing, and my tomb shall be then the more rich and renowned.' The original inscription reads as follows:

> Here, under the same stone, repose, of this monastery the founder, Peter Abelard, and the first abbess, Héloïse, heretofore in study, genius, love, inauspicious marriage, and repentance, now, as we hope, in eternal happiness, united. Peter died April 21st, 1142. Héloïse, May 17th, 1164.

16

Moslem and Jewish Philosophers and the Revival of Aristotelianism

In our account of the life and work of Aristotle, we have emphasized the extent to which Moslem thinkers were responsible for stimulating a new interest in the works of the master. Today we may tend to underestimate the part played by Orientals in precipitating a renaissance of Christian thought in the West. Between the death of Mohammed (632) and the tenth century, the Crescent had extended its Empire from Spain on the one hand to Turkestan on the other. This expansion without parallel in history of a militant religion was accompanied by a cultural renaissance no less remarkable. In course of time, the old division between the Christian West and the Moslem East lost its sharpness; for certain areas of Asia remained and still remain Christian, while Islam extended its influence to the borders of France. Greek thought infiltrated into the Orient by way of towns such as Edessa (the modern Urfa in Turkey), which was a veritable clearing-house of Hellenic culture. Baghdad was likewise a flourishing cultural centre where Oriental Christians engaged in Arabic translations of works on Greek science. In 832, the enlightened Abbasid Caliph, Al Mamoun, founded in that city a 'House of Wisdom': here learned doctors translated into Arabic the works of Plato, Aristotle, Euclid and Galen. At the heart of Islam there was an intellectual ferment which often brought about fierce conflict between the new spirit of enquiry and the upholders of Koranic orthodoxy. Men of learning proceeded to submit to the test of reason the most sacred articles of religion, thereby employing the pagan doctrines of Aristotle to disturb the consciences of the faithful. In general, the spirit of rationalism, often regarded as an exclusively Western product, proved a vital force in the Islamic world well before it began to play its part in the evolution of Christian theology.

Of the great Moslem students of Aristotle from whom the Western world derived profit, the most famous were Alkindi (*d.* 873), Alfarabi (*d.* 949), Avicenna (980–1037), doctor as well as philosopher, and finally Averroës (*b.* Cordova, 1126). Averroes, the 'Great Commentator', maintained that truth could be reached upon three separate planes: that of philosophy, which was in touch with absolute truth; that of religion, which sought to interpret truth in terms of mythical imagery; and that of ordinary common sense, which attained the truth through faith or natural piety. Origen, the Christian philosopher, had stated similar views several centuries earlier in relation to Christian thought.

The contribution of the Jews was no less important in assisting the emergence of the scientific spirit from within the bosom of religious mysticism and dogma. In Egypt, in Spain, in Morocco even, Jewish thought flourished, sometimes in close contact with Moslem thought, sometimes with that of Christianity or such pagan survivals as Neo-Platonism, rarely in isolation. The *Kabbala,* for instance, was in essentials the Jewish version of Neo-Platonic mysticism, in contrast to the Talmud, which was the orthodox commentary upon the Law. A most notable attempt to 'reconcile' science and philosophy with the teachings of the scriptures was made by a Jewish Rabbi, Maimonides, born (like Averroës) at Cordova in 1135. Maimonides likewise invoked the work of Aristotle, but for the purpose of giving rational basis to Holy Writ. He is thus the true precursor of Thomas Aquinas (1227–74), the greatest of the so-called 'Scholastic' philosophers.

The word 'scholasticism', which has been revived in our day, is frequently misunderstood. Scholasticism, as originally conceived, was not a dry quibbling about theological subtleties; it was an attempt, and on the whole a successful attempt, to demonstrate that Faith and Reason, Religion and Science, complemented each other. Previously, attempts had been made to demonstrate either that the two were opposed or that they were identical. Both arguments broke down. That St Thomas was able to effect a reconciliation (but not a compromise) was due to the extraordinary breadth of his mental outlook, his huge learning, and above all his sense of logic and precision, the latter being the fruit of a close study of Aristotle. Indeed, Scholasticism was the marriage between Christianity and Aristotelianism.

Today it is the practice of nations to 'export' their cultures, because each feels, rightly or wrongly, that it has something to give to the world. In the mediaeval period, it was rather the practice to 'import' culture, because in Europe at any rate the centre of culture was the Catholic Church, with its great and pervasive spiritual authority. The exaggeration of the mediaeval unity by some historians has given rise, especially in our day, to its belittlement by others; but to say that Europe was united by a common faith is not to say that it was free from dissension.

An international language manufactured from synthetic counters, such as has frequently been suggested in modern times as the cure for international misunderstanding, will fail of its purpose because it lacks roots; the international use of Latin in mediaeval times was based upon a common culture, uniting all Christians without distinction of nation or class. The mediaeval unity was an ideal unity, or a unity of ideals, from which there were in practice many departures; but at least the offender, in breaking the laws, knew that he was offending, the blasphemer that he was blaspheming, the heretic that he deserved the title of apostate. In this awareness, the orthodox structure was indirectly honoured and preserved. What politics divided, culture unified. And the unification of culture was made possible by a theology and philosophy which embraced, for the first and in some ways the last time, the whole of human experience.

17

St Thomas Aquinas

God is known through all things and yet apart from all things; and He is known through knowledge and through ignorance
Commentary on 'The Divine Names'

His Life

Thomas Aquinas was born in 1225 or 1227 at the castle of Rocca Secca, a few miles from the town of Aquino, after which he later took his name. Like Abelard, he came of noble stock. His father was Count of Aquino, a fief within the kingdom of Naples, and nephew of Frederick Barbarossa. His mother, Theodora of Theate, was descended from the old Norman Kings of Sicily. Thus Thomas came into the world blessed with every material advantage. Like Abelard in one other respect, he early signified his wish to renounce these inherited privileges and to devote himself exclusively to a religious calling.

Thomas's parents were resolved to give their son—the youngest and most promising of their seven sons—a thorough education. The youngster's uncle was Abbot of Monte Cassino, home of the Benedictine Order, and a name familiar to the present generation. To the care of this wise and learned man, Thomas was entrusted at the tender age of five. He did not prove exactly a brilliant pupil, if by brilliant we mean 'bright' or 'quick-witted'; he was rather a plodding, receptive, assiduous type of student, who, if we are to believe contemporary witnesses, never forgot anything once he had learnt it. Both his parents and his teachers were anxious that he should enter the University of Naples, for they felt that a great career lay before him either in the field of learning or in the ecclesiastical hierarchy; and at that period the vocation of scholarship, like that of the priesthood, was held in far higher esteem than it is today. So to Naples Thomas was sent at the age of fourteen.

By the time that Thomas Aquinas had reached the age of sixteen, his mind was quite made up on the subject of what he wanted to do. He wanted to acquire learning; but he wanted to acquire it in obscurity. Now a robust, large-limbed lad, almost a giant in stature, friendly in manner but not a social 'mixer' in the ordinary sense, he was neither unhappy nor misplaced at the University; but the kind of fraternity for which he longed was not that of scholars but that of the devout.

From the first moment of his acquaintance with it, the white and black habit of the Dominican Order, then commonly seen in the streets of Naples, had exercised a strong fascination over him: not for its austere appearance, but rather for the ideals for which it stood—chastity and poverty. A life of humble obscurity in the service of a Mendicant Order was not, it need hardly be said, the kind of ecclesiastical career to which his parents, in planning his future, had looked forward. On the contrary, they fancied him as a rich and powerful Church dignitary, achieving rapid and well-merited promotion, and perhaps ending up as the Supreme Pontiff at Rome. He had influence; he had the brains; if necessary, he had the means. Aquinas knew this. But he also knew his own mind. And so, without divulging his intention to his family, he quietly took the vow of mendicancy and joined the Dominican Order in 1244.

When his mother discovered what he had done, she was at first surprised, though not perhaps so displeased as her husband; but when she later found that she was not to be permitted to visit her son, her approval turned to open hostility. In banning visitors, the Dominicans were ensuring that their protégé should not be persuaded (as if he could be persuaded) to change his mind about his vocation; but Theodora was resolved not to allow them to monopolize the son upon whom she had set such hopes. Thomas had brothers in the upper ranks of the army of Frederick II. When their mother confided to them her fears about Thomas, they unanimously decided to remove him by force from the clutches of the monks. Although they succeeded in waylaying him on the road to Paris, they failed to shake his decision to remain attached to the Order. For more than a year they kept him a close prisoner in the castle of Rocca Secca. He did not object. He used the seclusion and ample leisure at his disposal for unremitting study of the Scriptures.

In trying to dissuade him from adopting the monastic life, his family had merely succeeded in making him more of a hermit than ever. Indeed, some of their attempts to divert him from his purpose were both frivolous and stupid. On one occasion they even resorted to the expedient of introducing an attractive and flashily-dressed young woman into his cell. The inmate, who was for once roused to fury, seized a flaming brand from the fire and drove her screaming from the room: after which, with two mighty strokes, he marked the door with the sign of the cross. This particular stratagem was not repeated.

In the end his mother repented of her thoughtless, if excusable, behaviour. Her son was so obviously fitted to be a hermit-scholar that it was better, as she now realized, to enable him to follow his inclinations in freedom rather than in servitude. One day, with her connivance, he managed to let himself down from the castle window by means of a rope, and make his way back to his Dominican friends. Outwitted, his brothers took no action. Besides, Thomas was as strong as an ox—a 'dumb ox', as he was called by one of his masters; and they did not fancy provoking him further. After a brief spell in Naples, he set out, this time unmolested, for Paris again, where his fame as a scholar soon grew.

In 1248, accompanied by Johannes Teutonicus, Thomas took the road to Cologne. The intention of the two scholars was to put themselves under the tuition of Albert of Bollstadt (1206–80). Albert, later named 'The Great', was a scholar of distinct originality. He was convinced that the difficulties encountered by the theological thought of his time could be solved only by reference to the work of Aristotle—that is, the 'complete' Aristotle. Perhaps the 'greatness' of Albert of Bollstadt lay in the fact that, while seeking to resurrect a pagan thinker, he lost hold of no single element of the Christian faith. For Thomas and Johannes the journey to Cologne was both long and tedious; it took them three months to accomplish. No sooner had Thomas begun to receive instruction from Albert, however, than the latter, discounting his pupil's bovine appearance, realized that he had met a genius. Master and pupil soon fell into that most perfect of scholastic relationships in which the 'roles' were reversible at any moment. In Albert, Thomas recognized a spiritual leader as well as a teacher. In Thomas, Albert recognized an original and even daring thinker as well as a disciple. Together they would effect the 'conversion' of Aristotle, defying the official ban on his works of 1215.

Not merely did Albert and Thomas recognize each other's ability; the university and other authorities at Cologne could not but perceive how ably they worked in unison. Universities in those days often needed capable spokesmen for both scholastic and diplomatic reasons; and the relationship between scholarship and diplomacy was a great deal closer than it is now, owing to the importance of maintaining theological orthodoxy. Thus it came about in 1245 that the Chapter of the Dominican Order at Cologne dispatched Albert and Thomas on a kind of academic mission to Paris, still the great centre of learning of Europe. Here they remained for as long as three years, during which time Thomas not merely eclipsed his master in reputation as a teacher but proved himself a great intellectual force among the youth of his day. Many other philosophers have held their audience spellbound with original and startling 'ideas'. Thomas Aquinas acquired (and still maintains) his great reputation by the exposition and demonstration of clear, dry, logical propositions concerning Nature, man and God, presented without verbal flourishes, purple passages, or personal allusions, and set out like a legal treatise or a scientific blueprint. So much for the 'reactionary' influence of Aristotle on the mediaeval mind!

Although his stay in Paris was successful beyond his expectations, he returned in 1248 without having had any degrees or honours conferred upon him. There was still much prejudice in high quarters about members of the Mendicant Orders. In 1252, however, he was encouraged to set out once more for Paris, ostensibly in order to obtain the official academic recognition that he deserved, but primarily in order to establish an independent school there. From this course he was soon diverted by a problem which seemed at the time to be of greater importance, if not for Thomas Aquinas, then at least for the Dominican Order. A bitter quarrel had broken out between the Mendicant Orders and the University of Paris concerning precisely that 'recognition' over which Thomas had already experienced a limited rebuff in the case of his own academic honours.

The Dominicans had decided, after careful consideration, to appeal to the Pope. This was a bold and usually expensive step, and no organization was advised to embark upon it unless it were either sure of its case or confident in the skill of the man it had selected as emissary. The Dominicans were doubly convinced. First of all, they had a good case; and secondly, they had a spokesman whose ability was universally recognized, not least by those who were called upon to put it to the test. For when the Dominicans asked themselves whom they should send to intercede with Pope Alexander IV, they had no hesitation in choosing the 'dumb ox', Thomas Aquinas.

Thomas's plea to the Pope was successful: so successful, indeed, that he was able to return in triumph to Paris in 1256, to be granted, without the least grudge on the part of the authorities, the degrees of Licentiate and Master in Theology. These honours were conferred in recognition of his brilliant teaching and theological studies, which already included a Commentary on the Bible and on the *Sentences,* or works of the Fathers, and the treatise *On Being and Essence* which scholars now regard as the key to his whole philosophical system.

Between 1259 and 1268, Thomas Aquinas, now occupying a status similar to that of Abelard in his day, lectured and composed treatises upon all the major theological topics of the age. He was now an international figure. To him, kings, prelates and men of learning referred the problems that confronted them, putting the great man to the kind of use that is not common in our day, when wise men write books in the hope of creating an audience or 'public' rather than in the knowledge that such an audience is ready to hand. Some modern philosophers—Earl Russell is the latest offender—enjoy pointing out the triviality and frivolity of some of the problems with which Aquinas concerned himself; but this is to forget both the origin of most of these problems and the necessity that Aquinas was under to deal politely and diplomatically with his correspondents or interlocutors. Most of these were sincere but some were clearly indulging in the favourite mediaeval game of heresy-hunting. In any case, the majority of Aquinas's pronouncements were masterpieces of diplomatic skill, and worthy to be compared, at least in their form, with the more celebrated utterances of the classical oracles.

When asked, for instance, whether the names of the elect were written by the hand of God in heaven and whether there was an equivalent list in hell, he answered simply: 'For all I can see, it does not seem to be true, but there is no harm done in saying it.' Given conundrums of such relative puerility, this was a typical reply. Naturally he was frequently consulted upon questions of more serious import. Hugh II of Cyprus requested him to lay down the duties of a ruler; the Duchess of

Brabant, faced with an age-old problem, consulted him upon the best way of handling Jewish subjects; the Pope repeatedly sought his advice upon matters of theology (it was at the request of Gregory X that he wrote the great *Summa Contra Gentiles,* as a compendium of arguments to be used against infidels). He had indeed become a kind of oracle. And in some quarters he is still treated as one.

To have written thirty large volumes in the space of forty-eight years was an achievement which, taking into account his heavy public duties and frequent journeys abroad, is almost without parallel. But Thomas Aquinas possessed the type of mind that is never at rest. His occupation was thought—directed, energetic thought, not reverie; his mysticism was a discipline, not a relaxation. His one aim was not to 'lose himself' in the divine but to find himself in it. There are anecdotes, indeed, concerning his absent-mindedness (a form, as Chesterton pointed out, of presence of mind). One day, it is recorded, he was dining with St Louis, King of France, in a great company of nobles and ecclesiastics. The problems of the *Summa Theologiæ* were at that period uppermost in his mind. After remaining for some time in a fit of abstraction, he suddenly pounded the table with his heavy fist and exclaimed: 'That settles the Manichees!' His companions, much embarrassed, nudged him to recall him to his outer senses; but St Louis, with great tact, put everyone at ease by summoning a secretary and begging Aquinas to record, for the benefit of Christendom, the idea that had occurred to him.

During these productive years, Aquinas taught at such centres of learning as Ostia, Viterbo, Anagni, Perugia, Bologna, and Rome itself. Pope Urban IV, who welcomed his presence, was determined to raise him to high office in the Church. It was not common that a scholar of such profound learning and original mind could be relied upon to uphold, whatever the problem under discussion, the orthodox point of view; it was less common still to find that, after such rigorous and logical enquiries, orthodoxy appeared more firmly entrenched than ever. Yet that was precisely the effect of Aquinas's analytical researches: he succeeded, as few have succeeded since, in enlarging men's capacity for orthodoxy. When, later on, the French philosopher Descartes set out to apply the sceptical method to every sphere of thought, he found that most theological writings failed to stand up to the strain imposed upon them. But there was one exception: the works of Thomas Aquinas. St Thomas appeared to have an answer to everything, for he had thought of every possible objection, pushed through it, and made his way out the other side.

Although every inducement was offered Thomas to accept high office, and although he undoubtedly possessed gifts of administration and leadership as far above the average as he excelled his fellows in scholarship, he steadfastly refused to seek such preferment. No doubt it was with his own case in mind that he remarked in his Sermon for the Feast of St Martin that the 'episcopal state, for all its greatness, is not to be sought out; if a man says "I want to be a learned man, that afterwards I may be the wise ruler of a great church", his plan is not good. Augustine says: "It is not fitting for a man to aspire to that high place which is needed for the governance of the people, even though he may occupy it fittingly ... If no man put upon you the burden of this charge, give your time to the search for, and the gathering of, truth."'

In 1268, we find him back once more in Paris. During the next few years he was engaged in high controversy with a number of persons of whose growing influence the Church went in fear; for a heretic, especially an eloquent heretic, is the most plausible of men. There were in fact two sorts of heretic whose errors Aquinas was invited, and indeed urged, to confute: those, like Siger of Brabant, who followed the ideas of Averroës to the point of placing the authority of Aristotle above that of divine truth, and those, like some of the Franciscans, who adopted a one-sided Augustinianism and thereby upset the balance between Faith and Reason. Both in effect were covertly destroying that unity and harmony of thought which the scholastic doctors were striving to preserve. Out of these resounding controversies issued that gigantic synthesis of Christian thought and apologetic, the *Summa Theologiæ,* in which Aquinas constructed a 'cathedral' of reason as perfect and comprehensive as the edifices of stone that were raised, by a like impulse, in his century.

Feeling that their champion had had enough of disputation, the Dominican Order recalled him—it is said at the wish of the King of Sicily, brother of St Louis of France—to teach once more at Naples. But a man's reputation, once securely established, will not let him be. Summoned by Pope Gregory X to the General Council of Lyon in 1274, Aquinas, accompanied by Reginald a brother of his Order, set out on muleback to put his wisdom once again at the service of the Church. This time his task was that of reconciling the differences between the Greek and Latin Churches, and also of organizing another Crusade. Although Aquinas was thoroughly overworked and already ailing, such business could not be neglected and he refused to send excuses. When they had reached the castle of Magenza, however (the property of his niece, the Countess Ceccano), the doctor underwent a sudden change. He fell into what his companions and hosts called 'an ecstasy' in which he remained absorbed for a considerable time; and when he came to himself, almost as if he were revisiting the earth, his health was observed to have broken down beyond restoration.

Of his failing condition he was as conscious as his friends; and he at once expressed an earnest wish to be allowed to die in a house belonging to his Order. An attempt was made to comply with this desire; but the party that escorted him, realizing that further travel would be useless, decided to stop at the Cistercian abbey of Fossa Nuova near Terracina, where he died on 7 March, 1274. Until the last moment, except for periods of rapt meditation, he was in full possession and exercise of his faculties. A demon for work, if for nothing else, he continued to dictate to his secretary a commentary upon *The Song of Songs,* which his hosts had requested him to undertake. He had reached the passage beginning '*Filiae Jerusalem dicite dilecto meo, quia prae amore morior*' ('I charge you, O daughters of Jerusalem, if ye find my beloved, that ye tell him that I am sick of love') when he suddenly collapsed and died within a few minutes.[1]

At the time of his death, the fame of Thomas Aquinas had become so widespread that different Orders quarrelled fiercely for the possession of his mortal remains. The chief dispute was between the Dominicans and the Cistercians; and this undignified squabble, so alien to the spirit of the man over whom it had arisen, was still continuing when, fifty years later, Thomas was canonized by Pope John XXII. Nor was the dispute over the body finally settled until Urban V, issuing a special Bull in 1368, ordained that the saint's remains should be handed over to the Dominicans of Toulouse. At Toulouse stood the mother church of the Dominican Order. Even so, the surrender was not complete: to the Convent of St Jacques at Paris, where both Thomas and his master Albert had once taught, an arm was presented.

More than two centuries after his canonization, Pope Pius V proclaimed Thomas Aquinas 'Fifth Doctor of the Church' (1567), thereby making his festival equal in rank with that of the four Latin Fathers, Ambrose, Augustine, Jerome and Gregory. Not until the nineteenth century, however, did the Roman Church pronounce the 'Thomist' philosophy to be the basis of Catholic theological teaching. Today, both Catholic and non-Catholic philosophers recognize in the enormous achievement of the 'Angelic Doctor' (as he came to be called) the most complete synthesis of speculation concerning the natural and spiritual world that has yet been constructed. Just as Dante had referred to Aristotle as 'the master of those who know', so also he referred to Aquinas, whom he naturally placed higher in status than Aristotle, as a 'flame of heavenly wisdom'. It is therefore fitting that at the close of Dante's journey, as unfolded in the third part of the *Divine Comedy,* both Thomas and Albert should be encountered among those nearest to the Divine Presence: 'I was of the lambs of the sacred flock,' Aquinas is made to say, 'that Dominic leadeth upon the way where is good fattening if there be no straying. This, who most neighboureth me upon the right, brother and master was to me, and he was Albert of Cologne, I Thomas of Aquino' (*Paradiso,* X, 94–99). Thus, while Beatrice is the guide upon whom Dante relies during his final journey, Thomas Aquinas and St Bernard are the real successors of Virgil, in that they fulfil the function of interpreter of the spiritual mysteries into which Dante is being initiated.

To the Middle Ages, the intellect was not a dead, lifeless instrument, but a light to wisdom and faith. Consequently, Aquinas, the philosopher and poet (he wrote some very beautiful hymns, of which the most famous is that contained in his Office for the Feast of Corpus Christi, written at the request of Urban IV), represents for Dante the

[1] After his death a rumour began to circulate that Aquinas had been poisoned by Charles of Anjou. Dante, who accepted Aquinas as his philosophic master, apparently believed this charge, for in the 20th Canto of the *Purgatorio* (line 67) he writes:

'Carlo venne in Italia, e, per ammenda, Vittima fe' di Curradino; e poi ripinse al ciel Tommoso, per ammenda.'

'Charles came to Italy, and, for amends, made a victim of Conradin; and then thrust Thomas back to heaven, for amends.'

human reason at its highest level of perfection. The philosophies of a later age, in which Reason is contrasted with Sense, Instinct or Intuition (as if the latter alone possessed warmth, life and radiance), would have been as unintelligible to Dante as to Aquinas himself.

His Thought

We have said that the aim of Scholasticism was to demonstrate the harmony or compatibility between Reason and Faith. What St Thomas succeeded in doing was not merely to prove such compatibility but to codify all knowledge in the light of it. Being an exceedingly careful and precise thinker, he avoids the pitfalls into which so many religious philosophers have sunk: he seeks not to 'spiritualize' everything, but, by recognizing what his modern disciple Maritain has termed the 'primacy of the spiritual', to define with accuracy the boundaries and 'rights' of the natural realm. Studying Aquinas for the first time, modern thinkers have been surprised and impressed to find that, austere and high-minded man though he was, he fully recognized the part played in human conduct and motive by such natural forces as sex. What he did not do was to attribute to such impulses a power and supremacy out of all proportion to their nature.

With the exception of the sermons, hymns and devotional works, the writings of St Thomas are composed upon a pattern which the ordinary reader may find a trifle uninviting: either they are short essays or *opuscula* upon a particular philosophical problem, which is 'argued out' much like a problem in mathematics, or they take the form of ten-volume treatises, divided into sections and subsections and resembling a legal digest rather than a work of literary exposition. Hence the student who—fired by what he has heard of the 'majesty' and 'profundity' of the Angelic Doctor—sets out to peruse what he actually wrote, will soon find himself wading through pages of syllogisms and propositions without encountering a single brilliant metaphor or anecdote; still less will he come upon anything resembling a personal confession or *cri de cœur*. Aquinas is a thinker; Augustine was a thinker who happened also to be a great literary artist. Hence those who refuse to study anything that cannot be 'read as literature' (which usually means read for its emotional rather than its intellectual appeal) will compare the humanity and warmth of Augustine with the cold, passionless intellectuality of Aquinas. The comparison is unjust. Aquinas is not without passion, but he is passionate in a different way from Augustine. And we know that the Thomist philosophy can inspire passion in others, for there is the *Divine Comedy* to prove it.

Not merely is the *form* of St Thomas's philosophy unfamiliar to most modern students; its *content* is also. As a result of certain developments of modern thought usually labelled 'idealist', philosophy has come to be regarded in many quarters as a vague, abstract, ethereal study, quite beyond the mental grasp of ordinary and (it is sometimes added) normal people. With St Thomas, philosophy was not like that at all. He begins at the beginning. We know something, and a thing is what we know; to deny that we have any reliable knowledge, as the sceptics do, is itself to make an affirmation and therefore to climb out of scepticism forthwith.

Aquinas follows Aristotle in asserting that the 'form' is that which gives being to a thing and makes it what it is; further, that all forms are in some way linked with matter, except the form of God, the Form of Forms. Thus we come to know God by and through the world of matter, which manifests a hierarchy of Forms; and since the more perfect a form is the more it increases its individuality, God is the supreme unity and supreme individual at once. For St Thomas, the natural sphere has both meaning and purpose. He is not the kind of philosopher who claims to know God in some direct fashion, and whose primary task is therefore to explain away the existence or 'illusion' of Matter.

St Thomas held that the human mind was committed to a standard which prevented our intellect from being converted into something different, and possibly mischievous. That standard was Reason. In the same way, the human will was committed to a standard which, as long as it remained uppermost, preserved the will as a free instrument. That standard was the Good. The onset of sin was due entirely to our natural and sensual nature rising up and suspending the will's operations. St Thomas refused to entertain the paralysing notion which Augustine came to embrace with excessive fervour: namely, that human souls were predestined to salvation or damnation. So great was his respect for Reason, and so ample his conception of it, that he held the Divine Will itself to be motivated by Reason. If there were any predestination to sin, it was not of the deterministic kind of Augustine; it was a moral predestination. The sinner ultimately comes to *choose* damnation. Otherwise it is not his sin that condemns him, but somebody else's; and that is to drift once more into the heresy of the Manichees.

Since the intellect necessarily has Reason for its guide, it can know and understand the world of nature without any illumination from outside; but as both the intellect and the world of nature are, as it were, orientated towards God, philosophy inevitably leads on to theology and is completed by it. Thus St Thomas wishes to apply his important (and in its origin Aristotelian) distinction between 'potentiality' and 'actuality' to every sphere of existence. Since nature is a hierarchy of Forms, each stage in the hierarchy is the 'form' of the stage next below it and the 'matter' of the stage next above it. Thus Matter is potential Spirit, the natural man a potential Christian, philosophy a potential theology, and the State a material version of the Church.

St Thomas did not complete the *Summa Theologiæ*. Great master of synthesis and codification as he was, he was content to leave his finest work unfinished, not because of age (for he died comparatively young), nor because of the sudden visitation of death, nor because of the magnitude of the task—he would often employ four secretaries at a time, dictating to each a different composition. It was because of his consciousness that no single book and no single man could attempt to embrace all the mysteries of nature and God; and also because, as he confessed to those friends who questioned him on this point, 'all that he had written so far appeared to him as nothing in comparison with the wonderful things that God had been pleased to reveal to him recently'. Hence it is clear that those critics, and also those over-fervid adherents, who believe that Thomism represents a 'closed system' of philosophical theology, not to be added to and not to be subtracted from, are possessed with an idea foreign to the intention of its author.

National Museum, Naples

Socrates
*c.*469–399 BC

Spada Museum, Rome

Aristotle
384–322 BC

St Augustine
354–430

Botticelli

Sir Francis Bacon
1561–1626

René Descartes
1596–1650

Benedict de Spinoza
1632–1677

Immanuel Kant
1724–1804

Picture Post Library

Georg *Wilhelm Friedrich Hegel*
1770–1831

John Locke
1632–1704

George Berkeley
1685–1753

Leibniz
1646–1716

The Florence Gallery
Picture Post Library

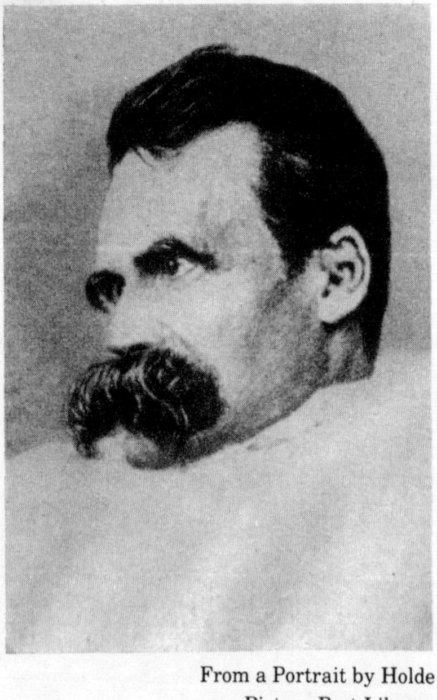

Friedrich Nietzsche
1844–1900

From a Portrait by Holde
Picture Post Library

18

Scholastic Decline and Scientific Advance

Those who have formed the impression that the Middle Ages were a time of order, unity and social stability have often been deeply distressed to discover, on inspecting the facts more closely, that this much-idealized period was in fact no less agitated, violent and confused than any other: with the result that they dismiss such works as Aquinas's *Summa Theologiæ* and Dante's *Divine Comedy* as exhibiting a purely fictitious unity, and end by transferring their affections to some other historical epoch, either before or since, which they proceed to endow with the characteristics of enlightenment or rebirth. Historical disillusion of this kind is due to a failure to perceive that every unity or order in society is engaged either in coming to be or in passing away; it never permanently crystallizes. Thus the mediaeval synthesis of reason and faith, Empire and Church, was at all times a precarious synthesis, it contained within itself, as every unity must do, the seeds of its own dissolution.

We soon pass, in other words, from the age of St Thomas to an age of open conflict and scepticism and infidelity. How was this change brought about? There were various long-term causes: the appalling strain and misery of the Hundred Years' War (1337–1453), the disintegration of the Empire, and the ecclesiastical schisms that deprived the Papacy of its power and reputation. Christendom was split up into principalities or nations; or rather, principalities or nations were the only authorities that survived the collapse of the European order. Not Christendoms but kingdoms became the centres of stability. We find lawyers beginning to argue seriously about the supremacy of the 'Royal power', so that kings (including the English Henry VIII) who wanted formal authority for their strengthened prerogatives found it already propounded for them by their own jurists. At the same time the prestige of the European universities was beginning to grow, chiefly perhaps because of their independent status and their wealth. At Oxford and at Chartres, for instance, distinguished schools of theology flourished, while the study of mathematics induced in such men as Robert Grosseteste, Bishop of Lincoln (1175–1253), and the monk Roger Bacon (*c.* 1210–1292) an appetite for exploring the secrets of the natural world which anticipated by several centuries the scientific humanism of the Renaissance.

Within the universities themselves a celebrated controversy arose, that between the 'Ancients' and the 'Moderns'. The Ancients clung to

Aristotle as the final authority upon most branches of knowledge; the Moderns, seeking to divest themselves of traditional theories, studied 'facts' alone. Duns Scotus (1274–1308), a Franciscan monk who was also professor of philosophy and theology at Oxford and a critic of Thomism, Raymond Lull (1234–1315) of Palma, theologian, naturalist, troubadour and devotee of Arabian mysticism, and finally William of Ockham (1280–1350), reflect each in their different ways the 'modern' spirit: and this tendency gave rise in turn to a new movement of Nominalism, according to which (as we saw in the work of Abelard) general terms or universals were held to be 'fictions'.

The rise of experiment and scepticism did not necessarily bring about a weakening of religious faith among the common people. While philosophy and theology, as today, were matters for the schools and universities, traditional beliefs and likewise superstitions maintained a firm hold upon the laity. But even traditional faith was stirring with new impulses, largely under the influence of the monks and friars. The aristocratic scholasticism of the intellectuals seems to have called into being, by way of reaction, a revival of mysticism and the cult of inner illumination. Eckhart (*d.* 1300) the Dominican, Tauler (*d.* 1361), one of Luther's teachers, Ruysbroeck of the Netherlands (1293–1381), and Thomas à Kempis (1379–1471), author of the famous *Imitation of Christ,* widened still further the division between Reason and Faith that opened as the influence of the Scholastic philosophy declined.

The reaction in so many quarters against Aristotelianism caused a revival of interest in Plato; but just as the Aristotle of the Middle Ages had been an Aristotle converted, without permission, to Catholicism, so the Platonism of the Renaissance, as manifested in the work of thinkers such as Nicholas of Cusa (1401–64), Marsilio Ficino (1433–99), Pico de la Mirandola (1463–94), and Paracelsus (1493–1541), was Platonism permeated with Christian ideas. Plato had regarded the natural world as a world of half-truths and imprecision; men such as Leonardo da Vinci (1452–1519) assumed that Nature obeyed uniform laws which the scientist could both descry and tabulate. This conception of an ordered, reasonable world was ultimately derived from Christian teaching: for God, having created the world, 'saw that it was good', *i.e.,* intelligible, harmonious and in conformity with the divine Logos or Reason.

The seeds of the new scientific spirit had been present, as we saw, in the speculations of the English Franciscan monk, Roger Bacon. In the work of his later namesake, Francis Bacon (1561–1626), Chancellor to King James I, the new spirit is in full bloom. Bacon was one of the first declared enemies of *verbiage*; he believed that science had hitherto been rendered sterile because it had occupied itself with definitions and distinctions of a purely abstract or verbal kind. Experiment was the clue to the *Advancement of Learning* (the title of one of his works). Having experimented, the task was to organize research, to promote team work among scientists; hence the *Novum Organum,* the new technique or logic designed to supersede that of Aristotle. To apply such a technique was to acquire control over Nature. Science for Bacon is not merely true knowledge; it is power. What Bacon asserted as a revolutionary fact we tend to accept today as a commonplace.

Bacon was a man of extraordinary learning and culture, as his *Essays* alone reveal; but he was an inspirer of ideas in others rather than a practitioner of what he preached. His experimentation was fragmentary and 'rule of thumb'. Dismissed from high office on a charge of corruption, the indefatigable old man died from a cold caught one day while carrying out an experiment in refrigeration by stuffing a chicken with snow.

Bacon had dreamed dreams of a New Atlantis, a scientific Brave New World; René Descartes worked out the theoretical principles upon which scientific progress has since largely been based. With the Cartesian philosophy, modern thought is born.

19

René Descartes

In our search for the direct road towards truth, we should busy ourselves with no object about which we cannot attain a certitude equal to that of the demonstrations of arithmetic and geometry.

His Life

Born at La Haye in Touraine on 31 March, 1596, Descartes was the third son of a doctor and of the daughter of a law officer of Poitiers.

His family included numerous men of learning; it is not now agreed (as used to be maintained) that he came of military ancestry. He was a thoughtful, delicate boy, to whom the nickname 'little philosopher' easily attached itself. At the age of eight he was sent to a school for which he ever after preserved an affection: the Jesuit college at La Flèche in Anjou. Here the Rector, Father Charlet, a relation, and his tutor, Father Dinet, supervised his studies with particular care. Descartes seems to have been a model pupil, though not a mere bookworm; he it was who, on the assassination of King Henry IV, was deputed to receive the royal heart for burial at the church of La Flèche (1610).

The Jesuits taught Descartes the classics and poetry for five years, after which he proceeded to ethics, logic, mathematics, physics and metaphysics. This order, based upon the *trivium* and *quadrivium* of mediaeval times, developed his sensibility along with his intellect, and must have aided the evolution of his superb power of literary expression. His health seems to have remained extremely delicate. Much of his time, then as later, was spent in bed. Here he learnt to meditate, developing the taste for reflection upon mathematical problems that never left him.

From school he went direct to the University of Poitiers, where in 1616 he graduated in Law. Contrary to expectations, he rejected the idea of a legal career. Instead he began to contemplate one for which his early training seemed to have rendered him least fitted, that of soldiering. Nevertheless, he proceeded to devote his time to both riding and fencing; and upon the latter art he was even moved to compose an essay. To gain practical experience, he left France for Holland and forthwith became a gentleman volunteer in the army of the Stadthalter, Prince Maurice of Nassau, at Breda. The change of scene and manner of life turned out to be most beneficial. The sickly youth was now mixing with men, and exercising both mind and body in an atmosphere free from constraint.

From another point of view, the career he had chosen gave him valuable and practical scope for his mathematical interests, as these were called into play by the problems in military engineering with which the officers were frequently confronted. In fact, the solution of tricky mathematical problems had become a popular pastime at Breda. The statement of a problem would be posted, for interest, upon one of the city walls, and anybody who wished could submit his idea of the solution. Descartes, though not yet proficient in Dutch, rarely missed an opportunity of exercising his ingenuity in this field.

One day, as he was puzzling out a particularly abstruse problem, he turned for help over the translation to a man who happened to be standing at his side. It proved to be the great Dutch mathematician, Beeckman. The latter challenged Descartes to go home, solve the problem, and bring him the answer. Descartes worked it out in two days, and as a result a great friendship was established. Two works of Descartes, an *Essay on Algebra* and a *Compendium of Music,* were dedicated to Beeckman about this time (1618), for the Frenchman had already developed the habit of pursuing his speculations along several different paths simultaneously. From Beeckman, Descartes derived something more than the incentive to pursue his mathematical researches; he derived, for the first time, friendship with a man of his own sympathies and of at least equal intelligence.

Pleasant as his life had been in Holland, Descartes soon realized that his military aspirations were simply a cloak for the desire to live at liberty with his own thoughts, and also for his impulse—often said to find satisfaction in a military career—to see the world. He formed a resolution to go to Germany. Whether owing to the sudden change of scene or to some inner compulsion which the move laid bare, Descartes now became conscious of a kind of acceleration of his mental processes, an intellectual excitement which he had not previously known.

At the start it took the form of mystical possession (he is said to have enrolled himself among the Rosicrucians at this time). Then on 10 November, 1619, being rapt in meditation of a deeper kind than usual, he conceived in a flash of inspiration the outlines of what he believed to be an entirely new science of nature and thought. An experience very similar to that which befell Archimedes, when he exclaimed 'Eureka' ('I have found it!'), followed. This moment of intense exhilaration in turn gave place to a series of prophetic dreams. In the first, so he records, he dreamt that he was lame and seeking shelter in a church after a storm. In the second, he was again aware of a violent storm, with thunder and also showers of sparks. In the third and last, he dreamt that, having opened a book of Ausonius, he came by accident upon the phrase: *Quid vitae sectabor iter?* ('Which way of life shall I follow?'). This series of inner illuminations exerted the most profound alteration in his outlook. He instantly made a vow to undertake a pilgrimage of gratitude to Our Lady of Loretto: a resolution that he fulfilled during a visit to Italy two years later.

The eight years following upon his mystical experience were years of deep, and for the most part solitary, meditation. He may have seen some action during his stay in Germany; but historians now incline to the view that he never took part in any serious military engagement. In 1624 we find him once more in Italy: but although he must have passed through Florence while Galileo was living there, no record exists of a meeting between the two. Back in France, now feeling the iron hand of Richelieu, he realized that a man of his tastes needed a settled life in a settled country. He therefore sold up his estates and left for Holland, calculating that he now had enough to support himself without hardship.

The record of his life in Holland is not very full, though this was the most productive period of his career. He seems never to have ceased to be a loyal member of the Catholic Church; but of his precise relationship with a woman called Hélène, who bore him a child in 1632 (it died five years later), we know little. We do know, however, that a second crisis in his mental life occurred in the following year. He had almost completed a treatise called *The World,* in which he had accepted the Copernican thesis that the earth moved round the sun, when the news reached him of Galileo's condemnation by the Inquisition. For motives which have been severely criticized, not altogether with justice, he immediately abandoned work on his book. He may have feared persecution; it is more likely that, as a devout Catholic, he was reluctant to offend ecclesiastical authority upon an issue which still needed clarification.

He did not altogether escape persecution himself. At Leyden, he published the famous *Discourse on Method* (1637) and *Meditations* (1641), which embody in clear simple prose the ideas he had been elaborating since his illumination. The reception was enthusiastic in many quarters, but the conservative thinkers attacked him viciously. He became involved in public and private controversy. A denunciation by one of his enemies finally brought a summons to appear before the Magistrates of Utrecht on the charge of atheism. Descartes did not attend in person, but sent a letter of explanation. There was a further summons; and the situation was looking ugly when some of his powerful friends came to the rescue. The magistrates, having taken up the issue, were now in a dilemma as to how they should retire without loss of face. A solution worthy of the ancient oracles was finally hit upon: the authorities solemnly proclaimed that, as regards the new Cartesian philosophy, nothing was to be published either for or against it. And so the hubbub mysteriously died down.

Among the good friends upon whose loyalty Descartes was able to count at this time was the talented and intelligent Princess Elizabeth, daughter of Frederick V of Bohemia, now exiled in Holland. To her, he dedicated his *Principles of Philosophy* (1644), and in her he found a kindred soul. The two were constantly in each other's company, when not engaged in learned correspondence; but there is no reason to suppose that their relationship was anything but Platonic, or rather Cartesian.

As a result of repeated invitations, Descartes decided in 1649 to go to Sweden. He had now lived in Holland for twenty years; but owing to the covert hostility of certain officials, both civil and ecclesiastical, his life had latterly become uneasy there. The invitation to Sweden originally came from the remarkable Queen Christina, and Descartes felt the honour all the more keenly as it indicated his growing international fame. The journey was nevertheless a risk. Descartes was not old; but after such intense intellectual labours he lacked the resilience of men even several years his senior. Upon arrival, he found the climate particularly trying. The timetable to which, as royal guest, he was expected to adhere was still more taxing. The Queen, having heard vaguely about the New Philosophy, insisted upon being given formal instruction in it. The philosopher was to be put to work. Regularly three times a week, at the unpropitious hour of five in the morning, Descartes was obliged to visit the Queen in her bedroom to expound his ideas. He started off with enthusiasm, fulfilling his engagements conscientiously; but after a few weeks of such exertion, combined with strenuous public engagements during the day, his health broke down. On 1 February, 1650, he fell desperately ill, and on the 12th he died. 'Well, my soul, we have to part company,' he is supposed to have murmured resignedly on his death bed. Descartes lived all his life a solitary; and patronage, when it came, was more than he could either comprehend or endure.

His Thought

The *Discourse on Method* was the product of Descartes's interior conflict. He felt a duty towards orthodox belief, and he felt a duty towards his own ideal of the Sage or *Savant*. In this short essay, deliberately written in French to enable it to be read by all (such works were usually in Latin), Descartes delivers an attack upon the Scholastic method, with its sacred texts, its authorities, and its subtle definitions. His aim is to demonstrate, by citing his own experience, how the ordinary individual should arrive unaided at truth. What, in other words, will both satisfy our minds and enable us to know that such satisfaction is identical with truth? Is there some *criterion* that we can adopt whereby our beliefs and ideas can be tested without reference to external authority?

Today these questions seem banal. They were not so in Descartes's time. They were revolutionary questions. To ask them, however politely and reasonably, was to incur the suspicion of the established organizations of society. For Descartes was inviting his readers to approach the great questions of philosophy from an angle diametrically opposed to that of orthodoxy. The Scholastics, especially the later ones, had tended to assume the truth of their dogmas and had then proceeded to classify and codify them; such doubts as they raised were stated for the purpose of spectacular demolition at the hand of skilled dialecticians. According to Descartes's New Method, the test of a truth was not whether it had been enunciated by Holy Writ, or St Augustine or St Thomas, or stated *ex cathedra* by the Supreme Pontiff, but whether it was coherent with itself and above all whether it was 'clear and distinct'. In other words, the Method which Descartes proposed to apply to every sphere of knowledge was that which was best exemplified in analytical geometry. The stages and procedure used in a geometrical problem could surely be made to yield results of equal certitude in the sphere of metaphysics, logic, and ethics. That was Descartes's conviction, and the substance of his mystical revelation.

What he was in fact struggling to work out was something very like a universal mathematics. The idea that everything was susceptible to measurement, and that what eluded measurement was unreal, had been stated for the first time by Galileo. 'Philosophy,' Galileo had observed, 'is written in that vast book which stands ever open before our eyes, I mean the universe; but it cannot be read until we have learnt the language and become familiar with the characters in which it is written. *It is written in mathematical language.*' Descartes, though he claimed to owe nothing to Galileo, would have approved that statement. In his time, such a view was both novel and heterodox. What recommended it to Descartes was the fact that it revealed the interconnection between everything in the universe. In spite of its apparent lack of system and its teeming detail, the world exhibited a fundamental order; and that order was a mathematical order.

Descartes claimed that his Method was not a something to be learnt by the mastery of a few rules; it was a thing to be lived, to be grown into. Reflection must become a habit. Men must discover, by disciplined thought, what ideas are fundamental to their minds in the sense of being 'innate', like those of mathematics; for such ideas are superior in status to those either derived from sense or conjured up by the imagination.

How, therefore, can we eliminate the unreliable, the vague, and the illusory elements from our minds? By systematic scepticism or, as Descartes called it, 'methodic doubt'. Take nothing for granted; demand the production of its identity card, and examine that too lest it should prove to be a forgery. To take nothing for granted, however, is still to take something for granted: namely, the fact that you yourself are engaged in thinking and reflecting. And that is simultaneously to take for granted the fact that you, the thinking and reflecting being, exist. 'I think, therefore I am.' Descartes climbs out of doubt by certifying his own existence as a doubter. That is the first step towards knowledge.

I exist, argues Descartes, but in the capacity of a doubter; I am an essentially imperfect being, and I realize it. But unless I possessed at the same time some idea of the infinite and perfect, I should not have acquired this consciousness of imperfection. My reason tells me, therefore, that I am the creature of an all-wise, all-seeing, all-powerful God. Without the certitude of God's existence, I should not possess any guarantee that the deliverances of my Reason were such as could be relied upon; 'an atheist cannot be a geometrist'.

By this argument, as we have seen, Descartes reverses the Scholastic method. The latter began with matter and sense and argued itself up to God; Descartes, as it were, begins with God and argues down to matter and sense. His repudiation of authority, his emphasis upon Reason, his insistence upon logical clearness and distinctness, his interest in the developing sciences of physics and physiology, make him one of the pioneers of the great scientific movement which, during the next two centuries, reshaped the world.

The *Discourse on Method* is the Charter of scientific humanism. No philosophical or scientific writer has escaped its influence. As for its effect upon the civilization of France, that has been incalculable. More than a century later it inspired another book of equal influence, Rousseau's *Social Contract;* and it is no exaggeration to say that the 'reasonableness' still associated with the French mind at its most cultivated level is by nature Cartesian.

Against Descartes's method there have been several reactions, even within France itself. A Frenchman of remarkable intellect, Blaise Pascal (1623–62), whose death was even more lamentably premature than that of Descartes, underwent an experience very similar to the mystical revelation of the latter but opposite in significance. A mathematician of genius, Pascal records that one night he beheld a vision in which it was made clear to him that the true God of religion was not a 'God of philosophers and mathematicians' but 'the God of Abraham and Jacob': a revelation which, as he recorded on a parchment which he caused to be sewn into his clothing, caused him to weep 'tears of joy'. Pascal helped to redress the balance between the Cartesian or rationalist viewpoint and the sensitive, intuitional approach of the poets and mystics: between the *esprit de géomètre* and the *esprit de finesse.* He is the greater character of the two; but Descartes excelled him in capacity for systematic and original thinking.

20

Benedict Spinoza

'This man, from his granite pedestal, will point out to all men the way of blessedness which he found; and ages hence, the cultivated traveller, passing by this spot, will say in his heart: 'The truest vision ever had of God came, perhaps, here.'

Renan, at the dedication of Spinoza's statue at the Hague, 1882.

His Life

The most remarkable fact about Spinoza is that although he was personally the most aloof and isolated of beings, his chief aim was to show how men could make the universe their home and acquire a feeling of kinship with all its creatures. Exiled at an early age from his own community, Spinoza sought communion with a society more permanent than that of man, and one which was based upon the order of Nature and of God. In return for his devotion to Nature and to God, however, he did not suppose that either the one or the other should condescend to take any particular interest in his own welfare. To expect such attention was to love selfishly: 'He who truly loves God cannot wish that God should love him in return.'

This was a new note in philosophy. Such, the reader might say, is the attitude not of a Cartesian philosopher, a lover of clearness and distinctness, a devotee of enlightened Reason, but of a mystic, or even a religious fanatic. That occasional remarks of Spinoza recall those of the Spanish mystic St John of the Cross (1542–91) has more than once been pointed out: the German philosopher Novalis (1772–1801) likewise once referred to Spinoza as *Ein gottbetrunkener Mensch*, 'a God-intoxicated man'. Certainly Spinoza lived a most pious, upright, and—except in this one particular—sober life. But his thought is the very reverse of vague or confused. It is as transparently clear as that of Descartes; if possible, it is expounded with greater economy of word. What makes Spinoza a difficult philosopher for some people is not so much the manner of his exposition as the conclusions which he urges his readers to accept. These conclusions were hard, frigid, and uninviting.

What were the origins of this strange man, perhaps the most solitary figure in the history of philosophy? A flood of light upon Spinoza's thought is thrown by the circumstances of his birth and upbringing. Born in Amsterdam on 24 November, 1632, he came of Portuguese–Jewish parentage. To be precise, his father and mother were not so much Jews as 'crypto' Jews: that is to say, they were descended from Jews whom the Inquisition had forced to accept the Christian faith. When Holland proclaimed toleration for all religions, many of these uneasy, badgered folk did their best to seek asylum there (from about 1593 onwards). They brought with them their trades and their wits; and so they prospered. But they were still not citizens in the full sense. They resided, but they did not belong. Their religion, which they now practised again openly, made such absorption impossible. Hence the peculiar isolation of their position: they were avoided, as men usually avoided those who have suffered prolonged persecution.

Spinoza was sent to the Jewish school at Amsterdam, which had been founded in 1638. Here his education was confined exclusively to Hebrew subjects: firstly, the Jewish sacred books, such as the Talmud and the Hewbrew Codes, and secondly, the Hebrew philosophers, such as Ibn Ezra, and Maimonides, whom we have mentioned as being a precursor of St Thomas Aquinas. Such was the basic education given to Jewish boys at the time. Outside school-hours, however, Spinoza received instruction in secular subjects, and for these he showed great powers of assimilation. He also proved quick at learning languages; besides Spanish, which was spoken in his home, he learnt Latin, Portuguese, French, Italian and Dutch.

The first notable event in his life, after leaving school, was the death in 1654 of his father, a wealthy and respected man in the Jewish community. This event gave rise to family troubles, as Spinoza's step-sister laid claim to the entire estate. In consequence of a law-suit, Spinoza was pronounced the rightful heir; but for reasons which seem to have been genuinely altruisitic, he waived the greater part of his claim in her favour, and prepared to work for his living. As an occupation, he chose the sedentary art of grinding, cutting and polishing lenses for spectacles, telescopes and microscopes; and in this art, to which he devoted the rest of his life, he came to exhibit considerable skill.

Although at school he had been given a thoroughly orthodox education, his reading of such philosophers as Maimonides had early stimulated his critical faculty. In his celebrated *Guide to the Perplexed*, Maimonides, besides drawing attention to a number of inconsistencies in the Bible, had implied that the ultimate court of appeal in theological matters was not so much Faith as Reason; that if verbal inspiration conflicted with what was reasonable, so much the worse (he hinted) for verbal inspiration; and that the faithful, however complete their devotion, were not absolved from treating the Scriptures as documents to be studied with discrimination and judgment. Spinoza, though a regular patron of the synagogue, boldly voiced his approval of this way of thinking. The Jewish leaders pricked up their ears. Such talk was doubly dangerous: it was calculated not merely to undermine the faith of the orthodox but to excite the suspicion of the Dutch Calvinists, at whose good pleasure the refugees were allowed to remain in Holland. For Spinoza was attacking beliefs common to both guests and hosts.

Although the Jews in Holland had fled from persecution, they exhibited a regrettable tendency, there as elsewhere, to persecute each other in exile. The leaders felt it incumbent upon them to suppress demonstrations of infidelity. Occasionally, in order to hush up a scandal, they would endeavour to buy the silence of a heretic by means of bribery. We have evidence to suggest that Spinoza was offered money in this way. His stubborn refusal to be silenced caused him to be excommunicated by his community in 1656. Allegedly this was because he advanced the view that God had a body (by which he was referring to the world of matter); that angels were probably figments of the imagination; and that the Bible had nothing to say upon the subject of immortality. As a precaution, his exclusion from the synagogue was formally reported to the Dutch civil authorities; and Spinoza, much against his will, was give a term of exile. He was barely twenty-four years old. It is said that at this time a fanatical Jew made an attempt upon his life.

During the years of exile, Spinoza made the acquaintance of a number of learned Christians, and through them came to study the new philosophy of Descartes. He also applied himself to physics and mathematics, and, like Descartes himself, probably familiarized himself with various types of theosophy. When he returned to Amsterdam in 1660, he already regarded himself, and was regarded by others, as a free-thinker; and although he is said to have put in an appearance at the Synagogue and even to have written an Apology for his so-called heresies, his speculative mind could now no longer be bound by a 'closed' system of dogma and ritual. Besides the trade which he had adopted, he supplemented his income by teaching; the subject most in demand at this time was Hebrew, since both Christians and non-Christians were becoming increasingly interested to discover, amid the disputes of religious sects, what the Bible 'really said'. That Spinoza should have supplemented his instruction by exposition of the meaning of the text itself, was inevitable; and he soon became a recognized leader of study circles at which religion, philosophy, ethics, and natural science were discussed with a freedom rarely permitted even in the comparatively enlightened atmosphere of Amsterdam. It is possible, perhaps, to trace the origin of what is today called the 'higher criticsm' of the Bible to these quiet, communal researches conducted by Spinoza.

Although he had studied the writings of Descartes with great eagerness, he was now beginning to experience a feeling of dissatisfaction with certain aspects of the new philosophy. A system of his own was simultaneously beginning to crystallize in his mind. Solitary as his manner of life had become, he felt the need for even more prolonged solitude; and the impulse to write down his thoughts in systematic form was becoming more insistent. He therefore moved to Rijnsburg, a town six miles from Leyden, where he took up lodgings with a doctor named Hermann Homan. Here, in congenial company, he wrote an essay entitled *A Short Treatise on God, Man and his Well-Being*, which was first discovered in 1852, and also began the book in which his genius is most fully manifest, namely, the *Ethics* (1661–65).

By his influence upon his distinguished friends and also by the letters he wrote to thinkers and scientists of the day, Spinoza slowly began to acquire a reputation abroad. His letters to the famous physicist Oldenburg, whom he met in 1661 and who later became associated with the Royal Society in London, brought him in touch with English scientists; and some years later he began a corresondence with Leibniz, from which the latter profited more than he cared to acknowledge. About the year 1663, he was given a pension from the great Dutch patriot John De Witt. The two remained fast friends until a terrible tragedy parted them.

Spinoza was engaged between 1665 and 1670 upon the composition of a work in which he evidently meant to dispose once for all of the accusation, so frequently levelled against him, of atheism. This was known as the *Tractatus Theologico-Politicus*, an essay in which he expressed his feelings with unaccustomed passion. Unhappily the very aim he had set before himself was frustrated; he bowed to the advice of his friends not to publish such inflamable material under his own name. The book therefore appeared anonymously in 1670, and went through edition after edition within a short period. In the year of its publication, Spinoza moved to Voorburg, near the Hague, where he finally took up residence in the house on the Paviljoensgracht belonging to the painter Van der Spijck, remaining there until his death. His life at Voorburg seems to have been that of a complete recluse; but although he rarely ventured out of doors, he enjoyed the company of visitors, and with his artist-host Spijck he appears to have been on terms of great intimacy.

Two events occurred in the brief interval before his death, either of which may well have had the effect of hastening the end. One was the brutal assassination of his great patron De Witt. For the first time in the experience of his friends, Spinoza became convulsed with indignation, and was with difficulty prevailed upon not to fix a notice containing the words *Ultimi barbarorum* upon the prison in which the outrage had been committed. The second event is still a source of some mystery to historians. The Prince of Condé, who had established his winter quarters not far from Utrecht, apparently invited Spinoza, under promise of safe-conduct, to pay him a visit. Although by the time Spinoza arrived Condé was away, someone with sufficient authority evidently received him and offered him a pension on behalf of Louis XIV. This he refused, as was to be expected in view of the state of hostilities between France and Holland; but he did not reckon upon the bitterly hostile reception his fellow-townsmen were to accord him upon his return. Denounced as a spy, the mob very nearly tore him to pieces; and although he managed to reach is house unhurt, Spijck expressed the fear that the place would be raided that night. Spinoza reassured him. If necessary, he would go out, face the people, and die the death of John De Witt. From what we know of Spinoza's character, it is probable that, if necessary, he would have done so.

The explanation of this episode may be that the Dutch, realizing Spinoza's international reputation, used him to conduct certain peace negotiations which they could later repudiate. His journey seems to have been known to certain high officials—or so Spinoza claimed at the time. Moreover, on the French side there was a certain Colonel Stoup, commander of one of Condé's Swiss regiments, who played an ambiguous part in the proceedings—some say in order to discredit Spinoza and cause his arrest by the Dutch as a traitor: in which aim he nearly succeeded.

As time went on, Spinoza's occupation, though congenial to one accustomed to meditate for hours together, began to have a deleterious effect upon his health. It is said that the glass-dust in his workroom injured his lungs and induced consumption. In November 1677 he suddenly became very ill. Schuller, his doctor friend, was summoned, but on the 20th of the month Spinoza died. It was later suggested that, fearing a lingering death, the philosopher had called Schuller in order to arrange for a euthanasia; but this is hardly compatible with the calm and brave character that we know Spinoza to have possessed.

The man who had renounced his right to his father's fortune in youth left so few material possessions at death that his sister did not trouble to put in a claim for them. As for his writings, they were on the whole vilified and condemned for at least a century afterwards. Only with Lessing, Goethe and Coleridge did the serene philosophy of the short, swarthy Jewish exile from Portugal and from Zion come fully into its own. And today Spinoza is universally regarded as one of the great philosophers of the Western world.

His Thought

To understand the philosophy of Spinoza is to appreciate its blend of Christian, mystical and Jewish thought; it is Christian in its serenity and compassion, mystical in its visionary character, and Jewish in its spiritual 'obstinacy': Spinoza resembles the Old Testament prophets in nothing so much as in his insistence that 'you cannot serve two masters'. If we are to love God, he maintains, there must be no compromise, no *quid pro quo*; but once we have surrendered ourselves to Him, we shall find that 'his service is perfect freedom'. In a sense, however, we have no choice in the matter. We are by nature linked with God, as 'modes' of the Divine Substance; to become *conscious* of this dependence is what is meant by freedom and liberation.

The object of the treatise on Ethics is to show, by a kind of mathematical analysis, how the soul of man is necessarily attached to its Creator. Although he rejects many of Descartes's conclusions and also some of his arguments, Spinoza retains the Cartesian Method, and the ideals of clarity as typified by the procedure of mathematics and physics. He describes his Ethical treatise on the title-page as being *ordine geometrico demonstrata* ('proved in geometrical order'); hence the aversion that some readers have shown for its aridity and coldness, as if philosophical arguments must necessarily be dressed up as fine literature before they can be accepted. By his emphasis upon necessity and the fact that man's duty is to pursue divine and not human ends, Spinoza seeks to explain—or explain away—the evil, ugliness and inexplicability that confronts us in the world. 'Whenever anything in nature seems to us ridiculous, absurd, or evil,' he writes in the *Tractatus Theologico-Politicus*, 'it is because we have but partial knowledge of things, and are in the main ignorant of the order and coherence of nature as a whole, and because we want everything to be arranged according to the dictates of our own reason: although in fact what our law pronounces bad is not bad as regards the order and laws of universal nature, but only as regards the laws of our own nature taken separately'. The last statement is an admirable summary of the philosophical attitude of Spinoza. When man 'takes himself separately', he takes himself solemnly and therefore creates triviality; whereas if he realizes his dependence upon what is greater than himself, he attains to true dignity and peace of mind.

Spinoza's theory of Substance has proved a stumbling-block to philosophical students. But the idea which he is trying to put forward is really quite simple. If, as he says, there exists a truly Substantial Being, that Being or Substance must be *causa sui*; that is to say, it cannot have been produced by something other than itself, or it would not be a true substance. Likewise it must be infinite; if it were not, it would be in some way limited, and such limitation would be due to the existence of other substances. In short, if there is a substance at all, it must both depend upon itself and provide the ground of everything else. Such a substance must therefore be equivalent to God, for only God possesses the characteristics of being at once self-caused and the cause of everything. God, therefore, is the entire universe, since everything that issues from Him is a part of Him; and so Spinoza is accustomed to refer to the one universal Substance as *Deus sive Natura*, God or Nature, according as to whether he wishes to refer to its spiritual or to its material aspect. Such a theory is called in technical terms *monistic*; what Spinoza was endeavouring to do was to overcome the Cartesian division, or *dualism*, between mind and body, whereby there existed two different substances, a thinking and a non-thinking one, giving rise to the tricky problem as to how they worked together in harness.

That freedom results from a clear and dispassionate awareness of our dependence upon universal and divine laws is the cornerstone of Spinoza's ethical teaching. Freedom and understanding are thus as closely identified for Spinoza as they are for Socrates. Obstacles to freedom of thought must be eliminated from society: for bigoted ecclesiastics are wrong in supposing that piety and morality will increase with the introduction of spiritual 'controls' and inquisitional practices. The object of the *Tractatus Theologico-Politicus* was precisely to show 'that not only is perfect liberty to philosophize compatible with devout piety and the peace of the state, but that to take away such liberty is to destroy the public peace and even piety itself'. And in the course of the same work Spinoza flares up suddenly with indignation at the thought of how the world has treated so many of its great men, and how it had nearly treated him. 'What greater misfortune for a state can be conceived than that honourable men should be sent like criminals into exile, because they held diverse opinions which they cannot disguise? What, I say, can be more hurtful than that men who have committed no crime or wickedness should, simply because they are enlightened, be treated as enemies and put to death, and that the scaffold, the terror of evil-doers, should become the stage where the highest examples of tolerance and virtue are displayed to the people with all the marks of ignominy that authority can devise?'

This passage, which might have come straight out of Plato's *Apology of Socrates*, reveals the *saeva indignatio* of a great but passionate nature. Few men have preached so uncompromising a doctrine and yet practised it so uncompromisingly himself. Spinoza is no hasty reformer; the way to blessedness, which is 'virtue itself', remains obscure. 'If the road I have shown to lead to this is very difficult,' he says at the conclusion of the *Ethics*, 'it can yet be discovered. And clearly it must be very hard when it is so seldom found. For how could it be that it is neglected practically by all, if salvation were close at hand and could be found without difficulty? But all things excellent are as difficult as they are rare.'

21

Gottfried Leibniz

You will find that when you are admitted to the heart of nature, the further you go the greater will be your delights, because you will be only at the beginning of a chain that goes on to infinity.

Philosophical Dream

His Life

Leibniz might have been a greater philosopher, and perhaps a greater man, if he had needed to struggle to greatness. As it was, he achieved reputation and honour, in more fields than one, with an ease that astonished his contemporaries, and in some respects turned his head. He was at one and the same time a mathematician, a lawyer, an historian, a diplomat—and a philosopher. Of the ignominy and obscurity that drove Spinoza into Stoic seclusion, he knew little until his last years. He never had cause to fear persecution, like Descartes and Locke. Even professional jealousy left few marks upon him. For he had enough confidence in his own powers not to feel it, and sufficiently established prestige never to become the objects of it. In short, with so many gifts and with such opportunities, he ought to have cut a great figure in the philosophical pantheon that he has done. In the 'best of all possible worlds' (to employ his own description of this earth), he ought to have become the best of all possible philosophers. There is something poignant about the opening of the essay from which an extract is given at the head of this chapter: 'I was happy to be among men, but not happy about human nature.'

Gottfried Wilhelm Leibniz was reared in an atmosphere of learned speculation. His father was Professor of Moral Philosophy at Leipzig. Born on 21 June, 1646, in the latter city, young Leibnitz displayed remarkable precocity; for his father, realizing the boy's appetite for learning, decided to give him the run of his library before the age of six, using the words *tolle, lege* ('take, read'). The little fellow not merely devoured the classical philosophers and historians, but even ventured upon the Fathers of the Church. At the age of twelve, he could read Latin and Greek with ease. The next subject to absorb his attention was Logic, in which he claimed to have introduced reforms at an early age, for he became immediately dissatisfied with the scholastic approach. His parents and overseers found this avidity for learning a trifle overwhelming. They feared that he would turn into a bookworm or pedant. But they were wrong. Leibniz wore his erudition lightly. If he was a scholar among courtiers, he was a courtier among scholars.

When Leibniz was fifteen, he entered the University of Leipzig as a law-student. The first part of his course, which occupied a period of two years, consisted chiefly of philosophy. His masters belonged to the old school; their pupil, already bursting with knowledge, soon found that he belonged to the new. He discovered, largely for himself, the works of Francis Bacon, Campanella (1568–1630), Galileo and, above all, Descartes. Admittedly, his revolt against Scholasticism was not accomplished without some mental turmoil. No subtle revolution of this kind ever is. Leibniz has left us an account of his final conversion, which, like most conversions, took place out of doors in the course of a walk (even Augustine had to run into his garden to be converted). 'I remember walking alone,' he writes, 'at the age of fifteen, in a wood near Leipzig called the Rosenthal, to deliberate whether I should retain the doctrine of substantial forms. At last mechanism triumphed and induced me to apply myself to mathematics.' Thus he joined the band, headed by Galileo, of those who believed that the book of nature was written by God in the language of mathematics. The next problem was to put himself under an efficient tutor in this difficult but fascinating subject. Most of the summer of 1663 he spent at Jena, and there took lessons from Weigel, whose reputation as a mathematics teacher was at its height; but this was only his initiation into a sphere of enquiry to which he was later to make some original contributions.

If Leibniz had been seduced by the subtle charms of mathematical philosophy, he did not remain wholly unfaithful to the law. Indeed, he had a particular reason for pursuing his legal training: for he had decided to adopt the profession of Assessor as being that most likely to fit his temperament and in particular to give him scope for private reflection. He therefore became a candidate in 1666 for the degree of Doctor of Law. His one handicap was his comparative youth; he was only twenty years old. There were candidates in the field much older than he; and it is to be feared that their covert opposition was responsible for the official refusal to grant Leibniz the honour which, in every other respect, he had merited. The affront nettled him. If his native town would not recognize his ability, he would see what redress could be obtained elsewhere. He left Leipzig—for ever, as it proved—and applied for admission to the University of Altdorf (the academic seat of the free city of Nuremberg). Here, as a result of a dissertation that won immediate approval from authorities more than three times his age, he was asked to stay and accept the vacant Professorship of Law. This was justice indeed. But the inviting gesture was all that Leibniz, at his time of life, wanted. He politely but firmly refused the offer; for he had by this time begun to entertain higher ambitions than could be satisfied by a mere professorship. He wanted to be an international figure.

At Nuremberg, where he now decided to stay, he began to move in society for which he was more suited. Like Descartes and Spinoza, he was for some while attracted to the doctrines of the Rosicrucians; and as Nuremburg was a Rosicrucian centre, he was able to mix freely in their society and even to take part in their activities. Of more material benefit to him, however, was his meeting with Johann Christian von Boineburg, who had had a distinguished career as first minister to the Elector of Mainz. Boineburg encouraged the young man to print some of his essays, above all that entitled *Nova Methodus docendi discendique juris*, with which he had been particularly impressed; and he suggested that the book should be dedicated to the Elector himself. Following this advice, Leibniz decided to present his work to the great man in person; and the Elector was so favourably struck with the young lawyer's ability that he forthwith offered him a government position revising the Statute Book. Such intricate work being well within Leibniz's capacity, he tackled it with confidence; but it soon became evident both to the Elector and his advisers that the new official was equal to much heavier responsibilities. Soon, therefore, he was commissioned with the task of doing battle, with his ready pen, on behalf of the candidature of a German prince for the throne of Poland, which had become vacant in 1669. This, his first political treatise, is unique in history as being the only diplomatic argument to submit mathematical proofs for its statements. Still it did not prevent the throne of Poland from being occupied once more by a Polish prince.

Another direction in which Leibniz was called upon to use his literary and forensic skill was that of exposing France's aggressive designs in Europe. In an essay entitled *Thoughts on Public Safety*, Leibniz advocated a 'Rheinbund' or league against Louis XIV for the defence of Germany, against which France seemed to be preparing for war. This document is interesting for a further suggestion that it contained: namely, that European nations, instead of attacking each other, should seek to revive the crusading spirit by uniting together in an expedition against some non-Christian state. What about Egypt, for instance, 'one of the best situated lands in the world'? Would not France do better to attack and conquer such a country than despoil her Christian neighbours? The French Secretary of State, commending this essay to Louis XIV, and deciding to solicit the author for further views on the subject, invited him to Paris. Leibniz set out, with great expectations, on 18 March, 1672. He never obtained the royal audience to which he was looking forward; but both his journey and the composition of a further treatise seem to have given Louis food for thought, and he might well have put Leibniz's grandiose plan into operation had not relations between France and Turkey (then in control of Egypt) suddenly taken a turn for the better. More than a century later, Napoleon, on entering Hanover in 1803, unearthed documents in the government archives relating to this scheme. He then made the interesting discovery that the idea of a French expedition to Egypt, such as he himself had undertaken in an atmosphere of tragi-comedy in 1797, had been proposed originally by a German philosopher.

Philosophically, if not politically, Leibniz profited from his journey. Politics and diplomacy were not allowed to crowd out mathematics and philosophy. In Paris he met the philosopher Malebranche, a religious Cartesian (1638–1715), Arnauld, the author of an anti-Cartesian treatise (1612–94), and the great philosopher and astronomer Huyghens (1629–93). To each he expounded his developing ideas and discoveries in such diverse fields as logic, natural philosophy, mathematics, mechanics, optics, and hydrostatics, together with his novel opinions on law and theology. Above all he outlined his famous philosophy of Monads, of which we shall speak later. His mind, now in its full maturity, seemed to be teeming with original suggestions, reforms, improvements, solutions. Nor were his ideas confined to the plane of theory or hypothesis. He showed himself to be an inventor too, having a peculiar genius for the construction of machines and gadgets. Most striking of his inventions at this period was a new type of calculating machine, which excelled that of Pascal to the extent of being able to multiply, divide, and extract roots. After having been exhibited at Paris, this machine was displayed on the premises of the Royal Society in London, of which Leibniz became a member in 1673. His election to the French Academy as a distinguished foreign member did not take place until 1700.

When in January, 1673, he came to London as the special envoy of the Elector of Mainz, Leibniz hastened to make acquaintance with the better-known English scientists and mathematicians. He met and (like Spinoza) corresponded with Oldenburg, then secretary of the Royal Society. He met the chemist Boyle and the mathematician Pell, who introduced him to the discoveries of Mercator as outlined in the latter's treatise called *Logarithmatechnica,* which to some extent Leibniz had himself anticipated. When he returned to Paris, he began to pursue his mathematical speculations with even greater energy, profiting meanwhile from the tuition of Huyghens; and in due course he worked out that system of differential and integral calculus, which is generally regarded as his particular discovery in the field of mathematics.

A change now came over Leibniz's fortunes which were thereafter to determine the course of his life. For some while he had been engaged in frequent and learned correspondence with Duke John Frederick of Brunswick-Lüneburg. In 1673, having entered the Duke's service, he went to Hanover (travelling, incidentally, via London and Amsterdam, which enabled him to pay a visit to Spinoza), and there assumed charge of the family library. Although he held the post of librarian for the next forty years, the work he was called upon to do went far beyond the confines of librarianship. He was expected to be at once champion of the rights of the Brunswick family and what amounted to Public Relations Officer for the State of Hanover. One of his numerous tasks, that of compiling a history of the Brunswicks, involved rummaging in the archives of towns as far separated as Vienna, Modena, Venice and Rome. In Vienna the wealth of material put at his disposal kept him occupied for nine months. In Rome, where his reputation had preceded him, he was diplomatically asked whether, assuming that he entered the Catholic Church, he would accept the custodianship of the Vatican library.

Although he was not disposed to change his creed, least of all on such a pretext, Leibniz had been much preoccupied in the past by the question of Catholic and Protestant reunion. It was not the least of his attempts to arrive at a unity transcending differences. To demonstrate that some sort of reconciliation between the two faiths was not merely desirable for feasible, he wrote in 1686 a *Systema Theologicum*, but this was not published until long after his death. At first he met with a good deal of co-operation and encouragement from elements on both sides; but when it came to thrashing out the real issues and discussing particular dogmas, the debate soon assumed a tone of bitter controversy, it being further realized that each side secretly hoped to achieve reunion by the wholesale reconversion of the other. When in 1688 the English revolution occurred and the Protestant Succession was established, the balance of spiritual power in Europe was permanently upset; nor did Leibniz fare any better in his attempt, made a little later, to bring about a working alliance between the Reformed and the Lutheran churches.

Despite these setbacks, Leibniz continued to prosper as few philosophers have prospered before or since In 1690, he was appointed librarian at Wolfenbüttel by Duke Anton of Brunswick-Wolfenbüttel, and increased a reputation already well established for learning, wisdom and inventiveness. He made close friendships at the highest social level. With the Electress Sophie Charlotte of Brandenburg and Princess Sophie of Hanover, her mother, he became so intimate that in 1700 he was invited to Berlin for the purpose of establishing there an Academy of Learning, plans for which he had been working upon for some years. The institution was formally opened on 11 July, Leibniz being elected its life-president. From then onwards public distinctions were conferred upon him with a liberality seldom enjoyed today except by successful politicians or sportsmen. The Elector of Brandenburg conferred upon him the title of Privy Councillor of Justice in 1700: which title he was to receive from a two other patrons, the Elector of Hanover in 1704 and Peter the Great in 1712 (Leibniz had sent him plans for an Academy at St Petersburg.)

At Berlin, Leibniz spent some of the happiest years of his life. Only the death of the Electress Sophie Charlotte, to whom he had taught philosophy in circumstances rather more congenial than those in which Descartes instructed Queen Christina of Sweden, put an end to his inner contentment, though it failed to halt his public advancement. He visited Berlin on the last occasion in 1711, after which he left for Vienna with the intention of setting up another Academy. Although the opposition of the Jesuits prevented him from making much headway, his services to learning were rewarded by two further honours, an Imperial privy councillorship and a barony of the Empire. From a material point of view there were not many worlds left to conquer. During his absence from Hanover, however, the Elector George

Louis had been invited to England to become king, and it was with genuine regret that Leibniz, his Brunswick researches still unfinished, was not permitted to join him. In fact he never completed the family history upon which he had laboured for so many years, and his huge manuscript was not published until 1843.

Until his death in November, 1716, Leibniz occupied himself with ceaseless correspondence, devoting his attention to almost every field of learning that scholars of the day considered worthy of cultivation. But the very success of his early and middle life were responsible for a contrasting negligence by the public as he grew older. His health began to give him trouble, and he was involved in futile arguments with critics, which exhausted his time and patience. It would be incredible, if it were not true, to say that he died practically unnoticed, even in the circles in which he had moved as a leader and guide. At his funeral, which took place at Hanover, his secretary Eckhart alone followed him to the grave. There never was a philosopher whose death presented so complete a contrast to his life; but in pondering that unlamented end we perceive that throughout the whole of his successful career Leibniz remained essentially a lonely figure, happy in a few attachments, which, once broken, left him, like the musician Schubert, with nothing but his genius. He was 'the man with a load of talent'; and we feel that he had not the opportunity, in one lifetime, to unpack and set in order all that he had brought with him.

His Thought

The difference between Descartes, Pascal and Spinoza on the one hand, and Leibniz on the other, is at bottom a difference in temperament. Of Spinoza we have used the word 'obstinate'. That quality of non-compromising obstinacy is characteristic of Descartes and Pascal, too; and it is not altogether absent from the work of Locke. Each of these thinkers wishes to accord universal applicability to a single principle—be it reason, intelligence or observation. This principle is regarded as the key to all problems. Being conciliatory by temperament and willing to learn from both sides, Leibniz displays a contrasting attitude. He seeks to maintain a standpoint in which justice is done to all extremes. To adopt a one-sided point of view is equivalent, in his opinion, to adopting a false one. Leibniz was as anxious to further the cause of unity within the theoretical sciences as he was anxious to further it in politics and religion. And for this reason he distrusted the rationalism of Descartes as being too productive of *distinctions*, of fissures and divisions in thought.

Leibniz employed a phrase in connection with the Cartesian philosophy which has become famous. He said that it represented the 'antechamber' of truth. The truth lay just beyond it, after a partition had been penetrated or broken down. To Leibniz, the philosophy of Spinoza was likewise open to objection, because Spinoza had merely clamped together in one Substance that which Descartes had forcibly separated. What needed to be revised, and if necessary jettisoned, was the current notion of Substance. Leibniz's theory of Monads was an attempt to replace this notion by something more satisfactory and in harmony with modern scientific ideas.

The true constituent of reality, argues Leibniz, is not so much a particle of matter as a centre of force. This centre of force he calls a monad. A monad is an individual thing capable of self-activity and self-subsistence; its very individuality and unity render it both independent of other monads and representative, as it were, of the whole world. Thus, in Leibniz's words, the monads composing reality, though 'without windows', form a 'mirror of the universe', just as a truly individual thing, simply because it is complete and self-sufficient, enjoys universal characteristics. For example, a real, complete, unified *personality* is a better representative of the genus Man than an unbalanced immature one.

Leibniz is careful to distinguish his monads from atoms, in the accepted sense. It is true that, in one of his works, he writes that 'the monads are the very atoms of nature—in a word, the elements of things'; but he does not understand them to be pieces, however tiny, of matter. They are not physical at all; they are rather metaphysical entities, local embodiments of force, varying one from the other in power. It is the graduation or hierarchy of monads, beginning with the simplest elements in nature and ending with God Himself, the Monad of Monads, that explains the universe in which we live. Cartesianism can never explain it, because Cartesianism invokes force from outside in the person of an intervening God.

According to Leibniz, even the simplest of monads is endowed with the faculty of perception. At first this perception is both elementary and confused; later it expresses itself more perfectly in thought and finally in self-consciousness. Similarly, every monad possesses its own *vis motrix* or motive force; and as we ascend the hierarchy, this motive force becomes first instinct and later will. Thought and will, operating in concert, produce freedom and therefore happiness; there is no happiness where there is uncontrolled submission to passion. Thus, Leibniz, like Spinoza, believes that man's highest goal is to render himself capable of *amor intellectualis dei*, the intellectual love of God.

Much that Leibniz asserted has been taken up, with renewed interest, by the philosophers of our own time. He started a great many hares, and could follow but few of them. One aspect of his system, however, has puzzled and dissatisfied even the most earnest of his disciples. So concerned is he to show that his universe of monads will not merely hold together but function dynamically by itself (whereas Descartes had dragged in God at every point) that he leaves us wondering how it is that the whole affair originally began. If the monads are 'windowless', individual, and infinite in number, they must clearly have started in good order, otherwise the result would have been not the 'best possible world' (as Leibnitz claimed) but the worst possible chaos. Who, therefore, lined up and graded the monads? God did, says Leibniz. He pre-established their harmonious arrangement. They continue to pursue, each in its own direction, their pre-ordained course. Consequently, they are a team, but without a conscious team spirit.

'According to my system,' writes Leibniz in his essay *The Monadology* (§ 81), 'bodies act as if there were no souls, and souls act as if there were no bodies, and both act as if each influenced the other.' In reality there is no interaction; merely the impression of co-operation as the result of God's original dynamic scheme.

This, the reader may say, is all very clever; but is it in fact very different from the gambit adopted by Descartes? Yes. Descartes said that God, with unceasing care, kept the world going. Leibniz said that God, with remarkable ingenuity, set the world going. Descartes postulated an active God in a passive universe; Leibniz's chief disciple, Christian Wolff (1679–1754), failed to recognize the importance of Leibniz's dynamic conception of the world; and perhaps that is why the philosophy of Leibniz, so soon to be over-shadowed by the gigantic structure of Kant, did not come into its own—if indeed it has yet come into its own—until a much later period.

22

Religious Conflict and the Rise of Rationalism

In the century that followed the death of Descartes, the European order underwent many violent changes. On the continent, the religious quarrel between Catholicism and Protestantism appeared no nearer solution, though Protestantism as a political force began slowly to gain the ascendancy. The problem for men was how to live, or to carry on social and international life, in a world thus racked and dislocated by religious passions: in short, the problem was one of toleration. Now an intellectual problem may well agitate a thousand or million minds at the same time; but only among a few, a sensitive and cultivated minority, will there be an awareness of that problem's true meaning. The philosopher is one who *abstracts* the real issue from the tangle of emotions that cling round it; consequently, as with the philosophy of Spinoza, his work often seems hard and cold, especially to those eager to plunge into battle armed with some provocative slogan or resonant war-cry. Such an apostle of calm and toleration was Pierre Bayle (1647–1706), a French Protestant, exiled, like Spinoza, in Holland; while another Frenchman, Fontenelle, distinguished from his fellow philosophers by his longevity (1657–1757), and inferior in versatility to Voltaire alone, did much to foster that new critical spirit which, as he claimed, would render the human mind capable of a gigantic 'spring forward', not least in the realm of the physical sciences. In this prophecy concerning the future of science he was not mistaken.[1]

There were those who, aware of the new critical forces at work, shied at the prospect of a great and perhaps disastrous intellectual upheaval. Thomas Hobbes, born in the year of the Great Armada (1588), delivered a counter-attack against the new libertarianism in his book of political philosophy, *The Leviathan* (1651). An apparent atheist, he feared, like many of his kind, the decay of those absolute standards in thought and life which religion formerly upheld. 'For if men were at liberty to take for God's commandments their own dreams and fancies, or the dreams and fancies of private men,' he writes (*The Leviathan*, Chapter XXVI), 'scarcely two men would agree upon what is God's commandment; and yet in respect of them, every man would despise the commandments of the Commonwealth.' That is true; but it was a

[1] His greatest remark was made on his deathbed. A friend enquired: *'Qu'est-ce-que vous sentez, Monsieur de Fontenelle?'* To which the old man replied: *'Je sens ... une certaine ... difficulté ... de continuer ... d'être.'*

risk which the advocates of toleration were prepared to run. At the close of the seventeenth century, indeed, a school of moral philosophers arose which openly preached a morality of personal sentiment. Shaftesbury (1671–1713), while agreeing with Hobbes that men were by nature egoists, yet posited the existence of a 'moral sense' which prevented them from becoming incurably anti-social. Hutcheson (1694–1746), pursuing this line of thought, endeavoured to represent the moral sense as being independent of all supernatural sanction, while Mandeville (1670?–1733), in a celebrated work entitled *The Fable of the Bees,* broke through the partition between private morality and public service by proclaiming the plausible but dangerous doctrine that the pursuit of private advantage was conducive to the public interest.

For the most part these are small men, skirmishers on the flank of the philosophical caravan. An Englishman, John Locke, stated the anti-Cartesian viewpoint more clearly and in a manner that influenced thinkers all over Europe.

23

John Locke

If I have anything to boast of, it is that I sincerely love and seek truth with indifferency whom it pleases or displeases.

Letter to his friend Anthony Collins

His Life

Born at Wrington in Somersetshire in 1632, Locke came of Puritan parents, and was for fourteen years educated in his own family circle—a little pocket of peace in a restive country soon to be plunged into civil war. In 1646, he went to Westminster School. Here, a Puritan in a Puritan stronghold, he might have been expected to flourish and distinguish himself. In fact he did neither. Judging from some of his observations in a later essay entitled *Thoughts on Education*, he was most unhappy at school, forming a poor opinion not merely of Westminster but of public schools in general.

At Oxford, whither he went in 1652 and stayed for many years, he found an atmosphere more congenial to his already precocious mind. John Owen, the Puritan, who was both Dean of Christ Church and Vice-Chancellor of the University, was appointed Locke's tutor at The House. Governed by Independents and crowded with Presbyterians, Oxford was becoming a hot-bed of fanaticism and heresy hunting; and although Locke was by upbringing favourable to Puritanism, he found a great deal less liberty in the new regime (especially in Presbyterian circles) than he had expected. 'The popular assertors of liberty,' he wrote of this period, 'were the greatest engrossers of it too, and not unfitly called its keepers.' Nevertheless, such men as Owen and Godwin were advocates of genuine religious liberty, and inspired in Locke that devotion to the idea of Toleration upon which he was later to write with such eloquence.

Recounting his early career to his patroness, Lady Masham, Locke later confessed that he was far from being a model student. Nevertheless, he studied in his own way, read widely, including the works of Descartes and Hobbes (*The Leviathan* had but recently appeared), met and corresponded with distinguished men of learning, participated in the chemical and meteorological experiments of the Royal Society, which was founded at Oxford in the Restoration Year (1660), began to study theology with a view (some say) to taking Anglican Orders, and finally, realizing that ecclesiastical advancement was not compatible with the kind of research that he favoured, decided to become a doctor. In his profession, despite his nickname 'Doctor' Locke, he obtained no academic distinctions; but he seems to have practised medicine at Oxford around the year 1666, abandoning it only when his own health broke down. Thereafter he never knew the meaning of physical vigour. He seems to have suffered from chronic asthma, and later developed some form of consumption, though neither seems to have curtailed his mental energy.

Indeed, he was ever seeking new outlets for this energy. Having accompanied Sir Walter Vane on a mission to Cleves in 1665, he developed a deep interest in diplomacy and politics. On his return to Oxford, he happened to meet Lord Ashley, afterwards famous as Earl of Shaftesbury. The two men formed an immediate and, as it turned out, lifelong friendship. Two years later we find Locke settled at Exeter House, the London residence of Ashley, as his private secretary. Locke was now caught up, for better or for worse, in the political life of more than one nation. In 1673, he emerged as a public figure, since in that year he was appointed, on Ashley's influence, Secretary to the Council of Trade and Plantations.

This immersion in public life was undoubtedly beneficial both to Locke and to philosophy; he was never to suffer from that ingrown academic mentality which afflicts so many scholars and otherwise able thinkers. At Exeter House, where he met persons of every sort, he could select at will those with whom he wished to form lasting associations. Like many others who are surrounded by a throng of people, he enjoyed best the company of a small group of intimates. Out of a little 'study circle' at Exeter House in 1671 developed the greatest enterprise of his life. 'Five or six friends' had assembled, at Locke's invitation, to discuss the 'principles of morality and religion'. They were soon baffled by 'difficulties that arose on every side'. Locke suggested that, as a prelude to such discussion, the members should think out for themselves the limits of man's capacity for knowledge. At first he believed it possible to jot down on 'a single sheet of paper' what these limits were; but he soon found the task more arduous than he could have dreamed possible. Thus 'what was begun by chance was continued by entreaty, written by incoherent parcels, and after long intervals of neglect resumed again as humour and occasions permitted'. Twenty years were to pass before the great *Essay Concerning Human Understanding* was finally completed, but such were its small beginnings.

Well might he describe this work as 'written by incoherent parcels'. Upon Ashley's fall from favour, Locke's career was seriously interrupted. He was obliged to go into retirement for a few years, choosing as his place of exile Montpellier and Paris, where he established a considerable reputation among men of learning. Here he jotted down more notes upon the human understanding, and looked after his precarious health. When in 1679 there was a change in the political atmosphere at home, Locke returned to London. It was a brief respite.

Shaftesbury soon got into trouble again, was placed in the Tower, released after trial and once more exiled (he died in Holland in 1683). Locke, who spent most of the time either at Beluton or Oxford, kept his mouth shut. He knew enough of political intrigue to realize that he was being watched closely by government snoopers. We know that this was so. A report from Oxford in 1682 says: 'John Locke lives a very cunning unintelligible life here'; and the Dean of Christ Church, writing to Lord Sunderland, confessed that 'there is not anyone in the college who has heard him speak a word against, or so much as censuring, the government'.

Finally, the strain began to tell even upon this 'master of taciturnity'. So in 1683 he quietly slipped over to Holland, still as much the land of freedom and home of exiled intellectuals as it had been in Spinoza's day. Bayle, the French philosopher, was an exile there at the time. Locke's sudden departure from England fanned the suspicion that his discreet conduct at home had served to allay. The British Government endeavoured to secure his arrest. He was deprived of his Studentship at Christ Church. Even his return to Oxford itself was prohibited by order of the King.

These cruel slights, which turned a voluntary into a compulsory exile, failed to reduce him to despair; they even roused him to greater exertions. He finished the *Essay,* contributed articles to Le Clerc's *Bibliothèque Universelle* (these latter were his first publications), and thus embarked at the age of fifty-four upon the career for which he had been so long preparing, that of authorship. It was the turn of the tide, both for Locke and for his country. In February, 1689, the philosopher experienced the exhilaration of returning home in the ship which brought the Princess of Orange to join her father, who had been crowned King of England the previous November.

The next two years were occupied in consolidating his fame. He had a large number of manuscripts ready for the press, which were issued one after another to a now eager and receptive public: the *Letters on Toleration,* the two *Treatises on Civil Government* (published anonymously), and the *Essay Concerning Human Understanding* Itself (1690). After the excitement of home-coming had subsided, Locke, partly from inclination and partly on account of his health (which the climate of London had never suited), decided to retire to the country. This was to prove the most pleasant exile of all that he had experienced. His hosts, Sir Francis and Lady Masham, were the embodiments of hospitality and, what was much to Locke's taste, of human understanding. And so Locke spent the last years of his life at the little village of Oates, conveniently situated twenty miles out of London, in the heart of Essex.

Retirement for Locke meant the reverse of idleness. Not merely did he spend much time in answering letters and pamphlets, many of them hotly controversial, concering the *Essay*; he also produced new works on economics, finance and theology. An essay entitled *The Reasonableness of Christianity as delivered in the Scriptures*, published at first anonymously in 1695, brought him into collision not merely with obscure rectors, anxious to demonstrate their polemical gifts, but with well-known bishops, anxious to preserve public orthodoxy. Among the latter was Stillingfleet, Bishop of Worcester, with whom he exchanged some of his most vigorous letters. In the following year Locke was obliged to interrupt his retirement by making regular visits to town in discharge of his duties as Commissioner at the Board of Trade, an office conferred upon him in recognition of his experience and ability in public work. Meanwhile, new editions of the *Essay* had to be prepared (the fourth appeared in 1700), and there were translations into French and Latin to be supervised.

As the century turned, Locke, now a very tired but on the whole a contented man, began to prepare himself for death. He abandoned public work, rarely ventured outside Oates, and spent most of his working hours meditating upon the Scriptures. When he heard that the authorities at Oxford had decided formally to condemn his *Essay*, he was not greatly distressed. The dignitaries of Oxford had once refused admission to his person; it was not surprising that they should now ban his masterpiece. (The University has since done full justice to his memory, and the John Locke Scholarship in Psychology is a much coveted award for those wishing to pursue higher studies in that subject.) Commenting on the academic anathema, Locke remarked to a local friend: 'I take what has been done rather as a recommendation of the book, and when you and I next meet we shall be merry on the subject.'

In 1704, while still engaged upon an answer to an attack upon his views on Toleration, he began to decline rapidly in health; by the autumn he was clearly dying, and the end came on 28 October. It was a peaceful release, and, to quote the words of his will, he died 'in perfect charity with all men, and in sincere communion with the whole Church of Christ, by whatever names'—a typical phrase, this—'Christ's followers call themselves'. He was buried in the parish church at High Laver, near the Masham family grave. Unhappily, the manor house at Oates no longer stands to commemorate the idyllic retirement of the man most distinguished in British philosophy for calm, sober, and solid jugement.

His Thought

It is frequently maintained that Locke, in endeavouring to analyse the human understanding from the point of view of common sense, was adopting a point of view typically British. The tradition of common-sense philosophy, which begins with Thomas Reid (1710–96) and the Scottish school of thinkers, and still flourishes in Britain, is something to which no other European country presents a parallel; but the very predominance of such a tendency at certain periods of history is indicative of an opposite movement, against which it is pitted and from which it derives its momentum. Thus the materialism of Hobbes and the criticism of Locke are counter-balanced, and from certain points of view overshadowed, by that extraordinary flowering of religious genius both in poetry and in prose—in Lancelot Andrewes and

Jeremy Taylor, as well as in Vaughan, Traherne, and Herbert—for which seventeenth-century England is famous. And it is impossible to understand the problems which Locke is tackling unless we realize the kind of world—the highly complicated world—in which he marshalled his thoughts.

No doubt it was from his study of medicine that Locke became convinced that the traditional methods of scientific enquiry needed to be overhauled. From the time of Plato to that of Descartes, the assumption had remained unchallenged that truth, or at least the truths of metaphysics, morals and religon, were somehow *innate* in the human mind; you had simply to examine your mind, to wait upon your thoughts, for the fundamental principles of life and conduct to disclose themselves. Socrates had not merely enjoined his fellows to 'know themselves'; he had declared that only by introspection could knowledge of any value be obtained. Plato invented the technique of Dialectic to bring such knowledge to birth; Aristotle, though more experimentally-minded, based his logic upon the same foundation. And what of Descartes himself and his so-called New Method? Even he, too, for all his distrust of Scholasticism and love of 'clearness and distinctness', had failed to dissociate himself altogether from an *a priori* attitude. His 'ladder' from self-knowledge to knowledge of God passed through a kind of intellectual limbo, never touching sense-experience at any point. No wonder Descartes was accused of having preluded his thinking by 'closing his eyes and stopping his ears'.

In his *Essay concerning Human Understanding,* Locke launches a frontal attack upon a *priori* thinking in general. If truth is native to our minds, he says, observation and experimental enquiry will lead us nowhere; at best they can merely confirm our knowledge, never add to it. And it is doubtful whether, taking the word confirmation literally, they can even confirm such knowledge; because an indubitable 'inner' conviction of the kind furnished by Descartes's *Cogito,* for instance, needs no additional evidence in its favour. In Locke's opinion, however, we arrive at knowledge by a method which is the reverse of that of the spider, who spins its web out of its own bowels. We do not nurture ideas from within; we acquire them from without. There are no 'innate ideas'. All our ideas (*i.e.* all our knowledge) are acquired through and in sensation.

Having laid down this challenging proposition, Locke proceeds to answer three questions that arise out of it. The first is: where do our ideas, if assumed not to be innate, come from? The second is: how do we know that our ideas, thus originating, are true? The third is: how much can the human understanding comprehend, and what sort of knowledge remains beyond its reach?

To 'know', in Locke's view, is to perceive a relation between ideas. Now ideas are of two kinds. There are first simple ideas, derived either immediately in sensation, or by a kind of 'inner' experience called reflection. Second, there are complex ideas, which are no more than combinations of the first. The mind or spirit of man originally resembles an empty tablet; experience is that which writes upon it.

Before we admit sensation, we cannot engage in thinking: *nihil est in intellectu quod non antea fuerit in sensu*—'there is nothing in the intellect which was not previously in the senses'.

That which causes an idea to be produced in our mind is, in Locke's terminology, the 'quality' of the external object. And here Locke introduces a distinction which has played an important role in all later philosophical thought.

Qualities such as solidity, extension, form, number, etc., are all constant qualities: to whatever alterations the body or object is subjected, these qualities suffer no change. Such qualities Locke calls 'primary'. They are to be distinguished from what he calls 'secondary' qualities, which, though not to be found in the object itself, are the result of the impact of some power in the primary qualities upon our sense-organs. Such secondary qualities are colours, odours, sounds, tastes, etc.; qualities occasioned by the object, but *produced* as a result of something which we, as observers, contribute. Without human sense-organs, colour and sounds, odours and taste would simply not exist.

Granted that we know all things from sensation, what guarantee have we that the object, the material body, the originator of all these ideas wherewith we form a picture of reality, is really *there*? That, admittedly, was a source of difficulty for Locke. It is part of his 'platform' that we have no immediate knowledge of anything but our own ideas. If experience simply means 'sensuous experience', the problems seems insoluble. Locke, to be fair to him, does his very best to provide a solution to this problem. He points out, for instance, that an actual sensation is accomplished by pleasure and pain. These are feelings which never attach themselves to the memory of that sensation, or, if so, with never the same degree of intensity. Moreover, we find by experience that one of our senses, if suspected of a 'false report', can be corroborated by the testimony of another. Perceiving a fire, a man awaits the report of his tactile sense before concluding that his visual sensation was genuine. These are indisputable facts; but as proofs of the existence of an object external to, and productive of, our ideas, they are frankly subjective; that is to say, they prove nothing at all, but merely suggest very great probabilities. And they suggest probabilities only if we are disposed, in the first place, to believe in the existence of an external world. Locke did so. But supposing we do nothing of the kind—what then? A most ingenious answer to that question was given, as we shall see, by Bishop Berkeley.

It is interesting to draw attention to two notions which Locke shared, however reluctantly, with the Cartesians. The first is the notion of cause. Locke assumes the existence of an object external to our senses, endowed with primary qualities and capable of stimulating in us secondary qualities. This means that he believes in the causal nexus: a relationship which, as we shall see, gave a good deal of trouble to later philosophers. Secondly, as he believes that our ideas are caused by *something*, that something must be a passive *substratum*, which, if endowed with primary qualities, cannot be resolved into such qualities. This is Substance; and we know nothing more about it than that it is an 'unknown somewhat' outside the scope of our faculties.

At this point, therefore, Locke sets up a kind of mental frontier commission. Philosophy, he says, must not presume to enquire into realms that cannot be explored by the well-tried scientific methods of observation and induction, comparison and experiment. The problem of Substance, the problem of Essence (*i.e.* what constitutes the inner character of a thing), remain outside the scope of philosophy. If a mediaeval science called Metaphysics claims to explore these things, then we should have nothing to do with the mediaeval science called Metaphysics. It has brought us nowhere. From now onwards we must adhere soley to the evidence of our senses: that is to say, we must be rigorous *empiricists*. In Locke, therefore, we have a modern restatement of the theory of Nominalism (*cf.* the chapter on Abelard) as first asserted by Roscellinus and developed by William of Ockham. And, in a sense, the controversies of the next two centuries on this subject were just as vigorous as those which agitated the ecclesiastics and heretics of the mediaeval Church. Nor are we, in the late twentieth-century, at the end of them.

24
George Berkeley

My speculations have had the same effect upon me as visiting foreign countries: in the end I return where I was before.

Commonplace Book.

His Life

The term 'freethinker', of which we hear a great deal today, became current, in England at least, during the latter half of the seventeenth century. Toleration was in the air. After 1688, England became, with the Dutch Republic, a refuge for the persecuted and the heterodox, the religious refugee and the philosophical sceptic. From that time onwards no one was obliged, though he has remained free, to leave England on account of his beliefs; and today it seems virtually impossible that so benign and moderate a spirit as that of Locke should ever have needed to go into exile.

The progress of free-thought in England can be judged to some extent from the titles of books published in the years following the so-called Glorious Revolution of 1688. There were John Toland's *Christianity not Mysterious* (1696), Arthur Collins's *A Discourse of Freethinking* (1713), Thomas Chubb's *A Discourse concerning Reason with regard to Religion* (1730), and many other significant titles, to mention only minor works. Some of this 'free-thought' was merely destructive and mischievous, though less mischievous perhaps for being permitted open expression; some of it was certainly the product of sincere thinking, directed towards combating both ignorance and superstition. In orthodox quarters it often provoked unmannerly replies, the more so as it reached its mark or touched a sore spot; but there were masterly counter-attacks as well, witness that of Bishop Butler (1692–1752), author of *The Analogy of Religion*, one of the finest theological treatises in any language.

The thinker best remembered for his wholesale and uncompromising attack upon materialism, however, is George Berkeley. In Berkeley, British philosophy possesses a figure as versatile and revolutionary as that of Descartes in French philosophy and Leibniz in German philosophy. It is a measure of the breadth of the British tradition that a thinker like Locke can be followed by a thinker like Berkeley, and that a thinker like Berkeley can be followed by a thinker like Hume, and that both kinds of thinker can claim to be speaking in the name of common sense. Nevertheless, Berkeley's extreme position—for it is an extreme, though not a preposterous, position—has given rise to much unnecessary mystification. The ordinary reader may feel, on reading his works, that he is being hoodwinked by someone much too clever to be allowed to run amok among fundamental truths. And, though Hume's reversion to brute materialism may not be any more attractive, the usual reaction is that it is preferable to a skylarking idealism.

Who was this extraordinary man Berkeley, and how did he come to the belief that there is no such thing as 'matter'? Was his disbelief in the independent world of nature just a pose, or was it based upon reasonable and logical argument? Was Bergson right to declare that modern philosophy begins not so much with Descartes as with Berkeley? Was this man an incurable dreamer and mystic, or was he in fact a person of sound sense and practical ability?

Although he was born at Dysert in the county of Kilkenny in Ireland (12 March, 1685), Berkeley came of an ancient English family. Of his early childhood in Ireland we know little, except that he entered the second class of Kilkenny School on 17 July, 1696. Four years later we find him enrolled as an undergraduate at Trinity College, Dublin. At Trinity he had a long and brilliant career. During the latter part of his twelve years' stay he was Fellow and Tutor of the College; and this is the period in which he conceived, wrote and published the most famous of his works on philosophy. We lack information about his private life during these busy, formative years. Judging from one anecdote that has been recorded, however, he was a man of extreme curiosity. One day, it appears, he saw a man hanged. When he returned to his lodgings, he persuaded a friend of his, Contarini, uncle of Oliver Goldsmith, to 'hang' him as an experiment. Being unloosed from the halter nearly unconscious, all he could murmur was: 'Bless my heart, Contarini, you have rumpled my band.' Apart from this incident, which may not be authentic, his life seems to have been singularly free from the grim and sordid, though not from disappointment.

During his years at the university, Berkeley kept a Commonplace Book. This volume was discovered long after his death and published in 1871. From it we see that as early as 1705 he believed himself to have arrived at a new philosophical principle—an answer, as he supposed, to the problems raised but not solved by Descartes, Locke, Spinoza and Leibniz. In 1705 he formed a Discussion Group at which these new ideas were debated. Four years later appeared his first important work, *An Essay towards a New Theory of Vision*, to be followed in 1710, when he was only twenty-five, by his *Treatise concerning the Principles of Human Knowledge*. The latter is a landmark in philosophical thought.

Since these urbane compositions contained many novel doctrines, Berkeley naturally expected them to make a considerable stir. The reception accorded them, however, was disappointing. Where they were not ignored, they were for the most part misunderstood. In order to present them in more attractive guise, Berkeley sat down to write the three *Dialogues between Hylas and Philonous*, which are among the most readable expositions of philosophical ideas. Here, more than anywhere else in his works, he displays his wit, his capacity for high controversy, and his translucent prose style. They are in some respects a reversion to the Platonic form of dialogue, except that they assume a rather more propagandist air, being directed primarily against 'Sceptics and Atheists'. Naturally they were directed also against persons of even greater respectability: for Berkeley was distressed to find that his new principle was travestied and misunderstood by persons for whose intelligence and character he had the highest regard.

For reasons of health and also because he wanted to broaden his horizon, Berkeley came to London in 1713. He quickly made a name for himself in intellectual circles, meeting Steele, Addison, Swift and Pope. To Swift, a fellow ecclesiastic with Irish associations, he owed his introduction to the eccentric but well-disposed Lord Peterborough, Ambassador to the King of Sicily and the Italian States, whose private chaplain Berkeley became on an extensive tour through France and Italy. Foreign travel proved much to the young philosopher's taste. In 1715 he was off again to Italy, this time as tutor to the son of Dr St George Ashe, Bishop of Cloyne, Clogher and Derry. His diary of the tour, together with a *History of Sicily*, have been lost; but we see from his correspondence that few things escaped his notice, whether the subject was some natural curiosity, such as the Tarantula spider, or a social or political problem. The 'dreamer' or 'visionary', as his critics were accustomed to call him, was by no means unaware of what was happening in the world about him. On returning to England in 1721, just after the South Sea Bubble incident, he showed the measure of his concern for the welfare of the country by writing an *Essay towards Preventing the Ruin of Britain*.

In the year of the publication of his essay, Berkeley returned to Ireland, this time as chaplain to the Duke of Grafton. His great intellectual gifts were soon put to use at the university again, where he became both divinity lecturer and official preacher. He took his D.D. on 14 November, 1721. Preferment swiftly followed in both the ecclesiastical and the secular spheres: in 1722 he became Dean of Dromore—an office that did not consume much of his time, even as Deaneries then went—and Senior Proctor of the University. Then, with his career mapped out before him, and his attention concentrated upon his new system of philosophy, an unexpected event occurred. A woman with whom he had come into contact but once—no less a woman in fact than Miss Vanhomrigh, Swift's friend Vanessa—bequeathed to Berkeley, without warning or explanation,[1] half of her considerable fortune.

Whatever else may be said about the sudden acquisition of money, it unsettles. Berkeley's wealth, soon to be augmented by the emoluments attaching to the Deanery of Derry (about £1,100 a year), turned his mind to schemes which were temporarily to deflect the whole course of his life.

[1] Possibly she was jealous of Swift's attachment to Esther Johnson ('Stella').

From 1724 onwards, then, Berkeley concentrated his mind upon a project which, though somewhat fantastic in retrospect, seemed to its originator eminently practical. Brieflly, the idea was to establish in the Bermudas a missionary college from which to conduct evangelistic campaigns in America, particularly among the negro population. Without Berkeley's enthusiasm and powers of persuasion, public interest in such a scheme could never have been enlisted; that Berkeley was able to extract a promise from the government of £20,000 towards meeting the expenses was even more remarkable. The money was indeed promised; four years passed but not a penny was handed over. Meanwhile Berkeley worked, persuaded, argued, canvassed, waited. Twice a week he attended the tea parties given by Princess (later Queen) Caroline, less for the enjoyment such functions gave him than for the opportunity they afforded of making contacts likely to further his project. How thoroughly he was in earnest may be judged from a passage from a letter written on his behalf by Swift to Lord Carteret.

> I do humbly entreat your Excellency either to use such persuasions as will keep one of the first men in this Kingdom for learning and virtue quite at home, or assist him by your credit to compass his romantic design, which however is very noble and generous, and directly proper for a great person of your excellent education to encourage.

Nothing, as regards material help, was forthcoming. Rather than abandon the project, however, Berkeley resolved to go without the money, feeling that if he could furnish more direct evidence that the scheme was feasible, he would be able to shame the government into honouring its promises. A Royal Charter for the College (to be called St Paul's) had already been granted; the royal bounty must surely follow. Resigning his rich Deanery, Berkeley set sail with his newly-married wife, daughter of Judge Forster, in the autumn of 1728. A small group of loyal friends accompanied him, all of them at some personal and material sacrifice.

Berkeley spent three years away from England. Pending a decision from London, he settled at Newport, on Rhode Island, where he purchased a farm of about 96 acres and built a house which he named, perhaps not without irony, Whitehall. Frustrated as he might be, he was not idle. In the intervals between drawing-up plans and reports, he continued his studies and worked on a philosophical dialogue directed against freethinking. This book, which he entitled *Alciphron, or the Minute Philosopher*, was a long essay in the style of the *Dialogues between Hylas and Philonous*. He wrote it at leisure, so he records, on a 'natural alcove' of rock on the island coast. It was not published until he returned home.

At length it became obvious, if not to the trustful Berkeley, then at least to his friends, that the government subsidy would never be paid at all. In a revealing letter, Walpole wrote that while as an official he was bound to say that the money, being already earmarked, would materialize, his advice as a friend was that Berkeley and his followers should dismiss the subject from their minds. We know now that the sum in question had already been diverted elsewhere. Disappointed, but not in despair, Berkeley resolved to return. Before doing so, however, he arranged for his large collection of books to be presented to Yale University, and for his farm to be sold for the purpose of founding scholarships there. And so he bade farewell to his pleasant homestead, his slaves (in whose material and moral welfare he had always taken the greatest interest), and the many friends that he had won during his residence. Typical of his character was his insistence, once back in London, that all the subscriptions which his enthusiasm and eloquence had drawn from private purses three years before should be returned.

Berkeley's imperturbable character, his warm and generous disposition, and his genius for friendship, had long won him the respect and admiration of the most hardheaded of men—and this was an age of hardheaded men. He was again received in high society; and soon the promotion which he had formerly renounced, if not forfeited, caused him to be raised to the Bishopric of Cloyne, which office he retained almost to the day of his death. Once settled at Cloyne, Berkeley decided to content himself with episcopal duties and meditation, and to plan no further excursions, save into the realm of theoretical philosophy. As for his office, he appears to have been a model Bishop. His private life was rigorous in its severity. He usually rose as early as three or four in the morning for purposes of study. His encouragement of local industries by patronizing the neighbouring workmen for all his needs meant dressing in the coarsest of clothes. He still devoted much time to literary work; in 1735 appeared *The Analyst*, an attack upon the extravagances of mathematical theorists, and shortly afterwards *The Querist*, which was concerned chiefly with questions of social reform. Then followed a pause of some years during which he turned his attention to a subject which, next to the Bermuda project, seems to have engrossed him more than any other, but in which posterity has been accustomed to see little but a waste of energy and talent. The result of his researches were finally published in a work for which there is no parallel in philosophical literature: *Siris: A Chain of Philosophical Reflections and Enquiries concerning the virtues of Tar Water, and divers other subjects connected together and arising one from another.*

Although a man of robust and handsome appearance, Berkeley's manner of life had not always been conducive to the maintenance of physical fitness; and it is clear that as he grew older he developed a tendency towards hypochondria. 'My own sedentary life,' he wrote in *Siris* (§ 119), 'has long since thrown me into an ill habit, attended with many ailments, particularly a nervous colic, which rendered my life a burden, the more so because my pains were exasperated by exercise. But since the use of tar-water, I find, though not a perfect recovery from my old and rooted illness, yet such a gradual return of health and ease, that I esteem my having taken this medicine the greatest of all temporal blessings, and am convinced that under providence I owe my life to it.'

In *Siris* Berkeley has not merely given us a treatise on medicine; he has produced at the same time a remarkable philosophical essay, for the 'chain of reflections and enquiries' leads him to speculate upon the nature of existence itself, beginning with the simplest considerations and ending with a mysticism which is both Christian and Platonic in inspiration. In the properties of tar, he claimed to detect the fundamental constituents of matter—or, if it is preferred, the vital elements which compose organic nature: thus he leaps from one subject to another, much as the spirit prompts him, throwing out a series of illuminating remarks rather than a consistently logical argument. *Siris* excited sufficient interest among a public always receptive of new 'cures' to prompt its author to issue, after an interval of eighteen years, an essay entitled *Further Thoughts on Tar Water*. Such was the measure of his confidence in that simple remedy.

In the year of the publication of this last essay, which was little more than a tract, Berkeley decided to remove to Oxford in order to be near his son George, who was an undergraduate there (his eldest son had died the year before). Although he was fully prepared to resign his Bishopric, he was granted special permission by the King to retain episcopal status. One Sunday evening in January, 1753, while listening to a sermon being read by his wife, he died peacefully. He was buried in Christ Church.

Two spontaneous testimonies from his friends sum up Berkeley's character and the influence it exerted. The first is from Francis Atterbury, Bishop of Rochester: 'So much understanding, so much knowledge, so much innocence, and such humility, I did not think had been the fashion of any but angels, till I saw this gentleman.' The second is from Alexander Pope, a man not much given to flattery: 'To Berkeley every virtue under heaven.'

His Thought

The history of Berkeley's reputation has been to some extent the history of the way in which he has been misunderstood. And the misunderstanding has arisen as much from the thoughtless admiration of friends as from the deliberate detraction of enemies. The question to be asked in outlining the thought of Berkeley is first—what did he in fact say? The second question, issuing out of the first, is—why did he say it?

First, then, as to what Berkeley actually said. Whereas Locke had introduced a distinction between 'primary qualities' and 'secondary qualities', maintaining that the latter inhered not in the perceived object but in the perceiving subject, Berkeley begins by declaring this distinction to be invalid. Just as a colour cannot exist apart from the sensation of a perceiving subject, so the 'primary qualities' of extension, form and motion are, in Berkeley's opinion, equally dependent upon perception. When we talk of an object, we are talking invariably of the object of a *subject*; the former cannot exist, and cannot be imagined as existing, without the latter. Now the object of the mind is, as Descartes, Hobbes, and Locke agreed, always an *idea*. Therefore, all objects, all 'things', indeed 'all the choir of heaven and furniture of the earth', are nothing but ideas. In spite of the difficulties inherent in his view, Locke had resolutely maintained that our ideas, to be true, must be 'of' something. Berkeley regards this as an absurdity. An idea, in his view, is not 'of' anything but another idea. The world is composed of minds on the one hand and ideas on the other. An 'outside' or 'external' world is therefore inconceivable.

So far, so good. But—and this is the point to be stressed—Berkeley never meant to assert that, as a consequence of the non-existence of matter, natural entities such as the earth, sun, stars, chairs and tables, were nothing but *illusions*. He was as completely aware of their existence as was Dr Johnson, who thought to dismiss Berkeley's philosophy by kicking a stone with 'mighty force' and saying 'I refute it thus!' In the *Principles of Human Knowledge* and again in the Dialogues, Berkeley does his best to clear himself of the charge of denying the *reality* of the natural world. 'I do not argue,' he explains, 'against the existence of any one thing that we can apprehend, either by sense or reflection. That the things I see with mine eyes and touch with my hands do exist, really exist, I make not the least question. The only thing whose existence we deny is that which philosophers call matter or corporeal substance. And in doing of this, there is no damage done to the rest of mankind, who, I dare say, will never miss it. The atheist indeed will want the colour of an empty name to support his impiety; and the philosophers may possibly find they have lost a great handle for trifling and disputation.'

Berkeley's position is as hard to refute as that of Locke is to prove. But there remains a difficulty for which there appears at first sight to be no solution: namely, if existence depends upon being perceived (*esse est percipi*), what happens to things when in fact no one is perceiving them? Berkeley, it must be admitted, was plagued with questions of this kind, which usually resulted from a failure to grasp the fundamentals of his position: but just as he held that we know reality *because* it is composed of ideas present to our minds and is inconceivable except as thus present, so he held that the world of nature is permanent *because* there is always in the last resort a mind to perceive it, namely, the mind of God. 'So long as (objects) are not actually perceived by me, or do not exist in my mind or that of any other created spirit, they must either have no existence at all or else subsist in the mind of some external spirit: it being perfectly unintelligible and involving all the absurdity of abstraction to attribute to any single part of them an existence independent of a spirit. To be convinced of which, the reader need only reflect and try to separate in his own thoughts the being of a sensible thing from its being perceived.' Berkeley's view is thus seen to approximate to that of Malebranche, who declared that 'we see all things in God'. Berkeley, incidentally, had visited Malebranche in his cell in Paris, and the two had engaged in some heated argument. The report that Malebranche died as a result of an illness brought on by the excitement caused by Berkeley's polemics is now generally discounted.

A philosopher of Berkeley's proved sincerity and eminence does not adopt an extreme view without good reason. In every generation there are wiseacres who enjoy bewildering the public with farfetched systems, just as there are poets and painters whose one ambition is to *épater la bourgeoise*. Berkeley did not try to bewilder and astonish; he was out to combat what he believed to be the most dangerous tendency of his age, namely, the drift towards materialism. Nor is it strictly true to say that he associated materialism merely with the belief in matter; what he regards as pernicious in the thought of his time is its addiction to *abstractions*. To Berkeley, the interposition of the artificial 'idea' between the perceiver and the object perceived is simply one among other examples of this abstractionist tendency. Thus empiricism, which claims to keep rigidly to the brute facts of experience, inevitably becomes involved in the most complicated word-spinning.

To those who accused him of making nonsense of such notions as the uniformity of nature and the sequence of cause and effect, Berkeley answered that such regularities were better explicable on his idealist view than on that of materialism: for 'whenever the course of nature is interrupted by a miracle, men are ready to own the presence of a superior agent. But when we see things go on in the ordinary course, they do not excite in us any reflection; their order and concatenation, though it be an argument of the greatest wisdom, power, and goodness in their creator, is yet so constant and familiar to us, that we do not think them the immediate effects of a free spirit: especially since inconstancy and mutability in acting, though it be an imperfection, is looked on as a mark of freedom.'

25

The Precursors of Hume

Berkeley had few disciples, for not many philosophers were vigorous enough to follow him all the way; and you cannot be a true Berkeleyan unless you follow the master all the way. His colleague, Arthur Collier, is perhaps the only other orthodox Berkeleyan: in 1713 he published a book entitled *Clavis universalis, or a New Enquiry after Truth, being a Demonstration of the Non-existence or Impossibility of an External World.* A thinker who owed nothing directly to Berkeley, and who had probably never heard of him, was the Italian Giambattisa Vico (1668–1744), an idealist of great originality who applied his theories to the problems of society and history, and outlined the principles of a New Science from which modern philosophers, particularly the Italian idealists Croce and Gentile, have drawn much inspiration. Vico, who laid stress upon the historical evolution of the human mind, lived an obscure but intensely busy life in Naples at a time when the chief centres of learning were London and Paris. Another contemporary, Montesquieu (1689–1755), a Frenchman, also set out to philosophize about society; but Montesquieu tended to look upon society as a mechanism with which human reason could at best 'tinker', not as the product of man's developing consciousness. His thought is static; that of Vico is dynamic. Meanwhile, thanks to the versatile Voltaire, France had been made acquainted with the ideas of Locke. Pushing empiricism to its logical conclusion, philosophers such as Condillac, Abbot of Mureaux (1715–80), and La Mettrie, the doctor-author of *L'Homme Machine* (1748) and *L'Homme Plante* (1748), ended up by denying the existence of mind altogether, and thereaby anticipated the theories of modern Behaviourism.

The French critic, Rémy de Gourmont, observed that 'very simple ideas are within the reach of very complicated minds only'. This is especially true of philosophy. We have seen how Berkeley, realizing that perception is always of the concrete and never of the abstract, concluded that perception and existence involved each other, and that in consequence there could be no such thing as a world outside or external to our minds. What makes Berkeley a thinker of such stature is not so much his original idea, however, as the way in which he sticks to it, analyses it and develops it. There is all the difference between the thinker possessed with an *idée fixe* which he enunciates as a dogma, and the thinker who, like Berkeley, is prepared to defend his thesis by argument step by step. As we know, Berkeley regretted that his critics should have shown such constant reluctance to cross swords with him; for while he was not seeking to provoke astonishment or dismay, he considered that his original notions deserved more than a passing gesture of contempt. A man of very different temperament from Berkeley, but resembling him in his addiction to an intellectual passion, was the Scotsman, David Hume. In spite of the hostility which his views have provoked (especially in orthodox circles), Hume deserves without question to be numbered among the important philosophers of the Western world. Berkeley's philosophy is a triumph of belief; Hume's philosophy is a triumph of disbelief. For if it is hard to believe, it is equally hard to maintain a consistent attitude of scepticism.

26

David Hume

If I must be a fool, as all who reason or believe anything certainly *are, my follies shall at least be natural and agreeable.*
Treatise of Human Nature

His Life

If we are right in assuming (as he himself assumed) that the family of Hume can be identified with that of the Homes, who had been associated for centuries with Ninewells, Edinburgh, David Hume came of a line of both substance and tradition. He was born on the 26 April, 1711. As for his early education, he tells us that he passed through 'the ordinary course with success'. We know that he matriculated, under the name of 'David Home', at Edinburgh in February, 1723, which is evidence of no mean ability. His first intention was apparently to study law; but already at the age of sixteen he had set his heart upon becoming a philosopher. By 'philosopher' he did not mean to imply a professor or instructor in philosophy—which is what a philosopher means today, if it does not mean a man who makes the best of a bad job, or takes the rough with the smooth; he meant to imply a devotee of the philosophical or contemplative *life*, a kind of religious or philosophical ascetic. The crisis came at the age of eighteen. It was then, as we learn from a letter written many years after (probably to the physician George Cheyne), that Hume believed himself to have arrived, like Berkeley at the same age and Descartes somewhat later in life, at a new discovery in thought, a new principle of philosophy.

Whatever the precise nature of this revelation, it was sufficiently compelling to cause him not merely to renounce the formal study of law but to embark upon research into the classics, English literature and philosophy itself. By 1729 the strain of such unremitting application had begun to affect his health. He suffered what we today call a nervous breakdown. Fortunately, he went the right way about curing it. He reformed his diet, took regular exercise, especially riding and walking—and, perhaps wisest of all, continued gently to pursue his studies. Such, we gather, was his manner of life for the next few years. Absorbed as he was in intellectual matters, he was still not absolutely sure what form his life's work should take: whether he should retire to some secluded spot and write down his thought in systematic form, or whether, having for so long studied in solitude, he should return to the world of men, and particularly of worldly men. He seems, at the critical moment, to have felt the 'pull' of society; we do not know precisely what were his motives in trying his hand for a period at commerce in Bristol. We may surmise, however, that this experience, though brief, decided him for good and all. It was now philosophy or nothing. In the summer of 1734 he was off to France. On 12 September he arrived at Rheims. Finally he decided to halt at La Flèche in Anjou, where for the next two years he was to make his home.

La Flèche, as the reader may remember, was a spot already sacred to philosophy, for it was there that Descartes had received his Jesuit education. There the New Method had germinated. Hume had not long settled in his new home when he experienced, with unconcealed delight, the first stirring of his creative powers—a moment for which he had waited so long as almost to have despaired of its arrival. The immediate stimulus (and there must always be an immediate stimulus) was an argument in which he became involved one day with a local Jesuit father. The subject was the reality of miracles. Dissatisfied with the orthodox view presented to him, Hume sat down to write a philosophical essay which, as he warmed to his theme, came to embrace most of the problems of natural and revealed religion. Admittedly it represented no more than an experiment, though an experiment worth making; but it cleared the stage for the more ambitious works upon which, now that his faculties were aroused, he felt ready to embark. The first of these works was entitled *A Treatise of Human Nature*, and Hume confessed that he intended by its composition to 'produce a total alteration of philosophy'. The claim, as it turned out, was not altogether extravagant. For some thinkers, of whom one at least was to prove Hume's superior, it came to represent a decisive turning-point in thought.

In return for £50 down and twelve bound copies, Hume agreed to have the *Treatise* issued anonymously in 1739. Meanwhile, having returned to Ninewells, he awaited publication with high hopes. He was confident that his views, displayed with tantalizing anonymity, would cause the kind of uproar for which all philosophers wish to provide occasion but so few arouse. Like Berkeley, he expected to precipitate a mild intellectual revolution; but, like Berkeley, he was sadly disappointed. A 'revolutionary' or 'advanced' author tends to forget that, being far ahead of the public, he must expect recognition only from those who, by great mental effort and adjustment, can keep up with him. From the public as a whole he must anticipate nothing but indifference or hostility, atoned for scarcely at all by the placid recognition of later generations. In Hume's own words, 'the book fell deadborn from the press'. Not that it was completely ignored; one reviewer paid him the doubtful compliment of comparing this first composition to the 'crude attempts' of a Milton or a Raphael. Deserved or not, the slight roused Hume to such fury that he is said to have considered challenging the writer to a duel; but the story is in keeping neither with what we know of Hume's character nor with his ideal of philosophical conduct.

At any rate he pushed ahead, still hopeful of success, with the second volume, which the firm of Thomas Longman agreed to publish in 1740. Again the work excited no particular interest. But the completed treatise, which was duly recognized to be a literary as well as a philosophical masterpiece, gradually began to make its way in the philosophical world: until, like the works of Locke and Berkeley, it came to form part of the tradition not merely of English but of European philosophy.

This does not mean that the philosophy of Hume is a satisfying philosophy. It is not. It does not even form a satisfactory philosophical *system* such as the work of Plato, Aquinas, or even Leibniz. Yet that, if nothing else, is the reason for its importance: it represents the first ambitious attempt to establish a basis from which other philosophical systems may be criticized. In short, it inaugurates the modern tradition of philosophy as a technique for the criticism of other philosophy, particularly that form which is known as metaphysics.

After the publication of the *Treatise of Human Nature*, Hume produced a number of shorter works which were later assembled under the title of *Essays Moral and Political*. An application for a professorship at Edinburgh was unsuccessful. Being in need of employment, he obtained in 1745 the lucrative but otherwise not very satisfactory position of tutor in the family of the Marquis of Annandale. The Marquis, who had already been declared by Chancery to be incapable of managing his own affairs, was almost a complete lunatic; nor was Hume slow to perceive that his estate, as supervised by a certain Captain Vincent, was showing good profits to everyone save its nominal master. Hume was not devoid of moral courage: and his plain expression of disapproval of what was going on cost him his job the following year. In these circumstances, he felt obliged to close with an offer, made soon after, to act as secretary to General St Clair for the duration of an expedition to Canada. This particular expedition did not materialize: instead it was diverted to an attack upon Port Lorient. Hume impressed his commander sufficiently to gain the appointment of judge-advocate. Soon afterwards he was appointed member of a diplomatic mission to Vienna and Turin, sporting a uniform which lent him the appearance, so it is said, of 'a grocer in the train-bands'. Hume seems never to have been wholly at ease in high society, and his manners possessed none of the grace and polish of his own prose style.

When, in 1749, Hume returned to Ninewells, he had in his pocket 'near a £1,000', not a bad capital sum in those days upon which to retire for the purpose of writing philosophy, which is not as a rule a paying business. Seclusion had once more exerted its attractions over him, and indeed the next few years proved that he had made the best use of it. In 1751 was published the *Political Discourses* and the *Enquiry concerning the Principles of Morals*. Upon a work of more controversial matter, to which he gave the title of *Dialogue concerning Natural Religion*, he had spent much labour; but realizing that its publication would draw upon him fierce accusations of infidelity and atheism, he finally decided to hold it back until such time as the public mood, easily disturbed in those days, grew calmer. As it was he became the object of a great deal of abuse, which he held chiefly responsible for his failure, for the second time, to obtain a university professorship.

In spite of these attempts to blacken his reputation (there was never any insinuation regarding his personal conduct), he finally succeeded in obtaining a position which, besides carrying a good measure of prestige, was to prove of great convenience to himself. This was the post of librarian of the Advocates' Library at Edinburgh, among the 30,000 volumes of which (it was the largest collection of its kind in Scotland) he was in his element. The pay, by contrast, was shocking: a bare £40 a year.

Although still as interested as ever in matters philosophical, and hoping one day to produce something more deserving of the name of 'system' than anything he had so far assembled, Hume had long been toying with the idea of writing a history of the United Kingdom. There have been several reasons suggested why, in middle life, his interest should thus have shifted from the theoretical to the practical, from the abstract to the concrete. That a professional thinker should 'change his direction' in this way is usually not an accident; there is some problem that he feels an urgent need to solve, and he will not rest content until he has devoted all his attention to it.

In the course of his travels abroad, as well as in his own country, Hume had developed an interest in public affairs. Being hardly at all adulterated by motives of ambition (for he did not aspire to shine in the world, other than as a figure of academic distinction), this interest was on the whole sincere. The difficulties and disturbances of his own age needed, in his view, first to be understood in order to be cured. When and how did these troubles begin? Hume realized that the key to the understanding of present social stress lay in history, in the chain of events that have led up to the present. And to pursue the kind of detailed research needed to satisfy his new mental curiosity, he could not have been better placed.

The first volume of what was to prove an epoch-making work appeared in 1754. It began with the reign of James I, which its author, after much reflection, pronounced to be the period from which the prevailing discontents dated, though he later saw reason to change his mind. This first volume had a poor reception. An author accustomed to initial disappointments ought not, on finding this first instalment a 'flop', to have allowed himself to be so dejected. The book represented, as Hume prided himself, a new departure in historical writing. The public does not collectively take to new departures. The public must be persevered with. Fortunately Hume pushed steadily on with his studies until, by the year 1762, he had completed five volumes. With gratification he began to realize that his patience was being rewarded. The copies began to melt from the bookshop shelves. Money flowed in steadily, increasingly: until Hume, who had never before believed such a thing possible, discovered that he was not merely a rich man, but something far more unique in those days, a man enriched by literary achievement. Hume's history was almost the first serious 'best-seller'.

For a good many years after its author's death, the *History of England* remained the standard work of its kind, the scholar's classic, enjoying the distinction common to such classics of being referred to not by its title but by its author. A man who declared that he was 'reading Hume' might confidently be supposed to be reading the History, not the *Treatise of Human Nature*, nor the *Enquiry concerning Human Understanding*. Today, such as is the changed estimation of these two branches of his work, the presumption would be otherwise, the History being relegated to the background and rarely consulted save out of curiosity. Nevertheless, it forms a landmark in historical writing in that it concerns itself as much with social and literary as with political affairs.

For reasons largely dictated by Hume's peculiar temperament, the more he progressed with his history the more he allowed personal bias to influence his judgments. Hume the philosopher stepped down some way to meet Hume the historian. Just as Dr Johnson confessed to have made sure, in writing his disguised parliamentary reports, that 'the Whig dogs had the worst of it', so Hume made no disguise in this book of his intransigent Toryism. Nor was he any kinder to the English people, whom he repeatedly accused of an anti-Scottish bias and a desire to ruin Scotland. Thus we have vituperative references to the 'barbarians on the banks of the Thames', and, on the party side, to 'the villainous seditious Whig strokes' or 'plaguey prejudices of Whiggism', which increased in violence as the story proceeded and infuriated a large section of the public. But the book still sold and sold, as infuriating books will do.

No doubt some of Hume's anti-Whig fury was due to his mounting hatred of Puritanism and bigotry. Royalism in the past seemed to have stood for a broader, more tolerant tradition, which he believed to be seriously in peril. Whatever his political views, however, he cannot by any stretch of imagination be described as orthodox in matters of religion. During the composition of the History, he turned aside more than once to write on philosophical subjects; in 1757, resuming the theme of his earlier *Dialogues concerning Natural Religion*, he produced a highly controversial study entitled *The Natural History of Religion*. His main contention was that polytheism represented the most natural, as well as the earliest, form of religious belief, while monotheism was the result of custom and habit not necessarily superior either to the former or to downright scepticism. In this work in particular, Hume, feeling moderately secure in his position, makes little or no attempt to conceal his own lack of faith. Not that he wished to advertise himself as an atheist; atheism, in his opinion, was a point of view to which no one wishing to avoid dogmatism could subscribe, for you could no more deny the possibility of a supernatural God than you could be sure that such a God existed.

Nevertheless, Hume could not resist the temptation to indulge in ridicule at the expense of orthodox and conventional religious beliefs, which in one place he describes somewhat uncharitably as 'sick men's dreams'; and in consequence his books have been listed by certain institutions as unfit for the devout. The truth is that Hume was temperamentally a man too much given to intellectual curiosity to find repose in any convenient formula of belief; but he recognized that in this respect he and his kind were not typical of the human race, and he was anxious not to disturb any man's convictions so long as they were free from fanaticism and intolerance.

The year after completing the History, Hume was invited to accompany Lord Hertford to Paris as secretary to the Embassy. He went in the capacity of a subordinate; by Parisian society, on the other hand, he was received as a man of the highest distinction, for his works were by then well known there. When the Foreign Office sent Hume to Paris, the French, quicker in these matters than other peoples, reminded England by their adulation what an important man she had chosen as representative. With Dalembert, the philosopher (1717–83), and Turgot (1717–81), the statesman–economist, Hume formed immediate attachments, for his point of view was very similar to their own.

In society itself (insofar as that could be separated from intellectual circles; the division was not so complete as it is now) the British philosopher shined less brightly. A contemporary witness has recorded how oddly his 'broad, unmeaning face' contrasted with the flower of French beauty, though Hume, as we shall see, now considered himself to be a dashing courtier, and lost no opportunity of participating in entertainments and charades for which his presence was requested by the ladies.

He made a good and discreet secretary; and when, later, General Conway wanted an assistant at the Foreign Office, Hume was considered the best man for the job. That was in 1767. After two years of responsible work, he began to feel that his interests and health required, as his pocket now permitted, a rest from professional labour, and a return to that part of the world in which he was most at home. He therefore decided to settle in Edinburgh, taking a house at the corner of St David's Street sufficiently large to enable him still to entertain the best society. He could well afford it. His pension and other earnings now brought him in £1,000 a year. He had comparatively few commitments, though he was exceedingly generous to friends and struggling authors. Smollett, the novelist, was one of those to whom he gave timely assistance.

The most ungrateful beneficiary was a man of established, indeed international, reputation, Jean-Jacques Rousseau. Rousseau, for whose writing Hume had a high regard, had been expelled from one country after another, as much because of his own quarrelsomeness as because he was a writer of 'dangerous' or seditious books. Hume was anxious for him to be given asylum in England. Arrangements were therefore made to bring Rousseau and his mistress, Therèse le Vasseur, over to that country, and Hume even went so far as to persuade the government to grant the Frenchman a small pension, on the understanding that the matter was to be kept secret. The ramifications of the story are very complicated; but it appears that Rousseau, learning of the proposed pension, and at once identifying secrecy with conspiracy and intrigue, wrote, as was his habit, a ferocious letter to the one man who had tried to help him. Hume, rightly indignant, replied asking Rousseau to explain himself. Once labouring under the delusion of persecution, however, the latter was beyond the control of any man and all but one woman; and the plan of providing him with an asylum of peace was wholly frustrated, though Rousseau spent long enough in England to write the first six books of his *Confessions*. As to Hume's handling of the affair, it was creditable throughout.

On 25 August, 1776, after an illness of some length which he bore without complaining, Hume died, having reached the age of sixty-five. He has left us his own view of his character and achievements which, allowing for a slight element of complacency, is as good a summing-up as he deserves at the hand of others. It is also a fine example of his supple, urbane, exquisitely clear prose, and with it we conclude this sketch of his life, almost as if he were speaking, disembodied, from behind that veil of sensation which he never thought to penetrate:

'I am, or rather was (for that is the style I must now use in speaking of myself, which emboldens me the more to speak my sentiments), I was, I say, a man of mild disposition, of command of temper, of an open, social, and cheerful humour, capable of attachment, but little susceptible of enmity and of great moderation in all my passions. Even my love of literary fame, my ruling passion, never soured my temper, notwithstanding my frequent disappointments. My company was not unacceptable to the young and careless, as well as to the studious and literary; and as I took particular pleasure in the company of modest women, I had no reason to be displeased with the reception I met with from them. In a word, though most men, anywise eminent, have found reason to complain of calumny, I never was touched, or even attacked, by her baleful tooth; and though I wantonly exposed myself to the rage of both civil and religious factions, they seemed to be disarmed in my behalf of their wonted fury. My friends never had occasion to vindicate any one circumstance of my character and conduct; not but that the zealots, we may well suppose, would have been glad to invent and propagate any story to my disadvantage, but they could never find any which they thought would wear the face of probability.'

His Thought

Although Hume differed in outlook from Berkeley as radically as a sceptic must necessarily differ from a convinced believer, there was one point upon which they were in whole-hearted agreement. This was the question of abstract ideas. Hume declared that of all the discoveries of modern thought, Berkeley's demonstration of the unreality of abstract ideas was by far the most important. But whereas Berkeley, criticizing Descartes and Locke, had argued that no idea was 'of' anything but another idea, thereby demonstrating the unreality of an external world, Hume introduced a distinction between ideas and what he called 'impressions'. The latter were defined as actual physical (or mental) *percepts*, i.e., things in their natural state as our senses perceived them. If, therefore, Hume had been asked to say what an idea was 'of', he would have replied that it was 'of' a previous impression. Any idea of which the previous impression or group of impressions could not be traced was to be judged a false or fictitious idea.

The multiplication of more or less subtle 'distinctions' has long been regarded, not without cause, as the curse of philosophy. When the spurious thinker runs up against a difficulty, he makes a distinction, thereby trying to encircle the obstacle on either side. If the two branches of enquiry do not manage to meet, a further bifurcation occurs, creating four questing antennae and so on until the enquiry has become altogether too involved for the lay mind to grasp. The great philosophers are distinguished for their capacity to keep their ultimate end in view; consequently when they introduce a distinction, it is usually with great care to explain why it should have been necessary at all, and upon what particular aspect of the enquiry it is designed to throw light. This applies above all to Hume's impression-idea distinction.

Having maintained that every genuine idea is a copy of a previous impression, Hume is still faced with the task of explaining how it is that we have, or appear to have, 'complex' ideas—genuine complex ideas, that is to say, as opposed to false or fictitious ones. It is here that Hume unfolds that part of his philosophy which has caused greatest controversy, and from which Kant, as we shall see, was to derive the stimulus to embark upon his own profound line of enquiry.

The transition, according to Hume, from our simple ideas to those of a complex character is not a logical or rational one at all: at least no logical or rational connecting-link has so far been traced. It is purely one of imagination association or habit. From the observed succession of certain ideas to others, or certain groups of ideas to other groups of ideas, we build up what we call our knowledge of matters of fact. The recurrence of these various successions impels us to attribute a greater or lesser measure of certainty to facts or events. This is true not merely of such facts as that the sun rises in the east and will set tonight, but of the observed succession of every set of 'effects' to an apparent set of 'causes'. All we are entitled to say is that we observe the *succession*, several times or continually repeated, of the latter to the former. Of the necessary connection or link between one and the other we have no impression at all. To assert that such a connection exists is to assert something for which there is no warranty in science and no justification save in custom.

If we bear in mind the theory of ideas advanced by Berkeley, we shall remember that he, like Hume, was obliged to explain how it is that our ideas, being the sole constituents of our minds and of the world itself, come to be arranged in a certain way, namely, the way in which we find them arranged. Berkeley's answer, perhaps the least satisfactory of all the explanations put forward by him in justification of a most ingenious theory, is that God has so arranged them. To this assertion Hume's reply is characteristic. If you believe in God, he says, well and good; your belief will permit you to believe in practically anything. But supposing you do not (and it is a matter of temperament, after all)? In that case, you can hazard no reasonable explanation as to why things are as they are. All you know is that in the course of normal living you come to rely upon events assuming direction, order, recurrence and regularity. Meanwhile, whether or not you discover the true explanation of such patterns, you must go on living as if such an explanation were forthcoming. Instinct will not wait for reason to catch up. Thus Hume would maintain that the entire assemblage of our knowledge—including the existence of an external world, the idea of personal identity, indeed the idea of knowledge itself—depends upon our trust in certain instincts. Against these, as he himself had good cause to know, the whole armoury of philosophical scepticism cannot prevail.

Believing as he does that 'all our reasonings concerning causes and effects are derived from nothing but custom, and that belief is more properly an act of the sensitive, than of the cognitive part of our natures', Hume comes to the conclusion that, as human creatures compelled to live and work as well as speculate, we must in essential matters, and for the greater part of the time, 'follow our instincts'. 'For I have already shown,' he observes, 'that the understanding, when it acts alone and according to its most general principles, entirely subverts itself, and leaves not the lowest degree of evidence in any proposition either in philosophy or in common life.' What, then, should we do to avoid intellectual suicide? If such are the consolations of philosophy, how has that exalted subject managed to acquire its reputation as a solace? Hume's reply reveals the kind of comfort philosophy may be expected to confer upon its devotees: 'Most fortunately it happens,' he says, 'that since reason is incapable of dispelling these clouds, nature herself suffices to that purpose, and cures me of this philosophical melancholy and delirium, either by relaxing this bent of mind or by some avocation and lively impression of my senses which obliterate all these chimeras. I dine, I play a game of backgammon, I converse, and am merry with my friends; and when after three or four hours' amusement I return to these speculations, they appear so cold and strained and ridiculous that I cannot find in my heart to enter into them any farther.' There are many to whom such sedatives, even if accessible, would be wholly ineffective. And there are many to whom the very idea of taking them would seem like intellectual cowardice. Hume's curiosity was extreme; but it was a broad rather than a deep curiosity. We can hardly imagine an Aristotle, a Spinoza, or a Kant speaking in this urbane but superficial manner.

In general it may be said that the materialism of Hume is nothing but the 'immaterialism' of Berkeley with the lights switched off. It was the *reductio ad absurdum* of what has been called, with reference to the course of philosophy from Descartes onwards, the 'way of ideas'.

Our natural reaction to the study of Hume is to conclude either that philosophy, *i.e.*, metaphysical philosophy, is nonsense, or that Hume's premises are seriously open to question. In both cases the reaction is bound to be somewhat violent. In England and France, many thinkers, rebelling against orthodoxy in both politics and religion, saw in Hume an apostle of liberation from superstition, an extirpator of absurd and outmoded fancies in theology and metaphysics. Others, less iconoclastic by temperament but genuinely desirous of salutory reform, were shocked thereby into rethinking their whole philosophical position from the beginning. Among these latter was a man of immense intellectual capacity and erudition: Immanuel Kant.

27

Encyclopaedists and Romantics

In fifth-century Athens philosophy was regarded as something in the nature of a divine gift. In the Middle Ages it became an intellectual discipline subordinated to its superior director, theology. In the sixteenth and seventeenth centuries it was an interesting, though sometimes also a dangerous, hobby. But in the eighteenth century it first became a profession.

Towards the end of the eighteenth century—one of the most crucial epochs of the world's history—a group of thinkers flourished in France under the title of 'philosophes'. A 'philosophe' was a man who, by proclaiming himself a thinker by profession, believed it his mission to apply reason to the problems of society, and to act as a kind of mental physician to the body politic. Among these apostles of reason were some who, though appalled by the flagrant abuses of the time, believed that the next few decades would see the establishment of a new form of society, based upon reason and justice, leading to a new order of civilization throughout Europe. With the object of compiling a modern equivalent to St Thomas Aquinas' *Summa Theologiæ,* and intending to codify the new knowledge at the disposal of enlightened men, these *savants* drew up plans for a gigantic Encyclopaedia. Hence the title 'Encyclopaedists', which was applied to a circle of writers of whom Denis Diderot (1713–84), founder of the Encyclopaedia project, was the acknowledged leader.

Diderot was a man of extraordinary versatility: philosopher, scientist, mathematician, and novelist (his remarkable story *La Réligieuse* would be regarded, if first published today, as a work of unusual sophistication and psychological precocity). His chief collaborator was Dalembert, with whom, as we have seen, Hume became acquainted during his stay in Paris. Excelling his contemporaries in breadth of vision and profundity, Voltaire (1694–1778), himself a contributor to the Encyclopaedia, directed the whole weight of his wit, learning, and eloquence against the ignorance, superstition and cruelty of his time. Sharing the current belief that the eighteenth century represented, at its best, the highest reach of which civilization was capable, he persisted in the hope that by the steady application of reason to the problems of society, public enlightenment might be achieved within the space of one or two generations. His attraction to British philosophy, increased by his own residence in England, was due to its emphasis upon experiment and practice, and its distrust of metaphysical abstractions. Voltaire's passion for exactitude, clarity, and order (characteristics of the French mind at its best) confirmed him in a prejudice against everything that was half-formed, in process of formation, or lacking in precision; and this slight mental inflexibility tended to blind him to two great factors in human development—firstly, the influence of sentiment and emotions in human conduct, and secondly the concept of evolution in history. The latter, he held, had no real place in a view of the world according to which all ages prior to the eighteenth century formed one long night of superstitious barbarism. For of darkness there can be no history; and if the millennium is due to dawn tomorrow, there is no scope for future eras of historical development.

To the apocalyptic visions of Voltaire, which the brave old man entertained to the end of his long life, when, as he declared, he 'left off dying' to come to Paris for the last time, Rousseau (1712–78) provided the most violent antidote. Instead of a millennium of reason, Rousseau preached the necessity of recapturing primitive innocence. This was possible, he held, only by recovering that spontaneity of sentiment which civilization and the progress of physical science had tended to desiccate. Rousseau's emphasis upon man's inner life of imagination and sentiment, as expounded in *Emile* and *Julie,* exerted the most powerful impression upon Kant, whose whole philosophical position might well have been different had he not, at an early and critical stage of his career, made acquaintance with Rousseau's writings. That Rousseau's temperament made him the most unmanageable of men, setting an example of romantic irresponsibility which cast its spell over many later generations, we have already observed. Hume, who received first-hand evidence of his incalculability, summed up the French writer succinctly: 'He has only *felt* during the whole course of his life. He is like a man who was stripped not only of his clothes, but of his skin, and turned out in that situation to combat with the rude and boisterous elements.'[1] Nevertheless, Rousseau must not be dismissed as an effeminate dreamer. Like many others who have preached the brotherhood of man, he could speak with the tongue of devils as well as angels (as his *Confessions* amply show), and he was a shrewd, if unbalanced, critic of his fellows. He was not in himself a particularly original thinker, even in *The Social Contract*; his function was rather to redress the balance of thought.

[1] *Cf.* 'You would say that my heart and my mind do not belong to the same individual. Feeling fills my soul more quickly than a flash of lightning; but instead of enlightening me it burns and dazzles me.' (*Confessions*, Book III.)

28

Immanuel Kant

You will not learn from me philosophy, but how to philosophize—not thoughts to repeat, but how to think. Think for yourselves, enquire for yourselves, stand on your own feet.

His Life

The story of Kant's life is so difficult to separate from his philosophy that we shall here revert to the method already adopted on occasion, and discuss the two together. Of the importance of Kant's contribution to thought, everyone who possesses the slightest knowledge of the history of philosophy is in some degree aware: if asked to give the names of five philosophers, or at least of more than three, the ordinary man will almost certainly include Immanuel Kant. There are at least two good reasons why Kant should be recognized as a great figure even by those who, if challenged to expound the essence of his thought, would be hard put to do so. One is that he made gigantic and lasting contributions to all the major problems of philosophy; the other is that he came very near, in his own individual way, to living the genuine philosophical life. The number of so-called 'practising' philosophers is not large: there is Pythagoras, there is Socrates, there is Aquinas, there is Spinoza—and there is Kant. If Spenser is the poet's poet, then Kant is surely the philosopher's philosopher.

The career of Immanuel Kant provides a striking demonstration of the capacity of genius to overcome limitations. At a time when it is an accepted axiom that 'travel broadens the mind', and that the 'conquest of distance' has tended to further international understanding, we may well ponder the fact that Kant, who knew so much and commanded (at any rate in his later years) such widespread public attention, never once crossed the frontiers of East Prussia, nor showed any inclination to make such an excursion in the interests of either recreation or learning. To speculate whether a more cosmopolitan Kant would have produced a system less rigid in certain of its aspects is futile; what we should find sufficiently remarkable is that his philosophy, thus conceived in a limited though active environment, has influenced thinkers in every part of the world.

Kant's father, Johann Georg Kant, was born in Memel but finally settled in Königsberg. He persisted in the belief, which his son shared all his life, that his family came originally from Scotland. This is not at all unlikely. There had been an influx of Scottish immigrants into

Poland during the seventeenth century, and Kant himself drew attention to the prevalence in East Prussia of such names as Douglas, Simpson, Hamilton, and others. Although some of the immigrant families accumulated power and riches, a great many pursued humble trades. Kant's father was a strap-maker, who, marrying the daughter of a fellow-craftsman, begot nine children of whom Immanuel was the second (born 22 April, 1724). The five children to survive were brought up in the extreme of austerity. According to Kant's own testimony, his father and mother were model partners. 'Never,' he says, 'not even once, have I had to hear my parents say an unbecoming word, or do an unworthy act.' Kant always speaks of his father with respect. To his mother he seems to have been particularly attached, and such early education as she was capable of giving him (and she seems to have taught him a great deal) moulded his outlook for life. By nature a devout woman, she was much influenced by the religious reform movements of the day. This was known as Pietism, and its emphasis was upon faith and sentiment as opposed to reason and dogma. The Pietistic movement was started in Germany by Jacob Spener about 1670; in Kant's day its chief representatives in Königsberg were J. H. Lysius and F. A. Schultz. The latter was both director of a college patronized by Freidrich William I and pastor of the church at which the Kant family worshipped. Ever willing to help the poorer members of his congregation, Schultz remained for many years a real friend to the Kant household. On one occasion Kant remarked that Schultz was perhaps the only person who really understood his philosophy: a high compliment indeed.

After a brief period at a local Hospital School, Kant entered the *Collegium Fridericianum* (the institution over which Schultz presided) at the age of eight, staying there until he entered the university in 1740. His schooling was as strict as the puritan foundation could make it; and the habits of regularity, punctuality, frugality and hard work thereby inculcated, combined with early home influences, to form a character almost too rigid and unbending to be attractive.

Kant's mother died of rheumatic fever when he was thirteen years old. Life thereafter proved very difficult for the family. The funerals of both parents were those of paupers, as the churchyard register shows. Kant's education thenceforth became a matter for his own exertions. From 1740 to 1746 he studied diligently at the university; and although he seems to have long remained uncertain of his true vocation, the influence of a remarkable young professor, Martin Knutzen, who put him in the way of the works of Isaac Newton, evidently first aroused his curiosity regarding metaphysics. Kant's associates during this period of preparation were students scarcely better off than himself. Two friends with whom he lodged, and in company with whom he is supposed to have earned a casual penny at billiards or cards, Wollner and Heilsberg (both Lithuanians), ended up the one as Finance Minister at Berlin and the other as War Minister. Kant also augmented his income in the way more usual to the indigent student, namely, by doing odd jobs of tutoring and finally by taking a permanent past as tutor. He lived with the family of a Reformed Church Pastor at Judschen, a village situated sixty miles from Königsberg, this being the absolute limit of his wanderings. He acted as tutor to two other families before becoming, in 1755, a licensed but unpaid lecturer at the university of Königsberg; by which time he had published sufficient papers on scientific and philosophical subjects to qualify as Doctor of Philosophy (the equivalent of our Master of Arts).

Largely owing to political intrigues, his efforts to obtain a professorship failed; but the government at Berlin, having heard of his ability as teacher and scholar, directed in 1766 that he should be appointed sub-librarian in the Schloss Library, the emoluments of which amounted to about £10 a year. Kant found the work trying, let alone ill-paid, and he soon resigned. Not that his work at the university, both official and unofficial, seemed likely to lead to prosperity. He was extremely hard up. He wore his clothes out until his friends, much embarrassed, begged him in vain to accept money to buy new ones. He moved from lodging-house to lodging-house, usually impelled to leave by the disturbances to which he was perpetually subject—at one house near the river it was the raucous boatmen, at another an intolerably vocal cock. Thus he struggled on, living so plainly as to succeed finally in accumulating a reserve fund of twenty sovereigns. By 1770, when he had reached the mature age of forty-six, he had established a reputation both as writer and as lecturer on such various themes as mathematics, physics, logic, metaphysics, ethics, geography, anthropology, and even military pyrotechnics and the science of fortification (the latter courses being attended by members of the Russian garrison). Like Francis Bacon before him, he seems to have made up his mind to 'take all knowledge for his province'. To have massed such a fund of knowledge and achieved such authority upon such meagre resources was to come near to being the most underpaid man in the world.

Twelve years after first applying for a professorship at Königsberg he was offered the Chair he had almost given up hope of obtaining, that of Logic and Metaphysics. His position was at last stabilized; and with stability came comparative financial ease—that is to say, his income rose to £60 a year (roughly what Wordsworth was earning at the height of his fame), together with some small 'extras' for academic services. Later he was given an additional subsidy, and at the end of his life his salary amounted to about £100 a year. The greater portion of this income he invested with an English settler in Königsberg, Green, at six (later five) per cent. The result of this judicious saving was that he left in his will the respectable sum of 21,539 thalers, and that in spite of his yearly outlay upon charitable purposes.

Professor Kant worked fully as hard as the earnest *privatdozent* who had been obliged to exercise such self-denial. But his work was more profitably distributed, and he had much more leisure. Nevertheless, his time-table remained extremely rigid, and for the next quarter of a century he rarely departed from it. Admittedly, he was occasionally indisposed, and one afternoon he missed his customary walk through absorption in Rousseau's newly-published *Emile*. If Blücher is said to have invented punctuality by arriving at the right time on the field of Waterloo, Kant may be said to have invented *routine* in the streets and lecture-rooms of Königsberg.

Kant's day, details of which have been carefully recorded, was planned as follows. Punctually at five minutes to five in the morning, his devoted servant Lampe, an old soldier from Würzburg, used to rouse him. At five o'clock sharp, the Professor, presumably in his dressing-gown, was installed at the desk in his study. While making notes for his lectures, he would drink a cup of tea and smoke one pipe. He was in the lecture-room promptly at seven, where he discoursed for an hour on Logic or Metaphysics followed by an hour on some less abstract theme. During the remainder of the morning he worked at his manuscripts. Halting at precisely 12.45, he announced the time to the cook, who would depend upon this verbal signal to make ready for lunch. Guests to the number of five (Kant's stock of plate would not accommodate more) might be expected daily, each invitation being issued that same morning in order to secure immediate acceptance or otherwise. Nor was any guest likely to receive a second invitation who appeared late for the first. Abstemious though he was in his habits, Kant enjoyed nothing better than to extend hospitality to his friends; and having sat down to a three-course lunch, he liked to linger as much as four hours over the dessert and the wine. He was himself a good conversationalist, and was not without a sense of humour, though he maintained high standards of decorum. It was his maxim that conversation at meal-times should pass naturally through the three stages of narration, discussion and jest. In his own case, the two themes upon which jest was debarred were metaphysics (a subject which, being the occupation of the rest of his life, was banned altogether from meals) and his own bachelor status, to which he rarely made reference. (The two women in whom he appears to have taken more than casual interest were, we gather, unable to preserve their single state long enough for the philosopher to calculate whether or not he should invite them to change it.) Once the conversation had passed the third stage, Kant did not hesitate to make clear to his companions that it was time for his afternoon walk. In the case of this regular promenade, the word 'constitutional' was particularly appropriate. Kant was far from being robust, and, like some other confirmed bachelors, he displayed a tendency to hypochondria. As he was convinced that every possible anti-germ precaution should be observed, he rarely departed from the practice of taking his walks unaccompanied, thereby enabling him to keep his mouth firmly closed. For the same reason he studiously refrained from indulging in exercise violent enough to induce perspiration, of which he had a particular dread. Thus, except towards the close of his life, he succeeded in keeping physically fit to a degree which, taking into account the intensity of his sedentary labours, was remarkable. The mind being in his case driven harder than his body, it was not surprising that the former should have been first to show signs of collapse.

His walk over, Kant would spend an hour or two reading the

newspapers—his very isolation from the world made him an avid collector of news—and also such books and journals as he considered worth a professional philosopher's scrutiny. Having refreshed his mind with new matter, he would turn once more to the particular philosophical problems which held his attention. In the winter season this reflective mood would seize him about the hour of darkness. It was then his custom to fix his eye, as an aid to concentration, upon the tower of Lobernicht Church, just as during his lectures it had been his habit to stare at a particular button on the coat of one of his regular pupils. One season, it appears, the rapid growth of some nearby poplar trees obscured the view upon which he had come to depend, just as one day the particular button he habitually kept in view was found to be missing. In both cases Kant suffered genuine mental torment; nor was his peace of mind restored until in the one case the trees were cut by the kindness of a neighbour and in the other the button was replaced.

It is not possible here to cite all the various idiosyncrasies that have been attributed to Kant: his habits of dress (and in particular the elaborate mechanism whereby his stockings were suspended) and his peculiar mannerisms. Suffice it to say that such details are all in keeping with his meticulous unbending character. The witty account by Heine (1799–1856), the German poet, sums up the impression made by Kant upon his fellow townsfolk.

'The life of Immanual Kant is hard to describe; he has indeed neither life nor history in the proper sense of the words. He lived an abstract, mechanical, old-bachelor existence, in a quiet remote street in Königsberg, an old city at the north-eastern boundary of Germany. I do not believe that the great cathedral clock of that city accomplished its day's work in a less passionate and more regular way than its countryman, Immanuel Kant. Rising from bed, coffee-drinking, writing, lecturing, eating, walking, everything had its fixed time; and the neighbours knew that it must be exactly half-past four when they saw Professor Kant, in his grey coat, with his cane in his hand, step out of his house door, and move towards the little lime-tree avenue, which is named, after him, the Philosopher's Walk. Eight times he walked up and down that walk at every season of the year; and when the weather was bad, his servant, old Lampe, was seen anxiously following him with a large umbrella under his arm, like an image of Providence. Strange contrast between the outward life of the man and his world-destroying thought. Of a truth, if the citizens of Königsberg had had any inkling of the meaning of that thought, they would have shuddered before him as before an executioner. But the good people saw nothing in him but a professor of philosophy; and when he passed at the appointed hour, they gave him friendly greetings—and set their watches.'

His Thought

Of Kant it may justly be said that the first half of his career was made up of two closely-interrelated struggles: the struggle to gain sufficient means to live and the struggle to set his mental house in order. As an unpaid lecturer, he devoted himself with great earnestness to the study of past and contemporary philosophers; and it was fully in the spirit of Galileo and Descartes—indeed of the 'new philosophy' in general—that he wrote that 'in every branch of natural science there is only so much strict and proper science as there is of mathematics'. Kant's study of Newton, together with his interest in scientific discovery in general, had gradually induced in him a deep dissatisfaction with the subject which, from 1770 onwards, he was obliged to teach. He was not even sure that metaphysics, divorced from the experimental sciences in general, had any right to exist. That such was his mood about the year 1765 may be judged from a remark made in the course of a letter to the young mathematical philosopher Johann Heinrich Lambert, who had written to him suggesting collaboration in tackling the new problems of thought raised by the progress of scientific discovery: 'After many and many a tack,' Kant wrote, 'I have at last reached a firm conviction as to the method which ought to be employed if escape is ever to be made from the illusory and pretended knowledge known as metaphysics.' What, we may well ask, was in his mind?

In maintaining that metaphysics, as commonly understood, represented nothing but 'illusory and pretended knowledge', Kant was not advancing anything original. As we saw in the last chapter, Hume had entertained a view of metaphysics very similar to this; and we have Kant's own admission that it was in consequence of his perusal of Hume's *Enquiry concerning Human Understanding*. (apparently he never set eyes on the *Treatise of Human Nature*, though the *Enquiry* was a re-issue of part of it) that he was 'awakened from his dogmatic slumber'. But whereas Hume was an avowed enemy of metaphysics in all its forms, Kant, concentrating upon the question as to what constituted true knowledge, refrains from dismissing metaphysical knowledge as utter nonsense. He leaves us always in some doubt as to how far he wishes to 'search for a proper method of metaphysics' and how far he wishes to supersede metaphysics by a new 'critical philosophy' of his own. In 1770, we find him again confiding to Lambert that 'It is nearly a year since, as I flatter myself, I reached a conception, which I feel sure I shall never change, though I may extend it: a conception which enables us to test all sorts of metaphysical questions by perfectly certain and easy criteria and to obtain a decision as to how far they are soluble or not.' In 1771, another 'year since', he wrotes to his friend Marcus Herz of Berlin that he is occupied with a work on the subject of the 'boundaries of Sense and Reason'. In February, 1772, again, he declares himself to be 'in a position to propound a criticism of the pure reason'. And so he goes on, making announcement after announcement, year by year, working on short essays and beginning longer ones, revising his views almost weekly, but always returning once more to the task of erecting what he well describes as 'an architectonic of pure reason', until, in 1780, at least a decade later than he originally intended, fearing that unless he marshalled his maturing ideas he would leave nothing to the world save a stack of miscellaneous notes written on the oddest scraps of paper, he devoted five busy months to the composition of the *Critique of Pure Reason*, one of the greatest, if least commonly read, of philosophical treatises. From the first edition of this substantial production, Kant received a payment of £30.

We have already hinted at the general problem with which Kant, in preparing for the *Critique*, was chiefly concerned; but a philosopher, like an artist, does not occupy his mind with a problem unless, in a sense, he is obliged to—unless, that is to say, it has become an 'irritant' that he feels the need to expel from his system, and unless his is endowed with the self-awareness to perceive what it is that, being troublesome, needs to be ejected. Moreover, the greater the thinker, the more he will reflect in his own individual experience the problems of his fellow-men: the more, indeed, he will think on their behalf and show them, by his superior gift of insight, what they themselves only dimly perceive.

If Hume may be called a 'rigorous' thinker, in what sense was Kant's approach more rigorous still? To study Kant's development is to observe that he was early perplexed by a contradiction in the thought of his time, which he realized must be resolved if philosophy were not to lay itself open to the charge of casuistry. The contradiction, in Kant's view, was between the thorough-going scepticism of Hume and the Newtonian view of the universe as a vast, intricate but fundamentally intelligible mechanism. Having begun to study Newton, Kant realized that the one principle or relation upon which the whole structure depended was that of cause and effect. Moreover, this principle, as understood by Newton himself, was nothing if not an *objective* principle. The relation really did operate and was observed at work in the world of nature. For Hume, on the other hand, the so-called relation of cause and effect was nothing more than a habit of our imagination. Instead of being a truth subsisting independently of our minds, a necessary and universal nexus based upon reason, the causal relation was a truth (if indeed it could be called as much as that) without any external foundation at all. Here was a violent contradiction between science and philosophy. Although by profession and inclination a philosopher, Kant was passionately interested in the methods and achievements of physical science. If, however, he was right to suppose, with Descartes and his successors, that a science became increasingly scientific the more it approximated to the condition of mathematics, then it followed that science was bound to affirm the objective certainty of the relation of cause and effect. Thus philosophy, having arrived at the parting of the ways, must choose between the way of Newton and the way of Hume.

Such was the problem which Kant endeavoured to solve in writing the *Critique of Pure Reason*. First of all, we may ask, why *pure* Reason? Kant's reply to this question was as follows. The primary task of philosophy since the time of Socrates, and even among Socrates' predecessors, was to arrive at a basis of certainty; to distinguish between the contingent and the necessary; to learn to distinguish the deliverances of reason from the deliverances of sentiment and emotion. Every age, every generation almost, views this crucial problem from a different angle. For Kant, the problem was to discover how the certain, necessary and universal judgments of science—the whole structure of scientific thought linked together by the causal relation—were *possible.* Hume had pointed out that such judgments could not be arrived at by mere analysis of our own ideas. Agreed; but that did not prove their irrationality or impossibility. Of their existence in experience there was no doubt; but, as Kant went on to observe, that which we observe to operate in experience need not itself have originated in experience. We must ask ourselves, as Hume never satisfactorily asked himself, what precisely we mean by experience. For the word is often employed very loosely. In short, there is a different between 'experience' used to connote 'all experience whatever' and experience used solely to connote 'sense-experience'. Failure to observe this important distinction has been responsible for much confusion and obscurity in modern philosophy.

Kant therefore begins the *Critique* by advancing the following proposition: the perception of objects—common, everyday sense-perception, that is to say—is not a direct process, but rather a process which demands that the object shall already have been subjected to what he terms, somewhat formidably, 'the *a priori* conditions of all scientific knowledge', including that of causation. This explanation may appear unnecessarily abstruse; but if we are sufficiently patient with Kant, our efforts will be rewarded. What does he mean by this novel account of the perceptive process? First of all, we must remove a possible misconception. He is not describing the physiological or psychological mechanism of perception. His enquiry is conducted a stage farther back. In order to analyse knowledge—knowledge in general—he naturally begins with the most elementary form of knowledge. And the point he is trying to make is that, during the act of perception, we are concerned with something already organized, already in a condition to be perceived, already 'worked up' into something *perceptible.* In other words, the object, in order to be an object at all, has to undergo such treatment as will give it sufficient rudimentary form to bring it within the purview of the higher faculties of our intelligence.

To provide this 'treatment' is the initial act of our sensibility. It is an act which involves a synthesis of what would otherwise be (and otherwise is) utterly formless, disparate, and miscellaneous—a 'manifold', as Kant calls it, without cohesion. Now the initial act involves a great deal more than setting things in good order; it effects a definite transformation, except that the latter word pre-supposes the exchange of one form for another, while this process consists in bringing order out of chaos. Here Kant introduces a new conception, which some have described as the most revolutionary discovery in modern philosophy. Our perception of objects as disposed in space and enduring through time is the first and most important achievement, he holds, of this initial act of sensibility. Space and time, that is to say, do not characterize the world, if it can be called a world, external to our minds; they are contributed by ourselves in our act of observing it. They are 'ideal' or subjective. In the framework that they provide, we build up, with the aid of our understanding, a coherent picture of the world.

The world, observe; not reality itself. Our understanding, resting upon the foundations laid by our sensibility, succeeds only in apprehending *phenomena*. To grasp the nature of things as they are in themselves is an entirely different matter. Kant does not deny that such apprehension is possible; all he maintains is that it is achieved, though rarely, by a faculty distinct from our ordinary understanding.

To sum up Kant's position: whereas philosophers have tended in the past to suggest that the mind's function is to 'conform to' reality, to register accurately and impartially what it perceives to be 'there' (*i.e.*, 'over there', in a world standing apart from the mind), Kant advances the view that the world of phenomena enjoys existence only in so far as we ourselves participate in its construction. (Such a view is very different from that suggested by Berkeley, who maintained not simply that the mind imposed form upon a chaos of impressions, but that the whole world of phenomena, consisted of ready-made ideas.) Hitherto, he says in effect, it has been contended that our knowledge is determined by the object; henceforth, as a result of his 'Copernican Revolution' in thought, it will be necessary to maintain that the object is largely determined by our knowledge.

Impressive as this philosophical revolution may be, we must bear in mind that we are still speaking of knowledge of phenomena, of appearances, of the outside of things. So far and no farther can our reason proceed. Let it once attempt to probe into deeper matters—for instance, the nature of the Self, or the problems of God, human freedom, and the immortality of the soul—and it will involve itself in untold difficulties. The history of philosophy is very illuminating in this respect. For centuries, Kant points out, philosophers and theologians have endeavoured, no doubt with the best of intentions, to unravel the deeper problems of life and thought according to a method which is frankly inadequate. To apply the methods of reason to that which by hypothesis evades reason at every turn; to apply intellect to spirit; to endeavour to rationalize religion—these, the aims of the great scholastic philosophers, Kant considers to have been gravely mistaken. By refusing to repudiate such aims, orthodox theologians had rendered a marked disservice to mankind. Being increasingly unintelligible to the masses, their teaching had provided an excuse for casuistry, clap-trap and pedantry. As for the humble and poor in spirit, they were usually content to accept a simpler faith. Hence the great rift of the Reformation, followed by the mushroom growth of 'inferior religions' of the heart instead of the head, of the emotions instead of the intellect. In the atmosphere of such popular illuminism Kant himself had been born and bred; and though not a regular churchgoer, his religion throughout life was in spirit identical with that of his humble parents. Thus his philosophy of knowledge, like his philosophy of ethics and of art, was essentially the product of his own experience. Of the intellectual problem, the mental 'irritant', with which he began, we have already spoken; but we must not forget that every intellectual problem, every conscious questioning, is shadowed by a deeper, emotional problem, of which it is an articulation. Naturally the degree of articulation or self-consciousness attained, depends upon the degree of genius with which the thinker is endowed.

His claim that human reason, operating alone, is incapable of understanding the nature of 'things-in-themselves' leads Kant to repudiate as outmoded and mischievous the traditional science of metaphysics. That is the reason why he refers to his own thought as 'critical philosophy'. Such a conclusion proved startling to many; even Kant himself appears to have found in it an element of paradox. He had set out to examine and exalt pure reason. He had ended by restricting the scope of that same faculty. He had set out to reform the science of metaphysics. He had ended by exposing it as a sham. Where, as a professional philosopher paid to give instruction in 'Logic and Metaphysics', was he to go for a solution to this dilemma?'

He was to go in a direction which, since his time and under his spell, many others have followed. For Kant's 'next step', whether a step in the right direction or a step in the dark, has affected the whole course of human thought.

Having quashed the claims of metaphysics (with whose fate he links that of theology) to penetrate reality as well as the world of phenomena, Kant adopts an attitude very different from that of Hume, who, having made a similar repudiation, merely throws his hand in. No one was a greater champion of the rights and powers of the human mind than Kant; and if he felt obliged, for the reasons we have cited, to circumscribe the powers of reason, he was the more persuaded that truth, ultimate truth, could be reached by another and deeper channel of intelligence. Here again Kant's pietistic upbringing asserted itself. What, he asks, is the most profound experience that we can have? In what sphere of life, for instance, do we feel ourselves to be in contact, however intermittently, with the essence of things? What is deeper than science and more compelling in its influence than art? Some philosophers would have answered 'love'. Kant, less sentimental, answers 'duty'—moral duty or the exercise of our ethical will. That, he says, is the channel whereby we make contact with the thing-in-itself. That is the experience in which we see beyond reason and enter the world behind appearances, the world of which metaphysics is dimly conscious but essentially ignorant.

Such is Kant's philosophy in outline in so far as it is expounded in the first of the Critiques. Its initial reception was moderate; it could be called disappointing only if Kant, who knew the meaning of obscurity, had been foolish enough to entertain excessive expectations. Like Hume's *Treatise of Human Nature,* the book made its way gradually, silently, creating its own audience in the manner, as Proust later maintained, of a great work of art. It received one or two appreciative reviews, followed by a long period of silence. Kant was as grateful for the latter as for the former, since, as he remarked a year later, 'this silence at any rate evinces a suspension of judgment, and a suspicion that after all, in a work which abandons every accustomed path and strikes into a new one which at first feels strange, there may be something calculated to give new life and fertility to an important, but now dead, branch of human knowledge—evinces, in short, an anxiety not to break off and to destroy the yet tender shoot by a premature judgment'.

The conclusions at which he had arrived in the *Critique of Pure Reason,* especially on the subject of moral judgment, prompted him to devote his attention next to ethical questions. In 1785 appeared the essay entitled *Foundation of the Metaphysic of Ethics* (a typical Kantian title: how many potential readers must this great man have alienated first by his titles and secondly by his terminology!). This, as well as his later ethical treatises, achieved something very like popularity; there was a zeal and fervour about their composition that made them more readable than his previous works, and their message was more easily intelligible.

The message was simple: a good act, says Kant, is one that can be 'universalized'—that is to say, if you are in doubt as to whether a course of action is good or not, ask yourself whether it could be made, without danger to mankind, a universal law. Secondly, treat every man not as a means, but as an end. And why an end? Because 'a good will is that by which alone man's existence can have absolute value; and in relation to it the existence of the world can have an ultimate purpose'. Duty, therefore, is a 'categorical imperative'. Do not ask *why* it should be obeyed: 'we cannot comprehend the practical unconditioned necessity of the moral imperative; we can only comprehend its incomprehensibility'. This was a stimulating doctrine in a day much given to moral lethargy and materialistic ethics. Moreover, it is a doctrine, Protestant in its inspiration, which has since influenced the lives of thousands to whom the name of Kant has meant little or nothing. Although the 'moral law' appears formidable and despotic in its operation, the existence in man of a moral consciousness, a sense of duty, is the surest evidence of his freedom. As an element of the world of nature, man is merely one among a number of other *phenomena*; as a member of the world of spirit, or of what Kant called 'the kingdom of ends', he is a free self-motivated being. In the one case, he is subject, like any other material thing, to the law of cause and effect; in the other case, he is his own master, endowed with self-consciousness, and bound by nothing but his own choice. Thus Kant found a 'way out' of the blind determinism of Hume.

His Last Period

Not until he had reached the age of sixty-six was Kant content to regard his exposition of the Critical Philosophy as complete. Two more Critiques, the *Critique of Practical Reason* (1788) and the *Critique of*

Judgment, a treatise on aesthetics (1790), followed that on Pure Reason. Now a rapidly ageing man, Kant confessed that 'it is only for between two or three hours in the forenoon that I can persistently devote myself to headwork'. Nevertheless, he continued not merely to lecture but to write papers on various philosophical questions. On one occasion he received an official rebuke for his supposed unorthodoxy from the Government at Berlin (1794). His reply was a trifle abject. Meanwhile, his reputation not merely in Germany but in the outside world was growing. To some it seemed as if the Kantian doctrine, especially as regards morality, was destined to become a new gospel, almost a successor to Christianity; 'In a hundred years,' one of his most enthusiastic disciples exclaimed, 'Kant will have the reputation of Jesus Christ.' At any rate, he was great enough and sufficiently well known to receive a fan-mail. From 1792 onwards, a certain Maria von Herbert, suffering from the effects of a love-affair and (judging from what is known of her) of a good deal else, wrote him a series of letters with the object of 'drawing him out' on the subject of love and marriage. In a year or two she was hinting at the desirability of a meeting, so that she might ascertain, among other things, 'whether it would not be worth your while to take a wife, or devote yourself to someone with your whole heart, and leave an image of yourself behind'. (The poor lady, given no encouragement in Kant's lifetime, committed suicide six months after his death.) Pilgrims, not less earnest but more philosophically inclined, visited the sage of Königsberg and have left us interesting accounts of him. Among these was a young man called Fichte, of whose work we shall later speak.

Kant abandoned his still heavy programme of lectures in the summer of 1795, but he continued to discourse for one hour each day on Logic and Metaphysics. Nor was he content thenceforth to sink into obscure idleness. On the contrary, he took greater interest than ever before in public affairs, especially in the course of the French Revolution, which he had hailed at its inception with as much enthusiasm as Charles James Fox: 'I can now say like Simeon,' he had exclaimed, '"Lord, let thy servant depart in peace, for mine eyes have seen thy salvation."' By 1795, it seemed as if, to use Tom Paine's phrase, a 'morning of reason' had dawned in Europe; and Kant, blind to the catastrophes to come, wrote an essay on *Perpetual Peace*, the prospects of which seemed then brighter than ever before. During the next two years he collected together a number of essays and lectures for publication, but in 1797 he decided to abandon public work altogether. This withdrawal from active academic life was marked by a special ceremony and procession. Forty-two years of continuous and active teaching could not be allowed to pass without some sign of appreciation from students, both young and old. Kant was wise to make this decision to retire. His faculties, and above all his memory, were showing signs of failure. He realized that while his life might be prolonged for some few more years, his brain was already worn out. It was better to spare an admiring public the sight of humiliating dotage.

Owing to the detailed memoirs of an old pupil, Wasianski, we know much more about Kant's last years than about his youth and middle-age. It is in many ways a pathetic story. We learn, for instance, how failing memory caused the great man to write everything down, however trivial, on scraps of paper. A scribbled sentence—'the name Lampe must be completely forgotten'—reveals, apart from the oddity of such a memorandum, how deeply he had been attached to his old servant, whom he was obliged eventually to dismiss for drunkenness and general unreliability, but whom he remembered in his will. A feeling of tension in his head grew more trying from about 1796 onwards. Attributing it to electricity in the air, Kant convinced himself that the forces responsible for his distress were identical with those reported to have caused the death of a number of cats in Germany about the same time. From such obsessions he could not be shaken, and his friends were obliged to humour him as best they could.

In a condition just short of complete senility he lingered on for several years. At moments he was perfectly himself again, though conscious of reduced vitality. 'Sirs, I am old and weak:' he said one day to a small gathering of friends, 'you must treat me like a child. I am not afraid of death. If I felt this night that I should die, I would lift up my hands, fall down and say, God be praised.' He lingered on, but several times his weakness nearly precipitated his end. One day he stumbled and collapsed in the street. Two ladies, running to his assistance, were surprised to receive from the old man, his balance scarcely restored, the rose he was wearing in his buttonhole. The regular supervision of his private affairs was now beyond his capacity. Wasianski assumed charge of the household, and a new servant, Johann Kaufmann, succeeded the unsatisfactory Lampe. Very occasionally the old man went out, or sat in his garden; but his nights were restless, and the enjoyment of life began to diminish with the onset of an old complaint, flatulence of the stomach. On 22 April, 1803, his birthday, he laboriously penned the words: 'According to the Bible our life lasts seventy years, and at the most eighty; and when it is at its best, it has been labour and sorrow.' That autumn he had become so utterly helpless that his sister, then living in an almshouse, arrived to look after him. She proved a very capable housekeeper; and Kant, while he grew no better, at least was able to make ready for the end in an atmosphere of domestic peace.

In the early part of 1804 Kant's faculties no longer displayed that recuperative power which had enabled him, even in his seclusion, to state his views on subjects of current interest, whether it was the composition of the university senate (from which an attempt was made to oust him), the virtues or otherwise of inoculation, or some moral problem about which his advice was sought. He became blind, partially deaf, and generally decrepit. On a sunny day on the 12 February he died. His body was placed on a bier in his own dining-room, and for sixteen days the mourners of is native city passed through to pay their respects. He was buried in the University Church in what is called the Professors' Vault. Some years afterwards his bust in marble was placed above his grave, to be moved later to the New University.

To conclude our account of Kant by lingering over his final dotage is to run the risk of forgetting what an extraordinary influence he exerted up to and even including his last years. Let us revert for one moment to those days of power and success, not forgetting that a thinker of Kant's type finds the rapt attention of a few more rewarding than the formal respect of a multitude. This, at least, is how he appeared to a young student as late as 1795: 'His delivery has quite the tone of ordinary conversation, and can scarcely be called elegant. Imagine to yourself a little old man' (Kant was not much above five feet in height) 'bent forward as he sits, in a brown coat with leather buttons, with wig and hairbag to boot; imagine further that this little man sometimes takes his hands out from the close-buttoned coat where they lie crossed, and makes a slight movement before his face as a man does when wishing someone else quite to understand him. Draw this picture to yourself and you see him to a hair. Though all this can scarcely be termed elegant, though his words do not ring clear, still, everything which his delivery, if I may say so, wants in form, is richly compensated by the excellence of the matter...'

Kant once remarked that two things in life moved him above all else: the first was 'the starry heavens above' and the second 'the moral law in my heart'. To those—and there are many—who find his writings ponderous, his arguments tortuous, and his conclusions repellent, the reply may be given that, whatever the difficulty of his works, they are monuments of sincerity, patience and application. He abhorred false simplification, without delighting in obscurity for its own sake. He attacked metaphysics not so much because he desired to abolish the study of ultimate reality as because he hated the mumbo-jumbo that often goes with 'transcendental' studies, the casuistry of the 'philosophaster'. At his best he speaks with a sublimity reminiscent of Plato himself, and his deepest words on the subject of the meaning of life (with which every philosopher worth the name is ultimately concerned) belong to what may be termed the *philosophia perennis*.

'It is difficult to suppose that a creature whose life has its first beginning in circumstances so trivial and so entirely dependent upon our own choice, should have an existence that extends to all eternity. As regards the continuance here on earth of the species as a whole, this difficulty is negligible, since accident in the individual case is still subject to a general law, but as regards each individual it certainly seems highly questionable to expect so potent an effect from causes so insignificant. But to meet these objections we can propound a transcendental hypothesis, namely, that all life is, strictly speaking, intelligible only, is not subject to changes of time, and neither begins in birth nor ends in death; that this life is an appearance only, that is, a sensible representation of the purely spiritual life, and the whole sensible world is a mere picture which in our present mode of knowledge hovers before us, and like a dream has in itself no objective reality; that if we could intuit ourselves and things *as they are*, we should see ourselves in a world of spiritual beings, our sole and true community which has not begun through birth, and will not cease through bodily death—both birth and death being mere appearances.'

29

German Romantic Philosophy from Fichte to Hegel

Kant was a thinker of such comprehensive vision that his disciples, of whom there were many, tended to concentrate upon and develop certain aspects of his system to the neglect of others. Such are the drawbacks of discipleship; the applause of enthusiastic followers drowns many a great man's true message. A philosopher whose emulation caused Kant some embarrassment during his lifetime was the young Fichte, to whom we have already been introduced. Fichte claimed to have developed Kant's theory of ethics in such a way as to transform it into a philosophy of action—of revolutionary action. Born in 1762, he was the son of a Saxon linen-weaver. In 1793 he was appointed Professor of Philosophy at the University of Jena; but was obliged in 1799 to resign his Chair as a result of charges, in themselves quite false, of atheism. For the next decade he lived from hand to mouth, barely earning sufficient to maintain his family; but in 1809, having regained popularity as a result of his *Addresses to the German Nation* (1807–08), he was made professor at the University of Berlin. Fichte's philosophy, not immediately easy to grasp, may be summarized as follows. Agreeing with Kant that man's will is the highest value in the universe, and that practical reason enjoys primacy, Fichte maintains that the business of mankind is self-realization. The thing-in-itself is not 'unknowable'; it is our own ego, our ideal self. To realize oneself is to become free. But freedom is not attained without struggle, opposition, conquest: the ego thus attains freedom by overcoming all that is not itself—the non-ego. The latter it creates in order that it may engage in such struggle. This non-Ego is mere appearance, phenomena; and while the understanding perceives and assists in constructing the world of phenomena, the Will or Ego uses it as a kind of improvised pontoon to reach the reality behind it. This dialectic, active in the individual, is also active in society and indeed in all history. History is nothing but the history of freedom, the story of man's struggle for liberation, the story of the vicissitudes of liberty. Fichte's *Addresses* to his countrymen, in which he expounded his ideas in words of great patriotic fervour, undoubtedly had a great deal to do with the uprush of German nationalism at a time when the French army, sweeping over Europe, had occupied and dismembered Prussia.

To Fichte's lofty idealism was opposed, as might be expected, a movement of practical scientific thought for which the German people have since been distinguished. Simultaneously, but again not unexpectedly, a remarkable revival of another kind took place. Schiller and Goethe are universal figures. Novalis, Friedrich Schlegel, Tieck and above all Hölderlin, are the great German romantic writers. Schelling and Hegel, at least at the beginning of their careers, were 'romantic' philosophers. And just as the Romantic writers of this period were the first, or among the first, to develop a new interest and insight into history, so Hegel, as his thought grew to maturity, turned his attention and that of all subsequent philosophy to the problems of historical development. Of the importance of this new vista of thought, hitherto explored only by the isolated genius of Vico, we shall have something to say later on. For it may be that the concept of History is that which is most characteristic of our era, as the concept of Nature was that most characteristic of the era preceding it.

The philosophy of Schelling (1775–1854); in its first phase, was a curious blend of mysticism, poetry, and almost magical science. He called it the Philosophy of Nature, and it would seem to have had its origins in the early speculations of the German-Swiss philosopher Paracelsus,[1] as well as in the more recent 'illuminism' of the 'unknown philosopher' Saint-Martin (1743–1803). At this stage Schelling was preoccupied with the problem of the reconciliation of 'contraries': in nature, the contraries whereby thought develops into consciousness, and in spirit, the contraries whereby thought develops into self-consciousness. In his second and revised view of philosophy—that to which he gives the name of the Philosophy of Identity—he explains this process of antithesis and synthesis in terms very similar to those employed by Fichte in his Dialectic. Here the goal to which the whole process is moving is the Absolute, which Schelling defines as something that survives all the changes manifested in nature and spirit (hence the use of the word 'identity' to describe it). In the Absolute, which is the highest manifestation of Will (and this distinguishes it from an entity such as Spinoza's God), the Ego and Non-Ego of Fichte, otherwise in combat, are reconciled.

Upon further reflection, however, his somewhat abstract standpoint satisfied Schelling as little as that with which he had begun: it dissatisfied him, indeed, because his development in the meantime had caused him to sacrifice the element of mysticism. At the close of his career, he came to the conclusion, as have so many of his kind, that the pursuit of mere speculative or rational philosophy led to profitless hair-splitting and futile argumentation; that it was useless as a guide to action; and that it failed even to stir the emotions. He therefore sought to evolve a philosophy which should grasp, instead of evading, reality, and which should have some message for the individual. Thus he turned his mind to the concrete thought of history: to the life of ordinary men, who, while philosophers are engaged in their lofty discourses, must meanwhile live, work and shape the future. Only by becoming concrete, full-blooded, historical and topical could philosophy henceforth justify itself. Having thus stated the problem, Schell-

[1] See page 348.

ing passed it, ripe for solution, to his young colleague, Georg Wilhelm Friedrich Hegel.

With Hegel, philosophy renewed itself. And no one is entitled to say that he understands modern philosophy unless he has grasped, at least in outline (for there is much detail of a less apprehensible kind), the thought of this 'Aristotle of modern times'. Hegel has received less than the justice due to him, especially in the English-speaking world, owing to the impression, current since the beginning of the First World War, that he is one of the forerunners of Prussianism and later Nazism; that he identifies might with right and therefore exalts the will to power; and that he was himself an obsequious, if learned, servant of the Prussian military hierarchy of his day. None of these accusations is altogether without basis: but their preferment has tended to obscure, if not for some people completely to obliterate, the great originality and value of the Hegelian system. In tracing so-called 'forerunners', it is easy to find in abundance what is being sought: a passage here, an emphasis there, a reported anecdote—and the case is considered proved.

One of the reasons why Hegel is so noteworthy a figure in philosophy is that he broke with the tradition of thought initiated by Descartes. Descartes, as we saw, claimed to have overcome scepticism by asserting his awareness of himself as a thinker. As a thinker, too, he recognized his contact with the truth by the clearness and distinctness of his own ideas. The Cartesian Method was the Charter of Human Reason; and Reason in the seventeenth century was regarded in much the same light as Faith during the Middle Ages: it was capable of moving mountains.

The result of the Cartesian approach was, as we said, a new attitude to knowledge and scientific method. This attitude can be summarized as follows: first ideas, then things—first thought, then action. And what was so very original about that? Do not we all think first and act afterwards, even if we think hastily and inadequately? Agreed: but behind this 'rhythm' of knowledge was an assumption that was not often brought into the light. The assumption was that ideas and things, thought and action, were somehow 'outside each other'; they acted and reacted one upon the other, but from different sides of the stage. It was also assumed, however covertly, that when (if such a thing were imaginable) the rhythm of knowledge came to a halt or a temporary rest, the two partners would retire to their separate spheres, the one to commune with itself in a world of spirit and the other to repose inert and lifeless in a world of matter.

This general idea was the result of an attempt, made by a process of abstraction, to arrive at the basic assumptions that men, when engaged in thought of any kind, are bound to make. A better word than 'assumption' would be 'presupposition'; a presupposition is that which a man holds to be true before he 'supposes' anything. The externality or mutual exclusion of thought and action was, we may therefore say, a presupposition of the thought of philosophers from the time of Descartes until the time of Hegel. We recognize this fact in everyday speech: the influence of 'mind' over 'matter' is a subject about which we never weary of talking.

To say that such a presupposition was entertained throughout the period we have specified does not imply that its limitations were never recognized. Spinoza, for one, recognized them. He therefore posited his single Substance which could be regarded, according to the point of view taken, as both thinking and non-thinking. Kant recognized them, and therefore advanced the view that human reason, in looking outwards, never contacted the 'object' at all but merely a set of 'appearances' in the construction of which it played a considerable part: it succeeded, that is to say, in acquainting itself with that which it had itself introduced. The thing-in-itself evaded it; and to weigh in, as Kant did, with the assertion that a faculty other than our understanding—namely our moral sensibility—was capable of penetrating to the heart of reality, much as heart speaks to heart, was, from a strictly philosophical point of view, somthing very like treachery. It was there that Hegel took up the challenge. With his assault upon the problem, a whole tradition of thought was brought to an end. Either reason enjoyed primacy, or it did not; but if it enjoyed primacy, it did not lie outside its object, it 'generated' that object.

30

Georg Wilhelm Hegel

One man has understood me, and even he has not.
Attributed to Hegel

His Life

Few thinkers have taken longer to arrive at maturity than Hegel; but few, having once developed, have exhibited such extraordinary insight into so many spheres of thought. Kant's outlook was astonishingly broad for one whose personal experience was in a sense so confined. Hegel possessed more than a wide outlook; he had grasp, or, if it is preferred, 'inlook', intuitive penetration into the spheres of science, art, philosophy, and above all history such as no later philosopher has possessed.

Born at Stuttgart on the 27 August, 1770, Hegel came of an unpretentious middle-class family. His father was a revenue officer; his mother, from whom it would seem that he inherited his chief abilities, was both well-educated and intelligent, and taught her little son all the Latin that he ever knew, which was quite considerable. Later he went to the grammar school at Stuttgart, where he remained, a scholar of average ability, until he had reached his nineteenth year. Without distinguishing himself, he was an industrious pupil, though busier at outside activities than at his prescribed lessons. Among his hobbies, for example, was the collecting of many hundreds of extracts, from books, newspapers, and other sources, which, with a hint of his future efforts at systematization, he arranged carefully in alphabetical order. We also know that from an early age he read the classics with mounting enjoyment and increasing understanding; and this love of the humanities, which Kant possessed to nothing like the same degree, may account for the quality of dignity and balance with which his work as a whole, in spite of serious defects of exposition, is graced.

It was as a student of theology that in 1788 Hegel entered the University at Tübingen. His choice of theology is not very easy to understand, because at this stage he showed no particular aptitude for the subject. Probably he put his name down for theology as some modern students put their names down for teaching; they can think of nothing better to do. No doubt Hegel excelled least at those aspects of his training upon which the greatest importance was placed; he seems to have made no great impression as a preacher, whatever the quality of his sermon-notes. Nevertheless, he plodded on with his studies, determined to complete the course and qualify for a degree. This he did, with fair success, in 1790. Nevertheless, the report upon his work and character given at the end of his stay at Tübingen was, if not absolutely damning, far from encouraging; and a less obstinate student would no doubt have been inclined to renounce academic aspirations for good and all. According to his supervisors, he was a young man of good ability, moderate industry, and average knowledge: the subject in which he exhibited least talent was, they took the trouble to emphasize, philosophy.

If Hegel was not a model student, he was at least a normal one. The beer-parties, escapades, and even the amorous adventures characteristic of undergraduate life occupied as much of his time as he needed rest from his work, but not more. He was a popular person, though not particularly youthful in either manner or appearance: his companions nicknamed him the 'old man'. As for his closest friends, some idea of his leanings and enthusiasms may be judged from the fact that he was almost immediately attracted within the cultivated circle of Schelling and Hölderlin, whose genius he recognized sooner than they recognized his. From Hölderlin especially he acquired considerable knowledge of the classical authors, thus increasing the regard in which he already held them.

Having left the university a certificated, adequately-trained, but in no way outstanding young man, convinced of nothing so much as his unfitness for the Ministry, Hegel was obliged to follow in the footsteps of Kant and secure a post as private tutor. The first position he obtained was with a family at Berne; but although he benefited from the change of scene, he hankered after the congenial company he had left behind. Being thrown for long hours each day upon his own resources, and deciding to engage in literary work and research, he soon completed a detailed treatise on *The Fiscal System of the Canton of Berne*. But as his real interests lay deeper than economics, he began to reflect seriously upon those subjects which, when imposed upon him as a duty at the university, had left him so completely cold. Encouraged to study Christianity from the original sources, he began to gather material for a new and original Life of Christ. At this period of his life he sought to eliminate as far as possible the miraculous element in Christianity, and to present Christ as merely the best of good persons. In the Christian faith he claimed to have found the answer to the problem for which even the greatest of Greek philosophers had discovered no solution: the problem, already spoken of in connection with Aristotle, concerning the exact relation between God and the world that He created. Only later did he perceive that this problem was insoluble save on the understanding that Christ was not merely the best of good persons, but the incarnation of the Divine Logos.

During his stay abroad Hegel has been careful not to lose touch with his friends. To Hölderlin he owed it that in 1797 he secured a more congenial post: this was with a Frankfurt merchant, Herr Gogol. Wherever he went he took the greatest interest in his surroundings, and thus we find him absorbed once more in economic problems. In order thoroughly to master the general principles of economics and politics, he had already made himself acquainted with the works of Hume (on economics), Montesquieu, and Gibbon, and had tried to keep abreast with social changes in other countries (he sought all the information he could, for instance, concerning the English Poor Law Bill of 1796). The result was a number of studies on European social problems, including one on the Constitution of Germany and another *On the Internal Conditions of Wurtemberg in Recent Times*; but the latter, owing possibly to its drastic criticism of the magistracy, did not get as far as publication. Not that he neglected his philosophical studies; he merely found, as have others, that philosophical problems have a way of working themselves towards a solution while the mind, at its topmost layers, is concentrated upon matters of quite another order. There are in existence a number of manuscript notes made by Hegel at this period which foreshadow, like Berkeley's Commonplace Book, the whole of his philosophical system.

When in 1799 his father died, Hegel inherited a sum of money which, though exceedingly modest, filled him with hopes of being able to continue his researches without slaving for a living as only a hack-tutor need slave. By 1801 he was already settled at Jena, at this period a centre of great cultural activity. Schelling himself, now grown to eminence as a philosopher with a 'message', was the social lion. Hegel, won over to philosophy for good, now began to seek an academic 'platform' from which to expound his own ideas; and finding much in the teaching of Schelling of which he thoroughly approved, he collaborated with the master (1802–03) in a periodical entitled *The Critical Journal of Philosophy*. Meanwhile, he submitted to the authorities an original essay, *De Orbitis Planetarum,* and was made a *privat-dozent* at the university. He was now on the first rung of the academic ladder.

It was a ladder that he was slow to climb. He was conscious of having something to say; he had not yet learnt how to say it. For four years he continued to expound philosophy; and although at the end of that period the number of his pupils had more than doubled, he had begun with eleven and he now had thirty! The future seemed to hold little promise of improvement. All this time, however, he was increasing his knowledge, especially of the ancient Greek philosophers; and if he failed to achieve popularity among the younger generation, he was steadily gaining the respect of his academic colleagues. The extent to which he had come to occupy a niche in the philosophical world, indeed, may be judged from the fact that in 1805, having made a formal application, he was appointed to the high post of Professor Extraordinarius at Weimar. Apart from the distinction of such an appointment, Hegel, now thirty-five years old, had the satisfaction of knowing that he was now able to command a regular income. His stipend amounted to one hundred thalers a year.

The new professor had occupied his Chair but a short time when political trouble broke out. Prussia, feeling her independence to be threatened by the formation of the Confederation of the Rhine, decided to declare war on Napoleon, with whom she had entered into alliance less than a year before. As a result, the French armies turned upon Prussia and inflicted upon her two simultaneous defeats in October, 1806, one at Jena and the other at Auerstädt. Hegel's reaction to this violent reprisal was very similar to that of Goethe. Without allowing national sentiment to becloud his judgment, he felt that the disaster was deserved. Of the bureaucratic system of Prussia, with its petty tyranny and corruption, he had always entertained a low opinion, and he did not trouble to conceal his satisfaction at the prospect of its being swept away. Loyalties at the period of which we are speaking were still not so much international as supernational. Beethoven dedicated his Eroica Symphony to the man who, if not an open enemy of his country, had done nothing to show himself its friend. And Hegel with the sound of the cannonade at Jena in his ears, could write of the 'world soul' emperor whose armies he frankly hoped would prevail over those of his own country.

The defeat at Jena, if welcomed by a minority of intellectuals, brought nothing but ignominy in its train. Two weeks later, Napoleon, having entered Berlin itself, was issuing the famous 'Decrees' wherein he announced his schemes for the defeat of the last enemy, Britain. Those who had somewhat recklessly displayed their admiration for the conqueror's 'civilizing mission' were not rendered more popular by the revelation of what that mission entailed; and Hegel found that such little popularity as he enjoyed was fast dwindling. Once more driven in upon himself, he worked hard upon the first book of any magnitude that he had projected, and in 1807 published the *Phenomenology of Spirit*.

His Thought

The *Phenomenology* was described by Hegel himself as his 'voyage of discovery'. It was a work of great originality and scope. Hitherto he had regarded himself as a devoted, if discriminating, pupil of Schelling. But the thought of Schelling was ceasing to satisfy him. The chief objection to a man with a 'message' is that he is constantly in receipt of new ones, each of which he feels obliged to pass on to his disciples with the same air of conviction. So it was with Schelling. He got through philosophies as a man might get through successive suits of clothes. What alienated Hegel was the manner in which he introduced, at the appropriate moment, an Absolute so comprehensive as to envelop the whole collection of problems that were awaiting analysis. This, in Hegel's view, was cheating. Philosophy must not expect outside aid from mysticism; it must work its own passage. And in the 'voyage of discovery', that is what philosophy was supposed to be doing.

The voyage was an adventurous one. From the most elementary forms of sense-experience, knowledge is shown as developing step by step to the highest form of consciousness, which, in Hegel's view, is philosophy itself. Never before had the *panorama* of knowledge been set out in such fullness and at the same time with such minuteness of detail. The *Phenomenology* is the dress-rehearsal for the astonishing performances of the *Logic,* the *Philosophy of Nature,* and the *Philosophy of Mind.*

As Hegel's thought was the most exciting thing in an otherwise comparatively uneventful and sedentary life, an account of how his system developed is here in place. The life of a statesman is an account of his diplomatic master-strokes. The life of an actor centres round his most successful roles. The life of a soldier is concerned with his successive battles, with special regard for his victories. The life of a philosopher, on this analogy, must include his adventures in speculation.

Hegel's early admiration for Schelling did not blind him to the fact that the last great philosophical leader was Kant. Kant had claimed to criticize metaphysics out of existence, or at least out of harm's way; and neither Fichte nor Schelling, acute though they were, had succeeded in rehabilitating that unpopular and frequently execrated science. To Hegel—the student so 'deficient' in (academic) philosophy—must be given the credit for restoring metaphysics to its rightful heritage. And to Hegel, for that same reason, must be given the credit for raising the prestige of philosophy higher than it had been for many years. To those who claimed that the meaning of life, the nature of existence, was a matter for science or for art or, as the sceptics and agnostics said, for dismissal as beyond human comprehension, Hegel replied that it was, as ever, a matter for philosophy. By philosophy he meant the science which, by taking all experience for its province, defined the limitations of the various 'sciences', exposed the presuppositions upon which they were based, and thereby freed the mind from the tyranny of *abstractions.*

In thus defining the task of philosophy or metaphysics, Hegel did not mean to imply that the individual abstract sciences represented so much hocus-pocus. On the contrary, he believed them to form necessary and indispensable steps on the road to self-knowledge. The error was to 'pause' at one or other of these stages, imagining the journey to have been already completed. The error, in short, was to mistake the abstract for the concrete. If, for instance, an artist believes that his imaginative world is the only real world, or a scientist that his measurable facts are the only facts of significance, the result will be disastrous. But let the artist and the scientist but realize that their particular medium affords an intimation of true knowledge—let them but realize that, in addition to being artist and scientist, they are human beings needing to be fed upon more concrete food than images and symbols—and they will preserve their sense of proportion and thereby their humanity. Kant criticized metaphysics by reference to the sciences; Hegel, more orthodox, criticized the sciences by reference to metaphysics.

The view of knowledge that Hegel began to work out in detail owed much to that of Plato. The latter had expounded the theory that knowledge, being a process of recollection, was achieved in a series of stages culminating in the soul's final communion with the Form of the Good. Between the state of primal innocence and that of final redemption lay the 'vale of tears' which is life on earth. Hegel's theory is based upon a similar assumption. What distinguishes his thought from that of Plato is the fact, not always sufficiently appreciated by modern philosophers, that he accepts as philosophically significant the Christian doctrines of the Fall, the Incarnation and the Redemption. There is a common impression that no great philosopher has ever adhered to an orthodox religious faith. Hegel's Christianity is not merely a private conviction but an integral element in his philosophical system.

One implication of the view that knowledge (*i.e.* self-knowledge) is achieved by stages is that the human mind is unable to know itself in a direct fashion. It is obliged, in consequence, to create for itself a series of spheres, each more 'transparent' than the last, through which it can bring itself, as it were, to a new and maturer vision of its nature. These spheres are precisely the 'forms' of knowledge with which we are familiar: art, science, history, etc. Our school *curricula* dimly reflect this necessity. The mind must pass through one sphere after another, surrendering itself temporarily to the influence of each, until it sees its own face in the mirror that it has constructed for itself. In a word, the mind learns to know itself through communion with its own spiritual offspring.

Hegel's terminology and method of exposition have not been calculated to endear him to the ordinary reader. Both are difficult, sometimes aggravatingly so. But the fact to which he is endeavouring, here and elsewhere, to draw attention is a very simple one. We come to know ourselves through contact with other people. As Hume took pains to point out, there is no direct or immediate knowledge of the Self. The chief source of difficulty in Hegel's theory, however, is that he is referring not so much to the ordinary, individual mind, as to Mind in general—the 'transcendental' Mind of which Kant spoke. Put a word in capital letters and use it always in the singular, and you will automatically scare half the readers in the English-speaking world. Nevertheless, if we are to understand Hegel, we must first discover what it is that he is trying to do. What Hegel was principally trying to do was to represent reality as the development, by a timeless process of dialectic, of an Absolute Mind, or, as he called it, the Idea. Only in the light of some such idealist theory, he claimed, could we understand both the relation between Nature and Mind and the whole course of human history. For that is the task which Hegel, in restoring to philosophy its legitimate subject-matter, had set out to accomplish. The *Phenomenology* is thus a great deal more than a cruise undertaken in home waters; it is a voyage through all the oceans of the spirit. The history and nature of civilizations, the characteristics of nationalities, the limitations and errors of thought in each epoch, crowd together in a work that is more ambitious in scope than the *Critique of Pure Reason*.

In a phrase that has since become famous, Hegel referred to the Absolute of Schelling, as 'a night when all cows are black'. A static, immovable, featureless concept of this kind was incapable, in Hegel's view, of explaining either the oppositions that Schelling wished to explain or the logical development of Nature and Mind. The Absolute is simply the God of philosophy, and as such must display the characteristics of Deity in intellectual guise. Now whereas Schelling sought to represent Nature and Mind as proceeding from an immobile Absolute, Hegel sought to represent the Absolute itself as active, not in the sense of being the principle of Nature and Mind but in the sense of being the very process whereby Nature and Mind turn the one into the other. The kind of view that he wished to avoid, in other words, was that which pictured Nature and Mind as a façade behind which the Absolute brooded in lonely majesty. Instead of being the principle from which things proceeded, the Hegelian Absolute or Idea was *the process itself*.

Another difference between the Absolute of Schelling and the Thing-in-Itself of Kant on the one hand and the Idea of Hegel on the other was concerned with the goal to which they were leading. Schelling's mystical Absolute and Kant's Thing-in-Itself transcended both reason and logic; Hegel conceived his Idea to be the very embodiment of such reason and logic. The Absolute and Reason were identical. The Process itself was the unfolding of Reason first in inorganic matter, then in living matter, and finally, having become self-conscious, in man. Unlike the eighteenth-century 'rationalists', for whom Reason implied merely a series of principles or rules of thought, Hegel looked upon Reason as permeating concrete things as well. For the Ideal Reason not only conceives things, it also generates things. The science of Reason is therefore the one universal science. Now Hegel gives this science a name. He calls it Logic.

In 1807, the year of the publication of the *Phenomenology*, Hegel was invited to become editor of the *Bamberger Zeitung*. He accepted the offer less because of its congeniality than because he wished to maintain his material position, now that the university was temporarily closed. So far as we know, he wrote little original work for the paper, and in the following year he resigned his post for one that seemed more attractive. This was the Rectorship of the Ægidien-Gymnasium in Nuremberg. As principal of the College, Hegel proved an unexpected success. For work of this kind his character and temperament showed themselves to be entirely suited. He kept order, but he permitted a greater measure of freedom than was customary in such institutions. Years of dogged perseverance, likewise, had greatly improved his ability as a teacher. He now began to 'hold' his audiences, and so to increase them. There was even talk of a second and greater Kant.

A free house and 1,500 guilders (about £130) a year income may have turned Hegel's mind to establishing what he lacked all his adult life, namely, a home. In 1811, he decided to get married. Marie von Tucher was twenty-two years younger than the prematurely aged, quiet but kindly man with whom she decided to share her fortunes. She gave him the home he wanted, two sons, one of whom became a well-known historian, and such companionship as a philosopher has rarely been allowed to enjoy. If we were engaged upon a history of sentiment, we might hazard the suggestion that Hegel's was the happiest marriage in philosophy. But among the great philosophers, only a minority have ventured upon the married state; for it would seem that thinking for thinking's sake is largely a celibate occupation.

Having reached the conclusions outlined on the subject of the Absolute Idea, it was natural that Hegel should next proceed to work out the details of that new science of Logic of which he had stated the general principles. In 1812 appeared the first two volumes of the *Science of Logic* (the third appeared in 1816), and this time the learned world sat up and took notice. Ponderous, turgid, abstruse, prolix—all these derogatory adjectives have been applied to this immense production; it is these and much more, especially for students obliged to read it in translation. But, allowing for such defects, the *Logic* remains a work of speculative genius ranking among the world's greatest philosophical treatises. To ignore its towering presence in the landscape of modern philosophy is like visiting a cathedral town and omitting to view the sacred edifice.

The central argument of the *Logic* is one of such abstract character that even the most persevering student is apt to find it baffling. In such a case, the best way of approach is to revert for a moment to Hegel's criticism of the inert Absolutes of both Kant and Schelling. The latter, it will be remembered, maintained that the Absolute (or the Thing-in-Itself) was unknowable by human understanding. To Hegel such a statement was absurd. The 'Thing-in-Itself', far from being inaccessible or unkowable, was easily the most knowable thing in all human experience. For the Thing-in-Itself was simply another word for Being as such, or Pure Being. But that is surely not such a familiar thing? Too familiar! Hegel would answer. For Being is everything, and everything is a mode or aspect of Being. Pure Being is simply that which is left when every possible qualification of Being has been removed. To imagine such an unqualified entity may be difficult; but that does not prove its unreality. The mind breathes the atmosphere of Being as the body breathes air. Being as such is therefore the common source of all the categories and concepts of our thought.

From this general root-idea Hegel builds up the hierarchy of concepts which forms the Logic. Having once and for all disposed of the scepticism which denies our capacity to contact Being—a scepticism which, if persisted in, makes nonsense not merely of philosophical thought but of thought in general (a fact which Kant failed to realize, though his ambiguous attitude to metaphysics implied that he half suspected what he had done, or left undone)—Hegel proceeds to ask the apparently simple question: how, if every single thing is a qualification or modification of Being, did the articulation of Being as such into individual 'beings' ever take place? A simple question indeed, and therefore in philosophy a question that may easily cause us trouble. Neither here nor elsewhere is Hegel discussing the problem of Evolution, which is a process in time; he is discussing a purely logical process, a process out of time. In short, he is asking how the multitude of entities both spiritual and material can be deduced from that undifferentiated ocean of Being which logically presupposes them all. (The

Evolutionist asks a similar question, but about things in time: and incidentally Hegel, to whom the problem presented itself more than once in the course of his *Philosophy of Nature,* dismissed as untenable the thesis elaborated by Darwin half a century later.)

Hegel's answer to this question introduces an idea fundamental to his thought, namely, the idea of contradiction. Why does anything turn into anything else? Because, says Hegel, it 'itches' to. In other words, there is an irritant or rift in it, which, once exasperated (to use Bergson's term), causes it to take measures to transform itself into something capable of healing that rift. In the sphere of thought, this rift takes the form of a contradiction. What contradiction is inherent in the idea of Pure Being that it should ever become anything else? The answer is simple. Pure Being is the most universal of notions; there is nothing so utterly and unequivocally comprehensive. But for that same reason it is the notion most completely deprived of content. There is nothing in it because everything has been removed from it. To be a house, or to be a green, or to be dishonest—to be all these things is to be *something*. But to be just Being is to be nothing at all. And that is the contradiction to which Hegel refers. Pure Being has only to be examined, to be pinned down, to be focused, to disclose the fact that there is nothing there. As we bring to bear our minds upon it, it slides away and vanishes.

A thing that simultaneously is and is not cannot therefore stay still. It must move on, budge, develop. The pitting of Being and Not-Being one against the other therefore generated a third notion, the notion of development itself, or Becoming. For what constitutes Becoming? Clearly two things: Being itself and Not Being in the sense of that which is not yet Being but will be. Becoming therefore 'contains' the two contradictory notions with which we set out, and in so doing resolves the tension between them. Within the new concept of Becoming they are now engulfed; but the truth is that they never enjoyed independent existence. They were, and will ever remain, abstract notions from what is *the first concrete concept,* Becoming. Thus we return to the central idea of Hegel's philosophy, which is the idea of Process as that which permeates and informs reality as a whole.

To trace the stages whereby Hegel mounts from the concept of Becoming to that of the Absolute Idea would take too long. All that we need to bear in mind is that each unity or synthesis, save the last of all, reveals an element of contradiction (the same contradiction but in a new form) which is in turn reconciled in a higher unity, and so on. Nor must we fall into the error of supposing that the contradictions are simply and solely in our minds (*i.e.,* that they are 'subjective'). They exist in the things themselves. Whereas Plato said that reality was a world of half-truths, Hegel said that reality was a world of conflicting truths.

To Hegel, then, the fact that Nature contained an element of contradiction proved not that Nature was not real but that it was somehow incomplete. It was incomplete because it was all the while undergoing the process of transforming itself into something else. This process of transformation was not something that would one day be finished; it was a perpetual transformation. That into which Nature was transforming itself was Mind. Nature kept on throwing up or precipitating Mind; Mind kept on being thrown up and precipitated by Nature. This was a logical and not a temporal process. To consider Nature apart from the fact of its being turned into Mind was to consider an abstraction. The reality was, as ever, the process itself, the process of Mind-manufacture. To use Hegel's own phrase, this development and passing away was a process that would never itself develop or pass away.

The dialectical process of 'thesis' versus 'antithesis' to be resolved in 'synthesis' was an exceedingly fruitful one; and Hegel was able to use it to illuminate many aspects of human experience. But it must be admitted that he tended to overdo it. This 'panlogism', as it has been called, has been responsible for much of the discredit into which the Hegelian philosophy, and the various schools that grew out of it, have since fallen. Nature, he maintained, is that phase in the development of the Idea (or God) in which the spirit 'externalizes' itself: that is to say (and this suggestion is a very original one), the natural world is the world in which everything is outside every other thing. But Nature, as we saw, is not merely engaged in externalizing itself; it is engaged simultaneously in the opposite process, a process of internalization, a process of becoming Mind. Now the process of becoming Mind is that at which a transition occurs between natural science and history; for whereas natural science is concerned with measuring and descrying order and uniformity in an external world, history is concerned with exploring the inward significance of human actions, which is an investigation of the internal realm of spirit. Such things as consciousness and freedom, which are characteristics of mind, do not bring history into being; they are themselves brought into being in history. What in Nature is mere instinct and blind passion becomes in history Reason and Will, which in turn give rise to Law and the State. But it is important to remember that since Nature never finally gives place to Mind, but is merely always engaged in turning into it, Law and the State never finally supersede instinct and passion, though they are always engaged in the attempt at such supersession.

So far, so good; but Hegel's attempt to apply the Dialectic to the course of history itself is not so fortunate. He ends up by proving that the Germanic world is the synthesis of the Oriental world and the Classical world; that Berlin is the centre of the earth; and that the State is the higher unity in which both the family and civil society are synthesized. This latter proposition is one that has exerted great influence upon political thought. We shall have more to say of it in connection with the two schools of Hegelianism which flourished after the master's death.

It is sometimes asserted that Hegel's philosophy culminates in the idea of the State. True it is that he defined the State as the 'march of God in the world'; but in the course of that divine progress much else of value was achieved. The human spirit, he rightly insists, is not satisfied with the activities of political life; it must go on to explore those realms which are more congenial to its nature. These are art, religion, and philosophy, regarded as purely intellectual activities: activities which, though possible only under good and strong government, are not the less individualistic and personal for that. For if history is that phase in the development of spirit in which the Idea 'turns back upon itself', it is likewise that phase in which for the first time it engages in self-communion. Such introspection discloses three fundamental ideals in the recesses of the soul: the ideal of the beautiful (art), the ideal of God (religion), and the ideal of truth (philosophy).

In art the human mind foreshadows the final triumph over matter but does not achieve it; or rather it achieves it in imagination only. Not that the artist will necessarily recognize this; he believes his world of imagination to be the only real world, and his work of art to possess a value in itself. This tendency to materialize the work of art, to set it up as an object of intrinsic value—a tendency particularly strong in the most primitive forms of art, but manifest at every level—is that which links the artistic impulse with the religious. The particular connection is idolatry. Whereas idolatry is characteristic of primitive religion, however, the higher religions begin with the elimination of idolatry. Hence the iconoclasm of Moses is the beginning of purified, spiritualized religion; but idolatry and superstition are continually creeping back into their former position, and can never be wholly abolished. Religion assumes many forms. There is the religion of the Hindu which exalts God and debases man. There is the religion of Greece, which exalts man and tends to debase God. Finally (we observe once more the use of the triadic form), there is the Christian religion in which the divine and the human, instead of being considered in separation, are synthesized in the God-Man, Jesus Christ. This is the Logos of which both Plato and Aristotle spoke and which the author of the Fourth Gospel interpreted in philosophical terms. Christianity, therefore, is the Absolute Religion.

What, in Hegel's view, is the difference between religion and philosophy? It is simply a difference in form. They are about the same thing: God or the Idea. But while there is in religion a necessarily authoritative element, philosophy can accept no authorities of any kind. It is the voice of Reason, and Reason ceases to be such unless it is free. Philosophy, therefore, states in *conceptual* terms that which religion, even the highest religion, states in imaginative terms. But we must guard against a possible misconception. Philosophy, with its conceptual approach, is not an abstract thing. It is a concrete thing, for it is an offspring of history. Philosophy is therefore best regarded as the History of Philosophy. We cannot think about the present unless we know that which has led up to it.

The Reputation

We have outlined the ideas of the *Logic* at some length because Hegel's whole philosophy is contained in it. Its first publication brought him immediate recognition as the foremost German philosopher of his time. Three universities, Erlangen, Berlin, and Heidelberg, offered him Chairs. After some deliberation, he accepted Heidelberg, where he stayed until 1818. During his time there he prepared a work of considerable size to which he gave the title of *Encyclopædia of the Philosophical Sciences*. This he wrote largely as an accompaniment to his lectures, which, though never rising to the level of great oratory (he was hampered by a chronic cough), were attracting more and more students by their wealth of learning and masterly exposition of difficult theories, not least his own. In 1818, the University of Berlin again extended its invitation; and Hegel, proud to succeed the last incumbent, Fichte (since whose death the Chair had remained empty), accepted it.

From his arrival at Berlin until his death, Hegel enjoyed a reputation without parallel in the history of modern philosophy. With the German government he was on the best of terms. No reprimand needed to be issued on account of heterodox thought; Hegel seemed to express the very sentiments of the new German imperialism. This may be seen in particular from his treatise on political theory entitled, *The Philosophy of Right* (1821). His lectures were now received as the final word on their respective subjects: Æsthetics, the Philosophy of Religion, the Philosophy of History, the History of Philosophy. These latter lectures were not issued by Hegel in book form; but from notes made by himself and his students they were later 'written up' and published. At the conclusion of the series on the Philosophy of History, the old man looked up from his desk (his snuff-box as usual before him) and declared roundly: 'Knowledge has reached *this point* in its development.' As the old distinction between 'facts' and 'theories' was one that he particularly abhorred, the final conclusions of his own thought constituted for him the latest information on the subject. There is a story told that on being informed that certain of his theories were incompatible with some new scientific facts that had been adduced, he replied characteristically: 'So much the worse for the facts!' It must be admitted that the great esteem in which he was held in his later years rendered him increasingly dogmatic; but in spite of this rigidity of thought, his mind was by no means closed to new influences. He speculated until the end.

That a man in his established position should have been seriously perturbed by the liberal movement which, never long in abeyance, rose up again in 1830, was to be expected. In *The Philosophy of Right* Hegel had set out to prove that the continuous life of the State was maintained not through parliaments but through the monarchy. He sincerely believed the Prussian absolute monarchy to be the most enlightened in the world. But, as he should himself have been aware, liberalism could not be prevented from asserting itself, for every 'positive' element will eventually make itself felt, if life is indeed the dialectical struggle that Hegel declared. It was nevertheless a worried, querulous old man who received from Frederick William II a decoration in 1831 for services to learning. A tired old man, too, who on being led out one calm, clear night to look at the stars, remarked that he found the sight 'boring'.[1]

Hegel's last work of importance was, interestingly enough, an essay on the British Reform Bill, passed in 1832. Considering his attitude towards Reform in his own country, it is odd that in this work he should have criticized the slowness with which the English Government had suppressed abuses. In the same year another disruptive and democratic force invaded Europe. This was the cholera. Hegel moved out of Berlin into the suburbs. The infection caught up with him. A day's illness and he died. It was at his own wish that they laid his body next to that of Fichte in the cemetery near the Oranienburg Gate.

[1] *Cf.* Carlyle in similar circumstances: 'Hech! it is a sad sight.'

31

The Marxist Philosophy

The Germany in which Kant was born was a 'crazy quilt' of more than three hundred independent States, each with its own particular system of government, its own tariffs, and its own army. The idea of a united Germany, even if entertained, was regarded as altogether outside the scope of practical politics. Such a man as Lessing (1729–81) could say with complete sincerity that 'the love of country is a sentiment which I do not understand'. Possibly the isolation of these little principalities encouraged the pursuit of abstract studies; for among the huddled roofs and spires of their picture-book towns there was usually a university, with its learned professors, its crowd of ardent students, and occasionally its genius. No wonder the saying arose that whereas England ruled the sea and France ruled the land, Germany ruled the clouds. The idea, still current, of metaphysics as a 'heady' nebulous subject is no doubt largely the result of its intensive cultivation in German seats of learning during the eighteenth and nineteenth centuries—the forced growth of so many academic hot-houses.

Over this busy, divided land, there appeared, to the foreign visitor at least, to hang an atmosphere of peace and almost smug contentment. When the remarkable Madame de Stael wrote her book on Germany, Heine, never uncritical of his country, described her as 'eddying about like a whirlwind through our tranquil Germany, exclaiming everywhere delightedly, "O how sweet is the peace that I breathe here!" She had got overheated in France and came among us to cool off. The chaste breath of our poets was so comforting to her boiling and fiery heart. She looked upon our philosophers as so many different kinds of ices; she sipped Kant like a vanilla sherbet and Fichte like a pistachio cream. "Oh what a charming coolness reigns in your woods!" She kept constantly exclaiming; 'What a ravishing odour of violets! How peacefully the canary-birds twitter in their little German nests!"'

But this tranquil country concealed beneath its surface much potential unrest. It was the liberation movement during the Napoleonic wars that first aroused the German people to a sense of nationality; for common humiliation is a powerful unifier. The movement in its intellectual aspect was led, as we saw, by a university professor. As Fichte told his countrymen, there existed in the German language no specific word for 'character', because to be German was automatically to be endowed with character. The Germans, he said, were an *Urvolk*, the Chosen People of Nature. There was no need for them to learn to be civilized; they had an obligation to teach others their own 'natural' civilization. To realize their world-mission, however, they must fulfil their mission as a nation; they must first become the nation that they naturally are.

The German Confederation formed after the Napoleonic wars, with Austria as its president, was little more than a group of absolute monarchies. One by one the liberties gained in the struggle against Napoleon were extinguished. Once you have liberated, you must govern; and to govern a liberated people is at once to come into conflict with the various 'resistance-groups' that were previously such an asset. Youth movements such as the *Burschenschaft*, formed to continue the struggle for liberty within the new political framework, were suppressed. Literature was censored. Even university professors—or, to speak more accurately, university professors in particular—were told to watch their step on pain of dismissal, fine, or imprisonment. In Prussia itself the Chief of Police was an agent of Metternich, whose policy of repression and reaction throughout the Confederation remained unchallenged.

As for Kant, he had received in his day but one official rebuke, and his answer, though dignified, was somewhat servile; he promised not to embark upon further public discussion about matters of faith. Such accusations of impiety were not infrequently made by secular bodies: for if it can be suggested that a man is already a moral reprobate, it becomes easier (if the occasion arises) to represent him as a public nuisance. Fichte was the victim of such persecution; Hegel, as we have just seen, was all that the secular authorities asked for, and more. But what was true of Hegel as a person was far from being true of the philosophical system that he left behind. As soon as the master was dead and the reconciling hand removed, all the latent ambiguities of that vast system of thought came creeping out of the clefts and cracks in its dialectic, and precipitated the most violent controversies, not all of which were confined to the plane of theory.

One of the presuppositions upon which Hegel's thought is based is that 'the real is the rational and the rational is the real'. Applied to political thought, this presupposition admits of two interpretations. If you say that the real is the rational, you are tending to imply that what exists is all that it should be: in which case you will do everything possible to maintain the status quo. This was the standpoint adopted by the so-called Right-wing Hegelians, or conservatives. If, however, taking the formula in its alternative phrasing, you maintain that 'the rational is the real', you are at liberty to suggest that the present system, not being rational, ought to be transformed into something that is. This was the standpoint adopted within a short period of the philosopher's death by the so-called Left-Wing Hegelians, or radicals. In their view, all the historical institutions regarded by Hegel as sacred and more or less eternal—the Prussian State and the Christian Church in particular—were considered as obstacles to progress. At first the controversy was conducted purely on the intellectual plane, centring around the theological criticism of Strauss, Feuerbach and

Bauer. All of these were opponents of orthodoxy and the last was a thoroughgoing sceptic. When Frederick William IV ascended to the throne of Prussia, however, he took steps to terminate the controversy, having decided that Hegelianism itself was a bad influence. Accordingly in 1841, he summoned to Berlin the ageing Schelling (at that time adviser to the ruler of Bavaria) for the purpose of obtaining guidance on the subject: an invitation which the veteran thinker is said to have accepted with some relish, presumably by way of reprisals for having been so long excluded from the limelight. But the controversy continued as bitterly as ever, and for a good reason. The very essence of the Hegelian philosophy is that no such thing as an absolute natural truth exists, and that no institution is perfect: truth and fact are not static but dynamic. Consequently Frederick William IV was not far wrong in supposing that the danger lay not with the Left-Wing Hegelians but with the Hegelians in general. And it might be added of Hegel himself, that though a Right-Wing Hegelian by temperament, he was a Left-Wing Hegelian by example.

In the Philosophy of History as Hegel conceived it, 'we have to do with individuals that are peoples, with wholes that are states'. Only one other thinker, Giambattista Vico, had turned his attention to this gigantic theme; but after Hegel had treated it (he remained ignorant of Vico's achievement), a great revival of historical studies took place in Germany, and thence elsewhere, which diverted and invigorated the whole course of modern thought. For the next century and more there were two marked but related tendencies in thought: a tendency to regard history from a philosophical point of view and an even more significant tendency to regard philosophy from a historical point of view.

While the study of history was being pursued upon the academic plane by such men as Ranke, and later Mommsen and Treitschke, a more practical attitude was being adopted by a group of Left-Wing Hegelians whose interests had brought them in contact with the common people to a degree not usually permitted to men of their origin. Of these, the two most famous were Frederick Engels and Karl Marx (1818–85), collaborators in the *Communist Manifesto* published in 1848. Engels was the son of a wealthy German cotton manufacturer. Marx, a German Jew of humbler origins, having taken part as a revolutionary in the uprisings of 1848, sought refuge in London in the same year, and remained there until his death. Living in lodgings in Bloomsbury and working daily in the library of the British Museum, he slowly amassed the material for the book which was to turn a great part of the world upside down. This was *Das Kapital*, the first volume of which appeared in 1867. A book need not be read, or read by more than a select few, in order to exert powerful influence; few books of Marx have enjoyed a large circulation and yet their collective impact upon their time and later has been incalculable. What they have done is to 'touch off' the impulses towards change in a few select and remarkable individuals; but at the same time—for these changes are never wholly the result of accident—they have themselves expressed in forthright terms the inarticulate feelings of the masses.

Das Kapital is a book almost as difficult to describe as it is to read. A text-book of history, a précis of government blue books, a prophetic denunciation of social evils; it is all these, and its style is successively the style appropriate to all these. It is therefore best read in extracts, as any other Bible is read by the faithful. For while its every word may be regarded as sacred, not even the most ardent disciple will regard it as evenly inspired. What is important for the student of thought is the general philosophy underlying it: and if it is agreed that the philosophy was a species of Hegelianism, the question arises as to how far its author can claim to have been an original philosopher.

Dialectical Materialism is today the official philosophy of much of the world, and Dialectical Materialism was the invention of Engels and Marx. How did it come to be formulated? A clue is to be found in an early work of Marx on the subject of Feuerbach. 'Philosophers,' says Marx, 'have hitherto interpreted the world in various ways; the thing is to change it.' The Real must be transformed into the Rational, if necessary by revolutionary action. What is wanted therefore is a philosophy of action, an active philosophy, a unity—hitherto never achieved—between theory and practice.

As a student of Hegel, Marx early began to ask himself the question: why should the process of nature and history necessarily be regarded as the finite reflection of a timeless dialectic of Spirit? What, in other words, is this transcendent Idea of which, Hegel assures us, the dialectic is merely the eternal self-revelation? Why all this metaphysical mumbo-jumbo about an Entity which, whatever it may mean to philosophers spinning their complicated systems in the seclusion of their studies, has no significance for the common man? Even if the common man knows or thinks he knows what is meant by God, he can neither know nor pretend that he knows what is meant by the Idea. In the interests of common sense and for the welfare of humanity, can we not bring philosophy down to earth, and if necessary plant it firmly there? Of the nature of the Spirit, we finite creatures know nothing. To us, the one demonstrably real entity is Matter. A realistic philosophy, and still more an activist philosophy, will be based upon the twin notion that Matter is the fundamental reality and that such changes as take place in the universe are primarily material changes. A realistic philosophy will be a dynamic—or, to continue to employ the favourite word of Hegel—a dialectical materialism.

This was Marx's so-called 'inversion' of the Hegelian dialectic. This was his way of bringing it down to earth. But it still remained a dialectic. Like the Idea, Matter underwent changes according to the process of thesis—antithesis—synthesis; unlike the Idea (and this is one of Marx's most radical departures from Hegelian orthodoxy), it underwent this process *in time*.

An understanding of the downtrodden, the persecuted, and the exploited came much more naturally to Marx than to Engels, because

Marx belonged to a race which knew at first hand the meaning of oppression, persecution, and exploitation. That section of mankind which was most completely enslaved to the machine, and whose lives were most heavily oppressed with material cares, was the proletariat, the workers of the world. Consequently, Marx found that his emotional sympathies and his intellectual interests tended to corroborate each other. Society was composed of a ruling class which, aided by the ecclesiastical hierarchy, held down the workers whose labour they ruthlessly exploited; but the basis of society was this very class of manual workers. In the same way, the universe of the philosophers was composed of a stratum of spiritual entities, more or less undefinable or (to use Kant's own term) unknowable, floating above a hard substratum of Matter: but whereas the philosophers had, with a few exceptions, assumed the greater reality of the spiritual entities, common sense dictated that Matter was the supreme reality. Hence materialism and socialism or proletarianism went hand in hand. The struggles of the working class throughout history were paralleled by the dialectical evolution of Matter: or, to speak more accurately, the historical manifestaton of the dialectical evolution of Matter was the struggle of the working class towards freedom. 'All history,' the *Communist Manifesto* declares, 'is the history of class struggle.'

Historical or Dialectical Materialism was a 'deterministic' system: that is to say, it represented the dynamic forces of society as evolving by a process which nothing could arrest. Individual men may have thought themselves to be in possession of free-will; but such an illusion of freedom, like the kindred illusions regarding immortality and divine benevolence, were nothing but 'ideology', or the terms with which men have hitherto sought to disguise from themselves the naked truth of material interest. What matters is not so much the action of individuals (the cult of 'great men' is a bourgeois myth) as the action of classes; the action of classes is dictated solely by class-interest. This is as true of the capitalist class as of the working class. The only difference is that the capitalist class, unaware that its historical mission is already discharged, seeks to maintain its position by even more intensive exploitation of the masses, hoping to divert their growing discontent by periodically mobilizing them for war. Here is the proletariat's opportunity. The workers should use the weapons placed in their hands not for fratricidal strife but for self-liberation from their exploiters. The expropriators must themselves be expropriated.

It should be observed at this point that Marx, if not always his disciples, has no quarrel with capitalist-bourgeois civilization as such. The *Communist Manifesto*, for all its violence and denunciation, goes out of its way to emphasize how great a contribution to knowledge and industry the bourgeois class has made. In the inevitable dialectic of history, the proletariat is poised, as it were, to assume the role of antithesis to the old bourgeois order. Nothing must be made to hinder the collision (the more delayed the more violent and bloody) out of which shall emerge the synthesis of a classless society. That is the crime of capitalism: not the crime of having taken the stage, but the crime of refusing to leave it.

Although Marx advanced a philosophy of life which appeared to deny all values as we understand them, he was himself a man of fastidious taste and high culture. One of his favourite poets was Dante. Many a later disciple of the Marxist faith, preaching a cold materialism and denouncing the bourgeois intelligentsia as allies of the capitalist exploiters, would have suffered a shock to meet the actual Karl Marx, with his air of Victorian respectability, his addiction to cigars, and his refined tastes in art. Mistaken as it is to picture Marx as a raucous demagogue, however, it is still not altogether correct to represent him as a respectable Victorian gentleman. He was also a prophet, perhaps the last of the great Hebrew prophets, the castigator of his generation, the herald of approaching Judgment. For whereas Hegel had preached the eternal recurrence of his dialectical process, Marx, by inserting the process in time, represented history as soon about to come to an end. With the attainment of the classless society, the last contradiction and source of conflict in society would have been once and for all removed. Consequently the Marxist view of history is what may be called a Messianic or Apocalyptic view. Its motive-force is not science but myth.

The development of the Marxist gospel supports this. The Chosen People becomes the Chosen Class. Faith becomes class-consciousness and solidarity. At the great Councils or Internationals, orthodoxy is proclaimed and heretics are excommunicated. The Marxist intellectuals exchange anathemas; and Lenin, in one of his politico-philosophical treatises, can accuse the philosopher Mach of 'betraying materialism with a kiss'. With the bourgeois spokesman beyond the pale, controversy becomes openly copro-logical; the protégés of the capitalist era are nothing but 'a generation of vipers'.

In spite of the extravagances and distortions to which Marx's ideas have been subjected, his thought remains of profound significance in the history of modern philosophy. To insist that a philosophy is something to live by is particularly salutary at a time when philosophies are assumed to have neither practical application nor even passing utility. Secondly, to have developed the habit of considering problems from the historical point of view, instead of from a purely analytical scientific point of view, is to have increased our understanding of both the past and the present. Thirdly, to have endeavoured to appeal to the masses of mankind, across frontiers and through different tongues, by means of a myth calculated to spur them to a collective endeavour, was at least to demonstrate that, whatever gospel men of thought have to offer, it must be a common gospel, a universal truth, and not the creed of a sect or party. But two paradoxes remain unresolved in Marx's thought, and time has served only to accentuate them. The first is connected with his notion of a *dialectical* materialism. If Matter is in fact the hard, dead thing that the nineteenth century imagined, how can it suddenly burgeon forth in the dialectical phases which Marx, recalling the unfolding of the Hegelian Idea, regarded as the stuff of history? The second is connected with his notion of ideology. If material interests alone dictate human conduct, and if ideologies (*i.e.* systems of ethics and religion) are merely the 'reflection' of these interests, how do we account for the fact that the Marxist theory has exerted such enormous influence upon the course of history? The answers to these questions may become apparent in the sequel.

* * *

The full effects of the Marxist gospel did not become visible until many years after its author's death. But instead of the social revolution occurring in the most highly developed of capitalist countries, America, as Marx confidently believed that it would, it occurred in the country in which the capitalist system was least developed of all, namely, Russia. Thus the highly sophisticated philosophy of Dialectical Materialism, with its origins in the speculations of German professors, has become in our day the official creed of a population which, though hardly touched by academic philosophy, is gifted with precisely that religious insight to which the so-called apocalyptic element in Marx's thought might be expected to appeal. In his early days, Marx was in the habit of pouring scorn upon those social propagandists who, if nominally socialist, were in fact unpractical dreamers: Proudhon, Fourier, Owen, Saint-Simon, etc. These men, he argued, were not revolutionaries at all; they were skirmishers on the fringe of the great Liberal Movement that was in spirit and method bourgeois. A sentimental offspring of capitalism, Liberalism was an attempt to delude the masses into believing that *laissez-faire* economics, though causing them temporary ills, was ultimately to their advantage. What enriched their masters must finally enrich them; and the system was in any case grounded in the nature of things. Progress must therefore come about inevitably.

Against such sweetly reasonable philosophy, Marx preached the class-war, the Law of Increasing Misery, the Law of Concentration of Capital, and the Theory of Surplus Value. Above all he preached anti-Liberalism. In this sense he takes his place among the great thinkers of the nineteenth century who attacked not merely the values of the day but the basis of that spiritual capital upon which Europe had been living since the Renaissance.

32

From Schopenhauer to Kierkegaard

No culture is all of a piece. Whereas it appears on the surface to be composed of homogeneous elements, it will always be found upon closer inspection to contain material of a totally different nature. As time goes on, these latter elements may work themselves to the surface and alter the whole structure. Thus beneath the apparently stable surface of nineteenth-century Liberalism, deep cracks and fissures developed through which a lava of new and revolutionary thought began to well up. And this process developed at a time when, to the superficial eye, the European order has reached its highest level of material prosperity.

The success of the machine naturally brought about a change in accepted values. Indeed, the so-called triumph of mechanism was best observed not so much in the multiplication of mechanical apparatus as in the triumph of the materialistic philosophy that went with it. Against this philosophy, the so-called 'intellectual' elements in society, above all the Romantic poets at the beginning of the century and the Art for Art's sake writers at the end, protested. But they were all the while engaged in fighting a rearguard action. The Churches protested too; and such developments as the Oxford Movement (paralleled in the political domain by Disraeli's Young England Movement) were attempts to wean the Established Church from connivance in what Keble termed 'national apostasy'. Having lost the first round, which materialism won largely as the result of the arrival of a timely ally in Darwinism, the writers retired to their Ivory Tower, the philosophers to the shade of their 'dreaming spires', and the ecclesiastics to a *via media* that often became a *via mediocrita*. The field was left to the scientists, who proceeded forthwith to occupy, without much opposition, all the territories of thought not previously overrun by them.

The above statement, like all generalizations concerning matters of thought, requires due qualification. There were, among the professional thinkers at least, certain men to whom neither escape nor compromise was possible. These men refused to budge. They were determined not to accept the new order. If necessary, they were prepared to go down fighting. Of this small band of diehards, only three can be mentioned: Schopenhauer, Kierkegaard, and finally Nietzsche, to whom the next chapter is devoted.

Arthur Schopenhauer, born at Danzig in 1788, was the son of a merchant father and an author mother, both of whom claimed aristocratic descent. The boy was thus early surrounded with material blessings, which may account for his growing up to thoroughly spoiled and irritable youth. It was assumed that he would carry on the family business, and this for a time he did; but after his father's death, which put him in possession of a considerable fortune, he threw up everything with the object of devoting himself to the study of the subject most dear to him, which was philosophy. For a time he studied under Fichte at Berlin; but during the war of liberation he went into premature retirement, there to occupy himself with the composition of his first and most remarkable book, *The World as Will and Idea*, published before its author had reached the age of thirty.

Although Schopenhauer ought not to have resented the cold indifference with which this youthful work was received, he was extremely indignant. Thereafter, except at the end of his life when recognition came to him in full measure, he never ceased to rail at his fellow-practitioners of philosophy, whose elaborate systems he ridiculed with (it must be admitted) some effect. The philosophical ideas to which he gave expression in his book, however, were too novel to command immediate popularity, and indeed they have never been popular. Schopenhauer's views on any subject are not such as to command moderate approval: they either fascinate or disgust.

Temperamental hypochondria and a close study of both Buddhism and such German mystics as Boehme, combined to infuse into Schopenhauer's thought a strong strain of pessimism. The fundamental reality, he maintained, is not Being but Will; but the Will that drives everything in the universe, whether animate or inanimate, is a blind Will. Not merely is it ignorant of where it is going, but there is nowhere for it to go; it is therefore also an aimless Will. Now a blind and aimless force in the universe will be the cause not merely of more unhappiness than happiness, but of the most poignant variety of unhappiness, that for which there is no explanation. Existence is therefore nothing but an infinitely prolonged and infinitely recurring evil. Happiness, if such a state could be imagined, would be the opposite of existence: not death, for that is merely the termination of existence, but non-existence, the opposite of all that we mean by existence—Nirvana.

If this were the whole extent of Schopenhauer's thought, it would amount to very little, and to the Oriental it would be mere commonplace; but Schopenhauer has some very original observations to make about the manner in which the world as we know it has come into being. He declares it to be the direct product of Will. Take, for example, our bodies: 'Teeth, throat and bowels are objectified hunger: the organs of generation are objectified sexual desire; the grasping hand, the hurrying feet, correspond to the more indirect desires of the Will which they express.' In this way the whole of Nature has been created, and indeed the whole universe. Does this necessarily show an evil or irrational Will? Yes, answers Schopenhauer, for the Will, in creating our bodies, endows them with insatiable desires. Nothing satisfies us. The moment one desire seems to be appeased, another springs from its bosom clamouring for attention. The world is sustained by this continuous uprush of creative desire, just as a ball may be held aloft by a fountain-jet; but each drop, once having reached its limit, immediately descends and is replaced by others. That same Will which sustains existence renders existence intolerable.

Is there any way out for us? Can we either make existence at least supportable, or escape from it, not into death, but into some other existence? Schopenhauer believes that both solutions are possible, though for most people they are extraordinarily difficult. The first way out is through the experience of art. Art, of which the purest form is music, implies pure contemplation, pure detachment, and is therefore a calmer of the passions. Without being a pain-killer in the literal sense, it is an anaesthetic. ('The world,' said Schopenhauer, 'is as much incarnate music as incarnate will': a theory to which Wagner, himself a philosophical influence in his day, subscribed.) Naturally we cannot live upon sedatives. At best they provide temporary relief, at worst they kill us, whereas we want something different from either distraction or extinction. The second way out provides the more satisfactory solution. Philosophical contemplation, if undertaken for its own sake, reveals to us the common plight of all beings, the universal bondage under which the whole of creation groans. This plight, this bondage, is simply the Will to Live. It must be eradicated from us. We must kill desire in our hearts, as the Oriental ascetic extinguishes his impetuous instincts. We must cease to desire happiness in order to arrive at a state of inviolability from which all agitation, whether of delight or care, has been removed. To commit suicide is neither prudent nor moral, because by so doing we have made no contribution to the eradication of the Will in others; we have merely shirked our task. Finally, we must realize that to help others to remove their burden of unhappiness is the best way of lightening our own. If the solution is to lose ourselves, let us do so in the service of our fellows.

Schopenhauer's philosophy is a mixture of querulous misanthropy (and misogyny: his views on women were almost pathological in their bitterness: perhaps his estrangement from his mother and his unfortunate love-affairs were responsible for this), acute perception, and sudden shows of wisdom, the whole being expressed in a literary style greatly superior to that of both Kant and Hegel and most of their contemporaries. As a personality, Schopenhauer was one of the few philosophers who may be called antipathetic. As a thinker, without being in the highest rank, he was original and disillusioned at a time when most thinkers were tending to drift with the tide. Like Marx, he was a bitter opponent of the idealism of the so-called Utopian thinkers (mostly Socialists); but, unlike Marx, he held out no vision of a New Jerusalem coming in the clouds and establishing the reign of justice upon earth. For him, such idealistic visions were merely part of the sustenance of that Will to Live which needed to be subdued. In the meantime—and in this respect he is a defender of the traditional values of Humanism—he bade his fellow-men cultivate the Stoic virtues and maintain their dignity in a world fast losing its standards in a general scurry for wealth and power.

More to be commended as a character but no less out of tune with the spirit of his age was the Danish philosopher and theologian Sören Kierkegaard (1813–55), whose thought has of recent years come to exert a profound influence throughout Europe. Like Schopenhauer, Kierkegaard exhibited the utmost contempt for all systems of thought, and in particular for such as represented the world as about to enter upon a new age of progress and enlightenment. He was therefore opposed to Hegelianism, because although Hegel went to great lengths to show that the dialectical process involved perpetual struggle, pain, and even anguish, he ended with the anti-climax of assuming an immediate consummation of his scheme to have been reached in the Prussian State of his day. To this trite and chauvinistic attitude, Kierkegaard opposed a thorough-going pessimism of which the source was an intense but somewhat tortured religious faith. The remedy for our ills and above all our itch for system-making was to turn our thought inwards, to cultivate an interior life, and to realize our utter insignificance and helplessness in the sight of God. All that was universal, objective, and impersonal was merely a facade created by our intellect to give us the illusion of freedom and independence.

These sombre views, which brought Kierkegaard into collision with the church of his country and deprived his personal life of all normal enjoyment, were indeed contrary to everything that so-called enlightened persons had assumed to be obvious and desirable. He was like a man who, deliberately lying down on the track, allowed the express train of progress to run over and crush him. In his emphasis upon the interior life, the life of feeling, he is akin to Rousseau; but he is a Rousseau to whom Original Sin is the greatest of all realities, the highest of all mysteries, and yet the fact of which the world of his day remained most obstinately unaware.

Kierkegaard's refusal to live upon illusions, his contempt and disgust for life at the level at which it is lived today, and his mental toughness and stringency, has excited the respect and sympathy of a generation—our own—which, in consequence of the upheavals of war and post-war disorganization, experiences a similar revulsion from the traditional values of Western civilization. For this reason the apostles of the philosophy or quasi-philosophy of Existentialism claim Kierkegaard as one of their masters, though they do not always follow him all the way. For Kierkegaard, modern man, cut off from the natural world by his pursuit of technics and removed from God by his naive humanism, is a 'displaced person': an individual with whom the world has had to reckon and whose psychology it does not yet wholly understand.

33

Friedrich Nietzsche

Only he that altereth remains unalterably mine.

The third enemy of decadence and degradation, and by far the greatest of the three, whose struggle to maintain his position proved fiercest, and who finally 'burnt himself out' (to employ his own phrase) in his own fire, was Friedrich Nietzsche. Of all the philosophers of the modern world he is the most tragic and in some ways the most terrifying figure. He is the one outstanding example in the whole history of thought of a man who, rebelling against the society of his time, took upon himself to do what society was too spineless to do, namely, to arrange his own martyrdom. In the fury of his contempt for the world of his day, his mental resistance gave way and he lost his reason. Neitzsche drove himself mad.

The family to which this extraordinary man belonged was that of the aristocratic Neitzkys, Protestant Poles who had settled in Germany in the eighteenth century. In spite of his admixture of German blood, Nietzsche never forgot his ancestry, and his features remained distinctly Polish. He could count among his forebears a large number of Christian ministers, a fact that is not without significance in view of his own mission as preacher of a gospel. As for mental and physical vigour, the Nietzsche family was particularly well-endowed; there is no record, however far back we go, of debility or mental oddity among them. Nietzsche's mother, also of a large and long-lived family, was eighteen year old when the most gifted of her three children was born. And she outlived his sanity by several years.

From his sister, who was later to write his Life and to assist in caring for him during his mental death, we learn that Friedrich was a good-looking, fair-haired boy, with exceptionally large dark eyes. At four years of age he could both read and write. He early showed signs of character; and although he was of quiet disposition, he would occasionally fly into a passion that startled everyone by its vehemence. But he was likewise capable of great feats of self-control: for instance, in order to demonstrate that the Roman Mucius Scaevola was not such a remarkable man after all, he several times held his hand in a flame without flinching.

After the death of his father (who fell down the steps of the parsonage one day and sustained injuries that finally killed him), the

Nietzsche family went to live at Naumburg on the Saale. Here the boy Friedrich went to the town school, mixing with all types of boy; but he did not blossom out, even though he seems to have made a very great impression upon his teachers. We learn that he was nicknamed 'the little parson'; that he found Greek very difficult (though his understanding of the Greek spirit in later years was profound); and that about the age of ten he developed the habit of writing poetry and composing music. He was likewise renowned for a kind of precocious piety.

The next educational establishment which Nietzsche entered was a school at Pforta. Here, though the discipline was extremely strict, he began to reveal for the first time his many intellectual talents; and it became obvious to his instructors that an immense creative energy was stirring within him. He took up the study of philology more as a mental discipline than as a deep interest, but his chief discovery at this time was the music of Wagner. There was thus a mounting tension in his breast which brought about something in the nature of a breakdown in 1862. Although his health was still as robust as ever, he began to be afflicted with headaches and eyestrain, and for a time he was obliged to take a complete rest from all formal study.

It was in the next year, 1863, that he underwent what we gather to have been his first and only genuine experience of love. A fragile little girl, the sister of one of his schoolfriends, became for him the object of a romantic devotion. Nothing resembling this experience ever recurred in later life, though on two occasions he contemplated marriage; and we have no reason to disbelieve his sister's rather sententious statement that 'my brother remained all his life long completely apart from either great passion or vulgar pleasure; his whole passion lay in the realm of knowledge, only very temperate emotions remained over for anything else'. Psychologists have been inclined to explain his final breakdown in terms of an incapacity for ordinary sexual expression; but in the case of a man of intense mental activity, what may be a normal outlet in others need not obsess him to the same degree. Nietzsche neither shunned the society of women, nor exhibited for them that contempt which Schopenhauer, with his sordid *amours*, came to display. It is probable that he knew more of the meaning of passion than some others of more demonstrative nature; but he also knew how easily such an instinct can be exploited. Years after, in his *Zarathustra*, he declared: 'It is better to fall into the hands of a murderer than into the dreams of an ardent woman.' Men who are total strangers to passion do not usually talk in that strain.

After leaving Pforta in 1863, he entered the university of Bonn. The change of atmosphere exhilarated him. He could now express himself freely. That he should proceed to abandon the traditional beliefs of his youth was not surprising; he had reached the stage at which such abandonment is, for most youths, almost automatic. The only difference was with what thoroughness he did it. Beginning to criticize all the assumptions upon which his former ideas were based, he resolved to devote his life to the task of freeing men from illusions. To this end he put all his energies into unremitting study, leaving little time for the normal recreations of an undergraduate. He neither drank nor smoked ('there is too much beer in the German intellect', he later remarked); he even denied himself food in order to attend concerts and plays. Perhaps it was his admiration for the Greek ideals of balance and moderation that prompted his lifelong abhorrence of rowdiness and excess. At the same time he was distinguished at Bonn for his physical robustness; and it was observed, when he left for Leipzig, that he was precisely the same height as Goethe, whose humanist ideals up to this point he shared.

At Leipzig the problem that began to obsess him was that of finding a secure philosophical standpoint from which to launch his critical bombardment upon the world. So great was his perplexity that he frequently prolonged his meditations far into the night and occasionally until morning. One day, browsing in a bookshop, he came upon Schopenhauer's *World as Will and Idea*, a work of which he had not then heard. On the spur of the moment he bought it. The reading of this book marked a turning-point in his life, for it thrust his mind forward in a way that he could not have conceived possible. It assisted him over the brow of the hill. On the purely emotional side, too, he made more discoveries in music, above all Wagner's *Mastersingers*, which caused 'every nerve and fibre' in him to thrill. In 1868 came another momentous event in his life, namely, his meeting with Wagner himself. It was as if two explosive forces had come together; but the detonation was to occur later, when disillusion had followed upon rapture.

He still pursued his studies in theology and, without displaying any particular enthusiasm for the subject, made sufficient progress to attract the attention of experts. A lecture on Theognis, the Greek poet (sixth century BC), brough him particular commendation, and in 1867 he was offered the Chair of Philology at Basle, which he accepted. To everyone's surprise, however, his first real publication was not an academic treatise but a remarkable philosophical work entitled *The Birth of Tragedy*, which he dedicated to Wagner.

This essay, which appeared in 1871, excited considerable discussion. Its argument was as follows. In Greek thought, two themes are ever present and perpetually in conflict: that associated with Dionysus, with its ecstatic intoxication, its intuitive principle, its emphasis upon singing, dancing, music, and lyricism, and that associated with Apollo, with its dream-like serenity and classic equilibrium. In combination, these two principles produce folk-song and finally tragedy, the highest achievement of Greek art. The tragic art began to disintegrate, however, with the popularization of the teaching of Socrates. Socrates, as we have seen, maintained that viciousness and evil were a consequence of thoughtless ignorance. 'More knowledge, more virtue,' was the essence of his teaching; and virtue was the chief promoter of happiness. Such optimism was, in Nietzsche's view, incompatible with the tragic view of life; and our continued acceptance of it, strengthened by the Christian teaching, has rendered our existence increasingly superficial. But now a new era is dawning. The art of Wagner is the beginning of a new Birth of Tragedy; for in Wagner's operas music is once more wedded to myth in the manner of the old tragedy. And this is the beginning of a resurgent German heathenism, which is to be the culture of the future.

Having so far departed in this work from strictly philological studies, Nietzsche was not surprised to find that his way to advancement was barred; but as his heart had never been in purely academic affairs, this hardly worried him. He knew he was making enemies. How could he expect otherwise? He was deliberately trying to overturn contemporary idols. Two of his 'heresies' in particular were the cause of public consternation and offence: first, his insistence that Socrates and Plato were perverters and diluters of the Greek tradition symbolized by Dionysus, and second, his assault upon Christianity. These two 'heresies' were of course interconnected. 'To ensure the eternal pleasure of creation,' he wrote, 'the eternal affirmation of the will to live, the eternity of birth-pangs is absolutely required. All this is signified by the word Dionysus. I know no higher symbolism than this Greek Dionysiac symbolism. In it the deepest instinct of life, of the future of life, the eternity of life, is experienced religiously: generation, the way to life, is regarded as a sacred way. Christianity alone, with its fundamental horror of life, has made sexuality an impure thing, casting filth on the beginning, the very condition, of our life.'

When in 1870 Germany defeated France, the event was regarded by many Germans (and some others) as the sign of the superiority and complete victory of German culture over that of France, so long reputed to be the highest in Europe and even the world. Nietzsche, it is interesting to note, did not share this view. Indeed, he poured more than his usual measure of scorn upon it. The Germans of his time were conspicuous, he said, for their lack of culture. Their thirst for information, their regimented efficiency, their coarse addiction to tobacco and beer was not so much culture as Philistinism. As yet they remained unworthy of the new ideals to which Wagner and his followers were giving expression; and the sabre-rattling of bragging soldiers was calculated to retard rather than to further their attainment of such sensitive life as true culture implied. In Nietzsche's view—and this is the central point of his book *Richard Wagner in Bayreuth*—art must go ahead to light the way; for art is a revolutionary force which, once accepted, will alter our whole conception of both education and morals. In a sense it simplifies life, is larger than life, and therefore serves as a guide to life: high enough to attract the most intellectual, yet broad enough to stir the most unpretentious. The secret of Wagner, as that of the Greek tragedians and of Shakespeare, was the secret of scope.

To a man of Nietzsche's sturdy individualism, a permanent attitude of hero-worship was not possible. Wagner was the hero so long as Wagner did what Nietzsche thought he ought to do. Their almost daily association at Basle had obscured the fact that each was developing upon different lines. To appreciate how much the other had changed, it was necessary for them to separate; and the separation came when Wagner left Switzerland. In 1876 there took place that momentous festival at Bayreuth at which the first performance of Wagner's *Ring of the Nibelungs* was held. Neitzsche was keyed up for what he assumed would be the climax of Wagner's creative life. He even wrote a prologue for the festival. It seemed to him, in fact, as if the whole gathering was to be in the nature of a 'sacred consecration of the morning of battle'.

When the *Ring* was enacted, with all is Teutonic splendour and oppressively barbaric mythology, Neitzsche realized with mounting distress that he had been horribly deceived. This, in the words of a modern poet, 'was not what he meant at all'. The very primitivism against which his heart and soul had been in rebellion was here displayed in gigantic, naked abandon. Wagner, who was to have been the prophet of a new life-giving cultural energy, had instead put the weight of his genius behind the movement towards Germanic barbarism, with Wotan as the symbol in place of Dionysus, and the Nordic blizzard as a substitue for the Hellenic calm. This was cultural apostasy of the most flagrant kind. Nietzsche, whose personal friendship for Wagner had been sincere (though Wagner was many years his senior), felt betrayed and humiliated. He flung away from the whole concourse in a mood bordering upon hysteria. A doctor-friend who was with him at the time recorded his opinion that Nietzsche was suffering from advanced neurasthenia.

Whatever his immediate reaction, he managed in time to pull himself together. The effort was still possible. And, having rallied, he decided that he must now eradicate from his being all the poisonous growth that had been allowed to fester there: the philosophy of Schopenhauer, the false mysticism of Wagner, and indeed all the morbid mushroom-philosophies of his day. It was like applying the handbrake in the middle of a race downhill—almost like trying to regain one's balance after gathering for a parachute-leap. In his next book. *The Case of Wagner*, he explained what he had tried to do for himself and what he summoned his contemporaries to do after him. Possibly it would have been better if he had taken Wagner's advice (given half in jest and half in earnest), that he should seek out a rich widow, marry her, and travel on the proceeds. A little less self-absorption might have enabled him to keep his balance; but a genius, especially the lonely genius that he was, rarely solicits sound practical advice, nor was Nietzsche likely to listen to the suggestions, however realistic, of the man largely responsible for his condition. Naturally, the attempt to turn his back upon old enthusiasms was not easy to make: and it was not perhaps altogether salutary that, instead of listening to Wagner, he should have turned for consolation to Bizet. A mighty opiate could be made to lose its attractions only by recourse to one of equal potency. The French culture that he so much admired offered no antidote of sufficient strength.

It says something for German academic tolerance at this time that Nietzsche was permitted the maximum of freedom in the interpretation of his duties, the more orthodox of which he by no means neglected. He was a popular and painstaking teacher, never revealing in his manner, which was always courteous, the mental turmoil within him. Like the punctilious Kant, he was greeted by his fellows (or most of them) with an unaffected geniality that betrayed no suspicion of the explosive gospel he was engaged in harbouring.

His retirement from Basle, which took place in 1880, was due to the state of his health, and he received thereafter a generous pension. Being now as free as he had ever been in his life, he devoted his time to European travel, writing a series of learned books at his leisure. One of his favourite haunts of study was the Piazza in front of St Mark's, Venice. It seemed on the whole that he was regaining the mental equilibrium which his break with Wagner had so rudely disturbed; and though appearances were deceptive, the publication in 1883 of his book *Thus Spake Zarathustra* suggested that he was then at the height of his powers, which was true. *Zarathustra*, undoubtedly Nietzsche's masterpiece, has very little to do with Zoroaster, the half-legendary prophet of Persia; but the symbolism of water and fire and the incantatory form in which the Master is supposed to speak were well adapted to Nietzsche's purpose, for he was able to use them to convey his own fragmentary ideas as if they possessed oracular significance. With *Zarathustra* Nietzsche ceases to be the apostle of Culture, a sort of German Matthew Arnold, and becomes a seer endowed with the capacity to see 'beyond Good and Evil' (the title of a later book). Nor is he any longer a mere critic, a satirist of petty vices and failings; he is the denouncer of morality itself (defined by him as 'the mob instinct working on the individual'), the castigator of man's stupidity in accepting the 'slave morality' of Christianity rather than the 'master morality' of which he claimed to be the prophet. The controlled passion of the earlier books, suddenly bursting its bonds, here (and still more later) pours out in torrential invective against modern ideas of right and wrong. Still clinging to the Dionysian symbolism, he rails at the trivial, comfortable doctrines of the bourgeois classes of his day, which betoken the 'plebeianization of Europe'. Never had such a terrific denunciation of human frailty been made in a style at once so majestic and so impassioned. And never had a modern writer indulged, apart from brief intervals of serenity, in such bouts of self-laceration and inward fury, as if he were working himself up to a kind of mental spontaneous combustion.

In writing *Zarathustra* and the books that followed, Nietzsche came increasingly to believe not merely that he had a mission but that his mission was the only one capable of saving mankind from spiritual anaesthesia. As his style became more didactic, and his opinions more dogmatic, so he developed a dangerous megalomania. Upon his literary works he placed a value which was, to say the least, extravagant: 'I have given men the deepest book they possess, my *Zarathustra*,' he remarked a little later. And there came a moment, just before—and no doubt heralding—the final collapse, when he seems to have regarded himself as embodying in his own person the genius of humanity. As his mind began to vibrate with even more tremendous throes of semi-prophetic fervour, he planned to write one last book—a super-Bible, a breviary of the Superman, the last will and testament of mankind's first human deliverer. It was never completed. It was never even begun.

The notion of insanity is not absent from Nietzsche's early works, but it is by no means obtrusive: his emphasis upon the Dionysiac symbolism reveals a preoccupation with an unfettered, uncontrolled individualism, but there have been as daring individualists before. The point at which he began to turn his back upon normality was the point at which he turned his back upon the whole complex of modern civilization—its art, its science, and above all its morality. In his first period, he denounces the 'slave morality' of his day as being a departure from the healthy robustness of Renaissance humanism; in his later work, he seems to be at issue with the whole of Western civilization, even including its pre-Christian founders, Plato and Aristotle. It is not enough for him to believe that by a process of natural selection and the survival of the fittest the Superman will automatically be born; he believes, like some other advocates of evolution, that the process must be given some assistance, that personal sacrifice is necessary, and that one man must die for the people, in order that the latter shall perceive its need of leadership and submission to authority. And he believes that he himself, to whom the 'joyful wisdom' has been given, must prepare for martyrdom—a martyrdom not so much of the body as of the mind. He will agree to 'take the strain' of that new morality or amorality to which man must in future learn to conform; and if the tension should prove unendurable, then he will accept the consequences, even if it should mean the ultimate collapse of his faculties.

And that is what in the end it did mean. Nietzsche had always been visited by strange dreams, and he likewise displayed a tendency to hallucination. One particular dream that he had as a boy was so vivid that he took the trouble to record it. He experienced the sensation, so he tells us, of being borne forward in company with others through the most beautiful country imaginable, with no sound save the sweet singing of birds. As he proceeded, it seemed that before him lay the whole of his life, a long vista of serenity and happiness. Then, to use his own words, 'suddenly a shrill cry reached our ears: it came from the neighbouring lunatic asylum'. This dream was merely the most outstanding of a number of others, but it was oddly prophetic. Not many years after the publication of *Zarathustra*, Nietzsche began to show signs of mental derangement. He became a prey to extravagant hallucinations. Writing to George Brandes, one of the first men in Europe to appreciate his genius, he signed himself 'The Crucified'. To the historian Burckhardt, he wrote under the name of Ferdinand de Lesseps. At Turin, where he was staying, he went about declaring that he was God. A friend, Professor Overbeck, to whom Burckhardt had spoken, hurried to Turin to see Nietzsche, and found him in a terrible condition, obviously on the verge of mental collapse, uttering extravagant opinions and spending his money in the most careless manner. He still continued to write, but evidence of insanity was increasingly apparent. On 27 December, 1888, in a letter to Overbeck, Nietzsche declared that he was engaged in drawing up a Memorandum to be sent to all the courts of Europe inviting them to form an Anti-German League. Explaining himself, he stated coolly that he wanted to see Germany encircled so that she should be provoked into declaring war upon the world. The psychologist will see in this an expression of his own neurotic condition. By the following year his senses seemed to have quietly slipped their moorings.

He survived twelve years. For some time he remained in a home in Basle and then at Jena. As he proved to be of gentle, almost child-like disposition, he was later taken to Naumburg to live with his mother, and after she died he was looked after at Weimar by his sister, whose account of him during that tragic period is the fullest record that we are likely to possess.[1] In spite of the general collapse of his intellectual powers, he could still enjoy music and literature, and he took pleasure in the conversation of friends. But it seemed that all recollection of his self-assumed mission—his war against the civilization of his day—had vanished beyond recall. On one occasion when a great author was mentioned in his presence, he observed mildly: 'I, too, have written some good books.' Nor did he seem to fret at the inactive, death-in-life existence that he was obliged to lead. Seeing his sister weeping one day, he said: 'Lisbeth, why do you cry? Are we not happy?' Perhaps he was for the first time in his life.

Nietzsche lost his reason out of loneliness and despair just at the moment when his name was becoming known all over Europe. 'A profound man,' he had remarked, 'needs friends, unless he has a God. And I have neither God nor friend.' Consequently, the solitude in his mind became unendurable. He departed from a world that had almost forgotten that he still inhabited it, on the 25 August, 1900, in the thirteenth year if his second childhood.

[1] Evidence has recently come to light that his sister later 'edited' his correspondence. First, in order to suggest that she was his only confidant, and secondly in order to give the impression that he was much more addicted to chauvinistic and 'racial' ideas than he really was.

34

Scepticism and Faith in Nineteenth-Century Philosophy

The lesson of Nietzsche may be summarized as follows: a philosophy is not something to be studied in a book—to be pondered in solitude and then, like any other book, shut up and put away—but something to be lived. Even if it exacts high or impossible standards, it must be tried and proved in action. The example of Nietzsche filled his contemporaries, as it has filled his successors, with something like awe and dread; but it is arguable that this revulsion was due as much to his insistence upon the importance of action and adventure ('A new world remains to be discovered—and more than one! Hoist sail, O Philosophers!'—the profession had rarely been addressed in such unorthodox terms), as to the perversity and paradox of his actual views. After Nietzsche, there was a scurry back to the study, the library, and even to that most sheltered of places, the laboratory, just as in literature and art there was concurrent flight to the Ivory Tower.

The contemporary thinkers upon whom Nietzsche vented his bitterest scorn were the English utilitarians, particularly John Stuart Mill (1806–73) and Herbert Spencer (1820–1903). The evil wrought by these thinkers was, according to Nietzsche, their *vulgarization* of the scientific spirit. They claimed to be apostles of Science; but all they did was to reduce Science to technics, and to use technics to make their already demoralized life more easy, more comfortable, more smooth—as if that were the way to produce Supermen! 'The best and wholesomest thing in science, as in mountains, is the air that blows there.' In spite of his claim that religions were extinct because 'God is dead', Nietzsche had not the slightest intention of exalting a purely materialistic philosophy. To him, the scientific spirit, the spirit of disinterested enquiry, was an aspect of that unquenchable human thirst for experience which the ancient wisdom had endeavoured to cultivate. To declare oneself a materialist, even an agnostic empiricist, was to betray science, since it revealed a lack of faith in science. This was the origin of Nietzsche's condemnation, along with modern Christianity, of that school of philosophy according to which all ultimate problems were dismissed as 'unknowable', the only 'realities' being sense-data, money, steam-power, and cheap labour. 'The air that blew' in that region was heavily polluted.

In spite of Nietzsche's admiration for France and French thought, the nineteenth-century philosopher who did most to make science an end in itself and therefore encouraged the growth of materialism was

Auguste Comte (1798–1857). But even Comte, who founded what he called the Positive Philosophy (according to which the scientific spirit evolved through three stages, the theological or mythical, the metaphysical or abstract, and the positive or concrete), failed to exclude altogether the mystical element: for at the conclusion of the exposition of his system, he introduced, as if by the back door, a brand new religion, the Religion of Humanity, which is the culmination and epitome of all other faiths. A somewhat similar development occurred in the thought of Herbert Spencer, an engineer by training, who was led to expound an evolutionary doctrine before Darwin published *The Origin of Species* (1859), but whose attempt to discern rigorous scientific laws in the universe and the development of nature concludes with the admission that behind the world of phenomena there lies, as Kant himself had maintained, an Unknowable realm. John Stuart Mill, a disciple of Comte but a less systematic thinker than Spencer, had likewise admitted to the existence of a 'final inexplicability' in all our speculations about the universe. Thus the shadow of Kant lay right across the thought of the nineteenth century, obscuring for many people the advances made by Hegel. Even a realist such as T. H. Huxley (1825–1895) was not immune from this influence: for Huxley and a good many of his followers (George Eliot is an example in the literary sphere), while believing that only the phenomenal world is knowable by science, clung desperately, and for reasons not always fully appreciated by themselves, to the moral ideas of the Christianity they had repudiated, thereby adopting the argument of Kant that the 'unknowable' Thing-in-Itself may yet be contacted in moral experience. In fact, we might go so far as to say that the reputation earned by the nineteenth century (perhaps not altogether deservedly) as an era of moral effort, self-help, thrift, and respectability was due to the prolonged hang-over of the Kantian ethic. The first Victorian, with his regalia of top hat, frock-coat and umbrella, was the Sage of Königsberg.

In his Philosophy of History Hegel had emphasized the role of struggle, effort, and contradiction in the development of nations and communities. With an insight that few of his predecessors had possessed, he sought to prove that stability in a society is a symptom not of calm but of tension: the orderliness and dignity most apparent to the superficial eye is purchased only by ceaseless struggle against forces making for disintegration and chaos. The placid surface of the nineteenth century, observed at an oblique angle, is thus seen to be stirring with restless forces barely held in check. And the reality is in the tension, just as a man's character, as distinct from his personality, is in the measure of his self-control: a nation, like an individual, is said to 'come out strong' when its character, put to the test, survives the shock intact. At perpetual war with the materialistic complacency of the last century were, first, the poets and imaginative writers, who conducted a kind of rear-guard action as they retreated into their isolated coteries (the last stand being made by Oscar Wilde and Walter Pater), and secondly, the apostles of a somewhat out-of-date humanism such as Matthew Arnold, who fought the Philistines without any very clear notion of what he would have substituted for their philosophy, and third the theologians and philosophers, whose solidarity had been somewhat weakened by the confusion caused by the Darwinian hypothesis, dividing them into those who refused to have anything to do with it and those who, impressed by the concept of Evolution, endeavoured to remould their faith in conformity with its tenets. Fundamentalism and Modernism were the two extreme reactions within the Anglican Church, and a similar division appeared, though less violent, within the ranks of Catholicism. In philosophy, the crisis was somewhat delayed by reason of the obsession of academic thinkers with points of detail. In the universities there had arisen a school of 'minute philosophers' (on the model of Berkeley's *Alciphron*), neo-Kantians, neo-Hegelians, authors of textbooks of Logic or monographs on some philosophical problem, polite sceptics, drawing-room agnostics, with bland 'scientific' arguments in their hands and dogmas up their sleeves. All this superficial pedantry seemed to have very little to do with ordinary life, and with the desires and aspirations of ordinary men and women. The Delphic maxim 'Know Thyself' meant little to an age in which the very possibility of Knowledge was held in doubt, and for which the Self, if it meant anything at all, was reduced to a fortuitous assemblage of instincts and impulses—a depersonalized ego, the wraith of Fichte's dynamic concept.

As long as Matter was regarded as being composed of hard 'billiard ball' atoms, invisible but assumed to be the ultimate constituents of Nature, over which were 'draped' all the qualities that the philosophers were accustomed to term 'secondary', materialism proved a reasonable and even a comfortable philosophy of life. Comfort and stability go together; materialism, if it did not permit men to sit down and dream, at least permitted them to stand secure. But just when it began to seem that all the traditional beliefs of mankind—their religion, their philosophy, their moral codes—were nothing but the products of imagination and fancy, survivals of tribal customs and taboos, maintained in large part merely by those (perhaps the capitalists or the churchmen) for whom their maintenance was a matter of self-interest, lo and behold! the solidity of Matter, its impenetrability and permanence, became the subject of doubt even among the materialists themselves. Before long the mechanical picture of the universe was being transformed, as through an X-ray, into a series of wave-like squiggles and curves, these being themselves the crude notation for forces inapprehensible by our senses and only inferred from the mysterious deflections of delicate instruments or from calculations beyond the capacity of all but mathematical experts. From being a comfortable faith, materialism was changed into something as incredible as the idealisms that it had claimed to supersede: indeed, it became a kind of idealism itself, for the more original of the scientists were daring to suggest that the only realities were the 'equations' whereby the universe (or what was left of it) was made intelligible, and that these existed only in the minds of mathematicians. They went further: if the only reality was a mathematical symbolism, the creator of that symbolism, God, must Himself be a mathematician, who 'thinks' the universe into being, and by thinking maintains it. And that was to return to the position of Bishop Berkeley.

It might have been expected that philosophy, observing the extremes to which science was being driven, would have exulted at the downfall or humiliation of a dangerous rival. But such celebrations were not at all appropriate. To speak of 'philosophy' and 'science' in this figurative manner is legitimate so long as we realize what we are doing: in fact it is not 'philosophy' that rivals 'science' but the human mind that seeks to reconcile two sides of its nature, the theoretical and the practical, the sensitive and the intellectual. At the period of which we are speaking (and we are not yet perhaps at the end of it), men came to realize that in relying upon the methods whereby physical science had been consistently pursued since the time of Descartes and Galileo, all that made life worth living—all the 'values' of existence—were being compressed into the ever-narrowing sphere of the irrational and the imaginary. The problem was no longer one of definition but one of salvage. The pursuit of knowledge, declared by Socrates to be the one road to happiness, had produced after all those centuries a state of mind that was incapable of serenity, since the knowledge most easily acquired had tended, like all scientific knowledge, to strip the world of its adornment. Sophia or Wisdom had demonstrated the folly of being wise. As a guide to truth, philosophy had done nothing (or so it seemed) but usher in illusion; as a guide to conduct, it had merely opened the way to a sterile utilitarianism. Perhaps the most complete revelation of the bankruptcy of thought, whether philosophical or scientific, was that contained in the work of the German philosopher Vaihinger entitled *The Philosophy of 'As If'*, according to which all human beliefs of a transcendental character were shown to be nothing but illusory wish-fulfilments, analogies without basis, or what Hume (himself a forerunner of this line of thought) had described as 'the playful whimsies of monkeys in human shape'.

In America a voice of protest was raised by William James (1842–1910), who bade his contemporaries forget the problem of abstract 'truth' and concentrate upon action; in 'pragmatism', or the identification of truth with what is effacious in practice, lies the hope of wandering humanity. He was followed by John Dewey and George Santayana, to whom we devote a special chapter. In England, a philosopher of fine sensitivity and perceptions, F. H. Bradley (1846–1924), questioned a view which reduced the world to 'a ballet of bloodless categories'. Finally, in France, affecting one of those sudden and salutary renewals of thought which fill humanity with hope, the philosophy of Henri Bergson shot through the intellectual gloom with the brilliance of a meteor.

34

Henri Bergson

In the Absolute we live and move and have our being.

His Life

Bergson died in 1941, in a country under the shadow of foreign occupation, an old and ailing man, one of a persecuted race whose humiliations he elected to share. His death, which marks the end of an era in European thought, had about it something of the nobility and dignity of that of Socrates. Consequently, it is appropriate that his achievement and example, which presented so marked a contrast to the faint-hearted ideals of his time, should be duly recognised.

Like Nietzsche, Bergson was of mixed origin: his family can best be described as Irish–Jewish of Polish extraction.[1] This may account for his extraordinary versatility: his poetic instinct, his grasp of science and mathematics, his extreme curiosity, and above all his mysticism. For that reason alone, he became at the height of his powers a public figure, a social lion, and for some the preacher of a new gospel of comfort and exhilaration. His greatness lay in the fact that this universal adulation—and occasionally execration; it springs from the same source—failed in any way to turn his head. After holding his audiences spellbound by his eloquence, he retired into seclusion for a quarter of a century to rethink his whole position in the light of an intensive study of history, anthropology and theology. Then, in spite of increasing ill-health, he produced what some have described as his masterpiece, a study of Religion and Morality. Nor was this the end of his labours. At the time of his death he was engaged in what we have reason to believe were even more profound researches; but of these we possess nothing but the barest hints.

Born in the Rue Lamartine, Montmartre, Paris, Henri Bergson went to school at the age of nine at the Lycée Condorcet (then called the Lycée Fontanes), which was situated not far from his home. He immediately distinguished himself as a pupil of extraordinary ability. Science, mathematics, and literature were his best subjects; but he seems to have been good at everything, except apparently geography. His school career ended at eighteen with a notable achievement: namely the solution to a mathematical problem for which a competition had been set, his version being thought worthy of publication in

[1] Bergson, it is interesting to recall, was a British citizen until after he had obtained his Baccalauréat.

the *Annales de Mathématique*. After such a display of virtuosity, it was natural that he should seriously consider taking up mathematics as a career; but, his Baccalauréat over, he decided that the choice must be between literature on the one hand and science on the other. In the end he decided upon a subject of study which partook of the nature of both. This, fortunately for the world, was philosophy.

Entering the École Normale Superieure in 1878, one of the Grandes Écoles of France, he studied for the next few years under three of the most able French philosophers of his day, Ravaisson, Boutroux, and, perhaps most distinguished of all, Jules Lachélier. These thinkers were all idealists; but the young Bergson, while attracted to a form of thought that exposed the errors of materialism, gave much attention to the close study of texts, especially those of the ancient Greek philosophers, in which he succeeded in making some important emendations. This period of absorption in the thought of ancient Greece, with particular reference to such pre-Socratic philosophers as Zeno and Heraclitus, was crucial; for his own speculations took their origin from certain of the problems with which those pioneers of philosophical enquiry were concerned.

Like most other young students of philosophy, Bergson, having to decide upon a career, chose that which seemed most likely to afford him opportunity, if not necessarily leisure, for further study; namely teaching. He first joined the staff of the Lycée at Angers in Anjou, where he remained for the next two years; and then proceeded by promotion to the Lycée Blaise Pascal at Clermont Ferrand, where, under M. Bourget, father of the famous novelist, he spent one of the happiest periods of his life. It was at Clermont Ferrand that his maturing thought took definite shape. As a teacher, he began to display qualities not merely of lucidity but of passionate eloquence which transformed his subject, philosophy, from a dull academic study to a burning issue, a living topic, something that affected his pupils personally. Nor did he confine his attention to conventional academic themes; he was willing at all times to throw light, if possible, upon topics familiar to all. Thus it was a notable occasion in the intellectual life of Clermont Ferrand when M. Bergson delivered a public lecture on the subject of 'Why do we laugh?' Sixteen years later, in his book entitled *Laughter*, the ideas advanced in this lecture were developed in conformity with the now famous Bergsonian system. Another fruit of his stay at Clermont Ferrand was a scholarly edition of *Lucretius*, with an Introduction (still of great interest) on the relation between poetry and philosophy, which has served as a textbook for half a century.

Apart from an article on Hypnotism published in the *Revue Philosophique* (1886) and no doubt inspired by some experiments carried out by Dr Montin in Clermont Ferrand, Bergson produced nothing of note until the two theses submitted in 1889 for his Doctorate. The first of these was in Latin; the second was entitled *Les Données Immédiates de la Conscience*, which was later worked up into a book and translated into English under the title of *Time and Freewill*. The latter, as we shall show, expounded a new and revolutionary theory of knowledge, which Bergson defended most ably in the oral part of his examination. He was accordingly made a Docteur-ès-lettres. Tiring of the provinces, he decided to move to Paris, where he obtained a post first at the College Rollin[1] and later at the famous Lycée Henri IV.

The articles that Bergson now began to write in philosophical magazines were attracting attention not merely in France but overseas. Apart from the fact that they were written in a style of pellucid charm, the subjects treated were fresh to most students of philosophy, and the conclusions to which they pointed, though only tentative, proved as exciting to the young and curious as they were alarming to the academically orthodox. That Bergson was no less able and charming a speaker than he was a writer became increasingly known. Moreover, his appointment in 1898 to the staff of the École Normale Superieure suggested that he was already making a name for himself in the educational world. In the same year appeared the first comprehensive statement of his philosophical position in a book entitled *Matter and Memory*. The public was able at last to take some measure of him.

His Thought

As to the new and revolutionary ideas that Bergson was putting forward, his own words speak for themselves. 'I set myself,' he later wrote, 'the following problem. What is it that modern psychology and pathology can teach regarding the time-honoured question of the relation between matter and mind?... When I began to study the subject I soon discovered that the problem could not be solved, even provisionally, unless it were narrowed down to that of memory.'

To explain how he arrived at this conclusion we must revert to the general assumptions upon which philosophers had relied since the time of Descartes. Not to repeat in detail what we have expounded elsewhere, it may be recalled that for the disciples of Descartes, and even in some degree for Kant himself, Mind and Nature were set over against each other in such a way that the problem for philosophical enquiry resolved itself into how there came to be any commerce between them. The conventional answer, as we showed, was that the mind made contact with nature by means of certain media called 'ideas'. Ideas, in fact, acted as a kind of currency whereby it became possible to effect transactions between the subjective and the objective spheres. The problem of knowledge, in short, was a problem of exchange.

One way of avoiding the complications arising from this theory of knowledge (and we have seen how Hume riddled it with criticism and then turned away with a shrug of his shoulders) was the way adopted by Hegel. Another was the way adopted by Bergson.

The point to which Bergson drew attention was that this whole 'picture' of the relation between Nature and Mind rested on a spatial metaphor. Naturally, if you place the Mind *here* and Nature *there*, leaving a gulf fixed between the two, the problem of how one esta-

[1] Now the Lycée Jacques Decour.

blishes connection with the other becomes insoluble; you have automatically rendered it so. But surely, it may be said, we need to picture the problem to ourselves somehow, and this seems the most natural way of doing so. Certainly it is, replied Bergson; but it is natural only for our *intellect.* That, indeed, is how the intellect works. It spatializes. If folds things out flat. It goes round its objects and maps them from the outside, delineating one aspect after another and then, if necessary, building up a composite photograph to represent the whole. Hence the capacity of the intellect to perform the most accurate feats of analysis: for what it has built up from small counters it can as easily take to pieces.

Now the capacity of the intellect to reduce things to spatial units and to interpret everything in such terms, including the mechanism of knowledge itself, would fully suffice for our needs if the reality with which it has to deal were an inert, static reality, presenting sharply disposed contours and features susceptible to measurement. But it is not. Reality is not static but mobile. And the change in which it is engaged is not a mere shifting, a rearrangement of parts (which is no change at all), but a transformation producing real novelty. Consequently, if we rely purely upon our intellectual faculty, we shall never grasp what reality is like; we shall merely gain a distorted chess-board picture of it. Reality in its ceaseless flow and perpetual change must ever evade our intellectual categories. To seize reality, to apprehend it in its fullness, to *know* it in the fullest sense (and to know authentically is to know that we know, as if by a kind of inner conviction), we must and do have recourse to another faculty altogether.

This faculty, Bergson holds, is Intuition. By intuition we do not go round the object, taking individual observations; we enter into it. Intuition is the means whereby we plunge into the stream of flux or Becoming and apprehend it from inside. Whether we realize it or not, we are constantly doing this, or we should become so completely divorced from reality as to perish of a kind of inanition. In certain of our experiences—and these are often the most valuable—we become perfectly conscious of such interior illumination. To know another person in the complete sense is to penetrate his mind with our own, to 'enter into' his enthusiasms and aspirations, to identify ourself with his attitudes. Nor is this experience confined to what is called, in technical terms, the specious present; it involves past states of mind as well, both our own and those of our companion. In other words, to know in the sense here employed involves an interpenetration of past and present in memory, a taking up into the present of the sum of our past experience and that of others, and the carrying it forward as a unified whole, accumulating at each moment ever richer experiences, much as a snowball (the simile is Bergson's own) increases in size as it moves.

This description of knowledge may strike some people as nothing but an excuse for Bergson to indulge his lyrical gifts. That he constantly illuminates his argument by striking and original metaphors is true. But his argument is still an argument, and he supports it not merely by decorative imagery but by cogent reasons.

To return for a moment to the problem of memory: how, we may ask, is this interpenetration of present and past possible? Does it not presuppose what is clearly absurd, namely, a reversal, however slight, of the time-series? That depends, says Bergson, upon what we mean by time. This introduces us forthwith to one of the most original elements in Bergson's philosophy, namely, his distinction between scientific time and what he calls 'real time' or Duration.

Scientific time—or, as Bergson sometimes calls it, 'clock time'—bears no relation to change in the true sense at all. That may seem a bold statement. But, to take an example: if the planets travelled twice as fast as they do, they would follow precisely the same course. Now this is true of all natural processes: speed up the process—speed it up, if you like, to such an infinite degree that everything happened simultaneously—and you would in no way alter the relation between one stage or event and another. In other words, time (and here Bergson follows Kant) is not a characteristic of the world of natural things; it is something that our intellect, in effecting one of its typical distortions, projects into the world. Temporal succession, in fact, with its placing of one event before or after another, is merely an example of the way in which our intellect 'spatializes' the reality that it apprehends in the interests of practical action. We must live; and our intellect is the instrument that makes life on this planet a practical proposition.

If, however, the essence of reality is change—continuous and everlasting change without there being (as Bergson is careful to insist, in contrast this time to Kant) anything permanent that changes—it follows that such real change must depend upon a kind of time deeper, older, and more dynamic than that just described. This time or Duration, which is merely another word for Change, has been defined by Bergson as 'the continuous progress of the past which gnaws into the future'. Consequently, it is the vehicle of perpetual novelty. It is not something that passes us by: nor is it something that we make use of for practical purposes. It is something that pulsates through our very being: indeed, it *is* our very being, for we are ourselves the conscious expression of the life-flow from which the whole universe has ultimately been derived. Matter, then, is congealed, lifeless Spirit, the hardened lava thrown up by the volcanic discharge of the creative principle or *élan vital*. The ultimate reality is Duration. Everything, as Heraclitus said, flows.

In expounding this theory, Bergson adduces a wealth of examples from all the sciences. He is not content to make dogmatic statements, as thinkers like Schopenhauer and Nietzsche tend to do: he advances nothing for which he is not prepared to produce factual evidence. In attacking the materialists' account of consciousness, he goes very thoroughly into the question of how far the brain can be considered to be the seat of mental activity; and the conclusion at which he arrives is that, while the brain may be a link in the process of consciousness, it neither originates nor contains consciousness. A brain can be subjected to quite severe mutilation before mental activity shows any sign of being affected, still less stultified; nor, as we know, will the most careful dissection of the cerebral cortex and brain cells provide clues to the nature of what, for want of a better term, we call mental states. Moreover, the common type of psychological phenomena—split personality, aphasia (loss of memory for words), and all the so-called subconscious activities upon which so much theory has recently been based—have never been related satisfactorily to any given physical condition of the brain. The function of the brain, then, is not to originate mental activity, but, so far as we can see, to canalize it; for the brain is the point at which consciousness or Duration enters into matter. Acting rather like a transformer, it reduces the pressure of the life-stream, admitting just so much of consciousness as our physical make-up can stand. Without the brain, we should be flooded with a volume of vital experience calculated to render action impossible. The brain, then, is an instrument not for remembering but for forgetting. What we call the Mind overflows the brain, and is exempt from its limitations.

Two years after the publication of *Matter and Memory*, Bergson was appointed Professor of Greek Philosophy at the Collège de France, and later, in succession to the philosopher and sociologist Tarde, Professor of Modern Philosophy. From now onwards he began to assume the role of a great intellectual force, a leader of thought, the preacher of a gospel—and a most eloquent preacher at that. His lectures, open to all, began to attract not merely the student working for his examinations but the men and women, as numerous then as now, who hungered and thirsted, if not for righteousness, then for certainty—the intellectual 'fringe' which, finding no solace in traditional religion and repelled by the cold materialism and relativism that claimed to have replaced it, clung at any straw of hope that might be borne by the latest wind of doctrine. In the philosophy of Bergson, no doubt partly because of the persuasiveness of its exposition, such people found comfort and inspiration, a new zest for life, an incentive to action, such as academic thought had in the past shown an incapacity to provide. There are few descriptions more moving than that given by Raïssa Maritain, wife of the Catholic philosopher, of the effect upon her wayward generation of a single sentence of Bergson, delivered with an earnestness and conviction impossible to reproduce, and to some extent rendered lame in English translation: 'In *The Absolute* we live and move and have our being.' The impact of this statement acted, as she says, like a sudden draught of fresh air, a mental tonic: more than that—a reviver of the spirit itself, so long deprived of healthy nourishment. For what Bergson was in effect doing was not merely to put man back into the universe from which he had so long been alienated, but to give him a rich and living universe in which to be replaced. The Bergsonian philosophy, whatever its shortcomings, effected the repatriation of the human spirit.

Like every other leader or pioneer, Bergson was often embarrassed and plagued by the attentions of admirers whose interest in his thought was frivolous and superficial. His audience contained its fair sprinkling of *demi-mondes* and society ladies to whom the *Elan Vital* and is spontaneous 'gushing forth of novelties' proved highly attractive, and who found it great fun trying to listen to the *ron-ron* of Duration pulsing through their delicate blue veins. As the new gospel was carried from *salon* to *salon*, so its author was bombarded with invitations, enquiries, personal disclosures, and requests for confidential advice; his mail, much of it carrying the scent of the boudoir, exceeded that of any living philosopher and also that of some film-stars. Importunate callers rendered his life so intolerable that, being obliged to make frequent changes of residence in Paris, he earned the title of 'The Wandering Jew'.

With the publication of his great work, *Creative Evolution*, in 1907, Bergson reached the height of his fame. In its pages, he seeks to show that 'reality is change, that change is indivisible, and that in an indivisible change the past is one with the present'; and his conclusion is that 'philosophy is not only the return of the mind to itself, the coincidence of the human consciousness within the living principle from which it emanates, an establishment of contact with the creative effort; philosophy is the deepening of becoming in general, the true evolutionism, and hence the true continuation of science'. In a word, it is 'seeing in time the progressive growth of the Absolute'.

His system apparently completed, Bergson spent the next fourteen years lecturing not merely in France but throughout Europe. At Bologna, at Oxford, at Birmingham, in London, in New York, the dapper figure in the cutaway coat, high collar and cravat poured forth a stream of silvery discourse, accumulating university degrees and honours and drawing huge audiences of enthusiasts. In 1914 he was elected to the French Academy. The war of 1914–18, exposer of so many reputations, left Bergson's prestige undimmed. Indeed, his philosophy received a kind of post-war boom which threatened to leave him without a moment's peace. In 1921, unable to endure the publicity in which he had become involved, he resigned his position at the Collège de France, retaining an honorary professorship there. In spite of ill-health, he had no intention of going into retirement, if retirement meant seclusion; he wished, as ever, to make himself useful. He therefore elected to serve on a number of committees for International Co-operation, and spent much time abroad. 'In recognition of his rich and life-giving ideas and the resplendent art with which they are presented', he became the recipient in 1927 of the Nobel Prize.

That Bergson's public activities in no way exhausted his energies, his closest friends knew well. Every minute of his spare time was devoted to intensive study. He was not trying to buttress an old reputation (he had, needless to say, many critics, from Julien Benda, a fellow Jew, to Jacques Maritain himself, who soon moved on to Catholicism); he was busy, though without ambition, establishing a new one. The subjects to which he devoted particular attention were history, ethnology, anthropology, sociology, and theology, particularly the great mystical writers. To the philosopher Höffding he had written in 1912 that 'I have not touched on the problem (of God) in my works; I believe it to be inseparable from moral problems, in the study of which I have been absorbed for some years'. Bergson went on being absorbed. Like the novelist Proust, whose cousin, Mlle Neuberger, he had married, he remained silent for more than twenty years, during which time his health deteriorated considerably. The outside world assumed that his creative powers were extinct; and meanwhile a new generation had grown up to whom the apostle of the *Elan Vital* was a back-number, deserving of a passing respect in academic circles simply because *on porte partout le cadavre de son grandpère.*

Then, without any prior advertisement or announcement, there was published in 1932 a book entitled *The Two Sources of Religion and Morality*. Packed with closely reasoned thought, and written with even greater dignity and serenity than any of his previous works, it displayed a new insight and immense, if lightly worn, erudition. Surveying the course of history, Bergson traced the evolution of two kinds of human society: that in which morality is imposed through 'pressure' and that in which it is imposed through 'attraction'. In the former, or 'closed' society, the moral life is a matter of conformity, automatism, submission; in the latter, or 'open' society, it is a matter of creative spontaneity and freedom. Thus the religion of the 'closed society' is a static religion, characterized by taboo and totemism, whereas the religion of the 'open society' is a dynamic religion of which the finest flower is mysticism. As in his early work Bergson had maintained that there were two ways of knowing, the way of intellect and the way of intuition, so in his last book he traced the development of the two forms of society, the one from intelligence and the other from instinct, twin forces whereby life expresses itself. In reality, however, the human consciousness does not operate upon two different levels. It is one process, but a process which, in striving towards ever higher modes of expression, is weighed down by a constant crystallization, a 'falling away', a degeneration into habit, which is matter.

In discussing mysticism, Bergson examined the technique and experiences of the Greeks, the Orientals, the Hebrew Prophets, and finally the Christians; and it is his considered opinion that in the latter alone we have the most complete consummation of the spiritual process which is called, at lower levels, life. From the evidence of the mystics, the spiritual leaders of humanity, Bergson deduces the existence of God; for just as we must take seriously the views of scientists about matter, so we must take seriously the views of mystics about divinity. If, he writes, the 'philosopher attaches himself to mystical experience, Creation will appear to him as God undertaking to create creators, that he may have, besides Himself, beings worthy of His love'. And in the end Bergson achieves a reconciliation between the dualism which runs through his work—between Intellect and Intuition, Thought and Action, Time and Duration; for as he says, 'man will rise above earthly things only if a powerful equipment supplies him with the requisite fulcrum. In other words, the mystical summons up the mechanical... We must add that the body, now larger, calls for a bigger soul, and that mechanism should mean mysticism...

Machinery will find its true vocation again; it will render services in proportion to its power only if mankind, which it has bowed still lower to the earth, can succeed, through it, in standing erect and looking heavenwards.'

His Last Years

In the years following the publication of *The Two Sources*, Bergson, now almost a complete invalid through arthritis, continued to pursue the line of thought which he had opened up in that book; but just as he had formerly disclosed the purport of his meditations to none but his intimate friends (and sometimes not even to them), so now he worked on in silence, in seclusion, and in pain. It was rumoured that he contemplated baptism into the Catholic Church; but the growing wave of anti-Semitism that swept Europe after 1933 moved him so deeply that he felt he must stand by and with his own people in the trials that lay ahead. From a passage in his will that Mme Bergson later disclosed, we learn that as early as 1937 he had quite made up his mind on this issue. 'My reflections,' he there confessed, 'have led me closer and closer to Catholicism, in which I see the complete fulfilment of Judaism. I would have become a convert had I not seen in preparation for years the formidable wave of anti-Semitism which is to break upon the world. I wanted to remain among those who tomorrow will be persecuted. But I hope,' he added, 'that a Catholic priest will consent, if the Cardinal Archbishop of Paris authorizes it, to come to say prayers at my funeral.' This was done.

After the defeat of France in 1940, the Vichy Government ordered that all Jewish employees should resign from State positions. Bergson was offered exemption, but he refused it. Likewise, he was invited to retain his honorary Chair at the Collège de France in view of his 'artistic and religious services to the nation'; but he submitted his resignation on 9 December, thus breaking an association of forty years' standing. Finally, when the Government stipulated that all Jews must submit to public registration, Bergson was again offered the chance of exemption, but again refused. And so, at the age of eighty-one, the practically bed-ridden philosopher, fulfilling his resolve, rose for the last time, and waited his turn outside the Registration Office, supported by two servants.

That last silent protest in the inclement weather, unnoticed and almost anonymous in its humble dignity, hastened the end. On 4 January, 1941, Henri Bergson died of pulmonary congestion.

36

John Dewey and George Santayana

It is a conventionally held belief that the United States of America is a new country. In one sense, this is obviously true; but in another sense it is far from being so. America is a country with a very ancient *ethos* or ideology. In that sense, it is unique among the nations of the world.

From the earliest times, man has dreamed of Utopias, or ideal societies in which people could dwell together in liberty and brotherhood; but not until the discovery of America—or rather its rediscovery in the late fifteenth century—did the possibility of actually establishing a Utopia on a grand scale arise. The Founding Fathers were practical idealists. Without idealism, they would never have been impelled to uproot themselves; without practical genius, they would never have succeeded in establishing a society on a far and untamed continent. The society which they set up was designed to be free, and if possible permanently insulated, from the corruption and tyranny of the old world. Even today, there is a feeling, especially in the Middle Western states, that the old world of Europe has an inveterate tendency to corruption and decadence. The Declaration of Independence of 1776 contains a clear statement of the principles on which the new society was to be based: 'life, liberty and the pursuit of happiness'. Never before had Utopia been launched on the collective plane. Moreover, the land to which the pioneers came was potentially rich beyond imagination.

Until quite recently, perhaps until the beginning of the last war, American culture was regarded, even by Americans themselves, as an offshoot of the culture of England and of Europe. A book such as *The Education of Henry Adams,* published in 1905, is infused with this idea, and it is reflected in the career of Henry James. The American intelligentsia might be described as partly resident outside the United States: witness the thousands of Americans who took up permanent abode in such centres of culture as Paris, Rome, and Florence. Gertrude Stein, herself a pupil of William James, wrote: 'So I am an American, and I have lived half my life in Paris, not the half which made me but the half in which I made what I made.' Henry James, brother of the philosopher, and later on T. S. Eliot solved the dilemma by renouncing their American nationality and becoming British subjects, though James did so only on his deathbed. Another American, Stuart Merill, not merely became a French subject, but virtually turned himself into a Frenchman and wrote poetry in the language of his adopted country. There was some tendency on the part of American intellectuals to ridicule and belittle American society, and to regard Europe as the only true source of cultural values. H. L. Mencken is the figure most closely associated with this tendency. There was even a time when, especially in the South, the profession of literature was not considered a respectable one: it is only recently, but with great effulgence, that Southern writers have attained eminence. This set up a tension in American writers, since, in view of their upbringing, they simultaneously despised the Europe which, in another part of their minds, they worshipped.

All this has now changed. The tensions are there, but transmuted. Others have arisen. But the American intelligentsia is no longer a kind of government in exile. Americans living and writing abroad have ceased to represent what might be called, in Toynbee's phrase, 'an external proletariat'. There is even a movement in the reverse direction. A genuine American literature, even when it is written by first-generation Americans, exists. Likewise, there is already a distinctively American tradition in philosophy.

If philosophy is the disinterested pursuit of truth, can the nationality of a philosopher affect his thinking? The answer is that it can and it does. The pursuit of any mental goal, not least the highest of all, must take as its point of departure the environment in which the thinker finds himself. And the further removed the goal, the more obviously will the thinker view it from his own standpoint, and with preconceived assumptions. We can detect a German, a French, a British, even an Indian approach to problems so apparently above or irrelevant to nationality as those of biology and psychology. The German will *tend* to adopt the *a priori* method; the British and American the empirical or mechanistic one. These particular slants will be no less present, if disguised, in subjects far more abstract in content. Metaphysics provides a good example. Perhaps the most elevated of enquiries, metaphysics is not so elevated as to have escaped bitter partisanship. On the contrary, metaphysics, its nature and its very legitimacy as an enquiry, has been subject to more controversy, especially in our time, than any other branch of thought. There are even thinkers who, far from discussing this subject in a non-partisan spirit, believe that metaphysics, especially in its more idealistic forms, is the result of an aberration of the German mind, a kind of Teutonic conspiracy against common sense. Not to confine such conspiracies to one nation, it might be argued that certain forms of extreme empiricism, such as Behaviorism, are conspiracies of the American mind.

One of the chief characteristics of American thought is that it presents a variety, a meeting of extremes, which results from the varied traditions which have gone to compose and to complicate the American character. In this chapter, we shall be discussing two thinkers who are as apparently different from each other as they are different from the thinkers of Europe, yet both of whom belong to a tradition distinctively American.

Dewey's Life and Thought

Born at Burlington, Vermont, in New England, on October 20 1859, John Dewey was descended from a pioneer family. His forebears probably came from Dorchester in the county of Dorset, England. The Dewey family sailed for America not many years after the *Mayflower* left Plymouth in 1620. The history of the English branch of the family has been subject to much research. It is possible that the family name was derived from the Flemish 'de Wei', meaning 'of the meadow', and that the Deweys were weavers from Flanders who, like many of their kind, took refuge in England from the persecution of their Spanish overlords. John Dewey's father, a farmer's son, owned a grocery business in Burlington. He was a man of some culture. We are told that he could quote Milton fluently, recite Burns in the Scottish dialect, and read Carlyle and the great Victorian novelists. His wife, from a well-to-do Vermont family and his junior by many years, was likewise both intelligent and resourceful. Their two sons, of whom John was the younger, were thus reared in a household where reading and study were encouraged. The boys developed an early interest in books. The Waverley Novels and Chambers Encyclopaedia were purchased from earnings from delivering papers and other odd jobs.

Dewey's schooldays were uneventful. He found school life boring, but he was not a bad scholar. He came under strong religious influence. The boys spent their holidays on the farm of their grandfather, and here they took their share of the heavy work. During the Civil War, the father joined a cavalry regiment in the Union Army. As the war dragged on, Mrs Dewey finally decided to move the family to Virginia in order to be near him. This proved to be the last winter of the struggle, and life was hard.

At fifteen, John Dewey graduated from high school and entered the University of Vermont. The transition was negligible, since the family home was situated almost next door to the university buildings. The subjects prescribed for study were of wide range. Dewey took Greek, Latin, ancient history, mathematics, and the natural sciences. The textbook prescribed for physiology was that of the great T. H. Huxley. Apart from the interest which such a book aroused, Dewey's mental outlook was broadened by what he was able to assimilate from periodicals from overseas. In his senior year, he embarked on philosophy. A capable teacher, Profesor H. A. P. Torry, took the students through Plato, Bishop Butler, Bain, and the Scottish school. Meanwhile, Dewey made acquaintance on his own with the English positivists through articles in the *Fortnightly Review*, and thus with the system of Auguste Comte. He finished his university career with high honours.

At this critical stage in his life, he lacked a clear idea of what he wanted to do for a living. As we have often observed in the foregoing pages, the uncertain student usually drifts into education. Perhaps 'drift' is the wrong word. The profession with which he has been in closest contact is that of teaching. Once his student days are over, he finds little difficulty in exchanging the 'passive' role for the 'active'; for teaching and learning are parts of a single process, if the teacher is not an automaton and the student is more than a receptive mechanism. By accident rather than by design, Dewey found himself teaching at a school in South Oil City, Pennsylvania, of which a cousin, Clara Wilson, was principal. After two years of plodding routine, he moved to a village school in Charlotte, not far from his home town of Burlington. These years of apparent obscurity were not without influence upon the future educational theorist. He experienced at first hand the grandeur and the misery of teaching. Meanwhile, he did not neglect his higher studies. He continued to maintain close contact with his old teacher, Torry. In 1882, he wrote his first essay in philosophy, a study of materialism. This he offered to a review of ideas, the only one of its kind in the States, called *Speculative Philosophy*, and was gratified by its prompt acceptance. The editor, W. T. Harris, was much under the influence of German thought, particularly that of Schelling and Hegel. His journal was one of several sources from which German philosophy obtained so strong a hold over the American academic mind.

Dewey at last felt that he had discovered his *métier*. Borrowing a sum of money from a relative, he entered Johns Hopkins University. This was in effect America's second university after Harvard; but at that time it was open only for graduate study. The new atmosphere proved exhilarating. In after life, Dewey confessed that he was heartily glad to leave Vermont. At Johns Hopkins, he met for the first time men of exceptional ability and originality. He had an opportunity for the free exchange of ideas not merely with his teachers but in such arenas of debate as the seminars. At that time the latter were almost unique to Johns Hopkins. In the realm of ideas, the greatest single influence upon his mind was that of Hegel. Against Hegelianism, he was later to react with a violence which carried him, together with many of his generation, to the opposite pole of thought; but he never underestimated the importance of the Hegelian 'moment' in his development. He described Hegelianism as an 'immense release or liberation'. In point of fact, he found in Hegel something more than a stimulus to profound and daring philosophical speculation. Then philosophy of Hegel provided a kind of substitute religion. The rather narrow evangelical beliefs of his youth had shown no obvious point of contact with his broadening outlook; and their renunciation took place with less violence in the context of a system which seemed to embrace all experience. Another influence upon his religious opinions, though probably antedating that of Hegel, was Coleridge's *Aids to Reflection*. This book had enjoyed great popularity in freethinking circles since its American edition was published in 1829. Dewey once told a friend that he had learnt from Coleridge all he ever was to believe on the subject of religion, but that he rarely referred to the fact because few people seemed interested.

It was at Johns Hopkins that, thanks to his teacher and later close friend George Morris, Dewey obtained some university teaching and later a fellowship. Soon after, he was offered an instructorship at the University of Michigan, where Morris held a professorship. Here, in

Ann Arbor, Dewey met his future wife. Alice Chipman was taking the university course on money she had earned as a teacher. She was from a Vermont family likewise descended from pioneers. Of strong character and independent mind, she was at that stage a good deal more progressive in outlook than the man she married in 1886. Dewey's increasing preoccupation with social problems, his interest in formulating a practical philosophy, and his respect for the religious outlook which he formally repudiated, may be attributed largely to her influence. She bore him six children, was his constant helpmeet, and died in 1927.

An academic career, even one covering so long a period as that of Dewey, does not usually provide material for vivid biography. Dewey held a succession of appointments. He spent a year at Minnesota. He went back again to Michigan, where he made perhaps the greatest philosophical friendship of his life, that with the original George H. Mead. He moved to Chicago in 1894, where he became Professor not merely of Philosophy and Psychology but of Pedagogy, and where he directed an experiment in education which came to be known as the Dewey School. The residence at Chicago was probably the most fruitful of all. Through his publications, he had already become well known as a progressive thinker; he was now afforded an opportunity of gaining practical experience of educational and social problems. One of the institutions in which he took a close personal interest was Hull House, the famous Chicago social settlement directed by a remarkable woman, Jane Addams. This settlement was open to people of every belief and of any social position. Its purpose was to conduct an experiment in democratic living. Dewey felt that such ventures might point the way to a truly democratic society, first on a national and ultimately on an international scale. Years after he had left Chicago, and despite differences of viewpoint over America's entry into the Great War, Dewey remained a loyal champion of Jane Addams and her social ideals.

A dispute concerning the school associated with his name terminated his residence at Chicago in 1904. Before taking up a post offered him at Columbia, he paid a long-planned visit to Europe. This interval of relaxation was darkened by the death from typhoid of one of his sons. The Deweys later adopted an Italian boy whom they had met on their trip. The decision proved a happy one; the boy grew up to become an educationalist after his foster father's own heart. The period at Columbia which followed was no less crowded with activity. To his academic work Dewey now added political activity and, through his friendship with the scientist and collector Albert C. Barnes, art. He became chairman of many committees and organizations, among them the League for Independent Political Action. He also helped to establish new ones, including the American Association of University Professors.

Although he was by no means a brilliant lecturer, and despite a style of writing that was often plodding, sometimes muscle-bound, and clogged with qualifications, Dewey was by now an acknowledged leader of American thought. His pragmatism or instrumentalism, of which we shall speak, was the kind of philosophy which lent form and respectability to the dominant mood of his country. As much by her exertions as by her example, America was rapidly becoming the world's most powerful and dynamic nation. Moreover, she represented a people who believed, and who daily saw evidence for their belief, that they had a mission. This mission was to teach the world the lesson of democracy in action. In contrast with the imperialisms of both past and present, America stood for a kind of moral imperialism. At the end of the First World War, she combined unrivalled strength, immense prestige, and, in the view of many of her people and not a few foreigners, the practical idealism often lacking in countries placed at such eminence. Of this practical idealism, Dewey proved to be the natural mouthpiece.

Chiefly through the diffusion of his progressive educational theories, he was now also becoming known abroad. Countries engaged in the task of reconstruction, as well as those embarking on nationhood, were seeking ideas on social matters which were not merely practical but flexible enough to be applied to their own problems. Modern technical civilization, a purely Western product, showed itself to be easily exportable. No other civilization had ever shown such capacity for rapid expansion, nor so powerful an effect in breaking down long-established custom. Measured by the standards of the West and particularly by those of the United States, half the world appeared *underdeveloped*. People conscious of this discrepancy in standards felt the need not merely for machinery and technical knowledge, but for the philosophy that went with them. Consequently, a form of thought which laid primary emphasis on growth, on the type of knowledge which led to practical results, and on the repudiation of tradition, hierarchy, and absolute values, was a philosophy likely to exert widespread appeal. No doubt this philosophy, or its crude equivalent, had already been tacitly exported along with the technical processes and know-how; Dewey merely gave it articulation. The first country to extend an invitation to Dewey was that which had been opened up by Americans in the previous century, Japan. By contrast, the countries in which Dewey's ideas made least impact, both then and after the Second World War, were those which had succeeded in reconciling tradition and progress: Great Britain, for example.

Dewey's reception in Japan in 1918 was enthusiastic; but the enthusiasm was manifest largely among those already acquainted with his views, or at least ripe to receive them—that is, a minority. He was under no illusions as to the contrary influences at work, the enormous power still wielded by militarists and traditionalists. In the years 1918–19, however, America's reputation in Japan was at its zenith; and most liberal-minded people, Dewey included, assumed that democracy would not merely triumph here and throughout the world, but that it must necessarily do so. Dewey's much longer and more rewarding visit to China was likewise the result of the enterprise of former students, among them the Chancellor of the National University of Peking. He travelled extensively, lecturing in most of the larger Chinese universitis. He saw the growing power of the student, that substitute in new nations for a bourgeois intelligentsia; the beginnings of female emancipation (Mrs Dewey was made Honorary Dean of Women at Nanking); and the awakening to modern ideas of a country gigantic in size and unparalleled in fertility. During the tour, one of his escorts was the Chinese Ambassador to the United States, Dr Hu Shih, who had studied at Cornell and Columbia. He left for Taiwan, and a change has come over Chinese affairs such as Dewey could not have foreseen.

Dewey also visited Turkey in 1924, the moment when Kemal Ataturk was consolidating his drastic, but beneficent, reforms. Two years later he went to Mexico. A visit to the USSR took place in 1928. Here Dewey was able to observe a process of social regeneration inspired by ideas sufficiently in line with his own to rouse his enthusiasm: for Soviet education was at least a co-operative activity, and its aim was to build a new world on the ruins of an old. Despite some of his statements on return, which caused him to be denounced as a Bolshevik, he was not deceived by the political aspects of this experiment in 'unanimous' democracy. The tour was an exclusively educational one, and today we can hardly say that the Soviet experiment, at least in its technical aspects, has failed. When many years later Dewey agreed to sit on a commission of enquiry into the charges brought by Stalin's government against Trotsky, he arrived, by an impartial study of the facts, at a more critical view of Communist ideals and practice. And if the facts were responsible for bringing about the later change of attitude, their earlier disclosure would not doubt have modified his initial enthusiasm. The *Soviet Encyclopaedia* of 1952 later retaliated by dismissing him as a 'reactionary bourgeois philosopher and subjective idealist (sic) . . . serving the interests of aggressive American imperialism'.

Dewey may be said to have reached the height of his eminence, as well as the climax of his powers, when in 1929 he delivered the Gifford Lectures at Edinburgh. The invitation to join so distinguished a company proved him to be among the most vigorous minds of his day. The lectures were published in the same year under the title of *The Quest for Certainty*. Together with *Human Nature and Conduct* (1922), this book represents in both thought and style perhaps the highest level of his work, and his most enduring contribution to philosophy.

Many years were still to be allowed him; and though he published no major work, with the exception of *Art as Experience* (1934), this did not imply that he had said all he had to say. He was a man of immense energy, and he lived his philosophy as much as any modern thinker may be said to have done. He lectured frequently and always drew large audiences. He became Professor Emeritus at Columbia in 1930. In 1931, he delivered the William James Lectures at Harvard, and in 1934 the Terry Lectures at Yale. As each decade passed, he was accorded the honour to which age and achievement entitle a man. A massive tribute was the publication in 1939 of the volume *The Philos-*

ophy of John Dewey, one of the distinguished compendia for which Professor Paul Schilpp has been responsible, and featuring essays by most of his distinguished colleagues, including Bertrand Russell and A. N. Whitehead. Another volume of essays in his honour was called *The Philosophy of the Common Man*, published in 1940 to mark his eightieth birthday. In 1946, he remarried. He died in 1952 at the age of ninety-three.

We have stated that Dewey's philosophy was above all a practical one; that it provided a liberation from much that philosophy currently stood for; and that it formed a fitting gospel for a new era. All this is true. What needs to be stressed, however, is its relation to the philosophy of the past, especially the immediate past. A thinker who seeks to break away from a tradition may at the same time be the last exponent of that tradition. That is the reason why a man who is hailed, or denounced, as an iconoclast in his day is often regarded by the next generation as already a back-number. The new generation, having absorbed from him all that was new, perceive retrospectively only the man who faces them, not the man whose back is turned to the past. A comparison with a figure of similar, if not much greater, stature may be illuminating. The generation in Britain which inherited the material advantages of the Welfare State tended to regard Bernard Shaw, who was perhaps its foremost ideological architect, as thoroughly *old hat*. In outlook and even in appearance, Shaw was indeed one of the last of the Victorians; and he achieved his impact by castigating Victorian standards. Dewey was in much the same position; and that is why the newest generation of Americans tends to find him pretentious and out-dated. Writing six years after his death, George Geiger remarks: 'This is a peculiar time to be writing about John Dewey. It is a time when almost every fundamental part of his philosophy seems to have been rejected.'[1]

The operation of this 'law of diminishing reputation' can be further illustrated with reference to Dewey's thought. After his initial addiction to Hegel, Dewey did not so much spurn the master as put his thought to a different use, exactly as Karl Marx did. Now, the foundation of Hegel's system is his Logic. Consequently, Dewey's early work, and that which may seem least remarkable to another generation, was concerned primarily with logical *reform*. Nevertheless, his approach and even his terminology remain those of Bradley and Bosanquet, the direct heirs of Hegel. The renewed interest at the time of writing in Bradley and Bosanquet, especially the former, is therefore part of a reaction against Dewey himself, who had endeavoured to push beyond these men.

Dewey published two major works in Logic, *Studies in Logical Theory* in 1903, and *Essays in Experimental Logic* in 1916, the original 'Studies' being included in the later volume. The title of this second book, besides emphasizing the current reaction against idealistic logic, revealed the philosophical direction in which he was moving. It represents something of a flourish, a challenge; for while logic itself is

[1] *John Dewey in Perspective* (1958), p. 3

hardly to be called experimental, the uses to which it is put may be so.

In talking of judgment, Dewey wishes to move away from the idealist position according to which a *mind* comes to know and entertain an *idea*. This he regards as too abstract a view. Judgment for Dewey is first and foremost a practical activity, a man judging: a difference of emphasis not without novelty in its day. Furthermore, the person engaged in judgment is doing so always in a concrete situation. He acts upon this situation, and only thus does he arrive at knowledge. For the situation is not to be understood in a mere environmental sense. A man's actions are part of his situation, and the 'transactions' between the two comprise his total experience. Judgment is that which turns unreflective experience into reflective experience: for if judgment is the acquisition of knowledge, there must first be something concrete to know.

This is a crucial point. Dewey is as much an enemy of pure or naïve empiricism as Bradley. It is the contention, or the tacit assumption, of the empiricist that our experience consists of a series of sensations. What are sensations? If they are the 'feeling of this' or the 'apprehension of that', one distinct sensation following another, they are much more sophisticated than our ordinary experience would suggest. These sensations are *not* what our experience contains. A 'stream of consciousness', in William James's sense, is by definition the opposite of an articulated procession. In other words, pure empiricism, far from viewing experience as it really is, presents us with an artificial blueprint. We might say that empiricism, simply by being the 'philosophy' of experience, is the philosophy of 'experience'. And this is as much as to say that there can be no such thing as empiricism *tout court*. When philosophers call themselves empiricists, they are employing a convenient and very general label. Consequently, the term, as used in philosophical argument, is almost always qualified. We have Hume's empiricism, or James's 'radical' empiricism, or the empiricism of the linguistic philosophers; and in each case we find that the view of experience so labelled is something different from what is called, perhaps with unintentional aptness, 'brute empiricism'.

If, however, unreflective experience takes the form of a stream, a continuum, how do we ever succeed in emerging from it in order to scrutinize or judge it? How does it become, in Dewey's phrase, 'an affair of history'? The answer is that the flux of experience, every now and then, is subject to disruption or arrest. A problem arises. We stop and think about it. The weight of our intelligence is brought to bear. We prescribe a remedy: that is to say, we consider what mode of *action* is best to adopt. Only when we have acted, when we have removed the barrier, can we be said truly to *know* what the situation is. The original plan of action is formulated partially in the dark: hence it is hypothetical. Knowledge, when we have it, is practical. The first is merely an instrument to knowledge; the second only is true judgment, and therefore knowledge itself.

This is the basis of Dewey's instrumentalism. As with all philosophical methods, a metaphysics lurks behind it. Dewey wishes, first of all, to dissociate his theory from those systems according to which knowledge 'makes no difference' to the thing known; but he is equally at pains to reject, or rather to reformulate, the standpoint which conceives of reality as being somehow moulded, even created, by the mind. Our intelligence, Dewey holds, does make a difference to what it knows, but only because it alters the *situation* which it has been called upon to judge. We pronounce judgment not in some abstract manner, but as responsible agents intent upon effecting changes for the better. Knowledge is not the passive contemplation of some higher object; 'philosophy will have to surrender all pretensions to be peculiarly concerned with ultimate reality'.[1] It is the active intervention in our immediate situation. This intervention not merely clarifies our thoughts. It is not mere 'analysis'. It is diagnosis: and its diagnosis, like all diagnoses, is a prelude to remedy.

The whole of Dewey's conception of ethics, education, and even aesthetics, is the logical consequence of his instrumentalist theory of knowledge. Ethics, or the science of conduct, is more than the analysis of concepts such as good, duty, interest, etc.; it is the act of passing from diagnosis to cure. It is practical reason at work. Education, in turn, is practical training, controlled growth. Art, finally, is the *élan*, the spirit of exultation, the sense of equilibrium, which accompanies all positive, fruitful activity; it 'celebrates with peculiar intensity the moments in which the past reinforces the present and in which the future is a quickening of what now is.'[2]

A crucial question next arises. How do we know that our knowledge, practical though it may be, is *true*? Such a question is one which gave Dewey a certain amount of trouble. He deals with it by making another plea for reformation. If 'true' means the conformity of the mind to reality, in some abstract fashion, the word is misleading. Dewey substitutes the phrase 'warranted assertibility'. It occurs for the first time in his *Logic, The Theory of Enquiry*, published in 1938, and owes its formulation to drastic criticism by Russell. But by what criterion is any statement warranted? By the warrant of the discipline most practical in method, namely science, with which philosophy must at all times 'take its stand'. Does this mean that science is infallible? Indeed not: the history of science is the history of error as well as of truth. In every assertion, we need to make allowance for an element of distortion and one-sidedness, just as we need to allow, in every warrant, for an element of inaccuracy, of faulty drafting. Then can we never arrive at truth? This again is a problem which Dewey associates with the traditional and superannuated philosophies of knowledge. To 'arrive' is to presuppose a settled and definite destination. It presupposes a reality at the foot of which the seeker after knowledge, having finished his course, bows down in reverence. To Dewey, reality is not of this nature. If we have the power to control our lives and our destiny, as is now the case, we can also control what used to be called Reality.

[1] 'A Recovery of Philosophy', from the symposium *Creative Intelligence: Essays in the Pragmatic Attitude* (New York, 1917), p. 12.
[2] *Art as Experience* (1934), p. 18.

The sciences of man, far from having completed their task, are every day making further progress. We 'live forward'. The future is 'implicated in the present', rather than the present being implicated in the past. And this is the best guarantee against error and illusion. Science goes on making mistakes, but it also goes on correcting them. Its 'going on' is the guarantee against mental sloth on the one hand, and rash claims to infallibility on the other.

In *The Quest for Certainty*, Dewey puts forward perhaps the most comprehensive and plausible case that has been made, at least in modern times, for a view of life which lauds risk, adventure, and experiment. Although the traditional philosophies were not deliberate attempts to evade the responsibilities of experiment, they tended inevitably towards a contemplative view of life. This was because, prior to the great discoveries of the sixteenth and seventeenth centuries, the notion of human control over nature did not arise. Man was passive by necessity. Apart from clockwork, windmills and waterwheels, he had no machinery for subduing nature. By contrast, we are the heirs of a great and continuing scientific revolution. We are risk-takers, instrumentalists, by adoption. Our quest for certainty is not a search for some haven of security. Having started out on our voyage, our only security lies in the seaworthiness of the craft in which we sail.

The great merit of Dewey's thought, and perhaps the reason for its influence on his time, lies in his conception of philosophy as *diagnosis* and *cure*. Philosophy has something to do. Logic is a weapon in our hands. The cultivation of these disciplines exclusively in some theoretical or academic 'reservation' is not the best way to preserve their efficacy; it is rather to encourage their deterioration. Granted, the books in a library must be well cared-for and accurately classified; but they must be also taken out and read. So it is with all the sciences. They require sedulous cultivation, if necessary in the laboratory and the study, but only for the sake of being applied and tested in the rough and tumble of life. This is true even of the most abstract sciences. We become convinced that certain mathematical equations are true not merely because they are coherent in themselves, but because they are compatible with the measures needed to put them into practice. For example, it was by no means certain, before the achievement of atomic fission, that a general destructive chain-reaction would not occur. Thus, before the crucial experiments undertaken in Germany, France, in Cambridge, England, and later in Chicago, no atomic physicist could be said genuinely to *know* what his theoretical formulae meant.

Exhilarated by a pragmatic philosophy which really worked, some followers of Dewey pushed his ideas to a point which he regarded as extremist. Pragmatism, it was realized, might be abused. If truth was that which worked—if the only legitimate ideas were those which promoted success in practice—the irresponsible pragmatist, or even the genuine but thoughtless one, might encourage conduct of an anti-social kind. What constituted success? Was it material gain? Was it the acquisition of power? Many comfortable philosophies were put forward within the shadow of pragmatism which defined success in the crudest terms. The test to which such philosophies appealed was frankly materialistic: a well-known book on the technique of winning friends and influencing people frequently quoted the impressive incomes of men who, according to the author, had practised his pragmatic ideas. William James would have been horrified, as were his followers, at Mussolini's claim that Fascism was based on the pragmatic philosophy of the American thinker. Even though the error was pointed out,[1] it cannot be denied that some such inference was, on the face of it, excusable. Like every theory which defined truth in a utilitarian manner, pragmatism was a doctrine depending at heart upon a system of values; and these values were necessarily non-utilitarian ones. The most persuasive exponent of utilitarianism, John Stuart Mill, was also the man who provided the most cogent of all its refutations. This was his declaration that it was 'better to be Socrates dissatisfied than a pig satisfied'. He even unconsciously added more force and universality to the refutation by later substituting 'a man' for 'Socrates'. Why was it better? How could dissatisfaction be valuable, unless satisfaction were measured by non-material standards?

Dewey was aware of this dilemma, and he discussed it at length in the chapter on values in *The Quest for Certainty*. It is doubtful whether he escaped from it. He speaks of the replacement of 'the older theory regarding the authority of the immutable and transcendent values by conceptions more congruous with the practices of daily life'.[2] We might ask whose daily life he had in mind. The practices of the daily life of Nero or Ivan the Terrible, or even of the ordinary man who pursues success and is entertained by portrayals of men and women in recurrent states of sexual excitement, depend on standards which every philosopher, save perhaps the hedonist Chinese sage Hsun Tze, would reject. Dewey's answer is that we should 'change from forming ideas and judgments of value on the basis of conforming to antecedent objects, to construing enjoyable objects by knowledge of consequences'; and he adds rightly enough that this represents a 'change from looking to the past to looking to the future', even though we must take into account past experiences as tools or 'intellectual instrumentalities'. One difficulty of this argument is that 'knowledge of the consequences' depends upon the 'construction of enjoyable objects' being itself past, in order that we may perceive what their consequences have been. Past experiences earn the title of 'instrumentalities' precisely because their consequences have been judged to be enjoyable: and that is why we are able to distinguish one set of instrumentalities from another, and to decide to what form of value or even enjoyment they have been instrumental. (One feels that Dewey does not always distinguish the enjoyable and the desirable.) In other words, instrumentalism as a 'philosophy of the future' depends upon instrumentalism as a 'philos-

[1] i.e., in an interview Mussolini gave in Rome to Professor Horace Kallen, a pupil of William James and successor to Dewey as President of the Conference on Methods in Philosophy.

[2] *Op. cit.* p. 257.

ophy of the past'; for the future must become past in order that we may know what it is. We 'look to the future', if we look at all, only to justify or judge the past, not to render it superfluous. We must, as Dewey admits, 'form the best judgment possible about what led us to like this sort of thing, and what has issued from the fact that we liked it'. Agreed: and this is to form 'the best judgment possible' of 'ideas and judgments ... conforming to antecedent objects'. Any method of thought 'congruous with the practice of daily life' which does not conform to this method would make daily life a precarious business. Moreover, Dewey's own philosophy, which we have sought to relate to its antecedents, must be judged by the same criterion.

The kind of philosophy preached by Dewey can be of value only if it is practised by men similar in integrity to its founder. Dewey was a man of firm character. He had all the solid virtues. He had common sense. Much of what he says on the subject of social life in *Human Nature and Conduct* is sound; but we sometimes feel that this wisdom springs from sources deeper than his philosophy. In quality though not in content, his thought is similar to that of Walter Pater. It is safe reposing in *his* hands, but it might prove corrupting in others. Just as certain forms of decadence resulted from the view that life should be, in Pater's words, 'a series of beautiful moments', so certain forms of vulgarization and materialism resulted from the view that life should be a repudiation of all 'immutable and transcendent values'. Indeed, the decadence consequent upon the latter, since it affects the practices of the daily life of the many, is potentially more dangerous than that of the former, since it affects only the practices of a few. Dewey saw the possibility that 'the force of new conditions will produce disruption externally and mechanically'; but this is hardly the kind of disturbance to constitute what he elsewhere called 'genuine danger'.

A danger to which he did not seem alive, possibly because of an intrinsic optimism of temperament, was that his new gospel might result in the kind of 'new decadence' which existentialist philosophy has sometimes encouraged; and this danger is the more likely in that his own belief, taken in its metaphysical aspect, has much in common with existentialism. The latter philosophy is equally a repudiation of 'immutable and transcendental values'; and there is some parallel between its view of man as being 'thrown into the world' and creating his own values, and Dewey's call to his fellows to 'throw themselves into the future' and work out their salvation experimentally. Existentialism admittedly has several varieties, and what is true of Sartre is not true of Marcel; but in his hostility to religion, Dewey is at one with the former rather than with the latter. Moreover, the chief difference between his own metaphysics (a word he was quite willing to employ, much to Santayana's disapproval) and that of Sartre is that the French philosopher, with a more powerful imagination and a mind wholly averse to the Protestant ethic, pushes his belief to a logical conclusion. Dewey, with his addiction to qualification, obscured the conclusion to which his thought pointed. He was probably too old to grasp the post-war versions of existentialism, even if he was sufficiently aware of them; but we may hazard the guess that had he studied them, he would have disliked them as much he disliked logical positivism. Yet the latter, with its liquidation of traditional philosophy, might be held to stem from his own particular brand of pragmatism. To declare a man responsible for the abuses or exaggerations of his beliefs would be unjust; but some measure of responsibility must be laid at his door if, in expounding them, he betrays no awareness of dangers other than the most superficial.

Even allowing for the resemblance 'on paper' between the instrumentalist and the existentialist philosophy, the defenders of Dewey might well draw attention to the complete dissimilarity between the robust patriarch of pragmatism, a figure more venerable even than William James, the preacher of manly virtues, the apostle of a muscular non-Christianity, and the morbid, febrile, almost haunted apostle of existentialism. Difference there is; and yet the comparison is not all to the advantage of Dewey. As Morris Cohen has stressed,[1] Dewey seems to have had little or no sense of what is called, in traditional thought, the problem of evil. He looked at life broadly, but not deeply. Evil existed; but it was identified with something which could be repudiated. To Dewey, as to most apostles of militant secularism, evil was 'the past', man's superstitious heritage. That is why we must turn our backs upon it. Now Sartre, who has himself no liking for the past, is a thinker morbidly aware of evil, even though he may not conceive it in conventional terms. Existentialist man, because he has been thrown into existence, has plumbed its depths. Even in his repudiation of values, the existentialist philosopher lives at the level at which the *sense* of values has become acute. Of Nietzsche we can say the same. To be 'beyond good and evil' is to live in a moral void, Sartre's *néant*; and to live in such a void, as Nietzsche knew, was to suffer a particular sort of agony, that of having 'neither God nor friend'. The agony was precisely to be aware of loss, as thirst becomes most acute in the desert. The more negative the philosophy, the more positive becomes its indirect message. Dewey's thought is lacking in this dimension. Indeed, he expressly repudiated it. He affirmed that the fate of the cosmos had nothing to do with the problems of education, politics, and morals. But, other matters apart, does not the fate of the cosmos have something to do with evolution? If evolution has no connection with education and morals, then what becomes of our trust in democracy, progress, and the future?

Santayana's Life and Thought

In the year of Dewey's decease, there died in seclusion in Rome a philosopher, seven years Dewey's junior, who, Spanish by birth, is regarded nevertheless as one of America's foremost thinkers, even though he had left the United States as far back as 1912. On December 16, 1863, George Santayana was born in Madrid, Spain. His family moved soon after to Avila, the birthplace of St Teresa, and a town pos-

[1] *American Thought* (1954), pp. 296–97, and *Studies in Philosophy and Science* (1949), pp. 139–63.

sessing to this day the atmosphere and much of the fabric of the sixteenth century. We know a good deal about Santayana's life, both as a child and as a man, from the lengthy autobiographical writings to which he devoted his later years. Yet he remains the kind of figure which it is conventional to call enigmatic. If a man spends so much time upon himself, it is likely that he is endeavouring either to discover who he is, or to put into circulation a view of his character which he feels may otherwise elude the biographer. This is especially the case if, as with Santayana, he likewise experiments with autobiography in the form of fiction. If *The Last Puritan* is 'A Memoir of the form of a Novel', his three-volume autobiography is, in great tracts, a novel in the form of a memoir. Such an approach does not necessarily imply insincerity, still less an attempt to conceal or manipulate facts. A man who has deliberately changed his cultural background, and who has all but changed his nationality, may need to write his autobiography, if he is to write one at all, in his own special manner. More than once in this book we have stressed how, by necessity, the most important part of the life of a philosopher is his thought; and since a man's thought includes his conception of who he is, his self-revelation may take a form totally different from that which the biographer, viewing the man from the outside, will present.

Before the marriage of which Santayana was the sole issue, his mother, who came from a Catalonian family, had married an American, George Sturgis. Sturgis was a Protestant merchant from Boston who had settled in Manila in the Philippines. He died in 1857 at an early age; and in accordance with his wish that his children should receive an education in the United States, where he owned property, his widow forthwith moved to Boston. In 1862, she revisited Spain on holiday. The stay became protracted, and in the course of it she renewed acquaintance with an old friend and finally married him. Her husband, Don Augustin Ruiz de Santayana, who had known Sturgis well, approved of her educating the children of her first marriage in America; and although Jorge, as he was called, was born the following year, he was left behind with his father when she returned to Boston six years later. The arrangement proved increasingly unsatisfactory. When George was nine years old, his father took him across the Atlantic, possibly with a view to settling permanently on American soil; but one severe winter in Boston was sufficient to induce him to return home. George remained with his mother.

At this time the boy knew no English. He tells us that he learnt the language wholly by ear. This he did in a kindergarten on Chestnut Street where, perhaps fortunately, no books were used, and the children were mostly younger than himself. This may have been responsible both for his perfect accent, and for his having assimilated the natural rhythms of a language of which he became a spoken and written master. He proceeded in due course to the Brimmer School, the Latin School, and finally to Harvard.

Despite his American education, Santayana always claimed that his spiritual roots remained Spanish, Latin, and Catholic. This is probably true, and the fact that he thought it so explains much of his outlook. His half-sister, Susana, to whom he remained devoted, instructed him in Catholic doctrine, and he attended mass from an early age. In the Unitarian atmosphere of the Sturgis family, however, he felt a stranger. He revisited Spain after his first year at the university. With his father's encouragement, he even considered entering the Spanish diplomatic service; but he found that he had become too American by training, if not in spirit, to do so, and also that his proficiency in Spanish had declined. If he deliberately assumed the cultural guise of his adopted country, it was, he claimed, for a special reason: he was enabled thereby to 'say plausibly in English as many unenglish things as possible'. Certainly he remained a critic of America all his life, as he was a critic of England; but in another sense his foreign roots, which he shared with many others in the United States, enabled him to say a good many 'English' things, especially those which may be labelled American.

At Harvard, Santayana's teachers were Josiah Royce and William James. In his *Character and Opinion in the United States* (1920), he criticized both, but the former more devastatingly than the latter. He was at first much attracted by James, and it was to James that he owed his appointment in 1889 to a post in the Department of Philosophy. In 1907, on Royce's death, he succeeded to the Chair of Philosophy. Santayana proved to be an admirable teacher and lecturer. Like Bergson, whom in this respect he resembled, he talked as gracefully as he wrote. There was no hesitation, no correction; his manuscripts are calligraphic models. He was aloof, but kind to students, finding their company more congenial than that of the faculty. Among his colleagues he was not especially popular. He declared later that he disliked academic teaching. He never showed it, except in so far as he chose to sever all university connections when, on his mother's death in 1912, he was able to travel freely overseas. He visited Germany in 1886 and France in 1905, but perhaps his most remunerative visit was that which took him to England for a year, on sabbatical leave, in 1896. He spent most of the time reading Greek with the English scholar, Henry Jackson, at Trinity College, Cambridge. This was a crucial stage of his life: for the study and meditation which he undertook in England, especially on Plato and Aristotle, provided much of the basis of his first great—some say his greatest—work, *The Life of Reason* (1905–1906).

Santayana's philosophical career, following the publication of this *magnum opus*, amounted to a series of commentaries on it, though as the years passed he slowly modified and even transformed his views. This applies as much to his novel, *The Last Puritan*, written in 1936, as to such works as *Winds of Doctrine* (1913), *Scepticism and Animal Faith* (1923), and *Platonism and the Spiritual Life* (1927). He wrote copiously. By way of compensating for his isolation, his literary meditations also served to deepen it. In a late essay, he spoke of 'the silly home poetry in which I talk to myself about everything'. He also produced much journalism, if the word can still be used to denote intelligent commentary on affairs and people: the *Soliloquies in England* (1922) is a masterpiece in its *genre*. He also wrote poetry, of which few have disputed his own modest estimate. At the age of eighty-eight, he published a book on politics and society entitled *Dominions and Powers* (1951). This study received a somewhat patronizing press. It was as if the critics were surprised not so much at its contents as at its having come from his pen at all; but it is not without value, and contains some original and constructive ideas. He was a prolific letter-writer; the collection published in 1956 under the editorship of his faithful disciple, Daniel Cory, is highly readable. His *Three Philosophical Poets* (Lucretius, Dante, Goethe), published in 1910, has exerted much influence on literary criticism. Of his autobiographical writings we have spoken.

To expound the main principles of Santayana's thought is no easy task. One obstacle is the seductive style in which they are written. His philosophy is borne in on the reader on wave after wave of limpid prose. Thought and style are commingled. If some have been inclined to dismiss the whole as a lyrical or (to use Santayana's own word) rhetorical *tour de force*, their reaction is understandable; but we feel that a man could not have launched so grandiose a display of fireworks unless he meant seriously to show us something, and to show us something more than a show. Santayana is on record as saying that he is a naturalist, a materialist, a Catholic, a behaviourist, a dreamer, a believer in happiness, a disillusioned man, and withal an apostle of reason. Furthermore, he is apt, as his argument proceeds, to give to each of these terms an individual twist: we have to read him as a whole to discover the meaning of the parts. The consistency, if he ever prided himself on such a quality, lies in the unflagging exposition. We become accustomed to a voice, persuading, sometimes cajoling, beating down opposition almost with the luminous wings of a Shelley, before we can reconcile ourselves to what is said. Or his style may be compared to a turning wheel. At first the spokes are visible and articulate. Then, as the revolutions speed up, it composes a pattern, vibrating finally on a thin note of ecstasy. The more naturalistic his theme, the more elevated becomes the style, and the more frequent the intrusions of the vocabulary of the transcendental—spirit, soul, eternity. On one brief page of his last autobiographical volume, *My Host the World*, he employs in a purely naturalistic context the words 'holy ghost', 'divine essence' and 'spirit', the latter several times. Never did the vocabulary of the spirit come so easily to the lips of this avowed materialist. Yet we have the uneasy feeling that, slowed down, the impression of exultation, which is so subtly communicated, will vanish; and so we shall find. Once we close the book, the intrusion of more human voices causes us to lose the thread.

The clue to Santayana's outlook is his attitude to religion. Whereas to Dewey religion was outmoded, a survival of a time when men looked to heaven for their salvation because they could not look anywhere else, Santayana regards religion, all religion, as a permanently valid human impulse, 'the head and fount of everything'. But here comes the paradox. The validity of religion lies not in its truth, still less in its falsity, but in its imaginative import. Religion is all symbol; and being all symbol, the source of every other symbolism, including that of science, it is universal, catholic. The human imagination alone is real, because it is the highest form of faith of which man is capable. Therefore we cannot accept any religion, any faith; we can accept only that which, by its elevation and inner consistency, can be trusted. Such trust is the product of much seeking, much pursuit, much disillusionment; for—and this is the final paradox—only when we have perceived that no religion, even the Catholic, is literally true, do we arrive at that *total* disillusionment or 'disintoxication' which is wisdom. We have to surrender conventional faith in order to arrive at that higher faith which, having created religion, transcends it. And this faith is imagination itself.

Once we have grasped this argument, upon which Santayana played variations all his life, the inner workings of his philosophy become clearer. That they become wholly clear is too much to claim. He bewilders us by proceeding, on the basis of his attitude, to employ all the terms with which philosophy has made us familiar. Of the traditional systems of thought, he observes: 'The philosopher ... must still ask whether any of these successive views were true, or whether the latter ones were necessarily truer than the earlier: he cannot, unless he is a shameless sophist, rest content with truth *pro tem.*[1] What does 'true' mean here? And what is the force of the word 'still'? He acknowledges that we must hold, as a matter of 'animal faith', that 'the conventional belief in the natural world' is valid; but this conventional view has itself been challenged by philosophers, and is therefore merely one of the 'successive' views which have been put forward *pro tem.* In our time to be the criterion? But that would be a parochialism from which Santayana would naturally recoil.

Santayana's standpoint is in one sense rendered difficult to criticize by his adoption of a position similar to that defined by a French thinker as 'the freedom of doubt'. He feels free to question everything; therefore he is free to assume anything. In one place he refers to truth as a 'mental fiction'.[2] We soon learn that when he speaks of truth, and more particularly eternal truth, he understand these words only within the context of imagination. 'My subject being the imagination,' he writes,[3] 'I was never called on to step beyond the subjective sphere. I set out to describe, not nature or God, but the ideas of nature and God bred in the human mind'. Yet there is a basis, objective enough, for these symbols and images, and this is revealed in the succeeding sentence. 'I assumed throughout that the whole life of reason was generated and controlled by the animal life of man in the bosom of nature'. In other words, he has what he calls a 'vital philosophy'; and a man

[1] 'A General Confession', *The Philosophy of George Santayana*, edited by Paul Arthur Schilpp (New York, 1951), p. 9. (All further references to this volume are labelled Schilpp.)

[2] *Apologia Pro Mente Sua* (Schilpp, p. 581).

[3] 'A General Confession' (Schilpp, p. 14).

may 'perfectly well cultivate more than one *Weltanschauung* if he has a vital philosophy of his own to qualify his adoption of each, so as to render them complementary and not contradictory'. Hence his apparent eclecticism. 'The movement of my mind among various systems of belief has tended merely to discover how far my vital philosophy could be expressed in each of them.' Thus Santayana has no system in the orthodox sense, the sense in which Plato, Aquinas, Hegel, even Royce, had a system; his is the truth of every system in so far as it promotes vital harmony.[1] And if we ask, what is harmony? He would answer, the Life of Reason, which is something we must cultivate.

With its evident circularity, this argument may seem to come dangerously near to solipsism. For a man who never steps out of subjectivity is nothing but a solipsist. If he does, and lives to tell the tale, he is no solipsist. Santayana recognizes this. He even says that the natural rhythm of the human mind is to oscillate between solipsism and pure scepticism, which he describes as 'the chastity of the intellect'.[2] To our protestations at this point, we can imagine him uttering the words of André Gide: *Ne me comprenez pas trop vite*! (Don't be too quick to understand me!) To be able to talk about solipsism, and to credit the mind with the ability to oscillate between it and scepticism, is to be outside both: Santayana is merely obeying his own edict to sample all systems, and to accept the dictates of animal faith. Again and again he falls back upon the inescapable fact that we are organic emergents of nature. Psyche and spirit are still further emergents, but how they emerge we do not know. Their origin is 'unintelligible only in the sense that all existence, change, or genesis is unintelligible'.[3] This, then, is the meaning at once of his scepticism and of his naturalism, his vital philosophy. We are a mystery. 'To execute the simplest action we must rely on fate: our own acts are mysteries to us.'[4] Scepticism, the natural propensity of the human mind to doubt, cannot touch mystery; it can only enhance it. The 'drawing-room' scepticism of the academic philosopher is a more superficial attitude; for it first asserts a concept—that of the external world, for instance—and then proceeds to deny or doubt it. This is a game that can be played *ad infinitum*, while the human animal goes about its business. Santayana underpins the *Cogito ergo sum* of Descartes with other *Cogito*, which is the affirmation of life. Before the human spirit can say 'I think, therefore I am', which is the culmination of a process of doubt, the animal has said its 'yes' to life. 'Animal faith ... requires no special philosophical evidence for its validity. All experience, all knowledge, all art, are applications of it, and reason has no competence to defend this faith because it is based on it.'[5]

The culmination of Santayana's first philosophical phase is best

[1] *Scepticism and Animal Faith*, p. vi.
[2] *Scepticism and Animal Faith*, p. 69.
[3] The process itself is outlined in the glossary of terms appended to Chapter I of *The Realm of Spirit*.
[4] *Reason in Common Sense*, p. 214.
[5] *Apologia* (Schilpp, p. 381).

mirrored in *Scepticism and Animal Faith*, perhaps his best known and most readable work. It forms likewise the introduction to his next and more rarefied phase. The volumes on the Realms of Being are highly metaphysical in character, though he would have repudiated the term. Dealing with Essence, Matter, Truth, Spirit, they form the 'Life of Reason' of his maturity, which has become the 'Life of Spirit'. It is Santayana who insists that he is a materialist; he even declares himself to be 'the only living one'.[1] But suggesting that he alone of a fairly large company is in step, he renders his claim suspect. To be a complete materialist would be to admit only one realm, the material, and not, as Santayana in principle does, a vast number. What Santayana would seem to mean, however, is that he rejects any view which conceives of spirit as descending upon matter like a logos, and *fertilizing* it. 'Spirit is incarnate by nature, not by accident'.[2] He has no use for the idealist or vitalist insertion of an occult principle, an entelechy, into matter. The Realms of Being are those which imagination generates from itself.

Thus when Santayana speaks of *essences*, which he does increasingly as his thought matures, he refers not to Platonic ideas or forms subsisting in a supernatural world, but to those qualities which imagination at its highest level, that of spirit, isolates for its own delectation and contemplation. In theory, there can be any number of essences. Every predicate, everything said of anything, is an essence. Santayana does not preach essential segregation: essences are not limited to what is refined or disinfected. Admittedly, spirit will by nature choose for contemplation certain essences rather than others; but this itself implies a vast field from which to select, for 'the potentialities of spiritual life are infinite'.[3] Nor are essences capable of action or influence upon everyday existence; they are merely pointers by which we may be guided, or, to use Peirce's term, 'indices'. The signpost does not usher us on our way; we merely take a cue from it.

A philosopher's importance cannot necessarily be measured by his influence. Indeed, it is difficult to speak of the influence of a philosopher who has been dead only a few years. It may take some decades, even generations, for him to acquire importance, or to lose such as he possesses. His contemporary impact is another matter. Santayana has had little influence in England, and almost none in France. The indifference may be due to his having little to contribute to immediate preoccupations in those countries. In empirical circles in Britain, 'literary' philosophies are unpopular; the charm of the style is considered to distract from, or to conceal, the argument. Santayana contended that he was by nature a scholastic, but that he abhorred disputation. 'Argument', he says in one of his letters, 'has never been, in my opinion, a good weapon in philosophy, because I feel that real understanding or difference in sentiment usually rests on hidden pres-

[1] *Scepticism and Animal Faith*, Preface.
[2] *The Realm of Spirit*, p. 43.
[3] *The Realm of Spirit*, p. 51.

uppositions and limitations that are irreconcilable'.[1] In only one essay, that entitled *Some Meanings of the World 'Is'*,[2] does he engage in analysis in the accepted sense; but even in that argument, the poetry is there, straining to be unleashed. In America, his thought received enthusiastic and prolonged attention. This is understandable, apart from the fact that he was in his way a great interpreter of Americanism. Both in thought and character, he provided an antithesis to Dewey. And that is a good reason for considering them together.

Dewey, obsessed with the need to reform society, eschewed cosmological speculations. Although Santayana devoted little or no attention to cosmology, he deplored Dewey's limited attitude, and argued that such indifference was incompatible with naturalism. Dewey, who was unable to follow Santayana into the realm of spirit, maintained that Santayana's naturalism was little more than a pose. Yet Santayana was surely right in his insistence that whatever ideals man may hold, however exalted his speculations may be, he remains an organic product of nature. If you ignore cosmology, you ignore not merely supernature but sub-nature; the cosmos is below as well as above. Where Santayana may appear to err is in his implied assertion that because man is pure nature, therefore he is no sense transcendent. Why cannot the natural, with all its potentialities, transcend *itself*? Indeed, when a man lays down his life for his friend or for a cause, is not this what he is doing?

When we try to determine Santayana's exact view of the aim of philosophy, we encounter first of all an olympian contempt for the preoccupations of other philosophers (with obvious exceptions like Spinoza), and secondly we discover to our surprise that philosophy is not the search for enlightenment at all. We began to wonder what philosophy if supposed to be about. In his essay on Royce,[3] Santayana holds his teacher up to ridicule for seeking *possession* of the truth. 'He longed', writes Santayana, 'to believe that all his troubles and questions, some day and somewhere, must find their solution and quietus: if not in his own mind, in some kindred spirit that he could, to that extent, identify himself with. There must not only be cold truth, not even cold truth personified, but victorious knowledge of the truth, breaking like a sun-burst through the clouds of error'. It is not only Royce who has entertained this view; he has had some distinguished predecessors. Without the common pursuit of truth, where would be the history of philosophy? Santayana, and not only Santayana but men wholly at variance with him, might well say: Look at it! Granted, what we see is not always edifying; but the impulse behind the delusions, the fallacies, even the verbiage, is more edifying to contemplate than the spectacle of men, some professedly philosophers, pursuing any lesser aim. A few pages later, Santayana concedes that 'this faith and this struggle' may be the 'supreme good'; but they can be good only if the

[1] To Professor Yolton, May 2, 1952.
[2] *Obiter Scripta* (1936).
[3] *Character and Opinion in the United States.*

goal is worth pursuing. Mere pursuit, mere activity for activity's sake, is futile and ludicrous. What, we may ask, is Santayana's 'life of spirit' which he claimed to be following, if not a faith and a struggle to uphold values in a world not prone to honour them? Why pursue philosophy if philosophy itself pursues a will-o'-the-wisp? In his 'General Confession', Santayana protests his recognition of 'the spiritual truth in the Neo-Platonist and Indian systems'; but these two systems have no end but the 'enlightenment' upon which he pours scorn. Finally, if, as he repeatedly says, spirit needs to be 'saved' or 'delivered', there must be a road to salvation, and philosophy, if it is to be of any use, must point us on our way.

There is another respect in which Santayana tries to eat his cake and have it. His attitude to Catholicism is ambivalent, to some exasperatingly so. While calling himself a Catholic for all official purposes, he makes it clear that he is a total unbeliever. He holds implicitly that all religious action, aspiration and sacrifice have been made not for a reality but for a symbol. Indeed, we suspect that one of the conditions for a form of thought to be worth while, so far as he is concerned, is that it can be shown not to be true. Yet he insisted on exactness in others: 'I always disliked mystics who were not definite in their logic and orthodox in their religion'.[1] Despite his rejection of dogma, he feels entitled to regard as his own, more freely than most believers, the entire emotional capital of the Catholic faith. His work reeks of the Liturgy. He writes 'General Confessions' and 'Apologias'. Although his last autobiographical volume is called *My Host the World*, it was the Church, not the World, at whose board he sat. In middle age, finding himself able to retire to any part of the world which took his fancy, he chose to settle not in the country which had nurtured him, America, nor in that for which he had so deep an affection, England, nor even in the country of which he remained a citizen, Spain, but in Rome itself. Moreover, when in old age the time came for him to withdraw still further into solitude, he took refuge in a Catholic hospital, to be cared for by nuns, the Sisters of the Little Company of Mary. Now this was an Order which, had Santayana's views prevailed, could never have come into being, nor Rome become the spiritual centre—*omnis urbis et orbis ecclesiam mater et caput*—to which Santayana, the unbeliever, gave so much devotion.[2] And he seemed symbolically to emphasize still further his allegiance by living as close as possible to the spiritual centre of Rome itself, namely the Vatican. Finally, at his own wish, he was buried in a Catholic cemetery, though in an unconsecrated plot.

The primary criticism of a view such as Santayana's, as of all those which venerate tradition purely for its symbolic value, is that it implies living on emotional or spiritual credit. Now credit has a way of running out. To say that everything has symbolic value is much like

[1] 'A General Confession' (Schilpp, p. 27).

[2] The volume in *The Life of Reason* entitled *Reason in Religion* is nothing but a sustained assault on Protestantism, though he regards scholasticism as the beginning of Catholic decadence.

saying that everything has exchange value; but this must depend ultimately upon a standard or principle which is valuable in itself. The symbols must ultimately be redeemable or 'cashed'. Difficulties will not arise so long as the symbols retain a measure of potency; but this cannot go on forever. If the symbols are not periodically re-charged, the faith in spiritual 'values' must inevitably decline. The life of the spirit, symbolically conceived, cannot be lived for more than one or two generations from orthodoxy. Moreover, there is little difference at bottom between a symbolic view of reality and a utilitarian or instrumentalist one: for what is a philosophy of symbolism but a kind of higher utilitarianism, a pragmatism for purists? When their thought is probed deeply enough, Dewey and Santayana do not seem so far apart as they or their disciples have supposed; and that is perhaps why each contended for the same title or naturalist. It is as if they were fellow passengers on the same ship, bound for the same destination, but in different classes. Nor is it necessary to specify which class each would have chosen.

Santayana's mysterious character, his love of solitude, his repudiation of conventional allegiances both spiritual and social, have been the source of much speculation. Bertrand Russell found him a trifle old-womanish; others found him a snob. He possessed a kind of genius for friendship; but what man or woman could have established an enduring relationship with a man who could write of his friends that 'it was only the *numen* in them that I loved, who, as I passed by abstracted, whispered some immortal word in my ear'? One could wish that occasionally this abstracted being could have been startled by the whisper of some mortal word. Yet he was not perhaps quite so aloof a man as he makes out. He had a taste in food and wine; he was a great traveller and observer of mankind; and of his personal kindness there is much evidence. His isolation was perhaps inevitable. He was a displaced person. Displacement has become associated with misery, destitution, and persecution; Santayana was a displaced person of means. Having repudiated his native country and her traditional religion, he was thrown back upon his inward resources. The truth was henceforth to be found within; there was no outward criterion. This perhaps accounts for the disproportionate amount of sheer personal writing for so impersonal a thinker. He is as self-exploratory as Nietzsche. Indeed, all his philosophy is a kind of interior dialogue, which we are privileged to overhear. Towards the end, his form of higher complacency seems for a moment to have been disturbed. He told reporters on his eighty-eighth and last birthday that 'I find things are not so simple to explain as I had imagined, and so I am not reconciled'. It is perhaps the only public utterance in which he reveals a lapse in self-assurance.

It is difficult to compare Santayana with any of his contemporaries. Among his Spanish compatriots, Unamuno perhaps resembles him most; Santayana had 'the Tragic Sense of Life'. Among Anglo-Saxon thinkers, he shows some kinship with an equally aloof figure, Havelock Ellis. Here was another gentle, spiritual mind that venerated, while repudiating, Catholicism, and who was incidentally a devotee of Spain. There is likewise some resemblance in the literary style of the two men. Allowing for obvious exceptions, we can imagine each to have written the other's books. Santayana could not have written the *Studies in the Psychology of Sex,* though he might have benefited from some of the experience with which it deals; but neither can we imagine Ellis writing *The Last Puritan,* though there is in Ellis something of the thwarted novelist. Being unconceptual but intuitional, the thought of the two men lends itself to the essay form, and to liberal quotation: we have Ellis's *Little Essays on Love and Virtue*, and we have the selection by Logan Pearsall Smith entitled *Little Essays Drawn from the Works of George Santayana.* Long after his contemporaries have been forgotten, the anthologies of English prose may serve to perpetuate Santayana's memory; and the style which his fellow thinkers dismissed as a mere ornament may turn out to be the means whereby his ideas, and not least the spirit which animated them, are handed on. The world of John Dewey, practical and democratic, has already come into being. Dewey himself witnessed its birth; for he lived into the future for which he had struggled. The world of George Santayana, ideal and aristocratic, will never fully come into being, and thus it may continue to haunt generation after generation with its elusive appeal.

37

Conclusion

Before closing, it will be useful to state, however tentatively, certain general conclusions: for the reader who has reached the present page will be aware of a thread of continuity running through the previous chapters. Three principal questions warrant our attention. In the first place, what are the basic differences between Oriental and Western thought? In the second place, what does the Western World owe to the thought of the East and vice versa? In the third place, to what extent is a *rapprochement* possible between the two worlds of thought, taking into account the great political and economic changes at present occurring in the Orient?

Twenty or thirty years ago such questions, particularly the last, might have seemed either trivial or irrelevant. The influence of 'thought' tended to be belittled: men were supposed to be the product of their economic circumstances. We now realize that it matters a great deal what people think: which accounts for the trouble to which leaders of men go to mould public opinion. The violent penalties with which dictators visit the sin of 'deviation', together with the daily evidence that such measures are by no means always effective, testify to a tough resilience, a spring of health in the human soul, a basic will to independent enquiry, which prevents mankind from descending to the level of mindless poltroons.

Oriental and Western Thought

It is tempting to embark upon a series of generalizations upon what it is that makes a great philosopher. Some readers will already have remarked upon the fact that our list contains the name of no woman; and the cynic may perhaps be tempted to say that this is not surprising, since the female character is that about which man philosophizes. In the words of a modern poet:

> You, madam, are the eternal humorist,
> The eternal enemy of the Absolute.[1]

But to turn away from fanciful speculations. Let us suppose, for the sake of argument, that all the works of all the philosophers were suddenly to be destroyed (as indeed many of them have already been): would the loss to mankind be very great, or would we carry on much as before?

[1] T. S. Eliot.

The answer, to put it bluntly, is that we should not be able to carry on at all. For 'philosophy' is not simply the collective works of great philosophers. Philosophy is an attitude of mind; at bottom it is nothing but that irrepressible impulse towards enquiry, that itch to probe at the meanings of things, which is the spur behind science itself. There are only Great Philosophers because there are little philosophers, and only little philosophers because there are little ironies and frustrations that need daily to be circumvented or overcome; and in the end the great philosopher will flourish only if there is general agreement among ordinary people that what he is doing is both legitimate and worth while. If the philosopher loses touch with society, then, like Nietzsche, he will end by losing touch with reason; and if society loses touch with those who engage in the disinterested pursuit of knowledge, then the people will perish for lack of vision. Today, as never before, we realize that the traditional view of the scientist as pursuing truth for its own sake, without fear or favour, is not something obvious or self-evident and therefore incorruptible, but a view which, in the last resort, is based upon a philosophical assumption, namely, that there are such things as absolute values. As a modern historian, Christopher Dawson, has observed: 'We cannot be sure that the world which science has made will be as favourable to the production of scientific genius as the world that made science'; for, to continue with the words of R. G. Collingwood: 'Science is a plant of slow growth. It will not grow (and for a plant the end of growth is the end of life) except where the scientist as the priest of truth is not only supported but revered as a priest-king by a people that shares his faith. When scientists are no longer kings, there will be (to adapt a famous saying of Plato's) no end to the evils undergone by the society that has dethroned them until it perishes physically for sheer lack of sustenance.'[1]

There are signs that both philosophers and non-philosophers—that is, both professional thinkers and those who are obliged to think without reflecting upon their thinking (or at least without reflecting systematically)—are alive to the serious issues which confront us today. Nothing less than civilization is at stake: not material civilization, but the attitude of mind which makes for that complete enjoyment, relish and worthwhileness of life without which material possessions are a mill-stone around the neck. First there is a coarsening of thought, an indifference to the finer values, and then, almost imperceptibly, a corruption, and finally a kind of *rigor mortis*—and some centuries afterwards a flock of visitors with guide-books contemplating the ruins. Today, however, in spite of every portent of decline, collapse, and even annihilation, there are reasons for hope that mankind will weather this, the most terrible storm that has broken over it. The demand for art, music, and poetry is greater and more insatiable than ever before. There may be some people who fear that popular manifes-

[1] It will be observed that we are using the word Science here to signify 'ordered knowledge' (Scientia): in other contexts we usually refer to 'natural science' or physico-mathematical science.

tations of enthusiasm will serve merely to vulgarize the high art of philosophical enquiry. That which is so easily vulgarized is neither high nor an art, and might as well be exposed, here and now, for the sophistry that it is. Philosophy began, as far as Socrates was concerned, in the open air; let it continue in the air, on the air, and by the fireside. Let it continue in plain language rather than jargon or recondite symbolism. Let it confound the dogmatic, expose the hypocrite, encourage the curious, and enlighten the bewildered.

It is the fashion today to belittle the idea of Progress. 'Progress', Wyndham Lewis has remarked in his *Time and Western Man*, 'may even bring Progress to an end.' If we accept a somewhat limited definition of progress, such a prophecy seems only too likely to be realized. In the course of two centuries the development of technical efficiency has wholly transformed a world that had remained stable for many thousands of years. We now live, as no other generation has lived, under the threat of sudden annihilation. If man is indeed the child of God, then God is in danger of assuming the role of a Frankenstein: a *dénouement* which it would be legitimate, if it were not presumably blasphemous, to describe as totally unforseen. Compared with this present crisis in both human and cosmic affairs, all other crises in history assume an aspect of triviality. To commit oneself to such a statement is by no means to indulge in mere rhetoric. Man at last knows his fate, because he has at last learnt to know the consequences of his power.

Given this unique situation, two interesting facts emerge, both of which have a direct bearing upon our subject. In the first place, you have only to ask any individual man whether, in his opinion, the great technical advances of the last two centuries have served to increase human happiness (not the 'sum of human happiness', because there is no such sum), and he will answer, unless he does not take the trouble to think, No. In the second place, you have only to ask him whether, in his opinion, the complete destruction of all human life would be such a deplorable thing, and he will likewise be tempted to answer (unless he thinks a little too carefully), No. In other words, it would seem to be the case that most men, reflecting on such matters cursorily, neither think very highly of human life nor consider that much can be done to improve it. Such pessimism is true of all save the young, who enjoy not so much life itself as the prospects that life seems to offer. And this may be the reason why our civilization, as shown above all in our modern educational systems, seems so intent upon perpetuating the conditions of youth and concealing by every device of propaganda the scandal of age: for this is its way of rendering life tolerable for a creature who, never particularly enthusiastic, now begins to show signs of regarding life with something approaching despair.

Whatever else may be said of history, it is full of the unexpected and the contingent. Prophecies of doom are heard in each generation. Evils come to pass, but not always the evils regarded as most imminent. To live under the threat of physical annihilation may not prove altogether unwholesome. Rapacity, cupidity, and complacency in all their forms are more likely to flourish at a time of increasing prosperity. Our age is one in which mankind, endowed with the means of self-destruction, may be prompted to enquire into the true value of that which he is about to throw away. This is particularly true of Western man, who, as we have often hinted, is by the circumstances of his material existence obliged to live at several removes from reality.

The social changes brought about by the Industrial Revolution in Europe impress us by their magnitude and their novelty. They should not blind us to the other changes that have taken place in Europe, as part of the normal rhythm of history. For Western civilization differs from any other in its dynamic character. This is the chief difference between Christian culture as fused with Greek and Roman ideals and any other culture. It has been the nature of Christian culture not so much to resist as to bring about social changes, even though many of these changes have been nominally 'secular' in character. The great social movements of the nineteenth century, for example, were parasitic upon the Christian ideal which in many cases they repudiated. We may suggest that the eradication of Christianity, which is in some places a deliberate policy, will bring to an end such revolutionary social movements, contrary to the belief of many secular reformers: for the eradication of Christianity will deprive the Western world of an element of tension without which society is likely to sink into regimented uniformity. The Christian social ideal has always been dynamic because it has never become identified with, still less dominated by, a political regime. Church and State, sacred and secular: these polarities, instead of involving the betrayal of the Christian Gospel, have been the conditions of its social effectiveness. An apparent exception is the Byzantine Empire, with its rigid theocratic structure. But the Byzantine Empire was rightly called the Eastern Empire, and its constitution was largely Oriental. For the norm of Oriental civilization is that of a social hierarchy from which evolution is excluded.

The fact remains that all the great world faiths have come from the East, above all that of Christianity. Even when, as so often in America, a new religion is founded, the elements and usually the vocabulary of the faith are inevitably Oriental: for the ordinary Western man feels, not perhaps without good reason, that the secrets of life, the arcana, are better known, if not always better practised, by the humblest Oriental than by the most learned of Western divines. Sometimes this respect for oriental wisdom assumes extravagant proportions. Thus Madame Blavatsky, a woman of remarkable personality, wrote such books as *The Secret Doctrine* (1888), and *Isis Unveiled*, in the course of which, having denounced the religion of the Western churches and in particular the Roman Church, she advocated the return to a more ancient and occult faith of oriental inspiration. To this faith she gave the name of the 'secret doctrine'. Now the trouble with the 'secret doctrine' is that no one is able, unless prepared to undergo forms of initiation involving (in the end) considerable expense, to discover what it is. Every faith has its core of mystery, or it would cease to deserve the name of faith. But a faith of mere mystery is both a religious parody and a logical absurdity: for it attempts to throw light upon the mystery of existence simply by declaring it to be inherently inscrutable.

A missionary gospel such as Christianity, though beset with pagan adversaries, is threatened most seriously by faiths bearing a superficial resemblance to its own. This is what happened to the early Church. Whereas the barbarians came to heel, the great rival to the Christian creed was another creed of similar oriental origin. To call it a creed is perhaps to give it greater definition than it either deserves or ever possessed: for, in spite of important researches and recent discoveries, we still know very little about the vague cluster of beliefs called Gnosticism. At present, almost all we know of Gnosticism is derived from the tracts written by Christian Doctors and Fathers attacking it. And it is the extreme virulence of these attacks, for which there is hardly a parallel even in ecclesiastical history, that affords us an insight into the danger which they constituted, or were thought to constitute, for the Christian communities. There are two reasons why Gnosticism is of interest to us here. In the first place, it represents a system of belief which owes much to the great Oriental religions of which we have written, so that it forms a kind of link between these faiths and Western Christianity. And in the second place, it represents a system of belief which, with due modifications, has flourished however obscurely, in every age, including our own. Perhaps, indeed, Gnosticism is nothing but that universal abstract 'religion' which public-spirited men in every generation, and also certain disillusioned rationalists, have been seeking as a means to the spiritual union of humanity. That would justify our having agreed, early in this book, to abandon so vague a word in treating the concrete faiths of the Orient.

Gnosticism is simply the religion of *Gnosis*, knowledge. Now what was the knowledge of which the Gnostics were in quest? It was suprasensible knowledge—that is to say, a knowledge of pure spirit. As far as we can see (though the belief assumed many forms), the Gnostics held the body to be evil, since it was immersed in a material world that was itself evil. Thus the way to salvation lay through *disincarnation*, an escape to the realm of spirit. Such an escape could be effected only by severe discipline and spiritual purgation; and as the technique of such discipline proved difficult, the seeker after salvation needed usually to be initiated into certain 'mysteries'. It is assumed that cults such as Orphism were training-schools for Gnostic disciples. Nevertheless, to sustain an interest and passion for pure spiritual apprehension is beyond the capacity of most men, and of no man for long at a time. While the mind is fixed upon an abstract One or All or *Brahman*, the passions, ignored and despised, muster for revolt. And as the mind in time tires from its labours, these grosser instincts may exact terrible reprisals. At its mildest, the cult degenerates into a trafficking with magic and sorcery (some of the newly-found Gnostic papyri provide evidence of this preoccupation): at its worst, the force of instinct transforms the faith from lofty spirituality into a witches' sabbath of depravity. Thus Gnosticism threw up, and continues to throw up, such heresies as that of Manichaeism, Catharism (at the beginning of the Middle Ages), Priscillianism (in Spain), the Albigensian heresy (in Provence), and that of the Bogamils (in Eastern Europe), as well as numerous other cults in Asia Minor and the Middle East. All these cults tended to be associated with gross practices consequent upon the desire, superficially logical in inspiration, to propitiate the forces of evil. The airborne devotee of the Absolute needs to return, even if only to refuel, to the world he shunned: and he need not wonder that the more frequent and prolonged his absences, the more this despised territory has become a prey to weeds, vermin, and decay.

It would be tempting, though hazardous, to see in Gnosticism a survival of that general movement of spiritual resurgence which is associated with the great names of Zoroaster, Buddha, Mahavira, Confucius, and Lao-Tze. That Gnosticism 'came out of Asia' is certain. It bears distinct traces of Buddhist influence in its dismissal of material nature as 'illusion'; of Persian influence in its conception of the struggle between Good and Evil as the opposition between light and darkness; of Egyptian influence (especially from the decadent period) in its truckling with magic, sorcery, and demonology.[1] Although on its most rarefied plane it is a faith likely to attract only the intellectual, we have reason to believe that it enjoyed considerable prestige among the common people. A vague cult of spirituality may attain its greatest reputation among the half-educated, especially the refined half-educated: witness the success of that modern diluted form of Gnosticism, Christian Science. A Gnosticism of a higher kind is that which Aldous Huxley and his colleagues used to preach with such eloquence from Los Angeles. Significantly enough, they regarded their mission as that of introducing Vedanta to the Occident.[2] Equally significant is the fact that Huxley's standpoint, though sympathetic to the Christian mystics, is definitely hostile to the Christian churches: a hostility that is reciprocated, especially by the Church of Rome.

Recent Western philosophy

For some years the philosophical world has been disturbed by a conflict which even today is by no means settled. This is a conflict between two conceptions of the function of philosophical enquiry. On the one hand, there is the school which, following Hume, distrusts everything in the nature of *metaphysical* speculation; and on the other hand there are a number of thinkers who, adopting a much wider and freer viewpoint, are seeking to recall philosophy to its traditional function,

[1] Five of the Gnostic papyri referred to above are said to have been written by Hermes Trismegistus ('Thrice-Greatest Hermes'), the Greek version of the Egyptian Thoth. The syncretic writings of this author, presumably a priest or group of priests, were composed in the third century AD. Gnosticism was not merely syncretic (i.e. a reconciliation of many different tendencies), but apt to borrow terminology from the faiths it opposed, possibly for the purpose of 'infiltration'.

[2] See *The Perennial Philosophy* by Aldous Huxley, and *Vedanta for the Western World*, edited by Christopher Isherwood.

which is to reflect upon the nature of reality as a whole. During the unsettled period between the two world wars, the former group achieved much notoriety; and it was a common experience for students of philosophy at that time to be instructed and harangued by teachers who, in spite of their official status as lecturers in philosophy, spent the major part of their time denouncing the whole subject as a fraud—the result, as one of them put it, of a disease of language. For such iconoclasts there was but one justification for philosophy, namely, that it should be reduced to logic, which in turn should confine itself to the 'analysis' of the meaning of ordinary propositions about matters of fact. In order to effect such delicate analysis a special technique was evolved, often introducing mathematical symbolism intelligible only to the expert; and it was tacitly, if not openly, assumed that all propositions about the world, or about anything whatever, which failed to yield to this specialized technique of dissection were nonsensical. So much for theology, metaphysics, poetry, and so forth.

What we were being invited to accept, and thus to condone, is nothing less than a 'closed shop' in philosophical speculation. Accept my language, my terminology, my assumption—in the one case, a purely 'rational' language; in the second case, a purely scientific terminology; in the third case, the assumption that only sensuous experience is genuine—or stop calling yourself a philosopher. Come in, or keep out: that, in sum, was the attitude of the apostles of 'analysis' and 'positivism', the contemporary enemies of metaphysics.

It was a mischievous attitude. For once you begin to introduce a distinction between two kinds of language—a specialist, esoteric, private language on the one hand, and ordinary common, everyday language on the other hand and announce that the first is the language of philosophers and the second the language of everyday life, then you are simultaneously dividing men into two kinds, the initiates and the outsiders, those who know the philosophical password and those who do not: in which case your final criterion is no longer truth or principle (as it has hitherto been) but something quite different, namely, class-distinction or 'snobisme'. Nor would this division prove so harmful to the cause of thought if the members of the specialist clique were not all the while engaged, as we have shown, in making an end among themselves of that which distinguished traditional philosophy; in showing that even if philosophy meant anything at all, it was frankly useless; and in suggesting that as it is nonsense anyway, the proper course for enlightened persons is to issue, from the recesses of their academies, brief communiqués to the effect that everything associated with philosophy in the past—above all, the Socratic belief that knowledge promotes virtue, that truth, goodness and beauty are absolute values, that reflection is superior to passion, and so on, down to the ordinary notions of what is right and decent—are purely matters of whim and expediency, subject to neither rules nor principles, or, to employ a more popular if more barbarous term, a mere floating 'ideology', concealing the brute facts of economic or material pressure. The situation is rather like that which would come about if, for example, the highest conclave of a Church, having met in secret session, had forthwith announced to its devotees that, for reasons which they could not be expected to comprehend, orthodox theology had been found to be based upon a misunderstanding, and that in consequence all the naïve piety upon which generations of devout persons were nourished had no foundation other than arbitrary sentiment; and that whereas people were at liberty to go on believing if they wished, they were in fact under no obligation to do so, though there were admittedly certain 'psychological' benefits to be derived from the disposition to believe, which might recommend that attitude to pedagogues, sociologists, youth leaders, probation officers, statesmen, and indeed all who were charged with the responsibility of keeping other people in order. Thus, to turn once more to our philosophers, one well-known enemy of metaphysics went so far as to say that while metaphysics, theology, poetry and so on are undeniably nonsensical, they represent, as compared with mere gibberish, a 'special kind of nonsense', to which even the enlightened person may be excused for giving some attention, since they exercise a therapeutic effect upon the nervous system and thereby provide some relief from the cold, dry universe that physical science offers for our acceptance.

We have dwelt at length upon this line of thought, because it is one with which almost everybody—certainly everyone who has had the patience to read this book—has at some time come into contact. We hear much talk about the 'decay of standards'. We are aware of a definite lowering of the canons of behaviour, not necessarily or exclusively moral behaviour but the ordinary behaviour of people with one another. We may infer a certain debasement of the idea of education not so much from the condition of modern schools and colleges as from the kind of press that people supposed to be educated choose to read. It is absurd to suggest that this observable decline in values is the result of treachery in high places; that those whose business it is to sustain our belief in the highest good are either shirking their job or mistaking it for something else; and that among these guardians (as Plato called them) our teachers of philosophy or metaphysics are not without their share of blame? Not that we should attribute our present wayward state of mind solely to the propagation, by those who should know better, of a neutral materialism. It is not so simple as that: for, as the American humanist Irving Babbitt aptly remarked, 'what is disquieting about the time is not so much its open and avowed materialism as what it takes to be its spirituality'. We are faced not so much with the denial of the spirit as with its repeated counterfeit.

In the foregoing pages we have several times indicated that where an age appears to exhibit a particular trend of thought, we can be fairly sure that this trend is all the time being dogged and shadowed by another movement, which, though recessive for the time being, may at any moment assume a dominant position. So it is today. Against the view of philosophy as a specialist technique, accessible only to the initiated, and of little more value than a parlour-game, there is a growing conviction that, of all the sciences, philosophy, the traditional science of sciences, should be open to everybody; that the attempt to demarcate its limits, to prescribe its rules, and to limit or 'screen' its devotees is precisely to indulge in the kind of dogmatism from which philosophy, in order to remain reasonable, must at all costs preserve itself; and that far from being a parlour-game—a superior amusement of superior people—it must reassume its former function as a guide to life, an incentive to right action, a light to widsom. In order to discharge these responsibilities, however, it must cease to busy itself solely with abstruse definitions and minute feats of analysis, and broaden its outlook to include all human experience. It must fight itself back to favour by re-occupying its former estates, now heavily mortgaged to mathematical science. For if philosophy fails to act as a guide to wisdom, there are a hundred other substitutes decked out to look like philosophy that will hasten to steal its custom.

Among modern philosophers, a man who did much to recall philosophy to a sense of its true vocation was Alfred North Whitehead (1861–1948). A mathematician by training and a man of immense learning and wisdom, Whitehead endeavoured to heal the wound opened first by Descartes with his unbridgeable distinction between mind and body,[1] and his consequent division of the world into two halves, a 'subjective half' (including the mind and the 'secondary qualities' which it originates) and an 'objective' half (including a substratum of matter characterized by the 'primary qualities' which are measurable by mathematics). This 'bifurcation of Nature' is, as Whitehead shows in his *Science and the Modern World,* the most vicious error that runs through modern thought. For consider what it implies. If your colours, and sounds, and scents are purely 'subjective', then what of such values as beauty? If beauty lies solely 'in the eyes of the beholder', then what of all the other values of life? They, too, must be 'subjective'. But if, as Galileo had maintained and as his successors believed, only that which is measurable is truly real, then it follows that every 'subjective' quality, being outside the scope of measurement, is unreal; and in consequence the whole of what we call culture or civilization (*i.e.* the values which we have been traditionally accustomed to uphold and venerate) has been lumped together with the intractable, unstable element in our minds, *i.e.* the emotions, passions, instincts, and impulses, with which no science claimed to have anything to do except psychology, so-called science of the irrational. This was indeed a paradoxical situation: the human intellect, having painfully built up a conception of the good, the true, the beautiful, and having devised an elaborate system of education to inculcate a respect for these values, proceeds forthwith to propound a philosophy according to which such values, however admirable, enjoy no objective existence at all. If there is such a thing as the Modern Dilemma, this surely is it. It is the dilemma of a split-man.

Whitehead refutes the subjective–objective distinction by pointing out that in the elementary case of a man looking at a rose, there are

[1] Unbridgeable' because it is doubtful whether much traffic can be got across the pineal gland, which Descartes declared to be the link between soul and body.

not two spheres—the mind of the man (or subjective sphere) and the primary qualities of the rose (objective sphere)—but a unity: namely, the man-seeing-a-rose. This single sphere Whitehead calls a 'society', and the whole of his philosophy as outlined in his most important book, *Process and Reality*, is an attempt to show that the universe is a hierarchy of such societies: the society of electrons that go to form an atom, the society of atoms that go to form a molecule, and so on up to human society and the even higher society of minds. In this hierarchical conception of the universe he was closely followed by the philosopher S. Alexander (1859–1942) in his great work *Space, Time and Deity*, and with certain modifications, by Field-Marshal Smuts (1870–1950), the philosopher-statesman, in his book *Holism and Evolution*. These three philosophers are therefore concerned with the branch of philosophy known as Cosmology, in which the human mind is given back the autonomy and freedom denied to it by the 'minute' philosophers. Moreover, in their work the conflict between Science and Religion, which so perplexed the nineteenth century but which is really Pascal's old problem of head and heart, is resolved in a conception which reveals the dialectical relation between the two.

A thinker of remarkable gifts who sought to analyse the above-mentioned relation from an original point of view was Robin George Collingwood (1889–1943), philosopher and historian, as well as artist and musician. Profiting from a study of the philosopher Benedetto Croce (1866–1952), the greatest of modern Italian thinkers and a vigorous defender of liberty under the Fascist régime (he was rescued by British parachutists when the Allied armies were advancing upon Naples), Collingwood outlined in his book, *Speculum Mentis*, what he called 'the map of knowledge'. The development of the human mind from imaginative gropings to complete self-consciousness may be conceived, he contended, as the dialectical development of art, or imagination, into successively religion, science, history, and philosophy: where by 'dialectical' he meant what Plato and Hegel meant, namely, the pitting of a thesis against its antithesis out of which developed a synthesis, which in turn provided the thesis for further development. Largely as a result of his archaeological investigations, Collingwood became more and more absorbed in the problems of historical knowledge, thereby pursuing the line of speculation begun by Giambattista Vico and continued by Hegel. In his *Essay on Metaphysics* and his posthumous *Idea of History*, he outlined a philosophy of history according to which metaphysics itself was shown to be a historical science, since 'all history is the history of thought'. The importance of Collingwood's work has yet to be appreciated, for it represents one of the most far-reaching attempts of modern times to demonstrate how philosophy can become of immediate use to men of action: this being possible, in Collingwood's view, by abandoning its three-hundred-year subservience to the method of natural science, which has led to increasing chaos in practical affairs as a result of the assumption that 'science is power', and its adoption of a method of understanding human affairs from the only point of view likely to shed light upon them, namely, by submitting them to the scrutiny of the historical imagination.

It would be an error to suppose that the movement of hostility to metaphysics has taken full possession of the Anglo-Saxon mind, or that it represents more than one current in the philosophy of the West. There are many such currents, and the deeper ones have not yet perhaps come to exert their full pressure. On the other hand, we must not underestimate the 'hygienic' value of the movement: it has swept away obscurantism and verbiage, and it has pricked the bubble of the conventional 'idealism' which for some people had come to be identified with 'philosophy'. Writing in the review *Mind* in 1952, Sir Isaiah Berlin spoke of 'the great logico-philosophical revolution of the last half-century initiated by Frege and Russell', and he went on to describe this as 'perhaps the most complete transformation of thought in this field since the seventeenth century'. Berlin might have added the name of another innovator: Ludwig Wittgenstein (1889–1951), who came to Cambridge from Berlin in 1912. With Bertrand Russell's help, Wittgenstein's *Tractatus Logico-Philosophicus* was published in 1922. This book exerted an enormous influence over modern philosophy, yet in his posthumous *Philosophical Investigations* (1953) Wittgenstein appeared to move away from his early radical position and to adopt a point of view almost mystical in character. Knowledge of ultimate reality, he affirmed, is incapable of conceptual expression. As the Taoist sage Lao Tze observed, our duty at the limits of thought is to remain silent, and it was Wittgenstein who said that 'Kierkegaard was by far the most profound thinker of the last century'. Latterly, too, British philosophers have begun to show wider sympathies and maturer judgment than some of the iconoclasts of the Thirties. There is a serene quality about some of A. J. Ayer's later writings, just as there is a markedly traditional quality about their subject matter. Although Gilbert Ryle's famous book *The Concept of Mind* (1949) appears to be a reversion to Behaviourism (the Italian translation is significantly entitled *Lo Spirito come Comportamento*), the author is aware that he is cultivating merely a plot in a vast field awaiting investigation. 'The time is not ripe,' he has said, 'for global syntheses'; but he added that 'a philosopher cannot invent conceptual stresses and strains; he has to feel them if he is to be irked into dealing with them.' One may hazard the opinion that life will prove sufficiently irksome during the next decade or so to impel philosophers to embark once more on the path of metaphysical speculation.[1]

Meanwhile, it is a paradox that the influence of Anglo-Saxon empiricism should have made itself felt in Europe and beyond at a moment when it had lost some of its impetus at home. Thus, in a book of considerable insight and interest we are told that 'philosophy . . . is simultaneously a name both for the conceptual confusions that arise in thinking about any subject and the attempt at the clarification of these confusions. . . . It is time that philosophers dispel the general impression that they are on intimate terms with Reality with a capital R,

[1] The quotations are from the symposium *The Nature of Metaphysics*, edited by D. F. Pears (London, 1957), pp. 156, 160.

and on hobnobbing terms with the Absolute and God Almighty'.[1] It is not easy to see how philosophy can be merely a name for its own confusions and their clarification, unless we are to assume that philosophical thinking, inherently prone to obscurantism, is also inherently endowed with the capacity to dispel it; for this would raise the question why, given this saving capacity, so many errors should have been committed. Nor is it evident that the greatest of thinkers (by whose standards the matter should be judged) were on such familiar terms with God and the Absolute as is here suggested. Most of them were distinguished for their humility. It is more often the sceptic, dismissing all traditional thought as 'nonsense', who assumes this arrogant pose. Happily, there is observable today a decline in what G. J. Warnock has called 'restrictive iconoclasm' among Anglo-Saxon thinkers. Meanwhile, philosophers like Radhakrishnan, Vice-President of the Republic of India, continued to expound the Vedanta tradition, and in Europe the influence of Oriental thought has made itself felt not merely in the brilliant writings of René Guénon, but in works not strictly classifiable as philosophical: we may cite the concluding volumes of Arnold Toynbee's *A Study of History* and his even more illuminating work *An Historian's Approach to Religion*. What seems to be needed is the fruitful exchange of ideas between Occident and Orient: for with the polished technique of argument perfected in the West and the grasp of profundities characteristic of the East, a philosophy might emerge not unworthy of the standards set by the great masters with whose thought we began.

No philosopher has so demonstrably reached the end of his tether as to maintain that his system of thought is a complete and closed one: that is why the 'closed shop' attitude of which we have spoken is the product not of philosophy but of sophistry. All the greatest philosophers have been conspicuous for an openness of mind, an honest candour, which has prevented them from becoming engrossed in such petty squabbles as make up the lives of the sophistical thinkers. That, incidentally, is the reason why all the great philosophers, with a few exceptions that must themselves be excepted at their highest moments, have been masters of their own language—artists in words as well as artists in ideas. The reputations of our poets and novelists undergo change with each generation. As long as our civilization lasts, the names of Socrates, Plato, Aristotle, Augustine, Aquinas, and indeed all the major figures of whom we have written in this book, will be remembered with undiminished and perhaps increasing veneration. However lacking in formal instruction, the reader who turns his attention to the lives and works of the great philosophers comes forthwith into possession of that which will last him all his life: faith in the ability of the human mind to grasp, in however fragmentary and fugitive a way, the essence and infinite variety of reality, and inspiration from the struggles of those who, in Whitehead's words, were 'individually powerless but ultimately rulers of the world'.

[1] Daya Krishna, *The Nature of Philosophy*, Calcutta, 1955, p. 233.

Rapprochement between Eastern and Western Thought

The question to which we should address ourselves is concerned with the possibilities of a *rapprochement* between Eastern and Western thought. Before embarking upon this difficult if popular subject, it will be as well to make one point clear. No *rapprochement* that is deliberately contrived, or that becomes the subject of pious resolutions at some international conference, or that takes the form of a common denominator of ethical teaching, is likely to prove effective. To belittle the efforts of men of goodwill to introduce harmony among conflicting creeds, or to remove minor misunderstandings, would be churlish; but it remains open to doubt whether the desperate attempt to find a basis for agreement (which can usually be made to yield to verbal formulation of some kind) is as profitable as an open statement of differences. Men are perhaps too disposed to demonstrate how much they agree, or, as commonly in politico–ideological discussion, how each is a better champion of a particular ideal (such as Democracy) than the other. In working together, *unanimity* is much less necessary, and indeed much less common, than is usually supposed. This is shown by the violence of criticism and often the strength of personal antipathies found within organizations which, to the world, present a united front. The most effective unions are usually those in which members agree to differ up to a point just short of scission: the least useful are thus eliminated before, instead of at, the moment of crisis. If, for the purpose of concealing the disunion of Christendom, the Churches were to form the habit of discounting their differences, there would be grave danger that the spirit of compromise might lead them, or some of them, into the most embarrassing liaisons: this happened in Nazi Germany. It is frequently complained of coalitions that, once the common danger is removed, they break up. But that is what coalitions should do. We know from experience what a dismal spectacle they present if they do not. It is better that materialism and false spirituality should be combated by Christians as Christians, Moslems as Moslems, and Buddhists as Buddhists, than that the followers of these faiths should combine to speak in the name of some vague entity called Religion, or Idealism, or even the Perennial Philosophy.

These observations, which are designed to discourage false attempts at concord, should not be construed as an invitation to each of us to retire into his separate phalanstery, thereby abandoning the effort of mutual understanding. Such a proposal would appear strange at the conclusion of a book of this kind. On the contrary, we should redouble our efforts to study other forms of belief, particularly those which appear to differ most widely from our own. There is a regrettable tendency, even so, to roam far afield in search of enlightenment, while neglecting that which is near to hand. If, as we have suggested, the study of comparative religion leads us to believe that certain forms of thought have flourished, with local variations, over wide areas, thereby indicating that civilized mankind *tends*, in the absence of some specific revelation, to embrace a particular kind of faith, we may profitably enquire whether, apart from the examples we have already cited, such a tendency is visible in the philosophical speculations of the present day. To pursue such an enquiry may at first sight seem vain: first because we have already ascribed to Oriental thought an indifference to the distinction between religion and philosophy, and secondly because academic philosophy in Europe seems, on a cursory inspection, to have so far divorced itself from religion as to exclude the possibility of such a tendency becoming manifest. The assumption is surely ill-founded; for a tendency can show itself just as effectively in a negative as in a positive fashion. And the impoverishment of much Western philosophy may be due precisely to lack of that form of alimentation from which, in previous centuries, it drew strength. Similarly, we may detect even in the etiolated systems or theories of the present day an impulse, often produced by debility, towards the kind of dogmatism hitherto associated with the 'superstitions' of the past.

The theory—for it makes no claim to form a system—of Logical Positivism was a case in point. Logical Positivism, as propounded by different exponents not all of whom are in agreement, enjoyed a vogue in England and to some extent in America which, given the aridity of its content, was nothing short of remarkable. This is not the place either to outline its history or to expound in detail its tenets; we must be content with a broad statement of its aims. The chief aim of Logical Positivism was to effect the 'elimination of metaphysics'. This was achieved by the application of a so-called Principle of Verifiability according to which all significant statements fall into two categories: either they represent statements that can be verified in fact or 'in principle', or they are tautologies. All sentences containing statements, or apparent statements, which fall into neither of these categories are to be dismissed as nonsensical.

This, as we have said, is a bald summary of Logical Positivism theory. Even by its most enthusiastic propounders it has been recognized to contain ambiguities. For example, once verification in fact needs to be supplemented by verification 'in principle', we have already taken off from the empiricist platform and may land anywhere. Nor is it easy to see what meaning can attach, on a theory which claims to have eliminated the concept of 'truth', to the overworked word *veri*fication. The point to which we wish to draw attention, however, is the following. If the Logical Positivist standpoint is correct, it follows that almost all the ideas propounded from the beginning of time by the spiritual leaders of mankind have been meaningless. These ideas, in fact, represent not intelligible concepts but emotional noises.[1] And such indeed was the conclusion to which Logical Positivists willingly stood committed.

If the Logical Positivist standpoint had been justified, it would have followed not merely that metaphysics and theology were illegitimate forms of enquiry, but that all the traditional values of our civilized life

[1] It would be as interesting to observe whether, in the event of a Logical Positivist being summoned for petty larceny, this form of defence would impress a magistrate, as what would happen to judicial procedure if all magistrates became Logical Positivists.

were nothing more than fictions. But you cannot fight superstition except from some particular standpoint, whether it be Reason or even Truth; and it is clear that, in spite of its elimination of absolute values, Logical Positivism is all the time concealing some such 'absolute' up its sleeve. Moreover, in declaring the statements of metaphysicians and theologians to be 'emotive nonsense', the Logical Positivists (as the asperity of their polemic amply demonstrates) were not above firing off a good deal of emotive ammunition themselves. Affirmations such as 'metaphysics is nonsense' produce their telling effect from the fact of their being 'war-cries' in a crusade against obscurantism and clap-trap. Finally, the Logical Positivist, in combating dogma, was not guiltless of adopting a dogmatic manner quite as formidable as that of his traditional adversaries.

The concealed Absolute

The reader will perhaps by now have grasped the point of this digression. The Philosopher, as opposed to the Sophist or the Casuist or the Charvaka or the Dialectician, is concerned with (to use the title of a well-known book on philosophy) 'interpreting the universe'. His business is with the meaning and values of life. And even if, for purposes of display, he shirks this task, the responsibilities of his vocation will still lie heavy upon him. He will be dogged by the very problems he is endeavouring to disown. What he 'eliminates'—what, like Mr Podsnap in *Our Mutual Friend*, he sweeps off 'the face of the earth'—will return to plague him. He is like a man who, transported on a misty day to the top of a mountain by a funicular railway or teleferic car, ridicules the exertions of those who painfully make the ascent on foot, and remains oblivious of the fact that the peak forms part of an impressive range of infinitely varied character. All he sees before him is a hand-made cairn of stones. What Bishop Berkeley called the 'minute philosophers' always adopt this parochial view of philosophy. The neat, ordered, logical system of their own construction is the cairn. But just as this cairn reposes not on the plain below but on the summit of a mountain and is a symbol of achievement, so the 'propositions' of our modern logicians represent the extreme abstraction from language in all its intellectual and emotional richness. They presuppose the existence of the 'mountain' of philosophy, which men in the past have ascended with toil in order that the present vantage-point shall have been prepared, and the various means of ascent devised.

The controversies surrounding Logical Positivism, the iconoclastic effect of its theories, and above all the warmth with which its partisans leap to its defence, suggest that it partook of the nature of a faith. And once we enter upon the realm of faith, an unfaith or 'armed scepticism' is as significant and instructive as a plain affirmation of belief. A simple or ingenuous error, once exposed, deserves quiet interment: we do not need to rant and rage over its tomb. But the opponent of metaphysics and theology sees in these things a potent means of capturing the human spirit. He sees them as the 'opium of the people'. Hence the venom of his denunciation, for he believes himself likewise to be an intellectual leader to whom the masses will one day be persuaded to listen. And so we are not surprised to hear the familiar plea of distinterestedness, though upon what philosophical grounds such pure devotion can be justified we are not told.

The theory to which we have drawn attention represents the extreme position adopted by Western thought in its flight from the 'idealism' of traditional philosophy in both West and East. The term 'idealism' is admittedly unsatisfactory in many ways; it has been associated for too long with a particular theory of knowledge. But the term 'spiritual' is not much better, and the term 'supernatural' is, for our purpose, perhaps worst of all. It remains true that all the great thinkers of mankind have observed a distinction between spiritual and material reality, and that they have attempted to explain the latter by reference to the former and not the other way round. 'We have tended to look to the lowest factor of explanation instead of the higher ones as the key to our problems. We explain mysticism in terms of medicine and pathology: the ancients explained the sensible by religion and by the highest philosophy of which they could think.'[1] We have seen that such scepticism and materialism appear at specific moments in every philosophical tradition, in India, in China, in Greece, in 17th-century Europe: the author has described this impulse towards scepticism and finally nihilism as the *anti-philosophia perennis*. If modern Europe had nothing to show for itself except this provincial doctrine, our penury would be extreme; but no one prepared to give attention to such matters can ignore the influence of another philosophical theory of much greater profundity, that known as Existentialism. Here again the schools were numerous, the controversy violent, and the general theory enmeshed in obscurities. Within Existentialism, as within any broad doctrine that aims at understanding existence, all the major trends of philosophical enquiry were visible, from the most spiritual to the most material: in contrast to a hidebound system such as Logical Positivism, where the spiritual elements remained in large part *recessive*. This circumstance, while it may cause the student to become sidetracked, testifies to a general direction in thought: and as this direction is towards an understanding of the meaning of life, which may possibly involve its demonstration to be meaningless, we have no alternative but to follow.

In his essay *What I Believe*, Tolstoy drew attention to a fact of which students of modern philosophical, sociological, and psychological works must finally become painfully aware: namely the absolute poverty of thought which, once the ponderous bulk of surmise and speculation has been shovelled away, remains visible. Immense atolls of fact, towered over by fantastic pagodas of theory, may have served for many years to obscure this deficiency; but it must be admitted that the 19th century, with all its achievements in the technical sphere, bequeathed little to mankind in the way of wisdom. And its general optimism, its self-assurance, its promises of liberty and prosperity,

[1] *The Mind and Heart of Love*, by M. C. D'Arcy, S. J., p. 34.

have been followed by two international explosions which could now culminate in a third. To the more sensitive minds of the time, these facts were apparent. The *Autobiography* of John Stuart Mill is perhaps the most moving and tragic document of the age. Brought to the brink of despair and suicide by the calculating Utilitarianism in which he had been educated, Mill found nothing upon which to fall back but the poetry of Wordsworth, and in old age a vague melioristic religion. A similar emotional crisis, though with a different issue, afflicted Tolstoy himself. More significant for our time, however, was the lonely duel with despair fought by Sören Kierkegaard, about whom we should say something more.

To Kierkegaard, the vague humanism of his time—and it is worth pointing out that he was born in 1813 and died in 1855—was renderd meaningless, deprived of all intelligibility even, by a single fact. This was the fact of death. To say that Kierkegaard was one of the few great thinkers to notice that men die would be to hold a strange view of what constitutes greatness. Other ages, and sometimes whole civilizations—such as Egypt and Babylon—have been preoccupied with the fact of death. But Kierkegaard's object—it would be too facile to say his desire—was to do more than confront his contemporaries with a *memento mori*; he was concerned to demonstrate that death, by constituting a full stop, made mockery of all the hopes and values upon which 19th-century civilization was based. In order to conceal the scandal of death, in fact, the 19th-century humanists and rationalists never ceased to hold out wild promises of an imminent triumph of science over mortality. This was to be achieved either by the manufacture of life itself or by the indefinite prolongation of human life; for next to the scandal of death came, as we have already observed, the scandal of old age.

To realize the true nature of existence, said Kierkegaard, is to be confronted with despair: for the most obvious fact of existence, namely its more or less abrupt termination, is not intelligible on the existential plane.[1] In existence we belong to something—a family, a society, a profession, a country, the human species; but in death we belong only to ourselves. We are therefore compelled to live in a condition of perpetual anguish (*Angst*), serving the group of which we are a member until the day of our death, but knowing that such a service is a matter of indifference to a society which, having registerd our disease, will continue much as before. All the elaborate measures of social service, above all 'cradle-to-grave' insurance, are illusory attempts of 'man the citizen' to persuade himself that society cares for 'man the individual'. In reality society does not care, because society, having no personality, is incapable of solicitude. The social-service State, which modern social idealists believe to be the greatest achievement of our epoch, is simply the official Receiver of the bankrupt ideals of humanism.

It is not merely death which renders life meaningless. The same is

[1] Possibly these truths become most forcibly apparent to those of delicate constitution. One is reminded of the remark of Maine de Biran, '*Seuls les gens malsains se sentent exister.*'

true, as indeed Schopenhauer had pointed out, of desire. And here the Existentialist point of view approximates to that of the great oriental sages, particularly the Buddha. On the natural plane, all love, even nominally requited love, is hopeless love, because it creates an image and promotes aspirations to which no human object is adequate. It was because of the impossibility of such attainment and possession that there grew up in Europe that cult of Eros which, as several modern writers have shown,[1] made a virtue of frustration and despair. There comes a moment in every love-affair when possession, satisfaction, or what the American sex-statisticians give an even more unattractive name, becomes something irrelevant; when 'no contact possible to flesh' can 'allay the fever of the bone'; when the original object is almost forgotten or, if recalled, found to be scarcely recognizable. To refuse to face such facts, or to dismiss them as romantic humbug, will not do. The attempt to consider passion unsentimentally, whether as a 'biological fact' or hygienic necessity, creates its own special anguish; for lust, with its terrible privacy, is a great deal less amenable to satisfaction than love. All lechers are solipsists.

Unlike most other contemporary apostles of despair, Kierkegaard found an answer to his problems in faith. Only in faith was the tension of existence rendered supportable or even intelligible; for men can learn to 'support' life in a variety of ways—there is a short-term solution to everything. Even those modern philosophers for whom Kierkegaard's solution is unacceptable at least face these ultimate problems with resolution. To insist, with Jean-Paul Sartre, that 'man is a useless passion' is at least to say something masculine, passionate, and therefore not wholly useless. It is not an accident that man alone can say these things; that he can affirm if only to deny; and that he can take the consequences of such affirmation and denial. In our survey, we have come upon thinker after thinker—the Egyptian Misanthrope, the sages Khekheperresoneb, Ipuwer and Amenemope, Zoroaster, the Hebrew Psalmists and Prophets, and the great spiritual leaders of India and China—who, often against all reason and unaided by revelation, have preached the 'divine connection', *Maat*, the *Tao*, the Way, with a unanimity impossible to confound with coincidence, and foolish to dismiss as illusion or poetry. It is not an accident that such men have been called Jainas, Nebiim, Buddhas, and Prophets, preachers of enlightenment and purveyors of wisdom; nor can we conceive of a time in which their teaching will have been rendered outmoded, unless men should at length choose to repudiate their humanity altogether. The Western World, having afforded the Orient some dubious specimens of its own wisdom, may well profit from deeper acquaintance with this great oriental tradition, thereby calling to mind the source of wisdom from which its own faith is derived. There are many to whom the apparent nihilism of oriental thought must always seem repulsive, and to whom the invitation to escape from nature and desire to a realm of spirit beyond conception is a fantastic example of human con-

[1] E.g. C. S. Lewis: *The Allegory of Love*, and Denis de Rougement: *Passion and Society* (translated by Montgomery Belgion).

ceit and self-delusion. Every man must choose from this storehouse that which answers his individual needs. Perhaps the teaching most accessible and attractive to our Western minds is that contained in the *Bhagavad-Gita*, with its emphasis on *Bhakti*, or devotion to a personal God. For it is in the revelation of Sri Krishna to Arjuna that we find the noblest message ever to have issued from the oriental world: the summons to face the future and its perils with humility, with awe, even with a touch of anguish, but without fear.

Suggestions for Further Reading

SOCRATES

Francis M. Cornford, *Before and After Socrates* (1932)
Benjamin Farrington, *Greek Science,* Vol. I, Thales to Aristotle (1944)

PLATO

R. C. Lodge, *Plato's Theory of Ethics* (1936)
David Ross, *Plato's Theory of Ideas* (1951)
A. E. Taylor, *Plato* (1927)

ARISTOTLE

Werner Jaeger, *Aristotle* (1934)
A. E. Taylor, *Aristotle* (1943)

FROM STOICISM TO NEO-PLATONISM

E. R. Beven, *Stoics and Sceptics* (1913)
Philip Merlan, *From Platonism to Neo-Platonism* (1953)
Paul Elmer More, *Hellenistic Philosophies* (1923)

ST. AUGUSTINE

A. Papini, *St. Augustine* (1930)
H. Pope, *St. Augustine* (1937)
A Monument to St. Augustine, Symposium (1930)

PETER ABELARD

J. Huizinger, *The Waning of the Middle Ages* (1955)
J. G. Sikes, *Peter Abelard* (1932)

MOSLEM AND JEWISH PHILOSOPHERS AND THE REVIVAL OF ARISTOTELIANISM

T. W. Arnold and A. Guillaume, *The Legacy of Islam* (1931)
E. R. Bevan and Charles Singer, *The Legacy of Israel* (1928)

ST. THOMAS AQUINAS

F. Copleston, *Mediaeval Philosophy* (1952)
M. C. D'Arcy, *St. Thomas Aquinas* (1930)
E. Gilson, *The Spirit of Mediaeval Philosophy* (1936)

SCHOLASTIC DECLINE AND SCIENTIFIC ADVANCE
F. H. Anderson, *The Philosophy of Francis Bacon* (1948)
S. C. Easton, *Roger Bacon and His Search for a Universal Science* (1952)
E. A. Moody, *The Logic of William of Ockham* (1936)

RENÉ DESCARTES
A. Boyce Gibson, *The Philosophy of Descartes* (1932)
S. V. Keeling, *Descartes* (1934)
J. Maritain, *The Dream of Descartes* (1944)
H. F. Stewart, *The Secret of Pascal* (1941)

BENEDICT SPINOZA
S. Hampshire, *Spinoza* (1951)
R. McKeon, *The Philosophy of Spinoza* (1928)
R. Roth, *Spinoza* (1929)

GOTTFRIED LEIBNIZ
B. Russell, *The Philosophy of Leibniz* (1937)
R. L. Saw, *Leibniz* (1957)

RELIGIOUS CONFLICT AND THE RISE OF RATIONALISM
Paul Hazard, *The European Mind* (1953)
J. Laird, *Hobbes* (1934)
A. E. Taylor, *Hobbes* (1908)

GEORGE BERKELEY
G. Dawes Hicks, *Berkeley* (1932)
G. Warnock, *Berkeley* (1953)
John D. Wild, *Berkeley* (1936)

THE PRECURSORS OF HUME
E. Cassirer, *The Philosophy of the Enlightenment* (1951)
B. Croce (translated by Collingwood), *The Philosophy of Giambattista Vico* (1923)

DAVID HUME
A. Basson, *David Hume* (1958)
H. H. Price, *Hume's Theory of the External World* (1940)
N. Kemp Smith, *The Philosophy of Hume* (1941)

ENCYCLOPAEDISTS AND ROMANTICS
E. Cassirer, *Rousseau, Kant, and Goethe* (1945)
Paul Hazard, *European Thought in the 18th Century* (1954)

IMMANUEL KANT
A. C. Ewing, *A Short Commentary on Kant's Critique of Pure Reason* (1938)
Roger Scruton, *Kant* (1982)

P. F. Strawson, *The Bounds of Sense* (1966)
T. D. Weldon, *Introduction to Kant's Critique of Pure Reason* (1945)

GERMAN ROMANTIC PHILOSOPHY FROM FICHTE TO HEGEL
A. D. Pringle-Pattison, *From Kant to Hegel* (1924)
E. B. Talbot, *Fundamental Principles of Fichte's Philosophy* (1906)

JOHN LOCKE
R. I. Aaron, *Locke* (1937)
D. J. O'Connor, *Locke* (1952)
A. N. Whitehead, *Science and the Modern World* (1926)

GEORG WILHELM HEGEL
B. Croce (translated by Ainslie), *What Is Living and What is Dead in the Philosophy of Hegel* (1915)
G. R. G. Mure, *An Introduction to Hegel* (1940)
W. T. Stace, *The Philosophy of Hegel* (1924)

THE MARXIST PHILOSOPHY
H. P. Adams, *Karl Marx and His Early Writings* (1940)
I. Berlin, *Karl Marx, His Life and Environment* (1948)
S. Hook, *From Hegel to Marx* (1935)

FROM SCHOPENHAUER TO KIERKEGAARD
F. Copleston, *Schopenhauer* (1953)
W. Lowrie, *Kierkegaard* (1938)
R. Thomte, *Kierkegaard's Philosophy of Religion* (1948)
H. Zimmern, *Schopenhauer, His Life and Philosophy* (1932)

FRIEDRICH NIETZSCHE
Crane Brinton, *Nietzsche* (1941)
F. Copleston, *Nietzsche, Philosopher of Culutre* (1942)

SCEPTICISM AND FAITH IN NINETEENTH CENTURY PHILOSOPHY
M. H. Carré, *Phases of Thought in England* (1949)
R. W. Church, *Bradley's Dialectic* (1942)
G. S. Carter, *A Hundred Years of Evolution* (1957)
F. R. Leavis, *Mill on Bentham and Coleridge* (1950)
E. Neff, *Carlyle and Mill* (1924)
R. B. Perry, *The Thought and Character of William James* (1936)
H. Peterson, *Huxley, The Prophet of Science* (1932)

HENRI BERGSON
I. W. Alexander, *Bergson* (1957)
A. D. Lindsay, *The Philosophy of Bergson* (1911)
L. Kalakowski, *Bergson* (1985)

JOHN DEWEY and GEORGE SANTAYANA
Max Black (ed), *Philosophy in America* (1965)

M. G. White, *The Origin of Dewey's Instrumentalism* (1943)
R. Butler, *The Mind of Santayana* (1955)
M. Cohen, *American Thought* (1954)
S. Hook, *John Dewey* (1939)
G. H. Mead, *The Philosophy of the Present* (1932)
A. Schilpp (Editor), *The Philosophy of George Santayana* (1940)
A. Schilpp, *The Philosophy of John Dewey* (1939)

CONCLUSION
A. J. Ayer and others *The Revolution in Philosophy* (1956)
A. J. Ayer, *Philosophy in the Twentieth Century* (1982)
Ivor Leclerc (Editor), *The Relevance of Whitehead* (1961)
M. Macdonald (Editor), *Philosophy and Analysis* (1954)
Bryan Magee (ed), *Men of Ideas: Some Creators of Contemporary Philosophy* (1978)
John Passmore, *A Hundred Years of Philosophy* (1968)
David Pears, *Wittgenstein* (1971)
D. Pole, *The Later Philosophy of Wittgenstein* (1958)
Radhakrishnan, *East and West* (1955)
G. Ryle, *The Concept of Mind* (1949)
John Searle, *Minds, Brains & Science* (1984)
C. L. Stevenson, *Ethics and Language* (1944)
E. W. F. Tomlin, *R. G. Collingwood* (1960)
A. J. Toynbee, *An Historian's Approach to Religion* (1956)
G. J. Warnock, *Modern Philosophy* (1956)

Index